RECREATION LAKES of CALIFORNIA

Since 1973

15th Edition

by Diane Dirksen & Jake Dirksen

Cover Photographs by Trevor Dirksen
Cartoons by Greg Dirksen

Recreation Sales Publishing
P O Box 1028
Aptos, CA 95001
Ph: (800) 668-0076
email: reclakes@comcast.net

Do you know what Lakes are on the front & back covers?
Check our website to find out.
www.rec-lakes.com

ISBN-13: 978-0-943798-23-3
Library of Congress 2009907370

Dedicated to the memory of

Jim Dirksen

with all our love

Jim Dirksen was the founder of the guidebooks, Recreation Lakes of California and Colorado River Recreation. He began research for these books in 1973 when he owned the Boat Warehouse in Walnut Creek, California. An avid sailor, he traveled thousands of nautical miles through the waters of Hawaii, Mexico, Newfoundland, Nova Scotia and throughout the Caribbean. During his life, he never was without a boat, large or small.

To a great Dad who taught us each to sail, fish and appreciate all the lakes in California, this 15th Edition has been published in your honor. We know you will be very proud.

Greg, Trevor and Jake Dirksen

INTRODUCTION

Each Lake is described according to location, elevation, size and facilities. The book is divided into three sections which are marked by black marks at the bottom of the page; the left is the North Section, the middle is Central and the right is the South Section of California. Campgrounds for tents and R.V.s, picnic areas, launch ramps, marinas and other facilities are located on each map. Also hiking, bicycle and equestrian trails are shown. While boating, fishing and camping are basic to most Lakes, we have also included swimming, hiking, backpacking and equestrian information. Cabins, resorts, boat tours, golf courses, airports and other attractions are shown. The maps also show major recreation areas near each Lake, such as State and National Parks, Wilderness Areas and the Pacific Crest Trail.

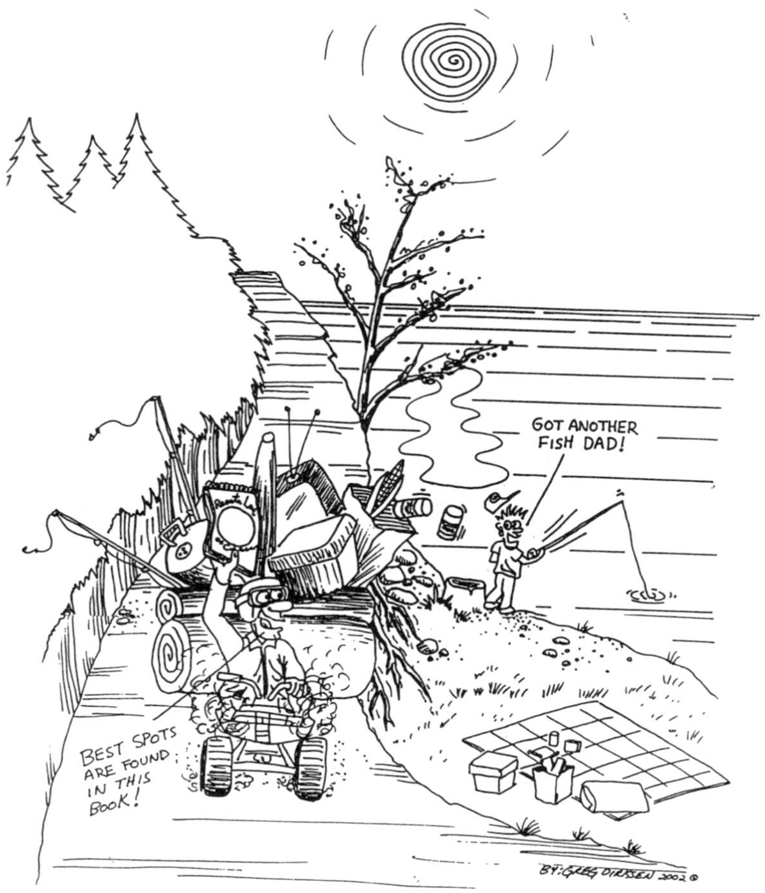
GOT ANOTHER FISH DAD!
BEST SPOTS ARE FOUND IN THIS BOOK!
BY: GREG DIRKSEN 2002 ©

We have made this book as accurate and current as possible at the time of publication. Phone numbers, fees and other information can change. *RECREATION LAKES OF CALIFORNIA* will help you enjoy the outdoor activities, spectacular scenery and unique environments this wonderful State has to offer.

The support of the US Forest Service, the Bureau of Land Management, Army Corps of Engineers, the California State Park System, the Department of Fish and Game is invaluable. Chambers of Commerce, Visitor's Bureaus and the many private owners and managers of facilities are equally supportive. We give our special appreciation to you, the reader. Your use of *RECREATION LAKES of CALIFORNIA* has made it a bestseller. Thank you!

MAPS ARE NOT TO SCALE
USE WITH STANDARD ROAD MAPS

INFORMATION IS PRESENTED AS IT APPEARS WHEN LAKES ARE AT FULL WATER CAPACITY
WEATHER CONDITIONS MUST BE CONSIDERED
ALL FEES AND INFORMATION ARE SUBJECT TO CHANGE.

TABLE OF CONTENTS

Lakes correspond to page numbers, divided into three sections: *North, Central* and *South*—areas of California. Each section begins with a Map illustrating that region, with an approximate location of each Lake in that area, referenced by a page number. Several maps include supplementary pages with information on campgrounds, resorts, marine facilities and other recreational opportunities.

*See **Index** at back of book for a complete alphabetical listing of Lakes.*

North Section

Central Section

South Section

Back of Book

North Section Lakes 1 - 60

Numbers around highways represent lakes in numerical order in this book. *See Index for complete listing.*

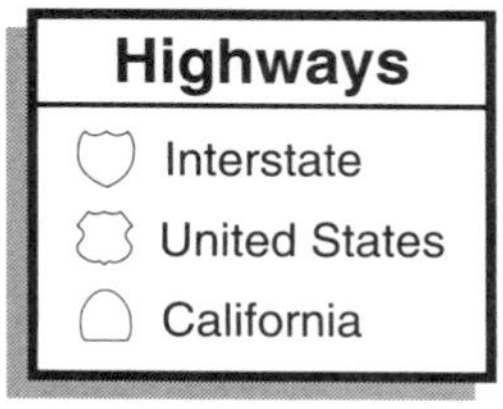
Highways
Interstate
United States
California

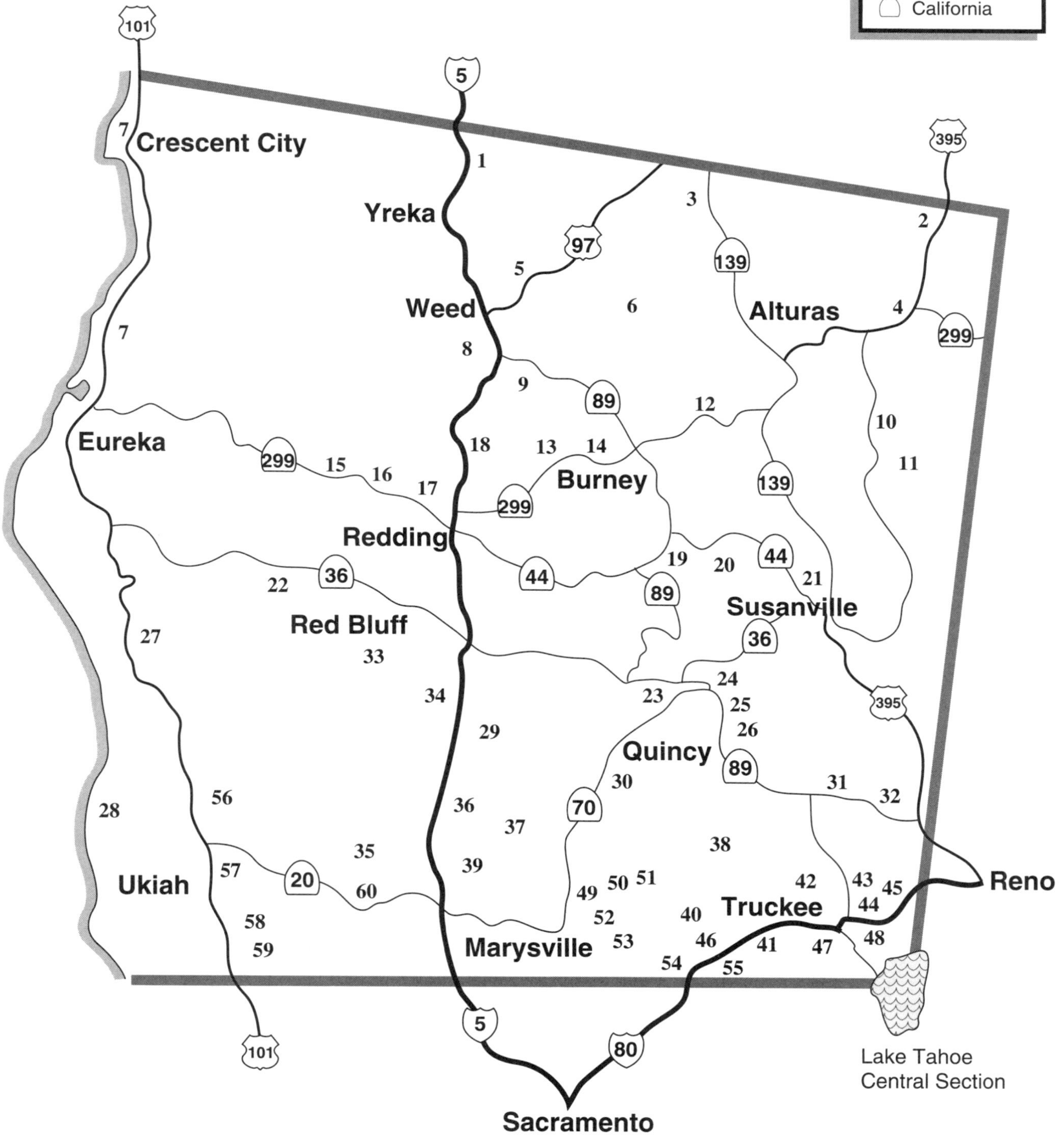
Crescent City
Yreka
Weed
Alturas
Eureka
Burney
Redding
Red Bluff
Susanville
Quincy
Ukiah
Truckee
Reno
Marysville
Sacramento
Lake Tahoe
Central Section
101
5
97
139
395
299
89
36
44
70
20
80

IRON GATE RESERVOIR and COPCO LAKE

Iron Gate Reservoir and Copco Lake are located east of Interstate 5 near the Oregon border. Iron Gate, elevation 2,343 feet, is 7 miles long and covers a surface area of 825 acres. Copco Lake, elevation 2,613 feet, has a surface area of 1,000 acres and is 5 miles long. The Wild Upper Klamath River above Copco Lake has native rainbow trout. Six fishing access areas with parking are available. From May through October, this is a popular part of the River for experienced whitewater rafters. You can put in at John Boyle Dam, go 17 miles and take out at Copco Lake. There is an abundant yellow perch fishery along with rainbow trout and large-mouth bass. The Klamath River has a good salmon and steelhead fishery.

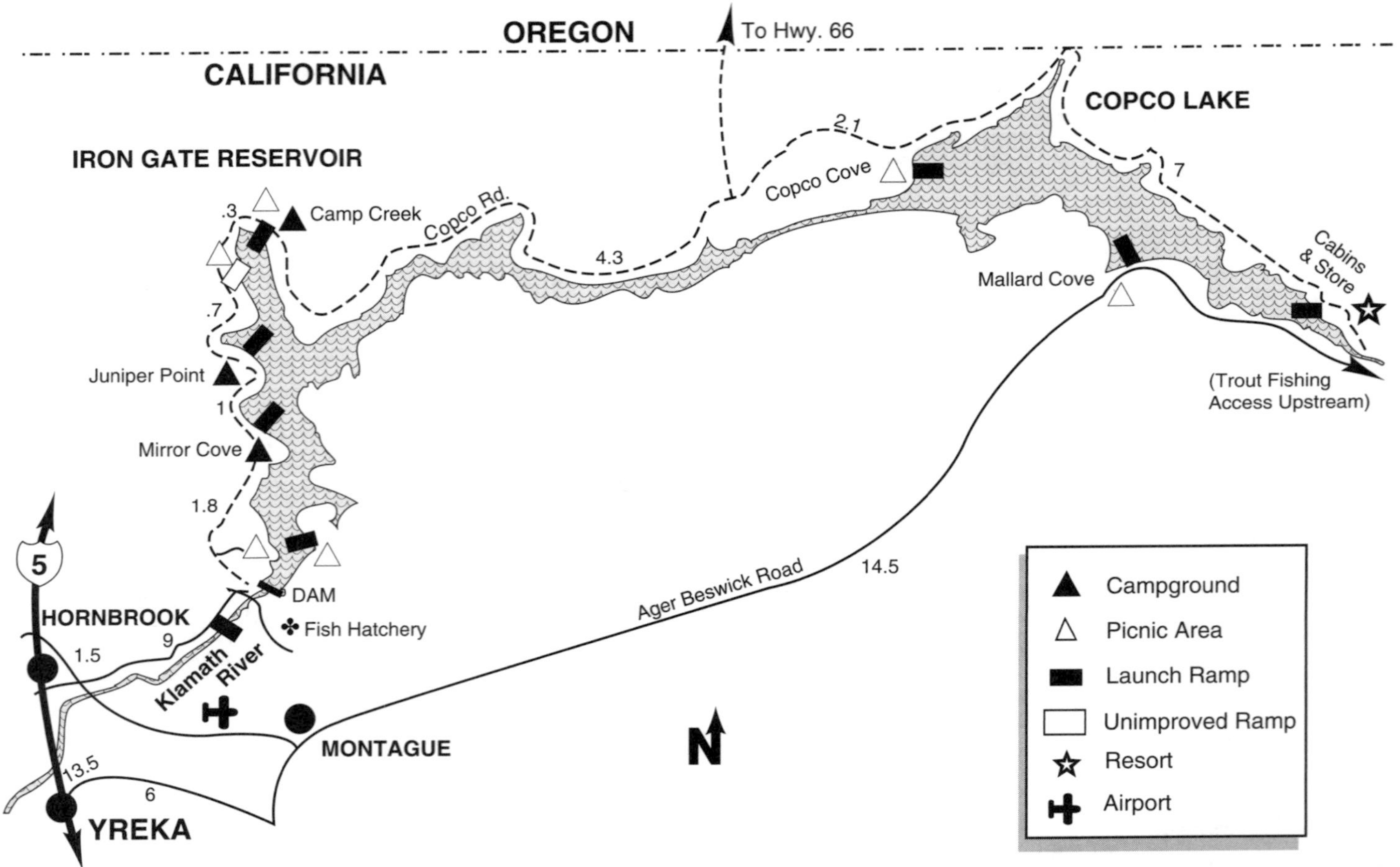
OREGON
To Hwy. 66
CALIFORNIA
COPCO LAKE
IRON GATE RESERVOIR
2.1
7
Copco Cove
Copco Rd.
.3
Camp Creek
4.3
Cabins & Store
Mallard Cove
.7
Juniper Point
(Trout Fishing Access Upstream)
1
Mirror Cove
1.8
5
DAM
14.5
Ager Beswick Road
HORNBROOK
Fish Hatchery
9
1.5
Klamath River
MONTAGUE
13.5
6
YREKA
N
Campground
Picnic Area
Launch Ramp
Unimproved Ramp
Resort
Airport

INFORMATION: Pacific Power - Recreation Department—Ph: (503) 813-6666

CAMPING	BOATING	RECREATION	OTHER
Iron Gate Reservoir: Camp Creek - 21 Sites for R.V.s Plus Large Overflow Area Juniper Point - 9 Sites, No Water Mirror Cove - 10 Sites, No Water	Power, Row, Canoe, Sail & Inflatable 10 MPH Speed Limit in Designated Areas Copco Lake - Upper 1/3 Set Aside for Fishing (No Wake) Launch Ramps Rentals: Fishing Boats with Motors - Copco Lake Store Only Docks	Fishing: Trout, Catfish, Crappie, Largemouth Bass, Yellow Perch, Salmon & Steelhead-Klamath River Swimming Picnicking Hiking & Equestrian Trails Whitewater Rafting	Copco Lake Store 27734 Copco Rd. Montague 96064 Ph: (530) 459-3655 Groceries, Bait & Tackle Nearest Gas - 20 Miles Full Facilities at Hornbrook River Flow & Reservoir Levels: Ph: (800) 547-1501

GOOSE, CAVE and LILY LAKES and FEE RESERVOIR

Goose Lake is on the California-Oregon border at an elevation of 4,800 feet. This shallow 108,800 surface acre Lake is used primarily for boating and wildlife viewing. Cave and Lily Lakes offer excellent fishing for brook and rainbow trout. Boating is limited to small non-motorized boats, canoes and kayaks. These two small mountain Lakes are neighbors at 6,600 feet elevation in the Modoc National Forest. Poor access roads limit use of trailers. Fee Reservoir, at 4,000 feet, can produce large rainbow trout. This remote Reservoir is operated by the Bureau of Land Management. Any facilities are 30 miles away.

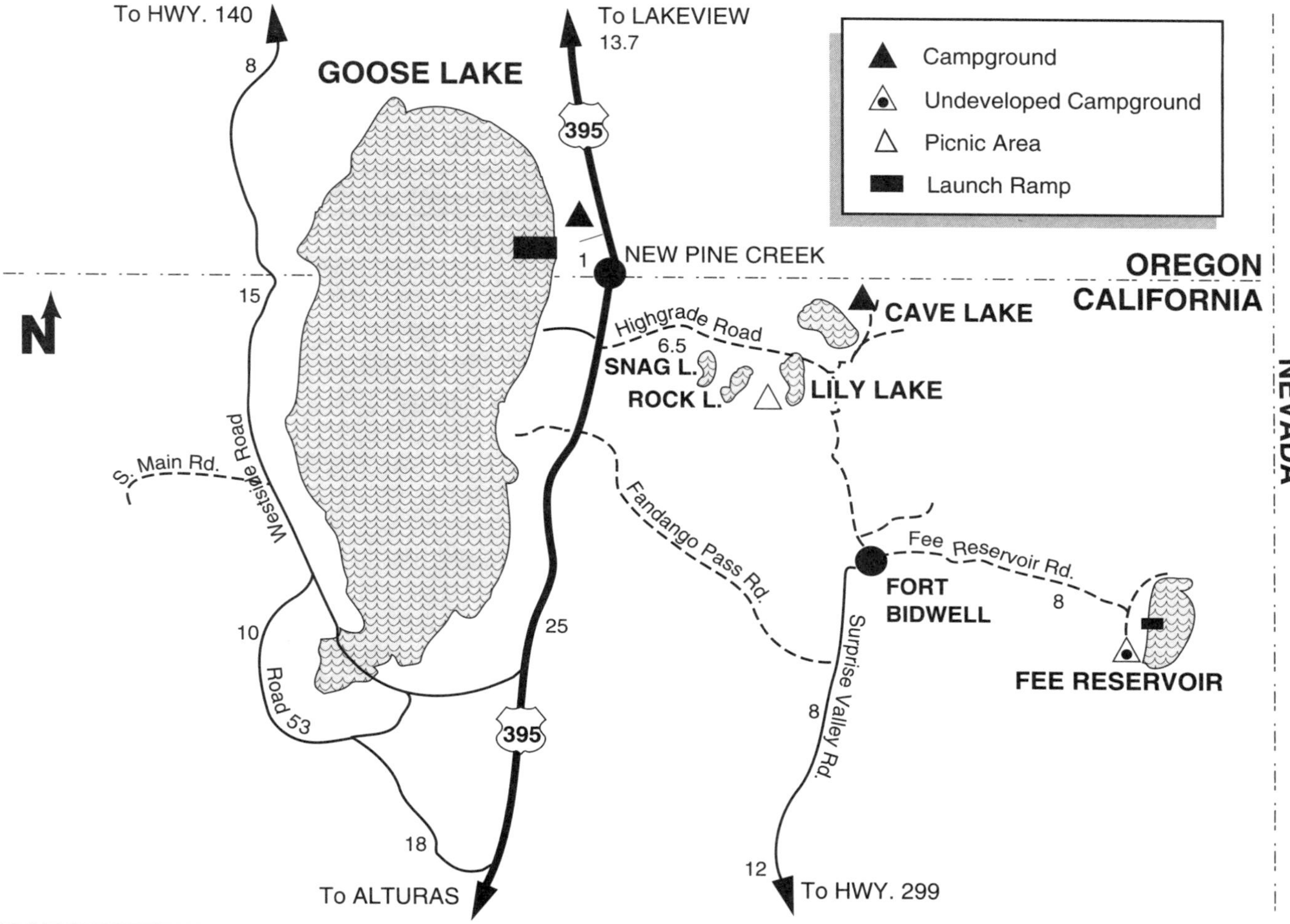

To HWY. 140
To LAKEVIEW
13.7
GOOSE LAKE
395
Campground
Undeveloped Campground
Picnic Area
Launch Ramp
NEW PINE CREEK
OREGON
CALIFORNIA
N
CAVE LAKE
Highgrade Road
6.5
SNAG L.
ROCK L.
LILY LAKE
NEVADA
Main Rd.
Westside Road
Fandango Pass Rd.
Fee Reservoir Rd.
FORT BIDWELL
8
FEE RESERVOIR
10
Road 53
25
Surprise Valley Rd.
395
18
12
To ALTURAS
To HWY. 299

INFORMATION: Goose Lake State Recreation Area - Oregon State Parks—Ph: (800) 551-6949

CAMPING	BOATING	RECREATION	OTHER
Goose Lake - First Come: Oregon State Parks 47 Tent/RV Sites to 50 ft. Electric Hookups Fees: $12 - $16 Disposal Station Cave Lake: 6 Tent/RV Sites - No Fee Fee Reservoir: 7 Undev. Tent/RV Sites to 24 ft. - No Water	Goose Lake: Open to all Boating Paved Launch Ramp Lily & Cave Lakes: No Motors Hand Launch Fee Reservoir: Launch Ramp Shallow Draft Boats Advised	Fishing: Brook & Rainbow Trout Picnicking - Lily Lake 6 Sites Hiking & Riding Trails Mountain Bike Trails Backpacking Nature Study Swimming Birdwatching	Cave Lake: Warner Mountain Ranger District 385 Wallace St. Cedarville 96104 Ph: (530) 279-6116 Fee Reservoir: Bureau of Land Management Surprise Field Office 602 Cressler St. Cedarville 96104 Ph: (530) 279-6101 Remote - Limited Facilities

LOWER KLAMATH, TULE and CLEAR LAKES—KLAMATH BASIN NATIONAL WILDLIFE REFUGES

This is waterfowl country. These Lakes are in the Klamath Basin National Wildlife Refuges, with some of the greatest numbers of migratory waterfowl in the world. Photography and wildlife observation are popular activities. Over 270 species of birds have been identified. The American bald eagle, golden eagle and peregrin falcon are among the birds that can be observed. Except for canoeing at Tulelake, boating is secondary to hunting. There is no fishing but this is a hunter's paradise. Rules and boundaries are strictly enforced. It is essential you have current information. Accommodations can be a problem, especially during hunting season so it is necessary to plan ahead.

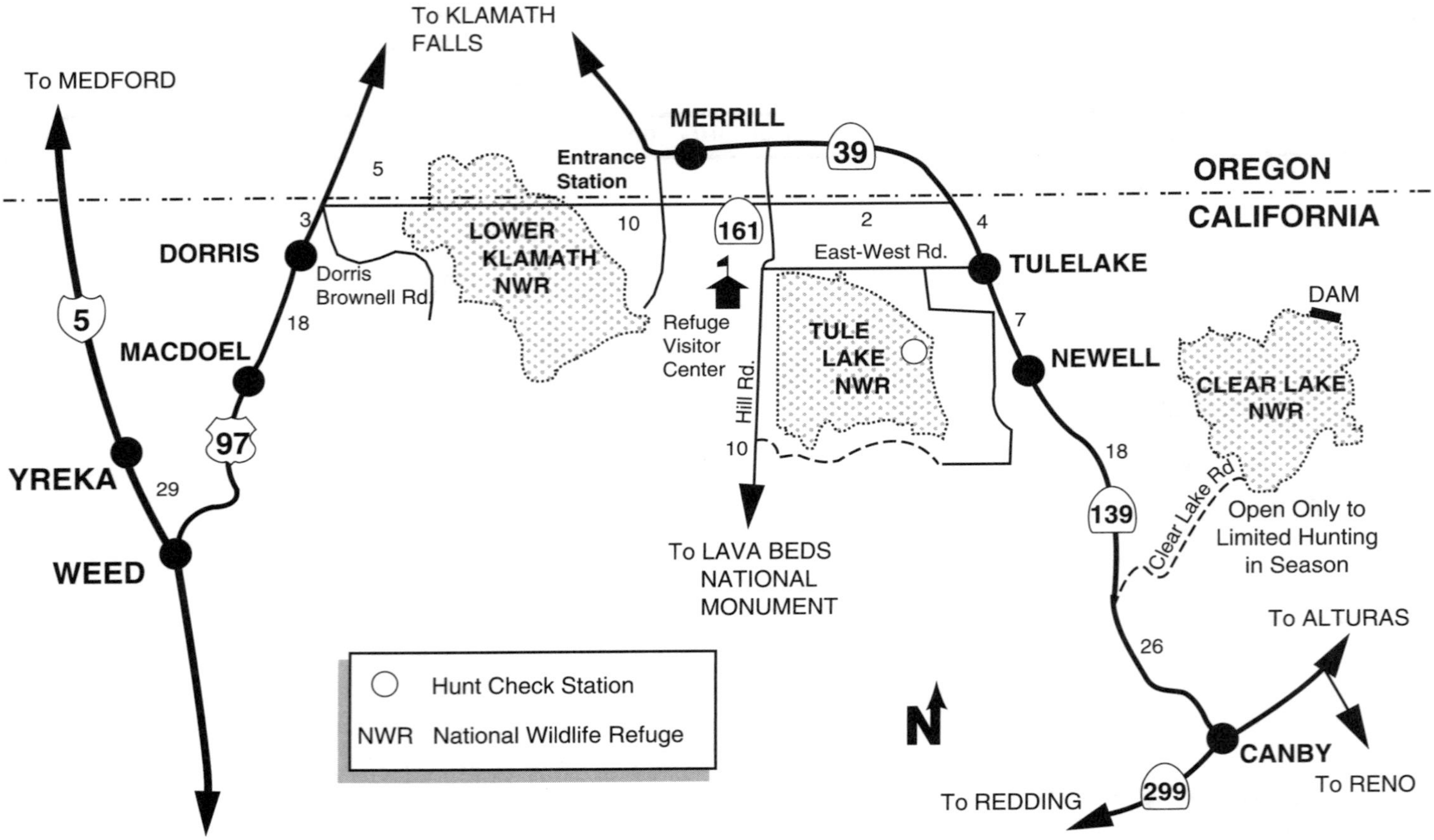
To KLAMATH FALLS
To MEDFORD
MERRILL
Entrance Station
39
OREGON
CALIFORNIA
5
3
10
161
2
4
DORRIS
LOWER KLAMATH NWR
East-West Rd.
TULELAKE
Dorris Brownell Rd
DAM
5
18
Refuge Visitor Center
TULE LAKE NWR
7
MACDOEL
NEWELL
CLEAR LAKE NWR
Hill Rd.
97
10
18
YREKA
29
Clear Lake Rd
139
Open Only to Limited Hunting in Season
WEED
To LAVA BEDS NATIONAL MONUMENT
To ALTURAS
26
Hunt Check Station
NWR National Wildlife Refuge
N
CANBY
To RENO
To REDDING
299

INFORMATION: Klamath Basin NWR, 4009 Hill Rd., Tulelake 96134—Ph: (530) 667-2231

CAMPING	BOATING	RECREATION	OTHER
Stateline R.V. Park: 30138 Lower Klamath Rd. Tulelake 96134 Ph: (530) 667-4849 55 R.V. Sites Full Hookups Tent Sites Other RV Parks in Area	Boats are Allowed Only During Hunting Season Except for Canoe Area at Tulelake NWR - Open July through September Air Thrust & Water Thrust Boats are Prohibited	Canoe Trails at Tule Lake Birdwatching Nature Study Photography Lower Klamath NWRS: Marked Auto Tours for Wildlife Viewing Photoblinds Visitor Center Hunting: Steel Shot is Required for Waterfowl & Pheasant Hunting	Refuge Visitor Center: Open Monday-Friday 8:00 am - 4:30 pm Open Saturday & Sunday 10:00 am - 4:00 pm Lava Beds Nat. Monument: 43 Tent/R.V. Sites Fee: $10 First Come, First Served Plus 1 Group Site by Reservation Ph: (530) 667-8100

BIG SAGE, "C", "F", DUNCAN, GRAVEN, BAYLEY and DORRIS RESERVOIRS—DELTA LAKE

Although facilities are limited, there are recreational opportunities at these Lakes in the Modoc National Forest and Modoc County. Big Sage Reservoir is at an elevation of 4,900 feet on a sage and juniper covered plateau. This 5,400 acre Reservoir is open to all boating and has a warm water fishery. Nearby Reservoirs "C", and "F" and Duncan provide a good opportunity to catch the large Eagle Lake trout. Dorris Reservoir is in the Modoc National Wildlife Refuge. It is closed during waterfowl hunting season. The angler will find trout and a warm water fishery. Graven, Bayley and Delta are shallow and muddy and primarily known for good catfishing. Caution is advised as the roads into these Reservoirs can be very rough.

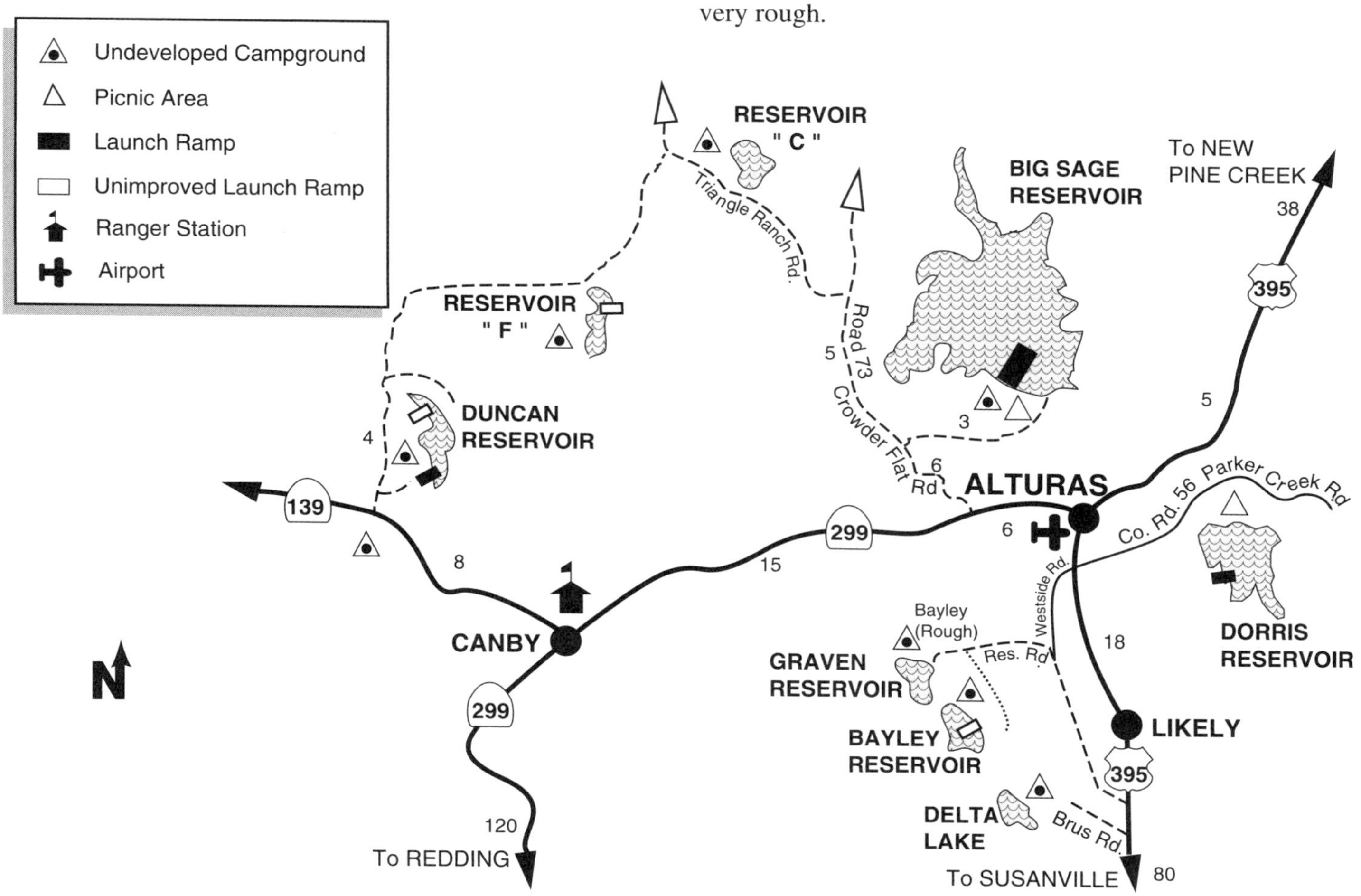

Undeveloped Campground
Picnic Area
Launch Ramp
Unimproved Launch Ramp
Ranger Station
Airport
RESERVOIR "C"
Triangle Ranch Rd.
BIG SAGE RESERVOIR
To NEW PINE CREEK
38
395
RESERVOIR "F"
Road 73
5
DUNCAN RESERVOIR
4
3
Crowder Flat Rd
6
ALTURAS
5
Parker Creek Rd
Co. Rd. 56
139
299
6
8
15
Westside Rd.
Bayley (Rough)
18
DORRIS RESERVOIR
CANBY
GRAVEN RESERVOIR
Res. Rd
N
BAYLEY RESERVOIR
LIKELY
299
395
DELTA LAKE
Brus Rd.
120
To REDDING
To SUSANVILLE
80

INFORMATION: Devil's Garden Ranger District, 800 West 12th St., Alturas 96101—Ph: (530) 233-5811

CAMPING	BOATING	RECREATION	OTHER
Undeveloped Campsites as Shown on Map No Drinking Water Limited RV & Trailer Access Dorris Reservoir: Walk-In Public Access February 1 to March 31 and Early October Before Waterfowl Season	Big Sage: Open to All Boating Launch Ramp Dorris: Boating: Apr. 1-Sept. 30 Waterskiing: June 1 - Sept. 30 No PWCs Launch Ramp *Underwater Hazards* Other Lakes Open to Small Hand Launched Boats	Fishing: Trout, Bass, Catfish & Panfish plus Eagle Lake Trout at Reservoir "C", Reservoir "F" & Duncan Hiking & Equestrian Trails Nature Study Birdwatching	Dorris Reservoir: Modoc National Wildlife Refuge P.O. Box 1610 Alturas 96101 Ph: (530) 233-3572 Graven, Bayley & Delta: Bureau of Land Management Alturas Field Office Ph: (530) 233-4666

INDIAN TOM, MEISS, JUANITA, ORR and SHASTINA LAKES

These Lakes along Highway 97 from Weed to the Oregon Border have a variety of recreational activities. The alkaline waters in Indian Tom support a unique Cutthroat fishery. Meiss Lake is within the Butte Valley Wildlife Area. Waterfowl hunting and wildlife observation are the main activities.

Juanita is a small mountain Lake at an elevation of 5,100 feet with 55 surface acres. There is a nice campground and trout fishing is good. Orr Lake is a USFS Lake open to the public for boating, fishing and wildlife viewing. Lake Shastina, a private facility, is open to all boating and good fishing.

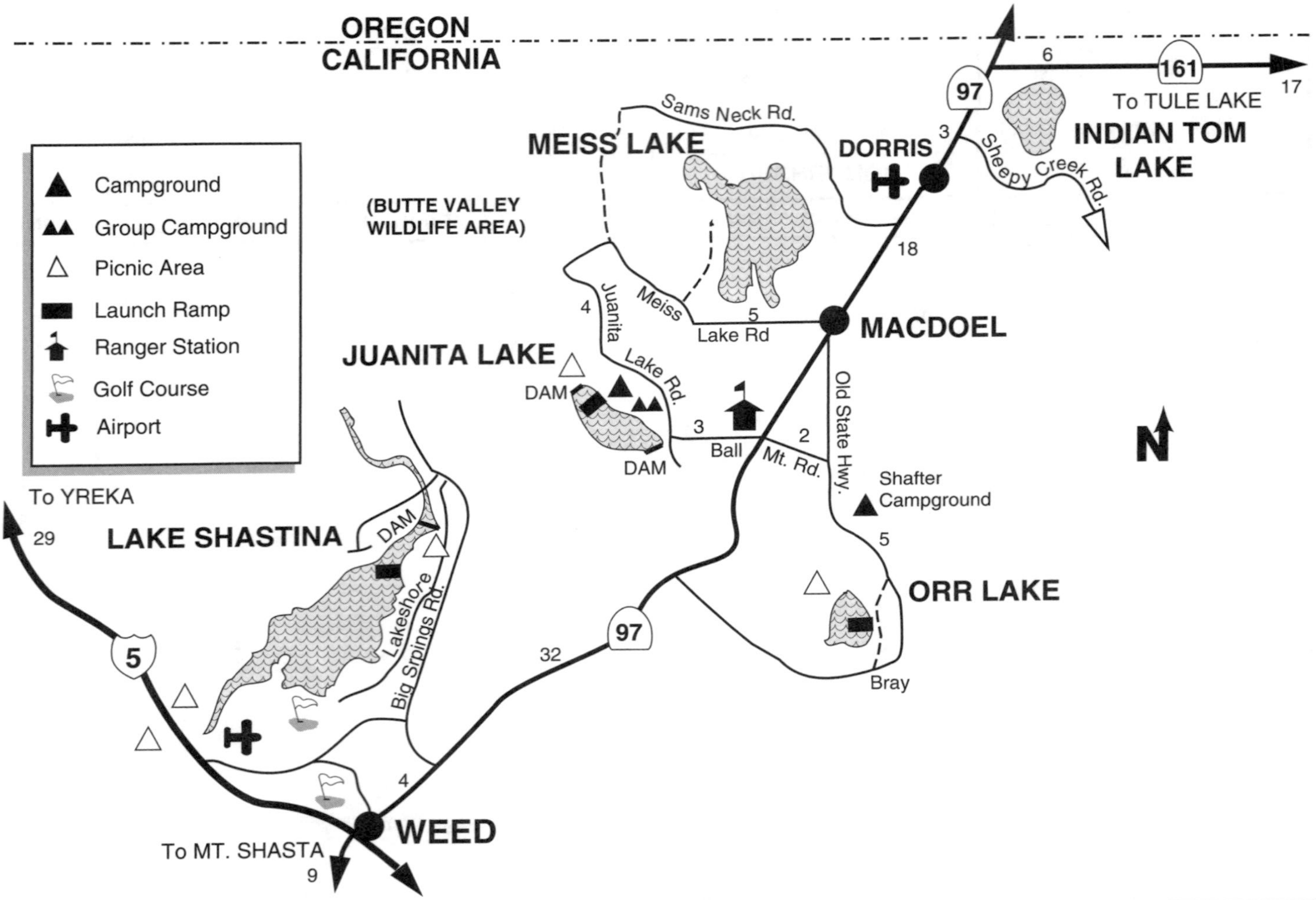

OREGON
CALIFORNIA
Campground
Group Campground
Picnic Area
Launch Ramp
Ranger Station
Golf Course
Airport
Sams Neck Rd.
MEISS LAKE
DORRIS
97
3
6
161
To TULE LAKE
17
INDIAN TOM LAKE
Sheepy Creek Rd.
(BUTTE VALLEY WILDLIFE AREA)
18
Meiss
Juanita
4
5
Lake Rd
MACDOEL
JUANITA LAKE
Lake Rd.
DAM
DAM
3
Ball
Mt. Rd.
2
Old State Hwy.
Shafter Campground
5
ORR LAKE
Bray
N
To YREKA
29
LAKE SHASTINA
DAM
Lakeshore
Big Srpings Rd.
5
97
32
4
WEED
To MT. SHASTA
9

INFORMATION: Goosenest Ranger Station, 37805 Hwy. 97, Macdoel 96058—Ph: (530) 398-4391			
CAMPING	**BOATING**	**RECREATION**	**OTHER**
Juanita Lake: 23 Dev. Sites for Tents & R.V.s to 32 ft. Fee: $10 Group Camp to 50 People Fee: $30 Reservations Required for Group Site Orr Lake: 3 Campsites Shafter Campground: 10 Campsites - $6	Juanita: Open to All Non-Powered Boating Launch Ramp & Dock Shastina: Open to All Boating Orr & Indian Tom: Small Hand Launch Craft - Max. 10 HP Meiss (State Fish & Game): Shallow Draft Non-Powered Boating	Fishing: Juanita: Brown & Rainbow Trout, Largemouth Bass, Bullhead Catfish Shastina: Trout, Silver Salmon, Bass, Catfish & Crappie Indian Tom: Cutthroat Orr: Rainbow Trout, Largemouth Bass Swimming Picnicking Hiking Trails	Full Facilities in Weed & Dorris Gas & Grocery Store at Macdoel Butte Valley Wildlife Area P.O. Box 249 Macdoel 96058 Ph: (530) 398-4627 Juanita Lake: 1-1/2 Mile Barrier Free Trail Around Lake

MEDICINE LAKE

Medicine Lake is in the Modoc National Forest at an elevation of 6,700 feet. Once the center of a volcano, this 640 surface-acre Lake has no known outlets and is 150 feet deep in places. The lodgepole pine-covered campgrounds are maintained by the U.S. Forest Service. Points of interest include Lava Beds National Monument, Glass Mountain, Burnt Lava Flow, Medicine Lake Glass Flow and Undertakers Crater. Although remote, this is a popular Lake for boating, waterskiing and sailing. The fishing is good from shore or boat. The small 5 surface-acre Bullseye Lake has a rainbow and brook trout fishery.

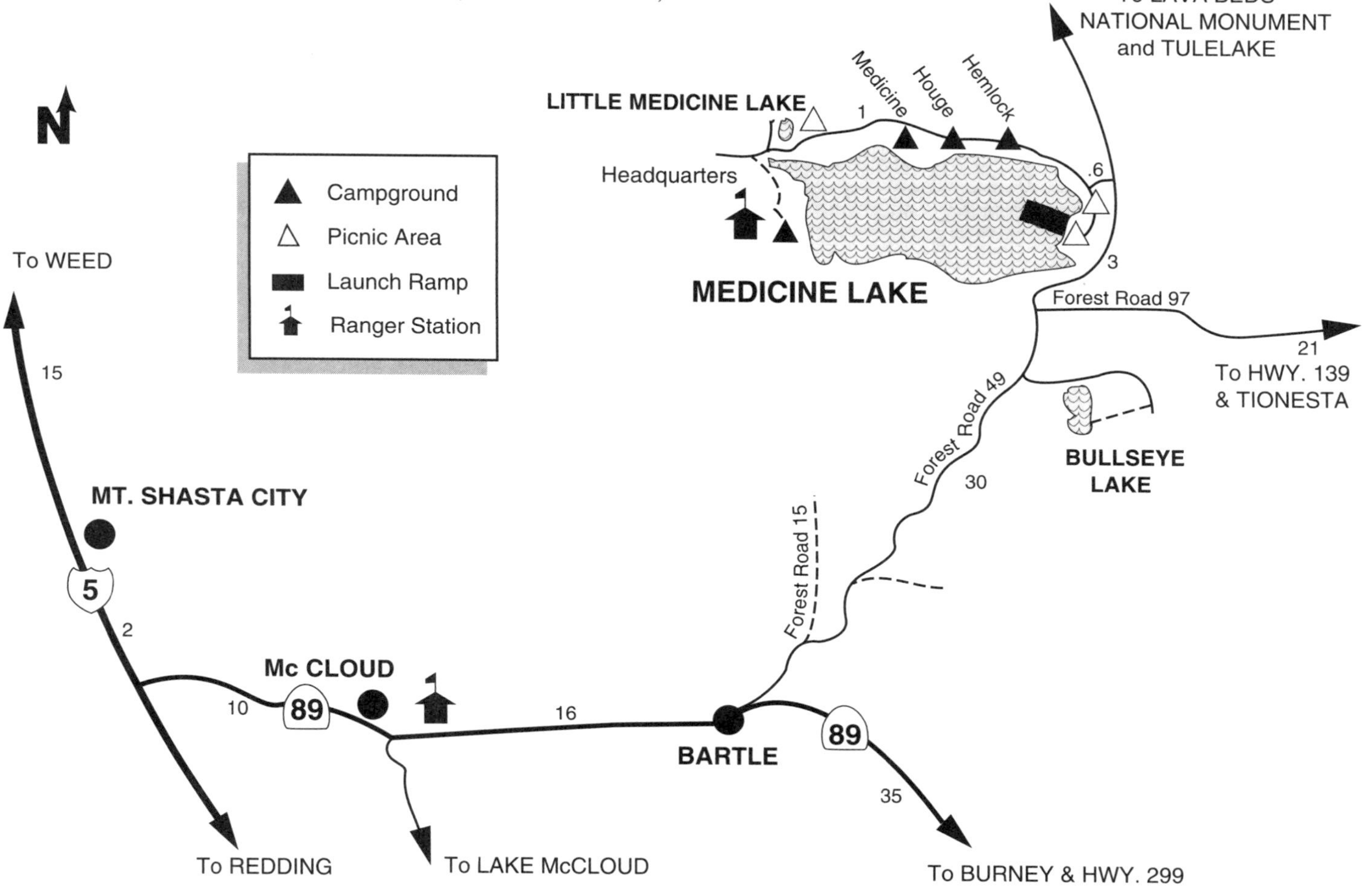
To LAVA BEDS
NATIONAL MONUMENT
and TULELAKE
Medicine
Houge
Hemlock
LITTLE MEDICINE LAKE
1
Headquarters
.6
Campground
Picnic Area
Launch Ramp
Ranger Station
To WEED
MEDICINE LAKE
3
Forest Road 97
21
To HWY. 139
& TIONESTA
15
Forest Road 49
BULLSEYE
LAKE
30
MT. SHASTA CITY
Forest Road 15
5
2
Mc CLOUD
10
89
16
BARTLE
89
35
To REDDING
To LAKE McCLOUD
To BURNEY & HWY. 299

INFORMATION: Doublehead Ranger District, P.O. Box 369, Tulelake 96134—Ph: (530) 667-2246

CAMPING	BOATING	RECREATION	OTHER
75 Dev. Sites for Tents & R.V.s Fee: $7 per Vehicle per Night No Hookups No Reservations	Power, Row, Canoe, Sail, Inflatable, Waterski, Jets Launch Ramp - Paved Courtesy Dock Bullseye Lake: No Motors Hand Launch	Fishing: Rainbow & Brook Trout Swimming Picnicking Hiking Horseback Riding Hunting: Deer, Bear, Grouse Accessible Disabled Facilities	Other Facilities: 14 Miles at Lava Beds National Monument & 35 miles at Tulelake Full Facilities: 33 miles at Bartle & 25 miles at Tionesta

LAKE EARL, FISH LAKE, FRESHWATER LAGOON, STONE LAGOON and BIG LAGOON

Big Lagoon and the smaller Stone and Freshwater Lagoons, are three of California's most unusual Lakes. Separated from the Pacific Ocean by a narrow strip of sand, these Lakes offer the angler a unique opportunity to fish for trout in fresh water and a few feet away, cast for surf perch in salt water. Lakes Earl and Talawa are part of the Lake Earl Wildlife Area.

These shallow water Lakes offer a variety of game fish as well as an abundance of waterfowl and animal life. Fish Lake, at an elevation of 1,800 feet, is a popular freshwater fishing spot. No motors are allowed on this small 22-acre Lake. The Forest Service maintains a campground amid fir and huckleberries. There are a variety of trails leading to Red Mountain Lake and on to Blue Lake.

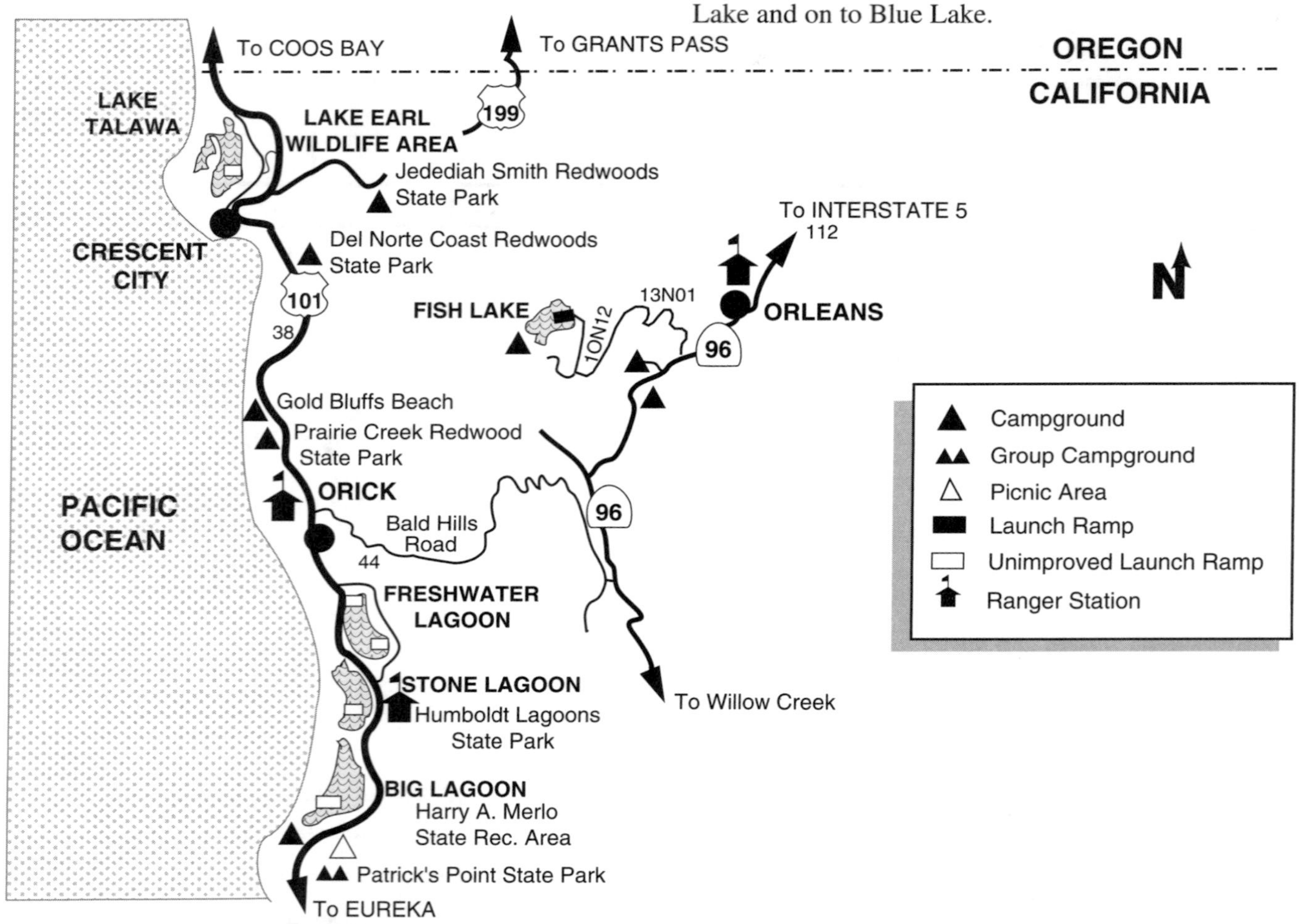

To COOS BAY
To GRANTS PASS
OREGON
CALIFORNIA
LAKE TALAWA
LAKE EARL WILDLIFE AREA
199
Jedediah Smith Redwoods State Park
To INTERSTATE 5
112
CRESCENT CITY
Del Norte Coast Redwoods State Park
101
38
FISH LAKE
10N12
13N01
ORLEANS
96
N
Gold Bluffs Beach
Prairie Creek Redwood State Park
PACIFIC OCEAN
ORICK
Bald Hills Road
44
96
FRESHWATER LAGOON
STONE LAGOON
Humboldt Lagoons State Park
To Willow Creek
BIG LAGOON
Harry A. Merlo State Rec. Area
Patrick's Point State Park
To EUREKA
Campground
Group Campground
Picnic Area
Launch Ramp
Unimproved Launch Ramp
Ranger Station

INFORMATION: Calif. State Parks, North Coast Redwoods, 3431 Fort Ave., Eureka 95501—Ph: (707) 445-6547

CAMPING	BOATING	RECREATION	OTHER
Redwood State Parks: Jedediah Smith Del Norte Coast Prairie Creek Gold Bluffs Beach State Parks: Patrick's Point Fees: $15 - $20 Reserve: Ph: (800) 444-7275	Lake Earl: Fishing Boats Beach Launch Stone Lagoon: Canoes & Fishing Boats Check Speed Limit Big Lagoon: Fishing & Small Sailboats Fish Lake: Non-Power Boats Only Launch Ramp	Fishing: Rainbow, Brown & Cutthroat Trout Stone Lagoon: Special Fishing Regulations Picnicking Swimming at Lagoons Hiking & Nature Trails Tidal Pools Redwood Groves Birdwatching	Fish Lake: Orleans Ranger Station P. O. Drawer 410 Orleans 95556 Ph: (530) 627-3291

LAKE SISKIYOU and CASTLE LAKE

Lake Siskiyou, a man-made Reservoir at an elevation of 3,181 feet, is located in the shadows of Mount Shasta. At the headwaters of the Sacramento River, the Lake has 437 surface acres surrounded by pine trees with 5 shoreline miles. There is a sandy swimming beach, a complete marina and store. The Pacific Crest Trail is located nearby and the fishing is good. Crystal-clear Castle Lake, 5,280 feet elevation, is located south of Lake Siskiyou. This is primarily a fishing Lake but swimming can also be enjoyed. There is a picnic area near Castle Lake and 6 campsites for tents.

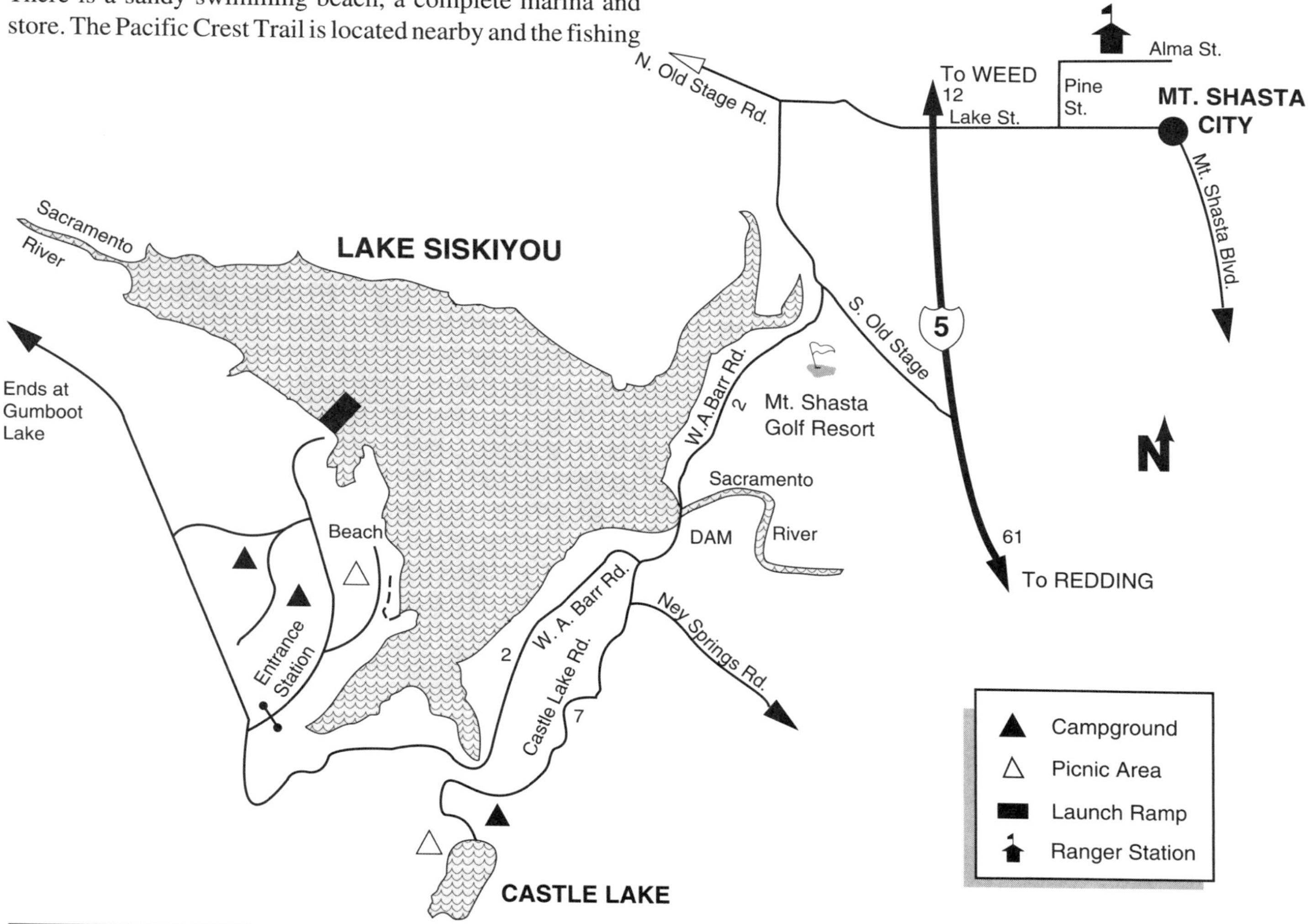
N. Old Stage Rd.
To WEED
12
Lake St.
Pine St.
Alma St.
MT. SHASTA CITY
Mt. Shasta Blvd.
Sacramento River
LAKE SISKIYOU
5
S. Old Stage
W.A.Barr Rd.
2
Mt. Shasta Golf Resort
Ends at Gumboot Lake
Sacramento
DAM
River
61
To REDDING
Beach
Entrance Station
W. A. Barr Rd.
2
Castle Lake Rd.
7
Ney Springs Rd.
CASTLE LAKE
N
Campground
Picnic Area
Launch Ramp
Ranger Station

INFORMATION: Lake Siskiyou, 4239 W.A. Barr Rd., P.O. Box 276, Mt. Shasta 96067—Ph: (530) 926-2618

CAMPING	BOATING	RECREATION	OTHER
363 Dev. Sites for Tents & R.V.s Full Hookups Fee: $20 - $29 Group Campsites Disposal Station Castle Lake: Mount Shasta Ranger District: Ph: (530) 926-4511 6 Tent Sites	Power, Row, Canoe, Windsurfing, Sail & Inflatables 10 MPH Speed Limit Full Service Marina Launch Ramp - Free Rentals: Fishing & Pedal Boats, Canoes, Kayaks & Pontoons Berths, Docks, Moorings, Dry Storage	Fishing: Rainbow, Kamloop, Brown, & Brook Trout & Smallmouth Bass Fishing Dock & Cleaning Station Swimming - Beach Picnicking Hiking & Backpacking Trails Playground Volleyball Court Free Family Movies Video Arcade, Horseshoes	Lakeside Cabins Rental R.V.s Groceries, Deli, Gift Shop Bait & Tackle Propane Community-Sized BBQ 2 Rec. Halls with Large User Kitchens For Further Information: Ph: (888) 926-2618

LAKE MC CLOUD

Lake McCloud is at an elevation of 3,000 feet. The surface area of this 520-acre Lake belongs to P.G. & E., and the surrounding land belongs to the Hearst Corporation. The U.S. Forest Service was deeded a narrow strip of land between the road and high watermark from the boat ramp to Star City Creek. The shoreline is steep and pine trees tower above the rocky terrain. This is a popular Lake for fishing. Forest Service campgrounds are located on the Upper and Lower McCloud River. The Pacific Crest Trail passes through this area. Friday's R.V. Retreat and Fly Fishing Ranch is an ideal place to stay with about 400 acres to explore.

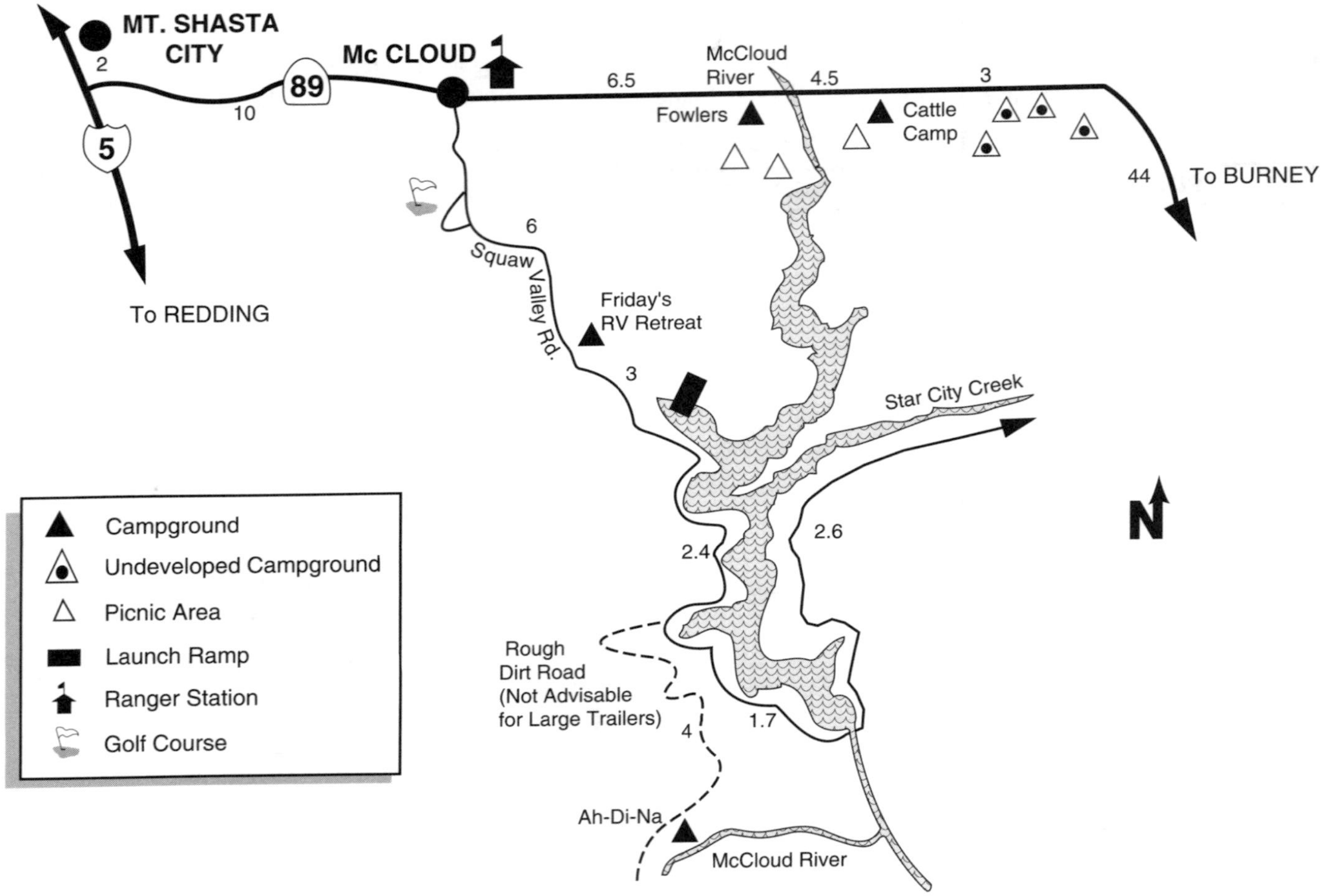
MT. SHASTA CITY
2
10
89
5
To REDDING
Mc CLOUD
6.5
McCloud River
4.5
3
Fowlers
Cattle Camp
44
To BURNEY
6
Squaw Valley Rd.
Friday's RV Retreat
3
Star City Creek
2.6
2.4
N
Rough Dirt Road (Not Advisable for Large Trailers)
4
1.7
Ah-Di-Na
McCloud River
Campground
Undeveloped Campground
Picnic Area
Launch Ramp
Ranger Station
Golf Course

INFORMATION: McCloud Ranger District, P. O. Box 1620, McCloud 96057—Ph: (530) 964-2184

CAMPING	BOATING	RECREATION	OTHER
Ah-Di-Na: 16 Camp Sites - Fee: $8 Trailers Not Recommended Due to Narrow Dirt Road Along Upper McCloud River: Fowlers: 40 Dev. Tent & R.V. Sites to 30 ft. Cattle Camp: 25 Dev. Tent & R.V. Sites to 32 ft. - Fee: $12 Undeveloped Sites	Power, Row, Canoe Launch Ramp	Fishing: Rainbow & Brown Trout Lower McCloud River: Designated Wild Trout Stream, Catch & Release Artificial Flies & Single Barbless Hooks Only Fly Fishing School and Ponds at Friday's RV Retreat Picnicking Hiking Trails Nature Study	Friday's R.V. Retreat P. O. Box 68 McCloud 96057 Ph: (530) 964-2878 30 Sites for Tents & R.V.s Full Hookups Fees: $17 - $25 Cabin Available Open May 1 to Oct. 15 Full Facilities in McCloud

WEST VALLEY RESERVOIR

West Valley Reservoir, with 970 surface acres, is located in the northeastern corner of California, off Highway 395 just east of Likely. Resting at an elevation of 4,770 feet, the 7 miles of shoreline is relatively sparse with only a few clusters of small trees. All types of boating are permitted including boat camping. Waterskiing is popular. Eagle Lake trout are the primary game fish and they are often good sized. There are also catfish and Sacramento perch. Support facilities are limited to a paved ramp and primitive campsite areas. This is a relatively remote Reservoir, but if you are a dedicated angler, give it a try. The Lake is usually frozen over from December to early March.

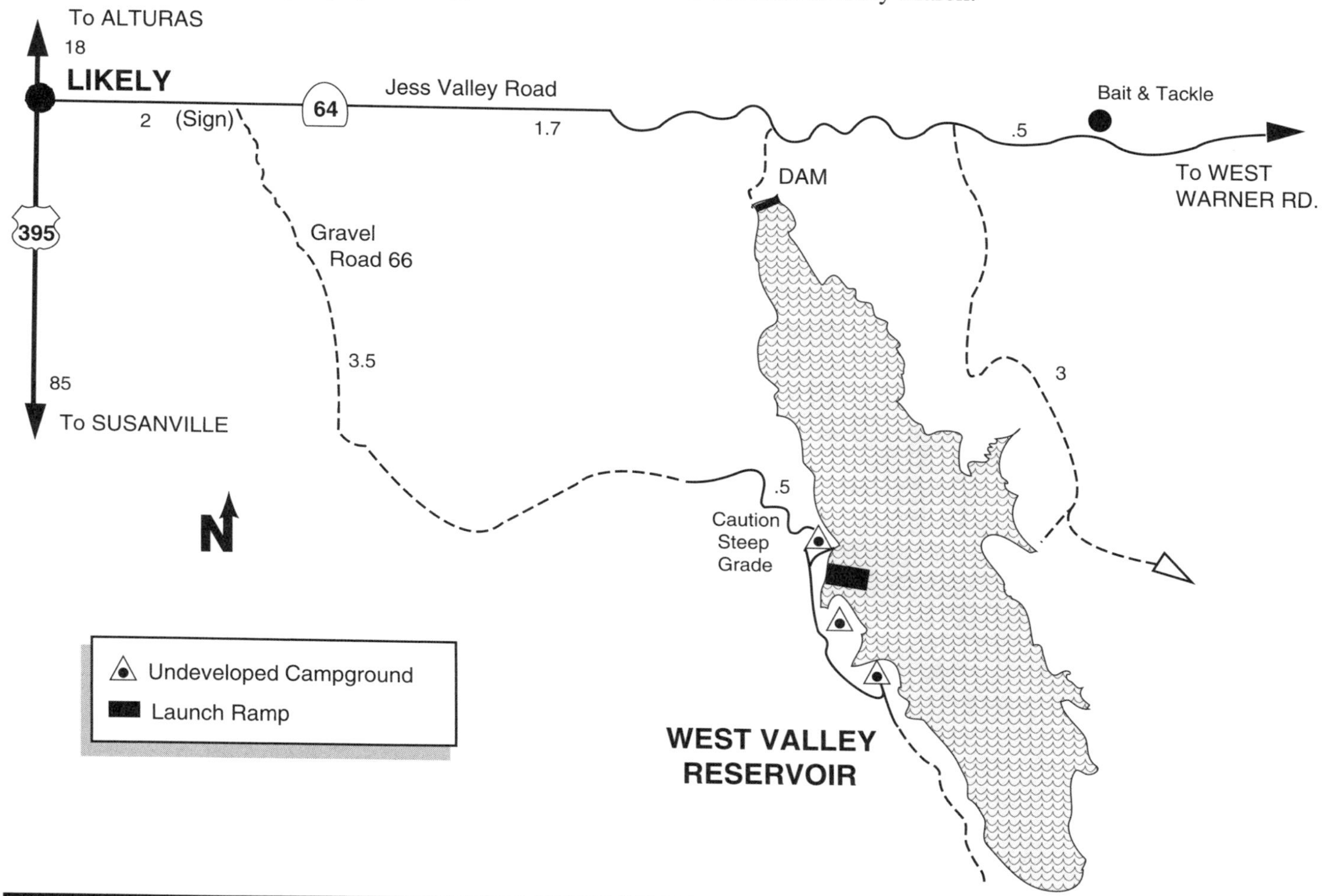

To ALTURAS
18
LIKELY
64
Jess Valley Road
2 (Sign)
1.7
Bait & Tackle
.5
To WEST WARNER RD.
DAM
395
Gravel Road 66
3.5
3
85
To SUSANVILLE
.5
Caution Steep Grade
N
Undeveloped Campground
Launch Ramp
WEST VALLEY RESERVOIR

INFORMATION: Bureau of Land Management Field Office, 708 W. 12th St., Alturas 96101—Ph: (530) 233-4666

CAMPING	BOATING	RECREATION	OTHER
Undeveloped Camping Areas with Fire Rings	Power, Row, Canoe, Sail, Waterski, PWCs, Windsurfing & Inflatable Overnight Camping In Boat Permitted Anywhere *High Winds Can Be Hazardous*	Fishing: Eagle Lake Trout, Catfish, Sacramento Perch Swimming Picnicking Hiking Backpacking [Parking]	Full Facilities - 6 miles at Likely

BLUE LAKE

Blue Lake, located 28 miles southeast of Alturas, is in the Modoc National Forest. This mountain Lake of 160 surface acres is surrounded by huge ponderosa pines, white firs and meadows at an elevation of 6,000 feet. This is a popular facility near the South Warner Wilderness area. Lake fishing is good for rainbow and brown trout. There are no boating facilities other than a paved launch ramp, but most boating is permitted with a 15 mph speed limit. For the hiker, backpacker, horseback rider or energetic fisherman, the South Warner Wilderness has good trails. You can fish from shore at Clear Lake.

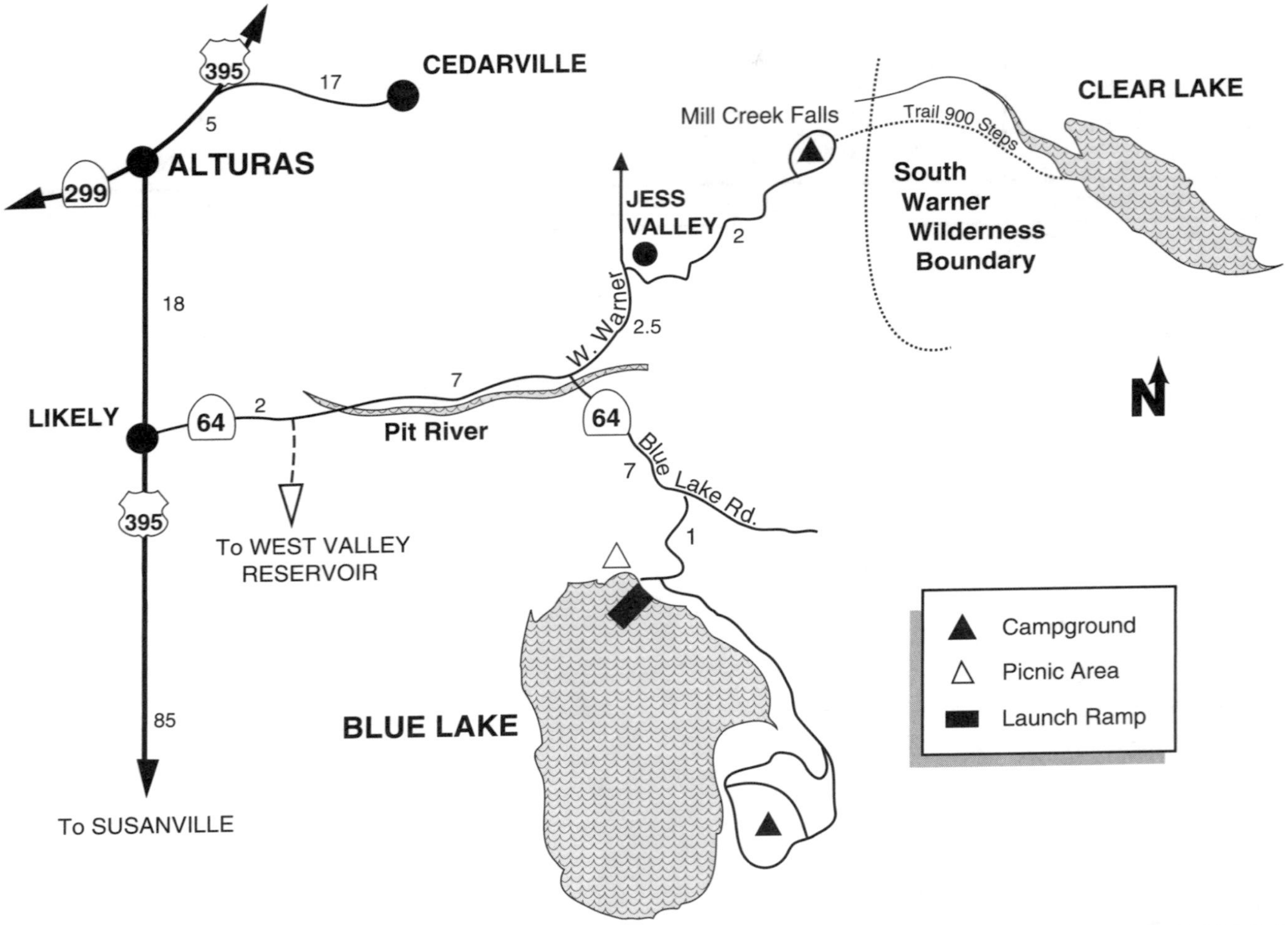

395
17
CEDARVILLE
5
ALTURAS
299
18
LIKELY
64
2
7
Pit River
395
To WEST VALLEY
RESERVOIR
85
To SUSANVILLE
JESS
VALLEY
2
W. Warner
2.5
64
Blue Lake Rd.
7
1
BLUE LAKE
Mill Creek Falls
Trail 900 Steps
CLEAR LAKE
South
Warner
Wilderness
Boundary
N
Campground
Picnic Area
Launch Ramp

INFORMATION: Warner Mountain Ranger District, Box 220, Cedarville 96104—Ph: (530) 279-6116

CAMPING	BOATING	RECREATION	OTHER
Blue Lake Camp: 48 Dev. Sites for Tents & RVs to 32 Ft. Fee: $7 Mill Creek Falls: 19 Dev. Sites for Tents & RVs Fee: $6	Power, Row, Canoe, Sail, & Inflatable 15 MPH Speed Limit *No Waterskiing or PWCs* Paved Launch Ramp	Fishing: Rainbow & Brown Trout Fishing Platform Picnicking Hiking Trails Blue Lake National Recreation Trail 1-1/2 Miles Swimming Bird & Wildlife Watching	Likely: Grocery Store Restaurant Gas Station Full Facilities - 28 miles at Alturas

EASTMAN, TULE, BIG, FALL RIVER, CRYSTAL and BAUM LAKES

The Fall River Valley is an angler's paradise. Nestled between the Sierra and Cascade mountain ranges, these Lakes are fed by Hat Creek, Pit and Fall Rivers. Baum has 89 surface acres and Crystal has 60 acres. Each of these Lakes are connected and support trophy-sized brown trout as well as rainbow and eastern brook. The warm water fisheries of Big, Tule, Eastman and Fall River Lakes are all contiguous. This area also has rainbow trout up to 4 pounds. The streams and rivers offer prime fishing. Hat Creek and Fall River are designated "Wild Trout" Streams which provide trophy-sized trout. Artificial lures must be used and other special rules apply.

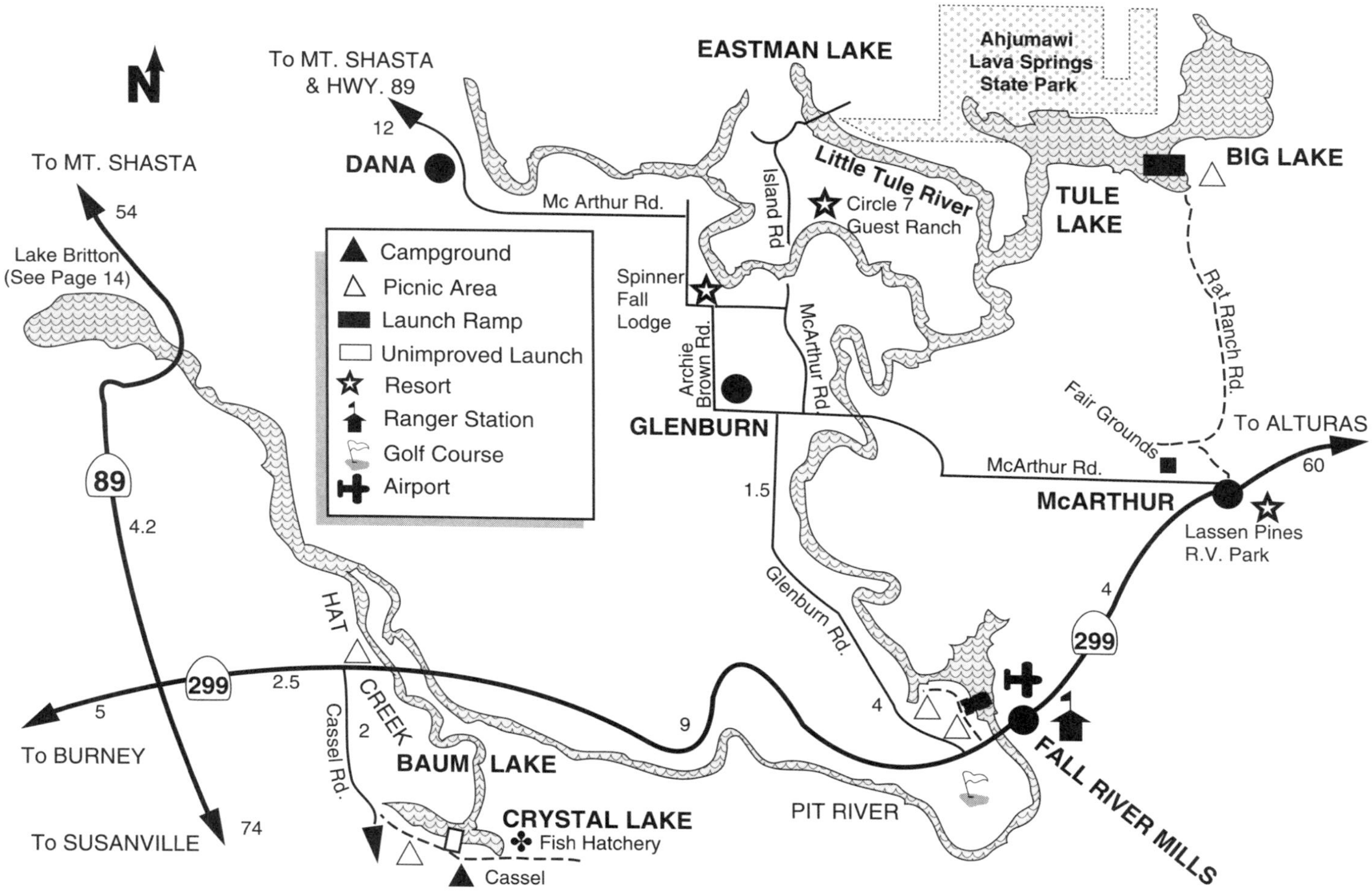

EASTMAN LAKE
Ahjumawi Lava Springs State Park
BIG LAKE
TULE LAKE
To MT. SHASTA & HWY. 89
12
DANA
To MT. SHASTA
54
Lake Britton (See Page 14)
Mc Arthur Rd.
Island Rd
Little Tule River
Circle 7 Guest Ranch
Campground
Picnic Area
Launch Ramp
Unimproved Launch
Resort
Ranger Station
Golf Course
Airport
Spinner Fall Lodge
Archie Brown Rd.
McArthur Rd.
Rat Ranch Rd.
Fair Grounds
To ALTURAS
GLENBURN
McArthur Rd.
60
MCARTHUR
Lassen Pines R.V. Park
89
4.2
1.5
4
Glenburn Rd.
299
HAT CREEK
299
2.5
5
To BURNEY
Cassel Rd.
2
BAUM LAKE
9
4
FALL RIVER MILLS
CRYSTAL LAKE
Fish Hatchery
PIT RIVER
To SUSANVILLE
74
Cassel

INFORMATION: Chamber of Commerce, P.O. Box 475, Fall River Mills, 96028—Ph: (530) 336-5840

CAMPING	BOATING	RECREATION	OTHER
See Lake Britton P.G. & E.: Ph: (916) 386-5164 Cassel - 1 mile South of Baum Lake - 27 Sites Fee: $10 Ahjumawi State Park Ph: (530) 335-2777 Above Big Lake 9 Primitive Sites Boat-in Access Only	Baum & Crystal: No Power Boating Other Lakes: 10 MPH Spinner Fall Lodge: Guest Boat Rentals Guides Available	Fishing: Largemouth Bass, Catfish, Green Sunfish, Brown, Rainbow & Eastern Brook Trout Hiking - Pacific Crest Trail Swimming: Fall River Lake & Big Lake Full Facilities at Fall River Mills	Lassen Pines R.V. Park Ph: (530) 336-5657 R.V. Sites with Full Hookups Spinner Fall Lodge: Ph: (530) 336-5300 Lodging, Bar, Restaurant Circle 7 Guest Ranch Ph: (530) 336-5827 Fully Equipped Cabins Fall River Hotel Ph: (530) 336-5550

IRON CANYON RESERVOIR

Iron Canyon Reservoir, at an elevation of 2,700 feet, is located in the Shasta-Trinity National Forest. This beautiful 500-surface acre Lake has 15 miles of shoreline. Larger boats with a deep draft are not recommended due to shallow Lake levels which vary greatly during the year, depending on weather and P.G. & E. power needs. There are some big trout and the fishing can be good. The Forest Service has a self-service campground providing a quiet atmosphere amid pine and fir trees. P.G. & E., in co-operation with the Forest Service, has a campground and paved launch ramp at Hawkins Landing.

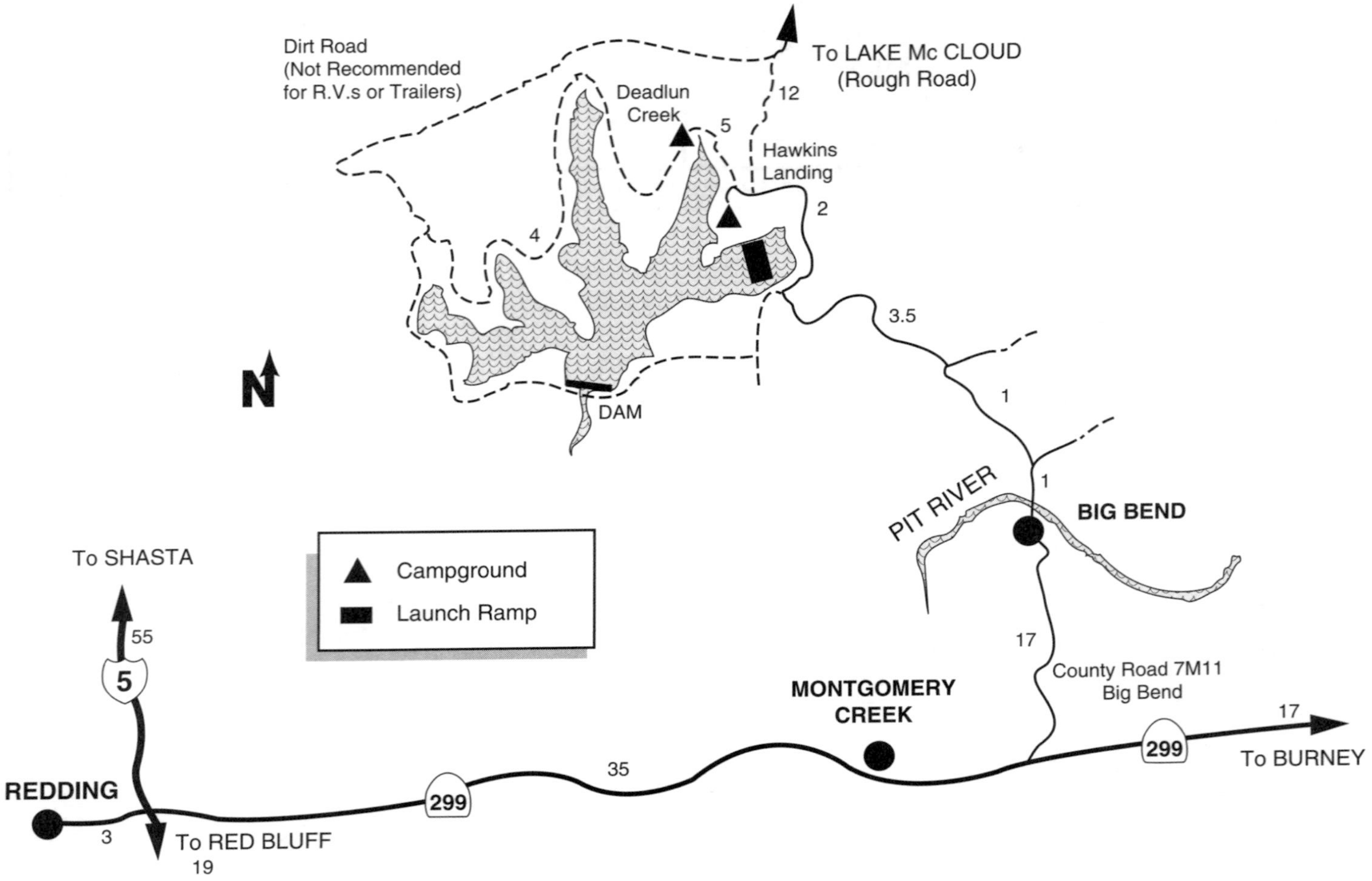

Dirt Road
(Not Recommended
for R.V.s or Trailers)
Deadlun
Creek
5
12
To LAKE Mc CLOUD
(Rough Road)
Hawkins
Landing
2
4
3.5
N
DAM
1
1
PIT RIVER
BIG BEND
To SHASTA
Campground
Launch Ramp
55
5
17
County Road 7M11
Big Bend
MONTGOMERY
CREEK
17
299
To BURNEY
35
REDDING
299
3
To RED BLUFF
19

INFORMATION: Shasta Lake Ranger District, 14225 Holiday Drive, Redding 96003—Ph: (530) 275-1587			
CAMPING	**BOATING**	**RECREATION**	**OTHER**
Deadlun Creek: 30 Dev. Sites for Tents & R.V.s to 24 feet No Fee Plus Undeveloped Camping Areas Campfire Permit Req'd. P.G. & E. Ph: (916) 386-5164 Hawkins Landing: 10 Dev. Sites for Tents/RVs Fee: $15	Power, Row, Canoe, & Inflatables No Waterskiing or PWCs Watch for Shallow Lake Levels Launch Ramp at Hawkins Landing Campground	Fishing: Rainbow, Brook & Brown Trout Swimming Picnicking Hiking Pacific Crest Trail Off Road Driving Trails Bird Watching Hot Springs at Big Bend	At Big Bend: Grocery Store Bait & Tackle Gas Station (Hours of Operation are Limited) Guard Station and Fire Station *Caution: Heavy Logging Truck Traffic at Times*

Lake Britton, located in the Shasta-Trinity National Forest, is at an elevation of 2,760 feet. This 1,600 surface acre Lake has 18 miles of shoreline and is nestled amid evergreen forests on the Pit River. The McArthur-Burney Falls Memorial State Park has over 900 acres stretching from Burney Falls along Burney Creek to the shoreline of Lake Britton. Burney Creek is planted with trout weekly in season. This park, established in 1920, is not only one of the oldest in the State Park System, but one of the best facilities in Northern California. There are also U.S. Forest Service and P.G. & E. campgrounds in the area. This is a good boating Lake although caution should be used as there can be floating debris and fluctuating water levels. Called by Teddy Roosevelt "the eighth wonder of the world," Burney Falls is the popular attraction in this area.

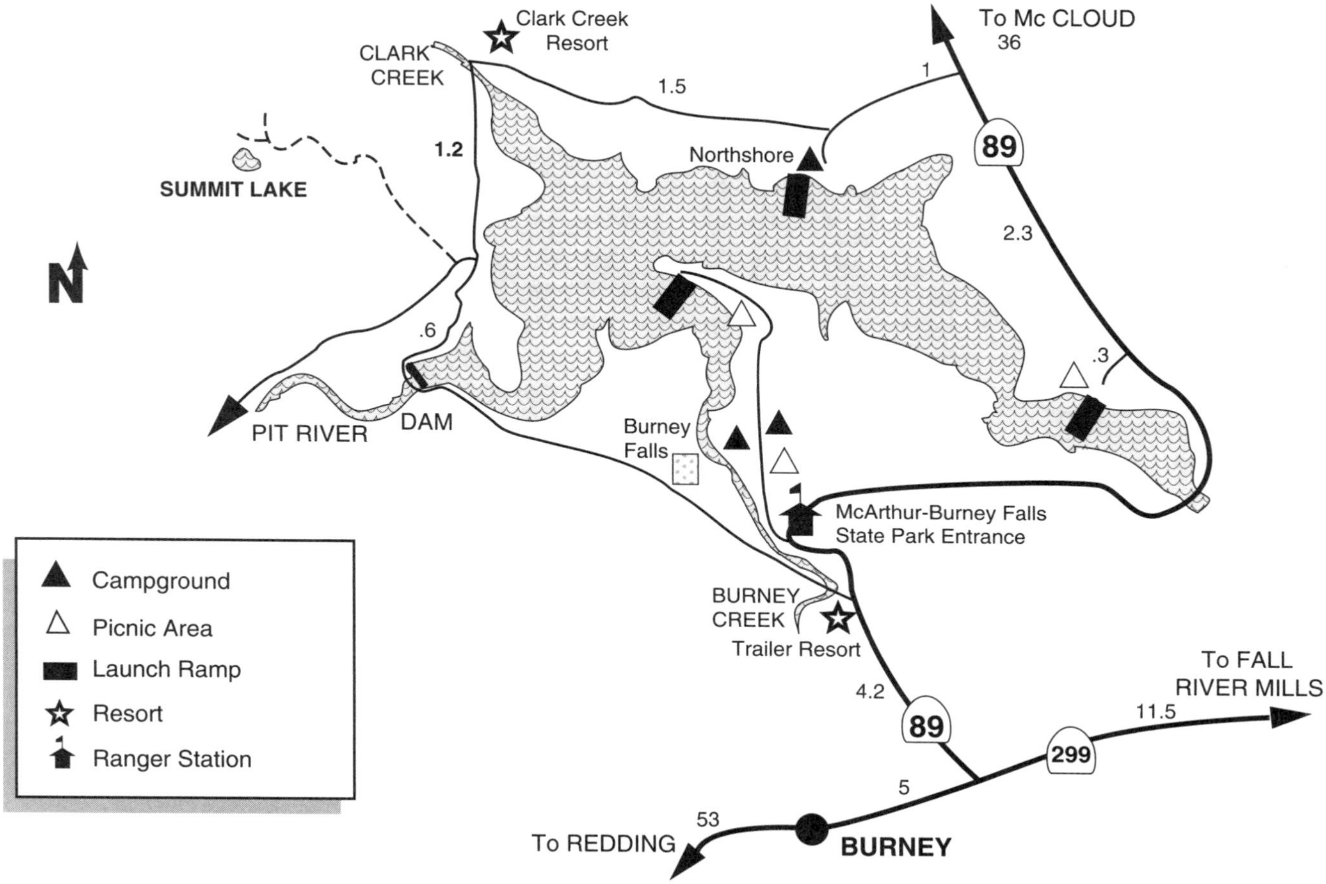
Clark Creek Resort
CLARK CREEK
1.5
To Mc CLOUD 36
1
89
1.2
Northshore
SUMMIT LAKE
2.3
N
.6
.3
PIT RIVER
DAM
Burney Falls
McArthur-Burney Falls State Park Entrance
Campground
Picnic Area
Launch Ramp
Resort
Ranger Station
BURNEY CREEK
Trailer Resort
4.2
89
To FALL RIVER MILLS
11.5
299
5
53
To REDDING
BURNEY

INFORMATION: McArthur-Burney Falls State Park, 24898 Highway 89, Burney 96013—Ph: (530) 335-2777

CAMPING	BOATING	RECREATION	OTHER
State Park Campgrounds: 121 Dev. Sites for Tents/R.V.s to 35 Feet Fee: $15 - $25 Reserve: Ph: (800) 444-7275 P.G.&E.: Ph: (916) 386-5164 Northshore: 30 Dev. Sites for Tents/R.V.s Fee: $15 Plus Group Sites	Power, Row, Canoe, Sail, Waterskiing, PWCs, Windsurf & Inflatables Launch Ramps - Fee Rentals: Fishing Boats, Canoes & Paddle Boats Ph: (530) 335-5713 Moorings Boat Storage	Fishing: Trout, Crappie, Bass Swimming Picnicking Backpacking Nature Trails Pacific Crest Trail Bird Watching Campfire Program	State Park: 24 Rustic 1 & 2 Bedroom Cabins Grocery Store Bait & Tackle Gas Station Clark Creek Resort: Ph: (530) 335-2574 Burney Falls Trailer Resort: Ph: (530) 335-2781 Full Facilities - 11 miles at Burney

TRINITY LAKE

Trinity Lake is at an elevation of 2,370 feet just below the rugged, granite peaks of the Trinity Alps Wilderness. This is one of California's finest recreation spots. A part of the Whiskeytown-Shasta-Trinity National Recreation Area, this 16,400 surface acre Lake offers prime outdoor opportunities. Houseboaters find the 145 miles of pine, cedar and oak-covered shoreline ideal for "getting away from it all." There are hundreds of quiet coves for the angler to tie up and catch a meal or better yet, catch a world-record smallmouth bass. Water levels may fluctuate in the late season which can create hazards but boaters will always find an expansive body of water for sailing or waterskiing.

...Continued...

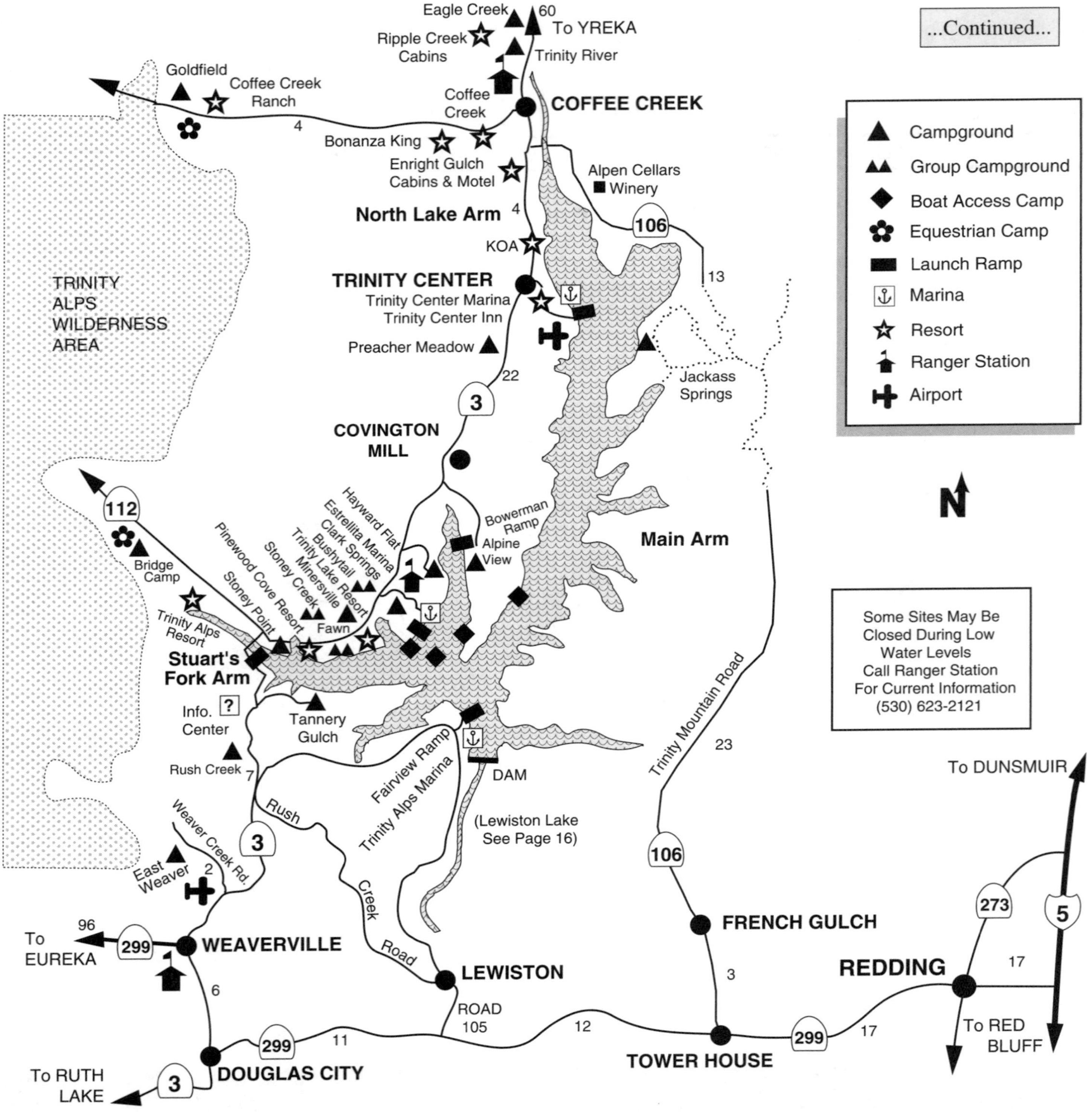
Eagle Creek
60
To YREKA
Ripple Creek Cabins
Trinity River
Goldfield
Coffee Creek Ranch
Coffee Creek
COFFEE CREEK
4
Bonanza King
Enright Gulch Cabins & Motel
Alpen Cellars Winery
North Lake Arm
4
106
KOA
13
TRINITY CENTER
Trinity Center Marina
Trinity Center Inn
TRINITY ALPS WILDERNESS AREA
Preacher Meadow
22
Jackass Springs
3
COVINGTON MILL
N
Main Arm
112
Hayward Flat
Estrellita Marina
Clark Springs
Bushytail
Trinity Lake Resort
Minersville
Stoney Creek
Pinewood Cove Resort
Stoney Point
Fawn
Bowerman Ramp
Alpine View
Bridge Camp
Trinity Alps Resort
Stuart's Fork Arm
Info. Center
Tannery Gulch
Rush Creek
7
Fairview Ramp
Trinity Alps Marina
DAM
(Lewiston Lake See Page 16)
Trinity Mountain Road
23
Rush
Weaver Creek Rd.
East Weaver
2
Creek
Road
106
96
To EUREKA
299
WEAVERVILLE
LEWISTON
FRENCH GULCH
REDDING
273
5
17
To DUNSMUIR
6
3
ROAD 105
12
11
299
17
To RED BLUFF
TOWER HOUSE
To RUTH LAKE
3
DOUGLAS CITY
Campground
Group Campground
Boat Access Camp
Equestrian Camp
Launch Ramp
Marina
Resort
Ranger Station
Airport
Some Sites May Be Closed During Low Water Levels
Call Ranger Station
For Current Information
(530) 623-2121

U.S.F.S. CAMPGROUNDS

Fees Subject to Change

STUART FORK ARM and South Area:

HAYWARD FLAT - 98 Sites, R.V.s to 40 ft., Beach, Fee: $17 - Single Family Sites, $23-Multiple, $5 Extra Vehicle
TANNERY GULCH - 82 Sites, R.V.s to 40 ft., Launch Ramp for Campers Only, Beach, Amphitheater, Fee: $17 - Single Family Sites, $23 - Multiple Family Sites, $5 Extra Vehicle
The Two Above Campgrounds: Reservations Ph: (877) 444-6777
CLARK SPRINGS - 21 Sites, R.V.s to 25 ft., Fee: $12 (Next to Clark Springs Day Area)
MINERSVILLE - 14 Sites, R.V.s to 36 ft., Fee: $13 to $24
STONEY POINT - 21 Walk-In Sites, Tents Only, Fee: $13
RUSH CREEK - 10 Sites, R.V.s to 20 ft., No Water, Fee: $7
EAST WEAVER - 11 Sites, R.V.s to 25 ft., Fee: $11
BRIDGE CAMP - 10 Sites, R.V.s to 20 ft., Fee: $12

MAIN ARM:

JACKASS SPRINGS - 21 Sites, R.V.s to 32 ft., Dirt Access and Interior Road, No Water, No Fee
PREACHER MEADOW - 45 Sites, R.V.s to 40 ft., Fee: $12
ALPINE VIEW - 53 Sites, R.V.s to 32 ft., Fee: $17 to $23, $5 Extra Vehicle, Wheel Chair Access

NORTH SHORE:

TRINITY RIVER - 7 Sites, R.V.s to 35 ft., Fee: $10
EAGLE CREEK - 17 Sites, R.V.s to 27 ft., Fee: $10

BOAT ACCESS ONLY SITES: Vault Toilets, No Water, No Fee
CAPTAIN'S POINT - 3 Boat-In Sites
RIDGEVILLE - 21 Boat-In Sites
RIDGEVILLE ISLAND - 3 Boat-In Sites
MARINER'S ROOST - 7 Boat-In Sites

GROUP CAMPGROUNDS - **Reserve: Ph: (877) 444-6777**
BUSHYTAIL - 11 Sites, R.V.s to 40 ft., Electric Hookups - Fee: $80, Wheel Chair Access
FAWN - Tent/R.V. Sites to 37 ft. - 3 Loops, 60 - 500 People, Fee: $100 Per Loop, Wheel Chair Access
STONEY CREEK - Tent Sites - 10 Units **-** 50 People Maximum, Fee: $75

(Additional Primitive Campsites around Trinity Lake)

...Continued....

INFORMATION: Weaverville Ranger Station, Box 1190, Weaverville 96093—Ph: (530) 623-2121

CAMPING	BOATING	RECREATION	OTHER
U.S.F.S. Dev. Tent/RV Sites Boat-In Sites 3 Group Campgrounds See Following Pages for Private Facilities	Open to All Boating Full Service Marinas Public Launch Ramps Launch Fees Rentals: Houseboats, Fishing, Pontoon & Ski Boats Annual General Passes: for Day Use Areas and All Boat Ramps	Fishing: Large & Smallmouth Bass, Bluegill, Catfish, Kokanee, Brown & Rainbow Trout Swim Beaches Picnic Areas Hiking & Equestrian Trails Backpacking	Complete Destination Facilities at Some Resorts and at Trinity Center Airports - Trinity Center, Weaverville

TRINITY LAKE............Continued

PRIVATELY OPERATED MARINAS & RESORTS

(Prices Vary - Call for Current Information)

TRINITY LAKE RESORTS & MARINAS - 45810 State Hwy. 3, Trinity Center 96091- (530) 286-2225 or (800) 255-5561- Restaurant & Lounge, Cabins, Full Service Marina, Launch Ramp, Fuel Dock, Propane, Mooring, Dry Storage, Rentals: Houseboats, Fishing, Waterski & Pontoon Boats, PWCs, Grocery Store.

TRINITY ALPS MARINA - P. O. Box 760, Lewiston 96052 - (530) 286-2282 - Launch Ramp, Mooring, Fuel Dock, Rentals: Houseboats, Fishing, Waterski & Patio Boats, Grocery Store.

ESTRELLITA MARINA - 49160 State Hwy. 3, Trinity Center 96091 - (530) 286-2215 or (800) 747-2215 - Launch Ramp, Rentals: Houseboats, Fishing, Waterski & Patio Boats, PWCs, Grocery Store, Fuel Dock, Propane, Moorings, Dry Storage.

RIPPLE CREEK CABINS - Box 4020, Star Rte. 2, Trinity Center 96091 - (530) 266-3505 - Housekeeping Cabins for 2 to 6 People, Secluded Area, Decks, Wood Stoves, Swimming, Hiking, Pets Welcome, Open Year Around.

COFFEE CREEK GUEST RANCH - 4940 Coffee Creek Rd., Trinity Center 96091 - (530) 266-3343 or (800) 624-4480 - Dude Ranch on Coffee Creek in the Trinity Alps, 16 Secluded Cabins, Pool/Spa, Horseback Riding, Hayrides, Wilderness Pack Trips, Stocked Fishing Pond, Gold Panning, Hiking, Summer Youth Programs, Square/Line Dancing, Conference Room, Handicap Accessible, Open Year Around.

BONANZA KING RESORT - 475 Coffee Creek Rd., Trinity Center 96091 - (530) 266-3305 - 7 Housekeeping Cabins for 2 to 8 People, Pets Welcome, Stalls for Your Horse, Open Year Around.

COFFEE CREEK CAMPGROUND & R.V. PARK, 4600 Sewall Rd., Coffee Creek 96091 - Ph: (530) 266-3534 - R.V. & Tent Sites, Electric & Water Hookups, Disposal Station, plus 1 Cabin, Pets Welcome.

ENRIGHT GULCH CABINS and MOTEL - 3500 Highway 3, Box 244, Trinity Center 96091 - (530) 266-3600 or (888)) 383-5583 - Housekeeping Cabins and Motel Units, Quiet Private Road Surrounded by National Forest, Hiking Trails, Grocery Stores, Restaurants and Marina Nearby.

TRINITY LAKE KOA RESORT - Box 70, Trinity Center 96091 - (530) 266-3337 - 136 R.V. Sites To 60 ft., Full Hookups, 80 Tent Sites, Cabins, Grocery Store, Gas, Propane, Snack Bar, Rental Boats, Private Dock, Slips, Swimming Pool.

PINEWOOD COVE RESORT - 45110 State Highway 3, Trinity Center 96091 - (530) 286-2201 or (800) 988-LAKE (5253) 84 Tent/R.V. Sites, 43 Full Hookups, Disposal Station, Grocery Store, Ramp, Dock, Slips, Propane, Game Room, Recreation Hall, Cabin Rental, Swimming Pool, Recreational Activities.

TRINITY ALPS RESORT - 1750 Trinity Alps Rd., Trinity Center 96091 - (530) 286-2205 - Rustic Housekeeping Cabins, Bar, Restaurant, General Store, Snack Bar, Hiking Trails, Volleyball, Basketball, Horseshoes, Bingo, Bonfires, Movies and Talent Shows, Tennis Court, River Swim Beach, Square Dancing, Open Year Around.

This is only a partial list of the private facilities around Trinity Lake. For further information contact:

TRINITY COUNTY CHAMBER OF COMMERCE
215 SOUTH MAIN ST.
P.O. BOX 517
WEAVERVILLE, CA 96093
(530) 623-6101 OR (800) 487-4648

LEWISTON LAKE

Lewiston Lake is at an elevation of 1,902 feet in the Shasta-Trinity National Forest. This scenic Lake is 5 miles long and has a surface area of 610 acres with 15 miles of shoreline. It is open to all boating but subject to a 10 mph speed limit. The very cold, constantly moving water flows into Lewiston Lake from the bottom waters of Trinity Lake providing an ideal habitat for large trout. Just below Lewiston Dam, the Trinity River, Rush Creek and other streams offer prize salmon and steelhead as well as trout. Lewiston Fish Hatchery is one of the world's most automated salmon and steelhead hatchery.

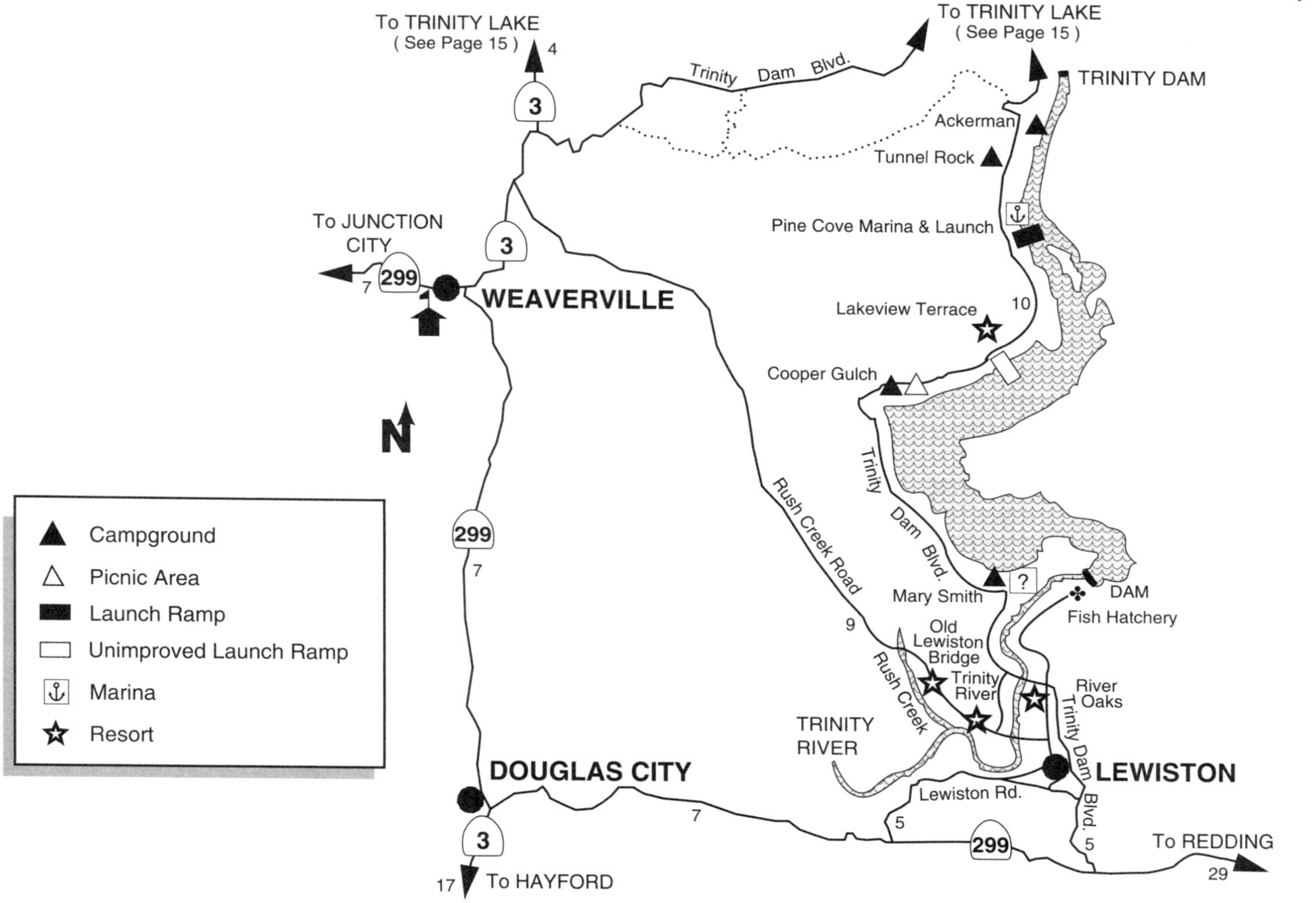
To TRINITY LAKE
(See Page 15)
4
3
Trinity Dam Blvd.
To TRINITY LAKE
(See Page 15)
TRINITY DAM
Ackerman
Tunnel Rock
To JUNCTION CITY
299
7
3
WEAVERVILLE
Pine Cove Marina & Launch
Lakeview Terrace
10
Cooper Gulch
Trinity Dam Blvd.
Rush Creek Road
299
7
Mary Smith
?
DAM
Fish Hatchery
9
Old Lewiston Bridge
Trinity River
River Oaks
Rush Creek
TRINITY RIVER
Trinity Dam Blvd.
DOUGLAS CITY
LEWISTON
Lewiston Rd.
7
5
3
299
5
To REDDING
29
17
To HAYFORD
Campground
Picnic Area
Launch Ramp
Unimproved Launch Ramp
Marina
Resort

INFORMATION: Weaverville Ranger Station, Box 1190, Weaverville 96093—Ph: (530) 623-2121

CAMPING	BOATING	RECREATION	OTHER
Ackerman: 66 Dev. Sites R.V.s to 40 ft. Disposal Station Fee: $13 Tunnel Rock: 6 Sites - R.V.s to 15 ft. No Water Fee: $7 Cooper Gulch: 5 Dev. Sites R.V.s to 16 ft. - Fee: $13 Mary Smith: 18 Sites Tents Only - Fee: $11 Additional Campsites at Private Resorts	Power, Row, Canoe, Sail & Inflatable Speed Limit - 10 MPH Full Service Marina Launch Ramps Rentals: Fishing Boats Docks, Gas Dry Storage	Fishing: Rainbow, Brook & Brown Trout, Kokanee Salmon Picnicking 5 Wildlife Viewing Areas	R.V. Resorts: Lakeview Terrace Ph: (530) 778-3803 Old Lewiston Bridge Ph: (530) 778-3894 Trinity River Resort Ph: (530) 778-3791 River Oaks Resort Ph: (530) 778-0220 Trinity County Chamber of Commerce Ph: (530) 623-6101 or (800) 487-4648

WHISKEYTOWN LAKE and KESWICK RESERVOIR

Whiskeytown Lake, at an elevation of 1,209 feet, has 36 miles of coniferous shoreline and is one of California's most diverse fisheries. Tree-shaded islands, numerous coves and 3,250 surface acres of clear blue water invite the watersport enthusiast. The boater will find complete marina facilities and over 5 square miles of open water. Houseboats or overnight boat camping are not allowed. The water is reasonably warm and there are some nice swimming beaches. Fishing is good from boat or shore for trout, kokanee salmon, bass and pan fish. The National Park Service maintains the facilities which include picnic areas and campgrounds. Approximately 50 miles of dirt roads and 40,000 acres of backcountry are open for visitor use. Keswick Reservoir, at an elevation of 587 feet, has a surface area of 630 acres. Fed by cold water released from Shasta Dam, Keswick provides the angler with large rainbow trout. Shore fishing at Keswick is difficult in some areas because of steep banks and heavy brush but access is good on the west side of the Reservoir.

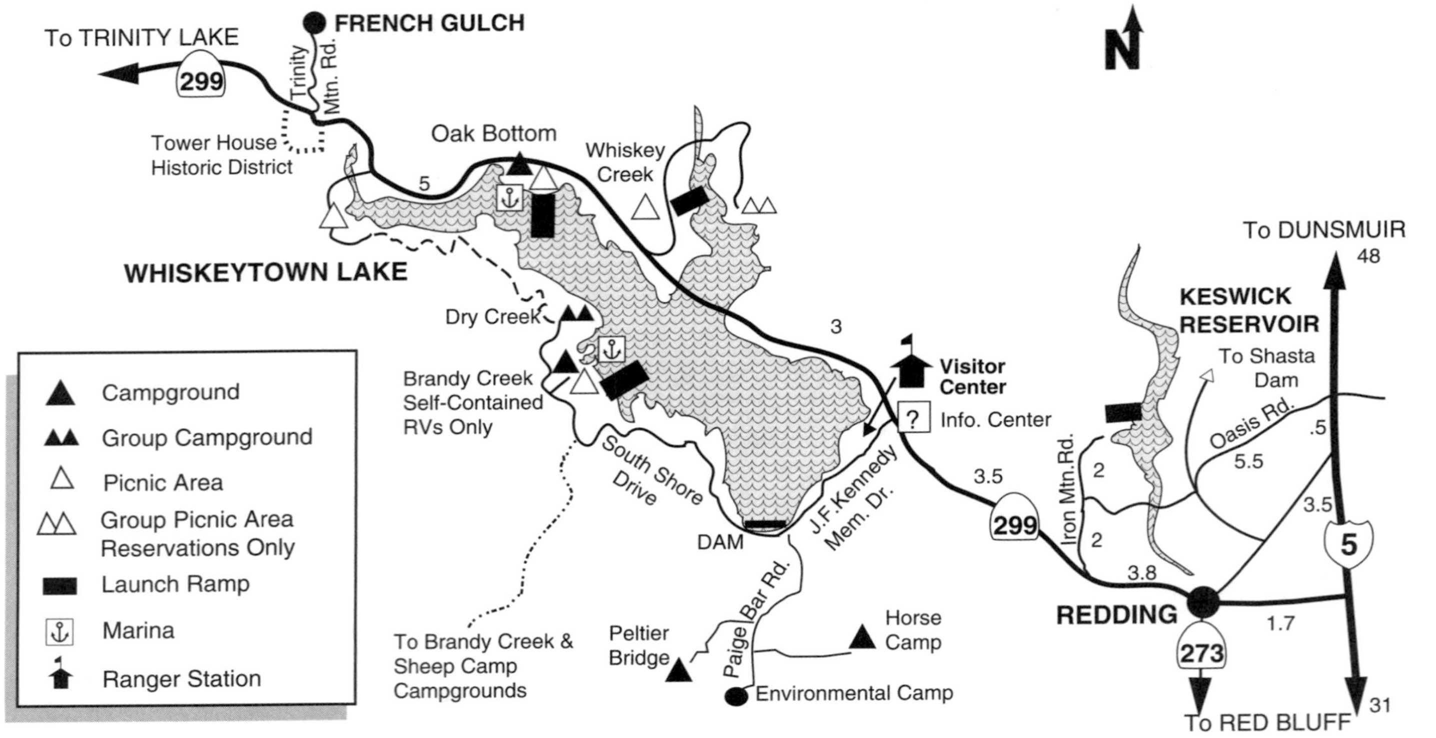
To TRINITY LAKE
299
FRENCH GULCH
Trinity Mtn. Rd.
N
Tower House Historic District
Oak Bottom
Whiskey Creek
5
WHISKEYTOWN LAKE
Dry Creek
3
Brandy Creek Self-Contained RVs Only
Visitor Center
Info. Center
South Shore Drive
J.F. Kennedy Mem. Dr.
DAM
3.5
299
Iron Mtn. Rd.
2
2
3.8
REDDING
273
1.7
To RED BLUFF
31
To DUNSMUIR
48
KESWICK RESERVOIR
To Shasta Dam
Oasis Rd.
.5
5.5
3.5
5
Paige Bar Rd.
Peltier Bridge
Horse Camp
Environmental Camp
To Brandy Creek & Sheep Camp Campgrounds
Campground
Group Campground
Picnic Area
Group Picnic Area Reservations Only
Launch Ramp
Marina
Ranger Station

INFORMATION: Whiskeytown National Rec. Area, P.O. Box 188, Whiskeytown 96095—Ph: (530) 246-1225

CAMPING	BOATING	RECREATION	OTHER
National Park - Oak Bottom: 100 Dev. Walk-in Tent Sites & 22 R.V. Sites to 36 ft. Fees: $10 - $18 Disposal Station Reserve: Ph: (530) 359-2269 Brandy Creek: 37 Self-Cont. R.V. Sites Fees: $7 - $14 Disposal Station Dry Creek: Group Camp to 100 People - Reserve: Ph: (877) 444-6777	Whiskeytown : Open to All Boats Except PWCs Full Service Marina Launch Ramps Rentals: Fishing, Ski, Sail, Canoe & Pontoon Boats Sailing Regattas Kayak Tours Keswick: Open to All Boats Launch Ramp	Fishing: Kokanee & Chinook Salmon, Brook & Rainbow Trout, Spotted, Small & Large- Mouth Bass, Bluegill, Crappie & Catfish Swimming Scuba Diving Picnicking - Groups Reserve (877) 444-6777 Hiking & Equestrian Trails Ranger Guided Tours Junior Ranger Programs	Whiskeytown NRA Day Use: $5 per Vehicle, $10/Week, $25/Year Campground Programs Gold Panning Camper Store Snack Bar Bait & Tackle Keswick Reservoir: Bureau of Reclamation 16349 Shasta Dam Blvd. Shasta Lake 96019 Ph: (530) 275-1554

SHASTA LAKE

Shasta Lake is one of California's prime recreation spots. It is located at the northern tip of the Sacramento Valley just off Interstate 5 at an elevation of 1,067 feet. The four main arms of this huge 30,000 surface-acre Lake converge at the junction of the Cascade and Klamath Mountain Ranges and are fed by the Sacramento, McCloud and Pit Rivers and Squaw Creek. When at full water capacity, there are 370 miles of wooded and sometimes steep, red-rock shoreline. Shasta is California's largest man-made Lake and one of the most popular. With quiet sheltered coves ideal for houseboating and wide-open areas to enjoy water sports, Shasta is a great vacation destination. In addition to the many private marinas, there are 6 conveniently located public launch ramps. The angler will find over 16 species of fish from several varieties of bass to trout or sturgeon. Shasta is operated under the jurisdiction of the U. S. Forest Service which provides many developed and boat-in campsites. In addition, shoreline camping is permitted. *As with all Lakes, call regarding possible low water levels.*

....Continued....

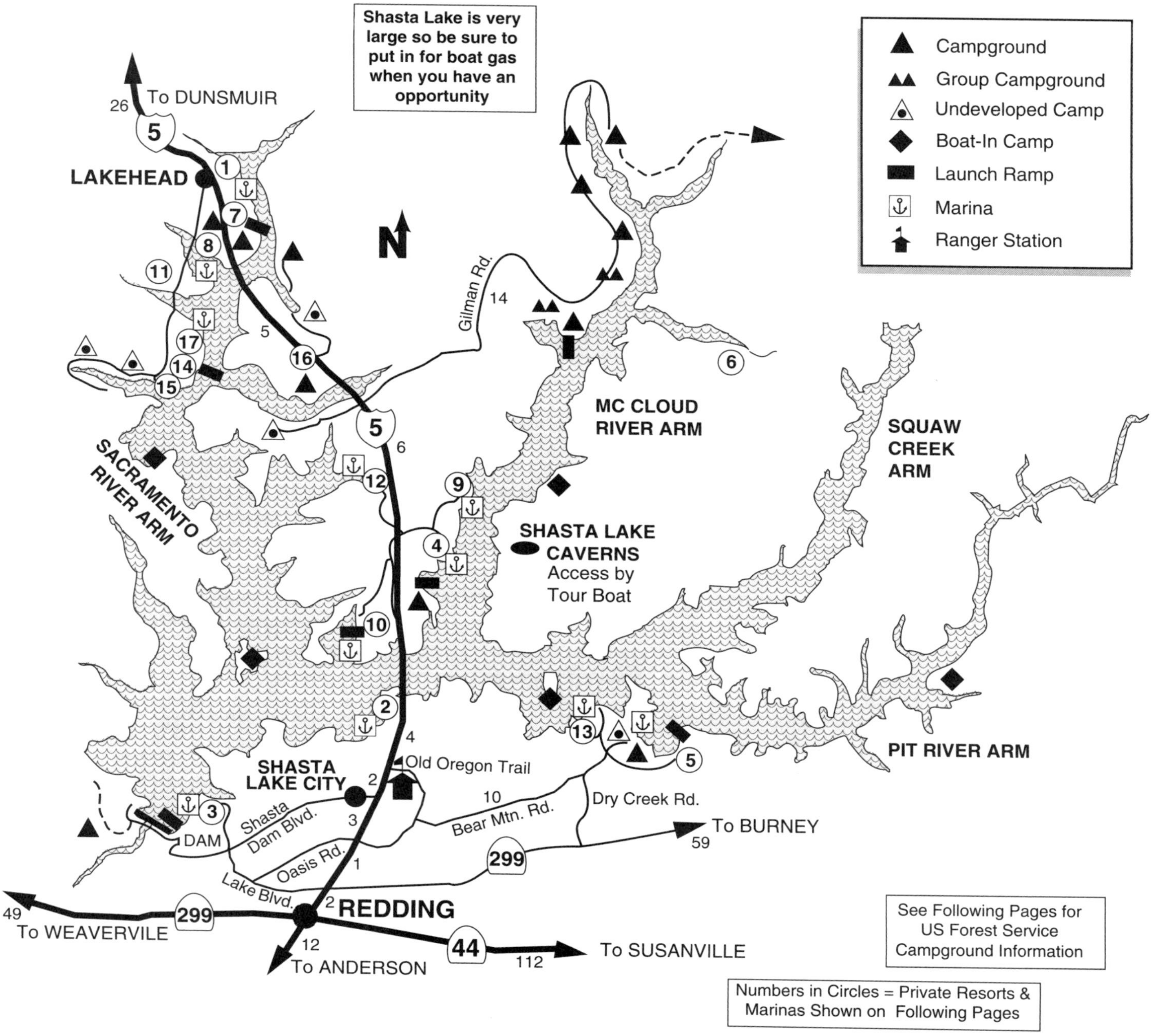

Shasta Lake is very large so be sure to put in for boat gas when you have an opportunity
Campground
Group Campground
Undeveloped Camp
Boat-In Camp
Launch Ramp
Marina
Ranger Station
To DUNSMUIR
LAKEHEAD
N
Gilman Rd.
MC CLOUD RIVER ARM
SQUAW CREEK ARM
SACRAMENTO RIVER ARM
SHASTA LAKE CAVERNS
Access by Tour Boat
PIT RIVER ARM
Old Oregon Trail
SHASTA LAKE CITY
Shasta Dam Blvd.
DAM
Oasis Rd.
Lake Blvd.
Bear Mtn. Rd.
Dry Creek Rd.
To BURNEY
REDDING
To WEAVERVILE
To ANDERSON
To SUSANVILLE
See Following Pages for US Forest Service Campground Information
Numbers in Circles = Private Resorts & Marinas Shown on Following Pages

SHASTA LAKE..............Continued

U.S.F.S. CAMPGROUNDS
Shasta Lake Ranger Station
14225 Holiday Rd., Redding 96003
Ph: (530) 275-1587

***Reservations at Many Sites:* Ph: (877) 444-6777**
Fees are Charged at all Campgrounds and Boat Ramps
FEES VARY WITH SEASON

Check Lake Level - Some Sites May Be Closed Because Of Low Water
There are no hookups or showers at Forest Service Campgrounds on Shasta Lake

PIT RIVER ARM:

From Interstate 5:
11 Miles NE - **Lower Jones Valley** - Tent/R.V. Sites to 30 feet, 10 Single, 3 Double - Fee: $18 - $30
Boat Access, Launch Ramp
Upper Jones Valley - 8 Tent/R.V. Sites to 16 feet - Fee: $14

McCLOUD ARM:

At O'Brien:
1 Mile E - **Bailey Cove** - Tent/R.V. Sites to 30 feet, 4 Single & 3 Double - Fee $18 - $30, Launch Ramp
At Gilman Rd.:
9 Miles E - **Hirz Bay** - Tent/R.V. Sites to 40 feet, 37 Single & 11 Double - Fee: $18 - $30, Launch Ramp
9 Miles E - **Hirz Bay Group Camp** - R.V. Sites to 30 feet
Camp #1 - Max. Capacity - 120 People - Fee: $110
Camp #2 - Max. Capacity - 80 People - Fee: $80
Reservations Required
10 Miles E - **Dekkas Rock Group Camp** - R.V. Sites to 30 feet - Max. Capacity 60 People - Fee: $110
Reservations Required
11 Miles E - **Moore Creek** - 12 Tent/R.V. Sites to 30 feet - Fee: $14 - Available as Group Campground
15 Miles E - **Ellery Creek** - 19 Tent/R.V. Sites to 30 feet - Fee: $14
16 Miles E - **Pine Point** - 14 Tent/R.V. Sites to 30 feet - Fee: $14 - Available as Group Campground
17 Miles E - **McCloud Bridge** - Tent/R.V. Sites to 35 feet, 11 Single, 3 Double - Fee: $18 - $30

....Continued....

INFORMATION: Shasta Lake Visitor Information Center, Mountain Gate/Wonderland Exit—Ph: (530) 275-1589

CAMPING	BOATING	RECREATION	OTHER
Dev. Sites for Tents & R.V.s Walk-In Sites Boat-In Sites Group Camp Sites *See Following Pages*	Power, Row, Canoe, Sail, Waterski, PWCs, Windsurf & Inflatable Full Service Marinas Launch Ramps Rentals: Houseboats, Fishing & Ski Boats Docks, Berths, Gas, Moorings, Storage Overnight in Boat Permitted Anywhere	Fishing: Trout, Bass, Catfish, Bluegill, Perch, Crappie & Kokanee Salmon Swimming - Lake & Pools Picnicking Hiking Trails Shasta Caverns Tour Cave Exploration	R.V. Resorts, Motels & Cabins *See Following Pages* Snack Bars Restaurants Grocery Stores Bait & Tackle Gas Stations Disposal Stations

U.S.F.S. CAMPGROUNDS: SACRAMENTO RIVER ARM

At Salt Creek:

1/2 Mile W - Nelson Point - 9 Primitive Tent/R.V. Sites to 40 feet - Fee: $9 - Available as Group Camp
3 Miles NE - Gregory Creek - 18 Tent/R.V. Sites to 30 feet - Fee: $14
Gregory Beach - Primitive Shoreline Camp Sites for Tent/R.V.s to 40 feet - Fee: $8
Lower Salt Creek - Primitive Shoreline Camp Sites - Fee: $9

At Lakehead:

1.7 Miles S - Antlers - Tent/R.V. Sites to 40 feet, 41 Single & 18 Double - Fee: $18 - $30
Launch Ramp, Adjacent to Resort with Full Facilities
2.5 Miles S - Lakeshore - Tent/R.V. Sites to 35 feet, 20 Single & 6 Double - Fee: $18 - $30
Adjacent to Resort with Full Facilities
4.6 Miles S - Beehive - Primitive Shoreline Camp Sites for Tent/R.V.s to 40 feet - Fee: $8

PUBLIC LAUNCH RAMPS are located at Antlers, Sugarloaf, Centimudi, Hirz Bay, Bailey Cove, Packers Bay & Jones Valley

BOAT ACCESS ONLY CAMPING

Pit River Arm: Arbuckle Flat - 11 Sites, Ski Island - 23 Sites, No Water
McCloud River Arm: Green Creek - 9 Sites
Sacramento River Arm: Gooseneck Cove - 8 Sites
Boat Launch Area Fee: $8

DISPERSED CAMPING:

Jones Valley Inlet, Mariner's Point, Gregory Beach, Beehive - $8 Parking Fee per Night per Vehicle
Contact Shasta Recreation Company for Further Information - Ph: (530) 275-8113

SOME FACILITIES: See Map for Numbered Locations - (in Circles)
(Prices Vary - Call for Current Information)

1 **ANTLER'S RV PARK N CAMPGROUND - P.O. Box 127, Lakehead 96051, Ph: (530) 238-2322 or (800) 642-6849**
Campsites, Hookups, Showers, Laundry, Store, Snack Bar, Bait & Tackle, Swimming Pool.

1 **ANTLER RESORT & MARINA - P.O. Box 140, Lakehead 96051, Ph: (530) 238-2553 or (800) 238-3924**
Full Service Marina, Bait & Tackle, Fuel, Moorage, Ice, Conference Room for Rent, Cabins, Swimming Pool for Cabin Guests, Rentals: Houseboats, Fishing, Ski & Patio Boats, PWCs & Canoes.

2 **BRIDGE BAY RESORT - 10300 Bridge Bay Road, Redding 96003, Ph: (530) 275-3021 or (800) 752-9669**
Full Service Marina, Ramp, Rentals: Houseboats, Fishing, Ski & Patio Boats, Motel, Restaurant, Lounge, General Store, Bait & Tackle, Swimming Pool.

3 **DIGGER BAY MARINA - P.O. Box 1516, Shasta Lake 96019, Ph: (530) 275-3072 or (800) 752-9669**
Full Service Marina, Ramp, Rentals: Houseboats, Fishing, Ski & Patio Boats, General Store, Bait & Tackle, Gas.

4 **HOLIDAY HARBOR RESORT - 20061 Shasta Caverns Rd., O'Brien 96070, Ph: (530) 238-2383 or (800) 776-2628**
Full Service Marina, Ramp, Restaurant, R.V. Hookups, Store, Gas, Rentals: Houseboats, Ski, Patio Boats, PWCs.

5 **JONES VALLEY RESORT - 22300 Jones Valley Marina Dr., Redding 96003, Ph: (800) 223-7950 -** Full Service Marina, General Store, Bait & Tackle, Rentals: Houseboats, Fishing, Ski & Patio Boats, PWCs, Canoes, Kayaks.

6 **KAMPLOOPS CAMP - Via Boat from Hirz Bay, P. O. Box 90133, Redding 96099, Ph: (530) 238-2472 -** Campsites, Showers, Group Camps Available with Cook Shack, Equipment Included, Docks, Seasonal.

7 **LAKEHEAD CAMPGROUND & RV PARK- 20999 Antlers Rd., P.O. Box 646, Lakehead 96051, Ph: (530) 238-8450,**
Campsites, Hookups, Disposal Station, Cabin & Trailer Rentals, General Store, Swimming Pool, Pavilion-Groups.

...Continued...

SHASTA LAKE............Continued

8 **LAKE SHORE VILLA R. V. PARK - 20672 Lakeshore Dr., Lakehead 96051, Ph: (530) 238-8688** - 92 R.V. Sites, Full Hookups, 15 Pull Throughs over 70 Feet Plus, Disposal Station, Showers, Docks, Propane, Game Room, Group Kitchen, Open Year Around.

9 **LAKEVIEW MARINA RESORT - 20720 Lakeview Rd., Lakehead 96051, Ph: (530) 238-2442 -** Full Service Marina, Private Boat Ramp, Rentals: Houseboats, Fishing & Ski Boats, Patio Boat, PWC's, General Store, Ice, Bait & Tackle.

10 **PACKER'S BAY MARINA - P. O. Box 1105, Bella Vista 96008, Ph: (800) 331-3137 or (530) 275-5570** Boat Ramp, Rentals: Houseboats, Boat Gas, Ice.

11 **SHASTA LAKE R.V. RESORT & CAMPGROUND - P.O. Box 450, 20433 Lakeshore Dr., Lakehead 96051, Ph: (800) 3-SHASTA or (530) 238-2370 -** 53 Full Hookup R.V. Sites, Secluded Tent Sites, Cabin Rentals, Store, Hot Showers, Laundry, Swimming Pool, Private Boat Dock.

12 **SHASTA MARINA RESORT - 18390 O'Brien Inlet Rd., Lakehead 96051, Ph: (800) 959-3359** - Full Service Marina, Private Boat Ramp, Gas, General Store, Bait & Tackle, Rentals: Houseboats with Ski Boats, Moorage.

13 **SILVERTHORN RESORT - P.O. Box 1090, Bella Vista 96008, Ph: (530) 275-1571 -** Full Service Marina, Launch Ramp, Houseboats, Cabins, Rentals: Patio, Ski & Fishing Boats & PWCs, Pizza and Pub, Grocery Store.

14 **SUGARLOAF COTTAGES - 19667 Lakeshore Dr., P.O. Box 768, Lakehead 96051, Ph: (530) 238-2448** - Lakeside Cabins, Free Moorage on Private Dock, Pool, Playground, Basketball, Volleyball.

15 **SUGARLOAF RESORT, 19671 Lakeshore Dr., Lakehead 96051, Ph: (530) 238-2711** - Full Service Marina, Launch Ramp, General Store, Bait & Tackle, Fuel, Rentals: Houseboats & PWCs.

16 **TRAIL IN Campground and Store, 19765 Gregory Creek Rd., Lakehead 96051, Ph: (530) 238-8533 -** Pull Through Campsites, Hookups, Pool, Laundry, Showers, Mini-Market, Playground, Bait & Tackle, R.V. Supplies.

17 **TSASDI RESORT - 19990 Lakeshore Dr., Lakehead 96051, Ph: (800) 995-0291 or (530) 238-2575** - Cabins, Cable TV, General Store, Bait, Heated Swimming Pool, Free Boat Slip on Private Dock, Playground.

*Full Service Marina = Boat Rentals, Moorage & Boat Gas

Shasta Lake Visitor Information
14225 Holiday Rd., Redding 96003
Ph: (530) 275-1589

Shasta Recreation Company
14538 Wonderland Blvd., Redding 96003
Ph: (530) 275-8113

Shasta Lake Chamber of Commerce
4249 Shasta Dam Blvd., Suite A
P. O. Box 1616, Shasta Lake 96019
Ph: (530) 275-7497

Shasta Lake Business Owners Association
P. O. Box 709, Lakehead 96051
Ph: (530) 275-1296

Shasta Dam Tours - Bureau of Reclamation
Ph: (530) 275-4463

MANZANITA, BUTTE, SUMMIT and JUNIPER LAKES and McCUMBER RESERVOIR

Manzanita, Butte, Summit and Juniper Lakes are within the 106,000 acre expanse of Lassen Volcanic National Park. All four types of volcanoes found in the entire world are represented in this Park - shield, plug dome, cinder cone and composite. There are over 150 miles of trails including a part of the Pacific Crest Trail for the hiker, backpacker and equestrian. Pets and vehicles are not allowed on trails. Pack and saddle stock must overnight in corrals by prior reservation and must have a Wilderness Permit for day use. Grazing is not permittted so you must pack in feed. McCumber Reservoir is a P.G.&E. facility with a small campground.

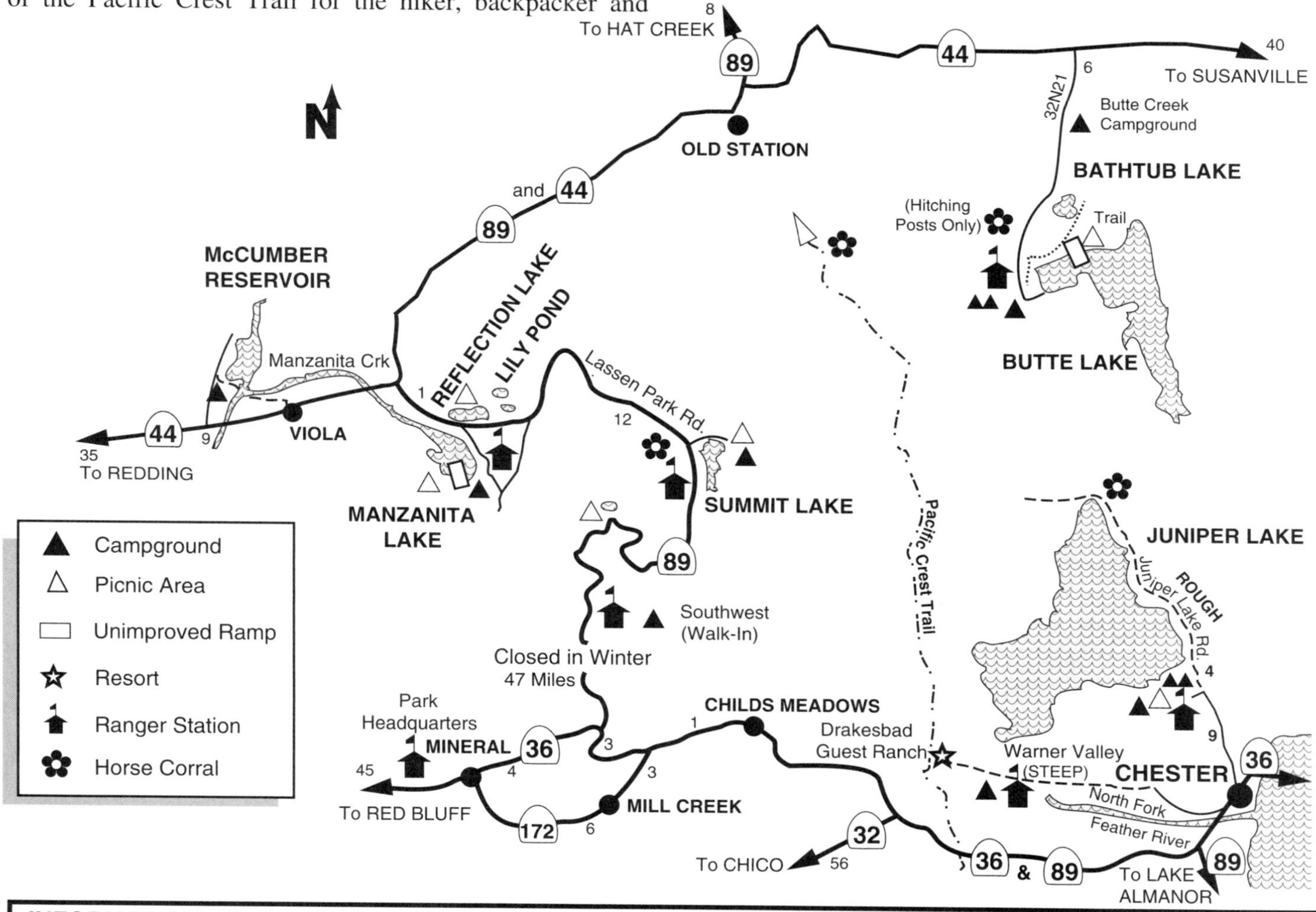

8
To HAT CREEK
89
44
40
To SUSANVILLE
6
32N21
Butte Creek
Campground
OLD STATION
BATHTUB LAKE
and
44
89
(Hitching
Posts Only)
Trail
McCUMBER
RESERVOIR
REFLECTION LAKE
LILY POND
Manzanita Crk
BUTTE LAKE
Lassen Park Rd.
1
12
44
9
VIOLA
35
To REDDING
MANZANITA
LAKE
SUMMIT LAKE
JUNIPER LAKE
89
Pacific Crest Trail
Juniper Lake Rd.
ROUGH
Southwest
(Walk-In)
Closed in Winter
47 Miles
4
Park
Headquarters
CHILDS MEADOWS
1
MINERAL
36
3
Drakesbad
Guest Ranch
Warner Valley
(STEEP)
CHESTER
9
36
45
4
3
To RED BLUFF
MILL CREEK
North Fork
Feather River
172
6
32
To CHICO
56
36
&
89
To LAKE
ALMANOR
89
Campground
Picnic Area
Unimproved Ramp
Resort
Ranger Station
Horse Corral

INFORMATION: Lassen Volcanic National Park, P.O. Box 100, Mineral 96063—Ph: (530) 595-4444

CAMPING	BOATING	RECREATION	OTHER
Manzanita: 179 Sites Tents & R.V.s to 35 ft. Fee: $18 Summit: 94 Sites Tents & R.V.s: $16 - $18 Equestrian Camp Juniper: 18 Sites Tents Only: $10 2 Group Sites for 10 - 15 People Each plus Equestrian Camp No Running Water	No Power Motors Row, Sail, Windsurf & Inflatables Only Unimproved Launch Ramps: Manzanita & Butte Only	Fishing: Rainbow, Brook & Brown Trout Manzanita: *Catch & Release* *With Barbless Hooks Only* Juniper: *No Fishing* Swimming - Picnicking Hiking, Backpacking Horseback Riding Trails & Corrals Campfire Programs: Summit & Manzanita Lakes	Butte Lake: 101 Sites for Tents & R.V.s to 35 ft. Fee: $16 Plus Group Camp Warner Valley: 18 Sites for Tents - Fee: $14 Southwest Walk-In 21 Tent Sites PG&E Ph: (916) 386-5164 McCumber Reservoir 7 Tent Sites - 5 Walk-In Fee: $15 *No ORV's*

CRATER, CARIBOU and SILVER LAKES

These Lakes are located in the Lassen National Forest. Crater Lake, at 6,800 feet elevation, has a surface area of 27 acres. This volcanic crater offers excellent fishing for trout. The Lakes near Silver Lake border the Caribou Wilderness, a gently rolling, forested plateau which can easily be explored by the hiker, backpacker or equestrian. Silver Lake and its neighbor, Caribou Lake, provide a quiet remote area for the small boater, camper and fisherman. Crater Lake has a small campground in a very scenic location. The roads are dirt and rough, especially into Crater Lake.

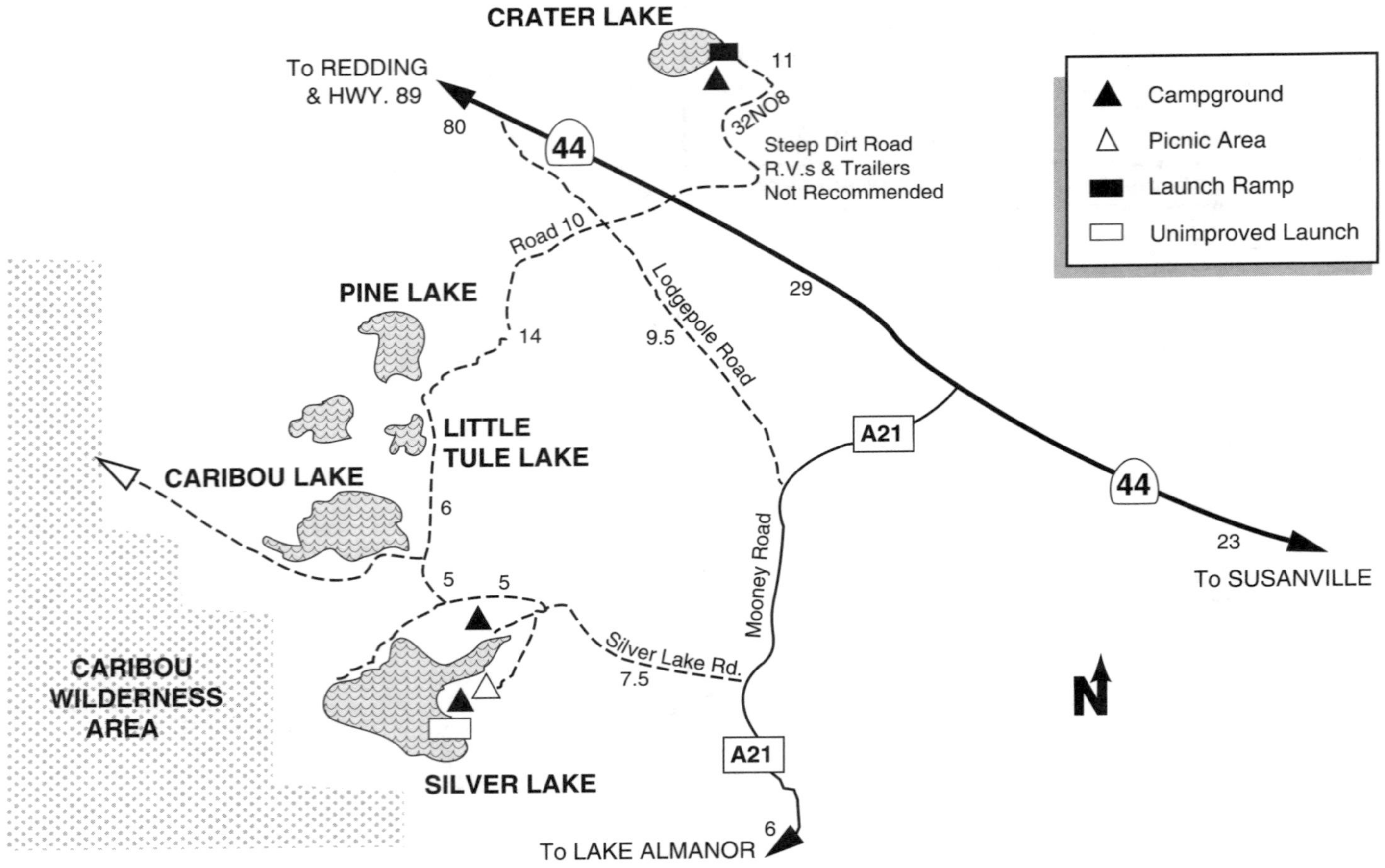
CRATER LAKE
To REDDING
& HWY. 89
80
44
11
32NO8
Steep Dirt Road
R.V.s & Trailers
Not Recommended
Campground
Picnic Area
Launch Ramp
Unimproved Launch
Road 10
PINE LAKE
14
9.5
Lodgepole Road
29
LITTLE
TULE LAKE
CARIBOU LAKE
A21
44
6
23
To SUSANVILLE
Mooney Road
5
5
Silver Lake Rd.
7.5
CARIBOU
WILDERNESS
AREA
N
A21
SILVER LAKE
6
To LAKE ALMANOR

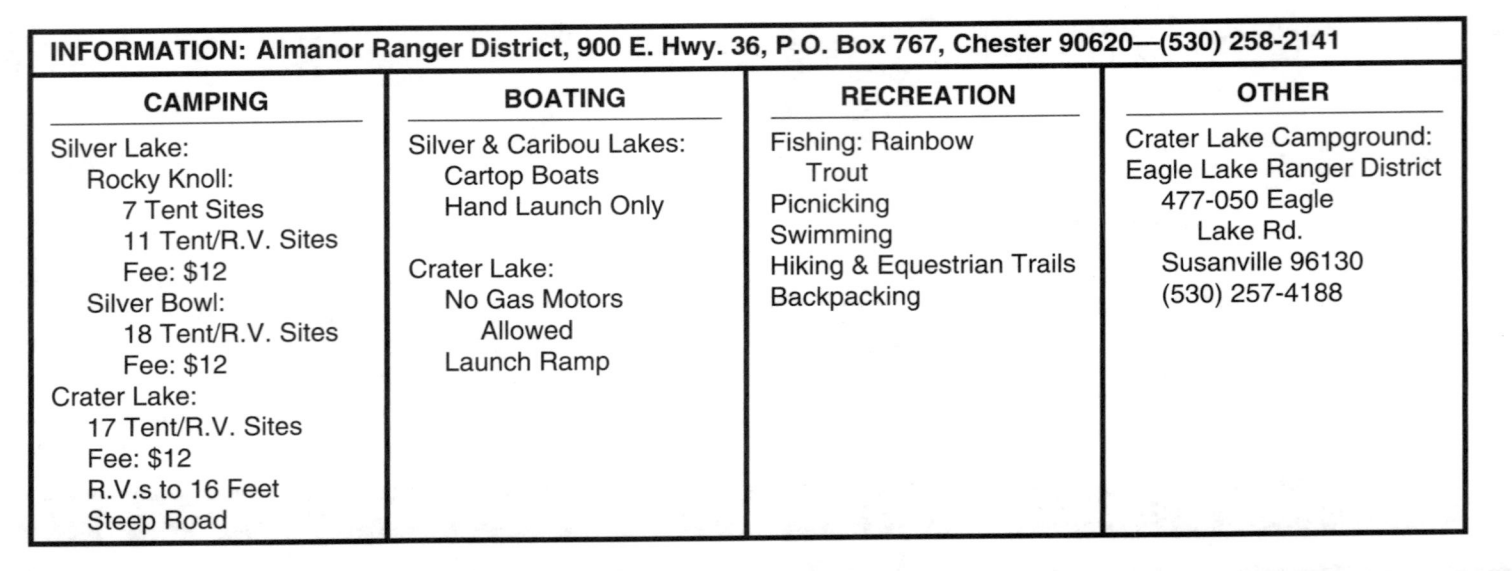

INFORMATION: Almanor Ranger District, 900 E. Hwy. 36, P.O. Box 767, Chester 90620—(530) 258-2141

CAMPING	BOATING	RECREATION	OTHER
Silver Lake: Rocky Knoll: 7 Tent Sites 11 Tent/R.V. Sites Fee: $12 Silver Bowl: 18 Tent/R.V. Sites Fee: $12 Crater Lake: 17 Tent/R.V. Sites Fee: $12 R.V.s to 16 Feet Steep Road	Silver & Caribou Lakes: Cartop Boats Hand Launch Only Crater Lake: No Gas Motors Allowed Launch Ramp	Fishing: Rainbow Trout Picnicking Swimming Hiking & Equestrian Trails Backpacking	Crater Lake Campground: Eagle Lake Ranger District 477-050 Eagle Lake Rd. Susanville 96130 (530) 257-4188

EAGLE LAKE

Eagle Lake is at an elevation of 5,104 feet in the Lassen National Forest. With a surface area of 27,000 acres and over 100 miles of timbered shoreline, it is the second largest natural Lake in California. The slightly alkaline water is the natural habitat for the famous Eagle Lake trout, a favorite of the fisherman for its size of 3 pounds or better. The water is warm and clear. There are numerous Forest Service campgrounds amid tall pines in this scenic area. Full hookups for R.V.s are located at Eagle Lake Park and Mariners Resort. McCoy Flat is a small Reservoir for fishing with brown and rainbow trout. *Contact USFS to check condition of McCoy as it may be dry.*

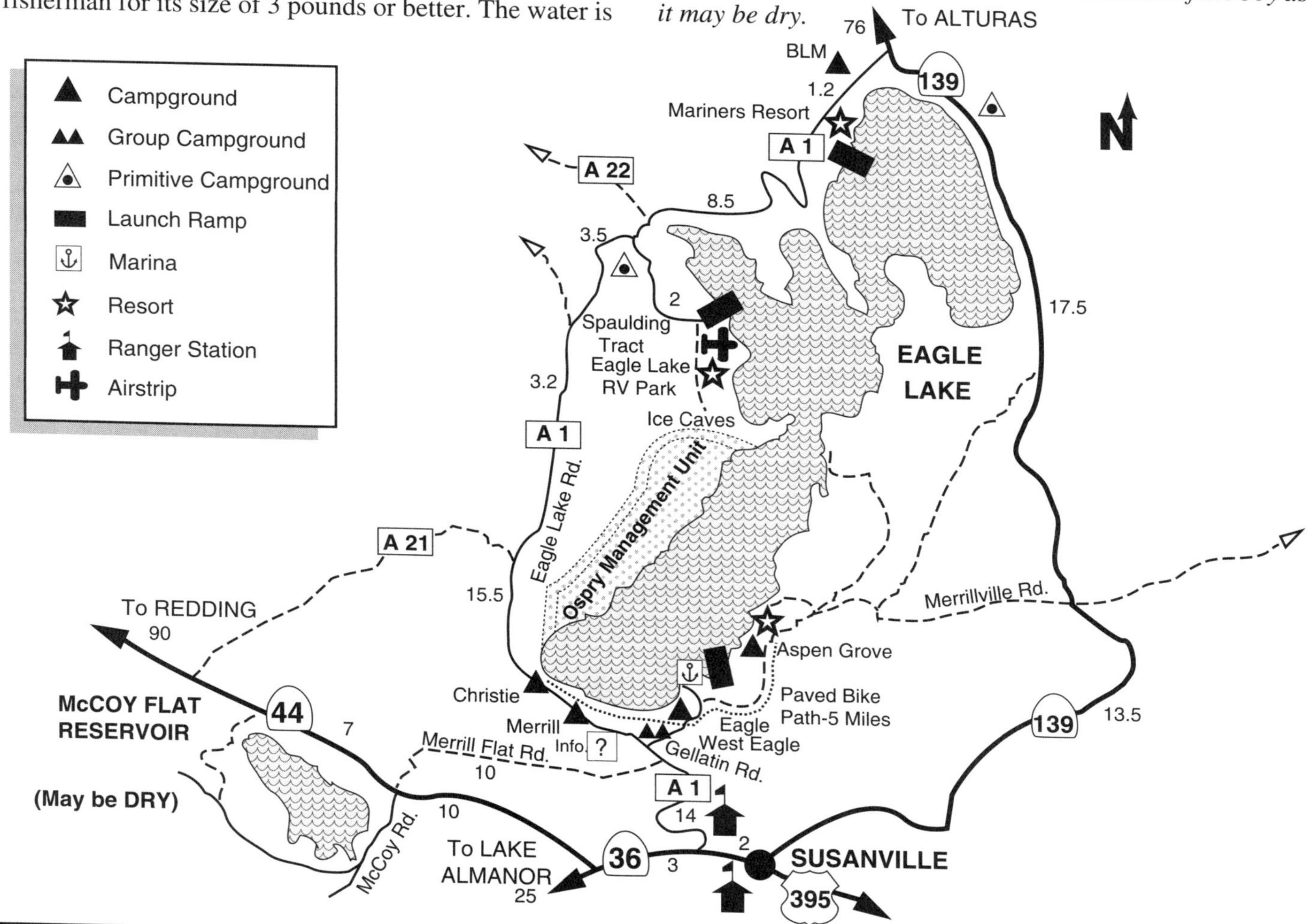

Campground
Group Campground
Primitive Campground
Launch Ramp
Marina
Resort
Ranger Station
Airstrip
76
To ALTURAS
BLM
1.2
139
Mariners Resort
A 1
A 22
8.5
3.5
2
Spaulding Tract
Eagle Lake RV Park
3.2
17.5
EAGLE LAKE
Ice Caves
A 1
Eagle Lake Rd.
Osprey Management Unit
A 21
15.5
Merrillville Rd.
To REDDING
90
Aspen Grove
McCOY FLAT RESERVOIR
44
7
Christie
Paved Bike Path-5 Miles
Merrill
Eagle
West Eagle
139
13.5
Info.
?
Merrill Flat Rd.
10
Gellatin Rd.
(May be DRY)
A 1
14
10
McCoy Rd.
To LAKE ALMANOR
25
36
3
2
SUSANVILLE
395

INFORMATION: Eagle Lake Ranger District, 477-050 Eagle Lake Rd., Susanville 96130—Ph: (530) 257-4188

CAMPING	BOATING	RECREATION	OTHER
USFS: Sites for Tents & R.V.s Christie: 69 Sites Merrill: 173 Sites Eagle: 50 Sites Aspen: 27 Tents Only Partial & Full Hookups Fees: $18 - $33 Plus 3 Group Sites Reservations: Ph: (877) 444-6777 Bureau of Land Management: 17 Dev. Sites	Power, Row, Canoe, Sail, Waterski, PWCs, Windsurfing, Inflatables Launch Ramps Full Service Marina Ph: (530) 825-3454 Rentals: Fishing Boats & Motors, Pontoons Docks, Moorings, Berths	Fishing: Eagle Lake Trout Swimming Picnicking Hiking Nature Trails 5 Mile Paved Bicycle Path Campfire Programs Amphitheater Birdwatching: Bald Eagles, Osprey, Grebes, Pelicans Airstrip	Mariners Resort 509 - 725 Stone Rd. Susanville 96130 Ph: (530) 825-3333 82 Full Hookups Cabins, Grocery Store Restaurant & Lounge Eagle Lake R.V. Park 687-125 Palmetto Way Susanville 96130 Ph: (530) 825-3133 46 Full Hookups Cabins & Grocery Store

RUTH LAKE

Ruth Lake is half way between Eureka and Red Bluff on Highway 36 within the boundaries of the Six Rivers National Forest. This is quite a drive on a narrow road at times but well worth the trip if you plan to stay awhile in this remote area. The Lake rests at an elevation of 2,654 feet and has a surface area of 1,200 acres. It was formed by damming the Mad River in 1962. This is now a popular recreation facility offering boating of all kinds, fishing and camping. The Mad River flows into and out of Ruth Lake and can provide good steelhead fishing. Call Ruth Lake Community Services for additional information.

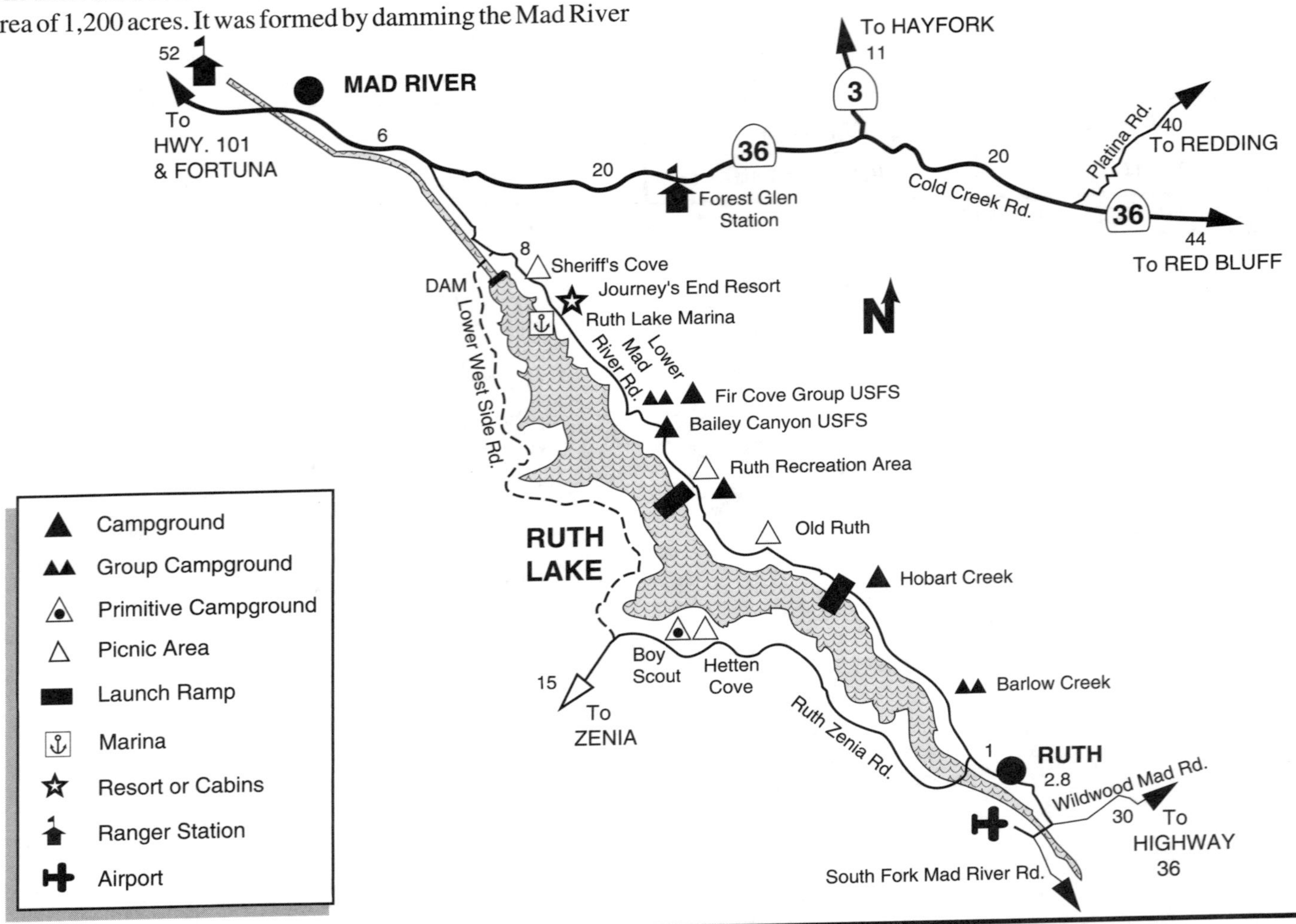
To HAYFORK
11
3
52
MAD RIVER
To
HWY. 101
& FORTUNA
6
20
36
Forest Glen
Station
20
Cold Creek Rd.
Platina Rd.
40
To REDDING
36
44
To RED BLUFF
8
Sheriff's Cove
DAM
Journey's End Resort
Ruth Lake Marina
Lower West Side Rd.
Lower
Mad
River Rd.
N
Fir Cove Group USFS
Bailey Canyon USFS
Ruth Recreation Area
Old Ruth
RUTH
LAKE
Hobart Creek
Boy
Scout
Hetten
Cove
15
To
ZENIA
Barlow Creek
Ruth Zenia Rd.
1
RUTH
2.8
Wildwood Mad Rd.
30
To
HIGHWAY
36
South Fork Mad River Rd.
Campground
Group Campground
Primitive Campground
Picnic Area
Launch Ramp
Marina
Resort or Cabins
Ranger Station
Airport

INFORMATION: Ruth Lake Community Services, P.O. Box 31, Mad River 95552—(707) 574-6332

CAMPING	BOATING	RECREATION	OTHER
U.S.F.S. Six Rivers NF: Fir Cove: 19 Dev. Sites & Bailey Cyn: 25 Dev. Sites for Tents & R.V.s - Fee: $12 Plus 3 Group Sites Reserve: (707) 574-6233 Ruth Lake Community: 118 Dev. Sites for Tents & R.V.s Fees Vary Barlow Group Camp & Picnic Area Reserve: (800) 840-9545	Power, Row, Canoe, Sail, Waterski, PWCs, Windsurf & Inflatables Full Service Marina Ph: (707) 574-6194 Launch Ramps - Free Rentals: Fishing Boats & Motors, Pontoons & Patio Boats Docks, Moorings, Slips Dry Storage	Fishing: Rainbow Trout, Kokanee Salmon, Large & Smallmouth Bass, Catfish Picnicking Hiking Trails Equestrian Trails Wildlife Viewing 4WD Adventure Trail	Journey's End Resort Ph: (707) 574-6441 Motel, Restaurant, Grocery Store Hetten Cove: Day Use Area Boy Scout Cove: Primitive Camp, No Water Annual Events: May: Trap Shoot, Kids Fishing Derby Bass Tournaments August: Rodeo & Summer Festival

Round Valley Reservoir, 350 surface acres, is at an elevation of 4,500 feet in the Plumas National Forest. Located 3 miles south of the historic town of Greenville, this small, secluded Lake is the town's water supply so water sports are limited to fishing. No body contact with the water is permitted.

Famous for black bass, Round Valley is an excellent warm water fishery. Good hiking, mountain biking, equestrian and nature study trails are numerous. For birdwatchers , there are over 100 species of birds that reside in the area.

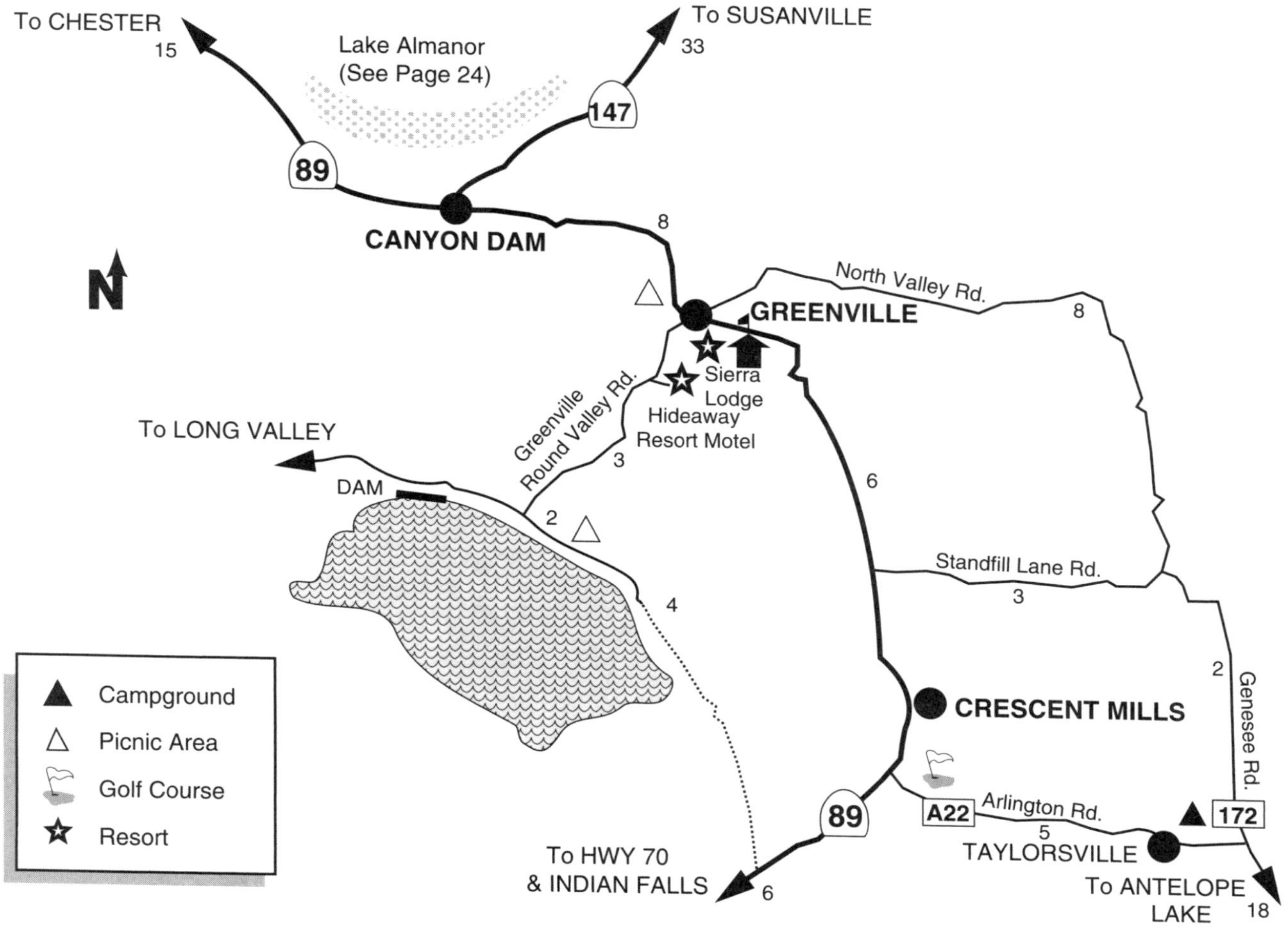
To CHESTER
15
Lake Almanor
(See Page 24)
To SUSANVILLE
33
147
89
CANYON DAM
8
N
North Valley Rd.
GREENVILLE
8
Sierra
Lodge
Hideaway
Resort Motel
Greenville
Round Valley Rd.
3
To LONG VALLEY
DAM
2
6
Standfill Lane Rd.
3
4
Campground
Picnic Area
Golf Course
Resort
CRESCENT MILLS
2
Genesee Rd.
89
A22
Arlington Rd.
5
172
TAYLORSVILLE
To HWY 70
& INDIAN FALLS
6
To ANTELOPE
LAKE
18

INFORMATION: Plumas County Visitors Bureau, 550 Crescent St., Quincy 95971—Ph: (800) 326-2247

CAMPING	BOATING	RECREATION	OTHER
No Camping At Round Valley Lake Taylorsville Community Camgrpound Ph: (530) 284-6646 200 Dev. Sites for Tents & R.V.s	Small Fishing Boats No Launch Ramp	Fishing: Black Bass, Catfish & Bluegill Picnicking No Swimming Hiking Trails Mountain Bike Trails Equestrian Trails Bird Watching including Bald Eagle & Osprey	In Greenville: Hideaway Resort Motel Ph: (530) 284-7915 Sierra Lodge Ph: (530) 284-6154 Plumas National Forest Mt. Hough Ranger District Ph: (530) 283-0555 Indian Valley Chamber of Commerce Ph: (530) 284-6633

LAKE ALMANOR

Lake Almanor is at an elevation of 4,500 feet in the Lassen National Forest. There is an abundance of pine-sheltered campgrounds operated by P.G. & E., the Forest Service and private resorts. The Lake is 13 miles long and 6 miles wide with a surface area of 28,000 acres. It is one of the largest man-made Lakes in California. Almanor's clear, blue waters offer complete boating facilities. Caution is advised because small islands are exposed during low water levels. Gusty winds can also make boating hazardous at times. Fishing can be excellent for a variety of species in the Lake. Nearby streams are also productive. Mountain Meadow Reservoir is a small fishing Lake in a scenic area near Westwood. There are no facilities but it is surrounded by numerous hiking and equestrian trails.

....Continued....

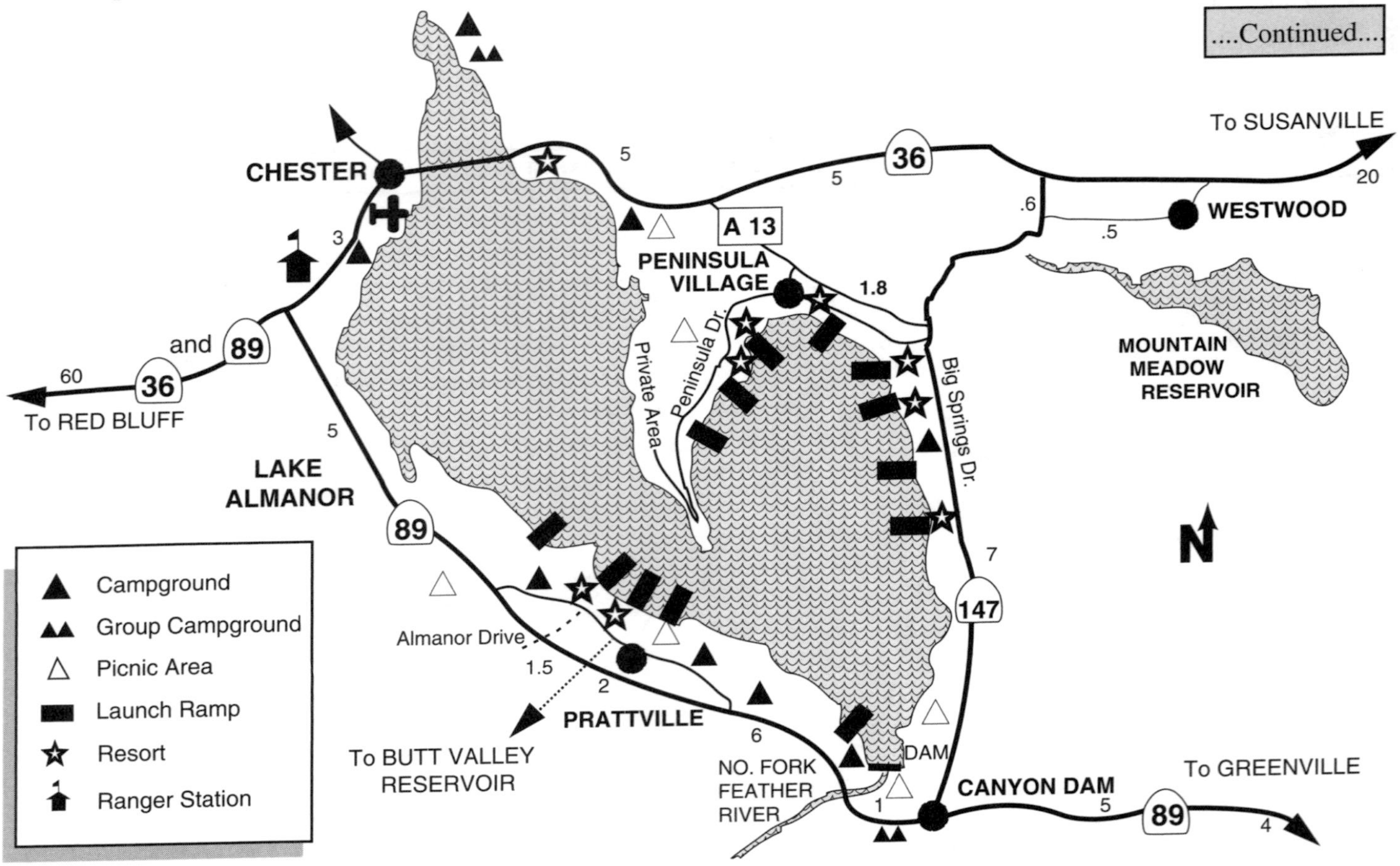

To SUSANVILLE
CHESTER
36
5
20
WESTWOOD
.6
.5
A 13
3
PENINSULA VILLAGE
1.8
MOUNTAIN MEADOW RESERVOIR
and
89
60
36
To RED BLUFF
Private Area
Peninsula Dr.
Big Springs Dr.
LAKE ALMANOR
89
7
N
147
Campground
Group Campground
Picnic Area
Launch Ramp
Resort
Ranger Station
Almanor Drive
1.5
2
PRATTVILLE
To BUTT VALLEY RESERVOIR
6
DAM
NO. FORK FEATHER RIVER
1
CANYON DAM
To GREENVILLE
89
4

INFORMATION: P. G. & E. Land Projects, 2730 Gateway Oaks Dr., Sacramento 95833–Ph: (916) 386-5164			
CAMPING	**BOATING**	**RECREATION**	**OTHER**
P.G. & E.: 131 Dev. Sites for Tents & R.V.s Fee - $15 Plus 30 Overflow Sites Group Camp to 50 People Maximum U. S. F. S.: 101 Dev. Sites for Tents & R.V.s Fee: $18 - $20 Private Campgrounds *See Following Page*	Power, Row, Canoe, Sail, Waterski, PWCs, Inflatables Full Service Marinas Launch Ramps Rentals: Fishing, Canoe, Patio & Ski Boats, Docks, Berths, Gas	Fishing: Rainbow & Brown Trout, Smallmouth Bass, Catfish & King Salmon Fishing Guides Swimming Picnicking Hiking Trails Equestrian Trails 9-1/2 Mile Recreation Trail - No Horses or Motorized Vehicles	Cabins & Motels Snack Bars Restaurants Grocery Stores Bait & Tackle Laundromats Disposal Stations Gas Stations Numerous Golf Courses Nearby Plumas County Visitors Bureau Ph: (800) 326-2247

P.G.&E. CAMPGROUNDS - **(916) 386-5164**

Rocky Point Campground - Off Highway 89 Westshore - 131 Tent/R.V. Sites - First Come, First Served
Yellow Creek Campground - Off Highway 89 Westshore - 11 Tent/RV Sites near Soda Springs Historic Site.
Camp Conery Group Camp - Off Highway 89 East of Dam.
50 People Maximum, Multi-purpose Utility Building with Cook Area, Grill, Refrigeration, Showers and 5 Bunk Houses, Swimming Beach and Picnic Area - Reservations Only.
Last Chance Creek Campground - 4 miles northeast of Chester on Juniper Lake Road.
13 Tent/R.V. Group Sites - Reservations Only & 12 Tent/R.V. Family Sites, Horse Camping.

U. S. FOREST SERVICE - ALMANOR RANGER DISTRICT
P. O. Box 767, Chester 96020, Ph: (530) 258-2141
Reservations: (877) 444-6777

Almanor Campground - Off Highway 89 West Shore - 15 Tent Only Sites, 86 Tent/R.V. Sites to 22 Feet.
Almanor Group Camp - Off Highway 89 West Shore - Groups to 100 People - Reservations Only.

SOME PRIVATE RESORTS - Call for Current Prices - Many are Seasonal

Almanor Drive

Plumas Pines Resort - 3000 Almanor Dr. West, Canyon Dam 95923, Ph: (530) 259-4343 - 50 R.V. Sites with Full Hookups, No Tent Camping, Motel, Housekeeping Cottages, Full Service Marina, Launch Ramp, Rentals: Fishing & Ski Boats, Pontoons & PWCs, Restaurant & Lounge, Store, Gas.

Wilson's Camp Prattville - 2932 Almanor Dr. West, Canyon Dam 95923, Ph: (530) 259-2267 - 34 R.V. Sites with Full Hookups, 8 Cabins, Marina, Launch Ramp, Docks, Cafe, Store, Bait & Tackle.

Highway 147

Vagabond R.V. Resort & Marina - 7371 Highway 147 East Shore, Lake Almanor 96137, Ph: (530) 596-3240 - 36 R.V. Sites with Full Hookups, Cabin & Trailer Rental, Marina, Launch Ramp, Dock.

Lake Haven Resort - 7329 Highway 147, Lake Almanor 96137, Ph: (530) 596-3249 - 25 R.V. Sites with Full Hookups, 8 Cabins, Launch Ramp, Dock, Slips.

Lake Cove Resort and Marina - 3584 Highway 147, Lake Almanor 96137, Ph: (530) 284-7697 - 50 R.V. Sites, Full & Partial Hookups, Disposal Station, 4 Tent Sites, Cabin, Launch Ramp, Slips, Rental Boats, Store, Bait & Tackle, Propane.

Peninsula Drive

Knotty Pine Resort & Marina - 430 Peninsula Dr., Lake Almanor 96137, Ph: (530) 596-3348 - R.V. Sites with Full Hookups, Fully Equipped Log Cabins, Full Service Marina, Boat Rentals, Launch Ramp, Boat Slips.

Almanor Lakeside Resort - 300 Peninsula Dr., Lake Almanor 96137, Ph: (530) 596-3959 - 12 Housekeeping Cabins, Marina for Guests, Picnic & BBQ Area, Restaurant & Groceries Nearby - No Pets.

Big Cove - 422 Peninsula Dr., Lake Almanor 96137, Ph: (530) 596-3349 - 51 R.V. Sites with Full Hookups, Launch Ramp.

Pine Cove - 410 Peninsula Dr., Lake Almanor 96137, Ph: (530) 596-3348 - R.V. Sites with Full Hookups

Chester

North Shore Campground - P.O. Box 1102, Chester 96020, Ph: (530) 258-3376 - 36 Tent Sites, 89 R.V. Sites, Water & Electric Hookups, Disposal Station, 3 Housekeeping Cabins, Store, Playground, Boat Rentals, Propane, Launch Ramp.

For additional information contact:
Chester - Lake Almanor Chamber of Commerce - (530) 258-2426 ..... or
Plumas Visitors Bureau - (800) 326-2247

BUTT VALLEY RESERVOIR

Butt Valley Reservoir is at an elevation of 4,150 feet in the Lassen National Forest. This picturesque mountain Lake is five miles long and three-quarters of a mile at its widest point. It is connected to Lake Almanor by a tunnel. Butt Valley Reservoir is the second level of P.G. & E.'s "stairway of power" which flows down the Feather River into Lake Oroville. This is a nice boating Lake with a launch ramp. There is a good fishery for planted rainbows as well as native brown and rainbow trout. The campgrounds and picnic areas are under the jurisdiction of P.G. & E.

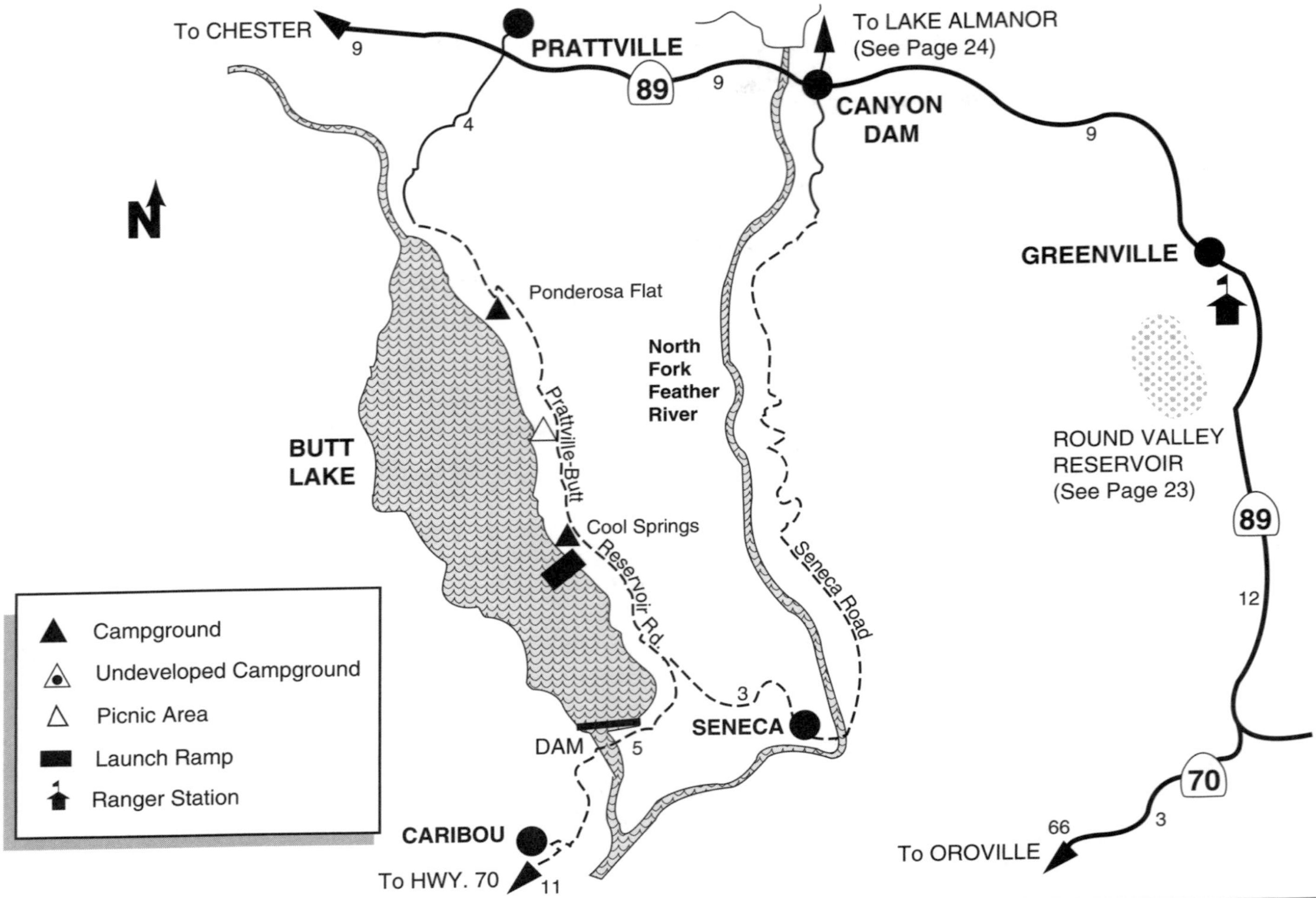

To CHESTER
9
PRATTVILLE
89
9
To LAKE ALMANOR
(See Page 24)
CANYON DAM
9
4
N
GREENVILLE
Ponderosa Flat
North Fork Feather River
Prattville-Butt
BUTT LAKE
ROUND VALLEY RESERVOIR
(See Page 23)
89
Cool Springs
Reservoir Rd.
Seneca Road
12
Campground
Undeveloped Campground
Picnic Area
Launch Ramp
Ranger Station
3
SENECA
DAM
5
70
CARIBOU
66
3
To OROVILLE
To HWY. 70
11

INFORMATION: P.G. & E. Land Projects, 2730 Gateway Oaks Dr., Sacramento 95833–Ph: (916) 386-5164

CAMPING	BOATING	RECREATION	OTHER
Cool Springs: 25 Sites for Tents & R.V.s 5 Walk-In Sites Fee: $15 Ponderosa Flat: 63 Sites for Tents & R.V.s Fee: $15	Open to All Boating Launch Ramp No Waterskiing	Fishing: Rainbow & Brown Trout, Catfish Picnicking Swimming Hiking Trails Nature Study Equestrian Trails	Full Facilities in Chester 9 Miles Plumas County Visitors Bureau Ph: (800) 326-2247

ANTELOPE LAKE

The Antelope Lake Recreation Area is at an elevation of 5,000 feet in the Plumas National Forest. The Lake has 15 miles of timbered shoreline and a surface area of 930 acres. The sheltered coves and islands make this beautiful Lake a boating haven. Forest Service campgrounds provide the camper with nice sites amid pine and fir trees. Good-sized Rainbow and Eagle Lake trout await the fisherman. Indian Creek, below the dam, has some large German Brown trout as well as Rainbows.

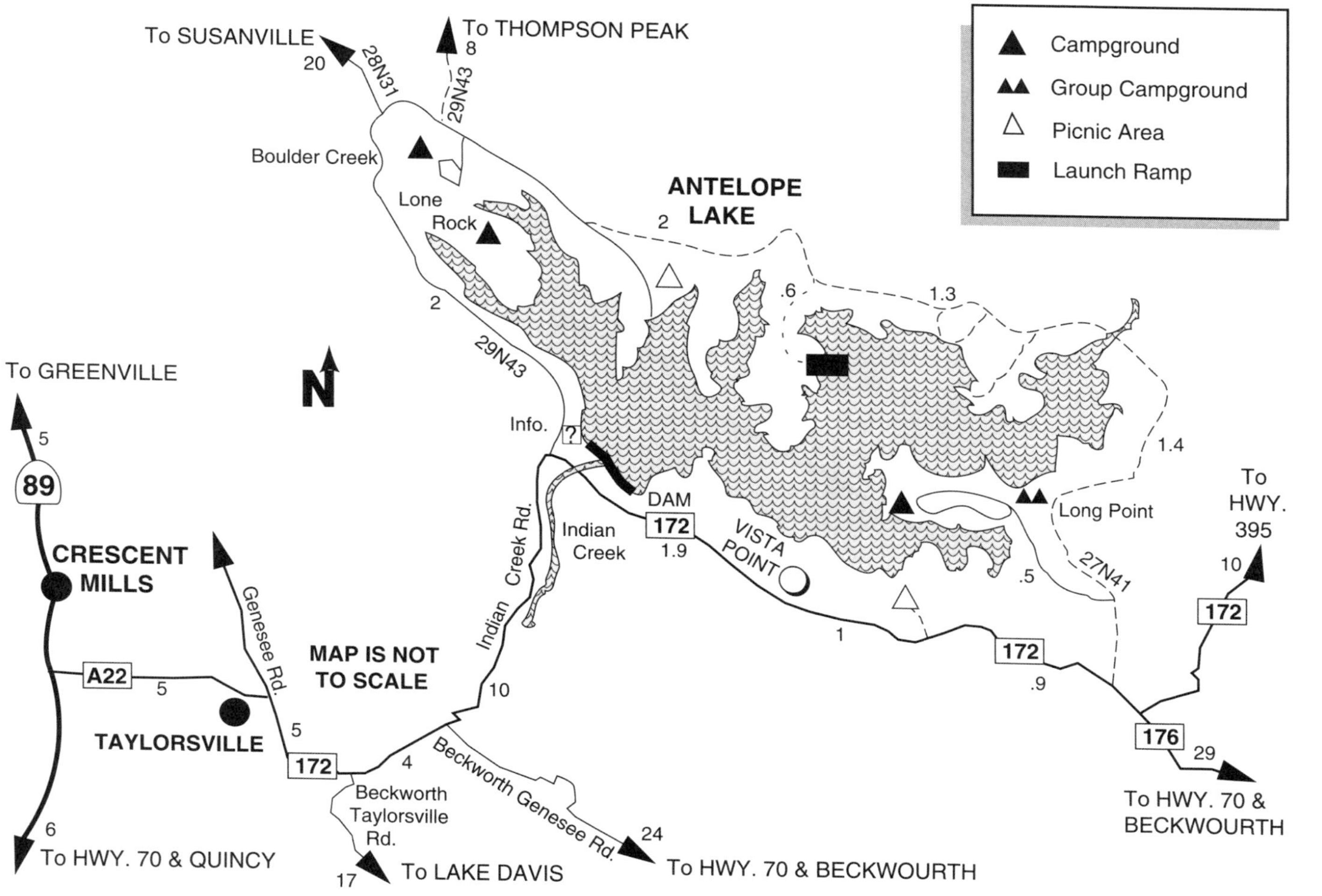

To SUSANVILLE
20
28N31
To THOMPSON PEAK
8
29N43
Campground
Group Campground
Picnic Area
Launch Ramp
Boulder Creek
Lone Rock
ANTELOPE LAKE
2
.6
1.3
2
29N43
To GREENVILLE
5
89
N
Info.
1.4
To HWY. 395
10
DAM
172
1.9
Indian Creek
VISTA POINT
Long Point
27N41
.5
CRESCENT MILLS
Genesee Rd.
Indian Creek Rd.
MAP IS NOT TO SCALE
1
172
172
.9
A22
5
10
TAYLORSVILLE
5
172
4
176
29
Beckworth Genesee Rd.
Beckworth Taylorsville Rd.
6
To HWY. 70 & QUINCY
17
To LAKE DAVIS
24
To HWY. 70 & BECKWOURTH
To HWY. 70 & BECKWOURTH

INFORMATION: Mt. Hough Ranger District, 39696 State Highway 70, Quincy, 95971—Ph: (530) 283-0555

CAMPING	BOATING	RECREATION	OTHER
Dev. Sites for Tents & R.V.s Boulder Creek: 70 Sites Lone Rock: 86 Sites Long Point: 38 Sites Fee: $18 - $20 Long Point Group Camp: 4 Sites - Fee: $33 No Hookups Disposal Station Reservations: Ph: (877) 444-6777	Power, Row, Canoe, Sail, Waterski, Windsurfing & Inflatables Launch Ramp Check for Current Road Condition to Launch Ramp	Fishing: Rainbow & German Brown Trout, Catfish & Largemouth Bass Picnicking Swimming Hiking Trails Nature Trail Campfire Program	Grocery Store Bait & Tackle Full Facilities - 26 Miles at Taylorsville Plumas County Visitors Bureau 550 Crescent St. Quincy 95971 Ph: (800) 326-2247 or Ph: (530) 283-6345

BENBOW LAKE

Benbow Lake State Recreation Area is at an elevation of 364 feet off Highway 101 in the Redwood Empire. This 230 acre Lake is created every summer by damming the South Fork of the Eel River. Boating is limited to small non-powered craft so this is a nice Lake for sailing and rowing. The California Department of Parks and Recreation maintains a 1,200 acre park with picnic areas, campgrounds and a swim beach. The Benbow Inn, adjacent to the Lake, is a lovely old hotel and restaurant. The Benbow Valley R.V. Resort offers 112 campsites with full hook-ups, cable TV, swimming pool and playground. A 9-hole golf course is adjacent to the R.V. Park.

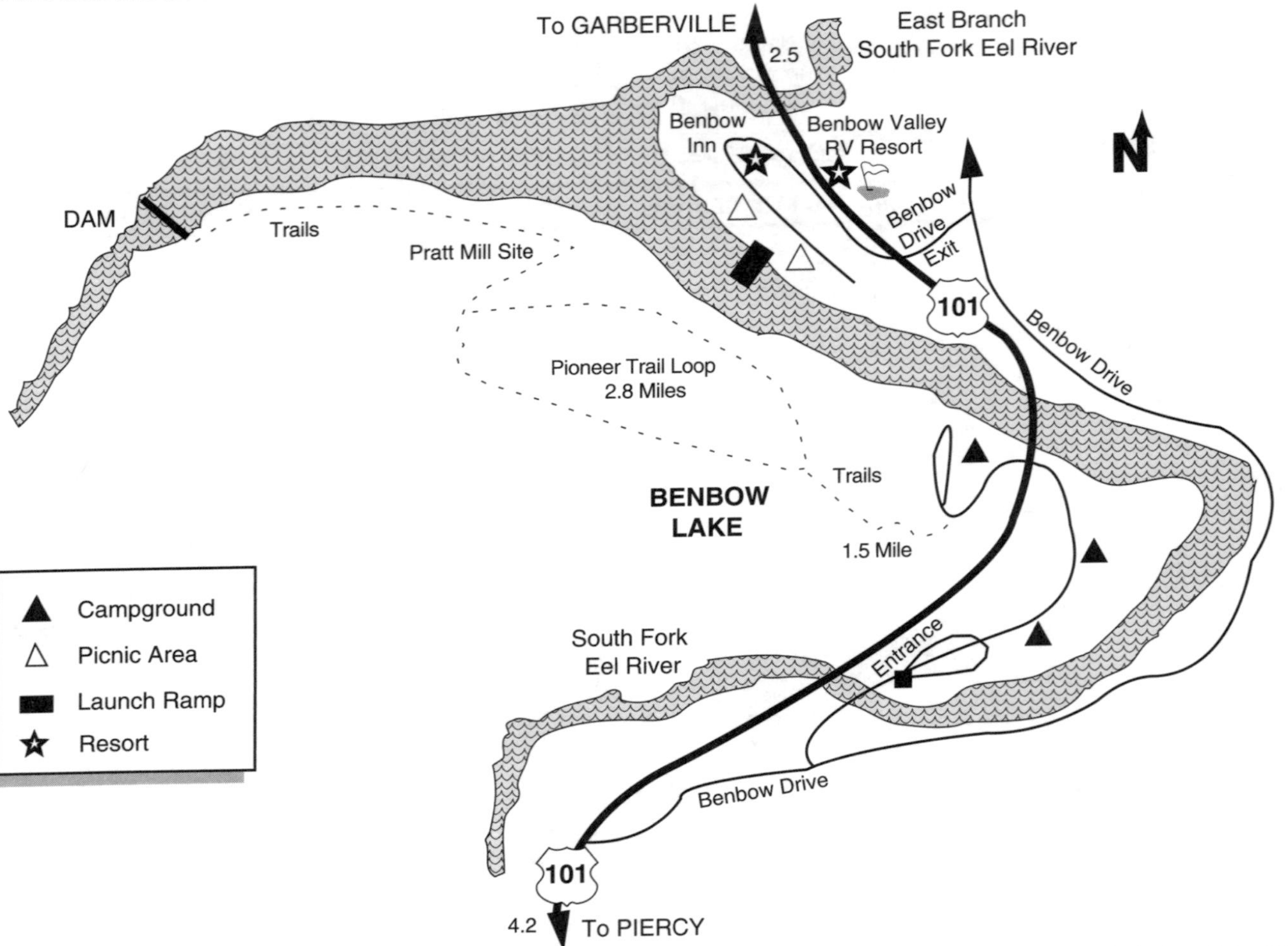

To GARBERVILLE
2.5
East Branch
South Fork Eel River
Benbow Inn
Benbow Valley RV Resort
N
Benbow Drive
Exit
101
DAM
Trails
Pratt Mill Site
Benbow Drive
Pioneer Trail Loop
2.8 Miles
Trails
BENBOW LAKE
1.5 Mile
Campground
Picnic Area
Launch Ramp
Resort
South Fork
Eel River
Entrance
Benbow Drive
101
4.2
To PIERCY

INFORMATION: Benbow Lake State Recreation Area, 1600 Hwy. 101, Garberville 95542—Ph: (707) 247-3318

CAMPING	BOATING	RECREATION	OTHER
State Park 77 Dev. Sites for Tents & Self-Contained Units including 2 Hookups Fees: $20 Hookups: $28 Disposal Station Reserve Ph: (800) 444-7275 Day Use - Fee: $6	Row, Sail, Canoe, Windsurfing & Inflatables No Motors Rentals: Canoes, Yak Boards Launch Ramp *Summer Only*	Fishing: Not Recommended in Summer due to Young Steelhead & Salmon Swimming Picnicking Hiking Trails Nature Study Campfire Programs 9 Hole Golf Course	Benbow Valley R.V. Resort & Golf Course 7000 Benbow Dr. Garberville 95442 Ph: (707) 923-2777 112 R.V. Sites-Full Hookups Fee: $30 - $49 Plus 3 Rental Cottages Benbow Inn & Restaurant Ph: (707) 923-2124 Full Facilities in Garberville

Lake Cleone is at elevation of 20 feet within the MacKerricher State Park. This park along the scenic Mendocino Coast provides a variety of natural habitats including forests, wetlands, sand dunes and a 6-mile beach. Although swimming is not advised due to cold, turbulent waters, the 500-yard black, sandy beach is a popular attraction. Lake Cleone, 40 surface acres, is open to shallow draft non-powered boating. The angler can fish for trout and an occasional bass at the Lake. Steelhead and salmon are in nearby rivers. Surf fish, rock fish and ling cod can be caught in the ocean. Skin divers enjoy the nearby coves. Hikers and naturalists will find trails around the Lake and along the beach.

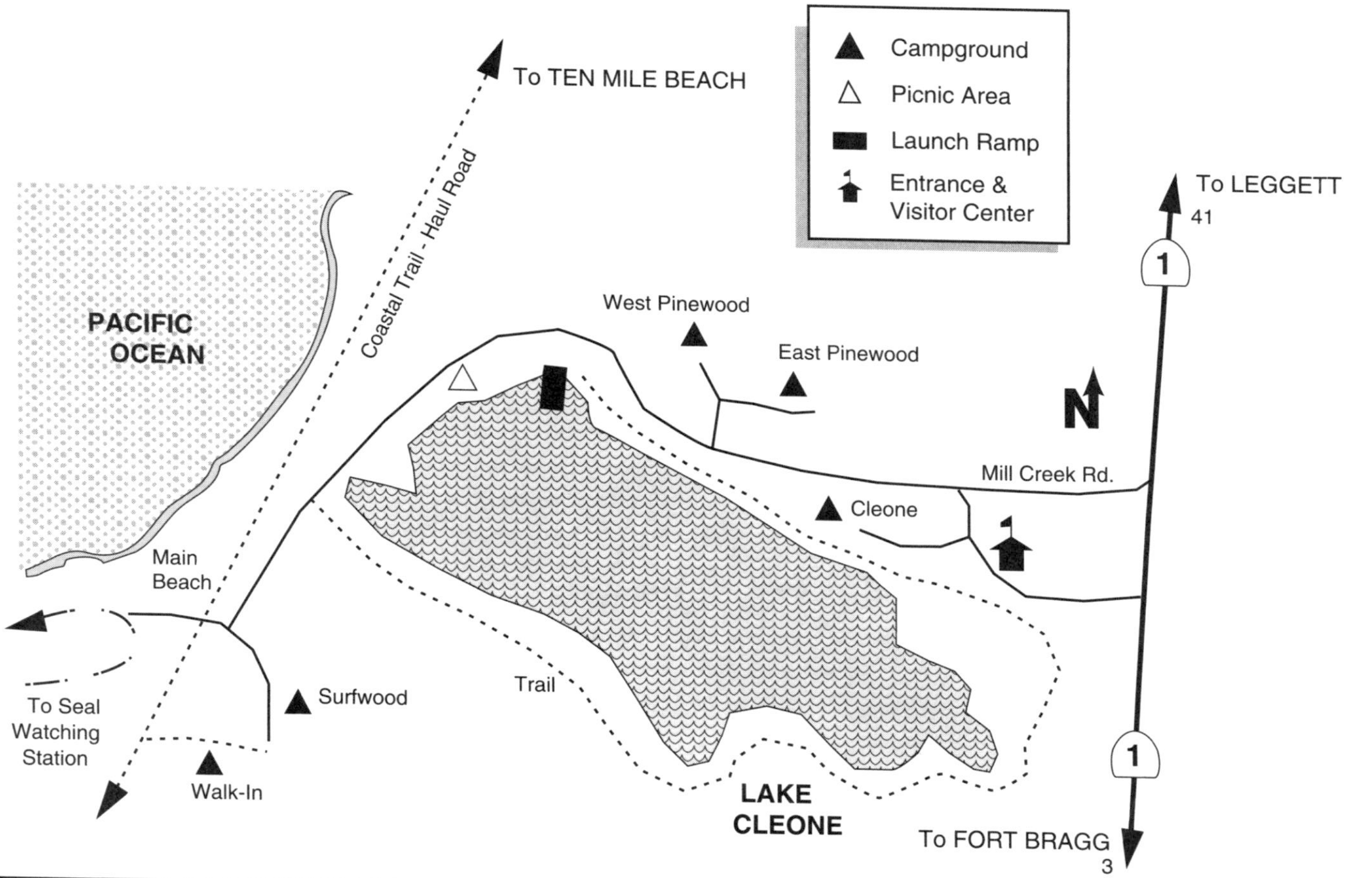
To TEN MILE BEACH
Campground
Picnic Area
Launch Ramp
Entrance & Visitor Center
To LEGGETT
41
1
Coastal Trail - Haul Road
PACIFIC OCEAN
West Pinewood
East Pinewood
N
Mill Creek Rd.
Cleone
Main Beach
To Seal Watching Station
Surfwood
Trail
Walk-In
LAKE CLEONE
1
To FORT BRAGG
3

INFORMATION: MacKerricher State Park, P. O. Box 440, Mendocino 95460—Ph: (707) 937-5804

CAMPING	BOATING	RECREATION	OTHER
148 Dev. Sites for Tents & R.V.s to 35 Feet No Hookups Fees: $20 - $25 Disposal Station 2 Group Camps 10 Walk-In Camps Reservations: Ph: (800) 444-7275	Open to Small, Shallow Draft, Non-Powered Boats Paved Launch Ramp	Fishing: Trout, Bass Picnicking Hiking & Nature Study Trails Equestrian Trails Campfire Programs Junior Ranger Programs Bird Watching Beach Combing Tidal Pools Skin Diving Seal Watching Station	Visitor Center Day Use Parking at Lake Cleone & at the Ocean Grocery Store Near Park Entrance Full Facilities at Fort Bragg

SNAG, PHILBROOK, De SABLA and PARADISE LAKES

These Lakes range in elevation from 3,000 feet at Paradise Lake to 5,000 feet at Philbrook Lake. Snag Lake does not have game fish but Philbrook is a good fishing Lake. Trailers, however, are not advised on this road. These two Lakes are part of the Lassen National Forest. P.G. & E. maintains a resort for its employees at De Sabla Reservoir but the public may fish for rainbow and some brown trout on the south and east sides of the Lake nearest Skyway Boulevard. A group picnic site is also available. Paradise Lake is popular for day-use fishing. The angler will find planted rainbows, some brown trout, bass, and channel catfish.

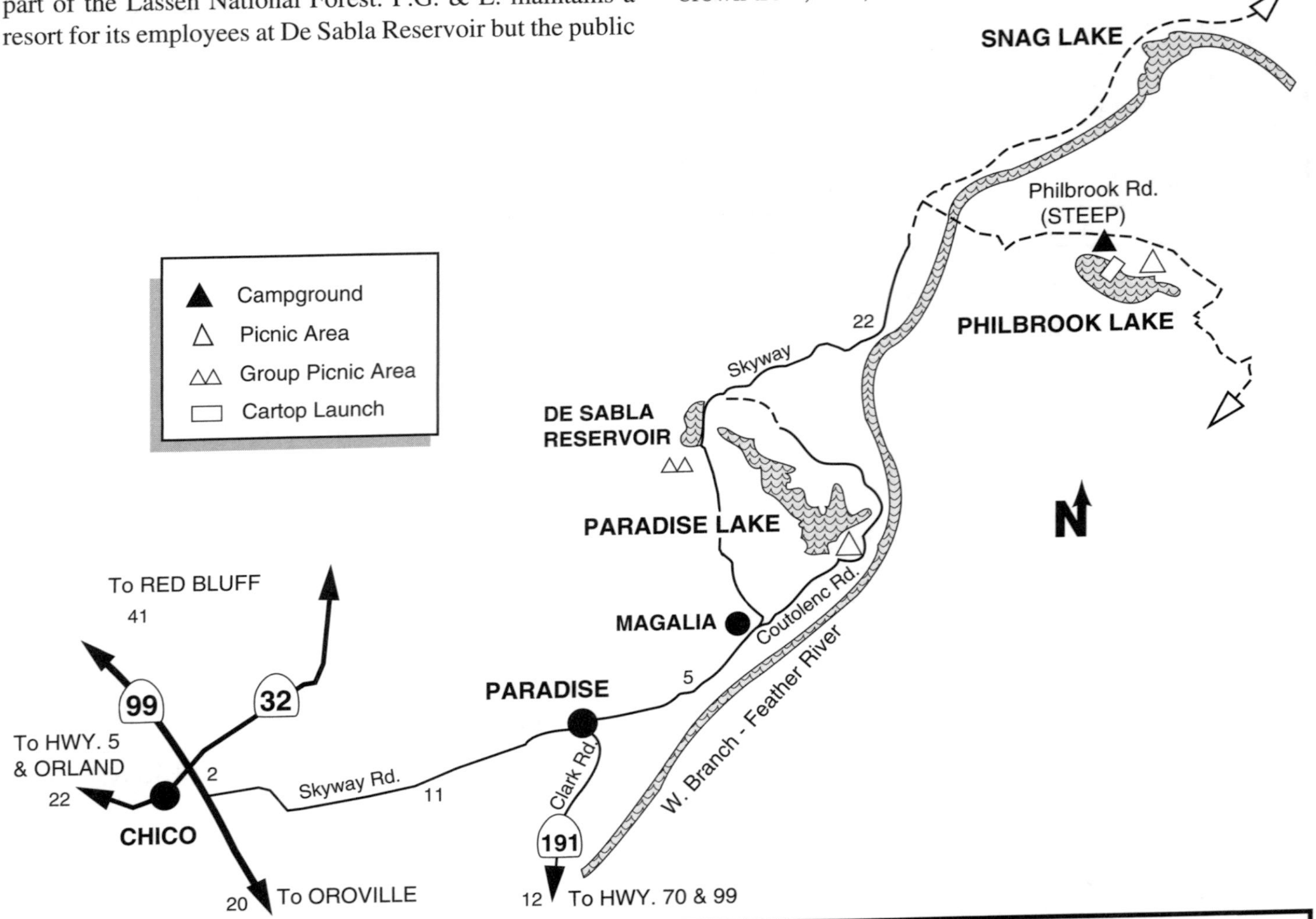

SNAG LAKE
Philbrook Rd.
(STEEP)
PHILBROOK LAKE
Campground
Picnic Area
Group Picnic Area
Cartop Launch
22
Skyway
DE SABLA
RESERVOIR
PARADISE LAKE
N
To RED BLUFF
41
MAGALIA
Coutolenc Rd.
W. Branch - Feather River
5
PARADISE
99
32
To HWY. 5
& ORLAND
22
2
Skyway Rd.
11
Clark Rd.
191
CHICO
20
To OROVILLE
12
To HWY. 70 & 99

INFORMATION: Almanor Ranger District, P.O. Box 767, Chester 96020—Ph: (530) 258-2141

CAMPING	BOATING	RECREATION	OTHER
P.G. & E.: Ph: (916) 386-5164 Philbrook Lake 20 Campsites Fee: $15	Philbrook: Cartop Launch Area Fishing Access Paradise Lake: Rowboats, Canoes & Electric Motors Minimal Facilities *Snag Lake is usually Drained Mid-Summer*	Fishing: Rainbow, Brown & Eastern Brook Trout, Small & Largemouth Bass, Channel Catfish Picnicking De Salba Reservoir: Group Picnic Area Reservations - PG&E: Ph: (916) 386-5164 Hiking & Backpacking Swimming - Philbrook Lake Only	Recreation Permits and Fees are Required at Paradise Lake

BUCKS, SILVER and SNAKE LAKES

The Bucks Lake Recreation Area in the Plumas National Forest is rich in wildlife and offers an abundance of outdoor recreation. Bucks Lake, at 5,155 feet elevation, has a surface area of 1,827 acres and holds State records for trout. There are facilities for all types of boating. Silver Lake, at 5,800 feet, offers excellent trout fishing. There is also good stream fishing. The Bucks Lake Wilderness Area of 24,000 acres and the Pacific Crest Trail are available for the hiker, horseback rider and backpacker to this area of gently rolling terrain, glaciated granite, forested meadows and perennial streams.

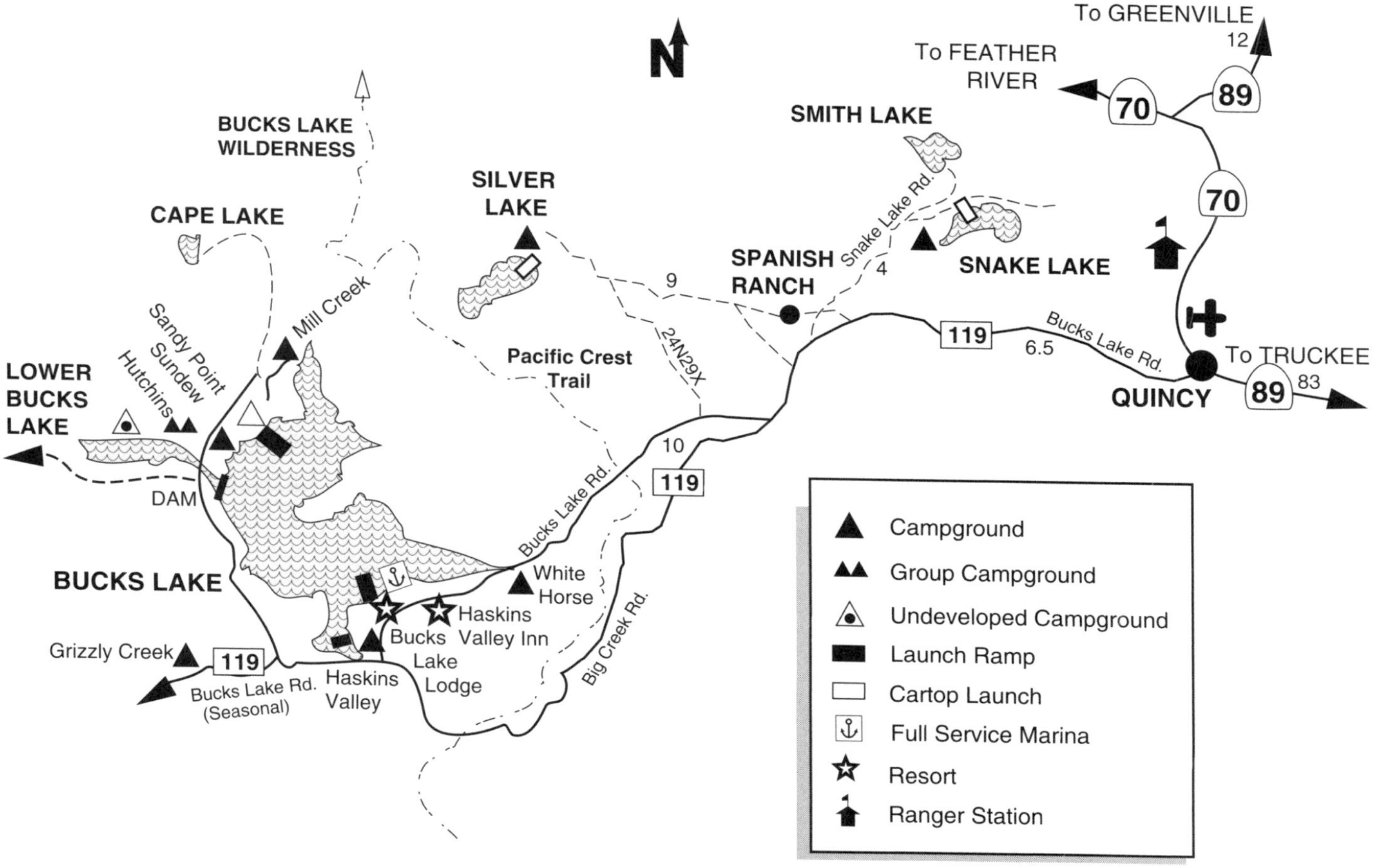

N
To GREENVILLE
12
To FEATHER RIVER
70
89
SMITH LAKE
BUCKS LAKE WILDERNESS
SILVER LAKE
CAPE LAKE
70
Snake Lake Rd.
SPANISH RANCH
4
SNAKE LAKE
9
Mill Creek
Sandy Point
Sundew
Hutchins
119
6.5
Bucks Lake Rd.
24N29X
Pacific Crest Trail
LOWER BUCKS LAKE
To TRUCKEE
QUINCY
89
83
10
119
DAM
Bucks Lake Rd.
BUCKS LAKE
White Horse
Haskins Valley Inn
Bucks Lake Lodge
Big Creek Rd.
Grizzly Creek
119
Bucks Lake Rd. (Seasonal)
Haskins Valley
Campground
Group Campground
Undeveloped Campground
Launch Ramp
Cartop Launch
Full Service Marina
Resort
Ranger Station

INFORMATION: Mt. Hough Ranger District, 39696 Highway 70, Quincy 95971—Ph: (530) 283-0555

CAMPING	BOATING	RECREATION	OTHER
U.S.F.S. - 64 Dev. Sites for Tents & R.V.s to 22 feet Plus Walk-in Sites Fees: $14 - $20 Hutchins Meadow: Reserve 3 Group Camps Ph: (877) 444-6777 P. G. & E. Ph: (916) 386-5164 Haskins Valley: 65 Dev. Sites for Tents & R.V.s City of Santa Clara: Grizzly: 7 Walk-In Sites	Bucks Lake: Open to All Boats Full Service Marina Ph: (530) 283-4243 Rentals: Fishing & Ski Boats, Pontoons, Canoes, Kayaks & PWCs Silver Lake: Rowboats & Canoes Only No Motors Hand Launch	Fishing: Rainbow, German Brown, Lake & Brook Trout, Kokanee Salmon Swimming & Ski Beaches Picnicking Hiking Trails Backpacking [Parking] Horse Rentals & Equestrian Trails	Bucks Lake Lodge Ph: (530) 283-2262 Cabins, Restaurant, Store, Gas Station Haskins Valley Inn Ph: (530) 283-9667 Timberline Inn Ph: (530) 283-2262 Lake View Cabins Ph: (530) 283-4243

LAKE DAVIS

The Lake Davis Recreation Area is located in the Plumas National Forest, 7 miles north of Portola. The Lake is at an elevation of 5,775 feet and has a total surface area of 4,026 acres. A concessionaire, under permit from the Forest Service, maintains three campgrounds on the eastern shore of the Lake as well as launch ramps around the 32 miles of tree-covered shoreline. Steady winds make this an ideal Lake for sailing although afternoon winds can be a hazard for small craft. Lake Davis is open to all boating but water skiing is not permitted. There is a good warm water fishery along with an population of both native and stocked trout. A threat to native trout and salmon are northern pike. The Department of Fish and Game are working to eliminate this problem. Call Beckwourth Ranger District for current information.

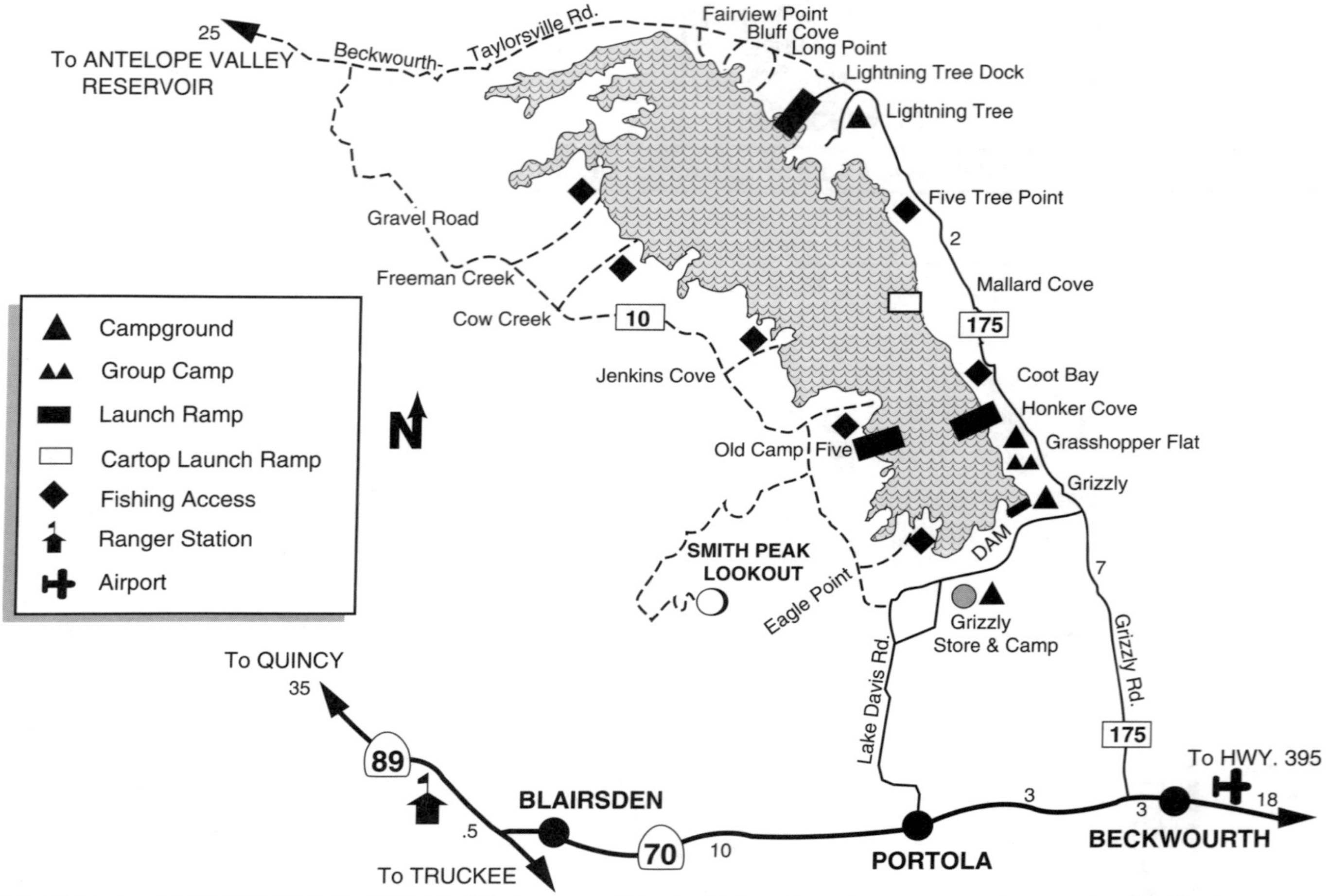

To ANTELOPE VALLEY RESERVOIR
25
Beckwourth-Taylorsville Rd.
Fairview Point
Bluff Cove
Long Point
Lightning Tree Dock
Lightning Tree
Five Tree Point
2
Gravel Road
Freeman Creek
Mallard Cove
Cow Creek
10
175
Jenkins Cove
Coot Bay
Honker Cove
Old Camp
Five
Grasshopper Flat
Grizzly
SMITH PEAK LOOKOUT
DAM
7
Eagle Point
Grizzly Store & Camp
Lake Davis Rd.
Grizzly Rd.
N
Campground
Group Camp
Launch Ramp
Cartop Launch Ramp
Fishing Access
Ranger Station
Airport
To QUINCY
35
89
BLAIRSDEN
.5
To TRUCKEE
70
10
PORTOLA
3
To HWY. 395
18
BECKWOURTH

INFORMATION: Beckwourth Ranger District, Box 7, 23 Mohawk Rd., Blairsden 96103—Ph: (530) 836-2575

CAMPING	BOATING	RECREATION	OTHER
165 Dev. Sites for Tents & R.V.s Fee: $18 Double Sites: $36 Grasshopper Group Site-$60 Disposal Station - Fee: $5 Reservations: (877) 444-6777 Grizzly Camp - Private: Ph: (530) 832-0270 34 Dev. Sites for Tents & R.V.s - Hookups Seasonal Rates	Power, Row, Canoe, Sail, Windsurf & Inflatables *No Waterskiing or PWCs* Launch Ramps Floating Boat Docks Cartop Boat Launch Areas	Fishing: Rainbow, Brown, Eagle Lake, Kamloop Trout, Bass & Catfish Numerous Fishing Access Sites Swimming Picnicking Hiking Trails No Off Road Vehicles in Recreation Area	Grizzly Store & Camp 7552 Lake Davis Rd. Portola 96122 Ph: (530) 832-0270 Store, Bait & Tackle Propane & Firewood R.V. & Boat Storage Airport & Facilities at Beckwourth

The Frenchman Recreation Area offers a variety of enjoyable outdoor activities from waterskiing to ice fishing in the winter. Frenchman Lake at an elevation of 5,588 feet, is within the Plumas National Forest. The 1,580 surface acres are surrounded by 21 miles of sage and pine-dotted shoreline. Five campgrounds are managed by a concessionaire under a permit from the Forest Service. There are also 15 picnic sites, 5 fishing access points and two boat docks around the Lake. All types of boats are permitted along with waterskiing and PWCs. Trout fishing can be very good.

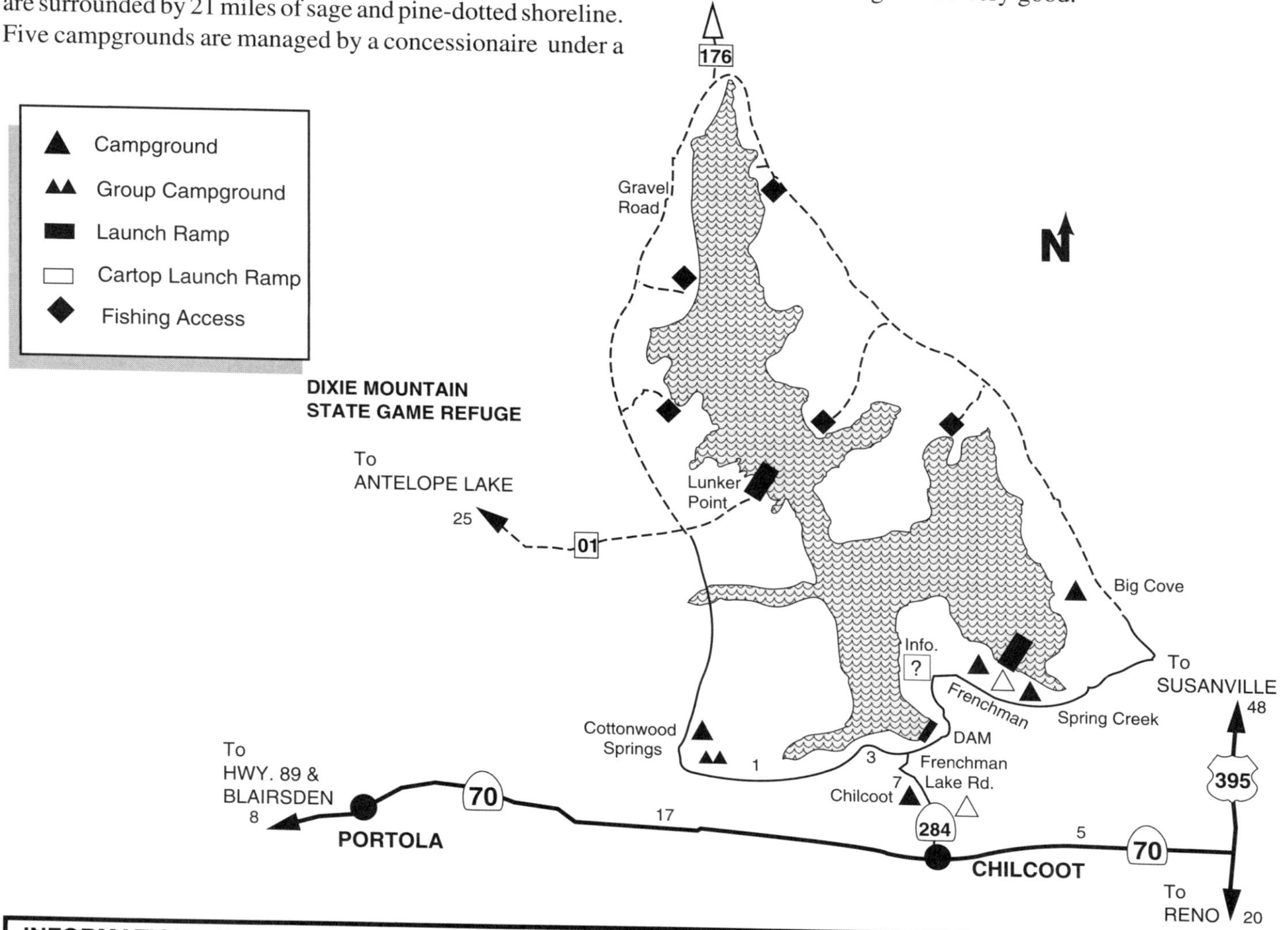
Campground
Group Campground
Launch Ramp
Cartop Launch Ramp
Fishing Access
176
Gravel Road
N
DIXIE MOUNTAIN
STATE GAME REFUGE
To
ANTELOPE LAKE
25
01
Lunker Point
Big Cove
Info.
?
To
SUSANVILLE
48
Frenchman
Spring Creek
Cottonwood Springs
DAM
1
3
Frenchman Lake Rd.
7
Chilcoot
395
To
HWY. 89 &
BLAIRSDEN
8
70
17
284
5
70
PORTOLA
CHILCOOT
To
RENO
20

INFORMATION: Beckwourth Ranger Dist. P.O. Box 7, 23 Mohawk Rd., Blairsden 96103—Ph: (530) 836-2575

CAMPING	BOATING	RECREATION	OTHER
Cottonwood Springs: 20 Single Sites-Fee: $18 2 Group Sites - 20 & 50 People - Fees: $70-$110 Chilcoot: 5 Walk-in & 35 Single Sites Spring Creek: 35 Sites Frenchman: 38 Sites Big Cove: 19 Singles & 19 Double Sites Fee: Single $18,Double $36 Reservations: Ph: (877) 444-6777	Power, Row, Canoe, Sail, Waterski, PWCs, Windsurf, Inflatables Launch Ramps with Docks *Check Current Water Levels*	Fishing: Brown & Rainbow Trout Swimming Picnicking: 15 Sites Hiking Trails No Hunting on West Side of Lake in Game Refuge No Off Road Vehicles in Recreation Area	Supplies at Wiggens Store 7 Miles in Chilcoot Plumas County Visitors Bureau Ph: (800) 326-2247

EAST PARK RESERVOIR - PLASKETT and LETTS LAKES

East Park Reservoir, with 25 shoreline miles, is operated by the Bureau of Reclamation. This warm water fishery is known for good bass fishing. All boating is allowed. Open primitive camping surrounds most of the Lake. Plaskett Lake, elevation 6,000 feet and Letts Lake at 4,500 feet, are within the Mendocino National Forest. These remote Lakes are good for trout fishing. Gas or electric powered boats are *not* allowed. Letts Lake is popular with hikers and backpackers who enjoy the Snow Mountain Wilderness. Summit Springs Trailhead is nearby. Trailers over 16 feet are not advised at Plaskett or Letts Lakes due to dirt access roads.

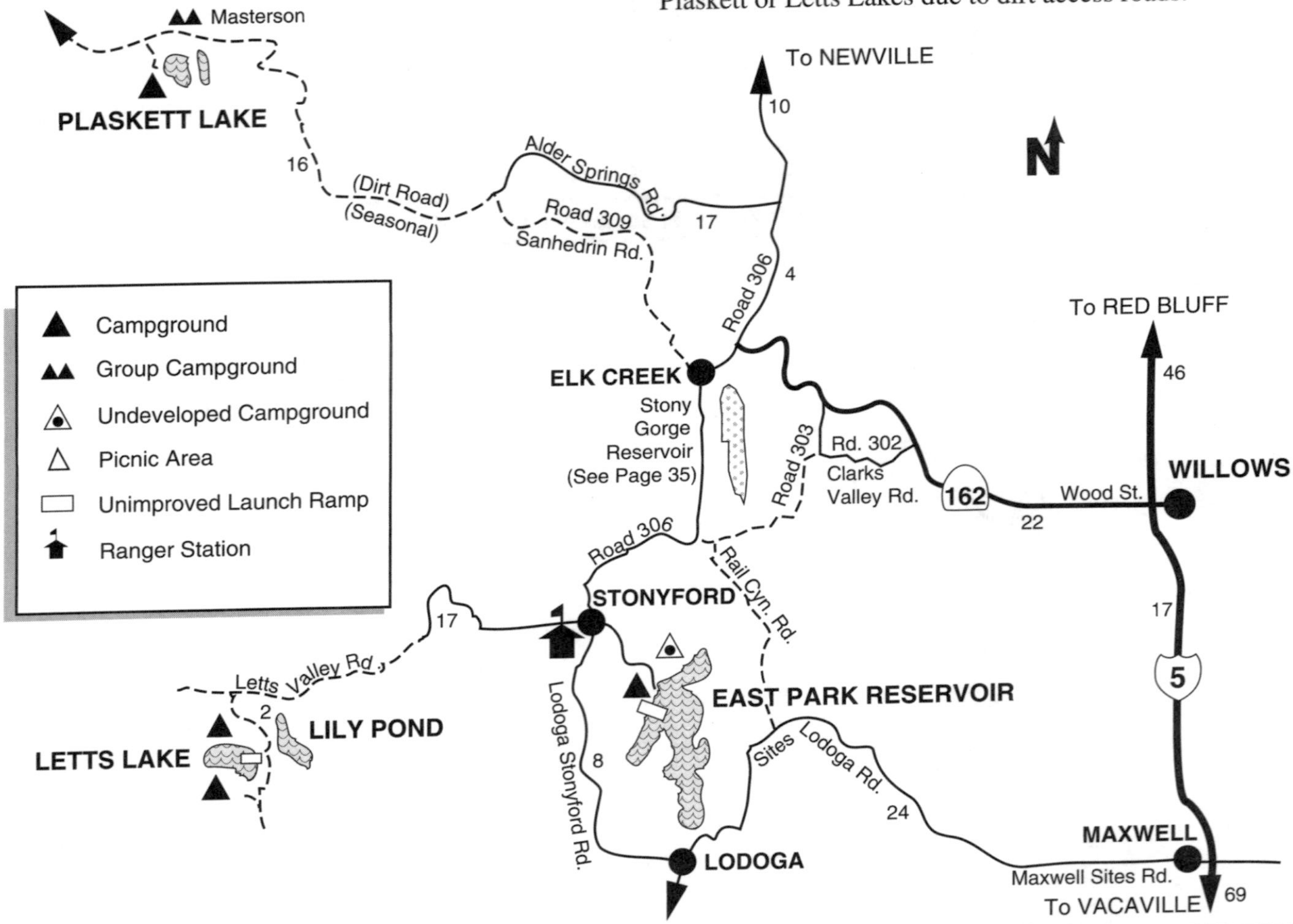

Masterson
PLASKETT LAKE
16
(Dirt Road)
(Seasonal)
Alder Springs Rd.
Road 309
Sanhedrin Rd.
17
To NEWVILLE
10
N
Road 306
4
To RED BLUFF
46
Campground
Group Campground
Undeveloped Campground
Picnic Area
Unimproved Launch Ramp
Ranger Station
ELK CREEK
Stony Gorge Reservoir (See Page 35)
Road 303
Rd. 302
Clarks Valley Rd.
162
Wood St.
WILLOWS
22
Road 306
Rail Cyn. Rd.
STONYFORD
17
Letts Valley Rd.
2
LILY POND
LETTS LAKE
Lodoga Stonyford Rd.
8
EAST PARK RESERVOIR
Sites Lodoga Rd.
24
5
MAXWELL
LODOGA
Maxwell Sites Rd.
To VACAVILLE
69

INFORMATION: East Park Reservoir, Bureau of Reclamation, P.O. Box 988, Willows 95988--Ph: (530) 934-7069

CAMPING	BOATING	RECREATION	OTHER
East Park Reservoir: Open Primitive Camping Around Most of the Lake No Water No Electricity Group Camp Available 15 Min. - 200 Max. Reservations	East Park Reservoir: Open to All Boats Subject to Low Water Hazards Unimproved Ramp 5 MPH Zone 100 feet from All Shorelines Boating Laws Strictly Enforced	Fishing: East Park Reservoir: Large & Smallmouth Bass, Bluegill, Crappie & Catfish Plaskett Lake: Trout Letts Lake: Bass & Trout Swimming Hiking & Nature Trails East Park: No Hunting & No ORV's	Plaskett & Letts Lakes: USFS - Stonyford R.D. P.O. Box 160 Stonyford 95979 Ph: (530) 963-3128 No Gas or Electric Boats at These Lakes Camping (Dogs on Leash): Letts - 42 Sites - Fee: $10 Plaskett - 32 Sites - Fee: $8 Masterson Group Site by Reservation - Fee: $50

Black Butte is surrounded by rolling hills with basalt buttes and open grasslands spotted with oak trees. It is at an elevation of 470 feet. This 4,500 surface-acre Lake has a shoreline of 40 miles. The U.S. Army Corps of Engineers administers the well-maintained campgrounds and facilities at the Lake. Water levels can change rapidly. Boaters are cautioned against possible hazards, such as sand bars, exposed during low water. This is a good warm water fishery especially in the spring when the crappie are hungry. There is abundant wildlife and the birdwatcher will find a wide variety of avian life.

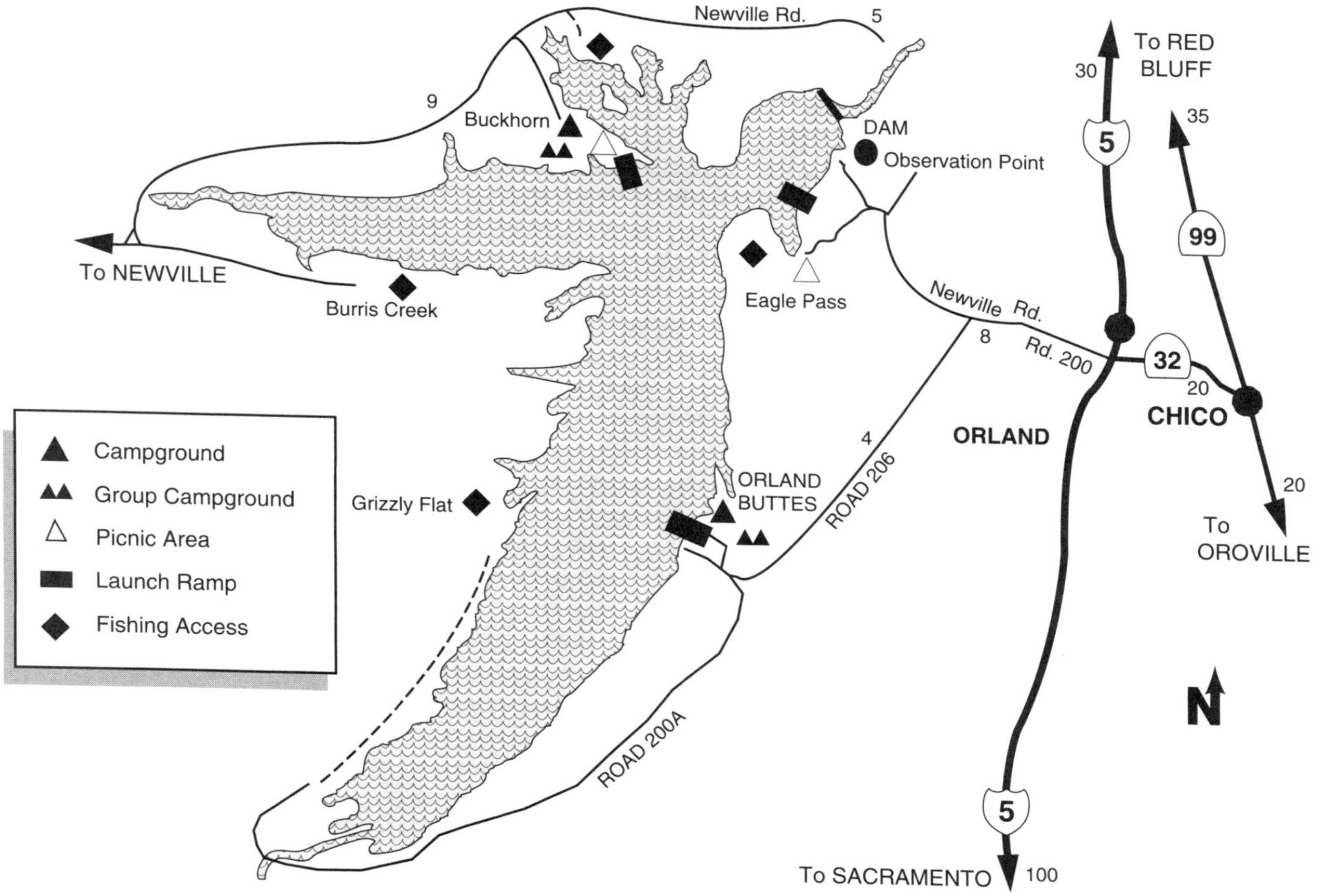
Newville Rd.
5
9
Buckhorn
DAM
Observation Point
To RED BLUFF
30
35
5
99
To NEWVILLE
Burris Creek
Eagle Pass
Newville Rd.
8
Rd. 200
32
20
CHICO
ORLAND
4
ROAD 206
ORLAND BUTTES
Grizzly Flat
20
To OROVILLE
Campground
Group Campground
Picnic Area
Launch Ramp
Fishing Access
ROAD 200A
N
5
To SACRAMENTO
100

INFORMATION: Park Manager, 19225 Newville Rd., Orland 95963—Ph: (530) 865-4781

CAMPING	BOATING	RECREATION	OTHER
Buckhorn: 65 Dev.Sites Tents & R.V.s-Fee: $15 Group Camp to 200 People - Fee: $120 Open Year Round Orland Buttes: 35 Dev. Sites Tents & R.V.s - Fee: $15 Group Camp to 100 People - Fee: $90 Open April-Sept. Disposal Station Reserve All Sites: Ph: (877) 444-6777	Power, Row, Canoe, Sail, Waterski, PWCs, Windsurf, Inflatables Launch Ramps - Fee: $4	Fishing: Large & Smallmouth Bass, Blue, White & Channel Catfish, Crappie, Bluegill & Green Sunfish Swimming Picnicking Hiking Trails Playground Campfire Programs	Full Facilities - 8 Miles at Orland

STONY GORGE RESERVOIR

Stony Gorge Reservoir is at an elevation of 800 feet in the foothills west of Willows in the upper Sacramento Valley. The Lake has a surface area of 1,275 acres and is under the administration of the U. S. Bureau of Reclamation. The rolling hills surrounding the 18 miles of shoreline are dotted with oak, digger pine and brush. Most of the shoreline is accessible. A number of campsites are relatively primitive. Boating facilities are limited to a 1-lane paved launch ramp which is not usable during late summer and fall . The fishing is good for warm water species in this scenic Lake.

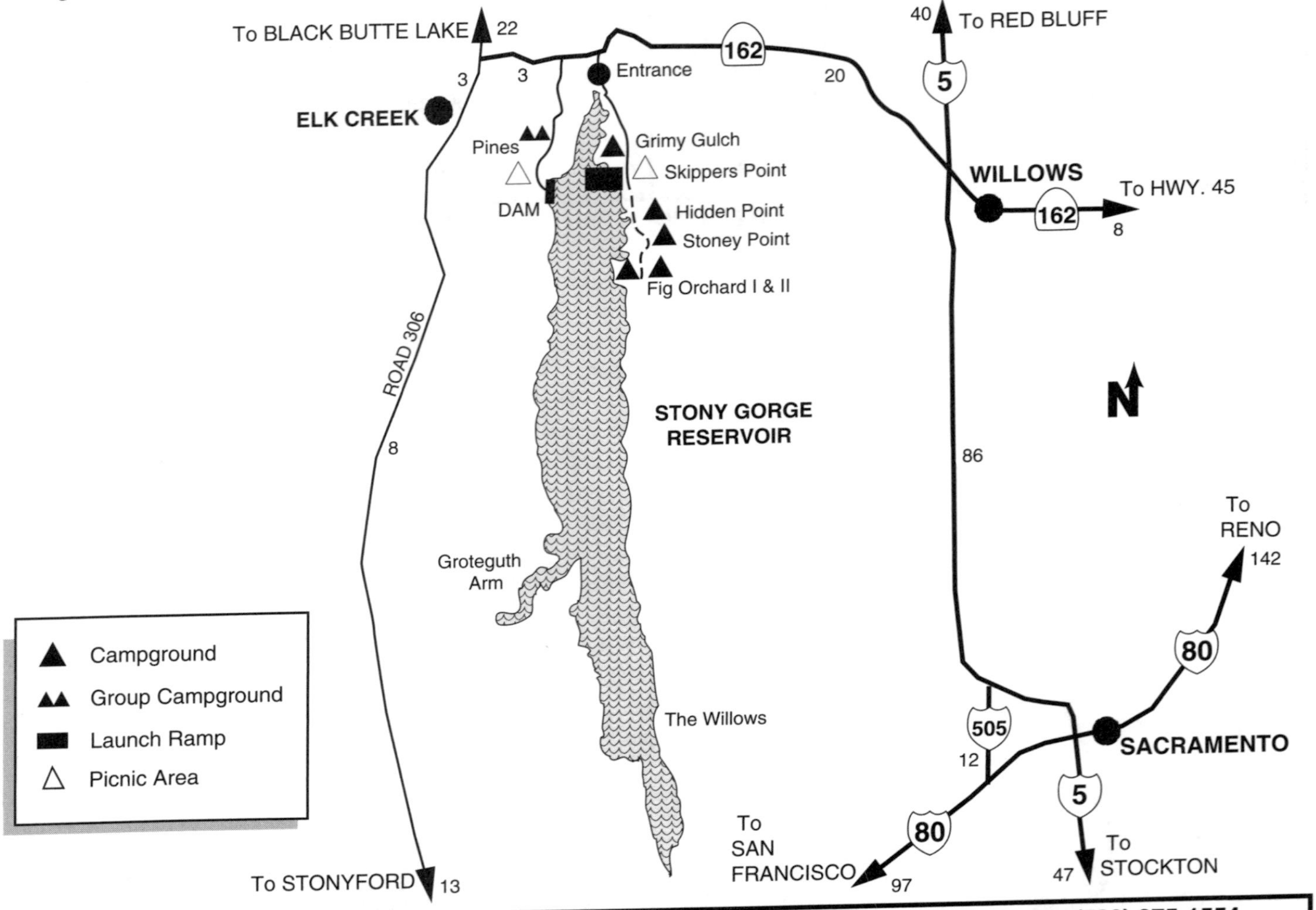
To BLACK BUTTE LAKE
22
3
3
Entrance
162
20
40
To RED BLUFF
5
ELK CREEK
Pines
Grimy Gulch
Skippers Point
DAM
Hidden Point
Stoney Point
Fig Orchard I & II
WILLOWS
To HWY. 45
162
8
ROAD 306
STONY GORGE
RESERVOIR
N
8
86
Groteguth
Arm
To
RENO
142
80
Campground
Group Campground
Launch Ramp
Picnic Area
The Willows
505
SACRAMENTO
12
5
To
SAN
FRANCISCO
80
97
To
STOCKTON
47
To STONYFORD
13

INFORMATION: Bureau of Reclamation, 16349 Shasta Dam Blvd., Shasta Lake 96019—Ph: (530) 275-1554

CAMPING	BOATING	RECREATION	OTHER
Primitive Sites for Tents & R.V.s No Fees Group Camp to 200 People Maximum Reservations No Electricity No Water	Power, Row, Canoe, Sail, Waterski, Windsurf & Inflatables No Houseboats Permitted Launch Ramp *Underwater Hazards Due to Fluctuation in Lake Level*	Fishing: Catfish, Bluegill, Crappie, Bass & Perch Swimming Picnicking - Group Site No ORV's	Elk Creek: Country Store Gas Station Full Facilities in Willows

LAKE OROVILLE

The Oroville Dam is the highest in the United States towering 770 feet above the City of Oroville. The Park encompasses 28,450 acres. Lake Oroville, at 900 feet elevation, has 15,500 surface acres with a shoreline of 167 miles. Although water levels drop late in the summer, the Lake offers unlimited recreation the year around. This is an excellent boating Lake with good marina facilities. Boat-in campsites and houseboat moorings are available for those who wish to spend the night on the Lake. The angler will find an extensive variety of game fish from smallmouth bass to king salmon. To the West, Thermalito Forebay includes 300 surface acres for boating, fishing and swimming.

....Continued....

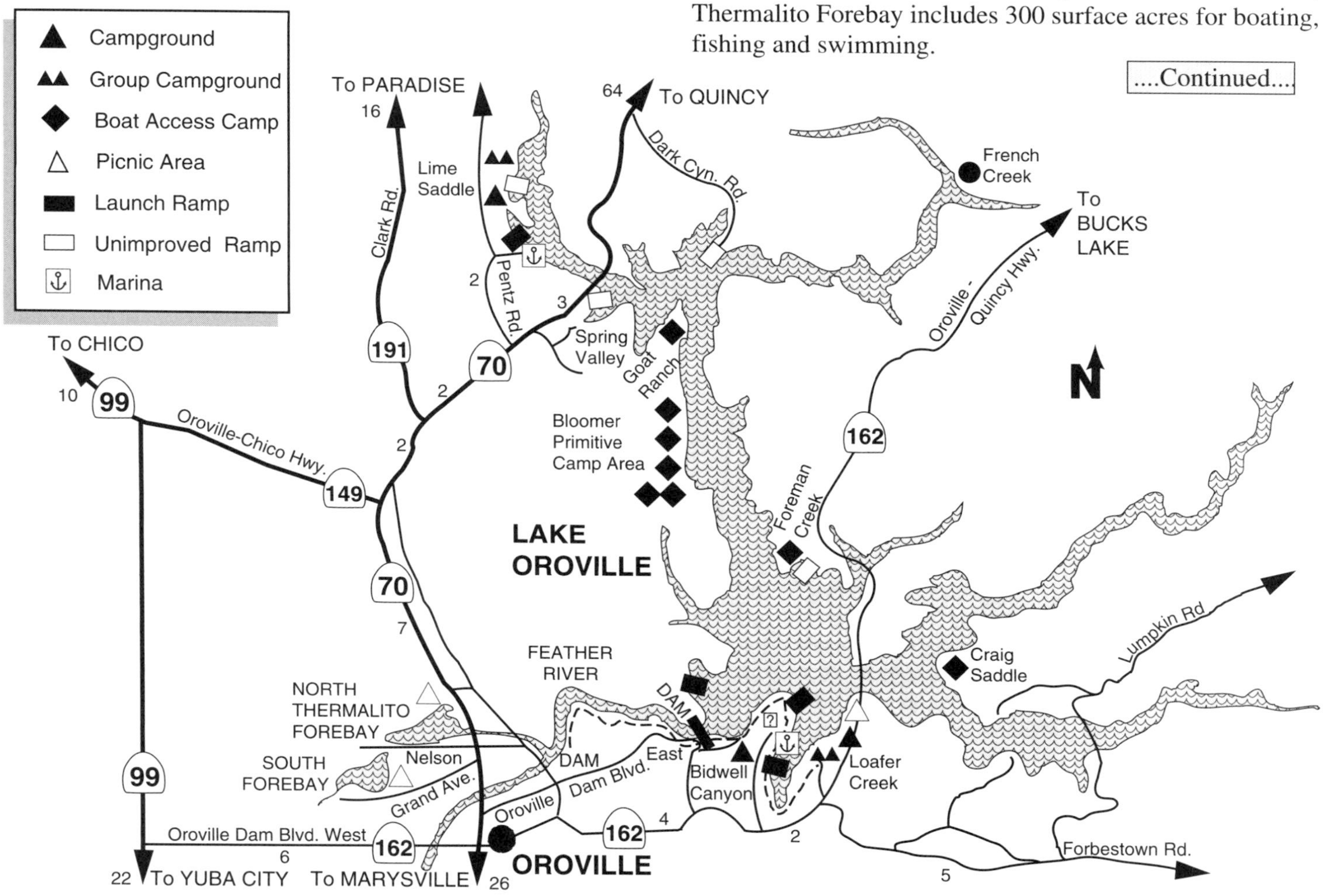

Campground
Group Campground
Boat Access Camp
Picnic Area
Launch Ramp
Unimproved Ramp
Marina
To PARADISE
16
To QUINCY
64
Clark Rd.
Lime Saddle
Pentz Rd.
Dark Cyn. Rd
French Creek
To BUCKS LAKE
Oroville - Quincy Hwy.
Spring Valley
Goat Ranch
To CHICO
10
99
Oroville-Chico Hwy.
149
191
70
Bloomer Primitive Camp Area
162
Foreman Creek
LAKE OROVILLE
70
FEATHER RIVER
NORTH THERMALITO FOREBAY
DAM
SOUTH FOREBAY
Nelson
Grand Ave.
DAM
East
Dam Blvd.
Oroville
Bidwell Canyon
Loafer Creek
Craig Saddle
Lumpkin Rd
99
Oroville Dam Blvd. West
6
162
162
4
2
5
Forbestown Rd.
22
To YUBA CITY
To MARYSVILLE
26
OROVILLE
N

INFORMATION: State Recreation Area, 400 Glen Dr., Oroville 95966—Ph: (530) 538-2200

CAMPING	BOATING	RECREATION	OTHER
Family Campsites R.V. Hookup Sites Boat-In Campsites Group Campsites Floating Campsites: 2-Story Structure Moored in a Cove Horse Camp Some Campsites: Reservations: Ph: (800) 444-7275 *See Following Page*	All Boating Allowed Full Service Marinas Paved Launch Ramps Hand Launch Ramps Docks, Berths & Moorings Rentals: Fishing, Waterski & Houseboats	Fishing: Large & Smallmouth Bass, Coho & King Salmon Rainbow Trout in the Forebay Picnicking Hiking & Equestrian Trails Bicycle Trails Swimming (No Diving) Visitor Center Fish Hatchery	Full Facilities in Oroville & Paradise Grocery Stores & Motels 7 Miles from Lime Saddle

LAKE OROVILLE..............continued

CAMPGROUNDS: On Season Rates: May 15 to September 15

LOAFER CREEK:
137 Sites for Tents & R.V.s to 31 feet - Fee: $18 On Season, $13 Off Season
Water, Showers, Laundry Tubs, Disposal Station, 100 Picnic Sites, Swim Beach, Launch Ramp.
Campground Ph: (530) 538-2217
Group Camps: 6 Well-Developed Group Camps Each Accommodating 25 People - Fee: $60
Campground Ph: (530) 538-2217
Equestrian Camp - Fee: $30 On Season, $25 Off Season

BIDWELL CANYON:
75 R.V. Sites to 40 Feet (Boat Trailer in Total R.V. length) - Full Hookups - Fee: $24 On Season, $19 Off Season
Launch Ramp, Boat Rentals, Full Service Marina - Ph: (530) 589-3165)
Grocery Store, Laundry Tubs, Snack Bar - Campground Ph: (530) 538-2218.
Reserve: Ph: (800) 444-7275

LIME SADDLE:
44 R.V. Sites to 40 Feet - Fee: Hookups $24 On Season, $19 Off Season,
Tents: Fee: $18 On Season, $13 Off Season, Disposal Station
Group Camps: 2 Sites with 4 Tent Pads Each Accommodating 25 People Each. - Fee: $20
Campground Ph: (530) 876-8516

BOAT-IN CAMPS: *NO Drinking Water Available*
109 sites at: Craig Saddle, Foreman Point, Goat Ranch, Bloomer,
Primitive Area - North Point, Knoll, South Cove, Bloomer. Fee: $12
Group Camp for 75 People Located at South Bloomer : Fees: $90
Reserve: Ph: (800) 444-7275

LAKE OROVILLE MARINA, 3428 Pentz Rd., Paradise 95969—Ph: (530) 877-2414
1-1/2 miles off Hwy. 70 on Pentz Rd.
Full Service Marina, 5-Lane Launch Ramp, Gas, Boat Shop,
Rentals: Houseboats, Ski Boats, Fishing & Patio Boats
Store, Bait & Tackle, Ice, Propane & Pumpout Station.

BIDWELL CANYON MARINA, 801 Bidwell Canyon Road, Oroville 95966—Ph: (530) 589-3165 or (800) 637-1767
Full Service Marina, Gas, Rentals: Fishing, Patio, & Water Ski Boats, Houseboats,
Overnight Moorings, Docks, Covered & Open Slips, Dry Storage,
Gift Shop, Grocery Store, Bait & Tackle, Ice, Pumpout Station.

PAVED LAUNCH RAMPS ALSO LOCATED AT:

SPILLWAY: 3-Lane Launch Ramp, Parking, Toilets, Overnight Camping for Self-Contained R.V.s.
ENTERPRISE: Free 2-Lane Launch Ramp, Cartop Launch During Low Water.

THERMALITO FOREBAY

The *North End of the Forebay* is for Day Use. There are 300 Surface Acres. Facilities include a 2-lane launch ramp, sandy swim beach, picnic tables, shade ramadas, potable water and many lovely trees. This area is for sailboats and other non-power boats only. *The Group Area is by Reservation at Park Headquarters.*
The *South End of the Forebay* has a 4-lane launch ramp. There is no shade or potable water.

Little Grass Valley, at 5,100 feet elevation, and Sly Creek, at 3,550 feet elevation, are scenic Lakes in the Plumas National Forest. Little Grass Valley, with 1,433 surface acres and 16 miles of shoreline, is a good boating lake. There is an abundance of developed campsites in this forested area. Numerous designated hiking, mountain biking and equestrian trails surround Little Grass Valley Recreation Area. Sly Creek Reservoir has 562 surface acres with facilities for boating and camping. Its neighbor, Lost Creek Reservoir, is primarily surrounded by private land except for a small portion of Forest Service land on the north side with steep slopes to the water.

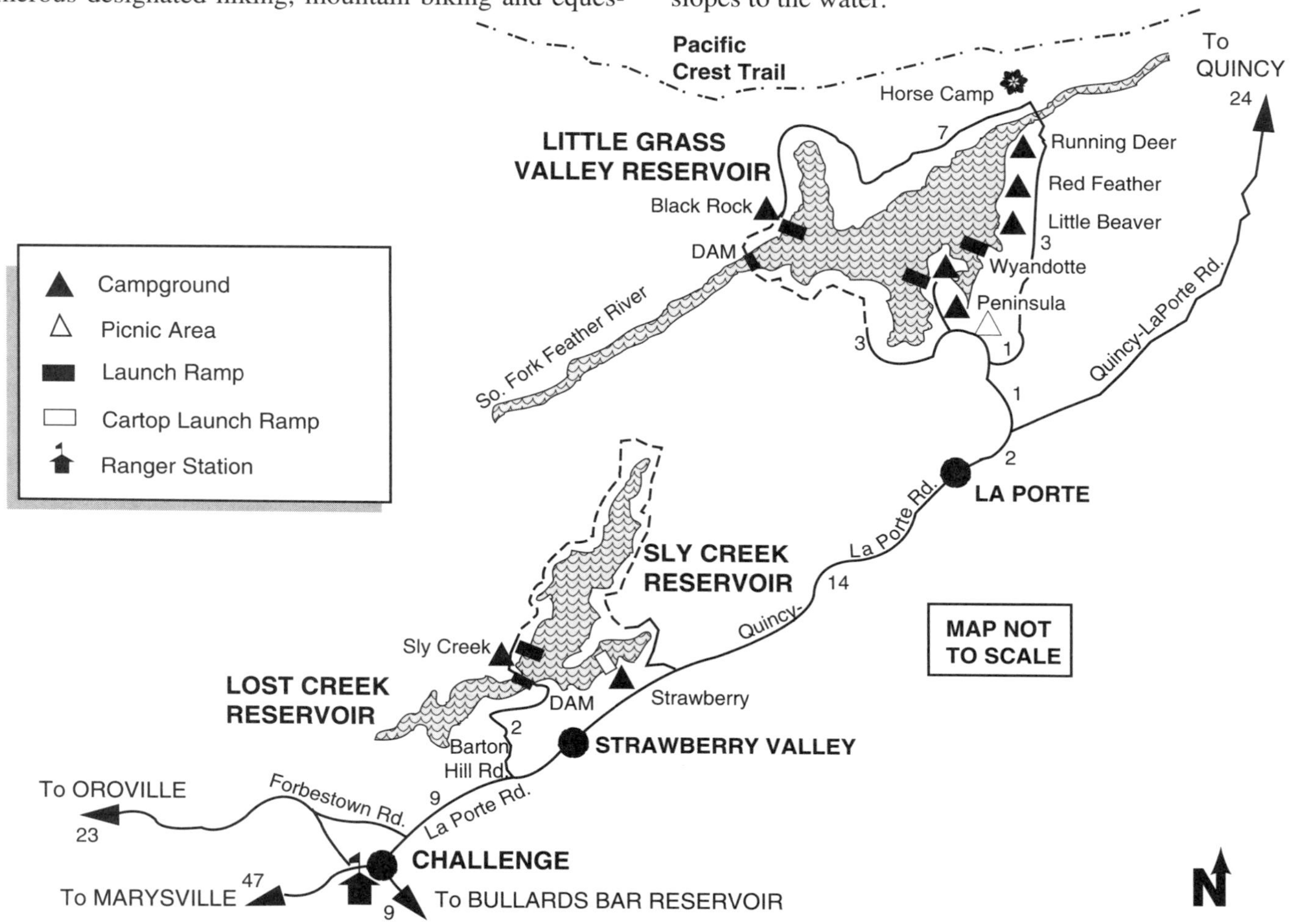
Pacific Crest Trail
To QUINCY
24
Horse Camp
LITTLE GRASS VALLEY RESERVOIR
Running Deer
Red Feather
Little Beaver
Black Rock
DAM
Wyandotte
Peninsula
So. Fork Feather River
Quincy-LaPorte Rd.
Campground
Picnic Area
Launch Ramp
Cartop Launch Ramp
Ranger Station
LA PORTE
SLY CREEK RESERVOIR
La Porte Rd.
Quincy-
MAP NOT TO SCALE
Sly Creek
LOST CREEK RESERVOIR
DAM
Strawberry
Barton Hill Rd.
STRAWBERRY VALLEY
To OROVILLE
23
Forbestown Rd.
La Porte Rd.
CHALLENGE
To MARYSVILLE
47
To BULLARDS BAR RESERVOIR
N

INFORMATION: Feather River Ranger District, 875 Mitchell Ave., Oroville 95965—Ph: (530) 534-6500

CAMPING	BOATING	RECREATION	OTHER
Little Grass Valley: 330 Dev. Sites for Tents & R.V.s to 40 feet Plus Equestrian Camp Fee: $18 - $20 2 Disposal Stations Reservations for: Horse Camp, Running Deer & Red Feather Ph: (877) 444-6777 Sly Creek: 53 Dev. Sites for Tents & R.V.s - Fee: $18	Little Grass Valley: Open to Small Boats 3 Paved Launch Ramps Sly Creek: Open to Small Boats 1 Paved Launch Ramp 1 Cartop Launch Ramp	Fishing: Rainbow, Brook & Brown Trout Swimming - Beaches Picnicking Hiking Trails Mountain Bike Trails Equestrian Trails Backpacking Nature Study ORVs with Restrictions	Facilities: 3 Miles at La Porte Abandoned Mining Towns Nearby Access to Pacific Crest Trail

GOLD LAKE and THE LAKES BASIN RECREATION AREA

Over 50 small glacial lakes and numerous streams filled with trout are located in this scenic area. Gold Lake is the largest. Elevations range from 5,000 to 7,000 feet. Many Lakes can only be reached by trail. This is a popular fly fishing area, especially along the Middle Fork of the Feather River which has been designated a natural Wild and Scenic River. The Lakes Basin is in both the Plumas and Tahoe National Forests. Part of the Pacific Crest Trail is through this area along with an extensive systems of hiking, mountain biking and equestrain trails. There are a number of resorts and facilities in this beautiful region.

....Continued....

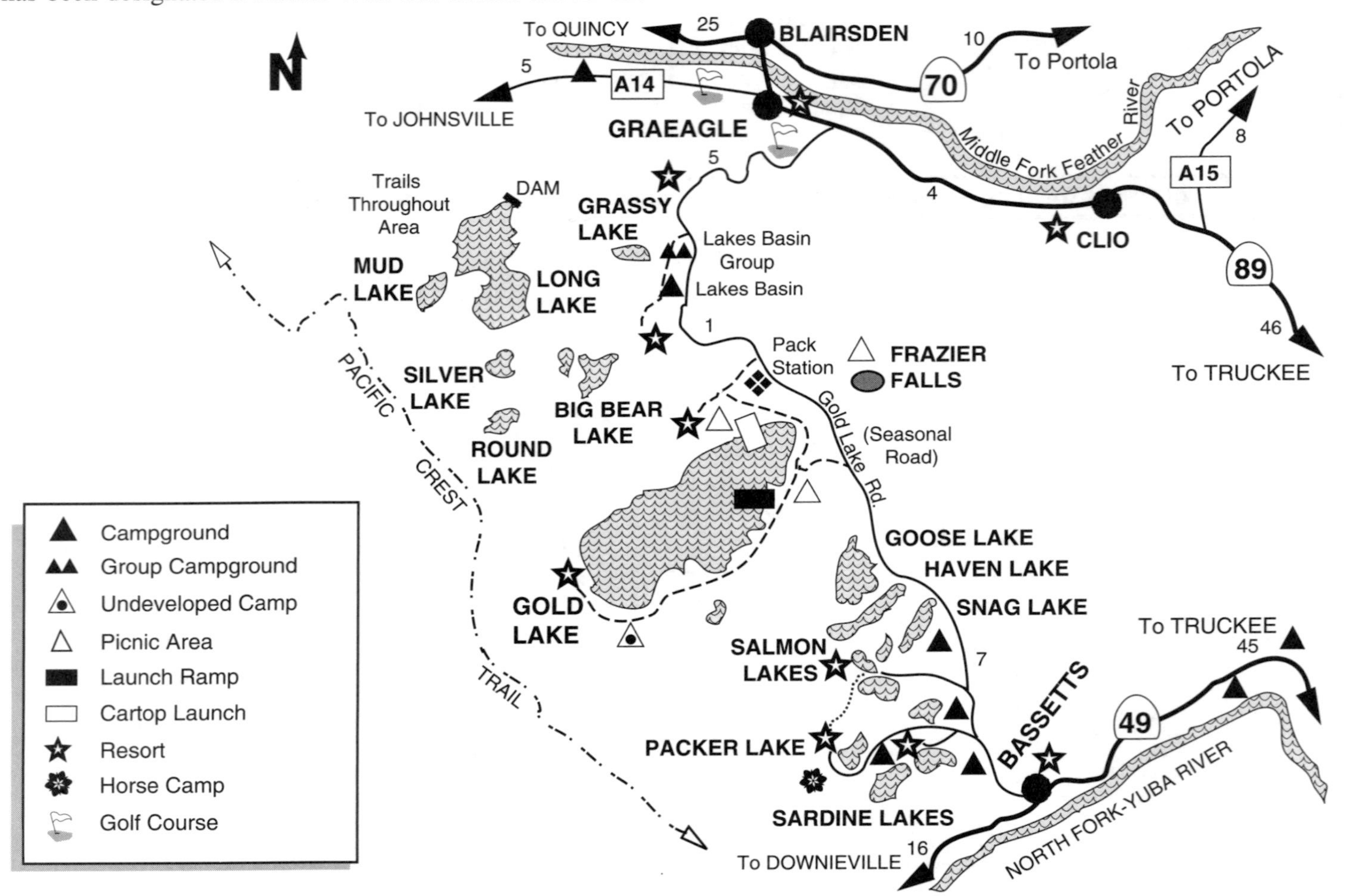

To QUINCY
25
BLAIRSDEN
10
To Portola
70
5
A14
To JOHNSVILLE
GRAEAGLE
Middle Fork Feather River
To PORTOLA
8
A15
4
CLIO
89
46
To TRUCKEE
N
Trails Throughout Area
DAM
GRASSY LAKE
5
Lakes Basin Group
Lakes Basin
MUD LAKE
LONG LAKE
1
Pack Station
FRAZIER FALLS
SILVER LAKE
BIG BEAR LAKE
PACIFIC CREST TRAIL
Gold Lake Rd.
(Seasonal Road)
ROUND LAKE
GOOSE LAKE
HAVEN LAKE
SNAG LAKE
GOLD LAKE
To TRUCKEE
45
SALMON LAKES
7
BASSETTS
49
PACKER LAKE
SARDINE LAKES
NORTH FORK-YUBA RIVER
16
To DOWNIEVILLE
Campground
Group Campground
Undeveloped Camp
Picnic Area
Launch Ramp
Cartop Launch
Resort
Horse Camp
Golf Course

INFORMATION: Beckwourth Ranger District, P.O. Box 7, 23 Mohawk Rd., Blairsden 96103—Ph: (530) 836-2575

CAMPING	BOATING	RECREATION	OTHER
North Area: Beckwourth Ranger District Ph: (530) 836-2575 South Area: North Yuba Ranger District Ph: (530) 288-3231 *See Following Page*	Gold Lake: Power, Row, Sail, Windsurfing & Waterskiing Launch Ramp with Dock Cartop Launch	Fishing: Rainbow & Eastern Brook Trout, Picnicking Hiking Trails Mountain Bike Trails Equestrian Trails Gold Lake Pack Station Ph: (530) 836-0940 Swimming Golf Courses: 9-Hole & 18-Hole ORVs Not Permitted in Recreation Area	Numerous Facilities & Resorts *See Following Page* Plumas County Visitors Bureau Ph: 800-326-2247 Sierra County Chamber of Commerce Ph: 800-200-4949

Plumas National Forest
Beckworth Ranger Station
Campgrounds:
Lakes Basin: 24 Dev. Sites for Tents & R.V.s - Fee: $16
Group Site to 25 People Maximum - Fee: $60
Reservations Ph: (877) 444-6777
Gold Lake 4 x 4 Camp: 16 Sityes No Water, No Fee,
No Reservations, 4 x 4 Entry Road

Tahoe National Forest
North Yuba Ranger Station
Undeveloped Campgrounds:
Berger: 10 Sites,
Diablo: 20 Sites,
Salmon Creek: 31 Sites,
Sardine: 29 Sites,
Snag: 16 Sites
Packsaddle: 20 Sites including Corral for Horses
No Reservations

The following is a list of a variety of some accommodations in the Lakes Basin Recreation Area, in alphabetical order. Many of the lodges and resorts are fully booked one year in advance in season so reservations are imperative. Phone Facility for Seasonal Information and Pet Restrictions

CLIO'S RIVERS EDGE R V PARK - Box 111, 3754 Highway 89, Clio 96106—Ph: (530) 836-2375
220 R.V. Sites to 45 feet, Full Hookups, Seasonal.

ELWELL LAKES LODGE - Box 68, Gold Lake Rd., Blairsden 96103—Ph: (530) 836-2347
10 Housekeeping Cabins, B&B Rooms, Recreation Room, Complimentary Boats for Guests, Creek-filled Swimming Pool, BBQ, No Pets, Seasonal.

FEATHER RIVER PARK RESORT, Box 37, Highway 89, Blairsden 96103—Ph: (530) 836-2328
35 Housekeeping Log Cabins, Weekly Rental Only from mid-June to Labor Day, 3 Swimming Pools, 9-Hole Golf Course, Lodge with Games & Snacks, Pets OK, Seasonal.

GOLD LAKE LODGE, Box 308, Graeagle 96103—Ph: (530) 836-2350
10 Cabins, Breakfast, Trail Lunch & Dinner Included, Lodge, Restaurant, Row Boats for Guests, No Pets, Seasonal.

GRAY EAGLE LODGE, Box 38, Gold Lake Rd., Graeagle 96103—Ph: (800) 635-8778
20 Cabins, Breakfast & Dinner Included, 3-Night Min., Lodge, Restaurant, Game Room, Pets OK, Seasonal.

HIGH COUNTRY INN, Highway 49 & Gold Lake Rd., Sierra City 96125—Ph: (530) 862-1530 or (800) 862-1530
4 Rooms, Views of Sierra Buttes & River, Deck, No Pets, Open All Year.

LITTLE BEAR R.V. PARK, Box 103, Blairsden 96103—Ph: (530) 836-2774
95 R.V. Sites to 40 ft., Full Hookups, Store, Seasonal.

MOVIN' WEST TRAILER RANCH, Box 1010, 305 Johnsville Rd., Graeagle 96103—Ph: (530) 836-2614
51 Tent & R.V. Sites to 40 Feet, Full Hookups, 2 Cabins, Seasonal.

PACKER LAKE LODGE, Box 237, 3901 Packer Lake Rd., Sierra City 96125—Ph: (530) 862-1221
14 Cabins, 8 with Kitchens, Complimentary Boat Included, Store, Restaurant, Pets OK, Seasonal.

RIVER PINES RESORT, Box 247, Highway 89, Clio 96106—Ph: (530) 836-2552 or in California (800) 696-2551
18 Housekeeping Cabins, Motel Rooms, Pool, Playground, Recreation Room, Restaurant, Open All Year.

SALMON LAKE LODGE, Box 121, Sierra City 96125—Ph: (530) 852-0874
10 Tent Cabins plus 4 Permanent Cabins, Central Utility House with Refrigerator & Showers, Bring Own Sleeping Bags, Pans & Groceries, Parking at East End of Lake, Barge Transports Guest & Baggage Across Lake, Fishing Boats, Kayaks and Canoes for Guests.

SARDINE LAKES RESORT—Ph: (530) 862-1196 - 9 Cabins, Lunch & Dinner by Reservations, Rental Boats.

BULLARDS BAR RESERVOIR

Bullards Bar Reservoir, surrounded by rugged countryside, is at an elevation of 2,000 feet in the Tahoe and Plumas National Forests. This beautiful Lake, with 4,700 surface acres, has 56 miles of shoreline. The area is heavily wooded so all campsites are shaded by trees. All boating is allowed. Waterskiing and wakeboarding is popular. Fishing is open year around for both warm and cold water fish. This is a prime Lake for Kokanee salmon. The Yuba County Water Agency and the U.S. Forest Service maintain 30 boat access camps as well as lakeside camping. Emerald Cove Marina is a full service facility offering rental houseboats and fishing boats, private houseboat moorings and other services. Bullards Bar Reservoir is a great place to visit for outdoor recreation.

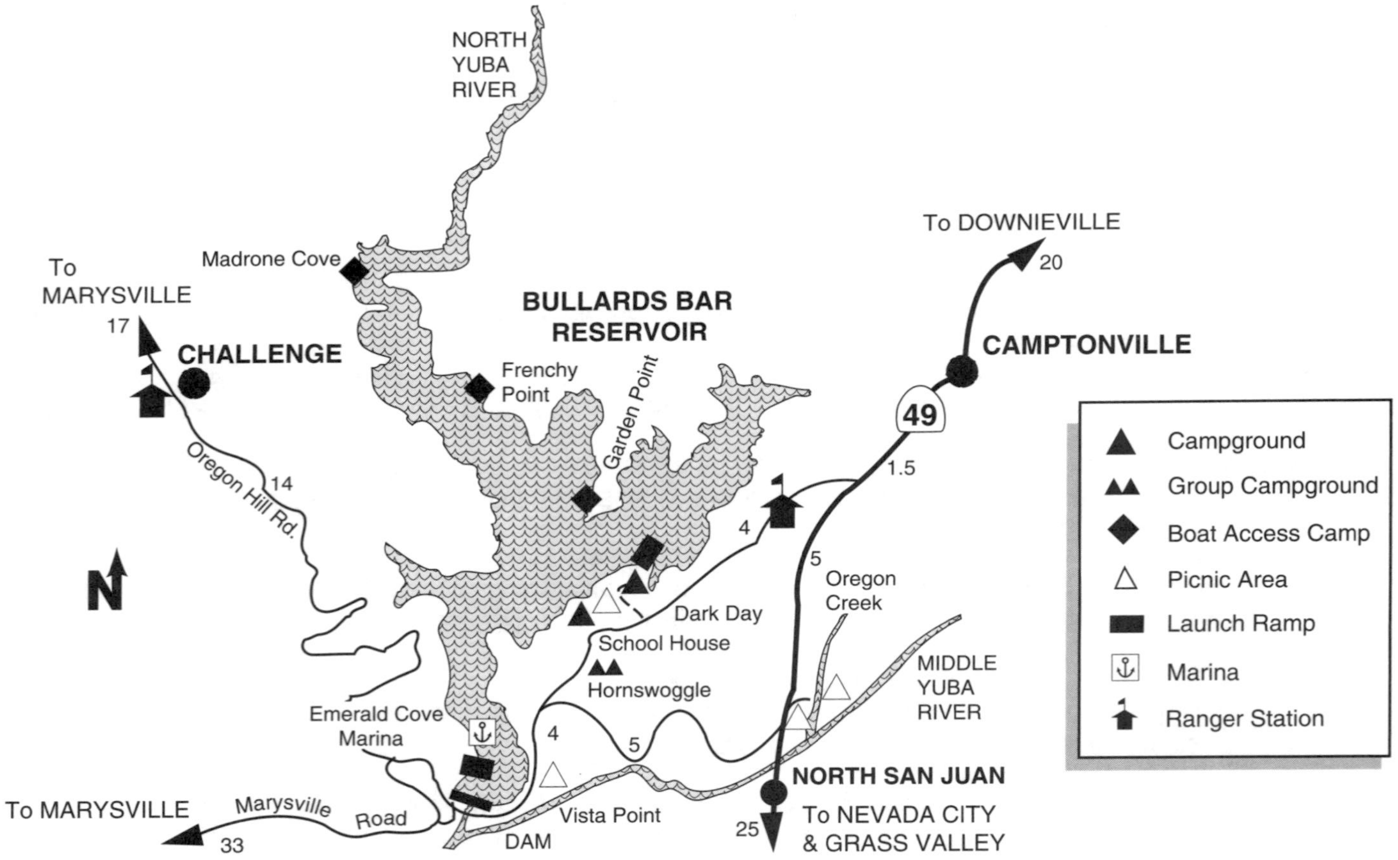
NORTH YUBA RIVER
To DOWNIEVILLE
20
To MARYSVILLE
Madrone Cove
17
CHALLENGE
BULLARDS BAR RESERVOIR
CAMPTONVILLE
Frenchy Point
Garden Point
49
Oregon Hill Rd.
14
1.5
4
5
Oregon Creek
Dark Day
School House
Hornswoggle
MIDDLE YUBA RIVER
Emerald Cove Marina
4
5
NORTH SAN JUAN
To MARYSVILLE
Marysville Road
33
Vista Point
DAM
25
To NEVADA CITY & GRASS VALLEY
N
Campground
Group Campground
Boat Access Camp
Picnic Area
Launch Ramp
Marina
Ranger Station

INFORMATION: Emerald Cove Marina, P.O. Box 480, Dobbins 95935—Ph: (530) 692-3200

CAMPING	BOATING	RECREATION	OTHER
Emerald Cove Resort: Accepts Reservations Dev. Sites for Tents & R.V.s - No Hookups Boat Access Camps Shoreline Camping Fee: $22 up to 6 People Hornswoggle Group Camps 4 Sites - 15-25 People Fee: $80 1 Site - 35-50 People Fee: $140 Dark Day: Tents Only	Open to All Boating Launch Ramps - No Fee Full Service Marina Gas - Propane Rentals: Fishing, Ski & Patio Boats, Wakeboards & Houseboats Private Houseboat Moorings Overnight Slips & Dry Storage	Fishing: Kokanee Salmon Rainbow & Brown Trout, Bluegill, Catfish, Crappie, Large & Smallmouth Bass, Swimming Picnicking Hiking Trails Mountain Bike Trails	Snack Bar Grocery Store Bait & Tackle USFS - North Yuba Ranger Station 15924 Highway 49 Camptonville 95922 Ph: (530) 288-3231

BOWMAN LAKE

Bowman Lake is the largest of several small Lakes in the scenic Bowman Road Area of the Tahoe National Forest. Bowman is 6 miles south of Jackson Meadow Reservoir and 16 miles north of Highway 20. These are often steep and rocky roads; 4-wheel drive or high clearance vehicles are advised. The Lakes range in altitude from 5,600 feet to 7,000 feet in beautiful high Sierra country. The Forest Service and PG&E maintain a number of campsites in the area but be sure to bring your own drinking water. Stream and lake fishing can be excellent in this rugged, remote and very scenic region.

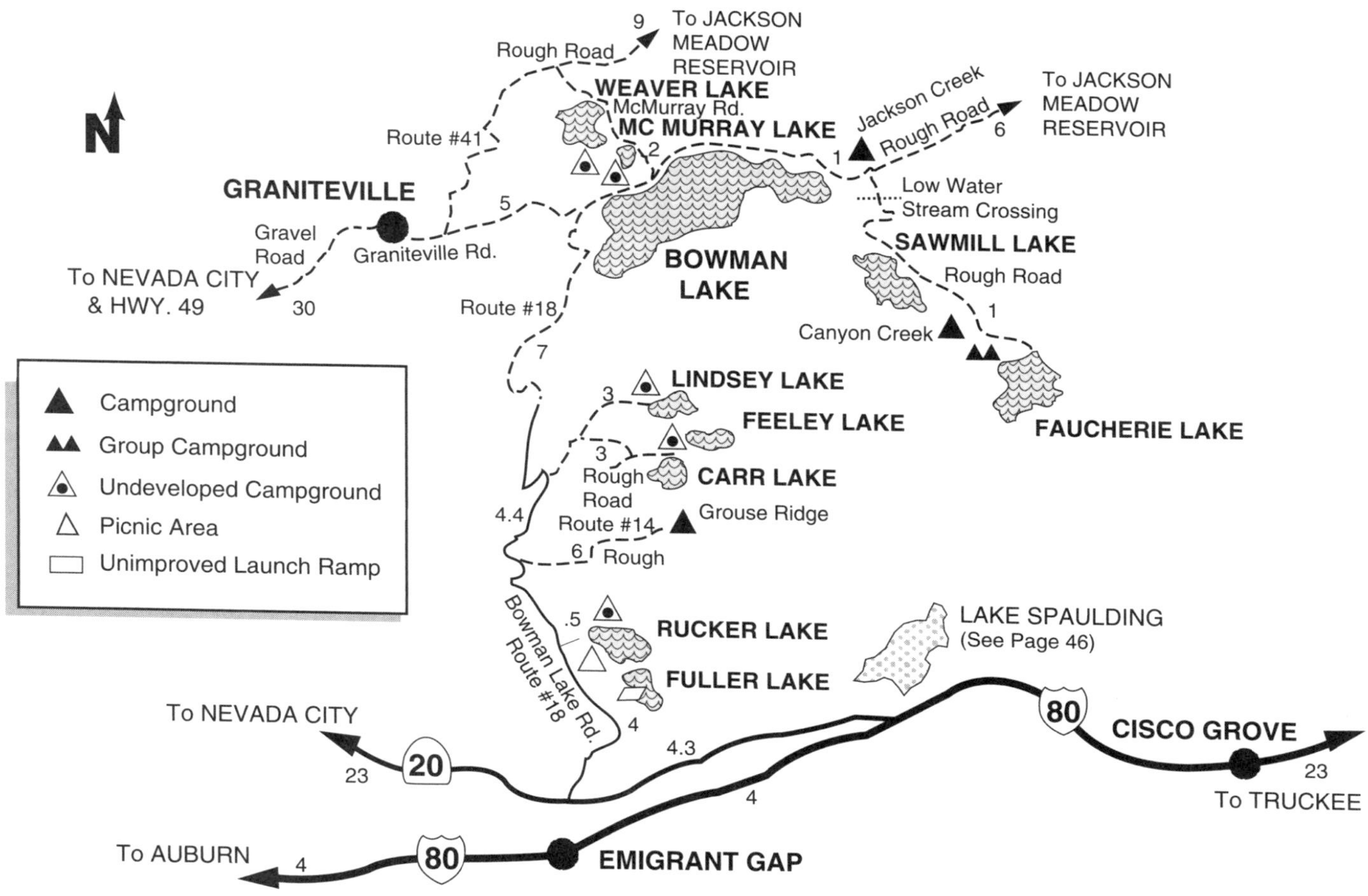

To JACKSON MEADOW RESERVOIR
Rough Road
WEAVER LAKE
McMurray Rd.
MC MURRAY LAKE
Jackson Creek
Rough Road
To JACKSON MEADOW RESERVOIR
Route #41
GRANITEVILLE
Gravel Road
Graniteville Rd.
To NEVADA CITY & HWY. 49
Low Water Stream Crossing
SAWMILL LAKE
BOWMAN LAKE
Rough Road
Route #18
Canyon Creek
LINDSEY LAKE
FEELEY LAKE
FAUCHERIE LAKE
Rough Road
CARR LAKE
Route #14
Grouse Ridge
Rough
Campground
Group Campground
Undeveloped Campground
Picnic Area
Unimproved Launch Ramp
RUCKER LAKE
LAKE SPAULDING (See Page 46)
Bowman Lake Rd. Route #18
FULLER LAKE
To NEVADA CITY
20
80
CISCO GROVE
To TRUCKEE
To AUBURN
80
EMIGRANT GAP

INFORMATION: Yuba River Ranger District South, 631 Coyote St., Nevada City 95959—Ph: (530) 265-4531

CAMPING	BOATING	RECREATION	OTHER
Primitive Camping In Area - No Fee Faucherie Lake: Group Camp - 2 - 25 People Units Maximum Fee: $50 Reservations: Ph: (877) 444-6777 Rucker Lake - Fee: $5 P.G.&E. Ph: (916) 386-5164 Lindsey Lake - Fee: $10 Carr & Feeley - Fee: $5	Small Boats Only 10 MPH Speed Limit Fuller Lake: Boat Ramp - Fee: $5 Rucker Lake: No Motors	Fishing: Rainbow, Brook & Brown Trout Swimming Picnicking Hiking Trails Mountain Bike Trails Equestrian Trails Backpacking Nature Study	Full Facilities in Truckee or Along Highway 80 *Rough Roads Not Recommended for Trailers or R.V.s 4-Wheel Drive Only*

FORDYCE, STERLING, EAGLE, KIDD, CASCADE, LONG and SERENE LAKES

These Lakes, off Interstate Highway 80 near Soda Springs, are at elevations of about 7,000 feet in the Tahoe National Forest. This beautiful high Sierra country offers a variety of recreational opportunities. Boating is limited to non-powered craft with limited facilities but rentals are available at Serene Lake. The angler will find trout and catfish. Numerous trails are available for the hiker, backpacker and equestrian to get away from it all in this remote natural area. The roads into Eagle, Fordyce and Sterling are not advised for any vehicles but 4-wheelers.

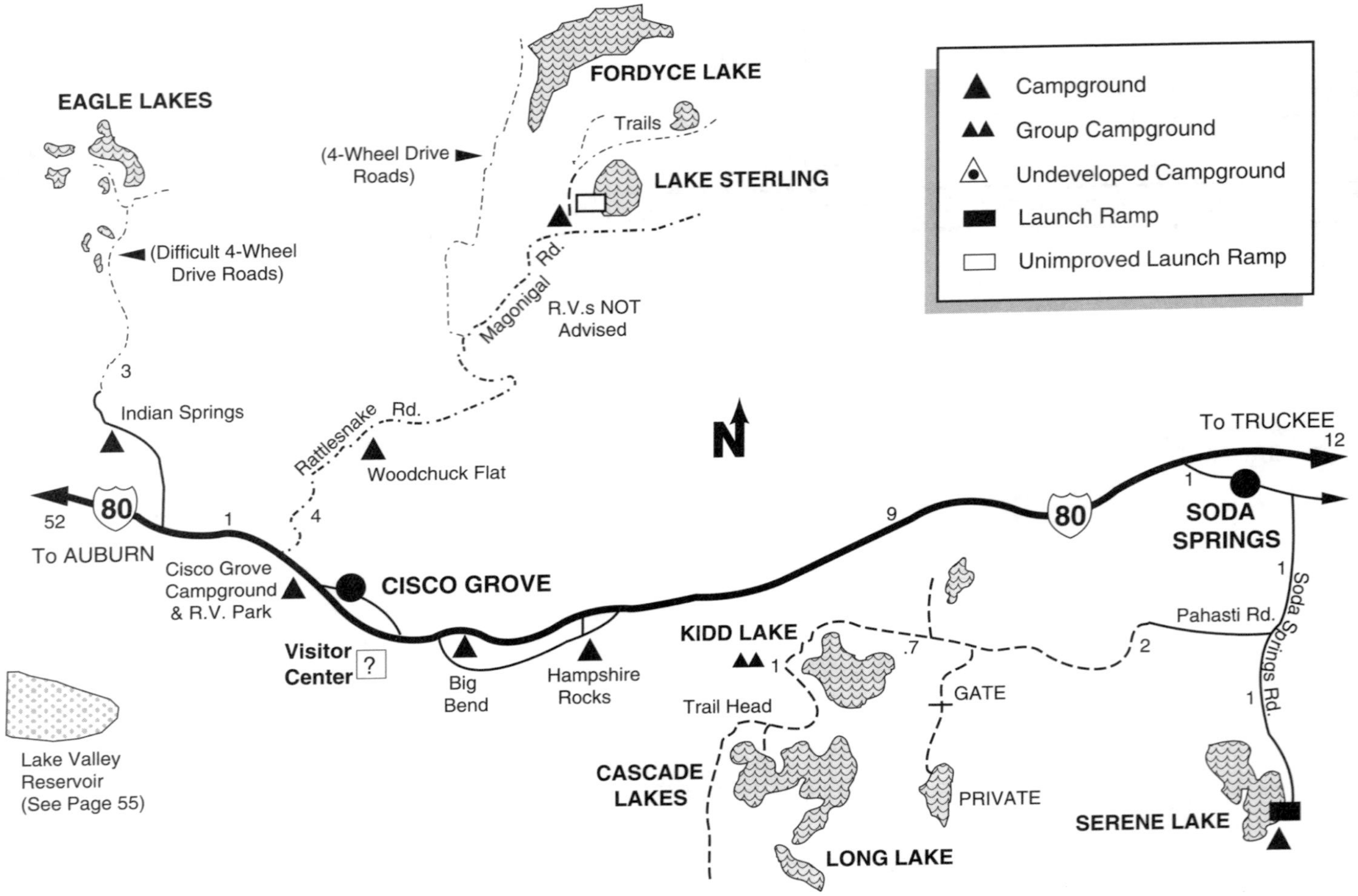
EAGLE LAKES
FORDYCE LAKE
(4-Wheel Drive Roads)
Trails
LAKE STERLING
(Difficult 4-Wheel Drive Roads)
Magonigal Rd.
R.V.s NOT Advised
3
Indian Springs
Rattlesnake Rd.
Woodchuck Flat
N
To TRUCKEE
12
80
52
To AUBURN
1
4
9
SODA SPRINGS
Cisco Grove Campground & R.V. Park
CISCO GROVE
Visitor Center
?
Big Bend
Hampshire Rocks
KIDD LAKE
Trail Head
.7
GATE
2
Pahasti Rd.
Soda Springs Rd.
Lake Valley Reservoir (See Page 55)
CASCADE LAKES
LONG LAKE
PRIVATE
SERENE LAKE
Campground
Group Campground
Undeveloped Campground
Launch Ramp
Unimproved Launch Ramp

INFORMATION: Yuba River Ranger District South, 631 Coyote St. Nevada City 95959—Ph: (530) 265-4531

CAMPING	BOATING	RECREATION	OTHER
U.S.F.S. Yuba River Ranger District South: Sites for Tents, Call for Fees P.G.&E. Kidd Lake: Group Campground to 100 People Maximum, 10 People per Site, Call for Fees, Reservations: Ph: (916) 386-5164	Electric Motors Allowed at Sterling Lake No Motors at All Other Lakes	Fishing: Trout & Catfish Swimming Hiking Trails Mountain Bike Trails Equestrian Trails Backpacking Nature Study	USFS Visitor Center at Big Bend Ph: (530) 426-3609 Cisco Grove Campground & R.V. Park Ph: (530) 426-1600, 406 Dev. Sites for Tents & R.V.s, Full Hookups, Fee: $32 - $35 Motel Rooms, Grocery Store Disposal Stations

JACKSON MEADOW RESERVOIR

Jackson Meadow Recreation Area, at an elevation of 6,200 feet, is located in the Tahoe National Forest. This area of forested slopes, alpine meadows, lakes and streams has an abundance of recreational opportunities. Along the 11 miles of shoreline at Jackson Meadow Reservoir, there are well-maintained campgrounds. Nearby Milton Reservoir and the Middle Fork of the Yuba River, between Jackson Meadow and Milton, are subject to specific artificial lures and size of fish limitations. Refer to the California Sport Fishing Regulations for details. The hiker, backpacker and equestrian will find a trailhead to the Pacific Crest Trail nearby.

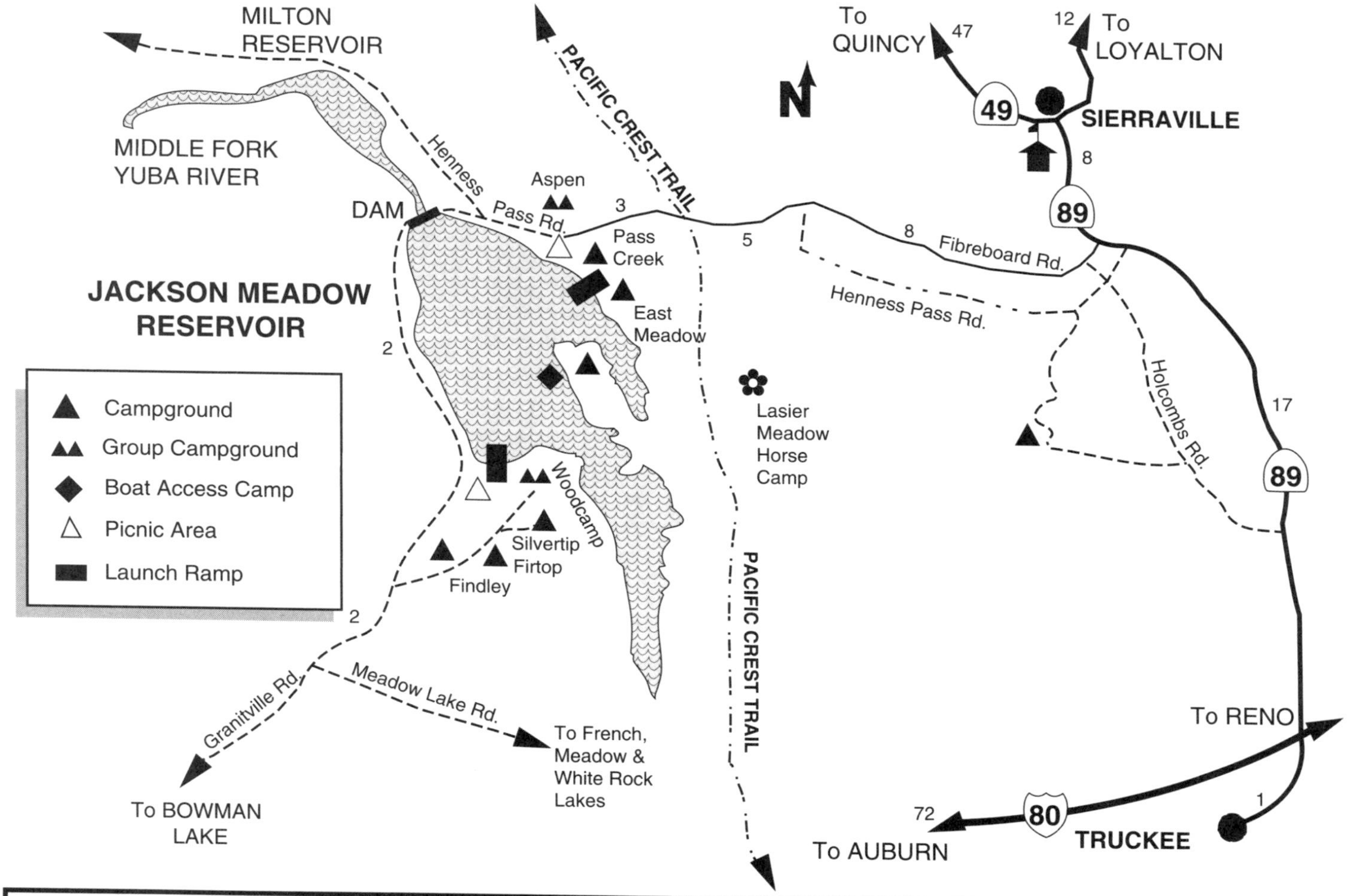

MILTON RESERVOIR
MIDDLE FORK YUBA RIVER
DAM
Henness Pass Rd.
PACIFIC CREST TRAIL
Aspen
Pass Creek
East Meadow
JACKSON MEADOW RESERVOIR
Campground
Group Campground
Boat Access Camp
Picnic Area
Launch Ramp
Woodcamp
Silvertip
Firtop
Findley
Lasier Meadow Horse Camp
Fibreboard Rd.
Henness Pass Rd.
Holcombs Rd.
To QUINCY
To LOYALTON
SIERRAVILLE
49
89
80
17
To RENO
To AUBURN
TRUCKEE
Granitville Rd.
Meadow Lake Rd.
To BOWMAN LAKE
To French, Meadow & White Rock Lakes

INFORMATION: Sierraville Ranger District, P.O. Box 95, Hwy. 89, Sierraville 96126—Ph: (530) 994-3401

CAMPING	BOATING	RECREATION	OTHER
130 Dev. Sites for Tents & R.V.s Fee: $11 - $13 2 Group Camps 2 - 25 People Max. $55 1 - 50 People Max. $111 Disposal Station Fee: $5 Reservations: Ph: (877) 444-6777 10 Boat-In Sites	Power, Row, Canoe, Sail, Waterski, PWCs, Windsurf & Inflatables 2 Launch Ramps No Gas Available	Fishing: Rainbow, Brook & Brown Trout Picnicking - 2 Beaches Hiking Trails Equestrian Trails	Full Facilities: Sierraville - 28 Miles Truckee - 31 Miles

STAMPEDE RESERVOIR

Stampede Reservoir is at an elevation of 5,949 feet in the Tahoe National Forest, northeast of Truckee. Stampede has a surface area of 3,440 acres with 25 miles of sage and coniferous covered shoreline. This large, open Lake has westerly winds for the sailor. Vast open waters can be enjoyed by the waterskier. Fishing is very popular and anglers will find rainbow and brown trout. A concessionaire, under permit from the Forest Service, maintains developed campsites near the Lake at Logger Campground. Water levels can be lower during the end of the season.

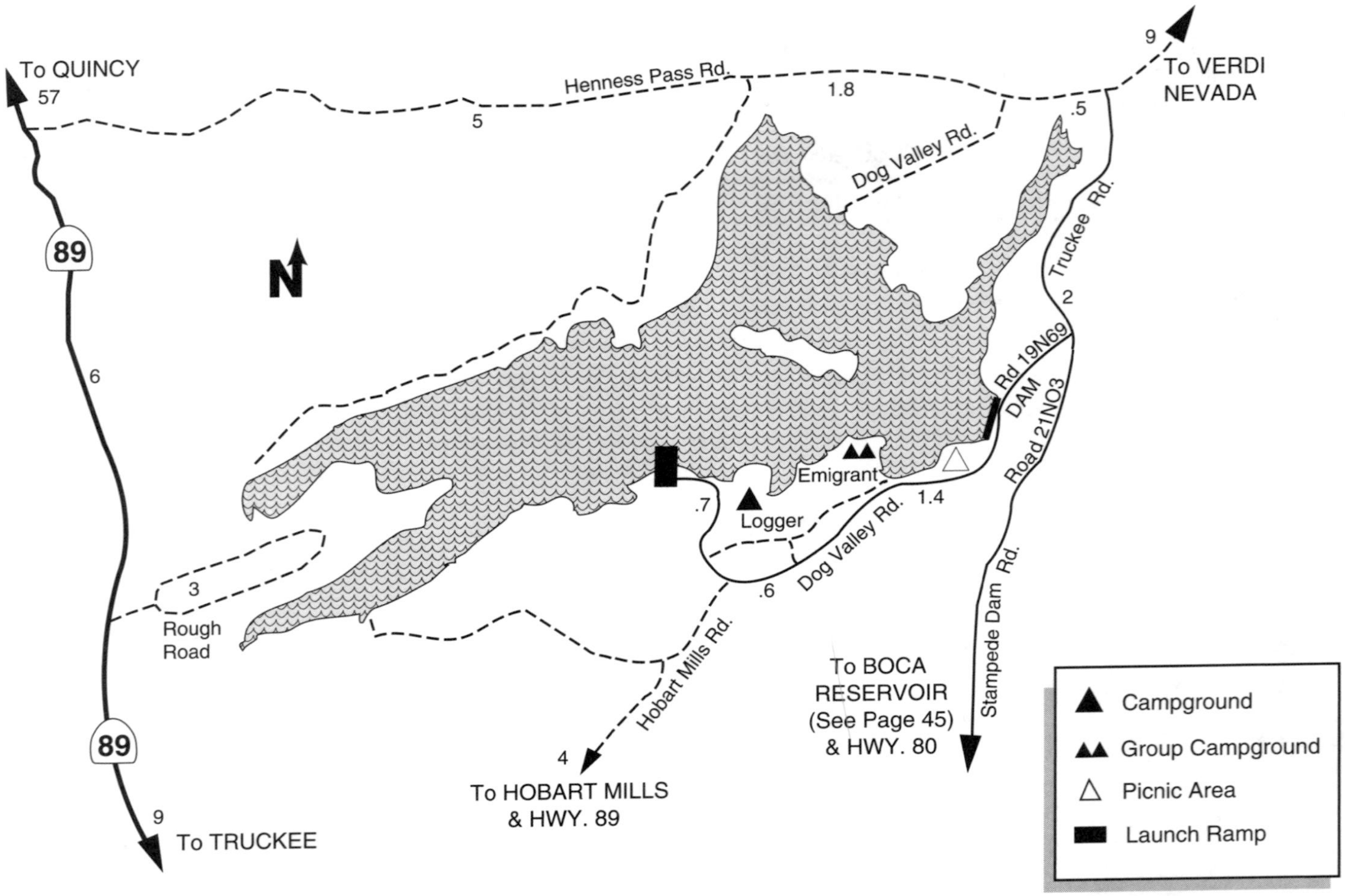
To QUINCY
57
Henness Pass Rd.
5
1.8
9
To VERDI
NEVADA
.5
Dog Valley Rd.
Truckee Rd.
2
89
N
6
Rd 19N69
DAM
Road 21NO3
Emigrant
Logger
.7
1.4
Dog Valley Rd.
.6
3
Rough
Road
Hobart Mills Rd.
Stampede Dam Rd.
To BOCA
RESERVOIR
(See Page 45)
& HWY. 80
4
To HOBART MILLS
& HWY. 89
89
9
To TRUCKEE
Campground
Group Campground
Picnic Area
Launch Ramp

INFORMATION: Truckee Ranger District, 9646 Donner Pass Rd., Truckee 96161—Ph: (530) 478-6257

CAMPING	BOATING	RECREATION	OTHER
Logger: 252 Dev. Sites for Tents & R.V.s Fee: $15 Disposal Station Emigrant Group Camps: 2-25 People - Fee: $63 2-150 People - Fee: $127 Reservations: Ph: (877) 444-6777	Power, Row, Canoe Sail, Waterski, PWCs, Windsurf & Inflatables Launch Ramp Extended for Low Water Launching	Fishing: Rainbow & Brown Trout, Kokanee Salmon Swimming Picnicking Hiking Trails Mountain Bike Trails	Full Facilities 14 Miles at Truckee

PROSSER CREEK RESERVOIR

Prosser Creek Reservoir is at an elevation of 5,711 located in the scenic Tahoe National Forest. This 740 surface-acre Lake rests in an open canyon surrounded by sage and coniferous-covered hills. The Donner Camp picnic area was the site of the Donner Party tragedy of the winter of 1846-47. Boating is limited to 10 MPH. Waterskiing, power boating and PWCs are not allowed at this facility. Launching can be difficult in the fall with low water levels. You can fish for trout and the scenery is beautiful with grassy open meadows at this high elevation Reservoir.

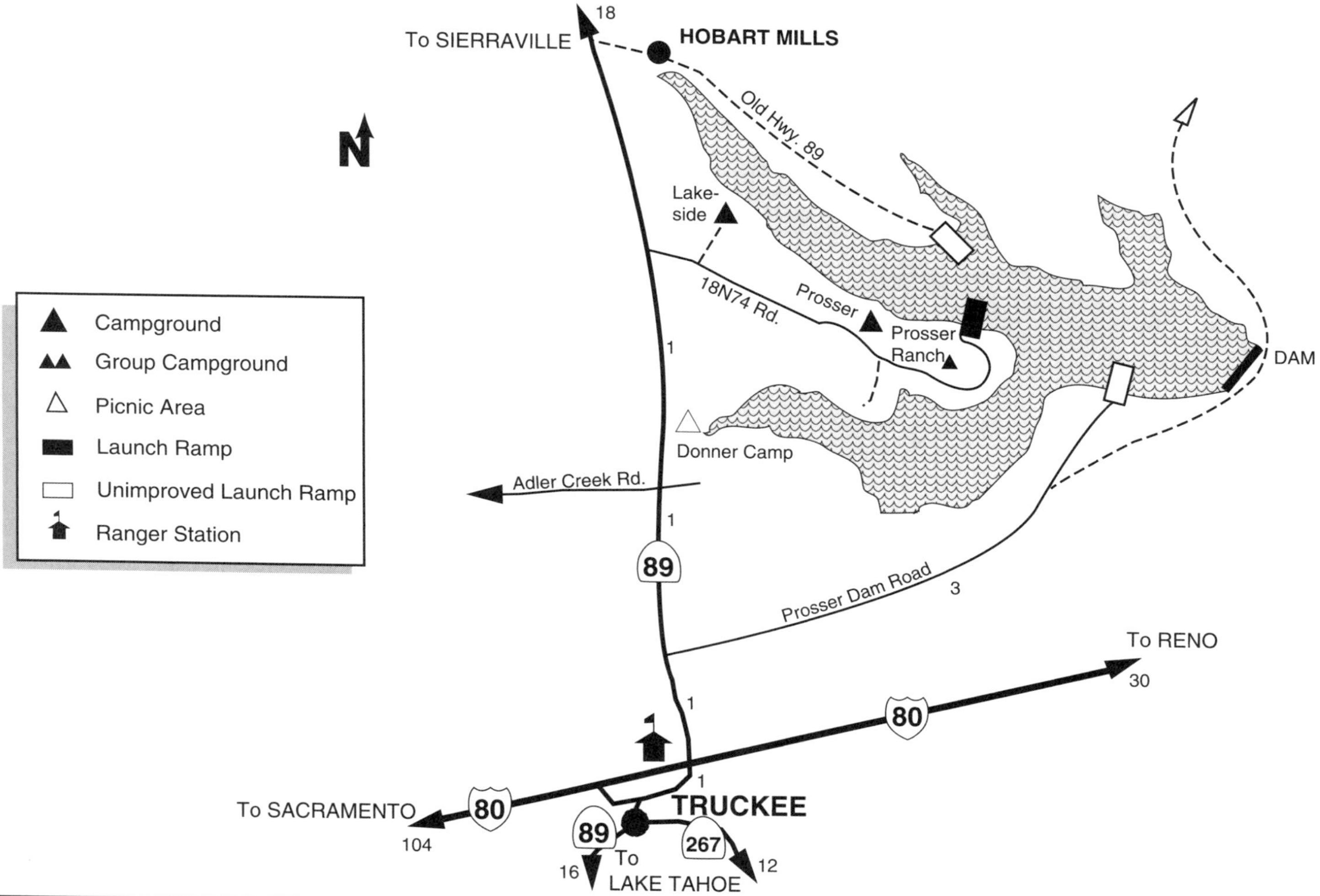

To SIERRAVILLE
18
HOBART MILLS
Old Hwy. 89
Lake-
side
18N74 Rd.
Prosser
Prosser
Ranch
DAM
Donner Camp
Adler Creek Rd.
1
1
89
Prosser Dam Road
3
To RENO
30
80
1
1
To SACRAMENTO
80
104
TRUCKEE
89
267
16
To
LAKE TAHOE
12
Campground
Group Campground
Picnic Area
Launch Ramp
Unimproved Launch Ramp
Ranger Station

INFORMATION: Truckee Ranger District, 10342 Highway 89 North, Truckee 96161—Ph: (530) 478-6257

CAMPING	BOATING	RECREATION	OTHER
Prosser Family: 29 Dev. Sites for Tents & R.V.s to 24 Feet Fee: $12 Prosser Ranch Group Camp to 50 People Fee: $86 Reserve: (877) 444-6777 Lakeside: 24 Dev. Sites for Tents & R.V.s Fee: $12	Power, Row, Canoe, Sail, Windsurf, & Inflatables Speed Limit- 10 MPH Launch Ramps	Fishing: Rainbow Trout Swimming Picnicking at Donner Camp Hiking Interpretive Trail at Donner Camp Mountain Bicycling Hunting: Deer	Full Facilities - 5 Miles at Truckee

BOCA RESERVOIR

Boca Reservoir is in the Tahoe National Forest at an elevation of 5,700 feet. The Lake has a surface area of 980 acres with 14 miles of shoreline. Steep bluffs and low grassy areas amid tall pine trees make for a scenic setting. Campgrounds are operated by the U.S. Forest Service. Many inlets and prevailing winds create a great atmosphere for sailing and boating.

The speed limit in all inlets is 5 mph. The water level lowers at the end of the season. Boca is fed by Stampede Reservoir, 5 miles above. *During drought conditions boat ramp can be completely out of the water. Always check water levels before making plans.*

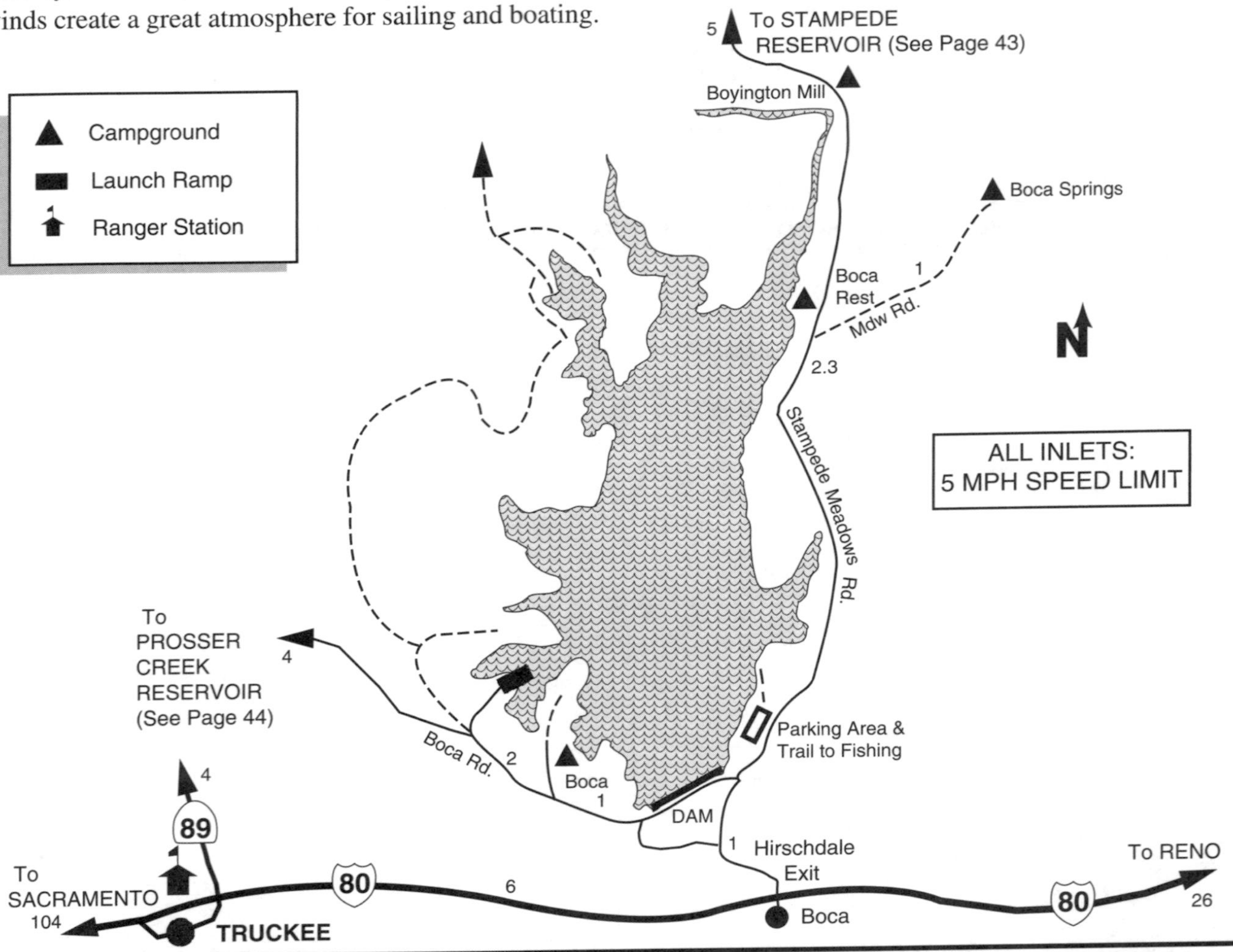

5
To STAMPEDE RESERVOIR (See Page 43)
Boyington Mill
Campground
Launch Ramp
Ranger Station
Boca Springs
Boca Rest
1
Mdw Rd.
2.3
N
Stampede Meadows Rd.
ALL INLETS:
5 MPH SPEED LIMIT
To PROSSER CREEK RESERVOIR (See Page 44)
4
Parking Area & Trail to Fishing
Boca Rd.
2
Boca
1
4
89
DAM
1
Hirschdale Exit
To RENO
To SACRAMENTO
104
80
6
80
26
TRUCKEE
Boca

INFORMATION: Truckee Ranger District, 10342 Highway 89 North, Truckee 96161—Ph: (530) 478-6257			
CAMPING	**BOATING**	**RECREATION**	**OTHER**
Boca: 20 Sites Fee: $12 - No Water Boca Rest: 25 Sites Fee: $12 - Water Boca Springs: 17 Sites Fee: $12 - Water Horses Permitted Boyington Mill: 13 Sites Fee: $12 - No Water Call USFS for R.V. and Trailer Access Information	Power, Row, Canoe, Sail, Waterski, PWCs, Windsurf & Inflatables Launch Ramp	Fishing: Rainbow Trout, Kokanee Trail & Parking for Fishing Access Swimming Picnicking Hiking Trails Equestrian Trails	Full Facilities - 7 Miles in Truckee Limited Facilities at Hirschdale Exit

Lake Spaulding is at an elevation of 5,009 feet in a glacier carved bowl of granite. The Lake has a surface area of 698 acres surrounded by giant rocks and conifers. Now a part of Pacific Gas and Electric Company's Drum-Spaulding Project, the dam was originally built in 1912 for hydraulic mining.

P.G. & E. operates the facilities at this scenic Lake which includes a campground and launch ramp. The Lake is open to all types of boating although launching large boats can be difficult. Fishing from the bank or boat is often rewarding. This is a good Lake for a family outing with a spectacular setting of granite boulders dipping into the clear, blue waters.

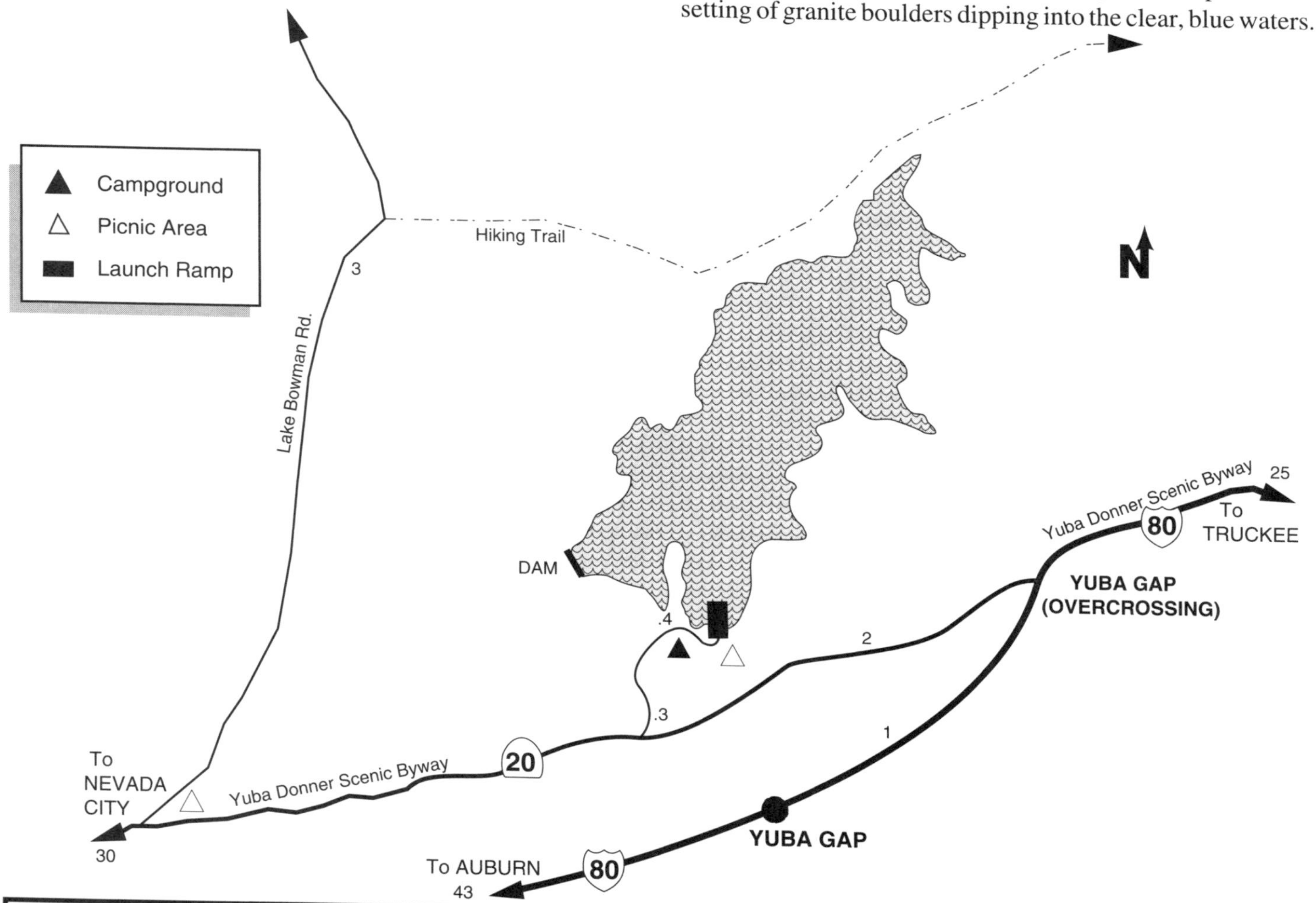
Campground
Picnic Area
Launch Ramp
Hiking Trail
3
Lake Bowman Rd.
N
DAM
.4
.3
2
1
Yuba Donner Scenic Byway
25
To TRUCKEE
80
YUBA GAP (OVERCROSSING)
20
To NEVADA CITY
30
Yuba Donner Scenic Byway
YUBA GAP
To AUBURN
43
80

INFORMATION: P.G. & E. Land Projects, 2730 Gateway Oaks Dr., Sacramento 95833–Ph: (916) 386-5164

CAMPING	BOATING	RECREATION	OTHER
25 Dev. Sites for Tents & R.V.s Fee: $15 Pets - Fee Plus 10 Overflow Sites	Power, Row, Canoe, Sail, Waterski, PWCs, Windsurf & Inflatables Launch Ramp - Fee Summer Use Only *Hazardous Rocks In Late Summer As Water Level Drops*	Fishing: Rainbow & Brown Trout Swimming - Beaches Picnicking Hiking Trails Backpacking [Parking]	Full Facilities at Nevada City

DONNER LAKE

Donner Lake is at an elevation of 5,963 feet in the Tahoe National Forest next to Interstate 80 and west of Truckee. The Lake is 3 miles long and 3/4 mile wide with a shoreline of 7-1/2 miles of high alpine woods. Donner has numerous private homes (no access) on the south shore and portions of the north shore. The Donner State Memorial Park, on the east shore, was named after the tragic Donner Party whose fate in the winter of 1846 attests to the hardships encountered by California's early settlers. This well-maintained park has 150 developed campsites with campfire programs and nature trails. The Emigrant Trail Museum is open daily from 9 a.m. to 4 p.m. The water in the Lake is clear and cold. A popular sailing Lake, Donner has its own local Sailing Club. *Beware of periodic afternoon winds that can be hazardous.*

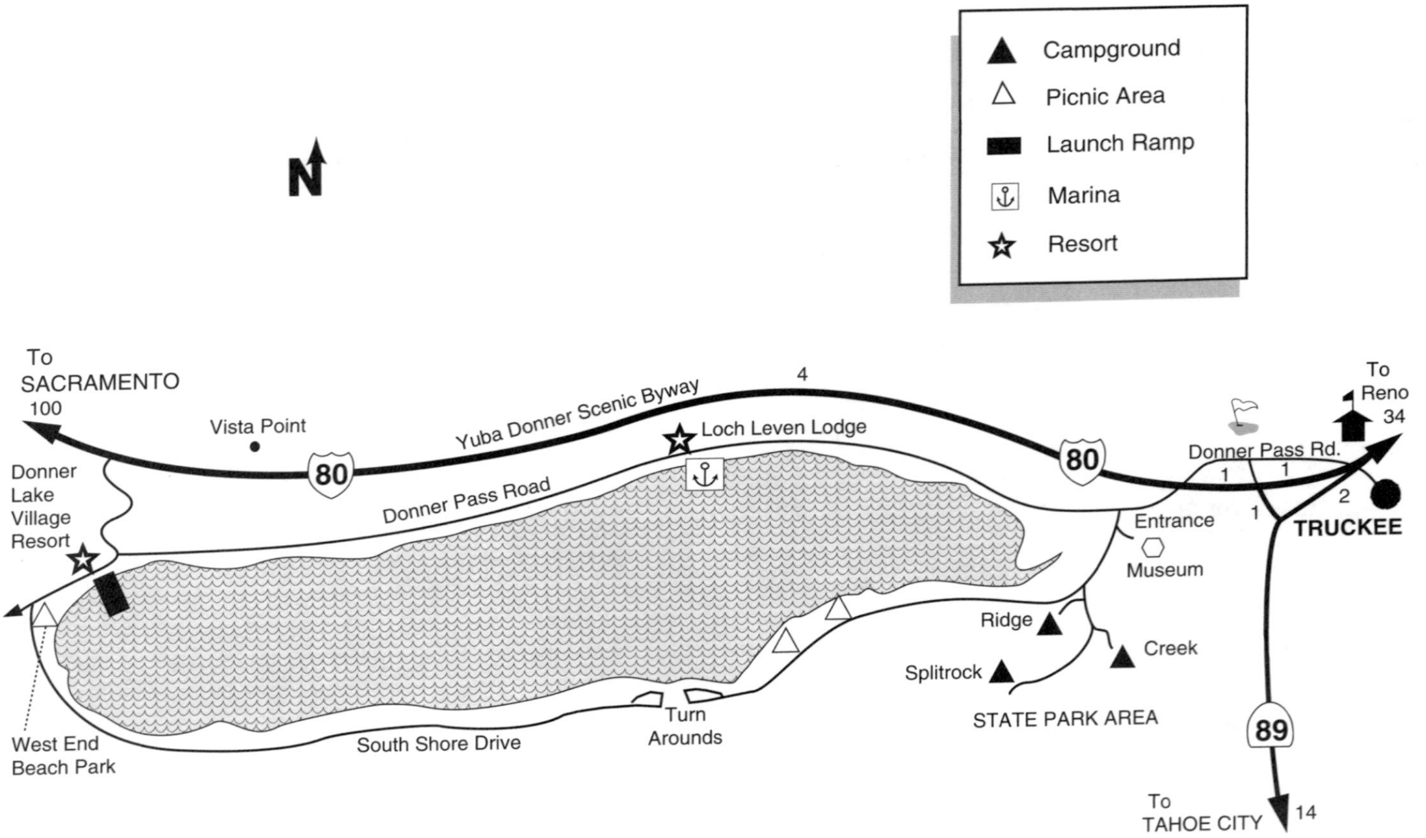
Campground
Picnic Area
Launch Ramp
Marina
Resort
N
To
SACRAMENTO
100
Vista Point
Yuba Donner Scenic Byway
4
Loch Leven Lodge
80
Donner Pass Road
Donner
Lake
Village
Resort
Donner Pass Rd.
To
Reno
34
1
2
TRUCKEE
Entrance
Museum
Ridge
Creek
Splitrock
STATE PARK AREA
89
To
TAHOE CITY
14
Turn
Arounds
South Shore Drive
West End
Beach Park

INFORMATION: Donner Memorial State Park, 12593 Donner Pass Rd., Truckee 96161—Ph: (530) 582-7892

CAMPING	BOATING	RECREATION	OTHER
Donner Memorial State Park 150 Dev. Sites for Tents & R.V.s Fee: $25 Ph: (530) 582-7894 (Summer Only) Reservations: Ph: (800) 444-7275 (On First Come Basis at Times) Day Use - Fee: $6	Power, Row, Canoe, Sail, Waterski, PWCs, Windsurf & Inflatables No Launching From State Park Public Launch Ramp At West End Rentals: Fishing, Pontoon & Paddleboats	Fishing: Rainbow Trout, Mackinaw, Kokanee Salmon Swimming - Beaches Picnicking Hiking Trails Bicycle Trails Campfire Programs Nature Study Tennis Golf	Motels & Cabin Rentals Snack Bar Restaurant & Lounge Grocery Store Bait & Tackle Gas Station Airport for Private Planes and Auto Rentals - 5 Miles Emigrant Trail Museum Ph: (530) 582-7892

MARTIS CREEK LAKE

Martis Creek Lake, 70 surface acres at minimum pool, was California's first "Wild Trout Lake" and one of its most unique. Originally built in 1972 by the U. S. Army Corps of Engineers for flood control and a water supply for Reno, this Lake was selected by the California Department of Fish and Game as an exclusive, naturally producing, trophy trout fishery for the endangered Lahontan Cutthroat Trout. Martis Creek is a trophy German Brown fishery in the catch and release program. The facilities and nearby 1,000 acre wildlife area are administered by the Corps of Engineers.

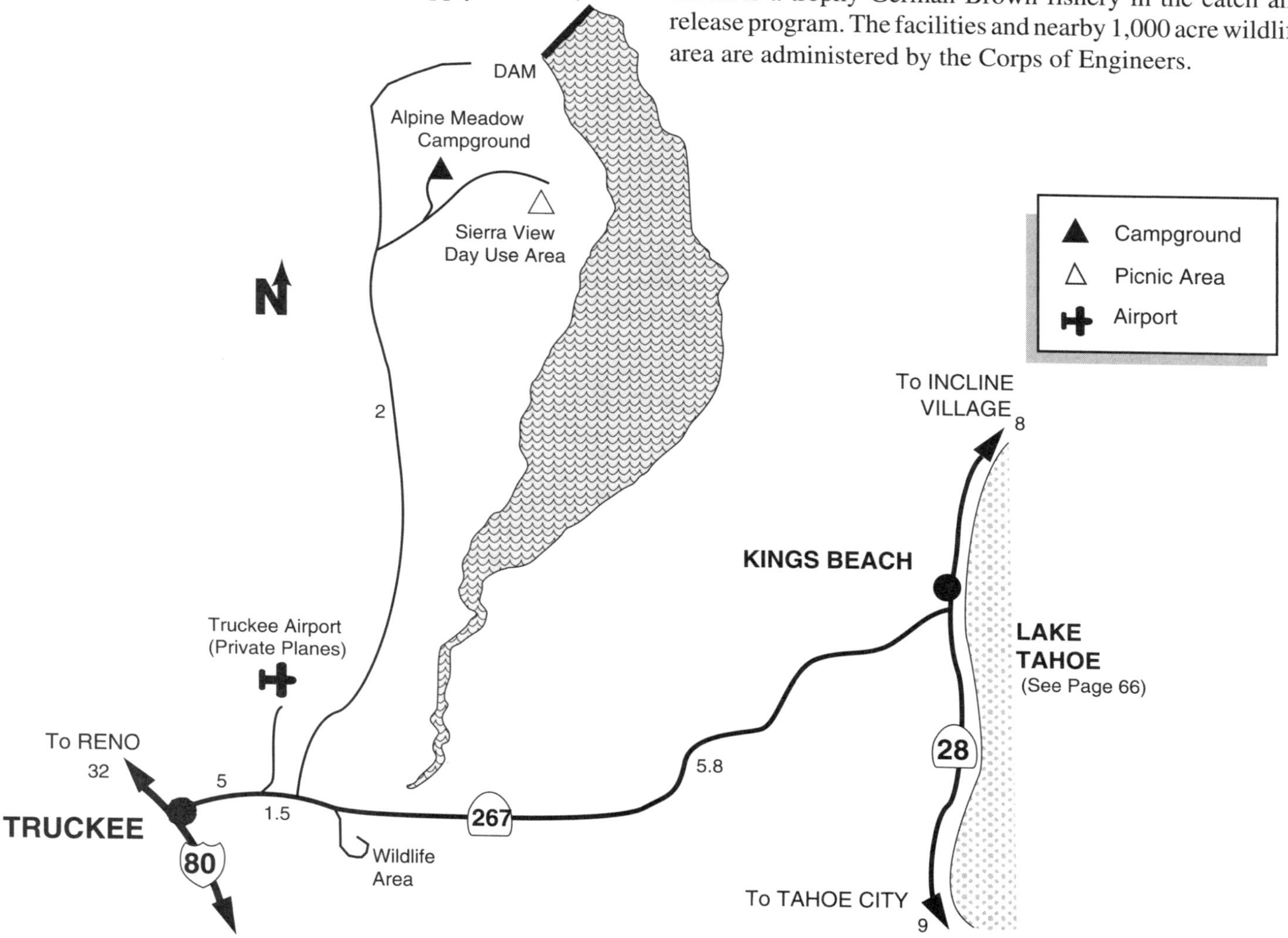
DAM
Alpine Meadow Campground
Sierra View Day Use Area
N
2
Campground
Picnic Area
Airport
To INCLINE VILLAGE
8
KINGS BEACH
LAKE TAHOE
(See Page 66)
Truckee Airport (Private Planes)
To RENO
32
5
1.5
TRUCKEE
80
Wildlife Area
267
5.8
28
To TAHOE CITY
9

INFORMATION: Park Ranger, P.O. Box 2344, Truckee 96160, Smartville 95977—Ph: (530) 587-8113			
CAMPING	**BOATING**	**RECREATION**	**OTHER**
25 Dev. Sites for Tents and R.V.s Fee: $14 First Come, First Serve 2 Accessible Sites May Be Reserved through Park Ranger Campground Open May 15 to Oct. 15 Depending on Weather	No Gas or Electric Motor Powered Boats Allowed Sail, Row, Canoe, Kayak & Inflatables Non-Motorized Boats Only	Fishing: Lahontan Cutthroat, Brown & Rainbow Trout *Artificial Lures and Flies Only* *Barbless Hooks* *Catch & Release Only* Picnicking Hiking & Biking Trails Birdwatching Campfire Programs	Park Manager P. O. Box 6 Smartville 95977 Ph: (530) 639-2342 Full Facilities 6 Miles at Truckee

MARLETTE & SPOONER LAKES, HOBART RESERVOIR

The Lake Tahoe Nevada State Park has jurisdiction over these Lakes and the surrounding backcountry spanning over 13,000 acres. Marlette Lake is one of the most beautiful in the Sierras. No fishing is permitted as it is a fish hatchery for rainbow trout. Fishing is allowed at Hobart Reservoir. Check for fishing conditions at Spooner Lake. This Lake is a trailhead for equestrians, hikers and mountain bikers with connections to the spectacular Tahoe Rim Trail - 165 miles. Numerous trails are throughout this entire area. For details contact the State Park. A great variety of wildlife and wildflowers can be viewed.

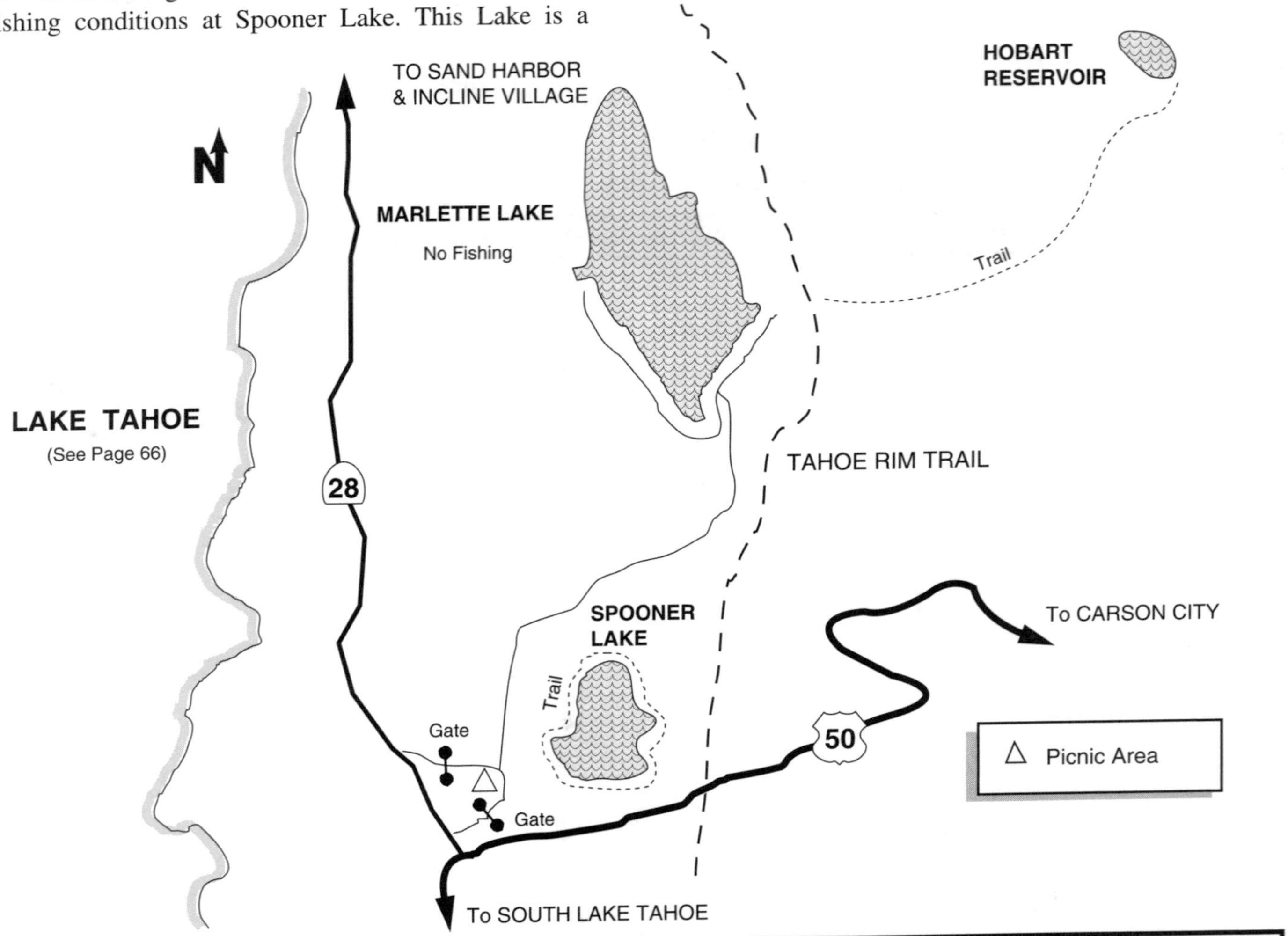
TO SAND HARBOR
& INCLINE VILLAGE
N
MARLETTE LAKE
No Fishing
HOBART
RESERVOIR
Trail
LAKE TAHOE
(See Page 66)
28
TAHOE RIM TRAIL
SPOONER
LAKE
Trail
To CARSON CITY
Gate
Gate
50
Picnic Area
To SOUTH LAKE TAHOE

INFORMATION: Lake Tahoe Nevada State Parks, P.O. Box 8867, Incline, NV 89452—Ph: (775) 831-0494

CAMPING	BOATING	RECREATION	OTHER
Backcountry Camping In Designated Areas 2 Overnight Cabin Rentals Mountain Bike Rentals Guide Service Ph: (775) 749-5349	No Boating Allowed For Lake Tahoe Boating Facilities See Page 66	Fishing: Trout Spooner Lake: Catch & Release Barbless Artificial Lures Only Fishing Clinics Hiking & Equestrian Trails Mountain Bike Trails 20 mph Max. 5 mph on Curves Picnicking Spooner Lake: 25 Sites	Tahoe Rim Trail Assn. DWR Community Non-Profit Center 948 Incline Way Incline Village, NV 89451 Ph: (775) 298-0012 Information for Volunteers Memberships Trail Maps

COLLINS LAKE

The Collins Lake Recreation Area is at an elevation of 1,200 feet in the scenic Mother Lode Country. The Lake has a surface area of over 1,000 acres with 12-1/2 miles of shoreline. The modern campground and R.V. Park are open year around and have well-separated sites under oak and pine trees. There is a broad, sandy beach and many family and group picnic sites. All boating is allowed but personal watercraft are *not permitted.* Waterskiing is allowed from May 15 to October 15. A designated fishing only area is at the north end of the Lake. One of the finest fishing Lakes in California, Collins is famous for trophy trout along with a variety of warm water species. There are zones for the exclusive use of fishermen throughout the year.

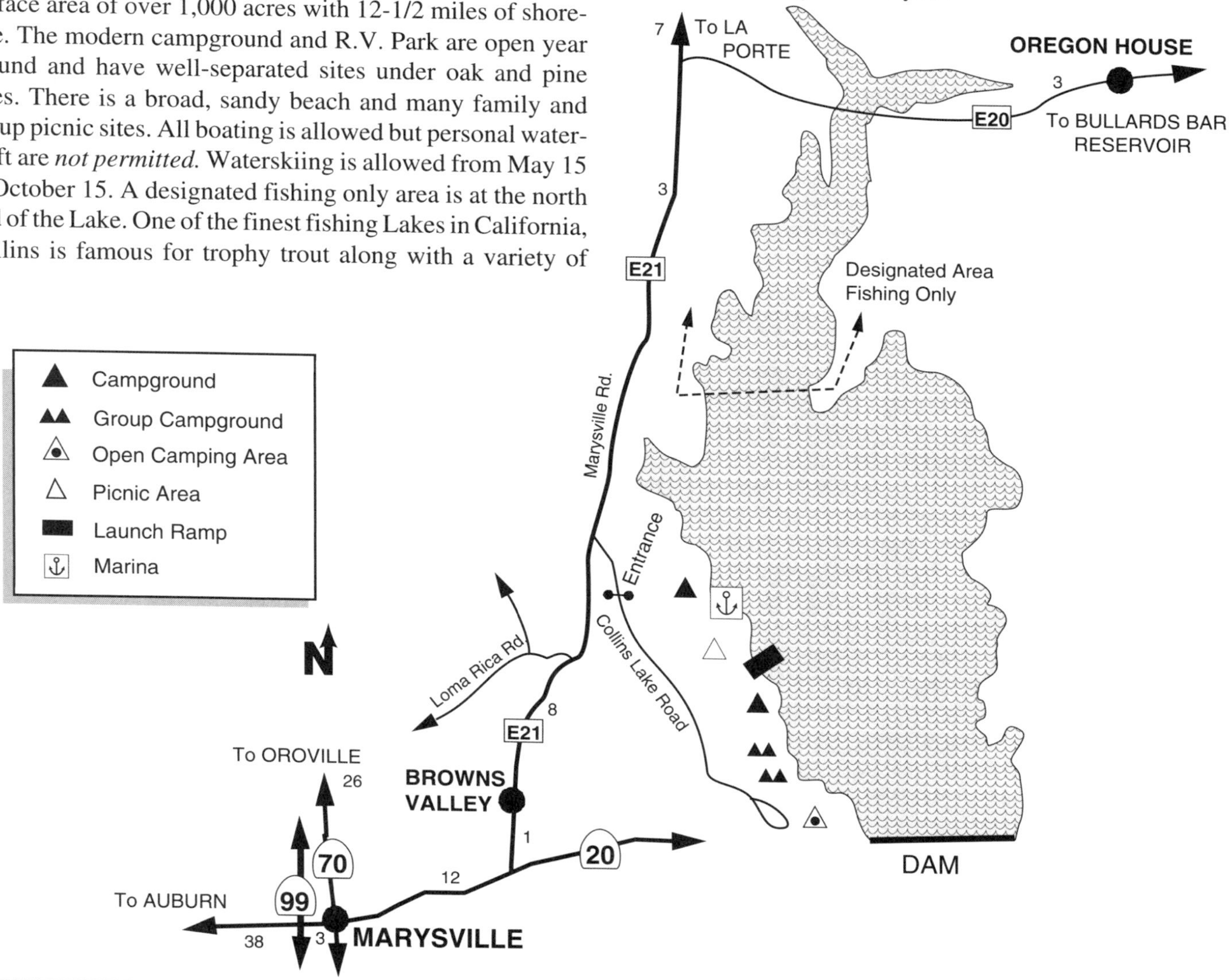

To LA PORTE
7
OREGON HOUSE
3
E20
To BULLARDS BAR RESERVOIR
3
E21
Designated Area Fishing Only
Marysville Rd.
Entrance
Collins Lake Road
Campground
Group Campground
Open Camping Area
Picnic Area
Launch Ramp
Marina
N
Loma Rica Rd.
8
E21
To OROVILLE
26
BROWNS VALLEY
1
70
20
12
To AUBURN
99
38
3
MARYSVILLE
DAM

INFORMATION: Collins Lake Recreation Area, P.O. Box 300, Oregon House 95962—Ph: (800) 286-0576			
CAMPING	**BOATING**	**RECREATION**	**OTHER**
183 Dev. Sites for Tents & R.V.s Fee: $24 - $45 Electric, Water, & Sewer Hookups Group Campgrounds Pets on Leash - Fee: $2 Reservations Recommended - Fee Open Camp Areas Along Shoreline Fee: $20 - $28	Power, Row, Canoe, Sail, Windsurf & Inflatables No PWCs or Unmuffled Boats Launch Ramp Fee: $8 Waterski Season: May 1 to Oct. 15 Rentals : Fishing & Row Boats, Kayaks, Paddle & Patio Boats Docks, Berths, Moorings, Dry Storage	Fishing: Trout, Catfish, Bluegill, Crappie, Bass Swimming - Sandy Beach Picnicking - Families & Groups Playgrounds	Cabins & Trailer Rentals Snack Bar Grocery Store Bait & Tackle Disposal Station Gas Station Propane Full Facilities Within 6 Miles

LAKE FRANCIS

Located in the foothills of the Motherlode country, Lake Francis is at an elevation of 1,700 feet. The Lake has about 40 surface acres. Only electric trolling motors are permitted for boating. The 32-acre Resort offers full vacation facilities including cabins and campsites for R.V.s and tents. Many campsites are amidst 100-foot pines, large oaks and madrones. Fishing can be excellent and the water is relatively warm for swimming. Canadian geese and abundant wildlife can often be seen at the Lake. There is a launch ramp and nice picnic areas next to the water. This is a good spot to bring the whole family.

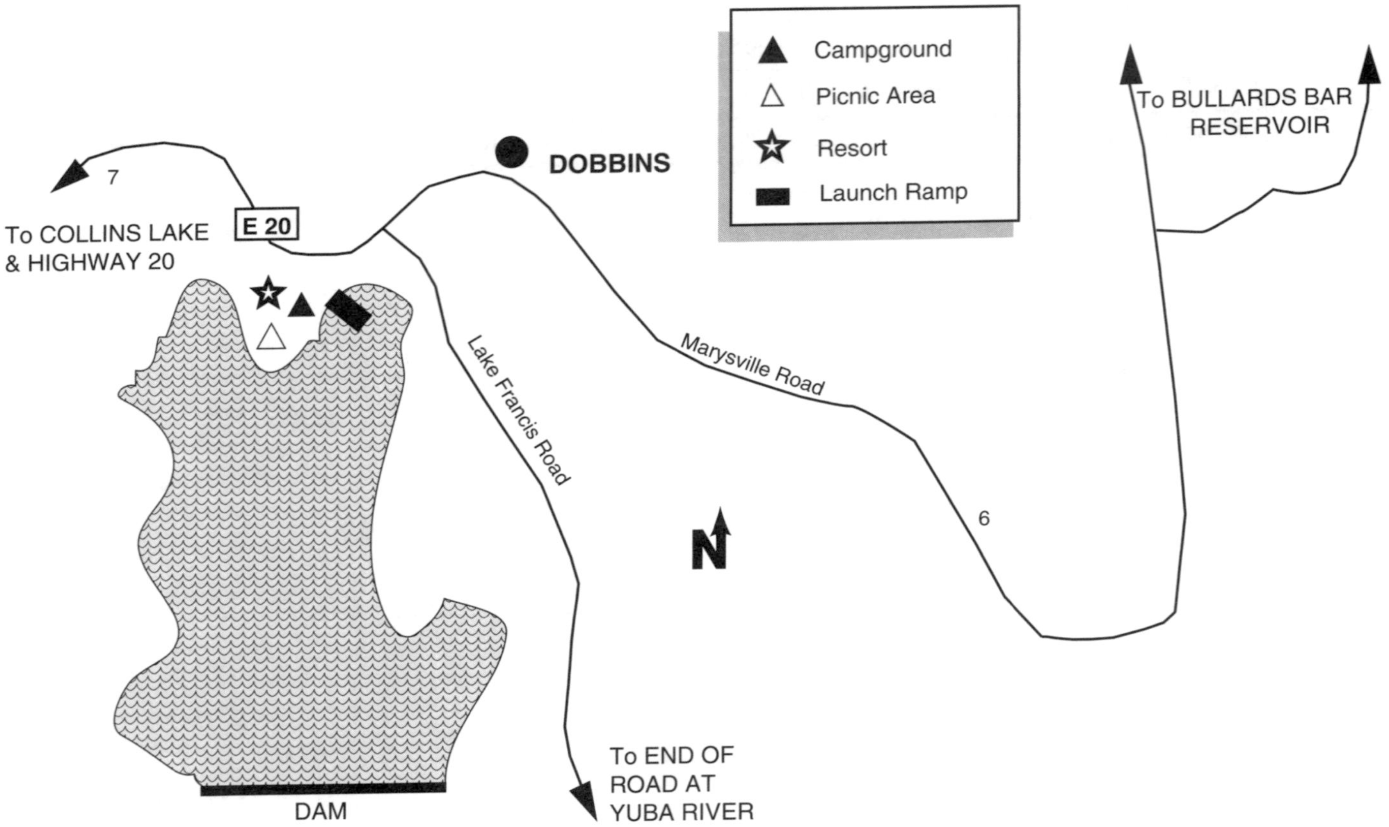
Campground
Picnic Area
Resort
Launch Ramp
DOBBINS
To BULLARDS BAR RESERVOIR
7
E 20
To COLLINS LAKE & HIGHWAY 20
Lake Francis Road
Marysville Road
6
N
To END OF ROAD AT YUBA RIVER
DAM

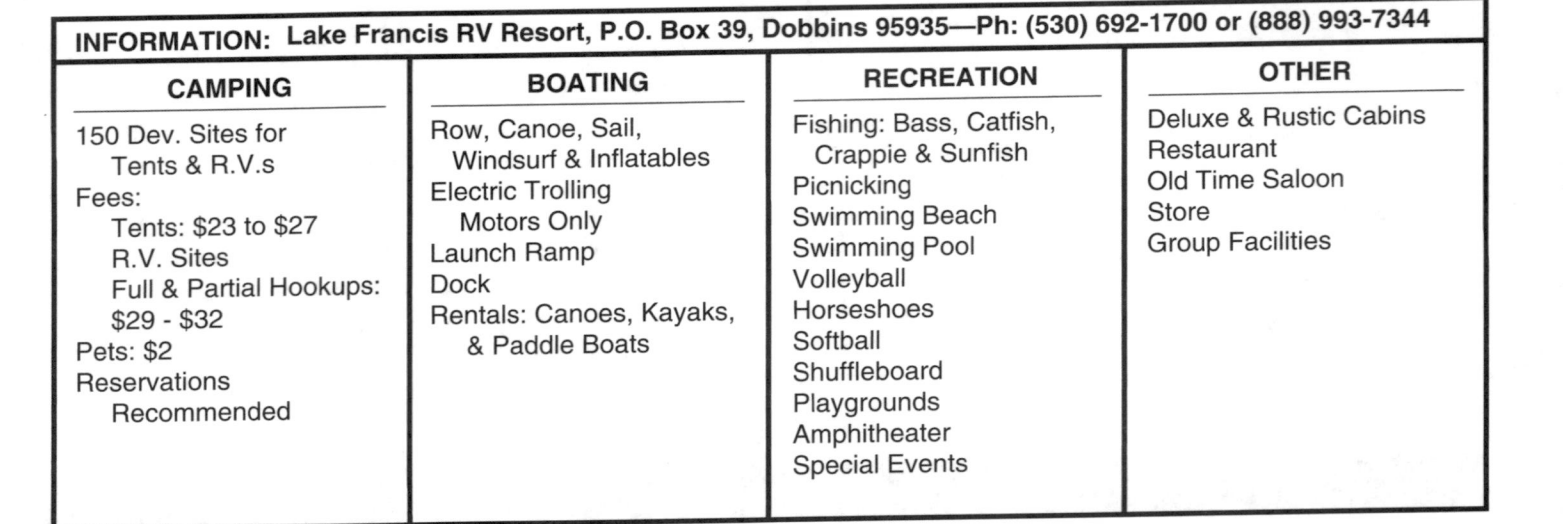

INFORMATION: Lake Francis RV Resort, P.O. Box 39, Dobbins 95935—Ph: (530) 692-1700 or (888) 993-7344

CAMPING	BOATING	RECREATION	OTHER
150 Dev. Sites for Tents & R.V.s Fees: Tents: $23 to $27 R.V. Sites Full & Partial Hookups: $29 - $32 Pets: $2 Reservations Recommended	Row, Canoe, Sail, Windsurf & Inflatables Electric Trolling Motors Only Launch Ramp Dock Rentals: Canoes, Kayaks, & Paddle Boats	Fishing: Bass, Catfish, Crappie & Sunfish Picnicking Swimming Beach Swimming Pool Volleyball Horseshoes Softball Shuffleboard Playgrounds Amphitheater Special Events	Deluxe & Rustic Cabins Restaurant Old Time Saloon Store Group Facilities

ENGLEBRIGHT LAKE

Englebright Lake, located northeast of Marysville, is at an elevation of 527 feet. The Lake has a surface area of 815 acres with a shoreline of 24 miles. Englebright is a boat camper's bonanza. Boats can be launched near the dam or at Joe Miller. A variety of boats can be rented at Skippers Cove. You can then proceed by boat up the Lake to a campsite. The shoreline is steep and rocky except at the campgrounds where there are some sandy beaches with pine and oak trees above the high water line. Fishing is good in the quiet, narrow coves. *Waterskiing is not allowed at the North end as noted on map.*

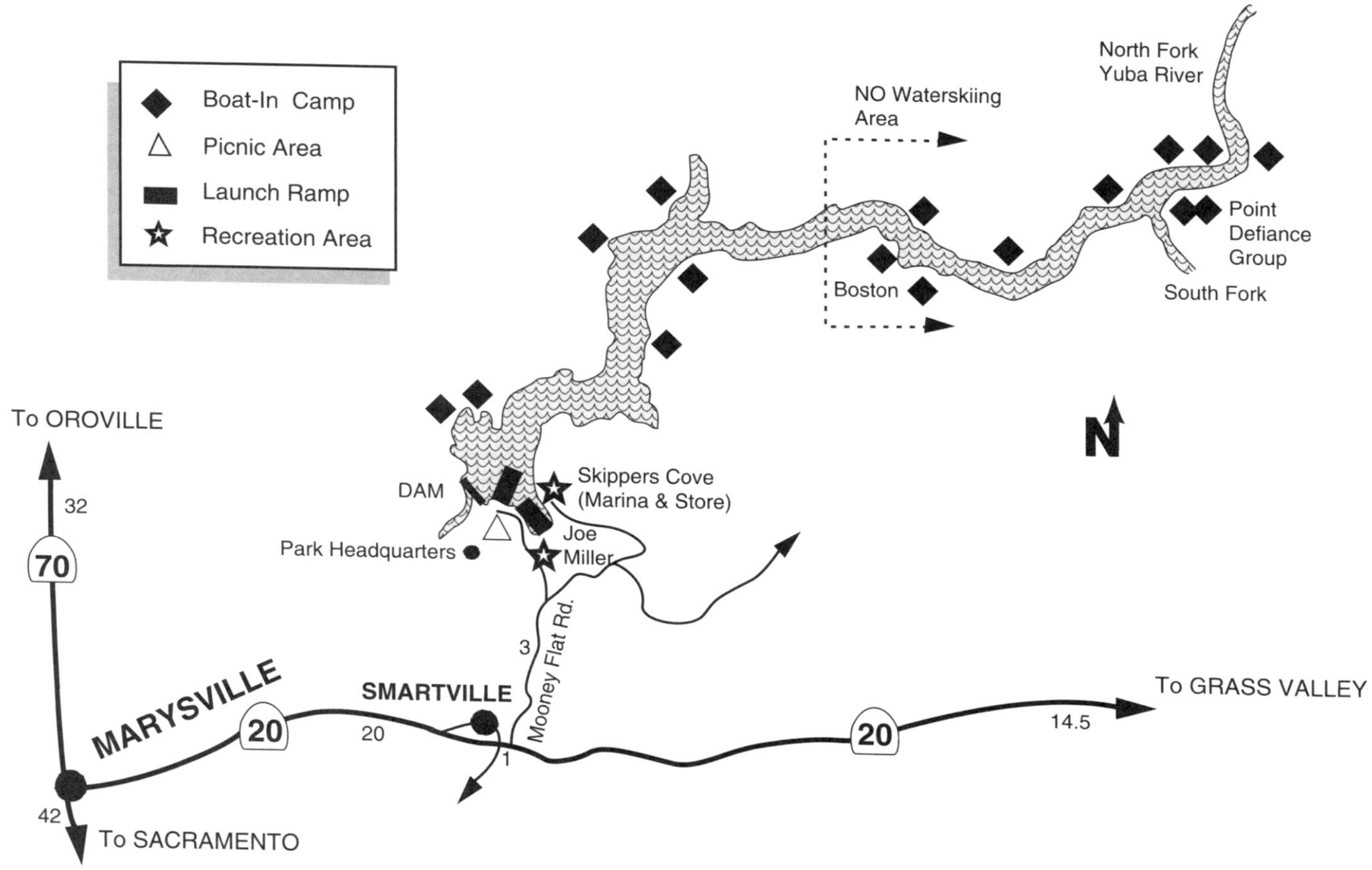

Boat-In Camp
Picnic Area
Launch Ramp
Recreation Area
North Fork
Yuba River
NO Waterskiing
Area
Point
Defiance
Group
South Fork
Boston
N
To OROVILLE
32
70
DAM
Skippers Cove
(Marina & Store)
Park Headquarters
Joe
Miller
Mooney Flat Rd.
3
MARYSVILLE
SMARTVILLE
20
20
20
1
14.5
To GRASS VALLEY
42
To SACRAMENTO

INFORMATION: U.S. Army Corps of Engineers, P. O. Box 6, Smartville 95977—Ph: (530) 432-6427			
CAMPING	**BOATING**	**RECREATION**	**OTHER**
100 Developed Boat-In Sites Fee: $10 First Come, First Served Group Campground at Point Defiance to 50 People Max. Reservations: Ph: (530) 432-6427 *Water levels may fluctuate Use caution when you boat camp as low water levels may occur overnight*	Power, Row, Canoe, Sail, Waterski, PWCs, Windsurf & Inflatables Full Service Marina Launch Ramps Fee: $4 Rentals: Fishing & Waterski Boats, Canoes, Houseboats & Patio Boats Docks, Berths, Moorings, Gas	Fishing: Trout, Bass, Catfish, Bluegill, Bass & Kokanee Fishing Trail Swimming Picnicking Group Picnic Site Reservations: Ph: (530) 432-6427 Hiking Trails	Skippers Cove Marina 13104 Marina Smartville 95977 Ph: (530) 432-6302 Grocery Store Hot Sandwiches Gas - Propane Bait & Tackle

SCOTTS FLAT LAKE

Scotts Flat Lake is at an elevation of 3,000 feet at the gateway to the Tahoe National Forest. The Lake has a surface area of 850 acres with 7 miles of coniferous shoreline. This is a good boating Lake with two launch ramps and complete marina facilities including boat rentals. Anglers will find trout, kokanee and warm water fish. Scotts Flat campground includes a picnic area, sandy beaches and a store. Open year around, this is a quiet, relaxing facility in a beautiful forested environment.

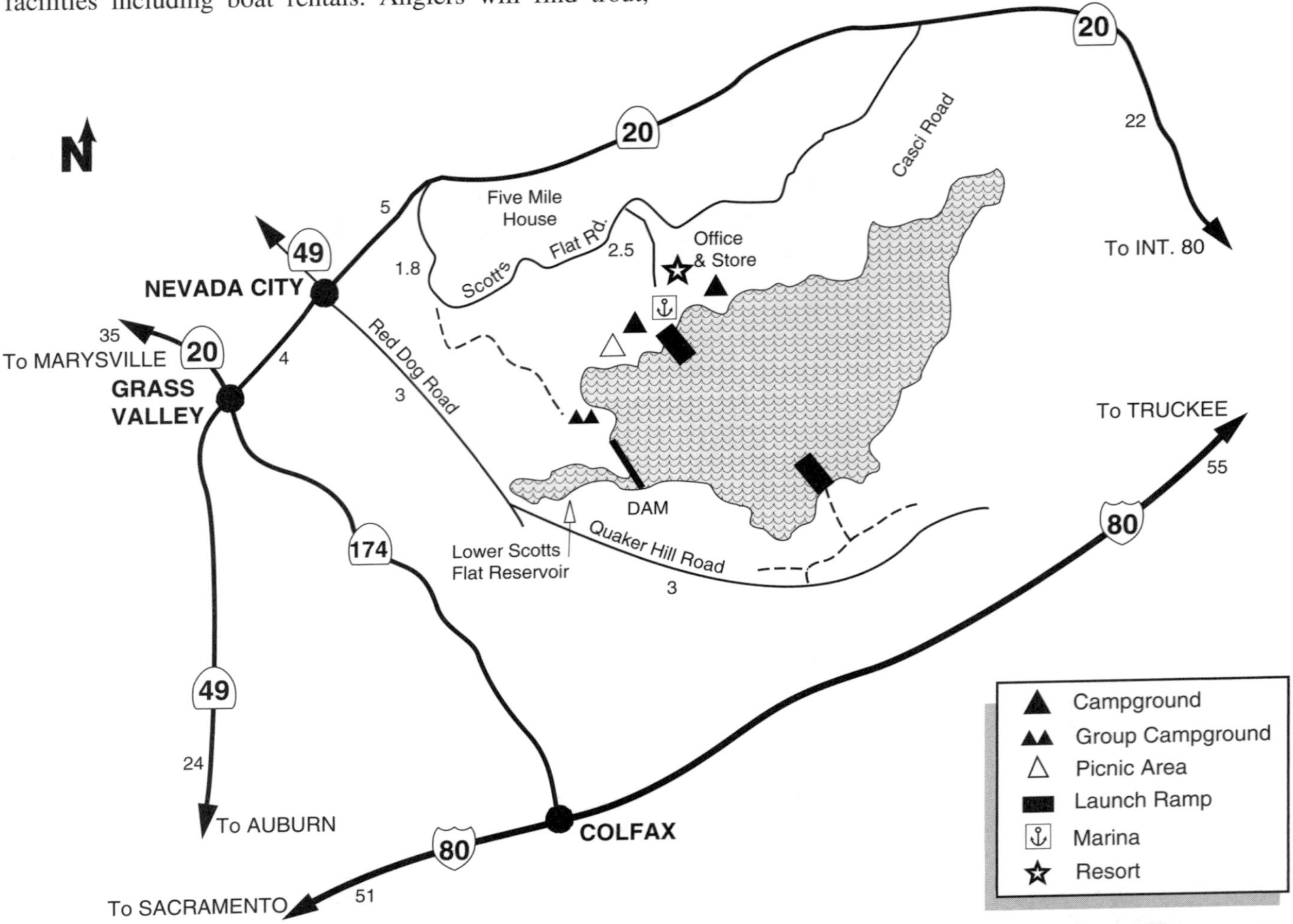

N
20
22
To INT. 80
Casci Road
Five Mile
House
Scotts Flat Rd.
2.5
1.8
5
Office
& Store
49
NEVADA CITY
35
To MARYSVILLE
20
4
GRASS
VALLEY
Red Dog Road
3
To TRUCKEE
55
DAM
80
174
Lower Scotts
Flat Reservoir
Quaker Hill Road
3
49
24
To AUBURN
80
COLFAX
To SACRAMENTO
51
Campground
Group Campground
Picnic Area
Launch Ramp
Marina
Resort

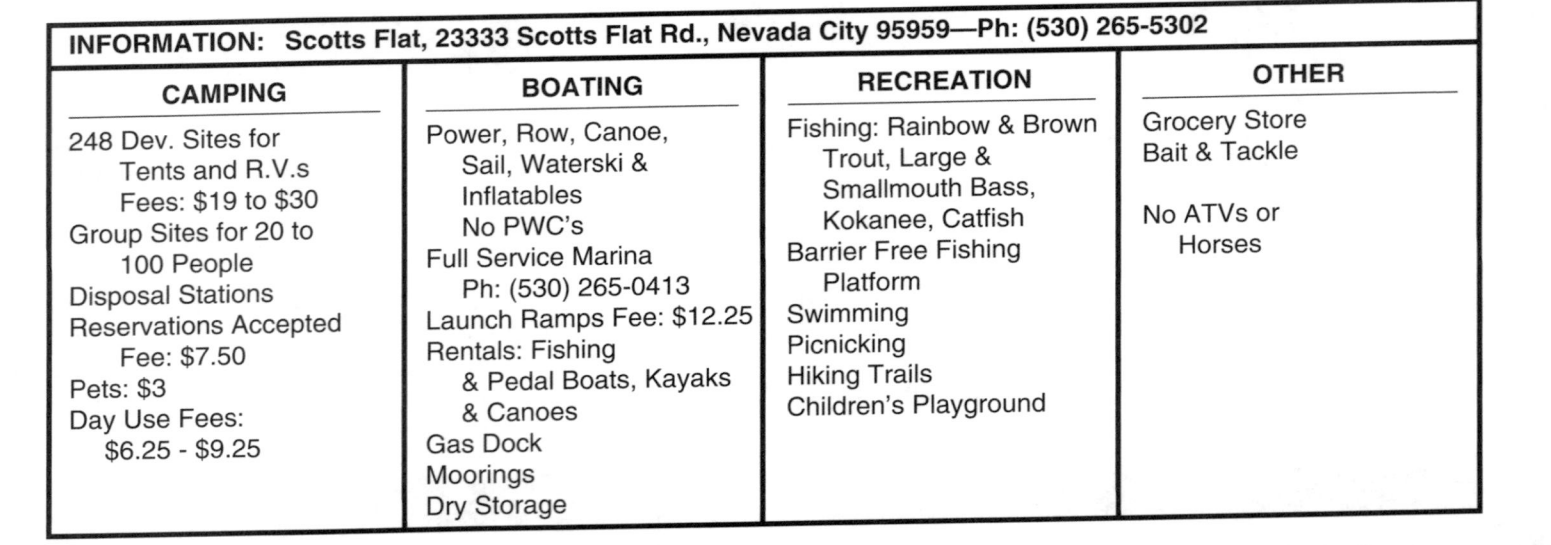

INFORMATION: Scotts Flat, 23333 Scotts Flat Rd., Nevada City 95959—Ph: (530) 265-5302

CAMPING	BOATING	RECREATION	OTHER
248 Dev. Sites for Tents and R.V.s Fees: $19 to $30 Group Sites for 20 to 100 People Disposal Stations Reservations Accepted Fee: $7.50 Pets: $3 Day Use Fees: $6.25 - $9.25	Power, Row, Canoe, Sail, Waterski & Inflatables No PWC's Full Service Marina Ph: (530) 265-0413 Launch Ramps Fee: $12.25 Rentals: Fishing & Pedal Boats, Kayaks & Canoes Gas Dock Moorings Dry Storage	Fishing: Rainbow & Brown Trout, Large & Smallmouth Bass, Kokanee, Catfish Barrier Free Fishing Platform Swimming Picnicking Hiking Trails Children's Playground	Grocery Store Bait & Tackle No ATVs or Horses

Rollins Lake, situated in the heart of the Gold Country at an elevation of 2,100 feet, is right off Interstate 80 near Colfax and Grass Valley. The Lake has approximately 840 surface acres of water and 26 miles of wooded shoreline. Rollins Lake offers 4 unique individual, family-owned and operated campgrounds. Each has their own convenience store, boat ramp, sandy beach and roped-off swim area. The individual campgrounds take their own reservations. Each arm of the Lake has many coves and long stretches of open water for boating and waterskiing. Water levels can fluctuate. Fishing is good from both boat and shore for a wide variety of trout and warm water species.

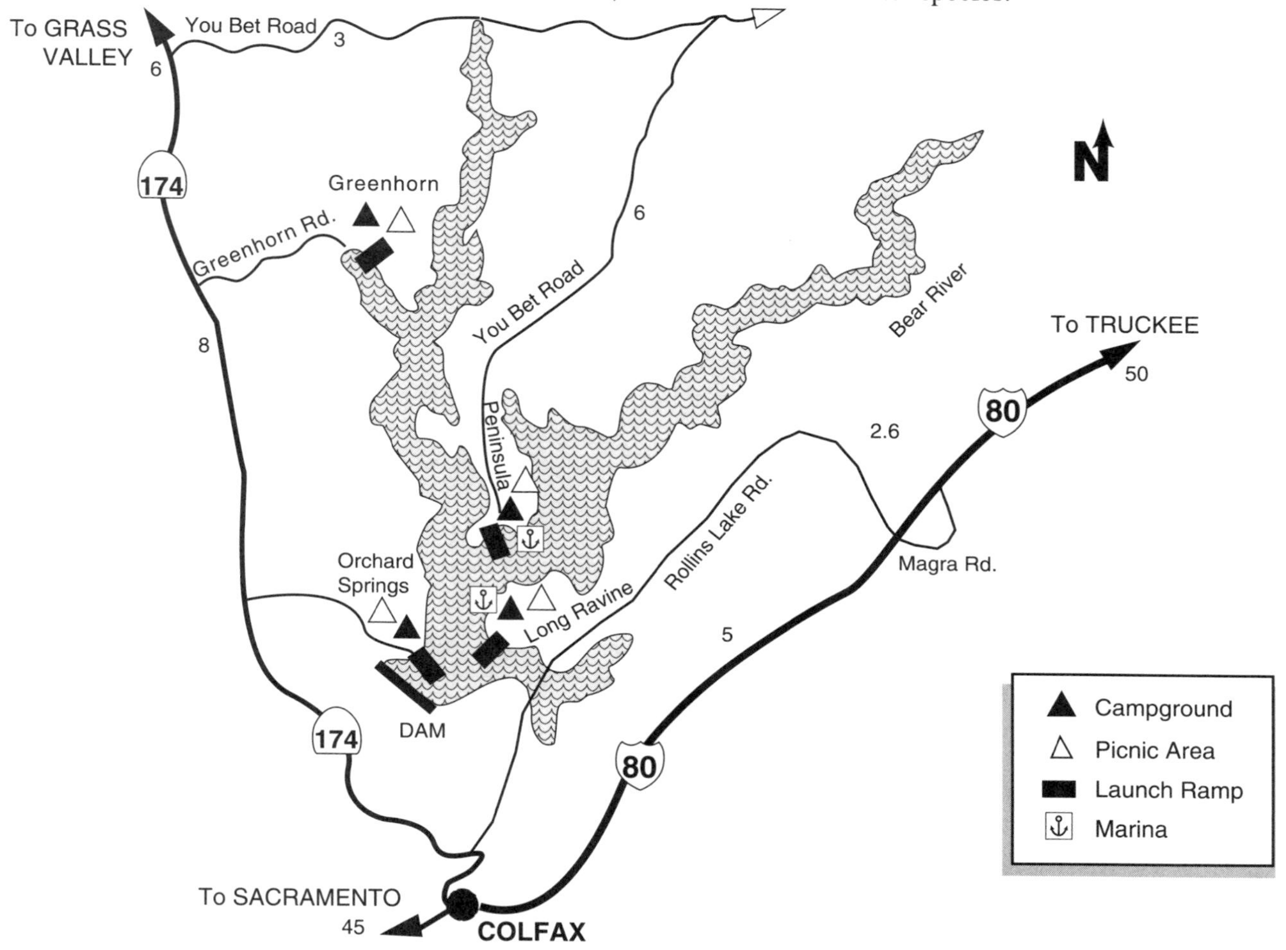
To GRASS VALLEY
6
You Bet Road
3
174
Greenhorn
Greenhorn Rd.
6
You Bet Road
Bear River
N
To TRUCKEE
50
8
80
2.6
Peninsula
Rollins Lake Rd.
Magra Rd.
Orchard Springs
Long Ravine
5
174
DAM
80
Campground
Picnic Area
Launch Ramp
Marina
To SACRAMENTO
45
COLFAX

INFORMATION: Rollins Lake - Each Campground has its own Phone Number - See Below

CAMPING	BOATING	RECREATION	OTHER
250 Dev. Sites for Tents & R.V.s Fees: $21 - $31 Full Hookups Group Camping - 16 to 40 People Fees: $95 to $150 *Reservations - Phone:* Greenhorn: (530) 272-6100 Orchard Springs: (530) 346-2212 Long Ravine:(530) 346-6166 Peninsula: (530) 477-9413	Power, Row, Canoe, Sail, Waterski, PWCs, Windsurfers Full Service Marinas Boat Gas Dock 4 Launch Ramps Rentals: Fishing Boats, Canoes, Paddle Boats Houseboat Mooring Boat Slips Dry Storage	Fishing: Rainbow & Brown Trout, Small & Largemouth Bass, Crappie, Catfish & Sunfish Picnicking - Boat-in Sites Swimming Bicycle Trails Hiking Trails Horseback Riding Volleyball Court	Camping Cabins Fee: $55 Snack Bar & Grill Restaurants & Lounge General Stores Bait & Tackle Fishing Licenses Disposal Stations R.V. & Trailer Storage

LAKE VALLEY RESERVOIR and KELLY LAKE

Lake Valley Reservoir, at an elevation of 5,800 feet, has 300 surface acres. The shoreline is surrounded by tall trees and granite boulders. The campsites are situated under the trees near the Lake and accommodate both tents and R.V.s. The steep shoreline combined with the steady west wind allows for good sailing. There are two islands in the Lake where you can stop for a picnic. Kelly Lake is a small day-use facility well worth a visit. 5 picnic sites, tables and firepits are available. Small boats without motors are allowed. Trout fishing can be excellent at both these High Sierra Lakes.

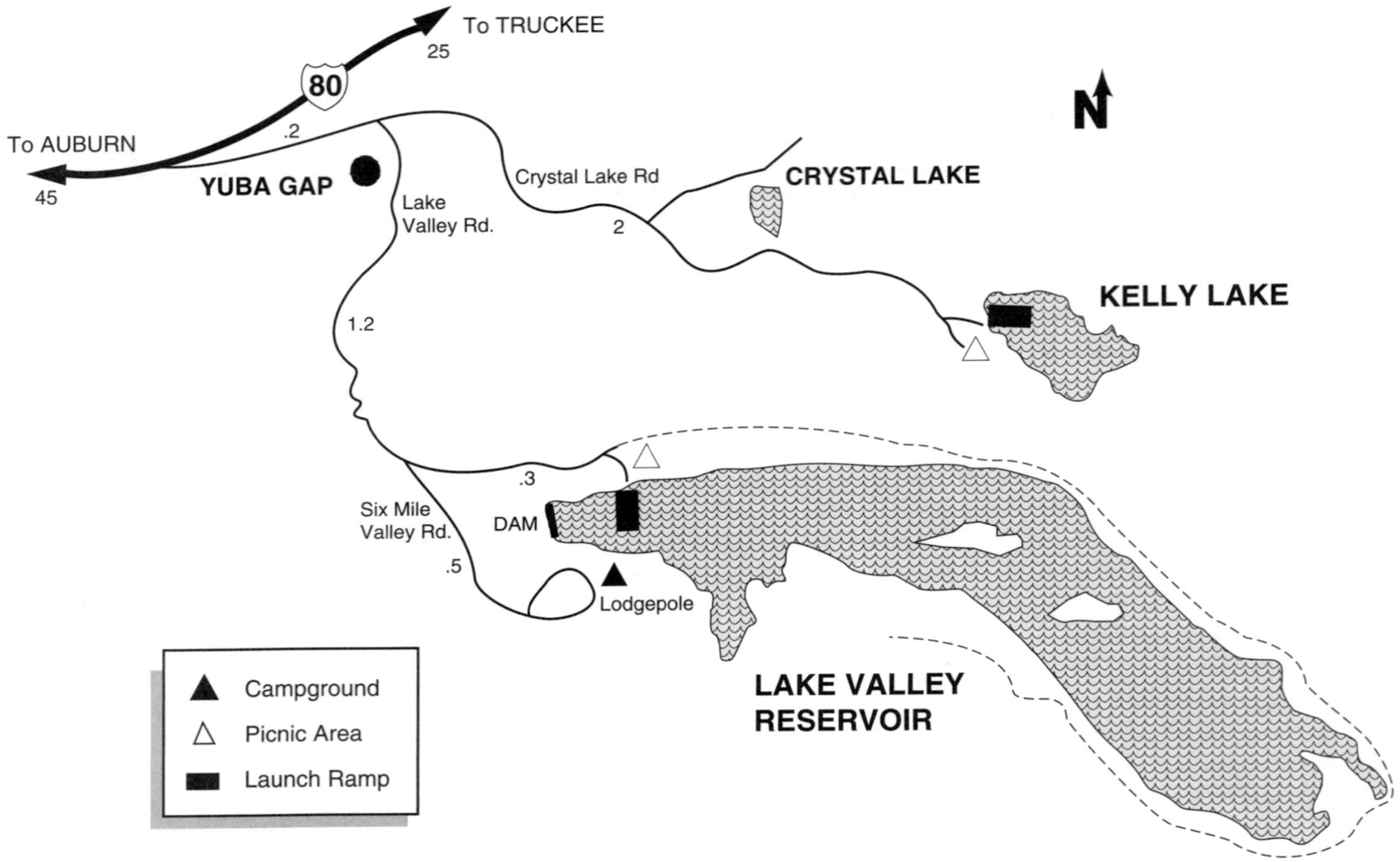

To TRUCKEE
25
80
To AUBURN
.2
45
YUBA GAP
Lake
Valley Rd.
Crystal Lake Rd
2
CRYSTAL LAKE
N
KELLY LAKE
1.2
.3
Six Mile
Valley Rd.
DAM
.5
Lodgepole
LAKE VALLEY
RESERVOIR
Campground
Picnic Area
Launch Ramp

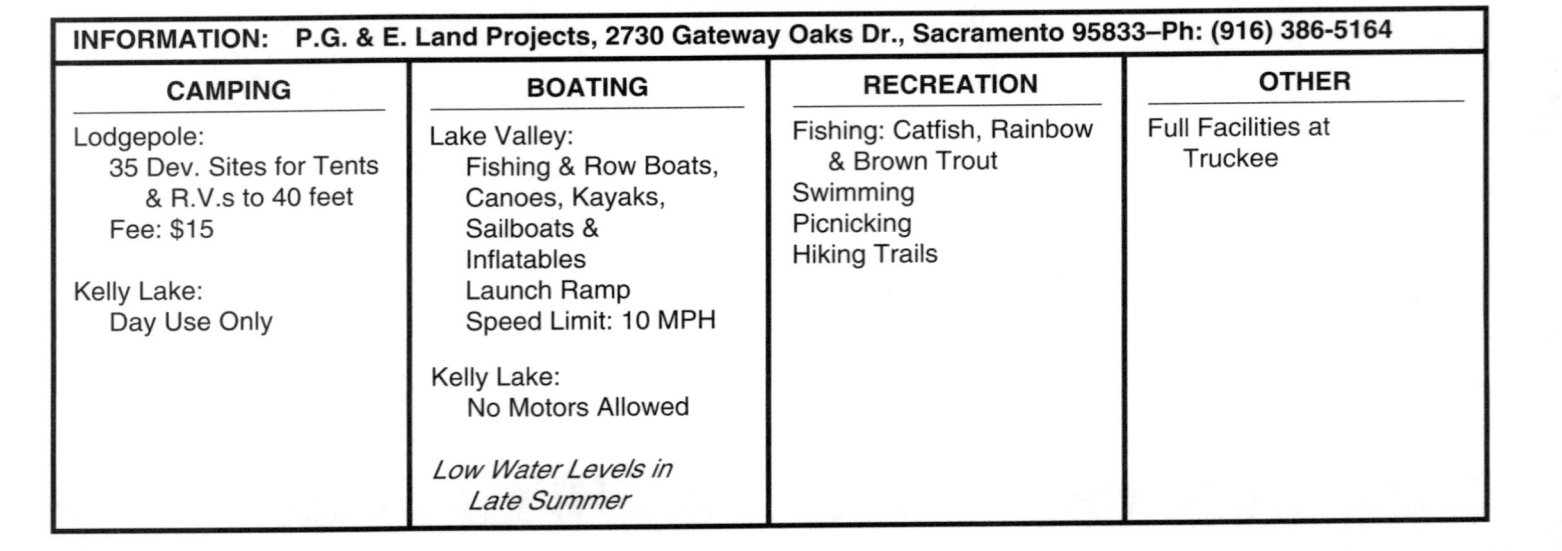

INFORMATION: P.G. & E. Land Projects, 2730 Gateway Oaks Dr., Sacramento 95833–Ph: (916) 386-5164

CAMPING	BOATING	RECREATION	OTHER
Lodgepole: 35 Dev. Sites for Tents & R.V.s to 40 feet Fee: $15 Kelly Lake: Day Use Only	Lake Valley: Fishing & Row Boats, Canoes, Kayaks, Sailboats & Inflatables Launch Ramp Speed Limit: 10 MPH Kelly Lake: No Motors Allowed *Low Water Levels in Late Summer*	Fishing: Catfish, Rainbow & Brown Trout Swimming Picnicking Hiking Trails	Full Facilities at Truckee

The Lake Pillsbury Recreation Area provides a wide range of outdoor recreation at an elevation of 1,832 feet. Located in a mountainous setting in the Mendocino National Forest, this 2,280 surface acre Lake has 31 miles of shoreline. It is open to all types of boating including boat camping in designated areas. Anglers will find trout, steelhead and salmon in season in the nearby Eel River and its tributaries. The Bloody Rock Area is popular with equestrians. Hang gliding at Hull Mountain (elevation 6,873 feet) offers spectacular views of the surrounding countryside. For further information: Lake County Visitor Center, 6110 East Highway 20, Lucerne 95458, Ph: (800) 525-3743.

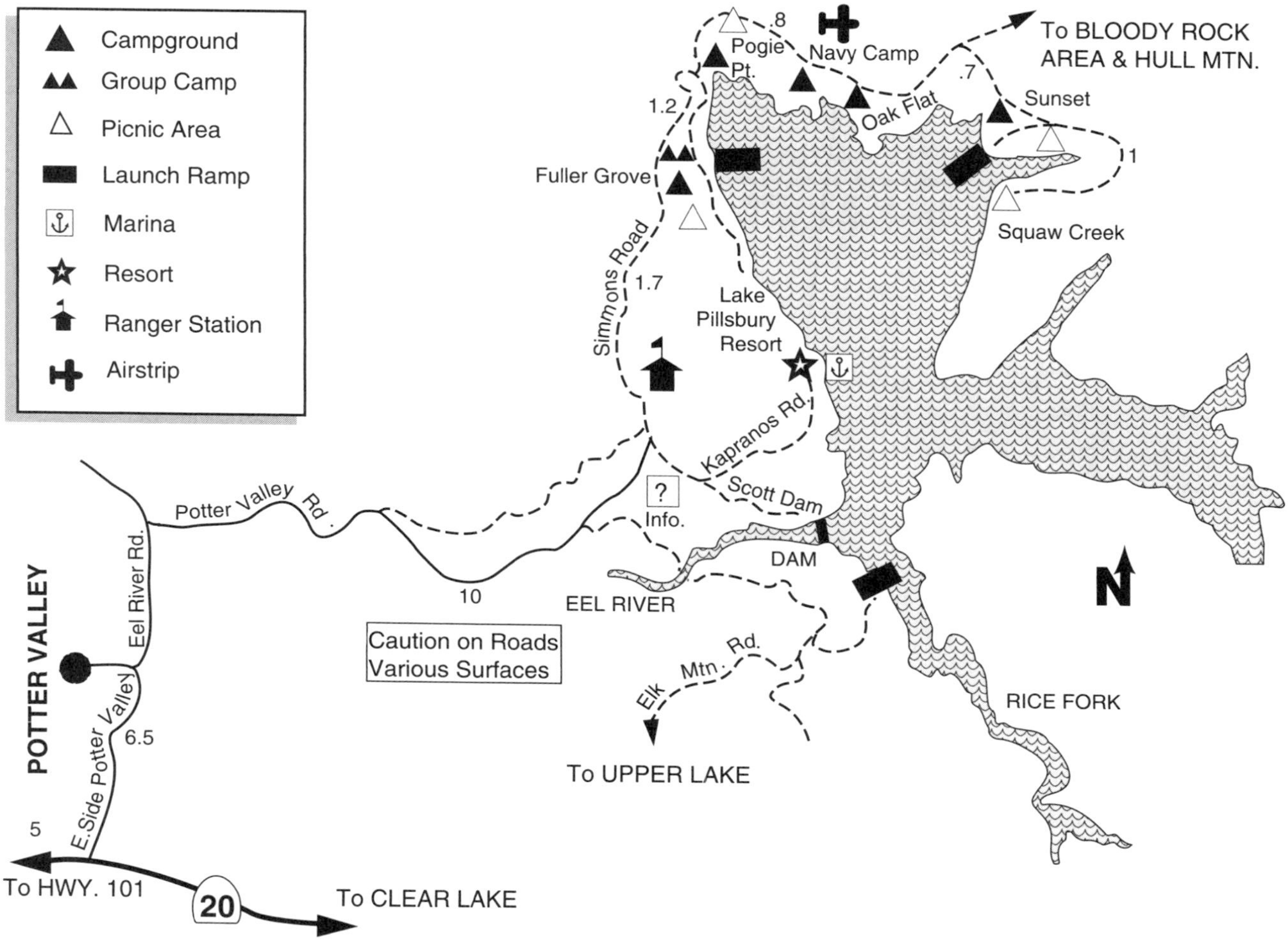
Campground
Group Camp
Picnic Area
Launch Ramp
Marina
Resort
Ranger Station
Airstrip
To BLOODY ROCK AREA & HULL MTN.
Pogie Pt.
Navy Camp
Oak Flat
Sunset
Squaw Creek
Fuller Grove
Simmons Road
Lake Pillsbury Resort
Kapranos Rd.
Scott Dam
Info.
DAM
EEL RIVER
RICE FORK
Potter Valley Rd.
Eel River Rd.
POTTER VALLEY
E.Side Potter Valley
Caution on Roads Various Surfaces
Elk Mtn. Rd.
To UPPER LAKE
To HWY. 101
20
To CLEAR LAKE
.8
1.2
.7
1
1.7
10
6.5
5

INFORMATION: Upper Lake Ranger District, 10025 Elk Mountain Rd., Upper Lake 95485—Ph: (707) 275-2361

CAMPING	BOATING	RECREATION	OTHER
Dev. Sites for Tents & R.V.s Operated by PG&E Fees: $13 Sunset: 54 Dev. Sites Navy Camp: 20 Dev. Sites Pogie Point: 50 Dev. Sites Fuller Grove: 30 Dev. Sites Plus Oak Flat Overflow: No Fee Fuller Grove Group to 60 People Max. $100 Reservations: Ph: (916) 386-5164	Open to All Boating Boat Camping in Designated Areas Full Service Marina Launch Ramps Rentals: Fishing Boats & Canoes Boat Fuel & Slips	Fishing: Largemouth & Black Bass, Rainbow Trout, Bluegill & Sunfish Swimming Picnicking Hiking & Equestrian Trails Backpacking Hang Gliding Nearby	Snack Bars Grocery Store Restaurant & Lounge Bait & Tackle Gas Station Lake Pillsbury Resort & Marina 2756 Kapranos Rd. Potter Valley 95469 Ph: (707) 743-9935 41 Tent & R.V. Sites Some Full Hookups 8 Cabins

LAKE MENDOCINO

Lake Mendocino is at an elevation of 748 feet above Coyote Dam on the East Fork of the Russian River. This beautiful wine country has many small valleys of vineyards and pear trees. The Lake has a surface area of 1,822 acres with 15 miles of oak-wooded shoreline. The U.S. Army Corps of Engineers maintain the facilities which include numerous campsites and picnic areas. Group picnic shelters each have a massive stone barbecue pit. There is a large protected swim beach and a 5-kilometer hiking trail. Equestrians will find a staging area and horseback riding trails. The fishing is good with channel catfish up to 30 pounds and stripers to 40 pounds. The Pomo Cultural Center, 3,200 square feet, overlooks the Lake. A Fish Hatchery is open to the public from November to March.

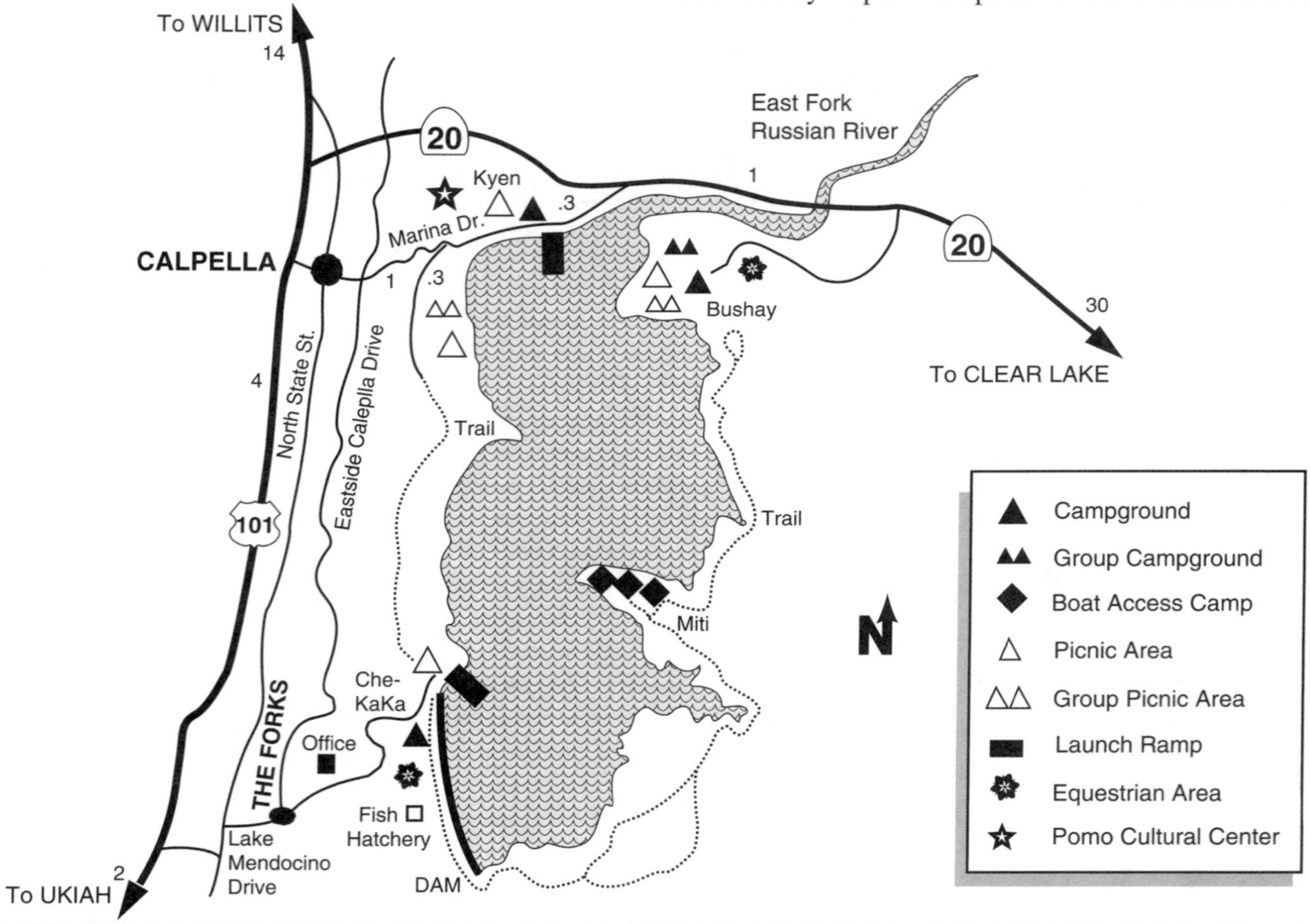

To WILLITS
14
20
East Fork
Russian River
1
Kyen
.3
Marina Dr.
CALPELLA
1
.3
20
Bushay
30
To CLEAR LAKE
4
North State St.
Eastside Calepella Drive
Trail
101
Trail
Miti
N
Che-
KaKa
Office
THE FORKS
Fish
Hatchery
Lake
Mendocino
Drive
DAM
2
To UKIAH
Campground
Group Campground
Boat Access Camp
Picnic Area
Group Picnic Area
Launch Ramp
Equestrian Area
Pomo Cultural Center

INFORMATION: Park Manager, 1160 Lake Mendocino Dr., Ukiah 95482—Ph: (707) 462-7581

CAMPING	BOATING	RECREATION	OTHER
Dev. Sites for Tents & R.V.s Bushay: 136 Sites to 40 ft. Chekaka: 20 Sites to 42 ft. Kyen: 101 Sites Fees: $16 to $22 3 Group Camps for 80, 120 & 130 People Fees: $140 to $200 Miti: 16 Boat or Walk-in Sites Only Disposal Stations Reservations: Ph: (877) 444-6777	Power, Row, Canoe, Sail, Waterski, PWCs & Inflatables Launch Ramps Fee: $3	Fishing: Catfish, Bluegill, Crappie, Large, Smallmouth & Striped Bass Swimming - Beaches Picnicking 10 Group Picnic Shelters Hiking & Equestrian Trails Horse Staging Area Mountain Bike Trails Disc Golf Course Playgrounds Amphitheater	Pomo Cultural Center Ph: (707) 485-8285 US Army Corps of Engineers Campfire Programs in Summer Full Facilities at Capella and Ukiah

The Blue Lakes are at an elevation of 1,357 feet off Highway 20 between Clear Lake and Lake Mendocino. Upper Lake has 73 surface acres and Lower Lake has 52 surface acres. These popular Lakes are nestled in a beautiful setting of dense groves of madrones, oaks and evergreens. They are spring fed and have existed for over 10,000 years. The clear blue waters and relaxed environment make this area a retreat for fishing, swimming and boating. The private resorts surrounding the Lakes provide complete vacation facilities including shaded campsites, cabins, restaurants, boat rentals, swim beaches and picnic areas.

...Continued...

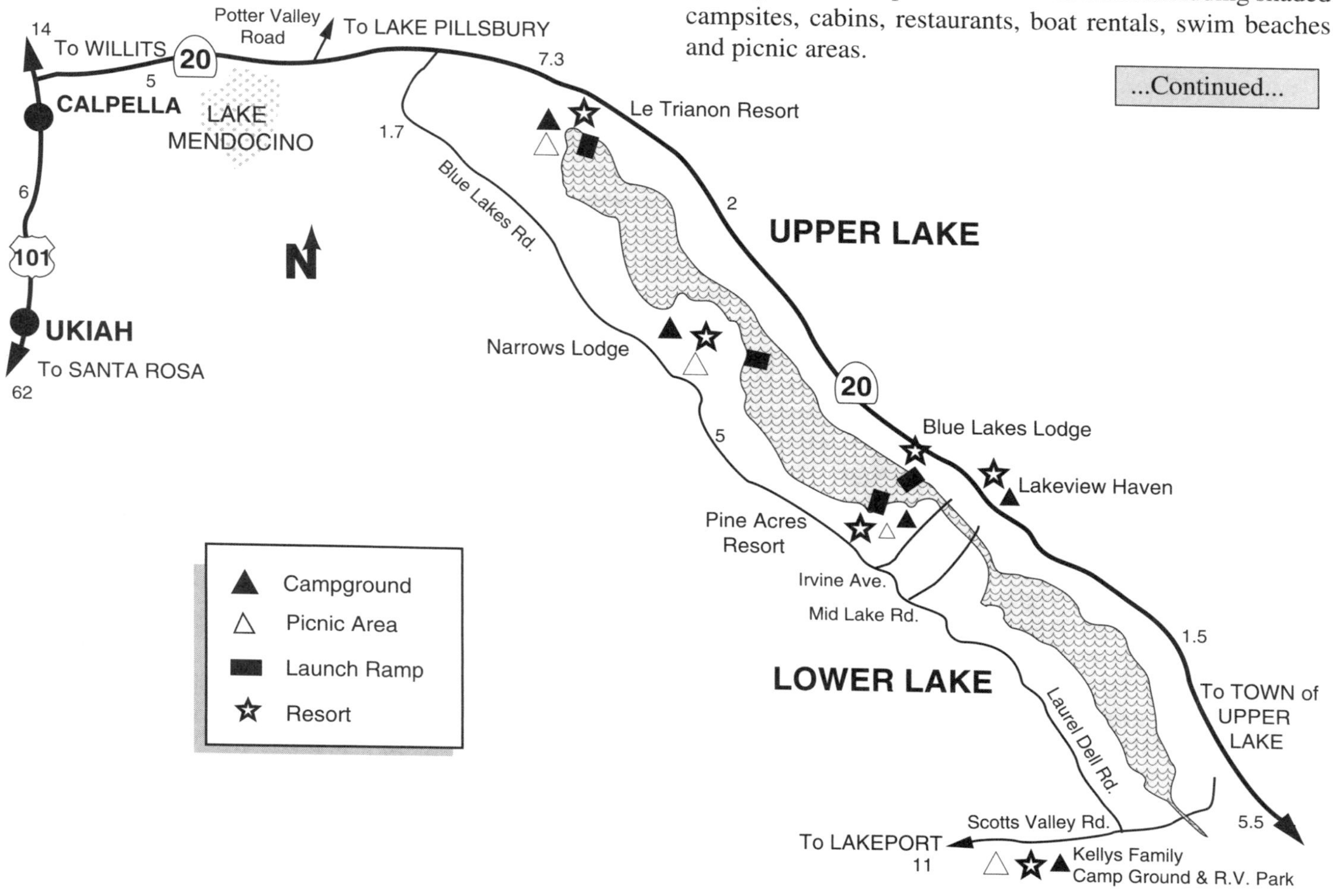

14
To WILLITS
20
Potter Valley Road
To LAKE PILLSBURY
7.3
5
CALPELLA
LAKE MENDOCINO
1.7
Le Trianon Resort
Blue Lakes Rd.
2
UPPER LAKE
6
101
N
UKIAH
To SANTA ROSA
62
Narrows Lodge
20
Blue Lakes Lodge
5
Lakeview Haven
Pine Acres Resort
Irvine Ave.
Mid Lake Rd.
1.5
Campground
Picnic Area
Launch Ramp
Resort
LOWER LAKE
Laurel Dell Rd.
To TOWN of UPPER LAKE
Scotts Valley Rd.
5.5
To LAKEPORT
11
Kellys Family Camp Ground & R.V. Park

INFORMATION: Lake County Visitor Info. Center, 6110 East Highway 20, Lakeport 95458—Ph: (800) 525-3743

CAMPING	BOATING	RECREATION	OTHER
Private Resorts: Sites for Tents & R.V.s See Following Page	Power, Row, Canoe, Sail, Windsurf & Inflatables 5 MPH Speed Limit Launch Ramps Docks Rentals: Rowboats, Motorboats, Canoes & Paddleboats See Following Page	Fishing: Trout, Largemouth Bass, Catfish, Bluegill, Swimming - Beaches Picnicking	See Following Page

BLUE LAKES - LAKE COUNTY............Continued

LE TRIANON RESORT: 5845 E. Hwy. 20, Ukiah 95482
Ph: (707) 275-2262

Le Trianon Resort has housekeeping cabins. The campground and the RV facilities are reserved for seasonal occupants and their guests. With a day pass you can use the beach, picnic area and playground. There is a launch ramp, dock, swim area, kayak and pedal boat rentals. A lakeside snack bar and grocery store are also available. No pets are allowed.

NARROWS LODGE: 5690 Blue Lakes Road
Upper Lake 95485—Ph: (707) 275-2718

The Narrows Lodge Resort has modern conveniences in a forest setting. There are fully equipped housekeeping cabins and motel units. The R.V. Park has 20 sites with complete hookups along with a disposal station. 10 sites have water and electric hookups. Tent sites are also available. The Resort has a launch ramp, fishing dock, swim area, BBQ's, picnic tables, disposal station, bait and tackle shop and game room. Rowboats, motorboats, kayaks, canoes and paddleboats can be rented. Open year around.

PINE ACRES RESORT: 5328 Blue Lakes Road
Upper Lake 95485—Ph: (707) 275-2811

Pine Acres Resort has a motel and fully equipped cottages. 30 R.V. sites are available, 23 with water and electric hookups and 4 with full hookups. There are shaded lawns, BBQs, picnic tables, horseshoe court, swimming beach with float, fishing pier, launch ramp, boat rentals, bait and tackle shop and disposal station. A clubhouse is available for pot lucks, square dancing, conferences, family reunions and other uses for R.V. groups. Open year around.

THE LODGE AT BLUE LAKES: 5135 W. Highway 20
Upper Lake 95485—Ph: (707) 275-2181

This Resort has deluxe rooms, some with a fireplace and jacuzzi along with rooms with kitchenettes. There is a free launch ramp for guests, fishing docks and a swimming pool. Kayaks and BBQ grill are also available at no charge. Facilities can be used for banquets, weddings or other group functions. Dogs are welcome.

Call Resorts for Current Prices

KELLY'S KAMP: 8220 Scotts Valley Road
Upper Lake 95485—Ph: (707) 263-5754

Kelly's Family Kamp Ground and R.V. Park has family camping on sites with frontage along Scotts Creek. There are 48 R.V. sites with water and electric hookups. Also available are the Kamp Store, laundromat, disposal station, firewood, picnic tables, fire pits and BBQ grills. Recreational facilities include a 2-acre swimming pond with floats, fishing, volleyball, basketball, horseshoes and hiking. A horseback riding trail is nearby. R.V. storage is available and a pavilion area with a built-in BBQ for large groups.

LAKEVIEW HAVEN R.V. PARK: 1057 W. Highway 20
Upper Lake 95485—Ph: (707) 275-2105

Lakeview Haven has a R.V. park with 45 sites including spaces up to 65 feet in length. Full hookups are available. There is a swimming pool, picnic tables with an area for large groups and a fishing dock. Boat rentals are nearby.

BAIT
BY: GREG DIRKSEN©

Clear Lake is at an elevation of 1,320 feet. With 43,000 surface acres, this is the largest freshwater lake that lies completely within California. The Lake has a shoreline of 100 miles and offers a huge variety of recreational activities. This was once the home of the Pomo and Lile'ek tribes who were drawn here by the abundant fish and game. Often called "Bass Capital of the West," Clear Lake has a productive warm water fishery. Boaters and waterskiers can enjoy miles of open water, many coves and inlets. This Lake is also known for excellent sailing conditions. Numerous launch ramps, marinas, beaches, campgrounds and resorts dot the shoreline. Nearby Highland Springs Reservoir offers warm water fishing, swimming and non-powered boating.

...Continued...

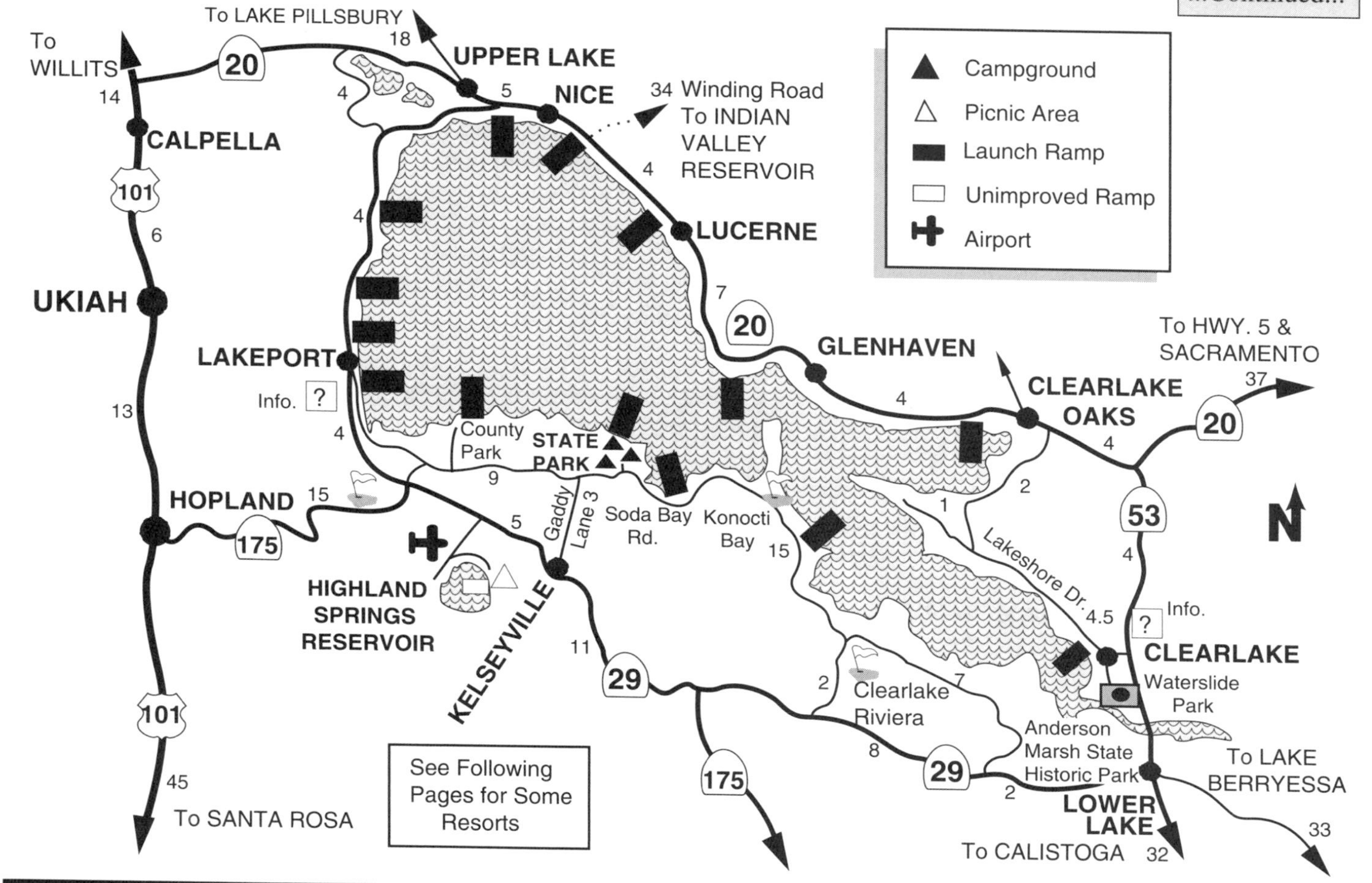

To LAKE PILLSBURY
To WILLITS
20
18
UPPER LAKE
5
NICE
34 Winding Road To INDIAN VALLEY RESERVOIR
4
14
CALPELLA
101
6
4
LUCERNE
UKIAH
7
20
GLENHAVEN
To HWY. 5 & SACRAMENTO
37
LAKEPORT
Info.
?
13
4
CLEARLAKE OAKS
20
4
County Park
STATE PARK
9
HOPLAND
15
175
5
Gaddy
Lane 3
Soda Bay Rd.
Konocti Bay
15
1
2
53
4
Lakeshore Dr.
4.5
Info.
?
HIGHLAND SPRINGS RESERVOIR
KELSEYVILLE
11
29
2
Clearlake Riviera
7
CLEARLAKE
Waterslide Park
8
29
Anderson Marsh State Historic Park
To LAKE BERRYESSA
101
45
To SANTA ROSA
See Following Pages for Some Resorts
175
2
LOWER LAKE
33
To CALISTOGA
32
Campground
Picnic Area
Launch Ramp
Unimproved Ramp
Airport
N

INFORMATION: Lake County Visitor Info. Center, 6110 East Highway 20, Lakeport 95458—Ph: (800) 525-3743

CAMPING	BOATING	RECREATION	OTHER
Clear Lake State Park 5300 Soda Bay Rd. Kelseyville 95451 Ph: (707) 279-4293 147 Dev. Sites for Tents & R.V.s to 35 Feet Fee: $12 Reservations Ph: (800) 444-7275 For Additional Campgrounds, See Following Pages	Open to All Boating Full Service Marinas Public Launch Ramps Boat Rentals: Fishing & Waterski Boats, PWCs & Pontoons Clear Lake Queen Cruise Boat	Fishing: Florida & Northern Bass, Yellow & Blue Channel Catfish, Trout, Crappie & Bluegill Swimming: Beaches & Pools Picnicking at State Parks Hiking & Bicyling Trails Equestrian Trails Disc Golf Course near Highland Springs Reservoir	Winery Tours Golf Courses Complete Facilities in Nearby Towns Anderson Marsh State Historical Park: Archeological Sites of Indian Villages and Sanctuary for Water Birds and Fish Gaming Casinos

CLEAR LAKE............Continued

THERE ARE OVER 50 PRIVATE CAMPGROUNDS AND RESORTS AT CLEAR LAKE.
THE FOLLOWING ARE RANDOMLY SELECTED FACILITIES, MANY WITH LAUNCH RAMPS
CALL RESORTS FOR CURRENT RATES

NORTHSHORE - NICE

HOLIDAY HARBOR MARINA & R.V. PARK
P.O. Box 26, 3605 Lakeshore Blvd., Nice 95464—Ph: (707) 274-1136
34 R.V. Sites, Full Hookups, Disposal Station, Full Service Marina, Launch Ramp, Marine Gas, Boat Slips.

DRIFT INN TRAILER RESORT
P.O. Box 8, 2730 E. Hwy. 20, Nice 95464—Ph: (707) 274-5501
17 R.V. & Tent Sites on the Lake, Full Hookups, Pier, Launch Ramp, Beach.

GLENHAVEN - CLEARLAKE OAKS

GLENHAVEN BEACH CAMPGROUND & MARINA
P.O. Box 406, 9625 E. Hwy. 20, Glenhaven 95443—Ph: (707) 998-3406
23 Tent/R.V. Sites, Hookups, Launch Ramp, Mooring, Slips, Fuel Dock, Groceries.

INDIAN BEACH RESORT
9945 E. Hwy. 20, Glenhaven 95443—Ph: (707) 998-3760
9 Cottages with Kitchenettes, On the Lake, Sandy Beach,
Pier, Launch Ramp, Docks, Boat Slips, Picnic Areas, Playground, Store, Bait.

LAKE MARINA MOTEL RESORT
10215 E. Hwy. 20, Clearlake Oaks 95423—Ph: (707) 998-3787
12 Units with Kitchenettes, Boat Launch, Pier, Fishing Area, Boat Rentals.

20 OAKS RESORT
10503 E. Hwy. 20, Clearlake Oaks 95423—Ph: (707) 998-3012
5 Cottages, 7 R.V. Sites, Full Hookups, Disposal Station, Picnic Area, Dock.

BLUE FISH COVE
10573 E. Hwy. 20, Clearlake Oaks 95423—Ph: (707) 998-1769
7 Cottages with Kitchenettes, On the Lake, Launch Ramp, Fishing Pier, Beach, Boat Rentals.

ISLAND RV PARK
P.O. Box 126, 12840 Island Dr., Clearlake Oaks 95423—Ph: (707) 998-3940
30 R.V. Sites, Full Hookups, Launch Ramp, Docks, Slips.

LAKE POINT LODGE
P. O. Box 708, 13440 E. Hwy. 20, Clearlake Oaks 95423—Ph: (707) 998-4350
40 Units, Swimming Pool.

CLEARLAKE - SOUTH SHORE

LAKEFRONT MOBILE HOME & R.V. PARK
P. O. Box 4115, 5545 Old Hwy. 53, Clearlake 95422—Ph: (707) 994-1194
15 R.V. Sites, Hookups, Launch Ramp, Docks, Fishing Area.

....Continued....

KELSEYVILLE - SODA BAY - KONOCTI BAY

EDGEWATER RESORT
1 Mile East of Clear Lake State Park
6420 Soda Bay Rd., Kelseyville 95451—Ph: (707) 279-0208
61 R.V./Tent Sites, Full Hookups, Sites up to 40 ft. with Slide Outs, 6 Cabins for 2-12 People, Full Kitchens, Picnic Area, Lighted Fishing Pier, Dock, Launch Ramp, Kayak Rentals, Swim Beach, Swimming Pool, Picnic Area, Clubhouse, General Store, Bait and Tackle, Volleyball Court, Ping-Pong, Horseshoes, Group Facilities, Pets on Leash Welcome.

FERNDALE RESORT & MARINA
6190 Soda Bay Rd., Kelseyville 95451—Ph: (707) 279-4866
19 Lakeside Rooms, Restaurant & Lounge, Full Serice Marina, Launch Ramp, Slips, Pier, Rental Boats, Bait & Tackle, Fuel Dock, Transportation to Konocti Harbor for Concerts.

KONOCTI HARBOR RESORT & SPA
8727 Soda Bay Rd., Kelseyville 95451—Ph: (707) 279-4281 or (800) 660-LAKE
250 Rooms including Beach Cottages, Restaurant & Bar/Nightclub, Indoor & Outdoor Concerts, 4 Swimming Pools, Tennis, Launch Ramps, Piers, Slips, Full Service Marina, Rentals: Waterski & Fishing Boats, PWCs, Kayaks, Paddleboats plus 15 Passenger Pontoon Party Boat and 80 Passenger Paddlewheeler Cruise, Conference Facilities.

RICHMOND PARK
9435 Konocti Bay Rd., Kelseyville 95451—Ph: (707) 277-7535
25 R.V. Sites, Hookups, Restaurant, Bar & Grill, Launch Ramp, Fuel Dock, Pier, Slips.

LAKEPORT

ANCHORAGE INN
950 N. Main St., Lakeport 95453—Ph: (707) 263-5417
34 Units with Kitchenettes, Swimming Pool, Launch Ramp, Docks, Fishing Pier, Ping Pong, Pool Table.

CLEARLAKE INN
1010 N. Main St., Lakeport 95453—Ph: (707) 263-3551
40 Units, Swimming Pool, Dock, Fishing Pier.

THE MALLARD HOUSE INN, 970 N. Main St., Lakeport 95453—Ph: (707) 262-1601
Housekeeping Units, Spa, Patios, Boat Dock with Electrical Outlets, BBQ Area, Fishing Pier.

SKYLARK SHORES RESORT/MOTEL
1120 N. Main St., Lakeport 95453—Ph: (707) 263-6151
5 Cottages with Kitchenettes, Lakefront Suites, Swimming Pool, Launch Ramp, Boat Dock, Picnic Area.

Along with other resorts not mentioned, there are public launch ramps shown on our map. The State Park is shown on the graph. For information on additional resorts and other attractions, contact:

Lake County Visitor Information Center
6110 East Highway 20, Lucerne 94358
Ph: (707) 274-5652 or 800-LAKESIDE (525-3743)

Lakeport Regional Chamber of Commerce
875 Lakeport Blvd., Lakeport 95453
Ph: (707) 263-5092

Clear Lake Chamber of Commerce
4700 Golf Ave., Clearlake 95422
Ph: (707) 994-3600

INDIAN VALLEY RESERVOIR

Indian Valley Reservoir, at an elevation of 1,476 feet, is under the jurisdiction of the Yolo County Flood Control District. The Bureau of Land Management is in charge of the Indian Valley/Walker Ridge Recreation Area. This very remote Lake has 3,800 surface acres and 39 miles of shoreline. The Lake is an excellent rainbow trout and warm water fishery.

Since there is a 10 MPH speed limit, this is a quiet place for sailing, canoeing and fishing. High winds, however, can occur, particularly in the afternoon. The area surrounding the Reservoir is an important winter habitat for bald eagles, golden eagles and waterfowl. It is important that you always check for current conditions before visiting Indian Valley Reservoir.

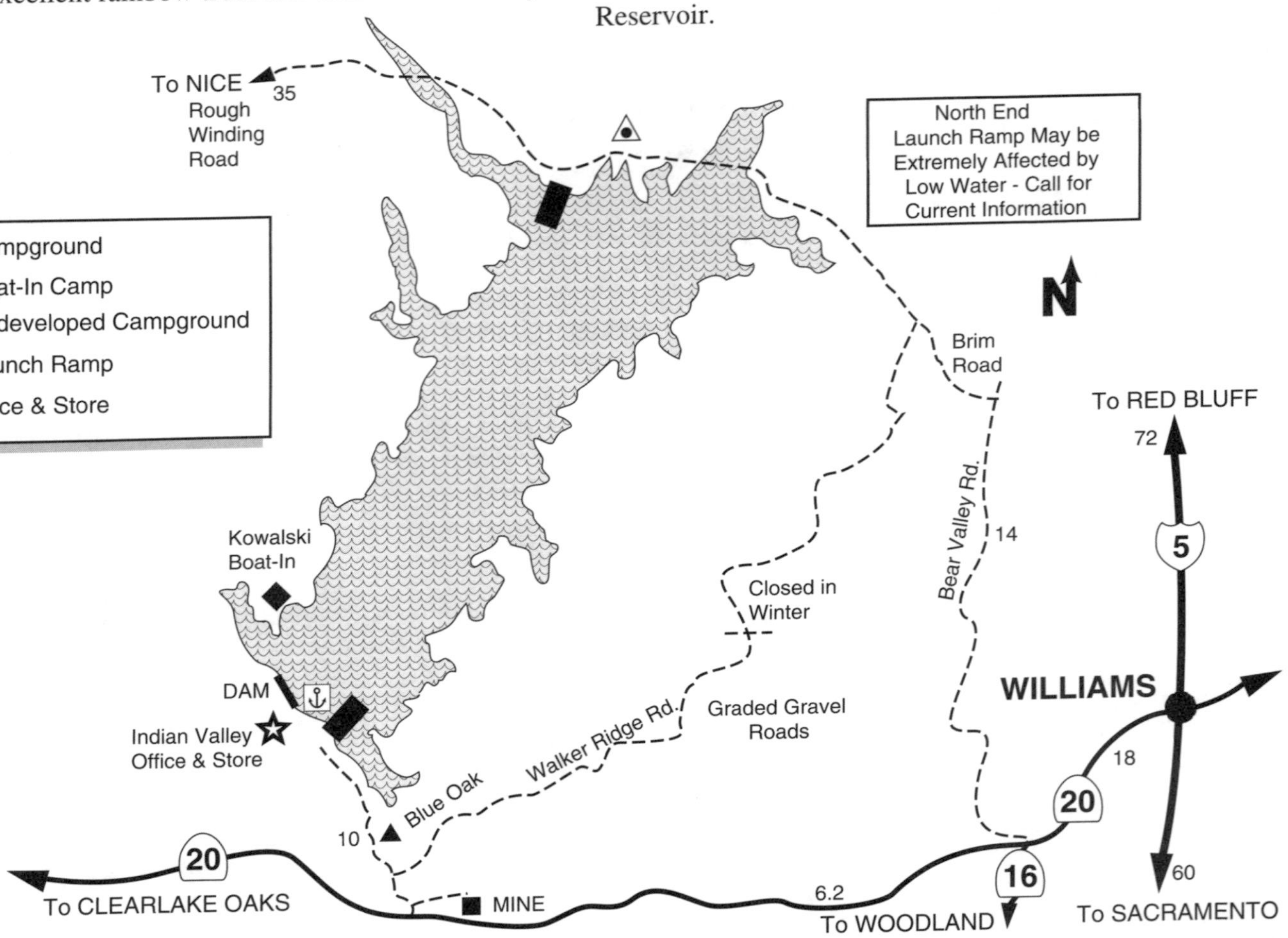
To NICE
35
Rough Winding Road
North End Launch Ramp May be Extremely Affected by Low Water - Call for Current Information
Campground
Boat-In Camp
Undeveloped Campground
Launch Ramp
Office & Store
N
Brim Road
To RED BLUFF
72
5
Kowalski Boat-In
Closed in Winter
Bear Valley Rd.
14
WILLIAMS
DAM
Indian Valley Office & Store
Walker Ridge Rd.
Graded Gravel Roads
18
20
Blue Oak
10
20
To CLEARLAKE OAKS
MINE
6.2
To WOODLAND
16
60
To SACRAMENTO

INFORMATION: Bureau of Land Management, 2550 North State St., Ukiah 95482—Ph: (707) 468-4000

CAMPING	BOATING	RECREATION	OTHER
Blue Oak: 6 Dev. Sites for Tents & R.Vs. No Hookups Kowalski: Boat-In Camping Only	Open to All Boating 10 MPH Speed Limit Paved Launch Ramp *Beware of Underwater Hazards and Afternoon Winds*	Fishing: Eagle Lake & Rainbow Trout, Kokanee, Large & Smallmouth Bass, Catfish, Bluegill, Picnicking Hiking, Bicyling & Equestrian Trails Hunting on Nearby Bureau of Land Management Area in Season	Indian Valley Store: Ph: (530) 662-0607 Groceries Bait & Tackle Propane Graded Gravel Roads Yolo County: Ph: (530) 662-0265

Central Section Lakes 61 - 150

Numbers around highways represent lakes in numerical order in this book. *See Index for complete listing.*

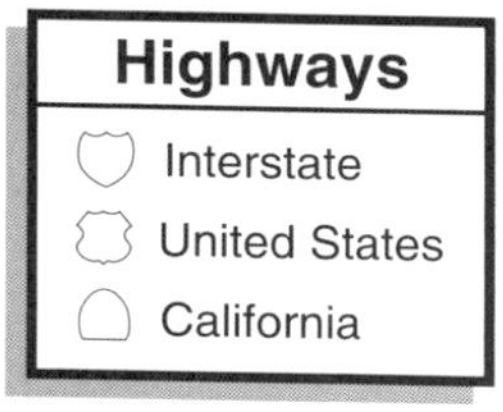

Highways
Interstate
United States
California

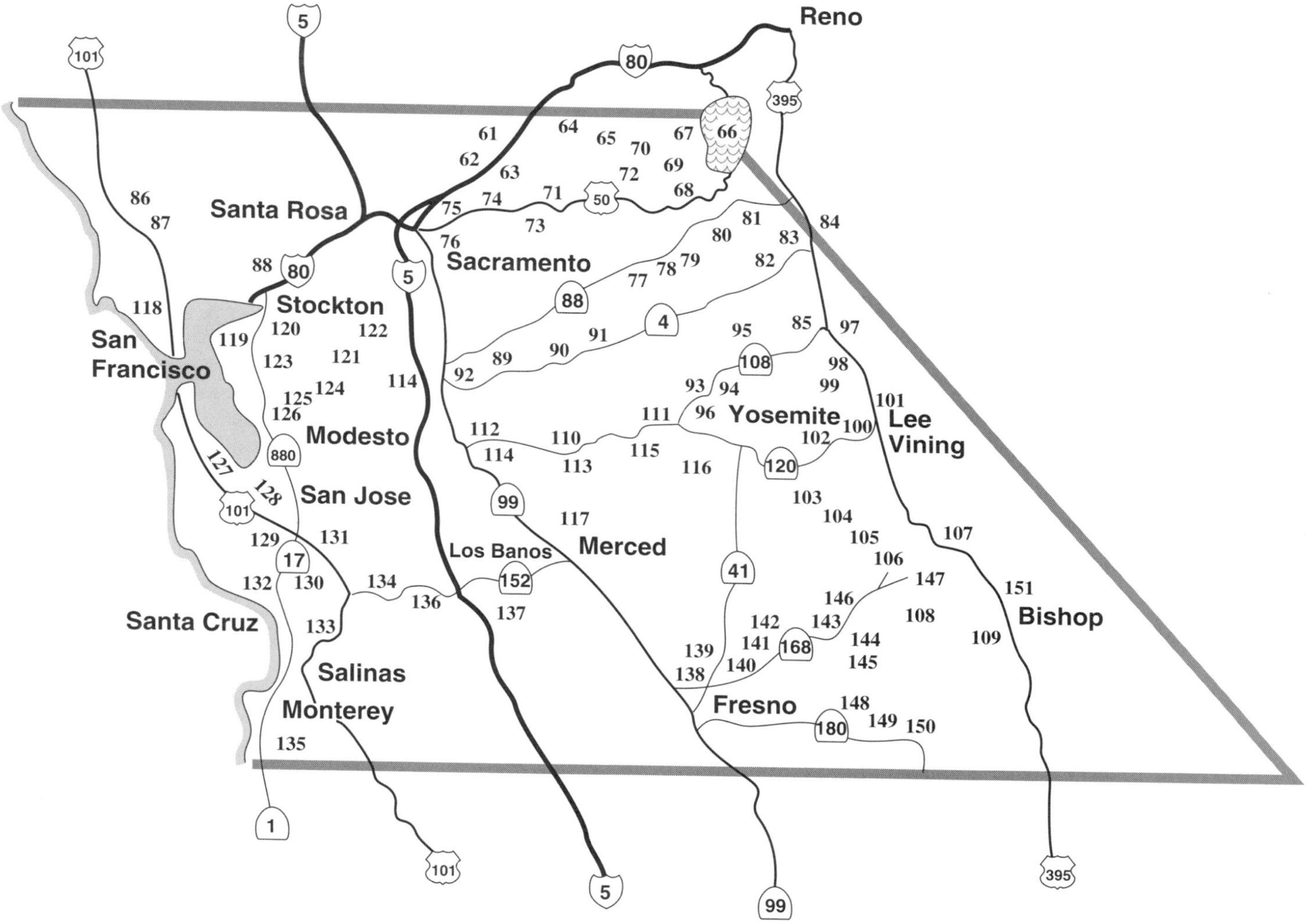

Reno
Santa Rosa
Sacramento
Stockton
San Francisco
Modesto
Yosemite
Lee Vining
San Jose
Merced
Los Banos
Santa Cruz
Salinas
Monterey
Fresno
Bishop

SUGAR PINE and BIG RESERVOIRS—LAKE CLEMENTINE

Sugar Pine Reservoir, at an elevation of 3,618 feet, has 160 surface acres and is located in the Tahoe National Forest. The campgrounds will accommodate R.V.s and trailers up to 40 feet. Big Reservoir, also called Morning Star Lake, is at 4,092 feet elevation. Facilities at this privately operated 80-acre Reservoir include Morning Star Resort. Down the road in the foothill canyons of the American River, Lake Clementine is a part of the Auburn State Recreation Area. The Lake is a 3-1/2 mile long stretch of the North Fork of the American River. Campgrounds are undeveloped but there is a launch ramp. This Lake is open to all boating with a 40 mph speed limit.

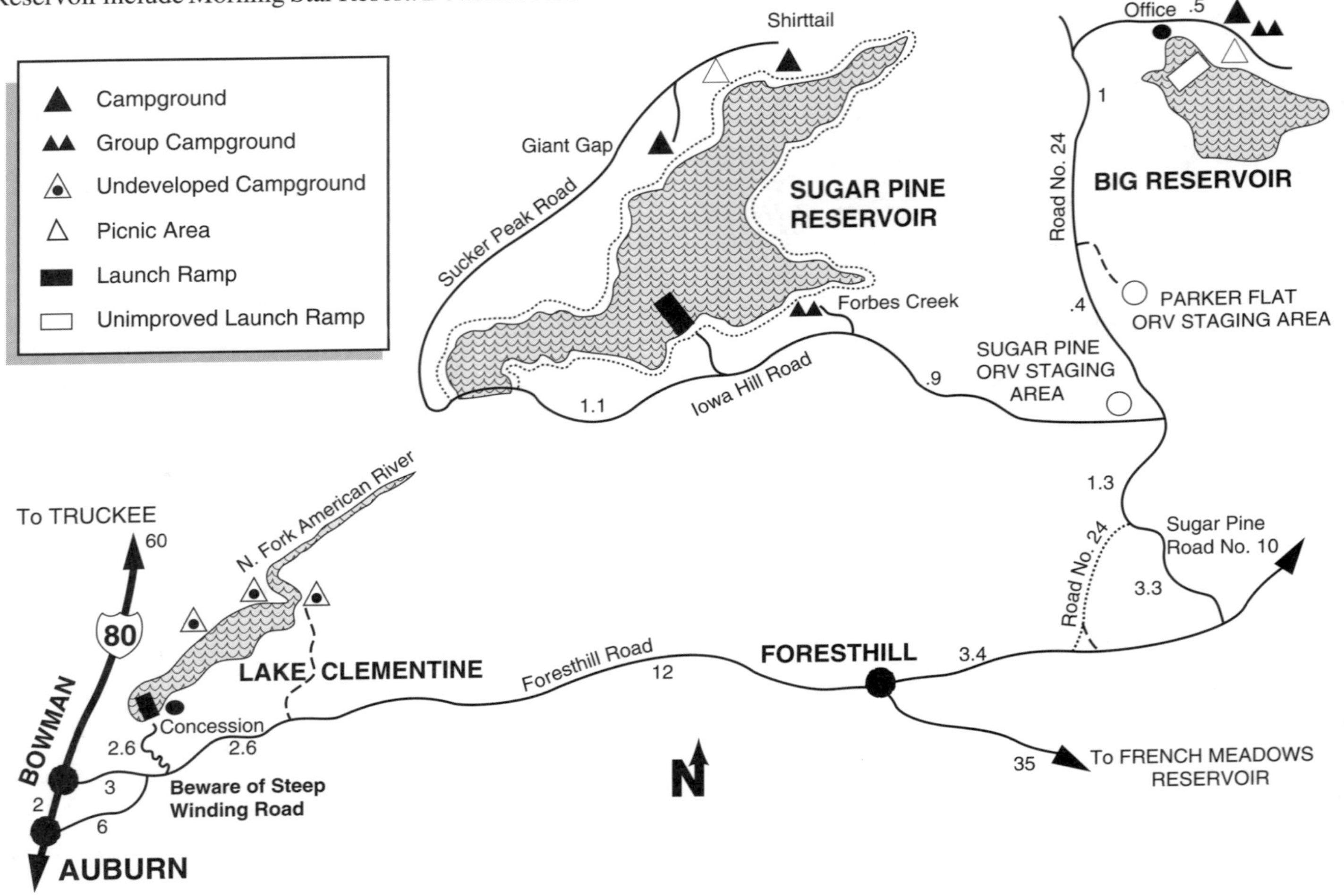
Campground
Group Campground
Undeveloped Campground
Picnic Area
Launch Ramp
Unimproved Launch Ramp
Shirttail
Giant Gap
Sucker Peak Road
SUGAR PINE RESERVOIR
Forbes Creek
Iowa Hill Road
1.1
.9
Office .5
1
Road No. 24
BIG RESERVOIR
.4
PARKER FLAT ORV STAGING AREA
SUGAR PINE ORV STAGING AREA
1.3
Sugar Pine Road No. 10
Road No. 24
3.3
To TRUCKEE
60
N. Fork American River
80
LAKE CLEMENTINE
Foresthill Road
12
FORESTHILL
3.4
BOWMAN
Concession
2.6
2.6
3
2
6
Beware of Steep Winding Road
AUBURN
N
35
To FRENCH MEADOWS RESERVOIR

INFORMATION: American River Ranger Station, 22830 Foresthill Rd., Foresthill 95631—Ph: (530) 367-2224

CAMPING	BOATING	RECREATION	OTHER
Sugar Pine: 60 Dev. Sites for Tents & R.V.s Fees: $18, $36, $54 Forbes Group Campground Reserve: Ph:(877) 444-6777 Big Reservoir: 100 Dev. Sites for Tents & R.V.s - Fee: $18 - $25 Plus 2 Group Sites for Tents Lake Clementine: Undeveloped Campground Fee: $24	Sugar Pine: Open to All Boating 10 MPH Speed Limit Launch Ramp Big Reservoir: Open to Non-Powered Boating Electric Motors Permitted Dock Lake Clementine: Launch Ramp 40 MPH Speed Limit	Fishing: Rainbow & Brown Trout, Black Bass, Bluegill & Perch Fishing by Permit at Big Reservoir Picnicking Swimming Hiking Trails - Paved & Unpaved ORV Trails Nearby	Morning Star Lake Resort at Big Reservoir P.O. Box 119 Foresthill 95631 Reservations: Ph: (530) 367-2129 Lake Clementine Auburn State Rec. Area 501 El Dorado St. Auburn 95603 Ph: (530) 885-4527 Facilities at Foresthill & Auburn

Camp Far West Lake is at an elevation of 320 feet in the Sierra foothills northeast of Roseville. The Lake has a surface area of 2,000 acres, 29 miles of shoreline plus 800 acres of camping, hiking, bicycle and equestrian trails. The water temperature rises up to 85 degrees in the summer when the climate can be quite hot although there are many oak trees providing ample shade. The Lake is open year around but the south entrance is closed at the end of summer. This is a good Lake for all types of boating and waterskiing. The boater should be aware of the rocky area as noted on the map. The water level of the Lake can fluctuate. There is a warm water fishery for landlocked smallmouth and black bass at the Bear River and Rock Creek Arms. A horse camp is available.

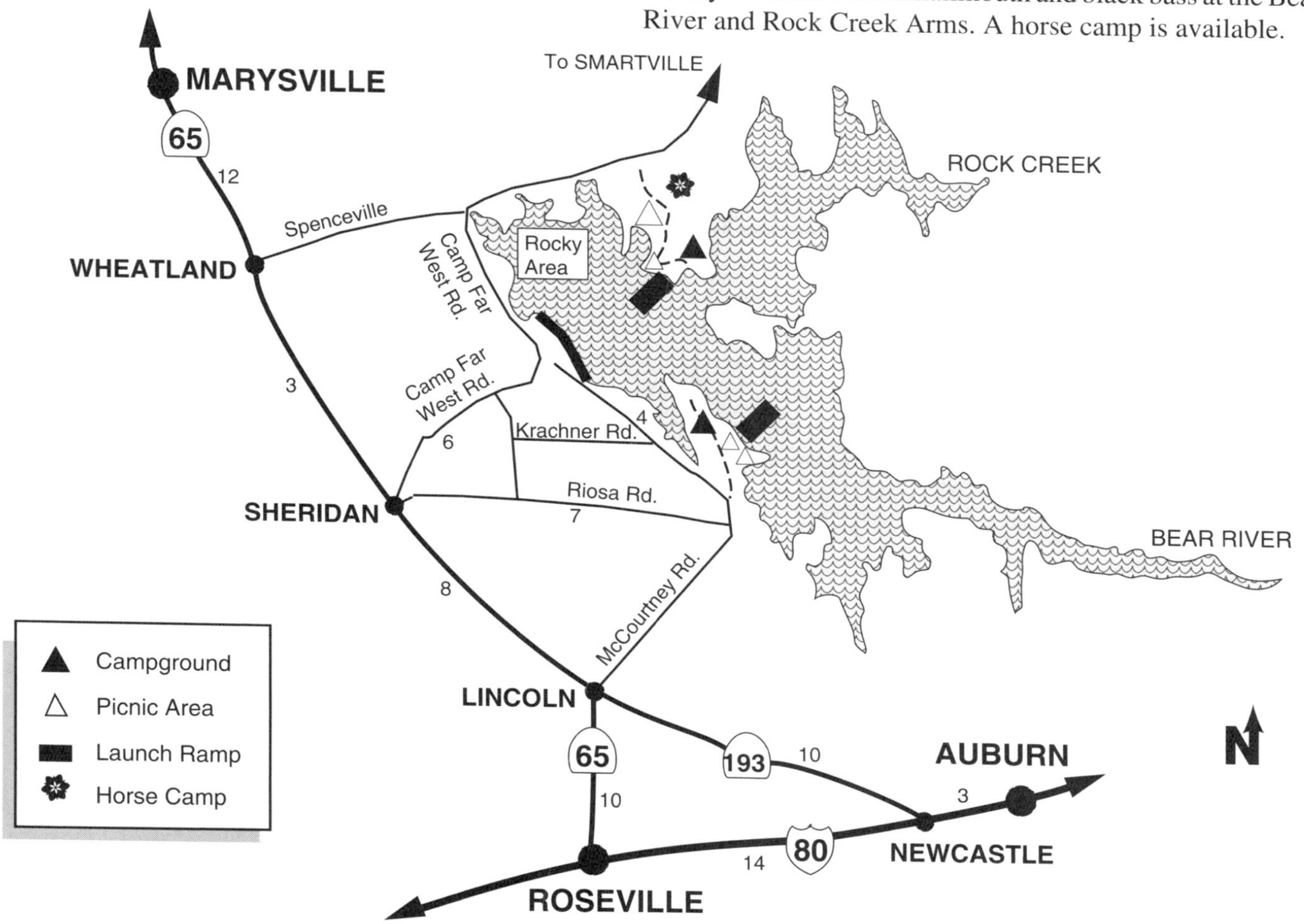
MARYSVILLE
To SMARTVILLE
65
12
ROCK CREEK
Spenceville
WHEATLAND
Camp Far West Rd.
Rocky Area
3
Camp Far West Rd.
4
Krachner Rd.
6
Riosa Rd.
7
SHERIDAN
BEAR RIVER
8
McCourtney Rd.
Campground
Picnic Area
Launch Ramp
Horse Camp
LINCOLN
65
193
10
AUBURN
N
10
3
80
14
NEWCASTLE
ROSEVILLE

INFORMATION: Camp Far West, 8176 Camp Far West Rd., Wheatland 95692— Ph: (530) 633-0803

CAMPING	BOATING	RECREATION	OTHER
143 Dev. Sites for Tents & R.V.s 10 with Full Hookups Fees: $20 - $35 Overflow Area Horse Camp Disposal Stations 3 Group Camps - to 250 People Reservations Accepted Day Use: $10 $15 with Boat	Power, Row, Canoe, Sail, Waterski, PWCs, Windsurf & Inflatables 2 Launch Ramps Gas Dry Storage Water Equipment Rentals at North Shore	Fishing: Florida Largemouth, Black, Striped & Smallmouth Bass, Crappie & Catfish Swimming Picnicking Hiking Trails Equestrian Trails Bicycle Trails Special Events	Grocery Stores Bait & Tackle North Shore: Open Year Around South Shore: Seasonal

FRENCH MEADOWS RESERVOIR

French Meadows Reservoir is at an elevation of 5,200 feet on the western slope of the Sierra Nevada. This man-made reservoir, 1,920 surface acres, is subject to low water levels late in the season. Although open to all types of boating, these low water conditions, along with underwater hazards, including tree stumps, make waterskiing and speed boating extremely dangerous. If the angler can suffer through the loss of tackle from these hazards, you are sometimes rewarded with a beautiful German brown or rainbow trout up to 7 pounds. The U.S. Forest Service maintains numerous campsites around the lake along with picnic areas and two launch ramps. There are several swimming beaches. This is a nice remote family camping area so plan on staying awhile.

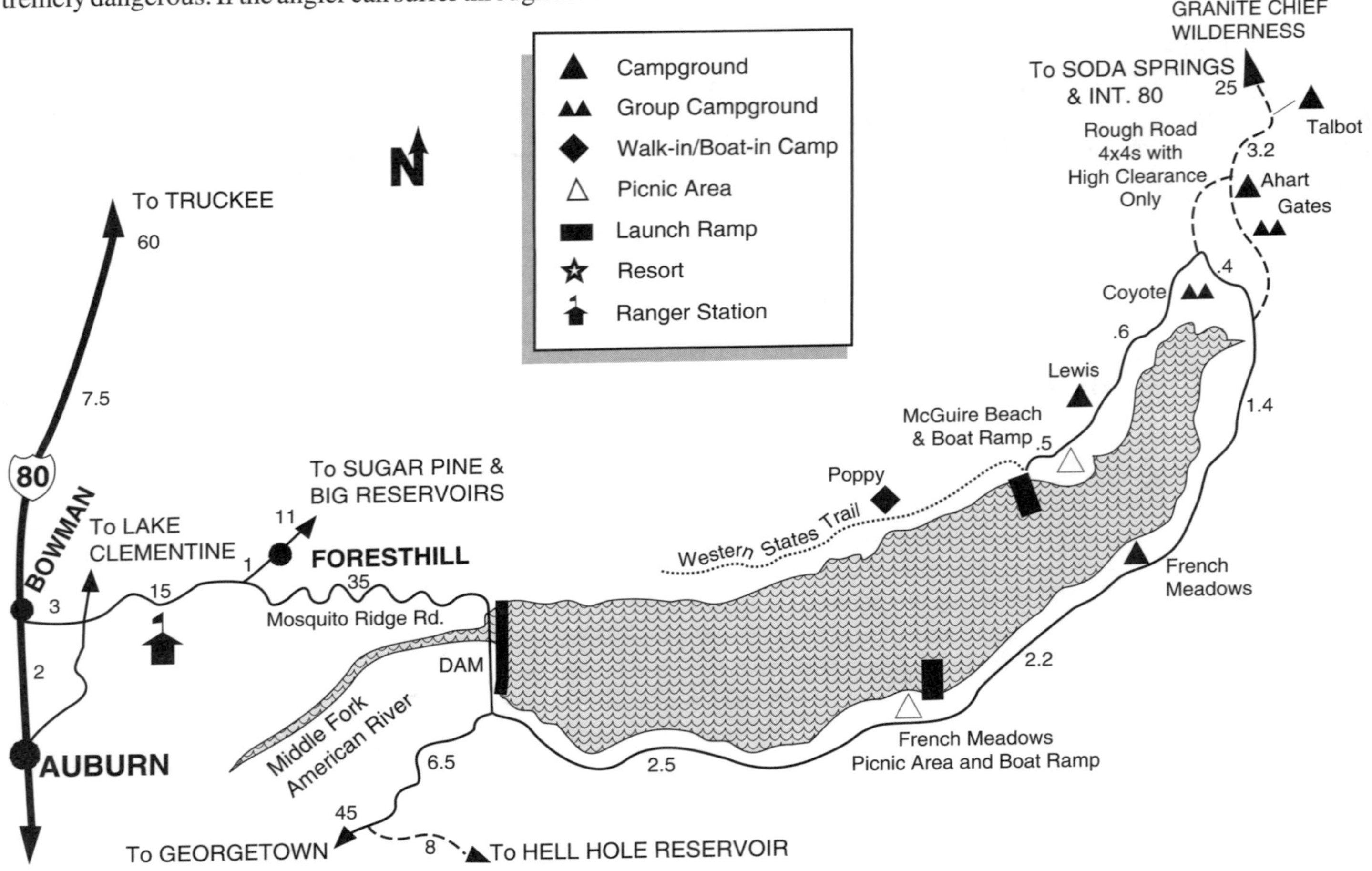
Campground
Group Campground
Walk-in/Boat-in Camp
Picnic Area
Launch Ramp
Resort
Ranger Station
N
To TRUCKEE
60
7.5
80
BOWMAN
To LAKE CLEMENTINE
3
15
2
AUBURN
To SUGAR PINE & BIG RESERVOIRS
11
1
FORESTHILL
35
Mosquito Ridge Rd.
DAM
Middle Fork American River
6.5
45
To GEORGETOWN
8
To HELL HOLE RESERVOIR
2.5
French Meadows Picnic Area and Boat Ramp
2.2
French Meadows
Western States Trail
Poppy
McGuire Beach & Boat Ramp
.5
Lewis
1.4
.6
Coyote
.4
Gates
Ahart
High Clearance Only
4x4s with
Rough Road
3.2
Talbot
To SODA SPRINGS & INT. 80
25
GRANITE CHIEF WILDERNESS

INFORMATION: American River Ranger District, 22830 Foresthill Rd., Foresthill 95631—Ph: (530) 367-2224

CAMPING	BOATING	RECREATION	OTHER
115 Dev. Sites Fee: $16 - $18 7 Group Sites Fee: $75 - $110 12 Boat or Walk-In Sites at Poppy No Fee Reservations for Group Camps: Ph: (877) 444-6777	Open to All Boats *Speed Boats & Waterskiing Not Advised Due to Submerged Hazards*	Fishing: Rainbow & Brown Trout Picnicking Swimming Hiking Trails Backpacking [Parking] Granite Chief Wilderness 7 Miles East No Mountain Bikes, Motorcycles or Mechanized Vehicles	Nearest Supplies and Facilities 39 Miles in Foresthill

HELL HOLE RESERVOIR and RALSTON AFTERBAY

Hell Hole Reservoir is in the Eldorado National Forest at an elevation of 4,700 feet. The facilities are operated and maintained by the U.S. Forest Service. Hell Hole is 15 miles south of French Meadows Reservoir in a rugged, rocky area along the Rubicon River. The Lake, 1,300 surface acres, is in a deep gorge surrounded by granite boulders with cold, clear water, creating a beautiful setting. It is especially scenic where the water leaves the power house and drops into the Lake. Be sure to bring a camera. Extreme water fluctuations can occur seasonally. Call for information on Lake levels. There are no facilities other than the launch ramp and campgrounds so come well supplied. Ralston Afterbay is on the Middle Fork of the American River with a nice picnic area and gravel launch ramps. Campers should be aware that bears inhabit this area.

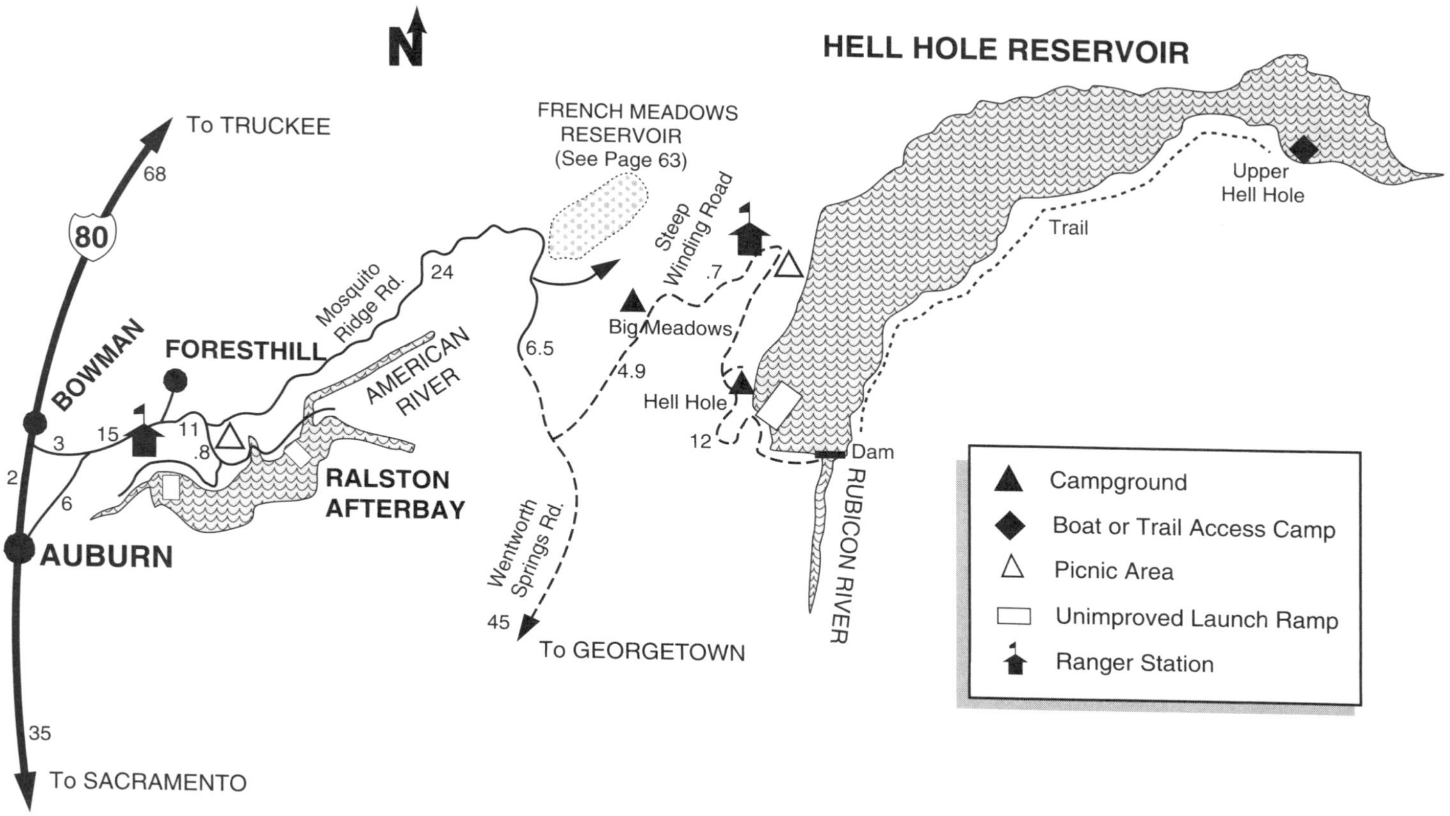

HELL HOLE RESERVOIR
To TRUCKEE
68
80
FRENCH MEADOWS RESERVOIR (See Page 63)
Steep Winding Road
Upper Hell Hole
Trail
Mosquito Ridge Rd.
24
.7
Big Meadows
BOWMAN
FORESTHILL
AMERICAN RIVER
6.5
4.9
Hell Hole
3
15
11
.8
12
Dam
2
6
RALSTON AFTERBAY
AUBURN
Wentworth Springs Rd.
45
To GEORGETOWN
RUBICON RIVER
Campground
Boat or Trail Access Camp
Picnic Area
Unimproved Launch Ramp
Ranger Station
35
To SACRAMENTO

INFORMATION: Georgetown Ranger Dist., 7600 Wentworth Springs Rd., Georgetown 95634—Ph: (530) 333-4312

CAMPING	BOATING	RECREATION	OTHER
Hell Hole: 10 Walk-in Tent Sites Fee: $10 Big Meadows: 54 Tent/R.V. Sites Fee: $17 Upper Hell Hole: 15 Boat Access or Hike-In Sites No Fee - No Water No Reservations Ralston Afterbay: No Campgrounds	Hell Hole: Power, Row, Canoe, Sail, Waterski & Inflatable Launch Ramp Caution - Afternoon Winds Can Be Hazardous Ralston Afterbay: Small Craft Only Hand Launch	Fishing: Rainbow, Brown, Cutthroat & Kamloop Trout, MacKinaw, Kokanee Salmon Picnicking Hiking Trails Backpacking Equestrian Trails 4 Wheel Drive Trails in Area	Nearest Facilities From Hell Hole Reservoir: 48 Miles at Foresthill

STUMPY MEADOWS RESERVOIR and FINNON LAKE

Stumpy Meadows is at an elevation of 4,260 feet in the Eldorado National Forest. This Lake has 320 surface acres and is surrounded by conifers. The water is clear and cold. Boating is restricted to 5 MPH so waterskiing is not allowed. The angler will often find German Brown and Rainbow Trout. Finnon Lake, at 2,420 feet, is a small Lake administered by the Mosquito Volunteer Fire Association and has a family campground for tents. Boating is limited to rowboats. Hiking and horseback riding trails are abundant. Lake levels can fluctuate so call for current information.

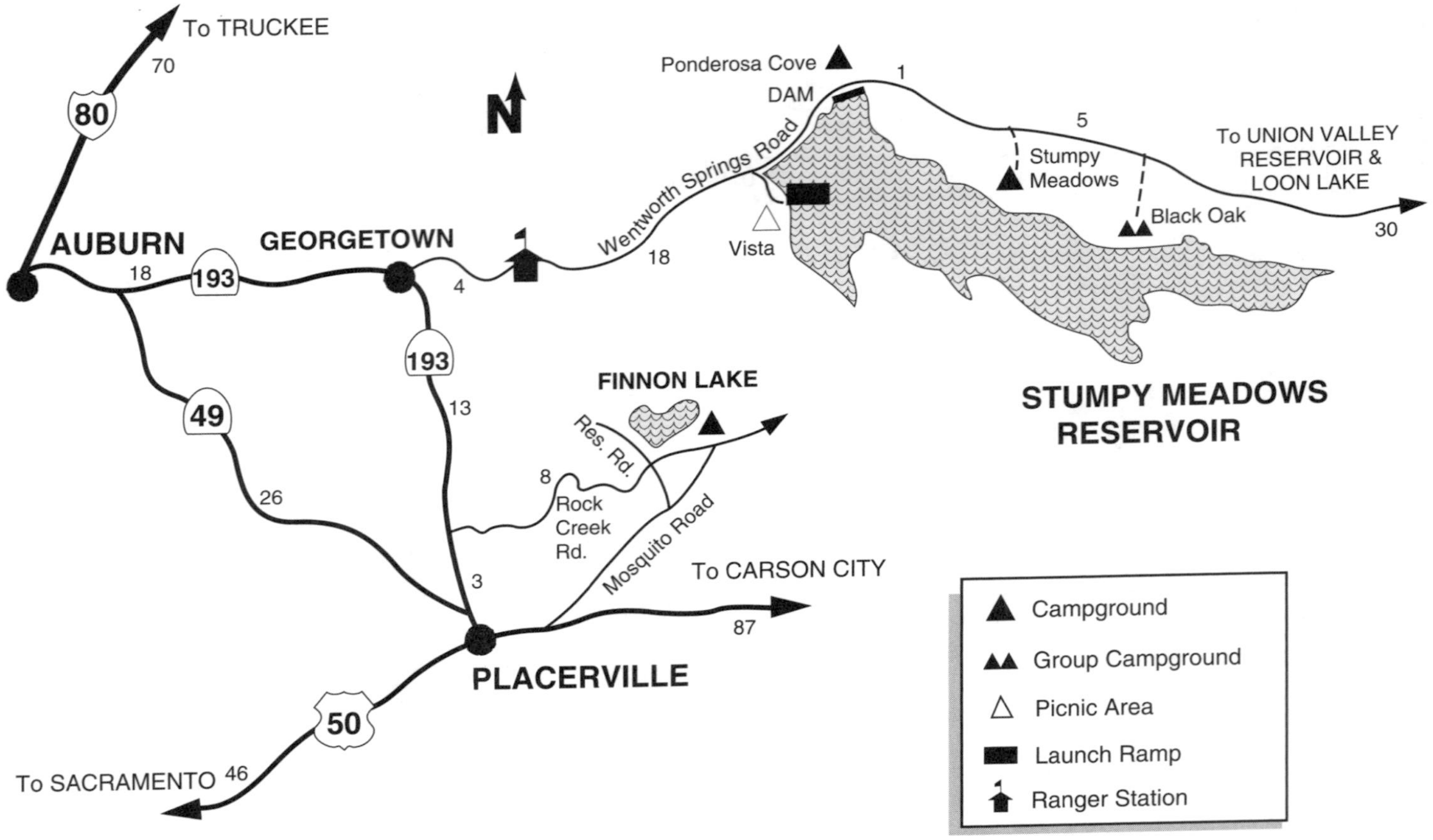
To TRUCKEE
70
80
N
Ponderosa Cove
DAM
1
5
Wentworth Springs Road
Stumpy Meadows
To UNION VALLEY RESERVOIR & LOON LAKE
Black Oak
30
AUBURN
GEORGETOWN
18
193
4
18
Vista
193
13
FINNON LAKE
STUMPY MEADOWS RESERVOIR
49
Res. Rd.
8
Rock Creek Rd.
26
Mosquito Road
To CARSON CITY
3
87
PLACERVILLE
50
To SACRAMENTO
46
Campground
Group Campground
Picnic Area
Launch Ramp
Ranger Station

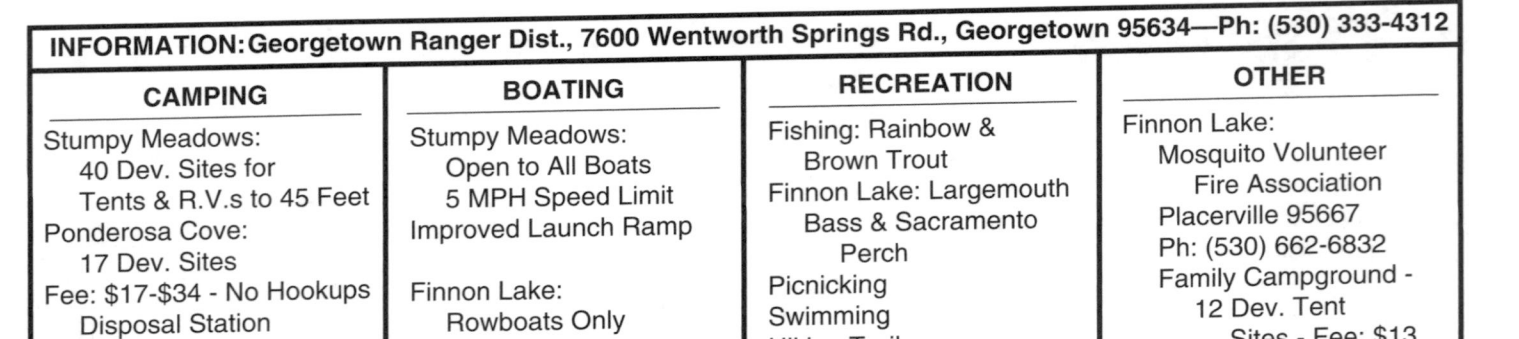

INFORMATION: Georgetown Ranger Dist., 7600 Wentworth Springs Rd., Georgetown 95634—Ph: (530) 333-4312

CAMPING	BOATING	RECREATION	OTHER
Stumpy Meadows: 40 Dev. Sites for Tents & R.V.s to 45 Feet Ponderosa Cove: 17 Dev. Sites Fee: $17-$34 - No Hookups Disposal Station Black Oak: 4 Group Sites - Fee: $50, $75 & $100 Reserve All Sites: Ph: (877) 444-6777	Stumpy Meadows: Open to All Boats 5 MPH Speed Limit Improved Launch Ramp Finnon Lake: Rowboats Only	Fishing: Rainbow & Brown Trout Finnon Lake: Largemouth Bass & Sacramento Perch Picnicking Swimming Hiking Trails Equestrian Trails Whitewater Paddling Nearby	Finnon Lake: Mosquito Volunteer Fire Association Placerville 95667 Ph: (530) 662-6832 Family Campground - 12 Dev. Tent Sites - Fee: $13 Large Group Camping by Reservation Day Use: $6 Restaurant

At 6,225 feet elevation, Tahoe is one of America's largest and most beautiful mountain Lakes. It is 22 miles long, 12 miles wide and 72 miles around. Tahoe is a prime recreation lake with a variety of facilities. Boaters, waterskiers and sailors make great use of the vast expanse of clear open water. The varied trout fishery ranges from planted rainbows to the huge lake trout or mackinaw and salmon. Hikers, backpackers and equestrians can enjoy the numerous trails, including the Tahoe Rim Trail, within the surrounding mountains and nearby Desolation Wilderness. Add these outdoor activities to the excitement and luxury of Nevada's casinos, "The Lake" has it all.

....Continued.....

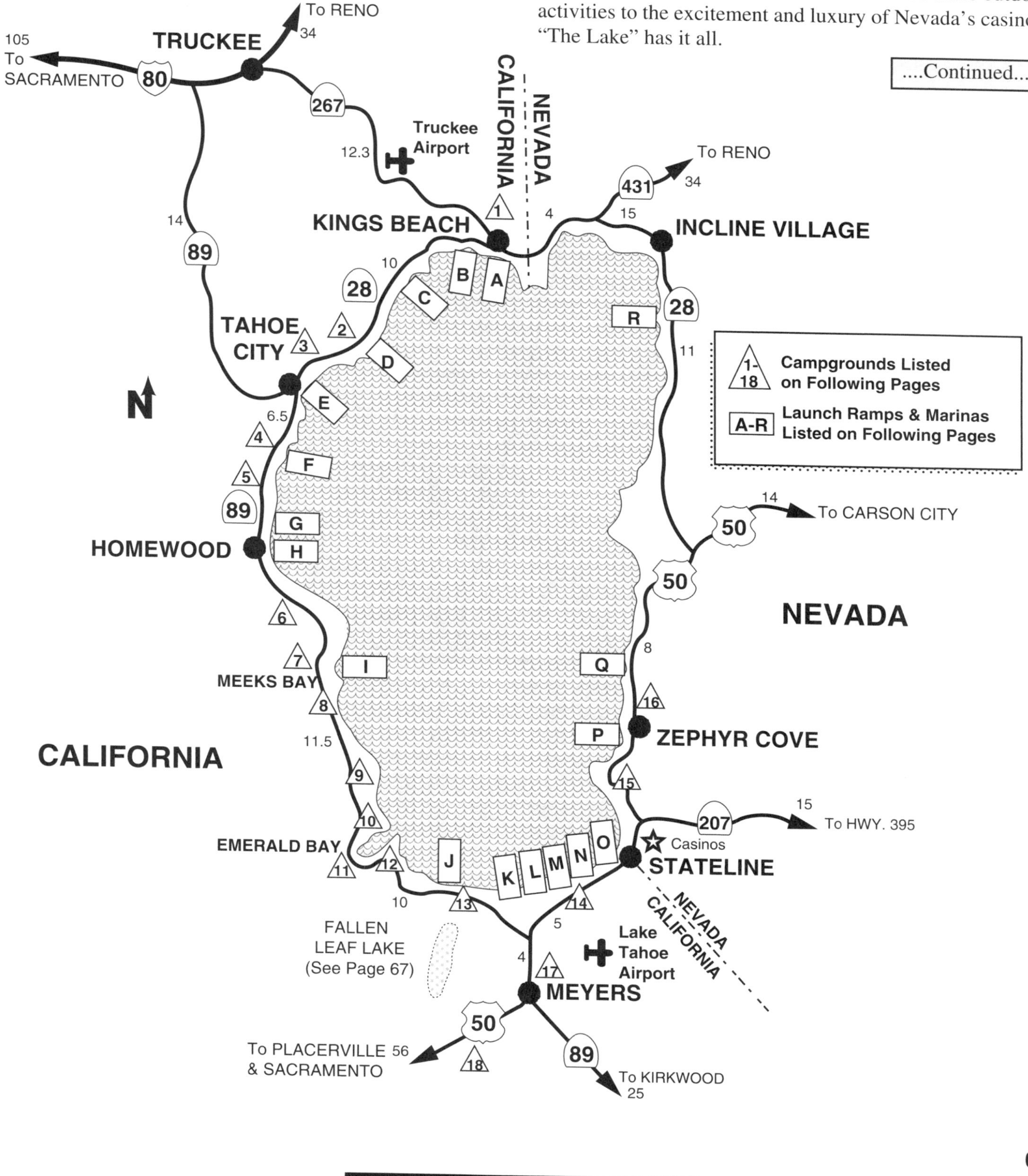

To RENO 34
105 To SACRAMENTO
80
TRUCKEE
267
12.3
Truckee Airport
CALIFORNIA
NEVADA
To RENO 34
431
15
4
KINGS BEACH
INCLINE VILLAGE
14
89
10
28
TAHOE CITY
28
11
Campgrounds Listed on Following Pages
A-R Launch Ramps & Marinas Listed on Following Pages
N
6.5
89
HOMEWOOD
14
To CARSON CITY
50
50
NEVADA
8
MEEKS BAY
ZEPHYR COVE
CALIFORNIA
11.5
207
15
To HWY. 395
Casinos
STATELINE
EMERALD BAY
10
5
FALLEN LEAF LAKE (See Page 67)
4
Lake Tahoe Airport
NEVADA
CALIFORNIA
MEYERS
50
To PLACERVILLE 56 & SACRAMENTO
89
To KIRKWOOD 25

LAKE TAHOE............Continued

Managed by California Land Management by Special Use Permit of the USDA Forest Service, Lake Tahoe Basin Management Unit Information Ph: (530) 543-2600
***Reserve the following Sites Except for Bayview* Ph: (877) 444-6777**

4. WILLIAM KENT - 2 Miles South of Tahoe City on Hwy. 89, - *Fee: $20* - 84 Tent/R.V. Sites to 40 Feet, Disposal Station, Swim Beach & Picnic Area Across Road. Ph: (530) 583-3642

5. KASPIAN - 4 Miles South of Tahoe City on Hwy. 89 - *Fee: $15* - 9 Walk-In, Bike-In Sites, Picnic Area. Ph: (530) 583-3642

8. MEEKS BAY - 2 Miles South of Tahoma on Hwy. 89, - *Fee: $20* - 40 Tent/R.V. Sites to 20 Feet, Swim Beach. Ph: (530) 525-4733

15. NEVADA BEACH - 3 Miles North of Stateline off Hwy. 50, -*Fee: $25-29* - 54 Tent/R.V. Sites to 45 Feet, Boat-In Picnic Area, Group Picnic Area to 100 People. Ph: (775) 588-5562

11. BAYVIEW - On Hwy. 89 at Emerald Bay - *Fee: $15* - 13 Tent Sites, No Water. Trailhead to Desolation Wilderness - Permit Required. Ph: (530) 544-5994

(Pets okay on Leash at Above Sites)

Operated by California State Parks
Reserve Ph: (800) 444-7275
Family & Group Sites - Reserve Up to 7 Months in Advance

3. TAHOE STATE RECREATION AREA - 1/4 Mile East of Tahoe City - *Fee: $20 - $25* - 27 Tent/R.V. Sites to 24 Feet, Pets - Free, Picnic Sites, Groceries, Fishing Pier - Information: (530) 583-3074.

6. GENERAL CREEK - SUGAR PINE POINT - One Mile South of Tahoma off Hwy. 89 - *Fee: $20 - $25* - 175 Tent/R.V. Sites to 30 Feet, Showers
Group Camps (Limit 6 R.V.s Over 15 Feet per Camp) - Fee: $75 - Open All Year.
All Camps can Accommodate up to 400 People - Information: (530) 525-7982.

9. D. L. BLISS STATE PARK - 3 Miles North of Emerald Bay, off Hwy. 89 - *Fee: $20 - $35* - 168 Tent/R.V. Sites to 18 Feet, Group Camp, Pets $1 a Day, Information: (530) 525-7277.

10. EMERALD BAY STATE PARK - 8 Miles North of South Lake Tahoe off Hwy. 89 - *Fee: $11 - $15* - 20 Tent Sites Boat-In Camp - First Come, First Served
Information: (530) 525-7277.

12. EAGLE POINT - Off Hwy. 89 at Emerald Bay-*Fee: $20 - $25* -100 Tent/R.V. Sites to 21 Feet, Pets $1 a Day, Information: (530) 525-7277

Operated by the City of South Lake Tahoe
1150 Rufus Allen, South Lake Tahoe, CA 96150
Information: (530) 542-6096
Open April through October

14. CAMPGROUND BY THE LAKE
2.3 Miles West of Stateline on
Hwy. 50 & Rufus Allen Blvd.

Fee: $23-$31 per Vehicle & 4 People per Night
157 Tent/R.V. Sites, 50 Sites w/ Electric Hookups,
Group Site to 30 People,
Disposal Station,
1 Cabin for Sleeping Only - No Facilities
Adjacent to Bicycle Paths

Bijou 9-Hole Golf Course Ph: (530) 542-6097

Operated by Tahoe City Parks and Recreation
221 Fairway Dr., P.O. Box 5249, Tahoe City 96145
Information: (530) 583-3796

2. LAKE FOREST CAMPGROUND
2 Miles East of Tahoe City
Fee: $15
18 Tent/R.V. Sites to 20 Feet
Boat Ramp, Swim Beach
Pets Okay on Leash.

....Continued....

PRIVATELY OPERATED CAMPGROUNDS: SEE NUMBER IN TRIANGLE ON MAP

1. SANDY BEACH - at Tahoe Vista, 6873 North Lake Blvd. off Hwy. 28 - *Fees: From $20-$25 - Ph: (530) 546-7682* - 27 Tent/R.V. Sites to 40 Feet, Hookups, Free for Pets, Showers, Boat Ramp one block away.

7. MEEKS BAY RESORT & MARINA, P.O. Box 787, Tahoma 96142 - 10 Miles South of Tahoe City - *Fees: From $25 Ph: (530) 525-6946 or Toll Free (877) 326-3357* - 22 R.V. Sites, Full Hookups, 12 Tent Sites, No Pets, Cabins & Lodge Units, Launch Ramp. (Under USFS Permit)

13. CAMP RICHARDSON HISTORIC RESORT & MARINA, P. O. Box 9028, South Lake Tahoe 96158 - 3 Miles West of of the intersection of Highway 50 and 89 - *Call for Fees - Ph: (530) 541-1801 or (800) 544-1801* - 333 Tent/R.V. Sites, Group Sites, Hookups, No Pets, Showers, Disposal Station, Lodge Units, Beach Motel, Groceries, Propane, Supplies, Boat Ramp, Horse Stables, Bicycle Rentals, Open All Year. (Under USFS Permit)

16. ZEPHYR COVE RESORT - P. O. Box 830, Zephyr Cove, NV 89448 - 4 Miles North of Stateline - *Fee: Winter from $28 - Summer from $65 - Ph: (775) 589-4981* - 150 Tent/RV Sites to 50 Feet, Group Sites, Pets OK, Showers, Cabins, Lodge, Marina, Groceries, Propane, Restaurant, MS Dixie II Paddlewheeler, Open All Year. (Under USFS Permit)

17. TAHOE VALLEY CAMPGROUND, P. O. Box 9026, South Lake Tahoe 96158 - 1/4 Mile South of Junction Highway 89 - *Fee: From $38-$58 - Ph: (530) 541-2222* - 413 Tent/R.V. Sites, Full Hookups, Group Sites, Pets OK, Disposal Station, Showers, Playground, Laundromat, Groceries, Propane, Recreation Room, Cable T.V., Open All Year, Swimming Pool in Season.

18. KOA KAMPGROUND, Box 550967, South Lake Tahoe 96155 - Off Hwy. 50 West of Meyers - *Fee: From $36-$71 Ph: (530) 577-3693* or *(800) 562-3477* - 16 Tent Sites, 52 R.V. Sites to 40 Feet, Full Hookups, Pets $5 a Day, Disposal Station, Showers, Laundry, Mini-Market, Propane, Swimming Pool, Recreation Room, Playground, Picnic Tables, Campfire Rings and BBQ Grills, Wooded Area.

LAUNCH RAMPS AND MARINA FACILITIES: SEE LETTER IN RECTANGLE ON MAP

A. KINGS BEACH STATE RECREATIONAL AREA - North Tahoe Parks & Recreation, P.O. Box 139, Tahoe Vista 96148 *Ph: (530) 546-7248* - *Call for Current Conditions of Launch Ramp* - 700 Feet of Lake Frontage.

B. NORTH TAHOE MARINA - 7360 N. Lake Blvd., Tahoe Vista 96148—*Ph: (530) 546-8248* - *Call for Current Fees* - Full Service Marina, Fuel and Repairs, Accessory Sales.

C. SIERRA BOAT CO. - 5146 North Lake Blvd., Carnelian Bay 96146—*Ph: (530) 546-2551* - *Gantry Launch - Hoist: $55 - $65 - Call for Other Current Fees* - Slips, Buoys, Fuel and Repairs, Supplies, Dry Storage.

D. LAKE FOREST BOAT RAMP - Hwy. 28 at end of Lake Forest Rd. near U. S. Coast Guard Station - *Ph: (530) 583-3440* - *Call for Current Conditions.*

....Continued....

LAUNCH RAMPS AND MARINA FACILITIES: SEE NUMBER IN RECTANGLE ON MAP

TAHOE CITY MARINA - 700 N. Lake Blvd., Box 6510, Tahoe City 96145—Ph: (530) 583-1039, Full Service Marina, Forklift and Travelift, Fuel, Repairs, Marine Accessories, Slips & Buoys, Boat Rentals & Storage, Boat Sales.

F. SUNNYSIDE RESORT - P.O. Box 5969, Tahoe City 95730—Ph: (530) 583-7200, Buoys, Pump Station, Fuel, Repairs, Restaurant, Ski & Boat Rentals, Ski School.

G. HIGH & DRY MARINA - P.O. Box 1735, Tahoe City 96145 @ 5190 Hwy. 89, Homewood —Ph: (530) 525-5966, Gantry Hoist (No Ramp), Fuel, Power Boat Rentals, Complete Service and Chandlery.

H. OBEXERS, 5300 West Lake Blvd., Homewood 96141—Ph: (530) 525-7962, Paved Ramp and Travel Lift, Fork Lift, Fuel, Marine Accessories, Boat Repairs, Groceries.

I. MEEKS BAY RESORT & MARINA - 7941 Emerald Bay Rd., Meeks Bay 96142—Ph: (530) 525-6946 or (877) 326-3357, Paved Ramp, Slips, Row, Power & Sail Boat Rentals, Groceries, Bait & Tackle, Snack Bar, Cabins, R.V. Park, Campsites.

J. RICHARDSON'S RESORT, ANCHORAGE MARINA - Off Hwy. 89, 2 Miles Northwest of "Y"—Ph: (530) 542-6570 - *Fees: Call for Information* - Launch Ramp, Gas, Supplies, Repairs, Rentals, Moorings.

K. TAHOE KEYS MARINA - 2435 Venice Dr. East, South Lake Tahoe 96150—Ph: (530) 541-2155 - *Fees: $30 Round Trip* Double Paved Ramp, 45 Ton Capacity Travel Lift, Paved Full Service Marina, Sail & Power Boat Rentals, Fuel, Repairs, Boat Supplies, Mini-Mart, 300 Slips, Largest Marina on the Lake, Overnight Parking, Restaurant.

L. EL DORADO BEACH PUBLIC BOAT RAMP - Hwy. 50 & Lakeview Ave., South Lake Tahoe 96150—Ph: (530) 542-6056, *Launch Fee: $13*, Public Use Facility, Paved Ramp, Swim Beach, Picnic Area with BBQ's, Campground across Street on Rufus Allen Blvd.

M. TIMBER COVE MARINA - 3411 Lake Tahoe Blvd., South Lake Tahoe 96150—Ph: (530) 544-2942 - *Fees: Call for Information* - Hoist, Mooring, Fuel, Repairs, Power, Sail Boat and PWC Rentals, Snack Bar, Gift Shop, Boat Charters.

N. SKI RUN MARINA - 900 Ski Run Blvd., South Lake Tahoe 96150—Ph: (530) 544-0200 - *Fees: Call for Information* - PWCs and Parasailing, Cafe, Beer Garden, On the Water Restaurant, Shops, Home of the Hornblower Cruises and Events, 500 Passenger *Tahoe Queen*.

O. LAKESIDE MARINA - Hwy. 50 at end of Park Ave., South Lake Tahoe - Ph: (530) 541-6626 - *Fees: $20 In - $20-Out* - Ramp Access - Boats Under 46 Feet Only, Slips, Gas & Moorings.

P. ZEPHYR COVE MARINA - 760 US 50, Zephyr Cove, NV 89448—Ph: (775) 589-4901, *Fees: Call for Information* - Moorings, Fuel, Power Boat & PWC Rentals, Parasailing and Full Resort Facilities, Picnic Area, Cabins, Campground, Restaurant.

Q. CAVE ROCK PUBLIC LAUNCH FACILITY - Off Hwy. 50, North of Zephyr Cove - Ph: (775) 831-0494 - *Call for Fees* - Paved Ramp, Swim Beach, Fishing Area.

R. SAND HARBOR - 4 Miles South of Incline Village - Ph: (775) 831-0494 - *Fees: Launch $15 - Day Use $8* - Paved Launch Ramp, Swim Beach, Picnic Areas, Group Use Picnic Area, Nature Trail.

....Continued....

GENERAL INFORMATION

Lodging and accommodations are extensive throughout the Lake Tahoe Basin. The casinos offer luxurious hotel rooms with complete facilities. Condominiums, bed & breakfasts, cabins and houses are available for rent. In addition to the enormous variety of lodging available, there are innumerable recreational and service facilities.

For Further Information Contact:

Lake Tahoe Basin Management Unit
USDA, Forest Service
35 College Dr.
South Lake Tahoe, CA 96150
Ph: (530) 543-2600

Eldorado National Forest
Headquarters
100 Forni Road
Placerville, CA 95667
Ph: (530) 622-5061

Humboldt-Toiyabe National Forest
Carson Ranger Station
1536 S. Carson Street
Carson City, NV 89701
Ph: (775) 882-2766

California State Parks
Sierra District
P. O. Box 266
Tahoma, CA 96142
Ph: (530) 525-7232

Nevada State Parks
Sand Harbor
P. O. Box 8867
2005 Highway 28
Incline Village, NV 89452
Ph: (775) 831-0494

Lake Tahoe Visitors Authority
169 Highway 50
P. O. Box 5878
Stateline, NV 89449
Ph: (800) AT TAHOE (288-2463)
Reservations
Ph: (530) 544-5050 - Information

North Lake Tahoe
Resort Association
P.O. Box 5459
Tahoe City, CA 96145
Ph: (530) 583-3494 - Reservations
Ph: (800) 824-6348 - Information

Chambers of Commerce:

South Lake Tahoe
169 Highway 50
Stateline, NV 89449
Ph: (775) 588-1728

North Lake Tahoe
P.O. Box 884
Tahoe City, CA 96145
Ph: (530) 583-3494

Lake Tahoe Incline Village
Crystal Bay Visitors Bureau
969 Tahoe Blvd.
Incline Village, NV 89451
Ph: (775) 832-1606 or
(800) GO TAHOE

Truckee-Donner
10065 Donner Pass Rd.
Truckee, CA 96161
Ph: (530) 587-2757

FALLEN LEAF LAKE

Fallen Leaf Lake, at an elevation of 6,400 feet, is part of the Lake Tahoe Basin Management Unit. The property around this Lake is divided between private and National Forest land. The shoreline is heavily forested with pine trees to the water's edge. It is within easy access to the Desolation Wilderness and near the numerous attractions at South Lake Tahoe with casinos at Stateline. The Forest Service maintains a campground on the north end of the Lake. Take the time to visit the Tallac Historic Site, once the summer retreat of three weathly families. The estates have been restored and many paths and most buildings are open to the public.

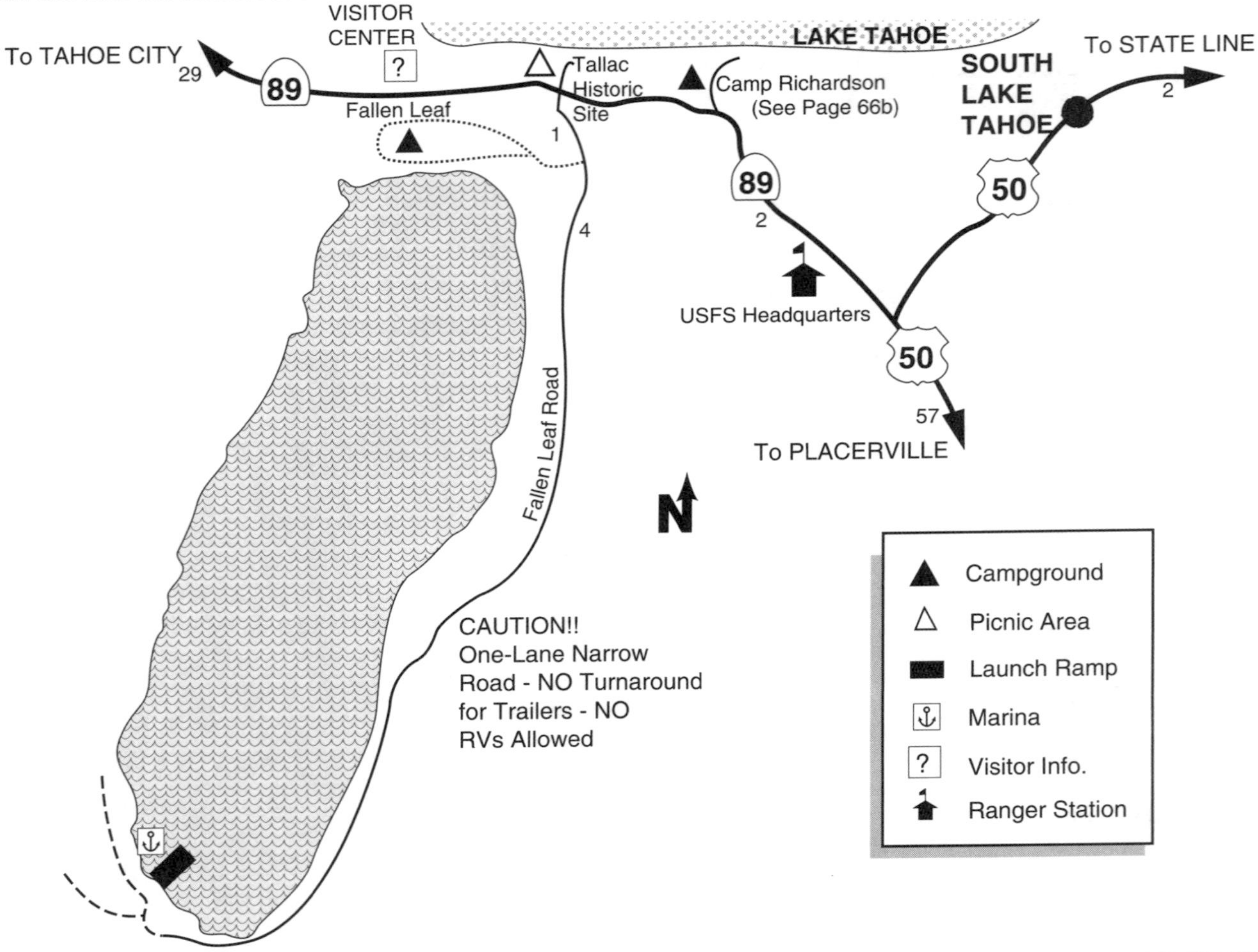
VISITOR CENTER
To TAHOE CITY
29
89
LAKE TAHOE
Tallac Historic Site
Fallen Leaf
1
Camp Richardson (See Page 66b)
SOUTH LAKE TAHOE
To STATE LINE
2
89
2
50
4
USFS Headquarters
50
57
To PLACERVILLE
Fallen Leaf Road
N
CAUTION!! One-Lane Narrow Road - NO Turnaround for Trailers - NO RVs Allowed
Campground
Picnic Area
Launch Ramp
Marina
Visitor Info.
Ranger Station

INFORMATION: USDA Forest Service, 35 College Dr., S. Lake Tahoe 96150—Ph: (530) 543-2600			
CAMPING	**BOATING**	**RECREATION**	**OTHER**
U.S.F.S. 205 Dev. Sites for Tents & R.V.s to 40 Feet Fee: $20 - $22 Further Information: Ph: (530) 544-0426 Reservations: Ph: (877) 444-6777	Power, Row, Canoe, & Sail Launch Ramp NO R.V.s on Road to Launch Ramp	Fishing: Rainbow, German Brown & Mackinaw Trout, Kokanee Salmon Swimming Picnicking Hiking Trails Backpacking Equestrian Trails Bicycle Trails Nature Study	Visitor Center on Highway 89 Tallac Historic Site & Baldwin Museum Ph: (530) 541-5227

Echo Lake is nestled at 7,414 feet in between high mountains near Echo Summit off Highway 50. This is one of the most beautiful natural Lakes in the High Sierra. All boating is allowed but waterskiing is not permitted on Upper Echo Lake. The bordering Desolation Wilderness Area, protected since 1929, covers over 60,000 acres of trails and streams. In addition, more than 50 lakes are easily accessible for the backpacker, equestrian and fisherman. Echo Chalet, the only facility on the Lake, provides a taxi service to the Upper Lake which shortens the hike into the Wilderness Area by 3-1/2 miles. The rustic housekeeping cabins are ideal for a relaxing summer vacation.

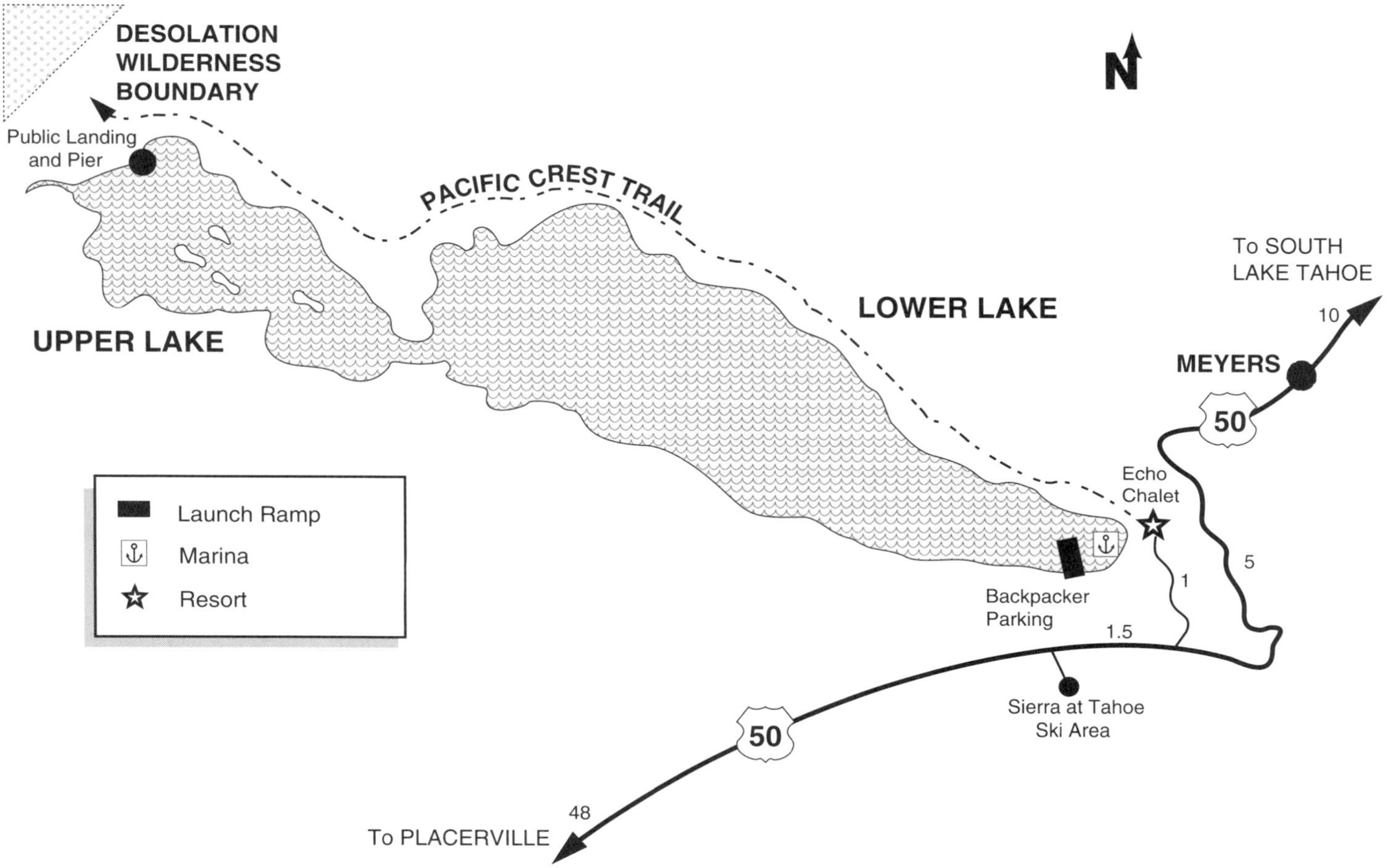
DESOLATION
WILDERNESS
BOUNDARY
N
Public Landing
and Pier
PACIFIC CREST TRAIL
To SOUTH
LAKE TAHOE
LOWER LAKE
10
UPPER LAKE
MEYERS
50
Echo
Chalet
Launch Ramp
Marina
Resort
5
1
Backpacker
Parking
1.5
Sierra at Tahoe
Ski Area
50
48
To PLACERVILLE

INFORMATION: Echo Chalet, 9900 Echo Lakes Rd., Echo Lake 95721—Ph: (530) 659-7207

CAMPING	BOATING	RECREATION	OTHER
No Overnight Camping or Trailers Allowed in Echo Lake Basin Camping Allowed in Desolation Wilderness Area with Permit from U.S.F.S	Power, Row, Canoe, Sail, Waterski, Windsurf & Inflatable Check for Restrictions Full Service Marina Launch Ramp - $20 Rentals: Fishing Boats, Canoes & Kayaks Docks, Berths, Gas, Storage	Fishing: Rainbow, Brook & Cutthroat Trout, Kokanee Salmon Picnicking Hiking Trails including Pacific Crest Trail Backpacking [Parking] Equestrian Trails Boat Taxi from Echo Chalet to Desolation Wilderness Area Trailhead	Housekeeping Cabins Snack Bar Grocery Store Hardware & Sporting Goods Bait & Tackle Fishing Licenses Gas Station Day Hike Permits to Wilderness Area Resort Open: Memorial Day through Labor Day Weekend

WRIGHTS LAKE

Wrights Lake has a surface area of 65 acres. At an elevation of 7,000 feet in the Eldorado National Forest, this is one of many Lakes in this area. The high Sierra setting is a unique retreat for the outdoorsman. Two Trailheads for Desolation Wilderness Area border the Lake, making it popular for the equestrian, hiker and backpacker. Wrights Lake offers good trout fishing. The other Lakes and streams in this vicinity are also great for the angler. Boating at Wrights Lake is restricted to hand launching. Motors are not allowed. Permits are required for entry into the Desolation Wilderness Area and can be purchased at the Pacific Ranger District in Pollcok Pines. Campgrounds include walk-in and equestrian sites.

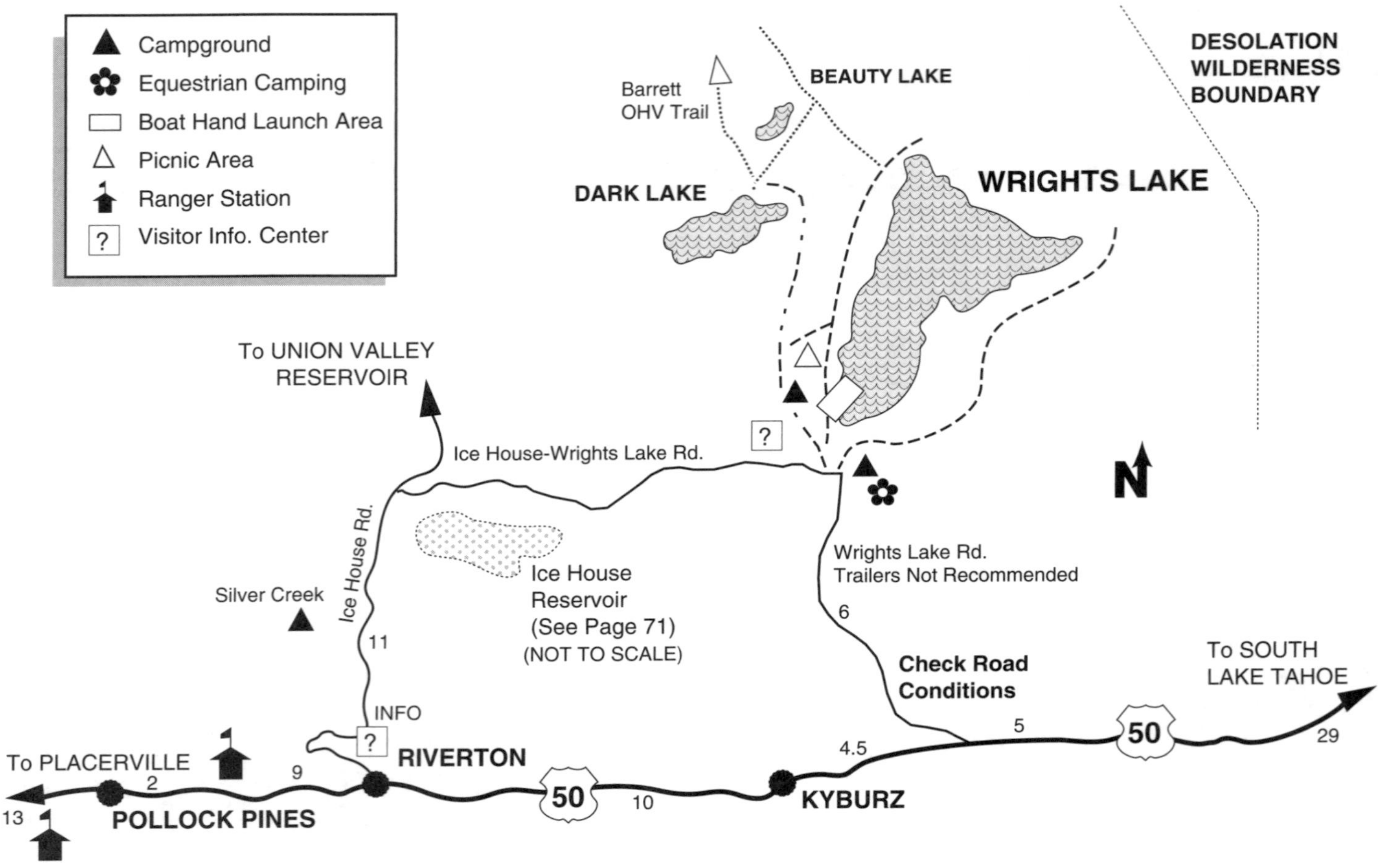

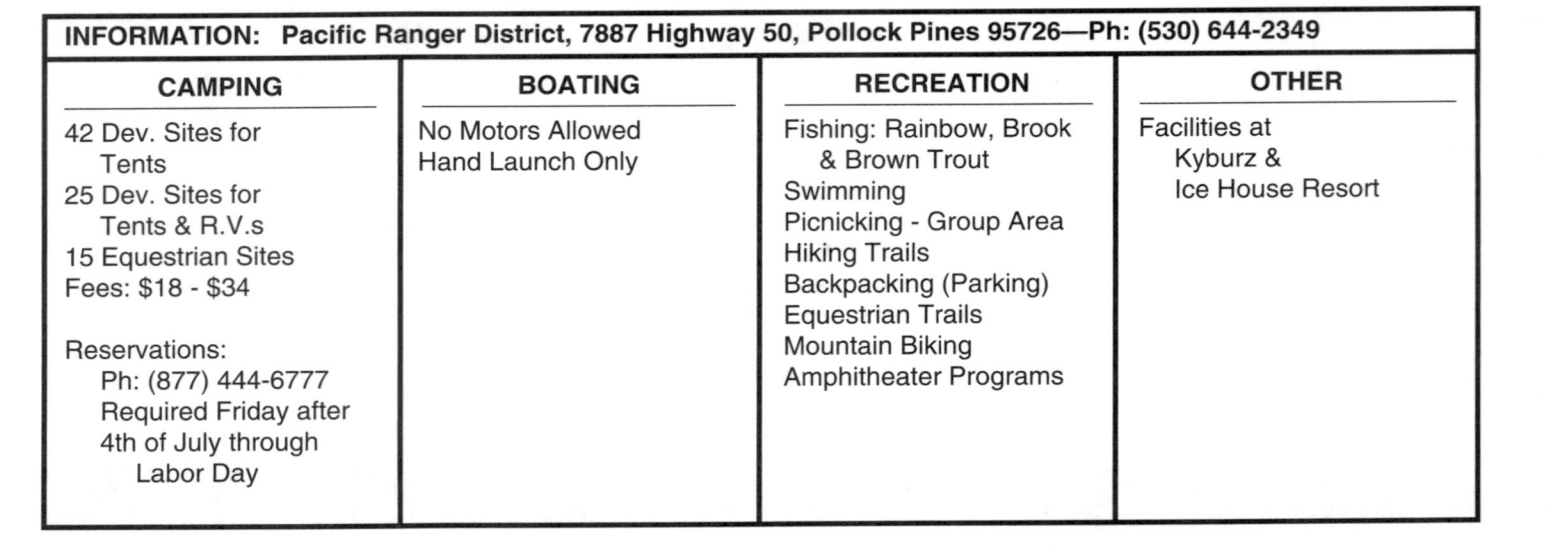

Campground
Equestrian Camping
Boat Hand Launch Area
Picnic Area
Ranger Station
Visitor Info. Center
Barrett
OHV Trail
BEAUTY LAKE
DESOLATION
WILDERNESS
BOUNDARY
DARK LAKE
WRIGHTS LAKE
To UNION VALLEY
RESERVOIR
Ice House-Wrights Lake Rd.
Ice House Rd.
Ice House
Reservoir
(See Page 71)
(NOT TO SCALE)
Silver Creek
Wrights Lake Rd.
Trailers Not Recommended
6
11
Check Road
Conditions
To SOUTH
LAKE TAHOE
INFO
RIVERTON
4.5
5
50
29
To PLACERVILLE
2
9
10
13
POLLOCK PINES
KYBURZ

INFORMATION: Pacific Ranger District, 7887 Highway 50, Pollock Pines 95726—Ph: (530) 644-2349			
CAMPING	**BOATING**	**RECREATION**	**OTHER**
42 Dev. Sites for Tents 25 Dev. Sites for Tents & R.V.s 15 Equestrian Sites Fees: $18 - $34 Reservations: Ph: (877) 444-6777 Required Friday after 4th of July through Labor Day	No Motors Allowed Hand Launch Only	Fishing: Rainbow, Brook & Brown Trout Swimming Picnicking - Group Area Hiking Trails Backpacking (Parking) Equestrian Trails Mountain Biking Amphitheater Programs	Facilities at Kyburz & Ice House Resort

Loon Lake is at an elevation of 6,500 feet in the Crystal Basin Recreation Area of the Eldorado National Forest. Crystal clear waters make this beautiful high mountain Lake appear carved out of granite. The Forest Service and a concessionaire maintain the campgrounds, picnic areas, paved launch ramp and a walk-in or boat-in campground. The Loon Lake Chalet can be reserved for up to 20 people. This is a good Lake for sailing and boating. Waterskiing is not advised due to extremely cold water and exposed rocks due to fluctuating reservoir levels. Fishing can be excellent for Rainbow and German Brown trout. There is trailhead parking for the Desolation Wilderness. Gerle Creek Reservoir has a 50-site campground and picnic area. No boats with motors are allowed at this facility.

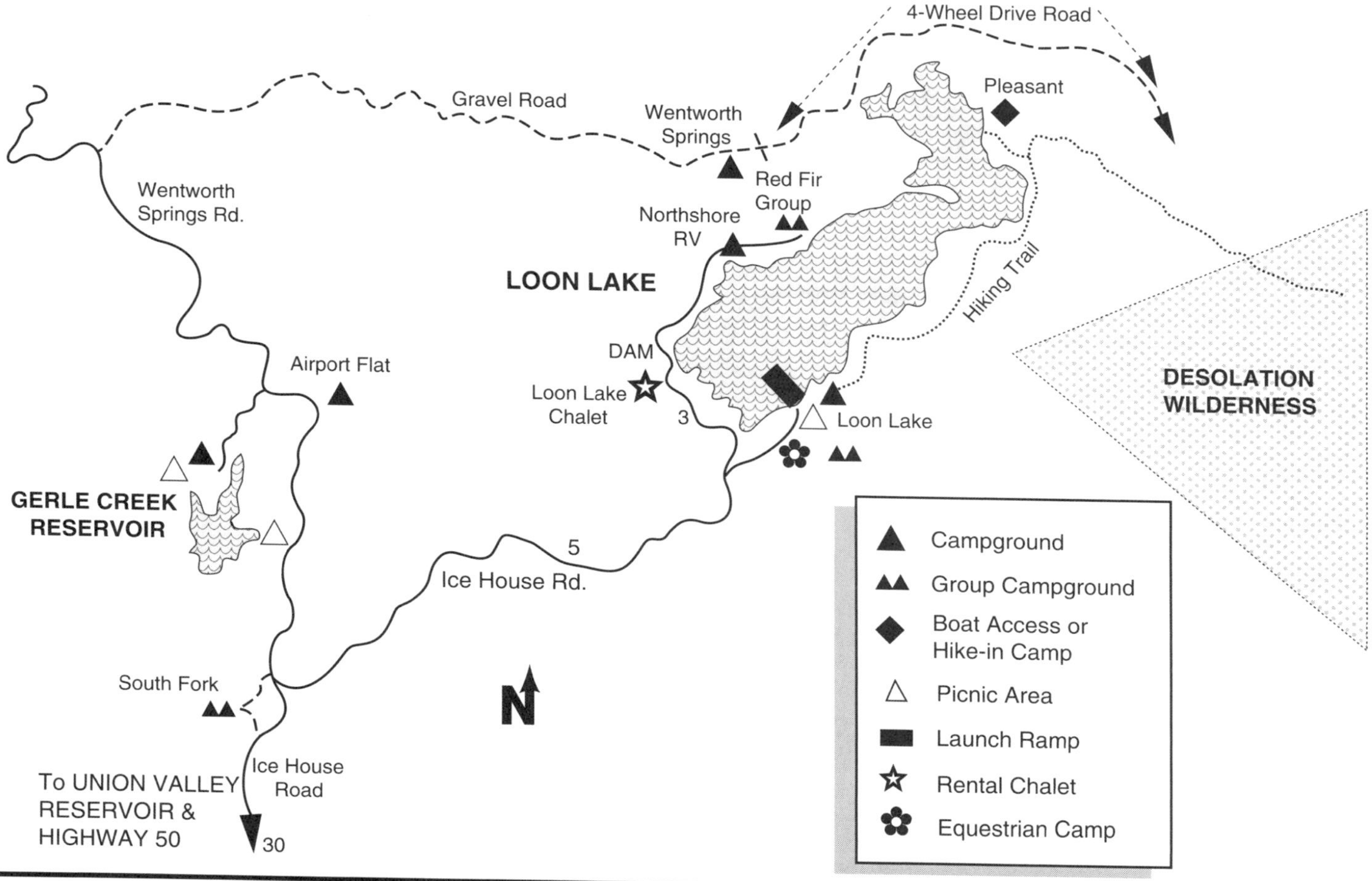
4-Wheel Drive Road
Gravel Road
Wentworth Springs
Pleasant
Red Fir Group
Wentworth Springs Rd.
Northshore RV
LOON LAKE
Hiking Trail
DAM
Airport Flat
Loon Lake Chalet
3
Loon Lake
DESOLATION WILDERNESS
GERLE CREEK RESERVOIR
5
Ice House Rd.
Campground
Group Campground
Boat Access or Hike-in Camp
Picnic Area
Launch Ramp
Rental Chalet
Equestrian Camp
South Fork
N
Ice House Road
To UNION VALLEY RESERVOIR & HIGHWAY 50
30

INFORMATION: Pacific Ranger District, 7887 Highway 50, Pollock Pines 95726—Ph: (530) 644-2349

CAMPING	BOATING	RECREATION	OTHER
Loon Lake: 43 Dev. Sites for Tents & R.V.s - Fee: $20 9 Equestrian Units: Fee: $20 3 Group Camps Plus 1 Equestrian Group Camp Fee: $80 - $120 Northshore: 15 Tents & R.V.s Fee: $8 - No Water Pleasant: 10 Boat-In Sites No Fee - No Water Red Fir Group: 25 People Tents Only - Fee: $40 Reserve Ph: (877) 444-6777	Power, Row, Canoe & Sail Launch Ramp No Waterskiing Gerle Creek Reservoir: No Motorboats	Fishing: Rainbow & German Brown Trout Picnicking Hiking Trails Backpacking [Parking] Desolation Wilderness: Permit Required Equestrian Trails ORV Trails Mountain Biking Disposal Station Near Loon Lake Campground	Gerle Creek: 50 Dev. Sites for Tents & R.V.s - Fee: $20 South Fork Group: to 125 People - Fee: $100 - No Water Reservations: Ph: (877) 444-6777 Airport Flat: 16 Units No Fee, No Water OHVs Allowed Wentworth Springs: 8 Sites 4WD - No Fee, No Water Full Facilities: 23 Miles

ICE HOUSE RESERVOIR

Ice House Reservoir is at an elevation of 5,500 feet in the Crystal Basin Recreation Area of the Eldorado National Forest. The surface area of this Lake is 678 acres with clear, cool water. The surrounding shoreline is covered with conifers. The Ice House campground, launch ramp and picnic facilities are run by a concessionaire. The Forest Service operates Northwind and Strawberry Point campgrounds. There are numerous swimming areas. The roads are paved and well maintained but beware of logging trucks. This is an great boating Lake especially for sailing. The Reservoir is stocked during the summer months and the angler will find good fishing for trout and Kokanee.

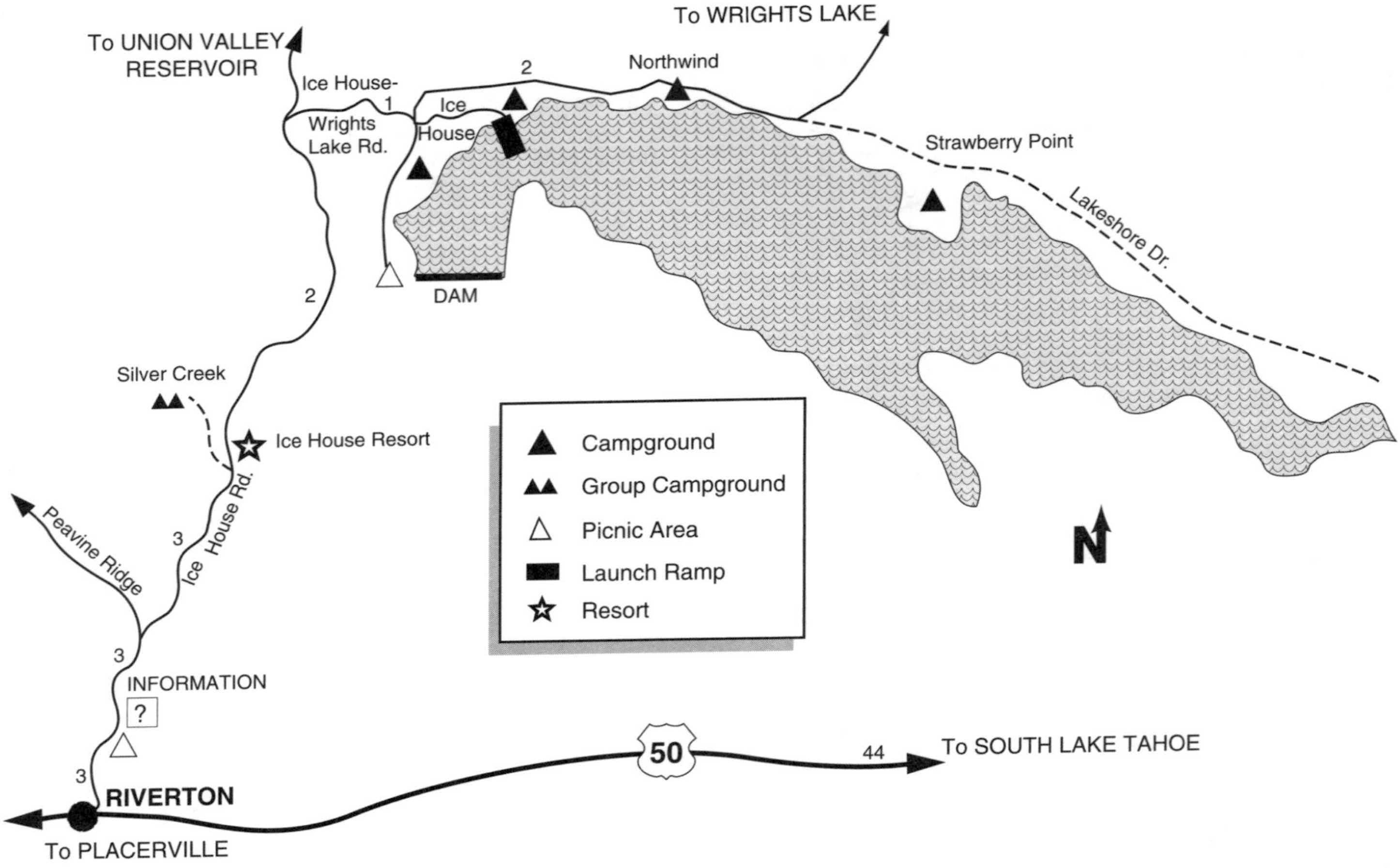
To UNION VALLEY RESERVOIR
To WRIGHTS LAKE
Ice House-Wrights Lake Rd.
1
2
Northwind
Ice House
Strawberry Point
Lakeshore Dr.
DAM
2
Silver Creek
Ice House Resort
Campground
Group Campground
Picnic Area
Launch Ramp
Resort
N
Peavine Ridge
3
Ice House Rd.
3
INFORMATION
?
50
44
To SOUTH LAKE TAHOE
3
RIVERTON
To PLACERVILLE

INFORMATION: Pacific Ranger District, 7887 Highway 50, Pollock Pines 95726—Ph: (530) 644-2349

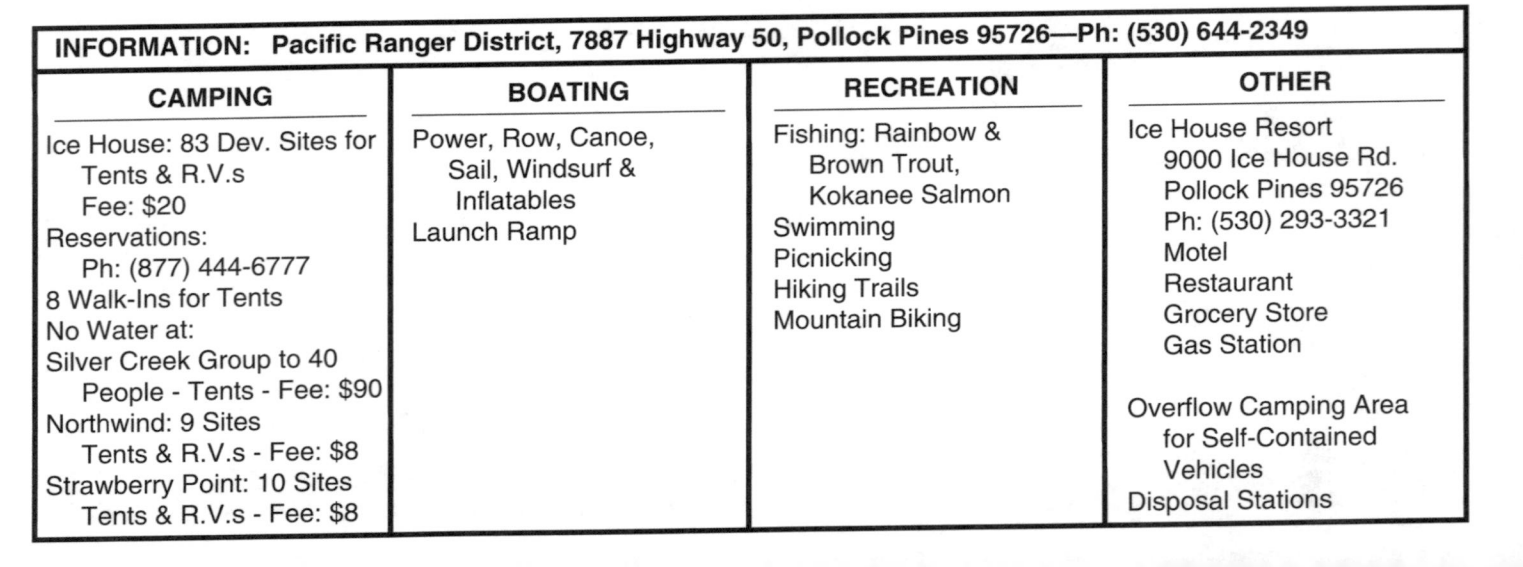

CAMPING	BOATING	RECREATION	OTHER
Ice House: 83 Dev. Sites for Tents & R.V.s Fee: $20 Reservations: Ph: (877) 444-6777 8 Walk-Ins for Tents No Water at: Silver Creek Group to 40 People - Tents - Fee: $90 Northwind: 9 Sites Tents & R.V.s - Fee: $8 Strawberry Point: 10 Sites Tents & R.V.s - Fee: $8	Power, Row, Canoe, Sail, Windsurf & Inflatables Launch Ramp	Fishing: Rainbow & Brown Trout, Kokanee Salmon Swimming Picnicking Hiking Trails Mountain Biking	Ice House Resort 9000 Ice House Rd. Pollock Pines 95726 Ph: (530) 293-3321 Motel Restaurant Grocery Store Gas Station Overflow Camping Area for Self-Contained Vehicles Disposal Stations

Union Valley Reservoir is located at an elevation of 4,900 feet in the Crystal Basin Recreation Area of the Eldorado National Forest. This area is in the pine and fir forests of the western Sierra and is dominated by the high granite peaks of the Crystal Range. The Reservoir has a surface area of 2,860 acres. The Forest Service maintains 3 launch ramps at the Lake along with a good variety of campgrounds and a picnic area. Union Valley is a great Lake for sailing and many clubs use this facility during the summer. Fishing can be excellent from your boat or along the shoreline.

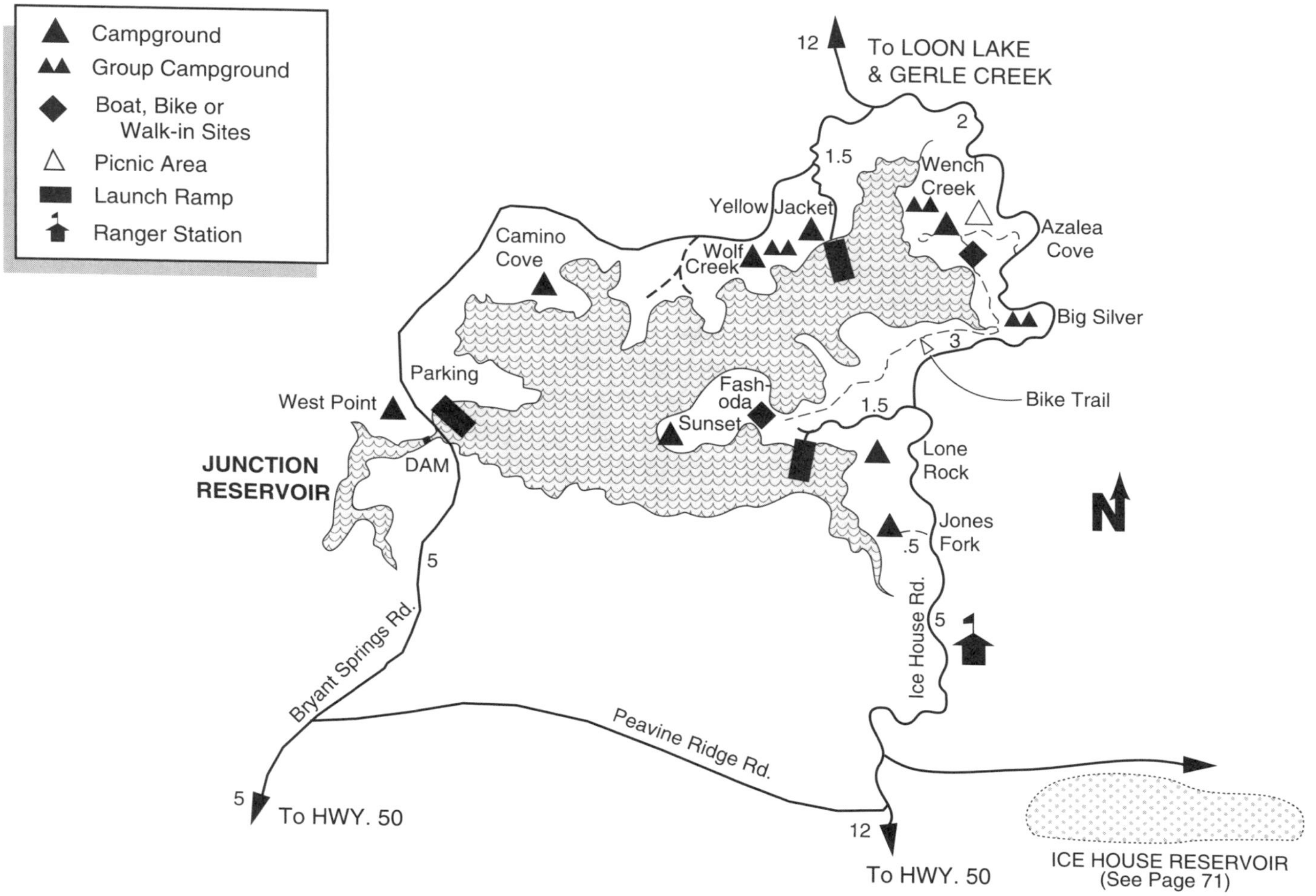
Campground
Group Campground
Boat, Bike or Walk-in Sites
Picnic Area
Launch Ramp
Ranger Station
12
To LOON LAKE & GERLE CREEK
2
1.5
Wench Creek
Yellow Jacket
Azalea Cove
Camino Cove
Wolf Creek
Big Silver
3
Bike Trail
Parking
Fash-oda
1.5
West Point
Sunset
Lone Rock
JUNCTION RESERVOIR
DAM
Jones Fork
.5
5
N
Ice House Rd.
5
Bryant Springs Rd.
Peavine Ridge Rd.
5
To HWY. 50
12
To HWY. 50
ICE HOUSE RESERVOIR
(See Page 71)

INFORMATION: Pacific Ranger District, 7887 Highway 50, Pollock Pines 95726—Ph: (530) 644-2349

CAMPING	BOATING	RECREATION	OTHER
Sites for Tents & R.V.s: Yellowjacket-40 Sites - $20 Wolf Creek-42 Sites - $20 Wench Creek-100 Sites-$20 Sunset-131 Sites - $20 Jones Fork-10 Sites No Water - $8 Group Sites: Wench Creek, Big Silver & Wolf Creek Boat, Bike & Walk-In: Fashoda - $20 plus Azalea Cove & Lone Rock Camino, W.Point-No Water	Power, Rowboats, Sail, Canoes, Windsurf, Inflatables Launch Ramps	Fishing: Rainbow & Brown Trout Swimming Picnicking Hiking Trails Bicycle Trails	Disposal Station Facilities - 7 Miles at Ice House Resort Reservations: Ph: (877) 444-6777 Yellowjacket, Fashoda, Sunset & Wolf Creek Plus Group Camps: Wolf Creek, Wench Creek & Big Silver Fees: $50 - $120 Other Sites: First Come Basis

JENKINSON LAKE - SLY PARK RECREATION AREA

Jenkinson Lake is at an elevation of 3,478 feet in the Sly Park Recreation Area south of Pollock Pines. The Lake has a surface area of 600 acres with over 8 miles of coniferous tree-covered shoreline. The Eldorado Irrigation District has jurisdiction over the various facilities at this scenic Lake including 2 launch ramps with floats. There are a variety of individual and group campsites, equestrian and handicapped areas. The water is clear and fishing can be good, especially in the coves. Winds are usually favorable for sailing. Waterskiing is in a counterclockwise direction in the central section of the Lake.

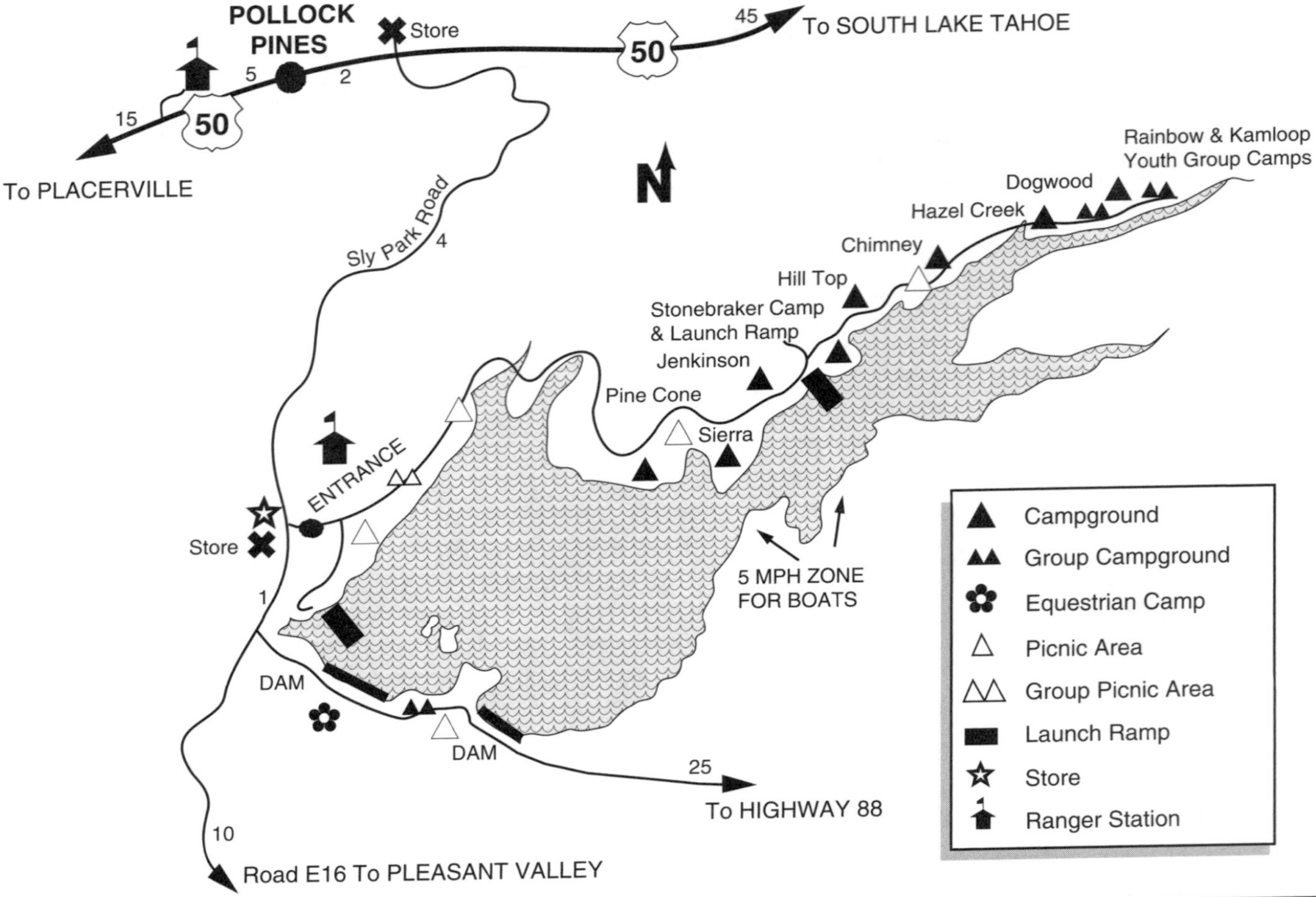
POLLOCK PINES
Store
To SOUTH LAKE TAHOE
45
50
5
2
15
To PLACERVILLE
Sly Park Road
4
N
Rainbow & Kamloop Youth Group Camps
Dogwood
Hazel Creek
Chimney
Hill Top
Stonebraker Camp & Launch Ramp
Jenkinson
Pine Cone
Sierra
ENTRANCE
Store
1
5 MPH ZONE FOR BOATS
DAM
DAM
25
To HIGHWAY 88
10
Road E16 To PLEASANT VALLEY
Campground
Group Campground
Equestrian Camp
Picnic Area
Group Picnic Area
Launch Ramp
Store
Ranger Station

INFORMATION: Sly Park Recreation Area, P.O. Box 577, Pollock Pines 95726—Ph: (530) 295-6810

CAMPING	BOATING	RECREATION	OTHER
191 Dev. Sites for Tents & R.V.s Fee: $28 - $40 Group & Youth Camp Areas Reservations Recommended for All Campsites	Power, Row, Canoe, Sail, Waterski, Windsurf & Inflatables *No PWCs* 2 Launch Ramps Fee: $8 Courtesy Docks Rentals - May - September: Motor Boats, Row Boats, Kayaks, Canoes & Pedal Boats	Fishing: Rainbow, Brown & Mackinaw Trout, Smallmouth Bass & Bluegill Swimming Picnicking Hiking & Bicycle Trails Equestrian Trails Nature Trails	Sly Park Store 4782 Sly Park Road Pollock Pines 95726 Ph: (530) 644-1113 Grocery Store Bar & Grill Bait & Tackle Gas Station R.V. Space Disposal Station Additional Facilities in Pollock Pines - 5 Miles

Folsom Lake State Recreation Area is one of the most complete recreation parks in California. This 18,000-acre facility offers campsites, picnic areas, swim beaches and extensive full service marina. With good waters for sailing and other types of boating, Folsom Lake has 11,930 surface acres with 75 miles of shoreline. You can camp aboard your self-contained boat but you must register at Browns Ravine Marina or at Granite Bay. This is a popular equestrian area with 80 miles of trails. The 32-mile American River Bike Trail links Beals Point to Old Sacramento. *Be sure to check water levels as some ramps and facilities may be closed.*

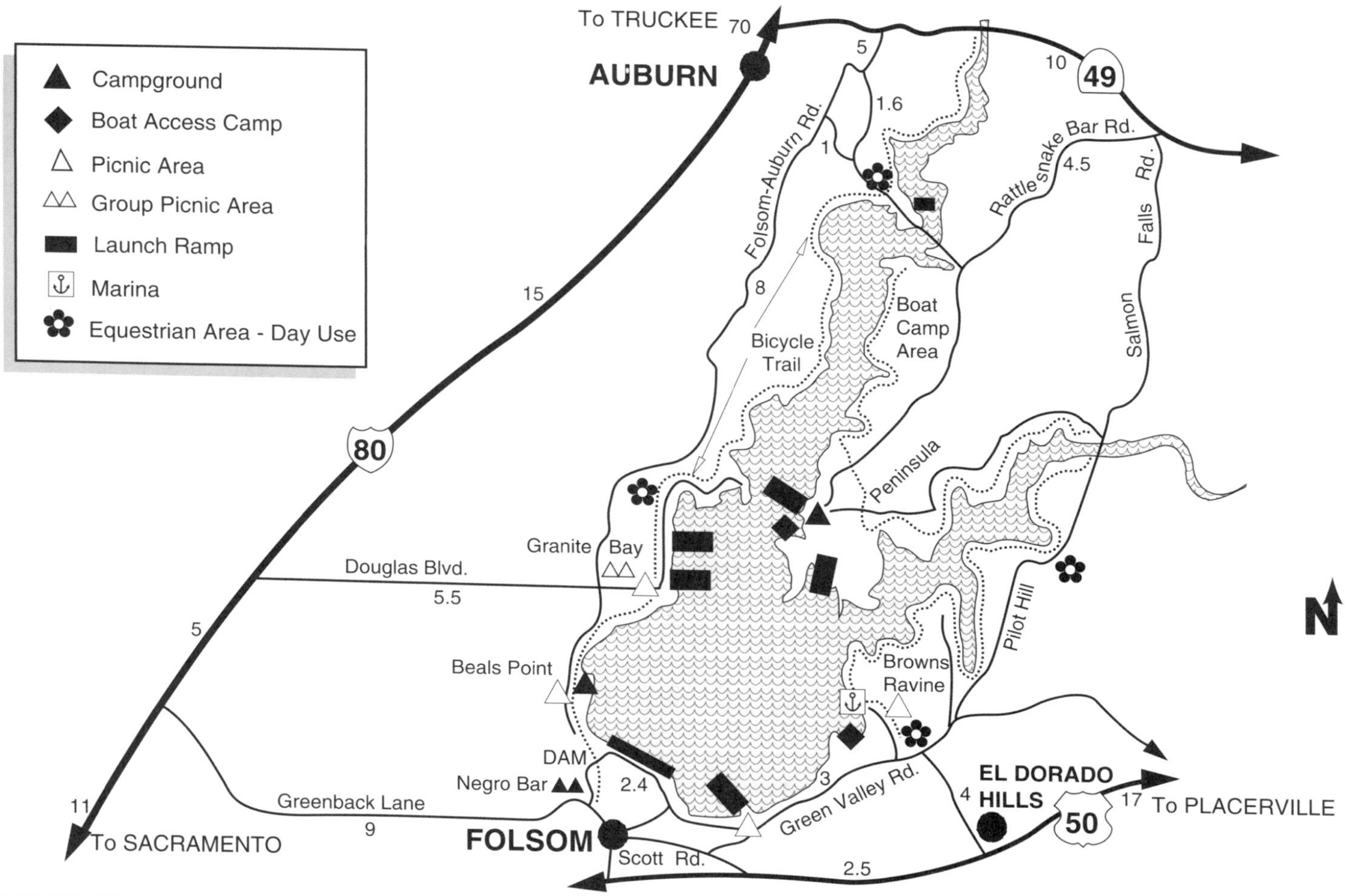
Campground
Boat Access Camp
Picnic Area
Group Picnic Area
Launch Ramp
Marina
Equestrian Area - Day Use
To TRUCKEE
70
AUBURN
5
10
49
1.6
Folsom-Auburn Rd.
1
Rattlesnake Bar Rd.
4.5
Falls Rd.
Salmon
15
8
Bicycle Trail
Boat Camp Area
80
Peninsula
Granite Bay
Douglas Blvd.
5.5
Pilot Hill
N
5
Beals Point
Browns Ravine
DAM
Negro Bar
2.4
3
Green Valley Rd.
4
EL DORADO HILLS
17
To PLACERVILLE
50
11
To SACRAMENTO
Greenback Lane
9
FOLSOM
Scott Rd.
2.5

INFORMATION: Folsom Lake, 7806 Folsom-Auburn Rd., Folsom 95630—Ph: (916) 988-0205

CAMPING	BOATING	RECREATION	OTHER
149 Dev. Sites Tents & R.V.s to 40 Feet Fee: $20 Group Campgrounds Reservations: Ph: (800) 444-7275 Boat Camping Areas Fees: $10 on Board $20 on Shore at Peninsula Equestrian Area up to 50 Riders & Horses Contact Park Hdqtrs.	Open to All Boating Full Service Marina Ph: 916-933-1300 10 Launch Ramps - *Check Water Levels* Boat Use Fees: $10 - $15 Docks, Berths, Dry Storage & Gas Rentals: Fishing, Waterski & Patio Boats, PWCs Low Water Hazards	Fishing: Rainbow Trout, Catfish, Bluegill, Large & Smallmouth Bass & Perch Picnicking Group Site at Granite Bay Swimming - Beaches Designated Bicycle, Hiking & Equestrian Trails Campfire Programs	Snack Bar Bait & Tackle Yacht Club Day Use Fee: $5 - $7 All Boats Must Register at Granite Bay or Browns Ravine Full Facilities in Folsom

LAKE NATOMA

Lake Natoma is a part of the Folsom Lake Recreation Area. At an elevation of 126 feet just below Folsom Dam, Natoma is the regulating Reservoir for Folsom Lake. The water is very cold and levels can fluctuate 3 or 4 feet in a day. This small Lake of 500 surface acres flows over dredger piles. The piles create a good fish habitat but they are a boating hazard. Fishing may be difficult, but for those who know the Lake, it can be rewarding. Good trails are available for the equestrian, bicyclist and hiker.

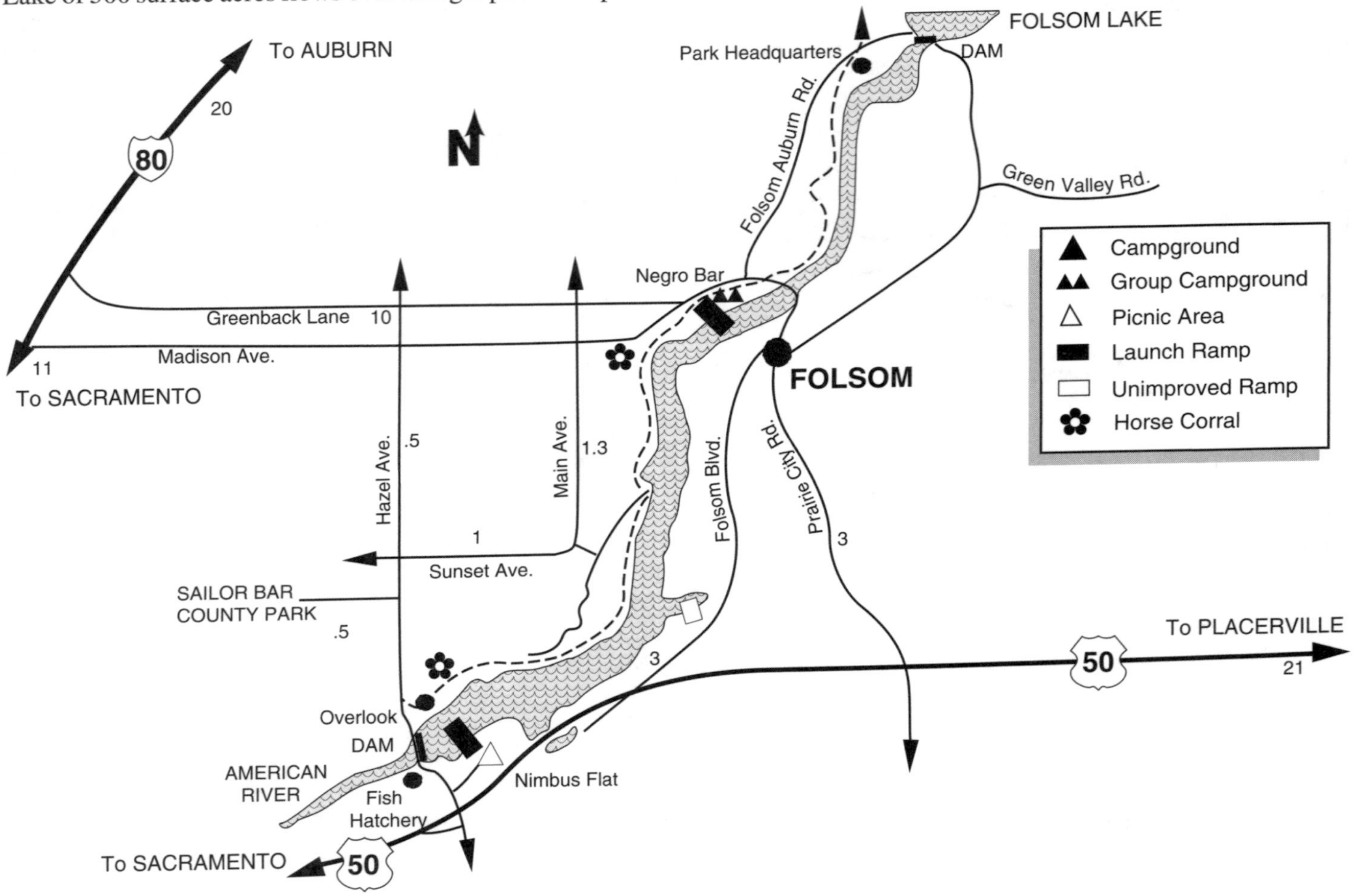
To AUBURN
20
80
N
Park Headquarters
FOLSOM LAKE
DAM
Folsom Auburn Rd.
Green Valley Rd.
Campground
Group Campground
Picnic Area
Launch Ramp
Unimproved Ramp
Horse Corral
Negro Bar
Greenback Lane
10
Madison Ave.
11
To SACRAMENTO
FOLSOM
Hazel Ave.
.5
Main Ave.
1.3
Folsom Blvd.
Prairie City Rd.
1
Sunset Ave.
3
SAILOR BAR
COUNTY PARK
.5
To PLACERVILLE
50
21
3
Overlook
DAM
AMERICAN
RIVER
Fish
Hatchery
Nimbus Flat
To SACRAMENTO
50

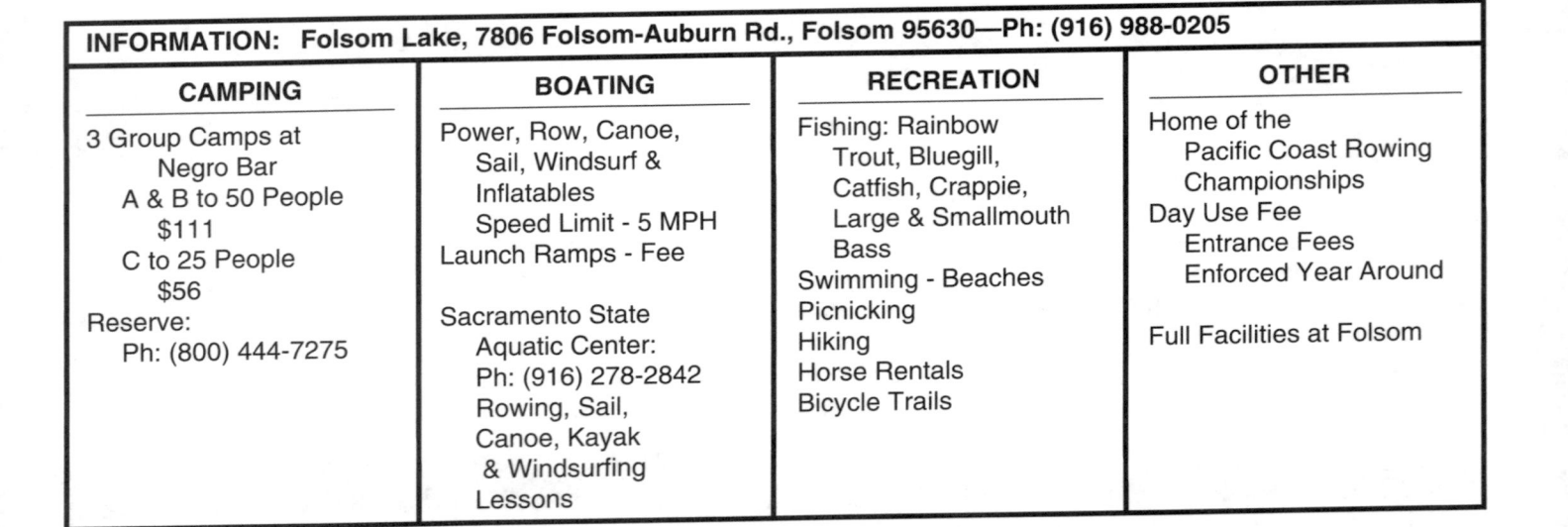

INFORMATION: Folsom Lake, 7806 Folsom-Auburn Rd., Folsom 95630—Ph: (916) 988-0205

CAMPING	BOATING	RECREATION	OTHER
3 Group Camps at Negro Bar A & B to 50 People $111 C to 25 People $56 Reserve: Ph: (800) 444-7275	Power, Row, Canoe, Sail, Windsurf & Inflatables Speed Limit - 5 MPH Launch Ramps - Fee Sacramento State Aquatic Center: Ph: (916) 278-2842 Rowing, Sail, Canoe, Kayak & Windsurfing Lessons	Fishing: Rainbow Trout, Bluegill, Catfish, Crappie, Large & Smallmouth Bass Swimming - Beaches Picnicking Hiking Horse Rentals Bicycle Trails	Home of the Pacific Coast Rowing Championships Day Use Fee Entrance Fees Enforced Year Around Full Facilities at Folsom

With all the qualities of a working ranch, Gibson Ranch County Park with 345 acres, is a unique facility. The County of Sacramento maintains this facility. The fishing lake and numerous equestrian activities and trails make it an ideal day-use area for families. It has 5 large group picnic sites. Elk Grove Park, 127 acres, includes a 3-acre fishing lake, swimming pool and numerous ball diamonds and picnic areas. This Park is maintained by the Cosumnes Community Services District. Under the jurisdiction of the Sacramento Municipal Utility District, the 400-acre Rancho Seco Recreational Area surrounds a 160-acre, warm-water lake fed by the Folsom South Canal. The water is recirculated daily and maintained at a constant level year around, providing ideal conditions for swimming, fishing, windsurfing and boating. No gas-powered motorboats are permitted. The camping facilities include a group campsite and reservations are available. There is a good swim area with a sandy beach and lifeguards on duty from Memorial Day through Labor Day.

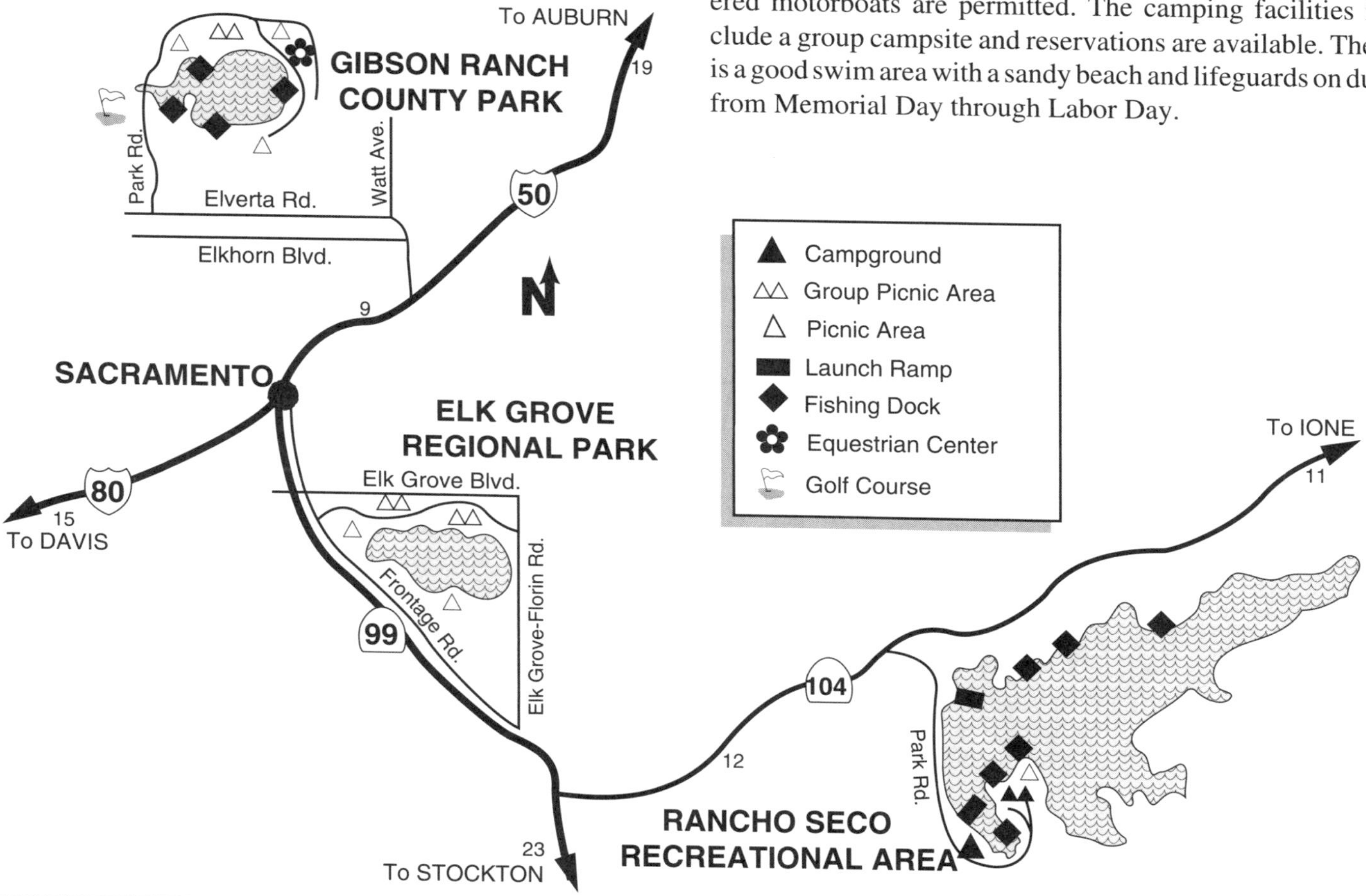
To AUBURN
19
GIBSON RANCH
COUNTY PARK
Park Rd.
Watt Ave.
Elverta Rd.
50
Elkhorn Blvd.
9
N
SACRAMENTO
ELK GROVE
REGIONAL PARK
Elk Grove Blvd.
80
15
To DAVIS
Frontage Rd.
Elk Grove-Florin Rd.
99
Campground
Group Picnic Area
Picnic Area
Launch Ramp
Fishing Dock
Equestrian Center
Golf Course
To IONE
11
104
12
Park Rd.
RANCHO SECO
RECREATIONAL AREA
23
To STOCKTON

INFORMATION: Gibson Ranch - County Parks, 3711 Branch Center Rd., Sacramento 95827—Ph: (916) 875-6961

CAMPING	BOATING	RECREATION	OTHER
Day Use Only: Gibson Ranch - Fee: $5 Elk Grove - Free Except for Special Events Rancho Seco Park: Sites for Tents & R.V.s Electric & Water Hookups Fees: $10-$15 Group Camping Area Disposal Station Reservations: Ph: (916) 732-4913	Gibson Ranch & Elk Grove - No Boating Rancho Seco: Electric Motorboats, Sailboats & Rowboats Rentals: Kayaks & Paddleboats 2 Launch Ramps	Fishing: Rainbow Trout, Bass, Bluegill, Sunfish, Catfish & Crappie Fishing Docks Trout Derby: March & Dec. Family & Group Picnic Areas - Reserve Swimming Pool - Elk Grove Swim Beach - Rancho Seco Horse Rentals & Hayrides - Gibson Ranch Ph: (916) 991-7592	Rancho Seco: Sacramento Utility District P.O. Box 15830 Sacramento 95852 Ph: (916) 732-4913 General Store Fish Cleaning Station Elk Grove Regional Park Cosumnes Community Services 8820 Elk Grove Blvd. Elk Grove 95624 Ph: (916) 405-5600

SALT SPRINGS RESERVOIR

Salt Springs Reservoir is at an elevation of 3,900 feet in the spectacular Mokelumne River Canyon of the Eldorado National Forest. This P.G. & E. Reservoir has a surface area of 961 acres. High afternoon winds may be hazardous for small boats. Fishing is often productive at the Lake, the Mokelumne River and other nearby streams. The Forest Service maintains three campgrounds along the river just below the dam. A trailhead into the 105,000 acre Mokelumne Wilderness is located just above the dam. *This is a high fire hazard area - NO campfires allowed - use portable stoves.*

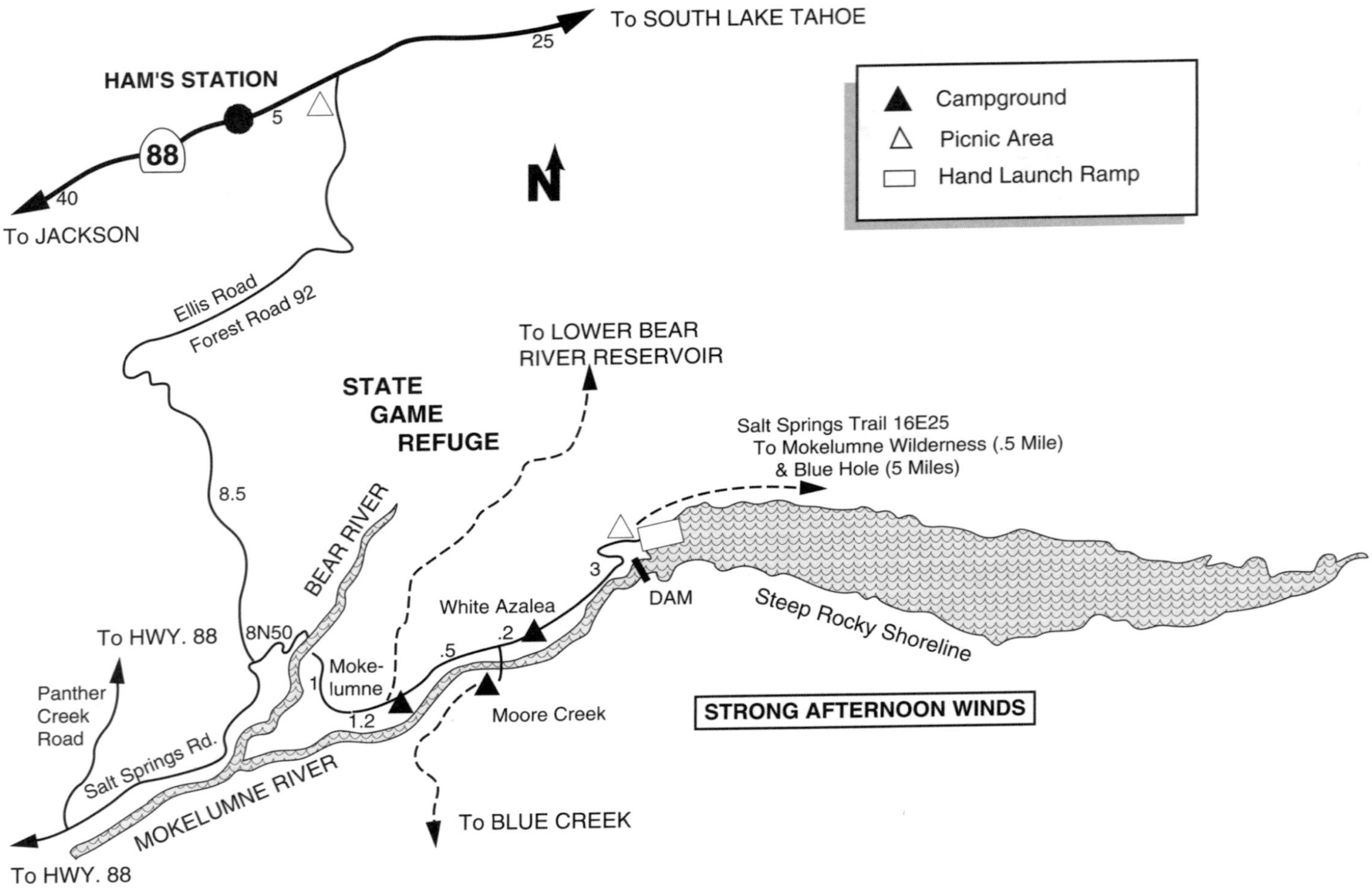
To SOUTH LAKE TAHOE
25
HAM'S STATION
5
88
40
To JACKSON
Campground
Picnic Area
Hand Launch Ramp
N
Ellis Road
Forest Road 92
To LOWER BEAR
RIVER RESERVOIR
STATE
GAME
REFUGE
Salt Springs Trail 16E25
To Mokelumne Wilderness (.5 Mile)
& Blue Hole (5 Miles)
8.5
BEAR RIVER
3
White Azalea
DAM
Steep Rocky Shoreline
To HWY. 88
8N50
.2
.5
Moke-
lumne
1
1.2
Moore Creek
STRONG AFTERNOON WINDS
Panther
Creek
Road
Salt Springs Rd.
MOKELUMNE RIVER
To BLUE CREEK
To HWY. 88

INFORMATION: Amador Ranger District, 26820 Silver Dr., Pioneer 95666—Ph: (209) 295-4251

CAMPING	BOATING	RECREATION	OTHER
22 Sites for Tents & R.V.s Mokelumne: 13 Sites Moore Creek: 8 Sites White Azalea: 6 Sites No Drinking Water No Fee	Power, Row, Canoe & Sail Hand Launch Only Difficult Water Access *Winds Can be Hazardous in the Afternoon*	Fishing: Rainbow, Brown & Brook Trout Swimming Picnicking Hiking Backpacking [Parking] Equestrian Trails	Nearest Facilities & Gas at Ham's Station *No Hunting in State Game Refuge* *No ORVs within the Mokelumne River Canyon below areas on Panther Creek and Ellis Roads*

LOWER BEAR RIVER RESERVOIR

Bear River Reservoir is at an elevation of 5,849 feet in the Eldorado National Forest. This scenic Lake, 727 surface acres, is surrounded by a coniferous forest reaching to water's edge. There are good vacation and boating facilities. Afternoon breezes are great for sailing. The Lake is regularly stocked and trout fishing can be exceptional. The Forest Service campgrounds are operated by a concessionaire. Overnight camping is limited to designated sites only. The Bear River Resort has complete camping and marina facilities with hot showers, groceries, bait and tackle, snack bar and deluxe rental units.

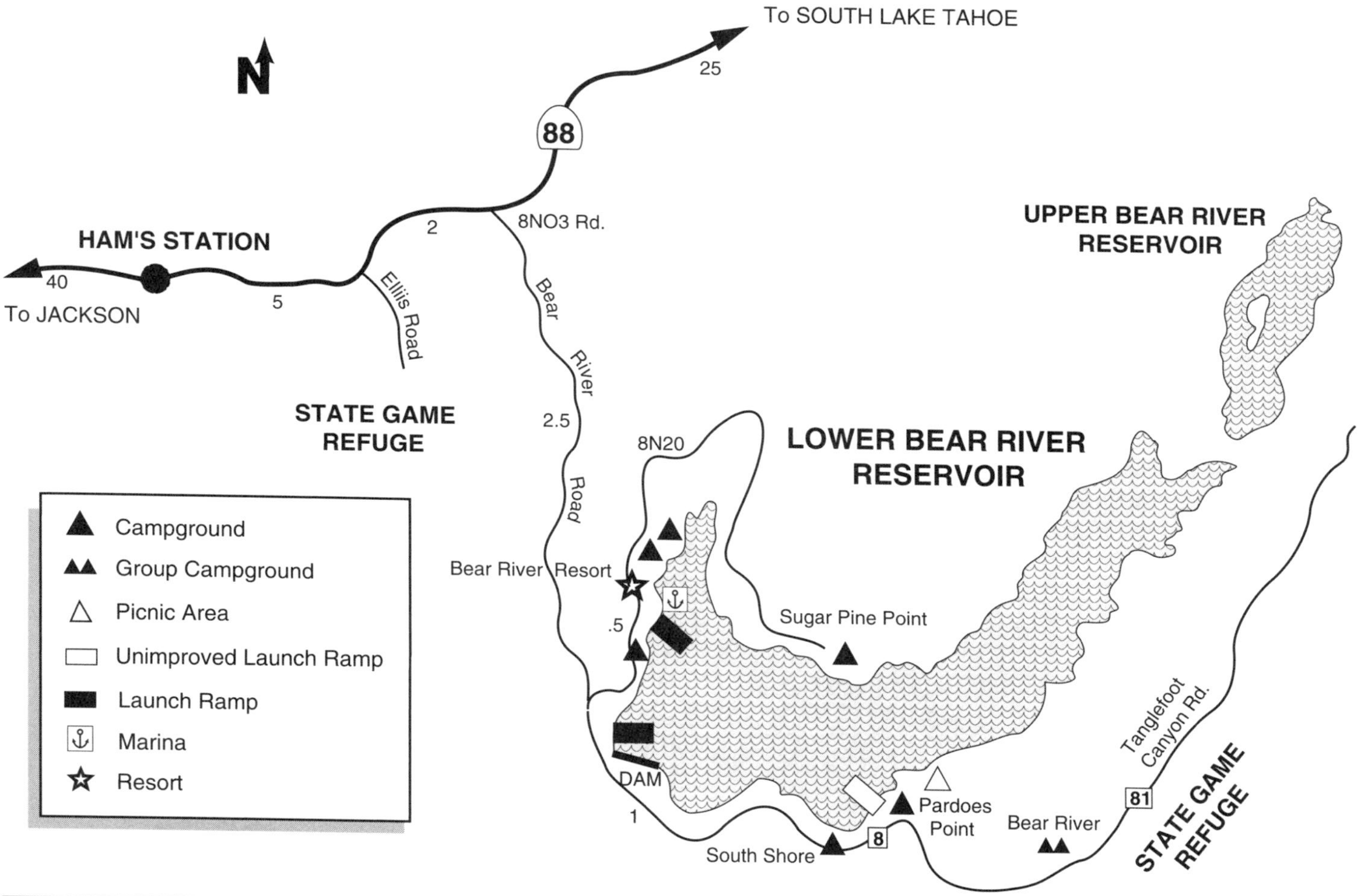
To SOUTH LAKE TAHOE
N
25
88
HAM'S STATION
2
8NO3 Rd.
40
To JACKSON
5
Ellis Road
Bear River Road
2.5
STATE GAME REFUGE
8N20
LOWER BEAR RIVER RESERVOIR
UPPER BEAR RIVER RESERVOIR
Campground
Group Campground
Picnic Area
Unimproved Launch Ramp
Launch Ramp
Marina
Resort
Bear River Resort
.5
Sugar Pine Point
Tanglefoot Canyon Rd.
DAM
1
Pardoes Point
Bear River
81
STATE GAME REFUGE
8
South Shore

INFORMATION: Amador Ranger District, 26820 Silver Dr., Pioneer 95666—Ph: (209) 295-4251			
CAMPING	**BOATING**	**RECREATION**	**OTHER**
South Shore: 22 Dev. Sites for Tents & R.V.s Fee: $19 - $38 - $57 Bear River Group Camps: 3 Sites - 25 People - $70 1 Site - 50 People - $140 Reservations: Ph: (877) 444-6777 Pardoes Point: 10 Sites Fee: $19 - $38 Sugar Pine: 8 Sites No Water-Fee: $17 - $34	Open to All Boating Launch Ramps Full Service Marina at Resort Rentals: Fishing Boats, Canoes, Kayaks, Paddle Boats Possible Low Water Hazards Late in Season	Fishing: Rainbow, Macinaw & Brown Trout Picnicking Swimming Hiking Trails	Bear River Lake Resort 40800 Hwy. 88 Pioneer 95666 Ph: (209) 295-4868 125 Dev. Sites with Hookups Fee: $31 - $47 Group Camp to 60 People - Fee: $250 Disposal Station Rental Units up to 4 People Each Restaurant, Store

SILVER LAKE

Silver Lake is at an elevation of 7,200 feet in a large granite basin just west of the Sierra Summit in the Eldorado National Forest. This exceptionally beautiful Lake was once a resting place on the Emigrant Trail leading to the gold fields. You can still see the trail markers carved in the trees. The descendants of Raymond Peter Plasse, who established a trading post in 1853, operate a good resort at the Lake from June through September. They offer campsites, horse camping and several recreational acitivties including horse rentals. A dining room and bar are also available. Silver Lake has been a popular recreation area for over a century, offering a variety of natural resources and facilities for the camper, angler, boater, hiker and equestrian.

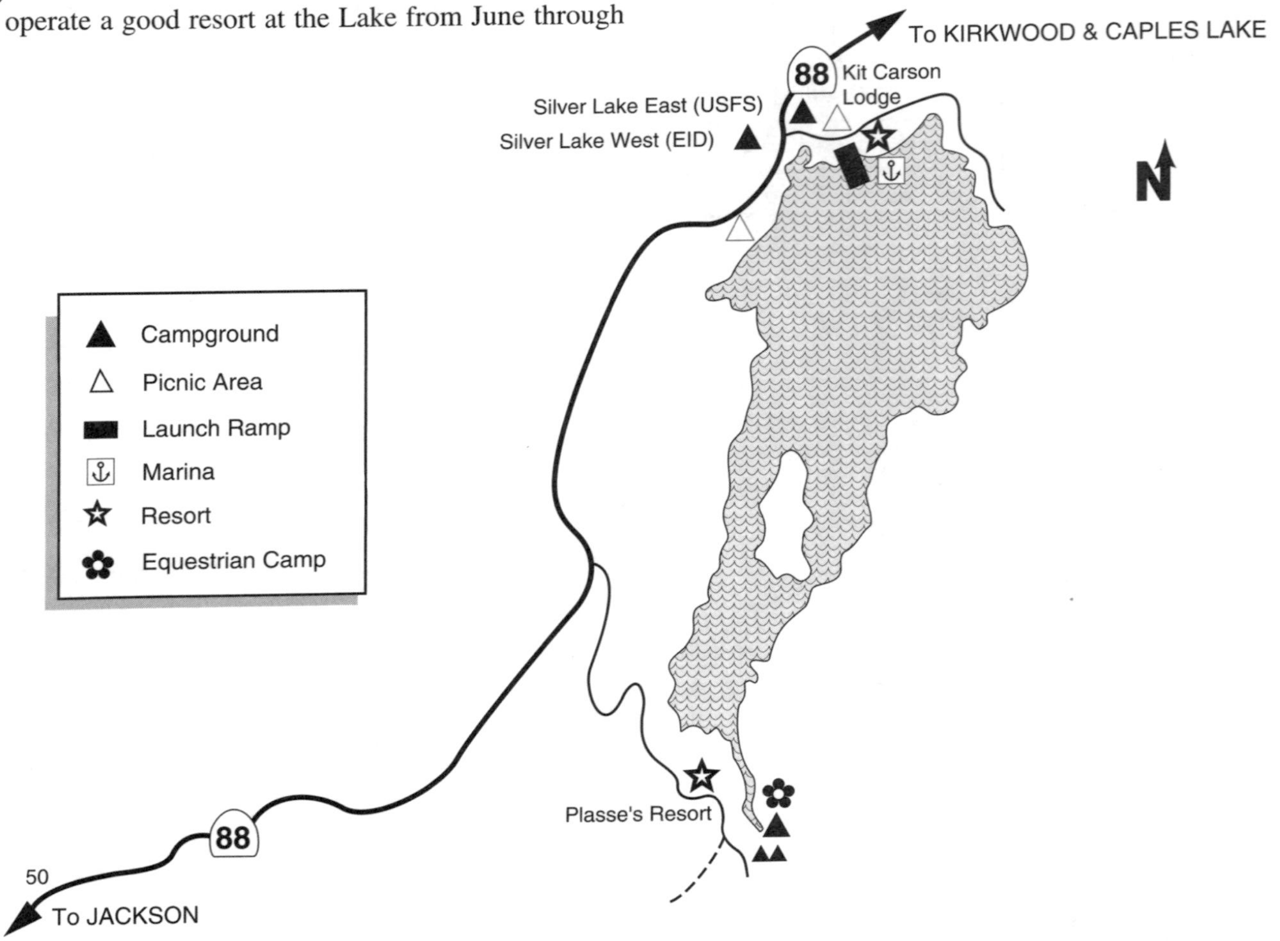

To KIRKWOOD & CAPLES LAKE
88
Kit Carson Lodge
Silver Lake East (USFS)
Silver Lake West (EID)
N
Campground
Picnic Area
Launch Ramp
Marina
Resort
Equestrian Camp
Plasse's Resort
88
50
To JACKSON

INFORMATION: Amador Ranger District, 26820 Silver Dr., Pioneer 95666—Ph: (209) 295-4251			
CAMPING	**BOATING**	**RECREATION**	**OTHER**
USFS - 62 Dev. Sites for Tents & R.V.s-Fee: $20-$40 Some Sites - Reservations: Ph: (877) 444-6777 Eldorado Irrigation District (EDI) Ph: (530) 644-1960 42 Dev. Sites for Tents & R.V.s - Fee: $24 Plasse's Resort Ph: (209) 258-8814 Dev. Sites for Tents & R.V.s Horse & Group Camps Fees: $27 and up	Power, Row, Canoe, Sail, Inflatables Full Service Marina Launch Ramps Rentals: Fishing Boats & Motors, Canoes & Kayaks Docks, Moorings	Fishing: Rainbow Trout Swimming Picnicking Hiking Trails Equestrian Trails Horse Rentals at Plasse's Resort	Plasse's Resort Ph: (209) 258-8814 Restaurant & Bar Grocery Store Disposal Station Canoe & Kayak Rentals Kit Carson Lodge Ph: (209) 258-8500 Housekeeping Cabins Restaurant Grocery Store Bait & Tackle Canoe & Kayak Rentals

CAPLES and KIRKWOOD LAKES

Caples Lake is at an elevation of 7,800 feet in the Eldorado National Forest near the summit of Carson Pass. The night and morning temperatures are cool and the water is cold in this 600 surface-acre Lake. Kirkwood Lake is 3 miles to the west of Caples Lake at an elevation of 7,600 feet. The road is not suitable for larger R.V.s or trailers. Gas or electric motor boats are not allowed on Kirkwood but you may use a motor up to 5 mph on Caples. Fishing is good for a variety of trout at these Lakes and other nearby lakes and streams. Trails lead into the Mokelumne Wilderness for the hiker or backpacker. Permits are required for overnight trips into the Wilderness year around. This entire area is a photographer's delight.

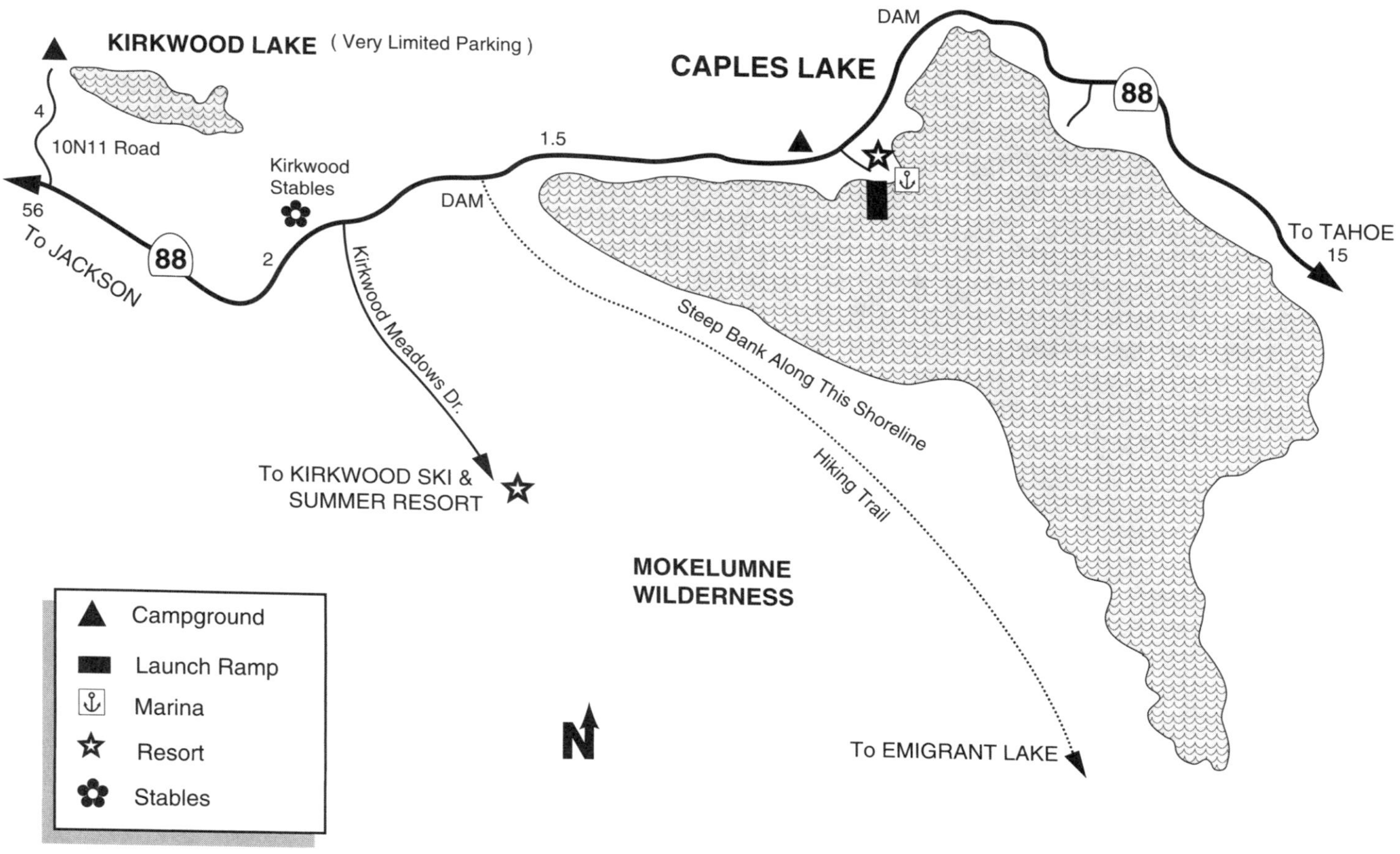
KIRKWOOD LAKE (Very Limited Parking)
CAPLES LAKE
DAM
88
4
10N11 Road
1.5
Kirkwood Stables
DAM
56
To JACKSON
88
2
Kirkwood Meadows Dr.
To TAHOE 15
Steep Bank Along This Shoreline
Hiking Trail
To KIRKWOOD SKI & SUMMER RESORT
MOKELUMNE WILDERNESS
Campground
Launch Ramp
Marina
Resort
Stables
N
To EMIGRANT LAKE

INFORMATION: Amador Ranger District, 26820 Silver Dr., Pioneer 95666—Ph: (209) 295-4251

CAMPING	BOATING	RECREATION	OTHER
Caples Lake: 34 Dev. Sites for Tents & R.V.s Including 5 Walk-in Sites Fee: $21 - $42 Kirkwood Lake: 12 Dev. Sites for Tents Fee: $19	Caples Lake: Power, Row, Canoe, Sail & Inflatables 5 MPH Speed Limit Launch Ramp Moorings Guest Dock Rentals: Fishing Boats, Canoes & Kayaks *No* Motors of Any Kind on Kirkwood	Fishing: Rainbow, Brown, Brook & Cutthroat Trout Swimming Picnicking Hiking Trails Backpacking Equestrian Trails Horse Rentals at Kirkwood Stables	Caples Lake Resort Ph: (209) 258-8888 Housekeeping Cabins Lodge & Restaurant Grocery Store, Bait & Tackle, Boat Rentals Kirkwood Resort Ph: (209) 258-6000 Lodge & Restaurant Condo Rentals Store, Gas Station Tennis Courts Mountain Bike Rentals

WOODS and RED LAKES

Woods Lake is at an elevation of 8,200 feet southwest of the Carson Pass in the Eldorado National Forest. This scenic hidden retreat, 2 miles south of Highway 88, has a US Forest Service campground and a picnic area at the water's edge. Fishing can be good from a hand-launched boat or along the shoreline and also in the streams throughout the area. Motorboats are not permitted on the Lake. Trails lead to Winnemucca, Round Top Lakes and other sites within the Mokelumne Wilderness. Permits are required for overnight trips into the Wilderness areas year around. The Pacific Crest Trail runs to the east of Woods Lake. Red Lake is with the 820 acres Wildlife Area owned by the California State Department of Fish & Game. No campground is available and facilities are limited.

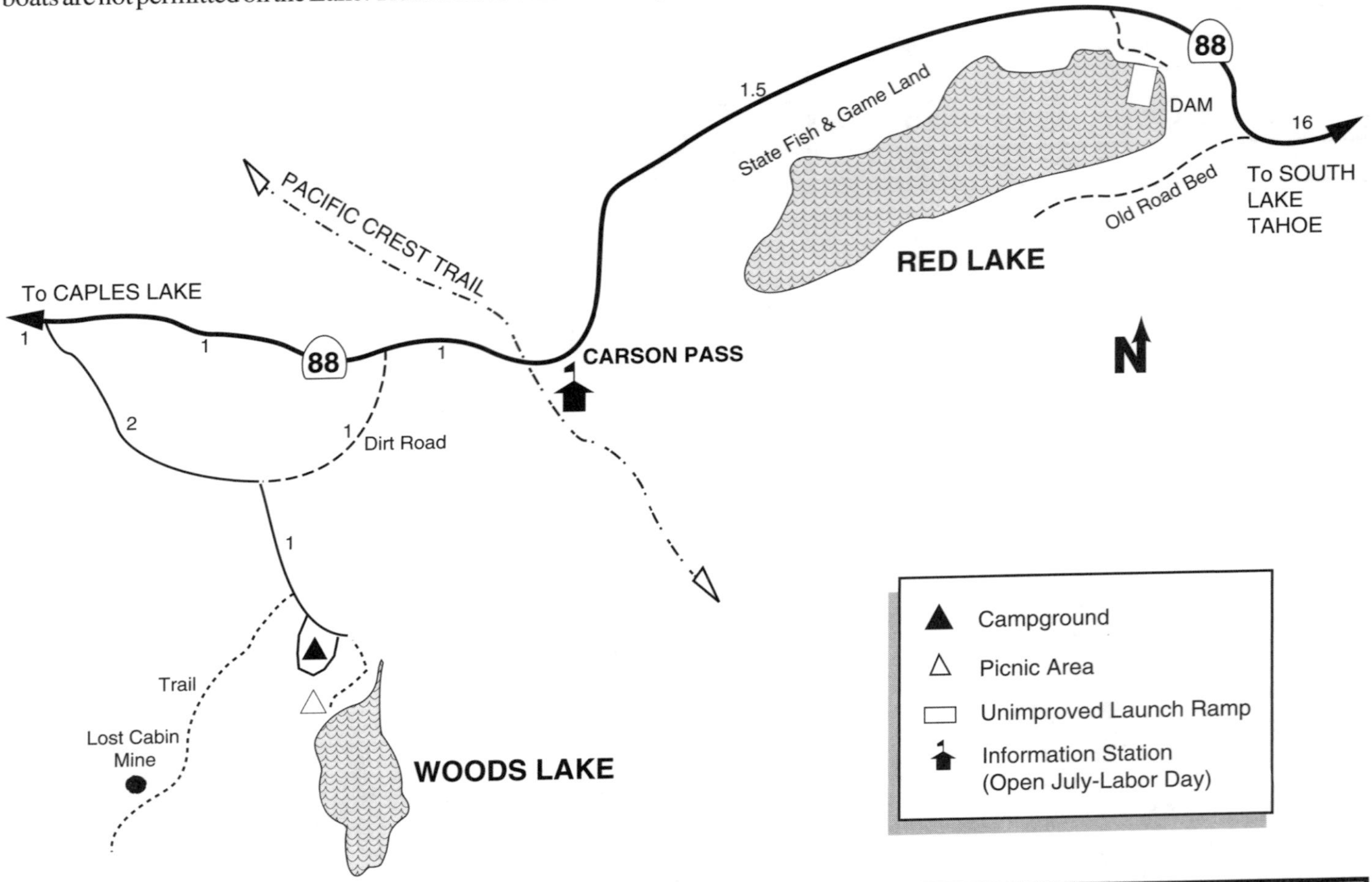

To CAPLES LAKE
1
1
88
1
CARSON PASS
2
1
Dirt Road
1
PACIFIC CREST TRAIL
1.5
State Fish & Game Land
88
DAM
16
To SOUTH
LAKE
TAHOE
Old Road Bed
RED LAKE
N
Trail
Lost Cabin
Mine
WOODS LAKE
Campground
Picnic Area
Unimproved Launch Ramp
Information Station
(Open July-Labor Day)

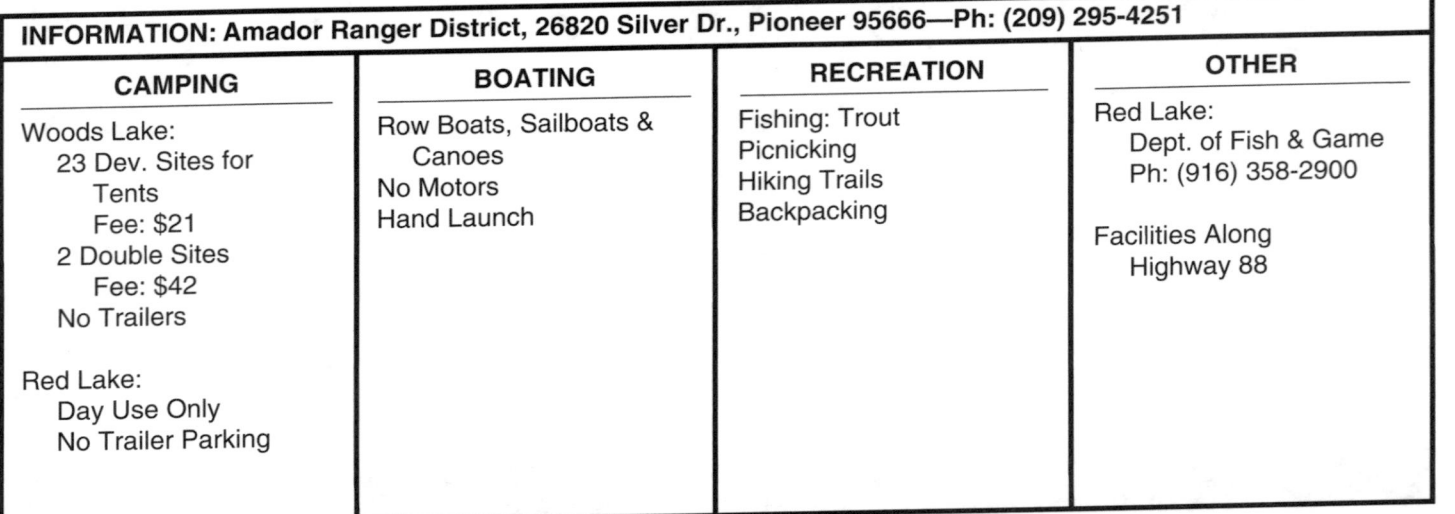

INFORMATION: Amador Ranger District, 26820 Silver Dr., Pioneer 95666—Ph: (209) 295-4251

CAMPING	BOATING	RECREATION	OTHER
Woods Lake: 23 Dev. Sites for Tents Fee: $21 2 Double Sites Fee: $42 No Trailers Red Lake: Day Use Only No Trailer Parking	Row Boats, Sailboats & Canoes No Motors Hand Launch	Fishing: Trout Picnicking Hiking Trails Backpacking	Red Lake: Dept. of Fish & Game Ph: (916) 358-2900 Facilities Along Highway 88

The Blue Lakes are at an elevation of 8,000 feet in this remote area of the Eldorado National Forest. The mornings and evenings are cool and the water is clear and cold. Boating is limited to small craft and fishing can be good. There are numerous hiking trails including the Pacific Crest Trail and those leading into the Mokelumne Wilderness. Campgrounds are maintained by P.G. & E. except for Hope Valley which is operated by the U.S.F.S., Carson Ranger District, Humboldt-Toiyabe National Forest. Two great resorts are in this area of Highway 88.

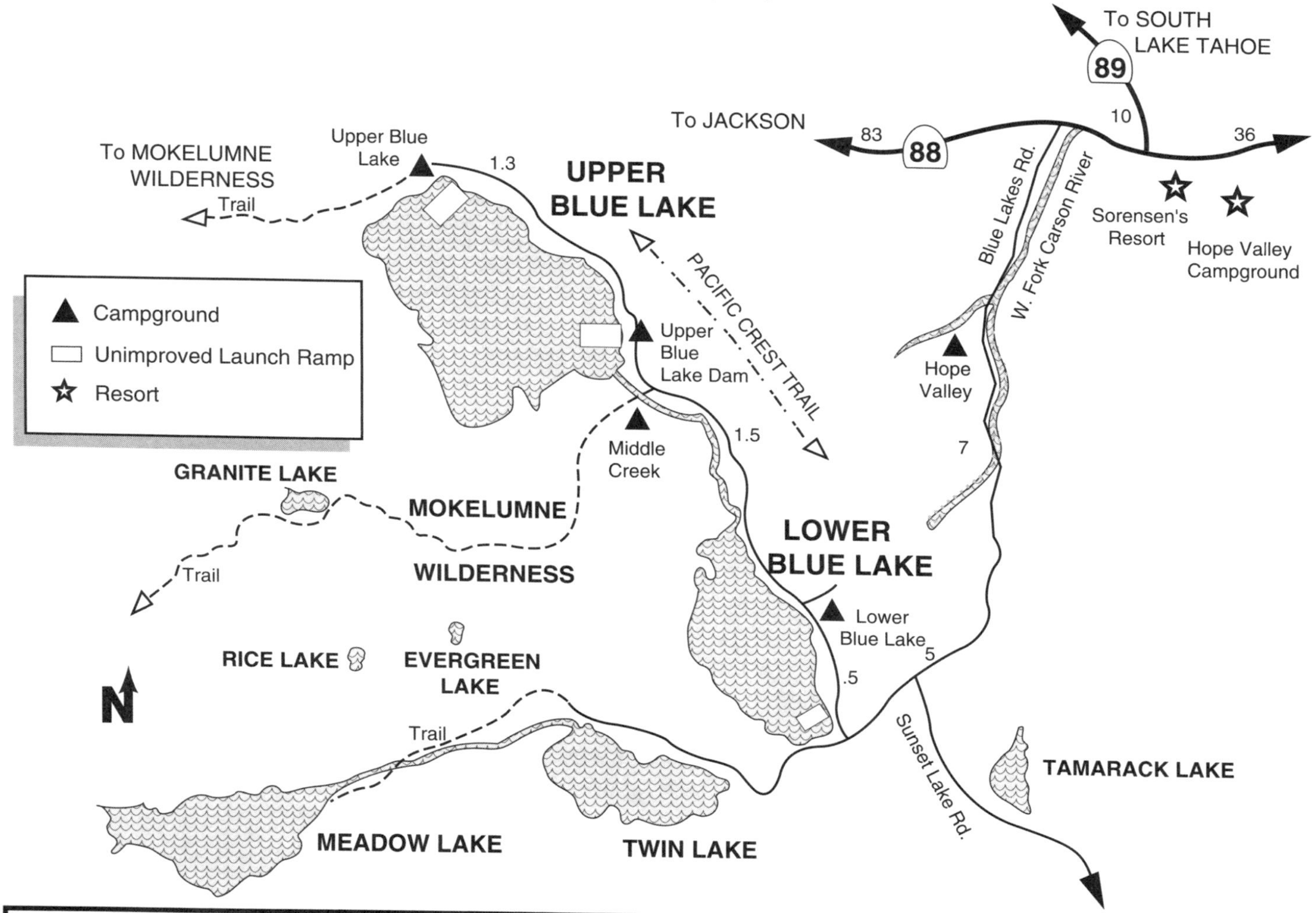
To SOUTH LAKE TAHOE
89
To JACKSON
83
88
10
36
To MOKELUMNE WILDERNESS
Trail
Upper Blue Lake
1.3
UPPER BLUE LAKE
PACIFIC CREST TRAIL
Blue Lakes Rd.
W. Fork Carson River
Sorensen's Resort
Hope Valley Campground
Campground
Unimproved Launch Ramp
Resort
Upper Blue Lake Dam
Hope Valley
Middle Creek
1.5
7
GRANITE LAKE
MOKELUMNE
WILDERNESS
Trail
LOWER BLUE LAKE
Lower Blue Lake
5
.5
RICE LAKE
EVERGREEN LAKE
N
Trail
Sunset Lake Rd.
TAMARACK LAKE
MEADOW LAKE
TWIN LAKE

INFORMATION: P.G.&E. Land Projects, 2730 Gateway Oaks Dr., Sacramento 95833—Ph: (916) 386-5164

CAMPING	BOATING	RECREATION	OTHER
Upper Blue Lake: 32 Dev. Sites for Tents & R.V.s Upper Blue Lake Dam: 25 Dev. Sites Middle Creek: 5 Dev. Sites Lower Blue Lake: 16 Dev. Sites Fees: $17 Plus Overflow Area	Small Boats Only Unimproved Launch Ramps Additional Campsites: Carson Ranger District 1536 S. Carson St. Carson City NV 89701 Ph: (775) 882-2766 Hope Valley: 26 Dev. Sites-1 Group Fee: $14 and up Reserve: (877) 444-6777	Fishing: Rainbow Trout Swimming Picnicking Hiking Trails Backpacking [Parking] Mountain Biking Carson River: Kayaking Rafting	Sorensen's Resort Housekeeping Cabins Restaurant Grocery Store Fishing Supplies Hope Valley Resort 25 Dev. Sites for Tents & R.V.s Full Hookups Fee: $18 - $40 Picnic Sites Reservations-Both Resorts: Ph: (800) 423-9949

INDIAN CREEK RESERVOIR and HEENAN LAKE

Indian Creek Reservoir is at an elevation of 5,600 feet on the eastern slope of the Sierras. The Bureau of Land Management maintains more than 7,000 acres in this beautiful area of Jeffrey and Pinon Pines. The 160 surface-acre Lake offers good fishing and small craft boating. Check current water levels. Nearby Heenan Lake, 129 surface acres, provides a good catch and release fishery by permit during a special fishing season. Only artificial lures and barbless hooks can be used. *Contact the California Department of Fish and Game at (916) 358-2900 for specific regulations.* A popular nearby attraction is Grover Hot Springs State Park where a hot mineral bath can be enjoyed. Camping reservations are advised.

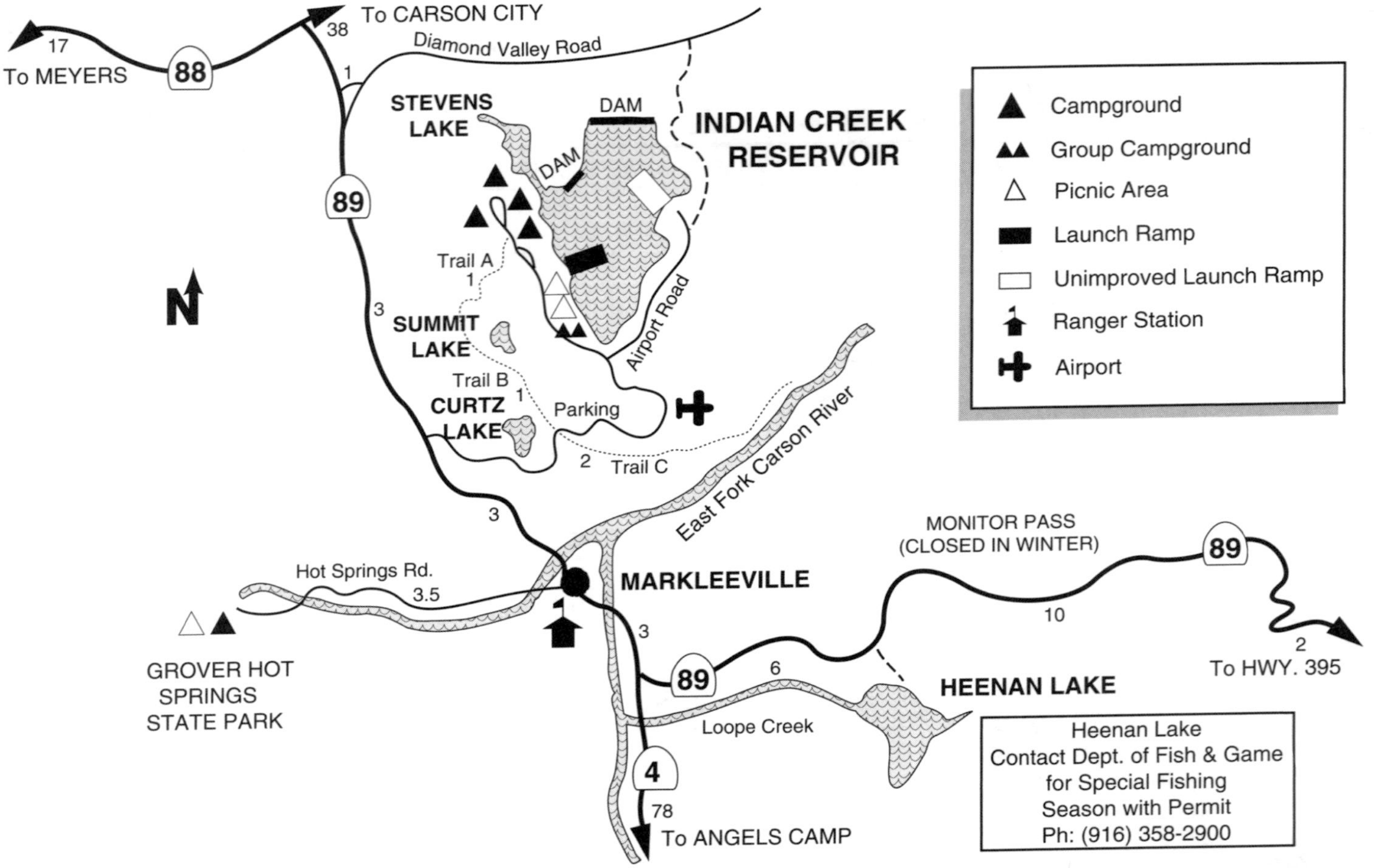

To CARSON CITY
38
17
To MEYERS
88
Diamond Valley Road
1
STEVENS LAKE
DAM
DAM
INDIAN CREEK RESERVOIR
89
Trail A
1
3
SUMMIT LAKE
Airport Road
N
Trail B
1
CURTZ LAKE
Parking
2
Trail C
East Fork Carson River
3
MONITOR PASS (CLOSED IN WINTER)
89
Hot Springs Rd.
3.5
MARKLEEVILLE
10
3
2
To HWY. 395
GROVER HOT SPRINGS STATE PARK
89
6
HEENAN LAKE
Loope Creek
4
78
To ANGELS CAMP
Heenan Lake
Contact Dept. of Fish & Game
for Special Fishing
Season with Permit
Ph: (916) 358-2900
Campground
Group Campground
Picnic Area
Launch Ramp
Unimproved Launch Ramp
Ranger Station
Airport

INFORMATION: Bureau of Land Management, 5665 Morgan Mill Rd., Carson City, NV 89701—Ph: (775) 885-6000

CAMPING	BOATING	RECREATION	OTHER
Indian Creek: 19 Dev. Sites for Tents & R.V.s to 34 Ft. Plus 15 Tent Only Sites No Hookups Fees: $14 - $32 No Reservations Group Camp to 40 People Fee: $50 Reservations: Ph: (775) 885-6000 Disposal Station	Indian Creek: Open to All Small Boats Launch Ramp Heenan Lake: Small Hand Launch Boats Only Electric Motors Only *Call for Specific* *Fishing Regulations* *Ph: (916) 358-2900*	Fishing : Indian Creek: Rainbow & Brown Trout Heenan: Lahontan Cutthroat Trout *Catch & Release* Picnicking Hiking & Nature Trails Backpacking Curtz Lake: Environmental Study Area	Grover Hot Springs P.O. Box 188 Markleeville 96120 Ph: (530) 694-2248 76 Dev. Sites for Tents & R.V.s to 24 Feet Fee: $20 - $25 Reservations: Ph: (800) 444-7275 Hot Springs Fee: $2 - $5 Alpine Chamber of Commerce Ph: (530) 694-2475

Topaz Lake is on the California-Nevada State Line at an elevation of 5,000 feet. This 1,800 surface-acre Reservoir is nestled amid sage-covered mountains and has 25 miles of sandy shoreline. The Lake is open to all types of boating, including boat camping. Be aware of potential heavy afternoon winds. California and Nevada Fish and Game Departments stock the Lake which is closed to fishing for three months beginning October 1. As a result, trophy-sized trout up to 8 pounds are no surprise. Half of Topaz Lake is in Nevada so there are nearby casinos to enjoy.

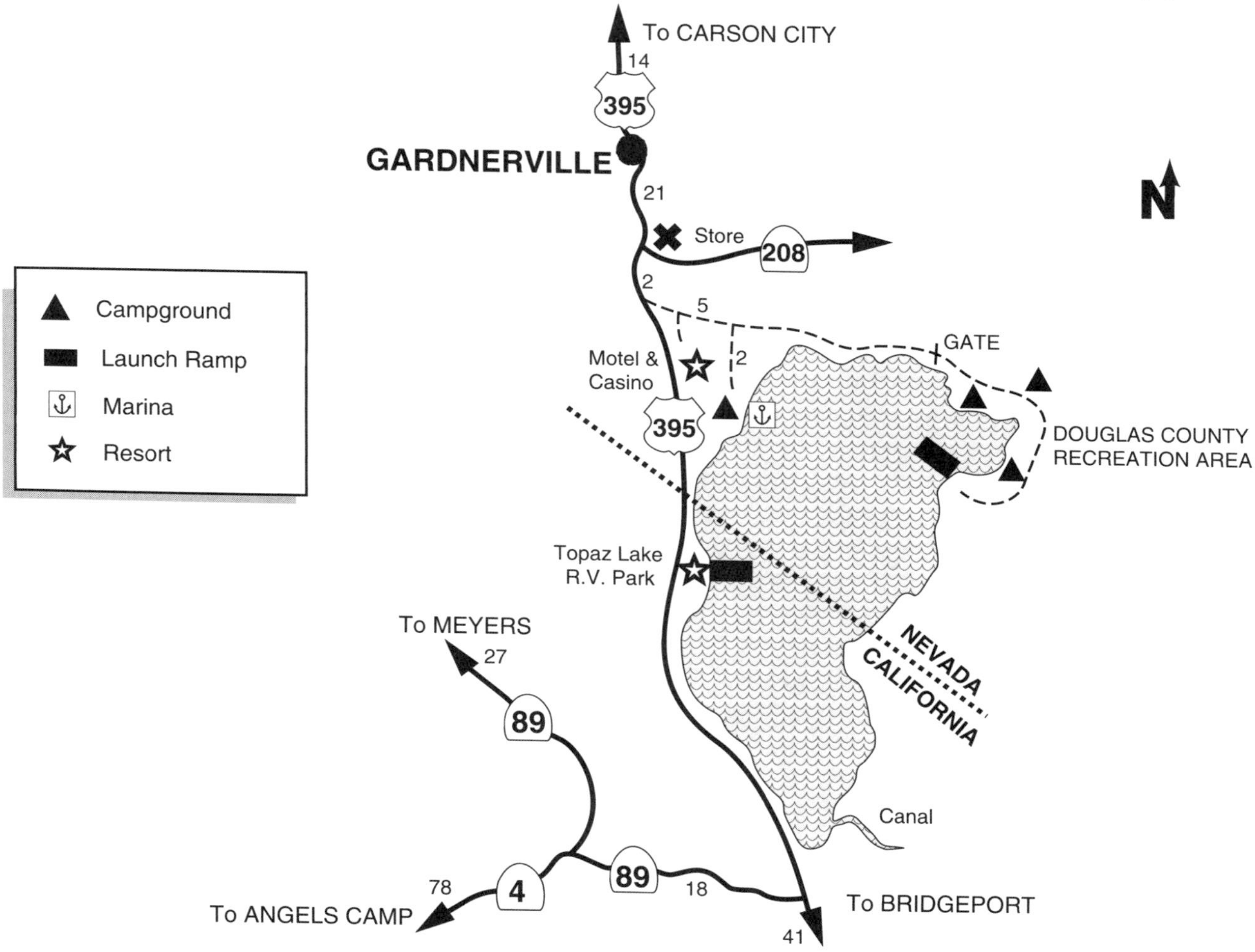
To CARSON CITY
14
395
GARDNERVILLE
21
Store
208
2
5
2
GATE
Motel & Casino
395
DOUGLAS COUNTY RECREATION AREA
Campground
Launch Ramp
Marina
Resort
N
Topaz Lake R.V. Park
To MEYERS
27
89
NEVADA
CALIFORNIA
Canal
78
4
89
18
To ANGELS CAMP
To BRIDGEPORT
41

INFORMATION: Douglas County Parks, 1325 Waterloo Lane, Gardnerville, NV 89410—Ph: (775) 782-9835

CAMPING	BOATING	RECREATION	OTHER
Douglas County Park: 15 R.V. Sites - Water & Electric Hookups - $18 42 Sites - Fee: $12 Disposal Station Topaz Lake RV Park: 69 R.V. Sites Full Hookups plus 40 Sites - No Hookups Topaz Marina: 28 Dev. Sites for Tents & R.V.s, Some Hookups	Power, Row, Canoe, Sail, Waterski, PWCs, Windsurf, & Inflatables Full Service Marina County Launch Ramp - $5 Rentals: Fishing Boats Docks, Berths, Dry Storage, Moorings & Gas Boat Camping	Fishing: Rainbow, Brown & Cutthroat Trout, Largemouth Bass, Catfish Use California or Nevada Fishing Licence Swimming - Beaches Picnicking Hiking Trails Playgrounds	Topaz Lake R.V. Park Ph: (530) 495-2357 Topaz Marina Ph: (775) 266-3236 Motel Restaurant & Lounge Casinos Bait & Tackle at Topaz Marina Reservations - Douglas County Park: Ph: (775) 782-9828

LAKE ALPINE

Lake Alpine is at an elevation of 7,300 feet in the Stanislaus National Forest. The Lake has a surface area of 180 acres and is regularly stocked with rainbow trout. The water is crystal clear and very cold. All boating is allowed within a 10 mph speed limit. The steady breezes make this a good sailing Lake. For the hiker and equestrian, there are trails leading to Carson-Iceberg Wilderness, located south of Lake Alpine, and to the Mokelumne Wilderness, a few miles to the north. The Forest Service maintains campgrounds near the Lake plus a special area set aside for backpackers. The historic Lake Alpine Lodge overlooks this beautiful Lake and the densely forested mountains.

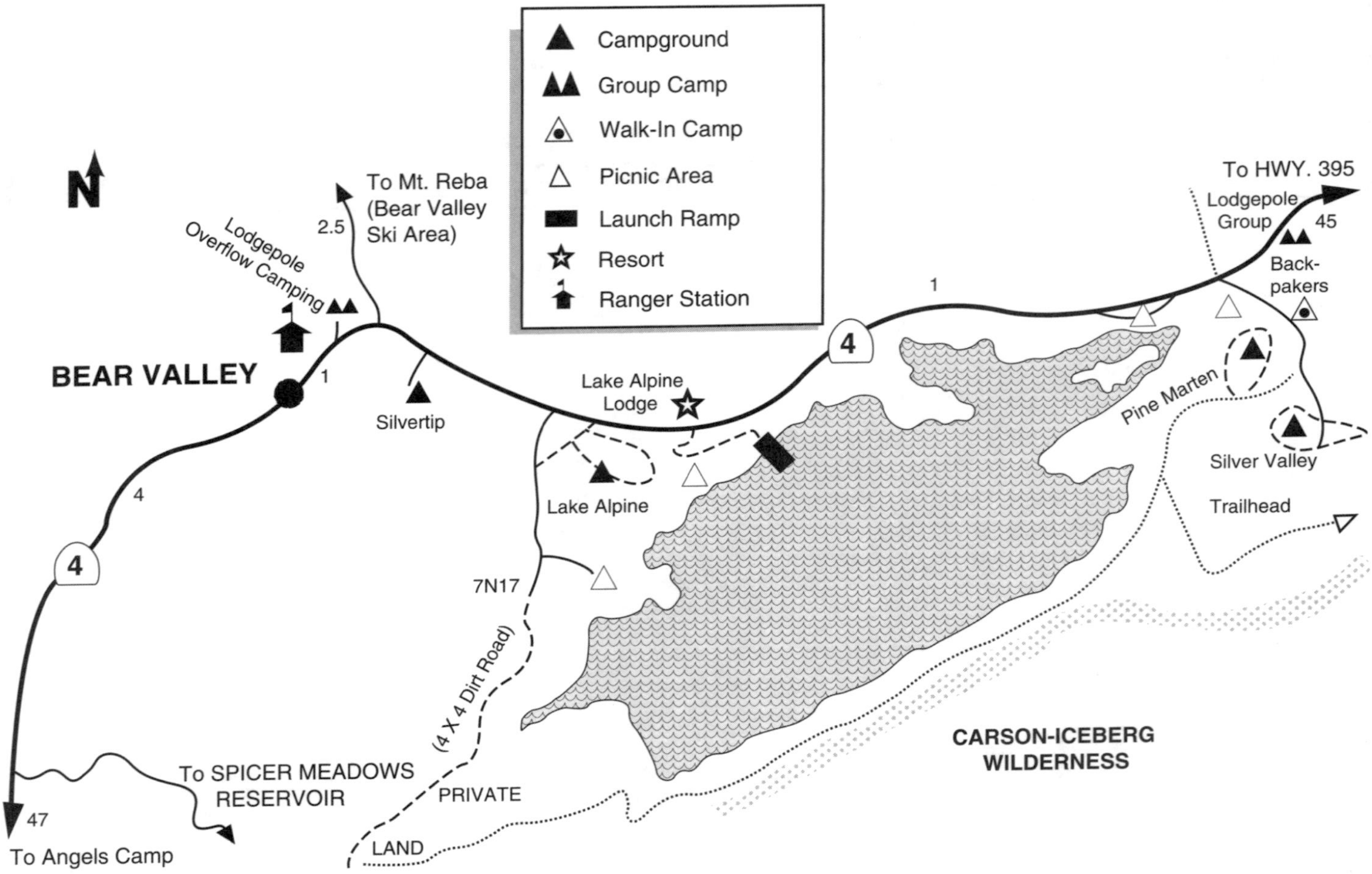
Campground
Group Camp
Walk-In Camp
Picnic Area
Launch Ramp
Resort
Ranger Station
N
To Mt. Reba (Bear Valley Ski Area)
2.5
Lodgepole Overflow Camping
BEAR VALLEY
1
Silvertip
Lake Alpine Lodge
4
Lake Alpine
7N17
(4 X 4 Dirt Road)
To SPICER MEADOWS RESERVOIR
47
To Angels Camp
PRIVATE
LAND
CARSON-ICEBERG WILDERNESS
To HWY. 395
Lodgepole Group
45
Back-pakers
Pine Marten
Silver Valley
Trailhead

INFORMATION: Calaveras Ranger District, P.O. Box 500, Hathaway Pines 95233—Ph: (209) 795-1381

CAMPING	BOATING	RECREATION	OTHER
Dev. Sites for Tents & R.V.s to 27 feet Fee: $20 Silvertip: 23 Sites Lake Alpine: 25 Sites Pine Marten: 32 Sites Silver Valley: 21 Sites Plus Lodgepole Group Camp to 100 People Fee: $73 Group Reservations: Ph: (877) 444-6777 30 Overflow Sites	Power, Row, Sail, Canoe & Inflatable Speed Limit - 10 MPH Launch Ramp Rentals: Fishing & Motor Boats, Canoes, Rowboats & Kayaks	Fishing: Rainbow Trout Swimming Picnicking Hiking Trails Backpacking [Parking] 4-Wheel Drive & Motorcycle Trails Mountain Biking Bike Trail from Bear Valley to the End of the Lake	Lake Alpine Lodge: P.O. 5060 Bear Valley 95223 Ph: (209) 753-6350 Cabins & Tent Cabins Full Services & Gas Station at Bear Valley

LAKE SONOMA

Lake Sonoma is nestled amid the rolling foothills of Northern California's coastal mountain range at an elevation of 451 feet. Located in the "wine country" just west of Healdsburg, this scenic Lake has 2,700 surface acres of prime recreational waters. There are many quiet, secluded coves for the boater, sailor or angler. Waterskiing is allowed only in designated areas. The U.S. Army Corps of Engineers has developed a variety of facilities. The 53 miles of oak-shaded hilly shoreline have almost 40 miles of lake access trails for the hiker, mountain biker or equestrian. There are primitive walk-in or boat-in areas with a total of 109 individual sites. The Liberty Glen Campground offers shaded, modern campsites. There is a 5-lane public launch ramp. The privately operated marina has complete facilities.

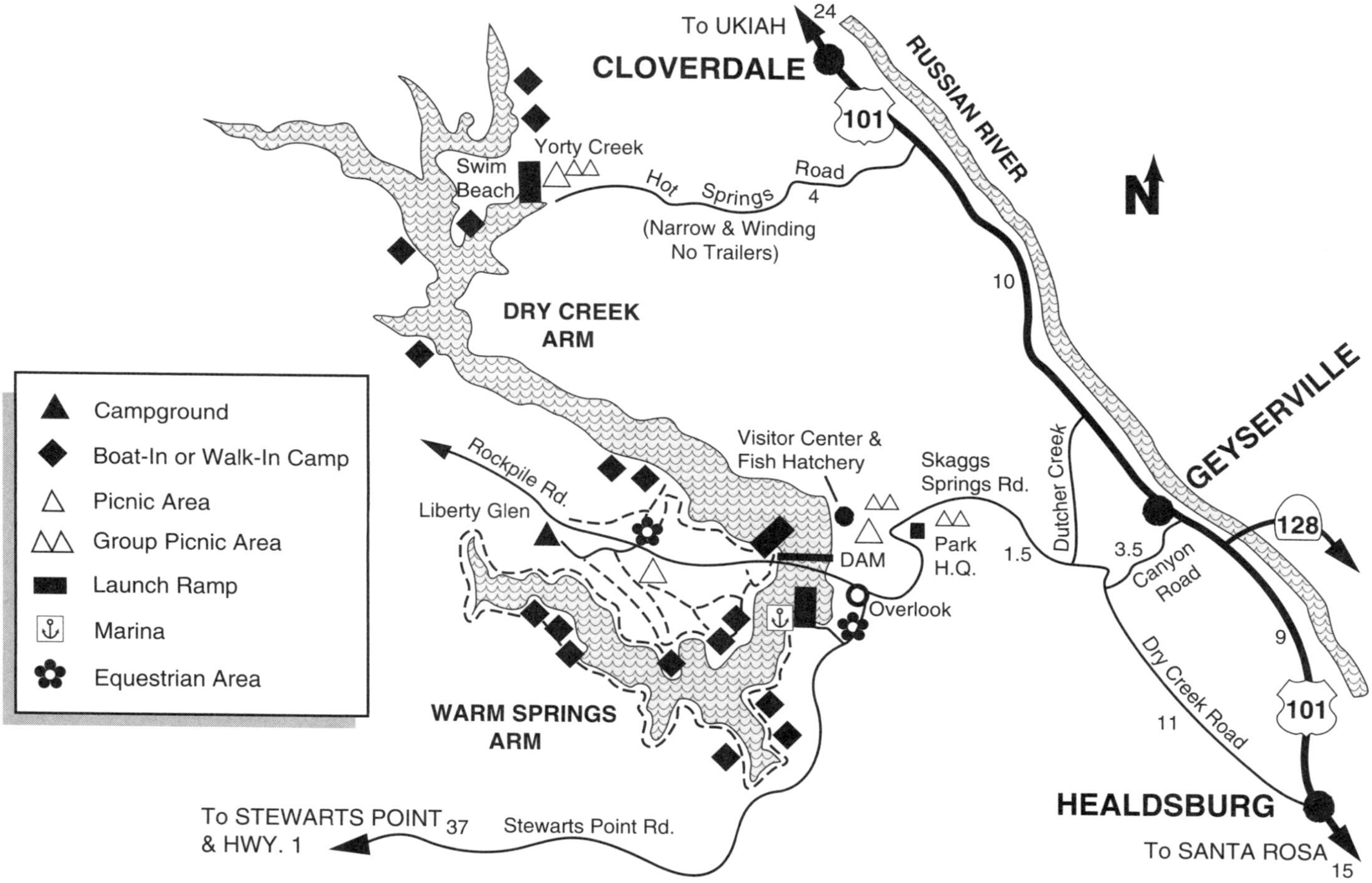

To UKIAH
24
CLOVERDALE
101
RUSSIAN RIVER
N
Yorty Creek
Swim Beach
Hot Springs Road
4
(Narrow & Winding
No Trailers)
10
DRY CREEK
ARM
GEYSERVILLE
128
Campground
Boat-In or Walk-In Camp
Picnic Area
Group Picnic Area
Launch Ramp
Marina
Equestrian Area
Rockpile Rd.
Visitor Center &
Fish Hatchery
Skaggs
Springs Rd.
Dutcher Creek
Liberty Glen
DAM
Park
H.Q.
1.5
3.5
Canyon Road
Overlook
9
Dry Creek Road
11
101
WARM SPRINGS
ARM
HEALDSBURG
To STEWARTS POINT
& HWY. 1
37
Stewarts Point Rd.
To SANTA ROSA
15

INFORMATION: U.S. Army Corps of Engineers, 3333 Skaggs Springs Rd., Geyserville 95441—Ph: (707) 431-4590

CAMPING	BOATING	RECREATION	OTHER
Liberty Glen:	Open to all Boating	Fishing: Large &	Lake Sonoma Resort/Marina
113 Dev. Sites for	Designated Areas for	Smallmouth Bass,	520 Mendocino Ave.
Tents & R.V.s	Waterskiing	Channel Catfish &	Suite 200
1st Come Basis	Public Launch Ramps	Redear Sunfish, Bluegill	Santa Rosa 95401
	Full Service Marina	Picnic Areas	Ph: (707) 433-2200
Reserve the Following Sites	Boat Gas	Group Picnic Sites	Snack Bar
Ph: (877) 444-6777	Slip Rentals	Reservations	General Store
2 Group Camp Sites	Boat Storage	Swim Beach	Beer & Wine Gardens
109 Boat-in or Walk-in	Boat Rentals	Hiking, Mountain Biking &	Bait & Tackle
Primitive Sites	Launch Ramp	Equestrian Trails	
No Water	Hand Launch at	2 Equestrian	Visitor Center &
Permits Required	Yorty Creek	Staging Areas	Fish Hatchery
Call for Fee Info.			

SPRING LAKE and LAKE RALPHINE

Spring Lake is under the jurisdiction of the Sonoma County Regional Parks Department. The 320-acre Park has an Environmental Discovery Center, campground, picnic areas, a summer swim lagoon and well-maintained trails. This is a popular equestrian area. The 72 surface-acre Lake is open to non-powered boating except for electric motors. Lake Ralphine is within the City of Santa Rosa's Howarth Park. This day-use facility has numerous children's attractions and various boat rentals. Lake Ralphine allows non-powered boating with sailing being a special attraction. There is a warm water fishery in addition to planted trout in the winter at Lake Ralphine. A bicycle path connects these parks.

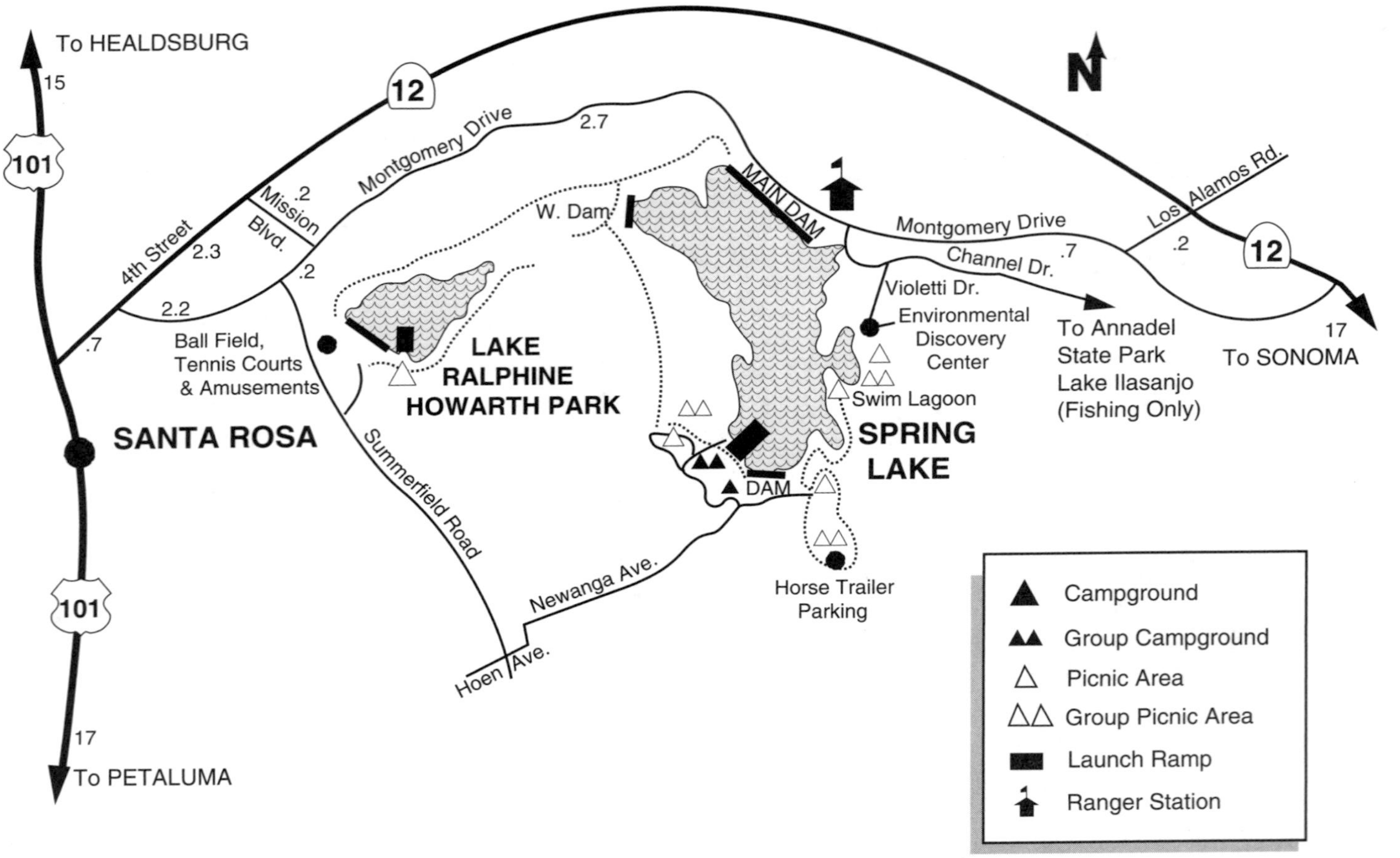
To HEALDSBURG
15
101
12
Montgomery Drive
2.7
N
Los Alamos Rd.
.2
Mission
Blvd.
4th Street
2.3
W. Dam
MAIN DAM
Montgomery Drive
Channel Dr.
.7
12
.2
2.2
.7
Ball Field,
Tennis Courts
& Amusements
LAKE
RALPHINE
HOWARTH PARK
Violetti Dr.
Environmental
Discovery
Center
To Annadel
State Park
Lake Ilasanjo
(Fishing Only)
17
To SONOMA
Swim Lagoon
SANTA ROSA
SPRING
LAKE
DAM
Summerfield Road
Newanga Ave.
Horse Trailer
Parking
Hoen Ave.
101
17
To PETALUMA
Campground
Group Campground
Picnic Area
Group Picnic Area
Launch Ramp
Ranger Station

INFORMATION: Spring Lake, 5390 Montgomery Dr., Santa Rosa 95409—Ph: (707) 539-8092

CAMPING	BOATING	RECREATION	OTHER
27 Dev. Sites for Tents & R.V.s - No Hookups Fee: $19 Open Daily in Summer Fri., Sat., Sun. in Winter Disposal Station Group Camp to 100 People No R.V.s Reservations: Ph: (707) 565-2267 Day Use Fee: $5 - $6	Spring Lake: Row, Sail, Canoe, Inflatables (2 Chamber), Electric Motors Launch Ramp Rentals: Row, Canoe, Paddle Boats, Sailboats (Summer) Lake Ralphine: Rentals: As Above Open Tues. - Sunday in Summer (Weekends in Fall & Spring)	Fishing: Trout, Bluegill, Redear Sunfish & Bass Swim Lagoon (Summer) Picnic Areas - Group Reservations: Ph: (707) 565-2041 Hiking & Equestrian Trails Paved Bicycle Trails Tennis Courts - Ralphine No Swimming in Lake Ralphine	Howarth Park: Santa Rosa Rec. & Parks Dept. Ph: (707) 543-3282 Day Use Only Miniature Steam Train Pony Rides Merry-Go-Round Land of Imagination Play Areas

Lake Berryessa is one of California's largest man-made Lakes, with over 13,000 surface acres and 165 miles of shoreline. Surrounding hills are covered with oak and madrone trees. Fishing is good year around and the angler will find trophy trout, three species of bass and a good warm water fishery. At this time, the Bureau of Reclamation is in the process of awarding new contracts for privately operated facilities on the west side of the Lake Berryessa. Lake Hennessy is off Highway 128 to the west. Under the jurisdiction of the City of Napa, this Lake is for day use only and has limited facilities. Lake Solano, southeast of Berryessa, is under Solano County jurisdiction. There are swim lagoons, picnic sites, boat rentals and a campground for tents and R.V.s. Non-powered boating and trout fishing are popular.

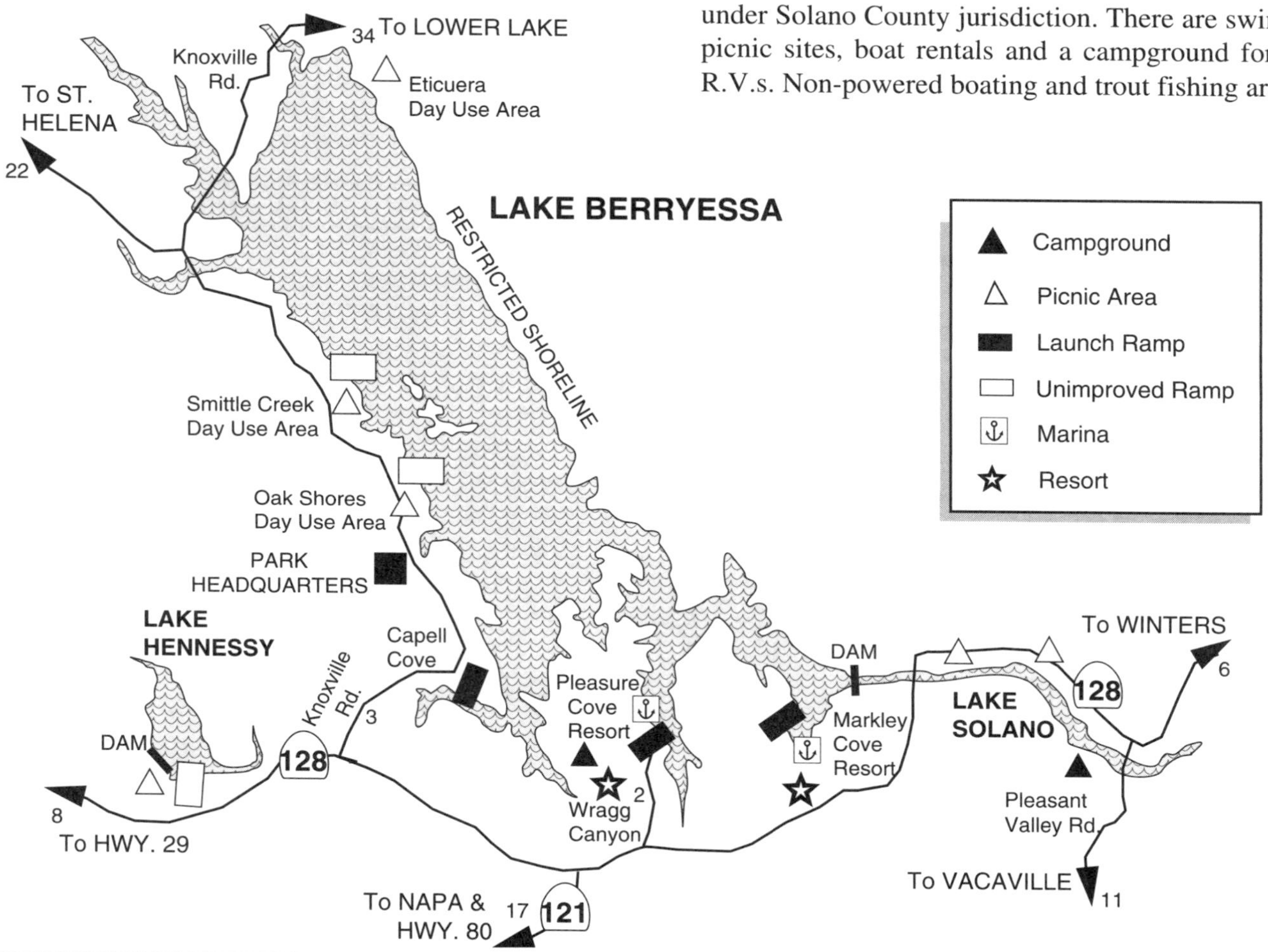
34 To LOWER LAKE
Knoxville Rd.
Eticuera Day Use Area
To ST. HELENA
22
LAKE BERRYESSA
RESTRICTED SHORELINE
Campground
Picnic Area
Launch Ramp
Unimproved Ramp
Marina
Resort
Smittle Creek Day Use Area
Oak Shores Day Use Area
PARK HEADQUARTERS
LAKE HENNESSY
Capell Cove
Knoxville Rd.
3
Pleasure Cove Resort
DAM
Markley Cove Resort
LAKE SOLANO
To WINTERS
6
128
DAM
128
8
To HWY. 29
2
Wragg Canyon
Pleasant Valley Rd.
To VACAVILLE
11
To NAPA & HWY. 80
17
121

INFORMATION: Bureau of Reclamation, 5520 Knoxville Rd., Napa 94558—Ph: (707) 966-2111

CAMPING	BOATING	RECREATION	OTHER
Pleasure Cove Resort & Marina 6100 Hwy. 128 Napa 94558 Ph: (707) 966-9600 140 R.V. & Tent Sites Full & Partial Hookups Fees: $30 - $35 Disposal Station Grocery Store Cabins	Lake Berryessa: Open to All Boating Full Service Marinas Launch Ramps, Boat Slips Rentals: Houseboats, Waterski Boats & PWCs Ph: (800) 255-5561 Lake Solano: Non-Power Boating Only - Launch Ramp Lake Hennessy: 10 HP Maximum	Fishing: Rainbow & Brown Trout, Large & Smallmouth Bass, Catfish, Bluegill Swimming Picnicking Hiking Trails	Markley Cove Resort 7251 Highway 128 Lake Berrryessa 94558 Ph: (707) 966-2134 Launch Ramp, Dock, Store, Boat & Tackle Lake Solano Parks Dept. 8685 Pleasant Valley Rd. Winters 95694 Ph: (530) 795-2990 90 R.V. & Tent Sites Full & Partial Hookups Picnicking

LAKE AMADOR

Lake Amador is at an elevation of 485 feet in the Sierra foothills, one mile east of the historic town of Buena Vista. The surface area of the Lake is 400 acres with 14 miles of shoreline surrounded by black oak-covered hills. Brush along the water's edge provides a thriving warm water fishery. Northern California records have been set for bass. Trout and catfish are also large and plentiful. This is a nice boating facility with good winds for sailing. No waterskiing or PWCs are allowed. The Lake is open to boating and fishing 24 hours a day and fishing boats with motors can be rented. Camping facilities include full hookups for R.V.s. Amador is a good family recreation area and the angler's dream.

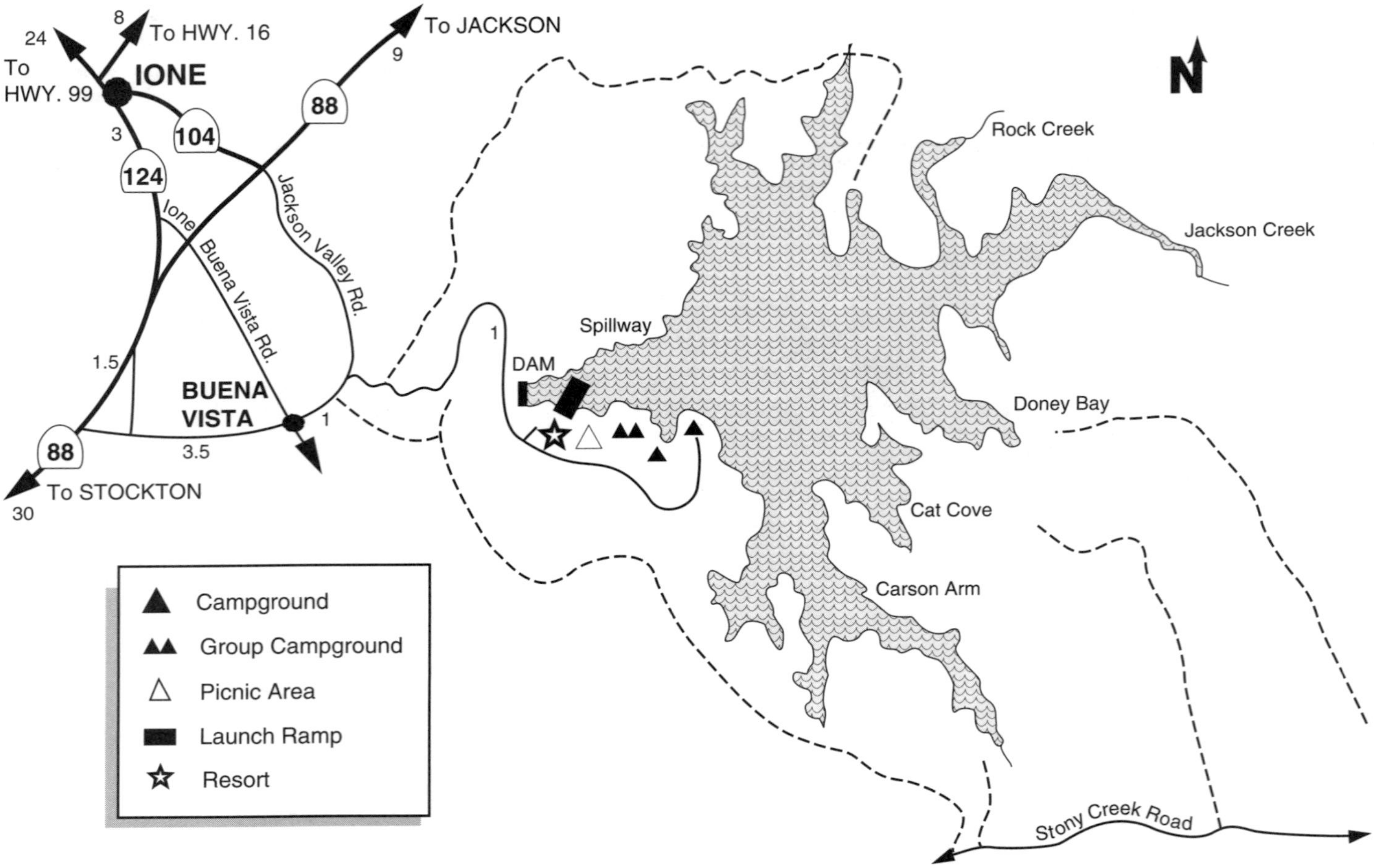
To HWY. 16
8
24
To
HWY. 99
IONE
To JACKSON
9
88
104
3
124
Ione
Buena Vista Rd.
Jackson Valley Rd.
1.5
BUENA
VISTA
1
3.5
88
To STOCKTON
30
1
Spillway
DAM
Rock Creek
Jackson Creek
Doney Bay
Cat Cove
Carson Arm
Stony Creek Road
N
Campground
Group Campground
Picnic Area
Launch Ramp
Resort

INFORMATION: Lake Amador Resort, 7500 Lake Amador Dr., Ione 95640—Ph: (209) 274-4739

CAMPING	BOATING	RECREATION	OTHER
150 Dev. Sites for Tents & R.V.s to 40 feet Partial Hookups Fee: $25 73 Full Hookups for R.V.s & Trailers to 30 ft. Fee: $30 Disposal Station Group Camp to 50 Vehicles Reservations for All Sites Suggested Reservation Fee: $5 Day Use Fee: $9	Power, Row, Canoe, Sail, Windsurf & Inflatables *No Waterskiing or PWCs* Launch Ramp - $7 Rentals: Fishing Boats	Fishing: Trout, Largemouth Bass, Catfish, Bluegill, Crappie & Perch Fishing Fee: $8 per Day per Person Swimming Picnicking	Restaurant - Seasonal General Store Bait & Tackle Propane R.V. Storage Club House & Recreation Room

LAKE PARDEE

Lake Pardee is at an elevation of 568 feet in the heart of the "Mother Lode Country" and the historic gold towns. Under the jurisdiction of East Bay Municipal Water District, this popular fishing Lake in the Sierra foothills has a surface area of 2,200 acres surrounded by 43 miles of rolling woodland. Trout and Kokanee are the primary gamefish. The angler will find a good smallmouth and largemouth bass fishery along with catfish. Waterskiing and PWCs are not allowed. The full service marina includes a 10-lane launch ramp. This is a nice family area with a large campground, two swimming pools (no lake swimming), picnic area and store.

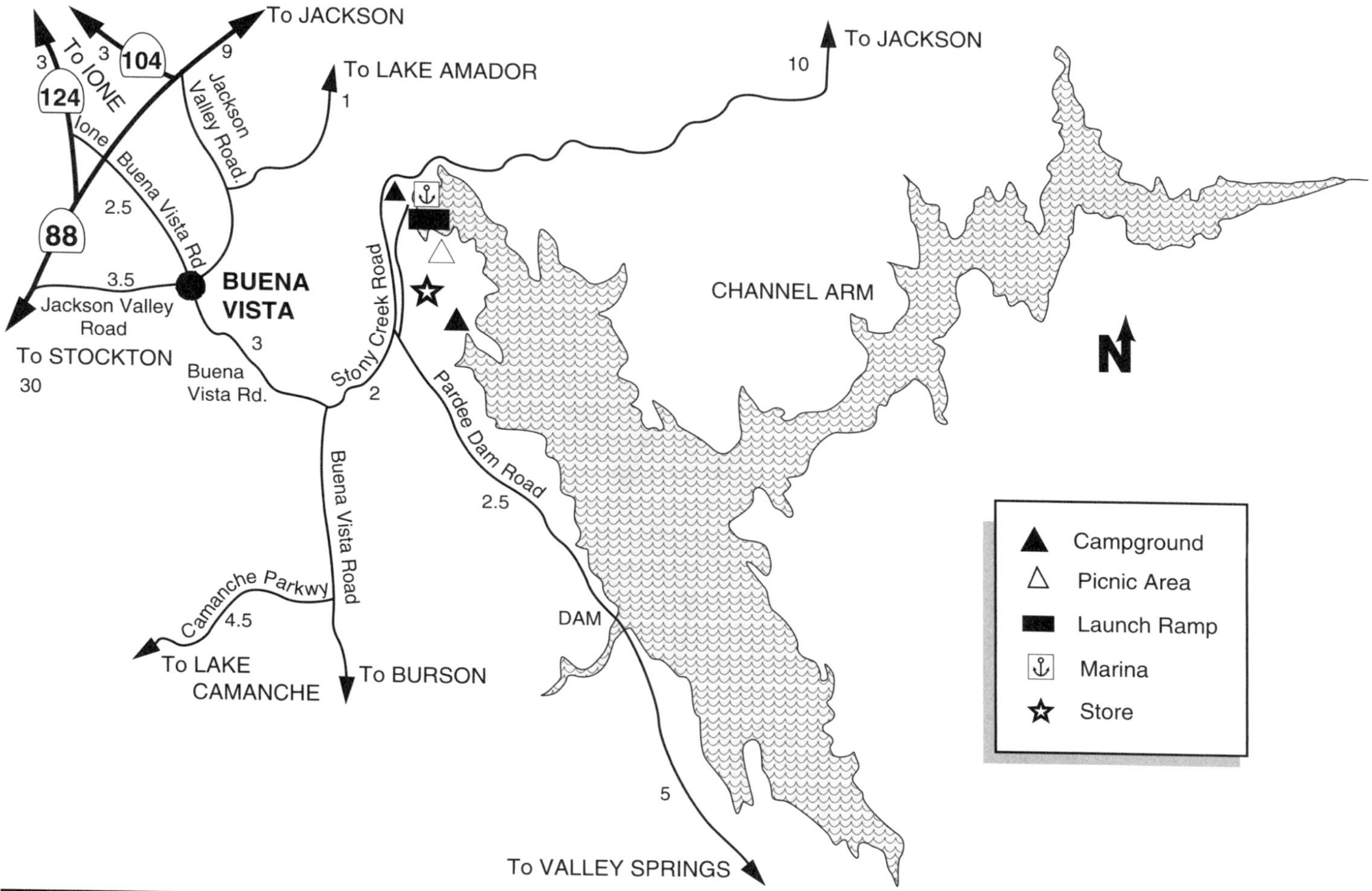
To JACKSON
To IONE
104
124
88
3
3
9
Jackson Valley Road
To LAKE AMADOR
1
To JACKSON
10
Ione Buena Vista Rd
2.5
3.5
BUENA VISTA
Jackson Valley Road
To STOCKTON
30
3
Buena Vista Rd.
Stony Creek Road
2
Pardee Dam Road
2.5
Buena Vista Road
Camanche Parkwy
4.5
To LAKE CAMANCHE
To BURSON
DAM
5
To VALLEY SPRINGS
CHANNEL ARM
N
Campground
Picnic Area
Launch Ramp
Marina
Store

INFORMATION: Pardee Lake Recreation, 4900 Stony Creek Rd., Ione 95640—Ph: (209) 772-1472

CAMPING	BOATING	RECREATION	OTHER
141 Dev. Sites for Tents & R.V.s Fee: $20 12 Dev. R.V. Sites With Full Hookups Fee: $29 Reservations Required Large Parking Area for Self-Contained R.V.s Disposal Station Day Use: $8	Power, Row, Canoe, Sail & Inflatables No Waterskiing or PWCs *Check for Current Boating Regulations* Full Service Marina Ph: (209) 772-8108 Launch Ramp: $7 Rentals: Fishing Boats & Pontoons Docks, Berths, Moorings, Gas Dry Storage	Fishing: Rainbow Trout, Kokanee Salmon, Catfish, Bluegill, Crappie, Small & Largemouth Bass Fishing Permit: $3.50 16 and Older Fishing Float Swimming - 2 Pools Picnicking Bicycle Trails	Snack Bar Coffee Shop Grocery Store Gas & Propane *No Body Contact With the Lake Water*

LAKE CAMANCHE

Lake Camanche is at an elevation of 235 feet in the foothills of the Sierra Nevada. This large Reservoir, part of the East Bay Municipal Utility District, has a surface area of 12 square miles with a shoreline of 53 miles. Camanche is located in the famous "Mother Lode Country," and panning for gold is popular in the spring when streams are high. Indian grave sites are visible along the shoreline. The water is warm and clear perfect for water sports. Known for bass fishing, there is also a variety of other good catches. The Resorts at Northshore and Southshore offer camping, marine and many recreation facilities. There are over 15,000 acres of park lands for the hiker and equestrian. Lake Camanche has complete facilities and is within easy access from the San Francisco Bay Area.

...Continued....

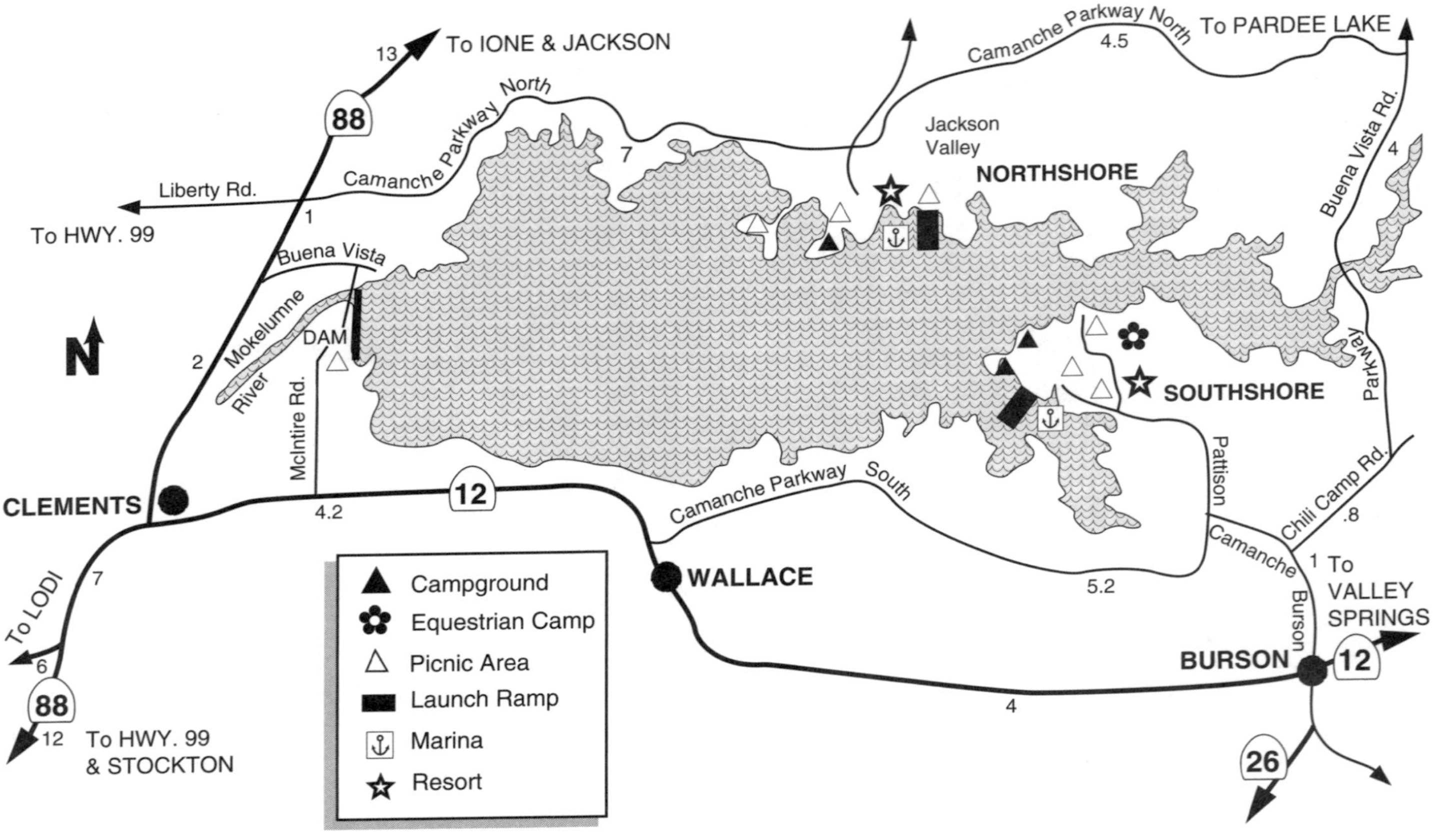

13
To IONE & JACKSON
88
Camanche Parkway North
4.5
To PARDEE LAKE
Jackson
Valley
NORTHSHORE
7
Liberty Rd.
To HWY. 99
1
Buena Vista
Buena Vista Rd.
4
Mokelumne
River
DAM
N
2
McIntire Rd.
SOUTHSHORE
Parkway
Pattison
Chili Camp Rd.
.8
CLEMENTS
4.2
12
Camanche Parkway South
WALLACE
5.2
Camanche
1 To
VALLEY
SPRINGS
Burson
BURSON
12
To LODI
7
6
88
12 To HWY. 99
& STOCKTON
4
26
Campground
Equestrian Camp
Picnic Area
Launch Ramp
Marina
Resort

INFORMATION: Camanche Recreation Company Northshore and South Shore - See Next Page

CAMPING	BOATING	RECREATION	OTHER
Over 600 Dev. Sites for Tents & R.V.s: $25 With Hookups at South Shore Only Fee: $38 Group Sites: 8 to 72 People Fee: $38 to $225 Equestrian Group Camp Boat-In Campsites Reservation Fee: $8.50 Disposal Stations	Power, Row, Canoe, Sail, Waterski, PWCs & Inflatables *No Waterskiing in* *Upper Lake* Full Service Marinas Launch Ramps: $7 - $8 Rentals: Fishing, Row, Motor Boats & Pontoons Fishing Rods & Reels Dry Storage Covered Slips	Fishing: Black Bass, Catfish, Bluegill, Crappie, Kokanee, Sunfish, Carp Trout Pond at South Shore Fishing Access: $4 Swimming Picnicking Tennis Courts Hiking & Equestrian Trails Horse Camp Clay Shooting Hunting Preserve	Rentals: Cottages up to 12 People $140 & Up Motel Rooms & Motorhomes $70 & Up Day Use Fee: $9.50 & Up See Next Page For Details

CAMANCHE RECREATION COMPANY
NORTH SHORE
2000 Camanche Rd., Ione, 95640
Ph: (866) 763-5121 or Ph: (209) 763-5121

219 Dev. Sites for Tents & R.V.s
No Hookups
Fee: $26 & Up
Group Campground - 1 for 12 People,
1 for 24 People & 2 for 72 People each.
Disposal Station, Trailer Storage, Playgrounds,
Store, Coffee Shop, Clubhouse.
Group Reservations for Camping or Picnicking.

Full Service Marina—Ph: (209) 763-5166
6 Lane Launch Ramp - Fee: $7 - $8
Boat Rentals: Fishing Boats & Pontoons,
Storage, Berths, Moorings.

Information—Ph: (209) 763-5166.
Housekeeping Cottages for 2 to 12 People
Motel Rooms & Mobile Home Rentals
From $70 and Up
Tennis Courts, Golf Courses, Wineries, Special Events.
Nearby: Bird Hunting Preserve and Club,
Two Mobile Home Parks.

CAMANCHE RECREATION COMPANY
SOUTHSHORE
11700 Wade Lane
Wallace, 95225
Ph: (209) 763-5178

263 Dev. Sites for Tents & R.V.s
Full Hookups - Fee: $26 - $45
120 Sites for Tents and Self-Contained R.V.s-Fee: $25
Group Campground to 64 People
Disposal Station, Store, Snack Bar, Clubhouse.
Turkey Hill Equestrian Group Camp
8 to 32 People and Horses
Paddocks & Horse Washing Station
Available for Youth Groups when not
Reserved by Equestrians

Full Service Marina
Ph: (209) 763-5915
6-Lane Launch Ramp - Fee: $7 - $8
Boat Rentals: Fishing & Pontoon Boats,
Storage, Berths, Moorings.

Housekeeping Cottages,
Tennis Courts, Trout Pond, Mobile Home Park.

NEW HOGAN LAKE

New Hogan Lake, about 700 feet in elevation, is located in the oak-covered hills east of Stockton. The U.S. Army Corps of Engineers has jurisdiction over the Lake, the marine and camping facilities. The surface area is 4,400 acres with 50 miles of shoreline. New Hogan is an ideal location for fishing, water sports and wildlife viewing. In addition to fishing at the Lake, catch and release trout fishing is available at the Calaveras River below the dam. Included in the facilities are the River of Skulls interpretive trail, an 8-mile equestrian trail and a 5-mile mountain bike trail. Over 200 campsites are located at the north end of the Lake. Boat access only sites are at Deer Flat campground on the east side of New Hogan.

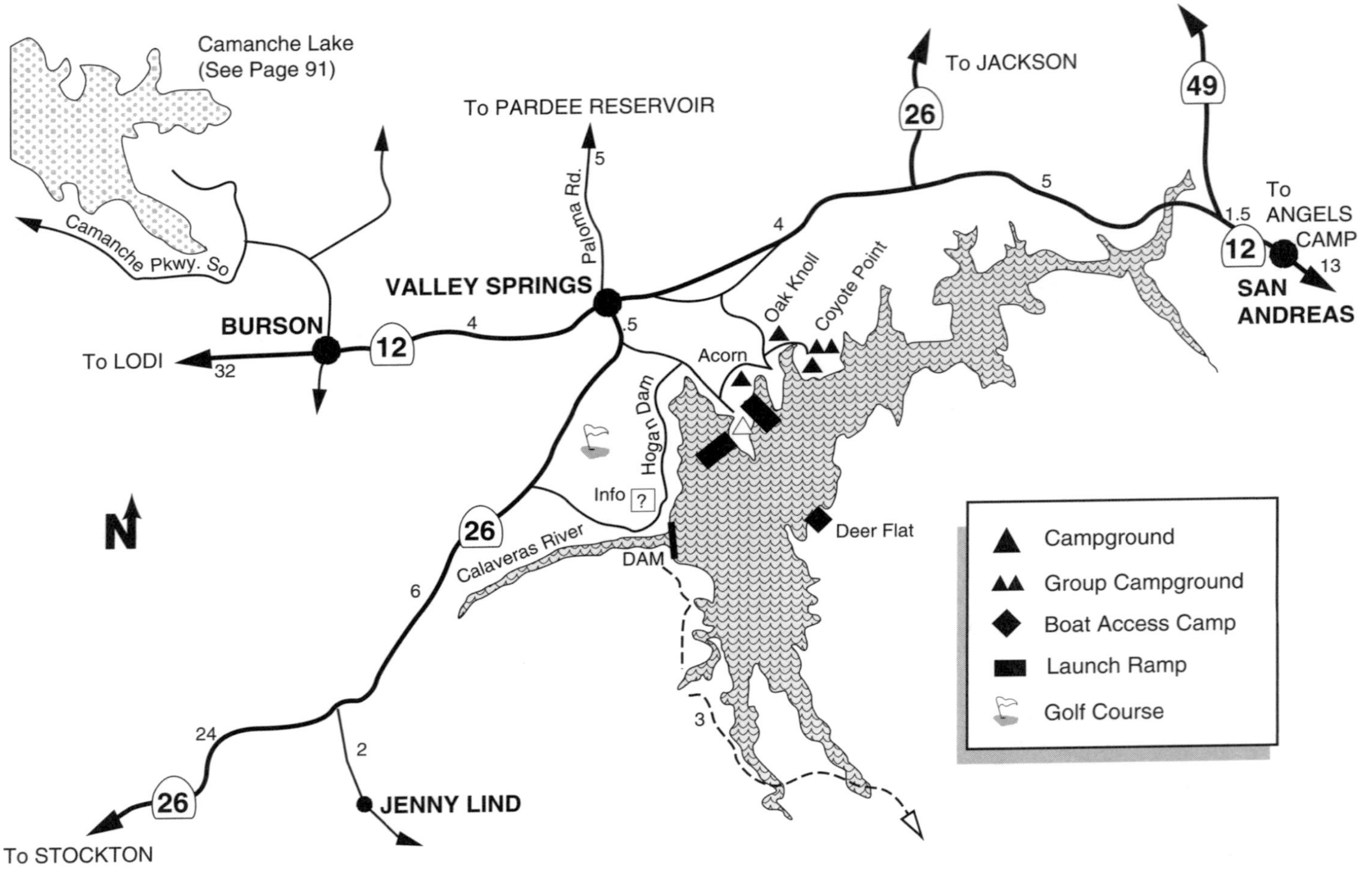

Camanche Lake
(See Page 91)
To PARDEE RESERVOIR
To JACKSON
26
49
Paloma Rd.
5
4
To
ANGELS
CAMP
1.5
12
13
SAN
ANDREAS
Camanche Pkwy. So
VALLEY SPRINGS
BURSON
12
To LODI
32
.5
Oak Knoll
Coyote Point
Acorn
Hogan Dam
Info
N
26
Calaveras River
DAM
Deer Flat
6
24
2
3
26
JENNY LIND
To STOCKTON
Campground
Group Campground
Boat Access Camp
Launch Ramp
Golf Course

INFORMATION: New Hogan Lake, 2713 Hogan Dam Rd., Valley Springs 95252—Ph: (209) 772-1343

CAMPING	BOATING	RECREATION	OTHER
Acorn: 129 Dev. Sites for Tents & R.V.s - $18 Oak Knoll: 49 Dev. Sites for Tents & R.V.s - $12 (No Showers) Group Camp Reserve: (877) 444-6777 Deer Flat: 30 Boat-In Only Campsites - No Water Fee: $8 No Vehicle Access	Power, Row, Canoe, Sail, Waterski, PWCs, Windsurf & Inflatable Night Boating: 15 MPH Launch Ramps Rentals: Fishing Boats & Motors, Patio Boats	Fishing: Catfish, Bluegill, Crappie, Black & Striped Bass Catch & Release Trout Fishing - Calaveras River Swimming Picnicking Hiking, Mountain Biking & Equestrian Trails Campfire Program Bird Watching	Disc Golf Course La Contenta Golf Course Nearby Full Facilities in Valley Springs

HIGHLAND and MOSQUITO LAKES - UTICA, UNION and SPICER RESERVOIRS

These scenic Lakes in the Stanislaus National Forest range in elevation from 6,460 feet to 8,730 feet at Ebbetts Pass. For those who enjoy a rustic and quiet environment, this area is a beautiful place to visit amid granite rocks and conifer forests. Mosquito and Highland Lakes have several campgrounds nearby. Spicer Reservoir, at 6,600 feet elevation, has a surface area of 2,000 acres. Facilities include campgrounds and a launch ramp. The eastern portion of this Reservoir is surrounded by the Carson-Iceberg Wilderness with numerous trails for the hiker and equestrian. Trout fishing can be excellent along the Mokelumne River near Highway 4 and at all the lakes and streams.

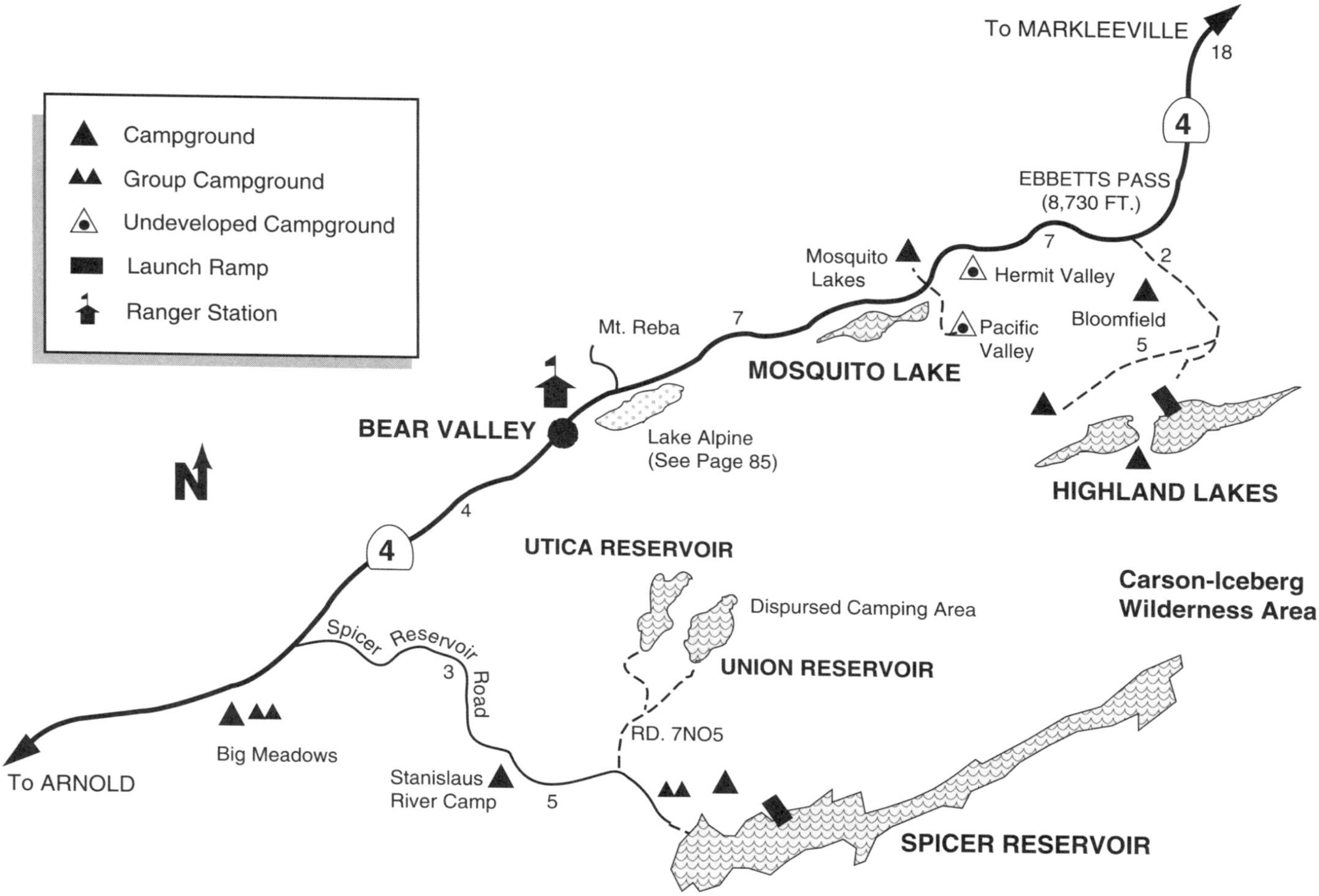

To MARKLEEVILLE
18
4
EBBETTS PASS
(8,730 FT.)
Campground
Group Campground
Undeveloped Campground
Launch Ramp
Ranger Station
Mosquito Lakes
7
2
Hermit Valley
Bloomfield
Pacific Valley
5
Mt. Reba
MOSQUITO LAKE
BEAR VALLEY
Lake Alpine
(See Page 85)
HIGHLAND LAKES
N
4
4
UTICA RESERVOIR
Carson-Iceberg
Wilderness Area
Dispursed Camping Area
UNION RESERVOIR
Spicer Reservoir Road
3
RD. 7NO5
Big Meadows
To ARNOLD
Stanislaus River Camp
5
SPICER RESERVOIR

INFORMATION: Calaveras Ranger District, 5519 Hwy. 4-P.O. Box 500, Hathaway Pines 95233—Ph: (209)795-1381

CAMPING	BOATING	RECREATION	OTHER
For Tents/R.V.s - Fees: $8 Highland Lakes: 35 Sites Bloomfield: 20 Sites Stanislaus River: 25 Sites Mosquito Lakes: 11 Sites No Water - Fee: $5 Big Meadows: 68 Tent/R.V. Sites to 27 feet-Fee: $17 & Group Campground Spicer: 43 Tent/R.V. Sites to 50 feet - Fee: $20 Hermit & Pacific Valley No Water - No Fee	Highland Lakes: Open to Boats But No Gas Motors 5 MPH Speed Limit Mosquito, Union & Utica: Small Hand Launch Only No Motors Spicer: Launch Ramp - Free Western Arm - 10 MPH Northern Arm - No Motorized Boating Canoes & Kayaks	Fishing: Rainbow, Eastern Brook & German Brown Trout Hiking & Equestrian Trails to Carson-Iceberg Wilderness Backpacking [Parking] No Swimming *Protect Fragile Shoreline Zone Camp at Least 100 Feet From Water's Edge*	Big Meadows Group Camp to 50 People Plus Some Single Sites Reservations: Ph: (877) 444-6777 Spicer Group Camp to 60 People Reservations: Ph: (209) 295-4512 Some Equestrian Camp Areas

PINECREST LAKE and LYONS LAKE

Pinecrest Lake is at an elevation of 5,600 feet in the Stanislaus National Forest. Also known as Strawberry Reservoir, Pinecrest has a surface area of 300 acres with 4 miles of mountainous, tree-covered shoreline. The USDA Forest Service operates over 300 campsites, a group camp, picnic sites, a paved launch ramp and a fishing pier. Pinecrest Lake Resort is a complete destination facility with extensive accommodations. This area has been a very popular vacation spot for families for many years. Reservations for Pinecrest and Pioneer Group Campgrounds are required during the summer season and all campsites are usually full. In season, trout are planted weekly. There are a number of lakes and streams within easy walking distance for the angler. A designated swim beach is adjacent to the picnic area. Lyons Lake, day-use only, is a separate facility operated by P.G.&E. There is a great hiking and fishing access trail along the Stanislaus River. *R.V.s and trailers not advised into Lyons Lake.*

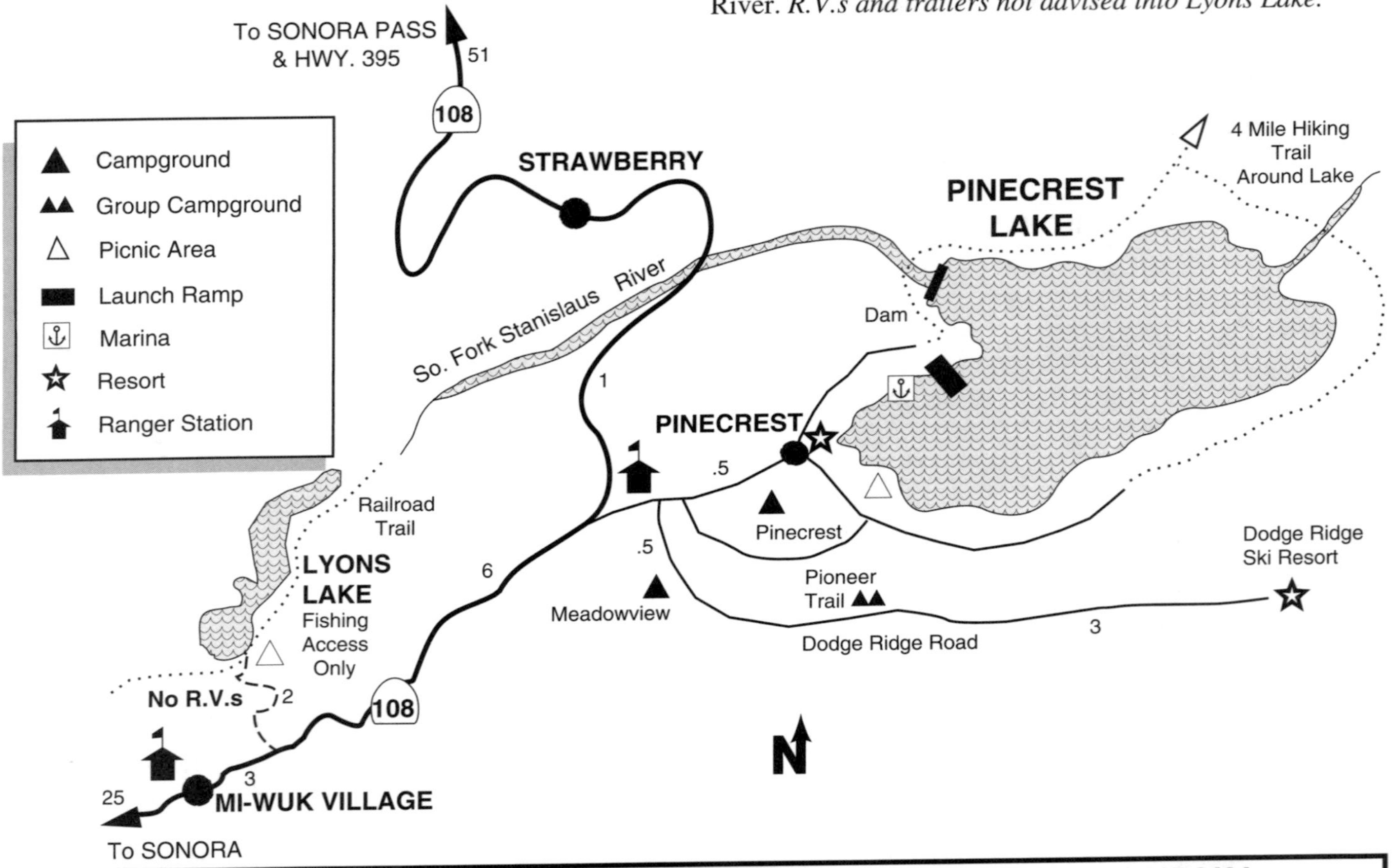

To SONORA PASS
& HWY. 395
51
108
Campground
Group Campground
Picnic Area
Launch Ramp
Marina
Resort
Ranger Station
STRAWBERRY
PINECREST
LAKE
4 Mile Hiking
Trail
Around Lake
So. Fork Stanislaus River
Dam
1
PINECREST
.5
Railroad
Trail
Pinecrest
.5
LYONS
LAKE
Fishing
Access
Only
6
Meadowview
Pioneer
Trail
Dodge Ridge
Ski Resort
Dodge Ridge Road
3
No R.V.s
2
108
N
25
3
MI-WUK VILLAGE
To SONORA

INFORMATION: Summit Ranger District, #1 Pinecrest Lake Rd., Pinecrest 95364—Ph: (209) 965-3434

CAMPING	BOATING	RECREATION	OTHER
200 Dev. Sites for Tents & R.V.s to 22 ft. Fee: $19 Pioneer Trail Group Camp 2 Sites - 50 People Each 1 Site - 100 People Reservations: Ph: (877) 444-6777 Meadowview - 100 Sites First Come Basis Fee: $14	Power, Row, Canoe, Sail, Windsurf & Inflatables *No Waterskiing or PWCs* Speed Limit - 20 MPH Full Service Marina at Pinecrest Lake Resort Launch Ramp Rentals: Fishing, Sail, Paddle & Motor Boats, Pontoons, Kayaks Docks, Slips, Gas *No Boating at Lyons Lake*	Fishing: Rainbow, Brown & Eastern Brook Trout Swimming - Beaches *No Swimming at Lyons* At Pinecrest Lake: Picnicking Hiking, Bicycling & Equestrian Trails Backpacking [Parking] Bicycle & Horse Rentals Amphitheatre: Campfire Programs & Movies	Pinecrest Lake Resort P.O. Box 1216 Pinecrest 95364 Ph: (209) 965-3411 Cabins, Condos & Motel, Restaurant, Snack Bar, Groceries, Bait & Tackle, Tennis Courts Lyons Lake - P.G.&E. Ph: (916) 386-5164 for Information Mi-Wuk Ranger Station: Ph: (209) 586-3234

BEARDSLEY and DONNELL RESERVOIRS, LEAVITT and KIRMAN LAKES

Ascending the western slopes of the Sierra Nevada above Sonora, these Lakes are along Highway 108 and range in elevation from 3,400 feet at Beardsley to 9,500 feet at Leavitt Lake. Many areas are difficult to reach. Donnell Reservoir is undeveloped with no facilities. The road into Donnell is rough and high-clearance vehicles are recommended. Beardsley Lake has picnic sites, a launch ramp and a campground on the northwest side of the dam. Facilities are limited. The road is steep and winding. These Reservoirs are within the Stanislaus National Forest.

Kirman is a designated Wild Trout Lake near the West Walker River. Barbless hooks are required and there is a two trout limit, minimum 16 inches. Numerous small lakes, including Leavitt Lake, are within the Humboldt-Toiyabe National Forest. Trails throughout the area are ideal for the equestrian, hiker and backpacker. Trout fishing is usually excellent. This all is beautiful high Sierrra country.

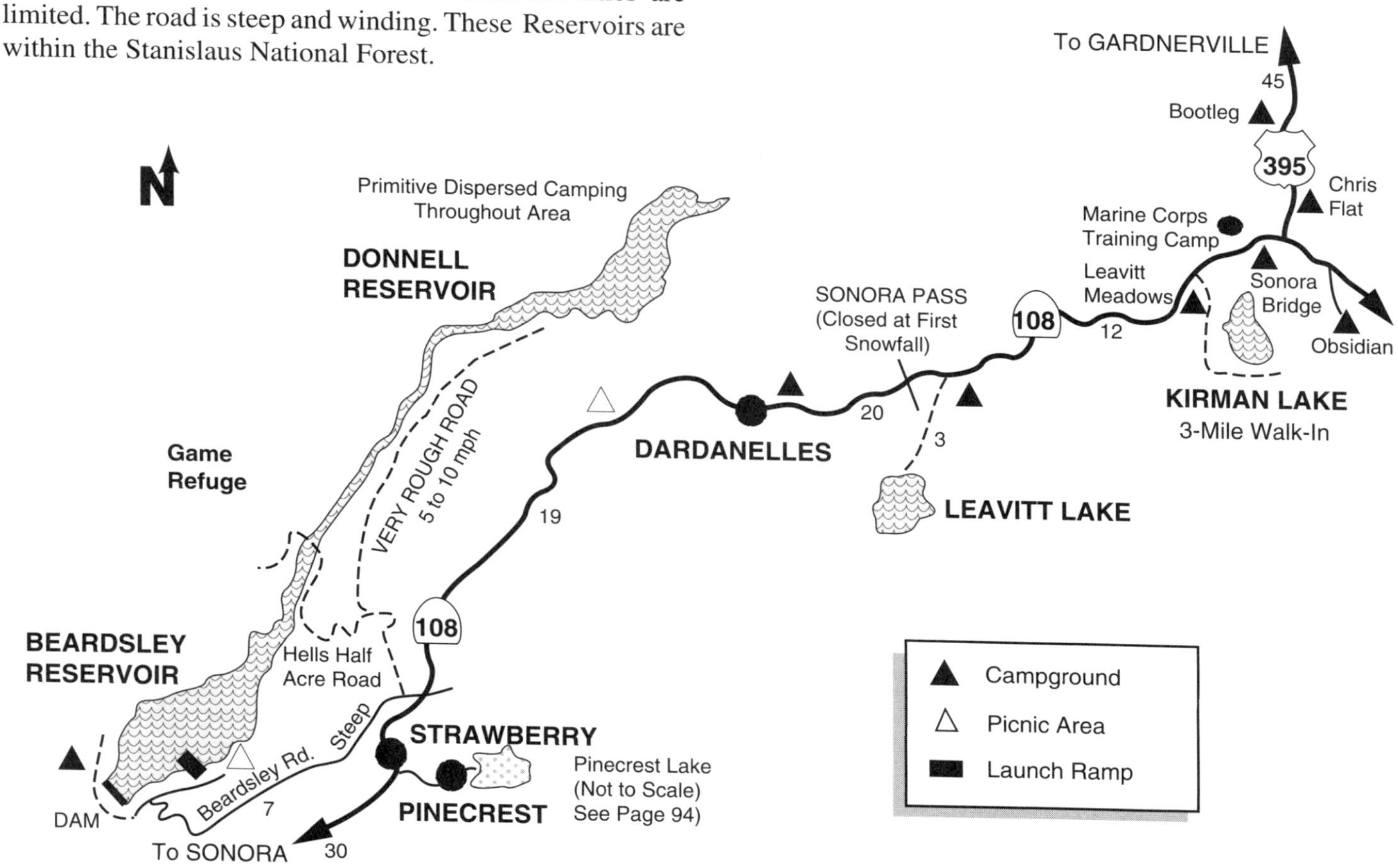

To GARDNERVILLE
45
Bootleg
395
Chris Flat
N
Primitive Dispersed Camping Throughout Area
Marine Corps Training Camp
DONNELL RESERVOIR
Leavitt Meadows
Sonora Bridge
SONORA PASS (Closed at First Snowfall)
108
12
Obsidian
KIRMAN LAKE
3-Mile Walk-In
20
3
DARDANELLES
Game Refuge
VERY ROUGH ROAD 5 to 10 mph
LEAVITT LAKE
19
108
BEARDSLEY RESERVOIR
Hells Half Acre Road
Campground
Picnic Area
Launch Ramp
Steep
STRAWBERRY
Beardsley Rd.
Pinecrest Lake (Not to Scale) See Page 94)
7
PINECREST
DAM
To SONORA
30

INFORMATION: Summit Ranger District, #1 Pinecrest Lake Rd., Pinecrest 95364—Ph: (209) 965-3434

CAMPING	BOATING	RECREATION	OTHER
Beardsley: 16 Primitive Sites for Tent/RVs to 22 ft. No Water - No Fee Dardenelle: 28 Dev. Sites for Tents/RVs to 28 ft. Fee: $18 Dispursed Camping in Area Cabins: Kennedy Meadows Resort Ph: (209) 965-3911	Beardsley Lake: Open to All Boats 2-Lane Paved Launch Ramp Leavitt Lake: Small Hand-Launch Boats Donnell: Boating Not Advised Difficult or Impossible Access	Fishing: Rainbow, German Brown & Brook Trout Picnicking Swimming Hiking & Backpacking Trails Equestrian Trails Mountain Bike Trails Pacific Crest Trail Through This Area Game Refuge Sonora Pass Closes at First Snowfall	East of Sonora Pass: Humboldt-Toiyabe N. F. Bridgeport Ranger District Ph: (760) 932-7070 Leavitt Meadows: 16 Sites Sonora Bridge: 24 Sites Fees: $15 Bootleg: 63 Sites - On the Walker River Chris Flat:15 Sites Fees: $17 Obsidian: 13 Sites Fee: $10 - No Water

CHERRY LAKE

Cherry Lake, sometimes called Cherry Valley Reservoir, is at an elevation of 4,700 feet in the rugged back country of the Stanislaus National Forest. This large, remote mountain Lake has a surface area of 4 square miles when full. This is a good trout fishery. Boating is limited and launching is subject to low water levels. This is truly a place to get away from it all. There is a campground, launch ramp and picnic area but no other facilities. Boat camping is permitted along the east side of Cherry Lake. Numerous small lakes and streams are within hiking distance and trout fishing can be exceptional. Backpackers will enjoy the expanse of this area. Roads in are winding and long so extra caution should be taken.

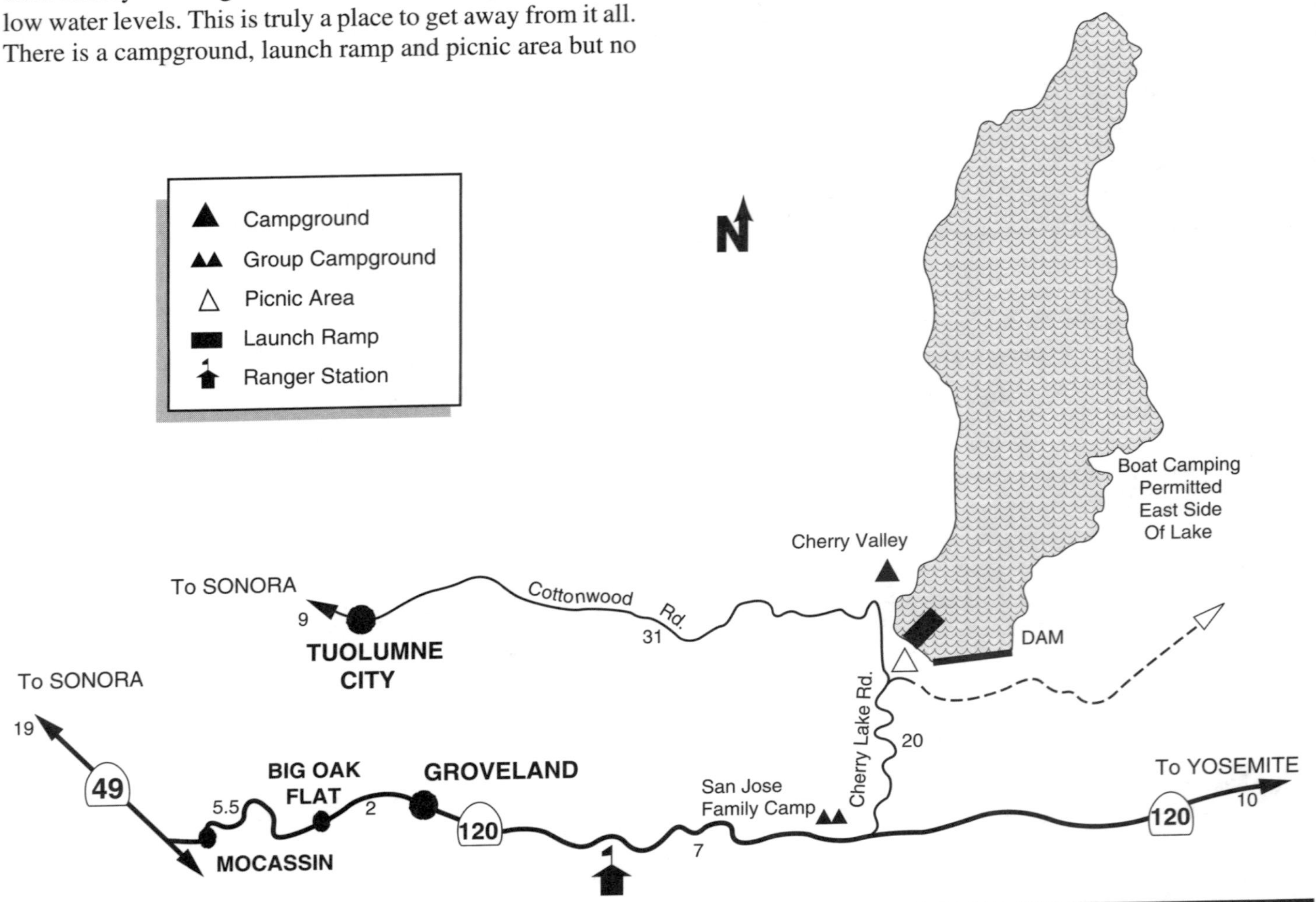

Campground
Group Campground
Picnic Area
Launch Ramp
Ranger Station
N
Boat Camping Permitted East Side Of Lake
Cherry Valley
DAM
To SONORA
9
TUOLUMNE CITY
Cottonwood Rd.
31
To SONORA
19
49
5.5
BIG OAK FLAT
2
GROVELAND
120
MOCASSIN
7
San Jose Family Camp
Cherry Lake Rd.
20
To YOSEMITE
120
10

INFORMATION: Groveland Ranger District, 24545 Highway 120, Groveland 95321—Ph: (209) 962-7825

CAMPING	BOATING	RECREATION	OTHER
46 Dev. Sites for Tents & R.V.s to 22 feet Fees: $17 - $34 Boat Camping Allowed on East Side of Lake	Power, Row, Canoe & Sail Paved Launch Ramp High Water Only	Fishing: Rainbow Trout Swimming - Designated Area Picnicking Picnic Sites Also Along Highway 120 Backpacking Hiking Trails Equestrian Trails	San Jose Family Camp Ph: (408) 871-3820 60 Tent Cabins - Some with Electricity Cafeteria-Style Meals No Services Available at Cherry Lake Full Facilities at Groveland, Tuolumne City and Yosemite National Park

LAKES ON HIGHWAY 395 FROM BRIDGEPORT TO BISHOP

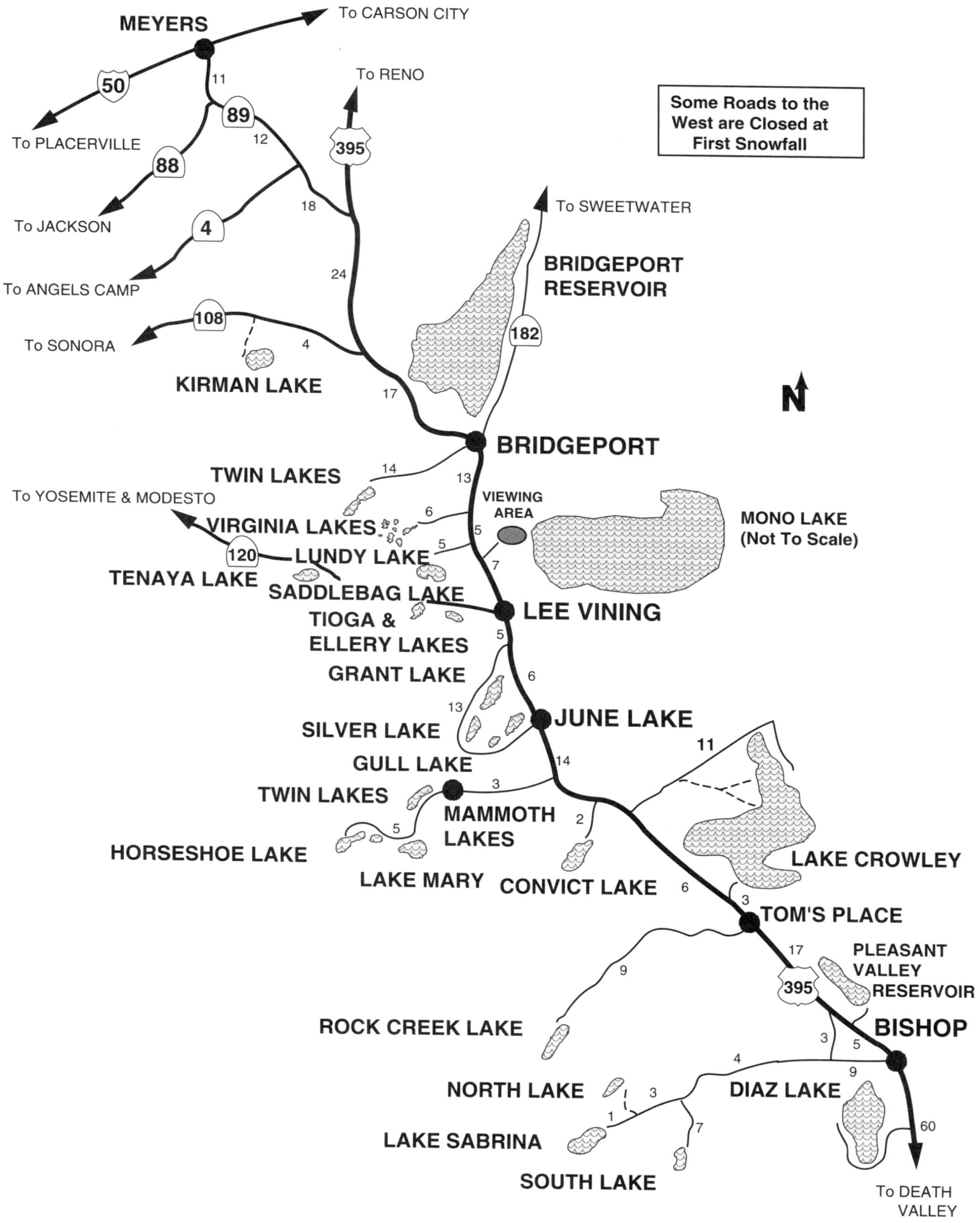

MEYERS
To CARSON CITY
50
11
To RENO
89
12
To PLACERVILLE
395
Some Roads to the West are Closed at First Snowfall
88
18
To JACKSON
4
To SWEETWATER
To ANGELS CAMP
24
BRIDGEPORT RESERVOIR
108
To SONORA
4
182
KIRMAN LAKE
17
N
BRIDGEPORT
TWIN LAKES
14
13
To YOSEMITE & MODESTO
VIEWING AREA
6
MONO LAKE (Not To Scale)
VIRGINIA LAKES
5
5
120
LUNDY LAKE
7
TENAYA LAKE
SADDLEBAG LAKE
LEE VINING
TIOGA & ELLERY LAKES
5
GRANT LAKE
6
13
JUNE LAKE
SILVER LAKE
11
14
GULL LAKE
3
TWIN LAKES
MAMMOTH LAKES
2
5
HORSESHOE LAKE
LAKE CROWLEY
LAKE MARY
CONVICT LAKE
6
3
TOM'S PLACE
17
PLEASANT VALLEY RESERVOIR
9
395
ROCK CREEK LAKE
BISHOP
3
5
4
9
NORTH LAKE
3
DIAZ LAKE
1
7
60
LAKE SABRINA
SOUTH LAKE
To DEATH VALLEY

BRIDGEPORT RESERVOIR

Bridgeport Reservoir is at an elevation of 6,500 feet in a large mountain meadow. This expansive Lake, over 4,000 surface acres, is famous for large trout, especially when trolling early in the season. In addition to the Reservoir, the angler will find 35 lakes and streams within 15 miles. The East Walker River, designated as a Wild Trout Stream, is considered prime waters for large German Browns. Artificial lures or flies are required. 18-inches is the minimum size with a 1-fish limit from the Dam to the bridge and a 2-fish limit from the bridge to the Nevada Border. The Lake is open to all boating. In addition to the facilities at Bridgeport Reservoir, the U.S. Forest Service operates campgrounds in this area.

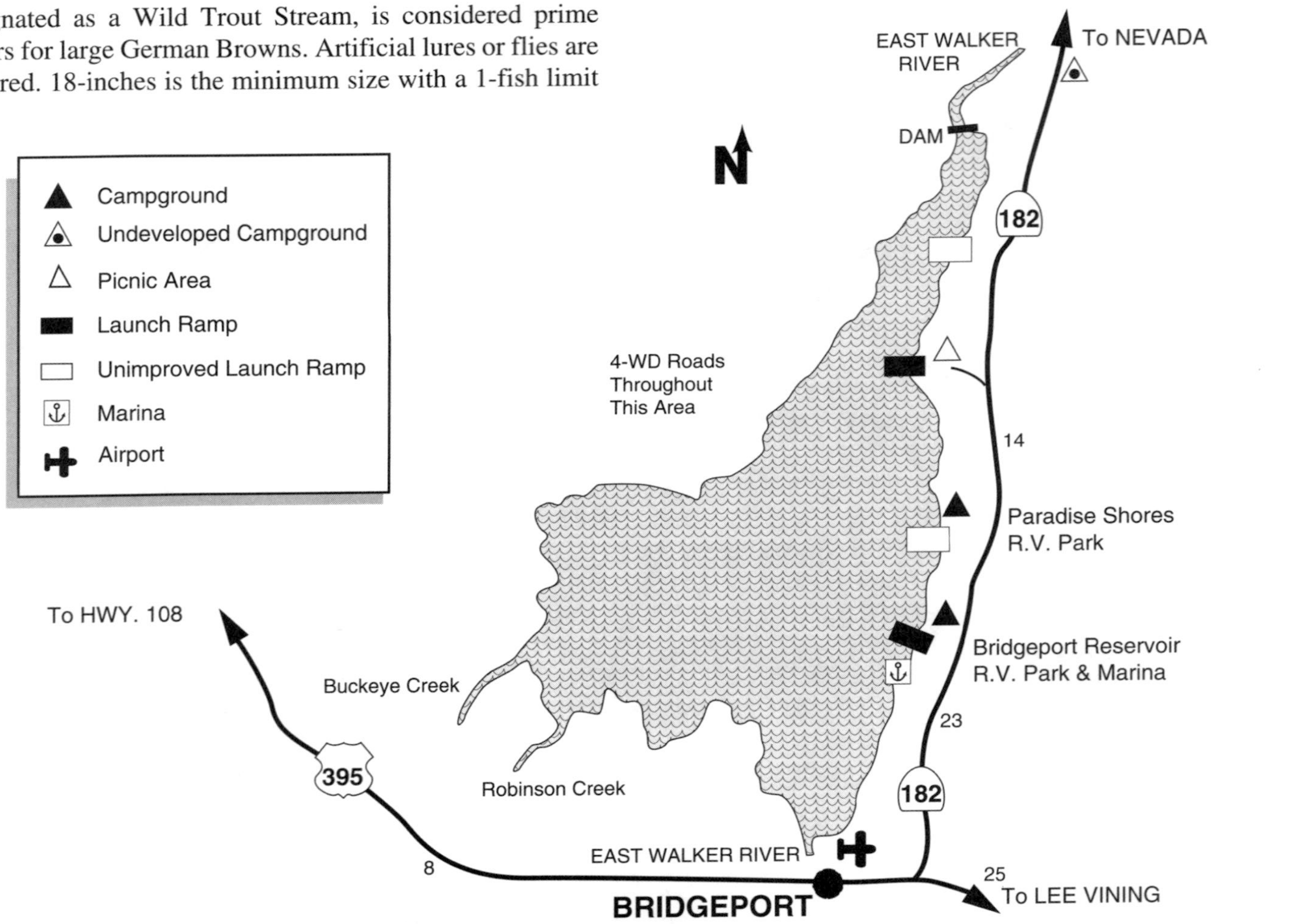
Campground
Undeveloped Campground
Picnic Area
Launch Ramp
Unimproved Launch Ramp
Marina
Airport
EAST WALKER RIVER
To NEVADA
DAM
N
182
4-WD Roads Throughout This Area
14
Paradise Shores R.V. Park
Bridgeport Reservoir R.V. Park & Marina
To HWY. 108
Buckeye Creek
395
Robinson Creek
23
182
EAST WALKER RIVER
8
25
To LEE VINING
BRIDGEPORT

INFORMATION: Bridgeport Reservoir R.V. Park & Marina or Paradise Shores Park - See Below

CAMPING	BOATING	RECREATION	OTHER
Bridgeport Reservoir R.V. Park & Marina 20 Tent/R.V. Sites - $18 14 R.V. Sites with Full Hookups - $30 Paradise Shores R.V. Park 37 R.V. Sites with Full Hookups - $30 Plus Tent Sites & 1 Fully Equipped Rental Trailer	Power, Row, Canoe, Sail & Inflatables Full Service Marina 2 Improved Ramps 2 Unimproved Ramps Rentals: Fishing Boats & Motors Docks, Berths, Moorings, Storage Overnight in Boat Permitted Anywhere	Fishing: Rainbow, German Brown & Cutthroat Trout & Sacramento Perch Swimming Backpacking [Parking] Bicycle Trails Horse Corrals at Bridgeport Reservoir R.V. Park	Bridgeport Reservoir R.V. Park & Marina P. O. Box 447 1845 Hwy. 182 Bridgeport 93517 Ph: (760) 932-7001 Paradise Shores R.V. Park P. O. Box 602 2399 Hwy. 182 Bridgeport 93517 Ph: (760) 932-7735

TWIN LAKES

Twin Lakes are 12 miles southwest of Bridgeport in the Eastern Sierra at an elevation of 7,000 feet. Campgrounds at the Lake and along Robinson Creek are part of the Humboldt-Toiyabe National Forest. Complete resort and marine facilities are available at Twin Lakes Resort at Lower Twin Lake and Annett's Mono Village Resort at Upper Twin Lake. The Hunewill Guest Ranch is a working cattle ranch offering accommodations, food and excursions on horseback into this beautiful area. These Lakes provide great fishing for large rainbow and brown trout. The backpacker can enjoy the nearby Hoover Wilderness with its many scenic trails, lakes and streams. This is one of the most beautiful areas in California and a great place for a vacation.

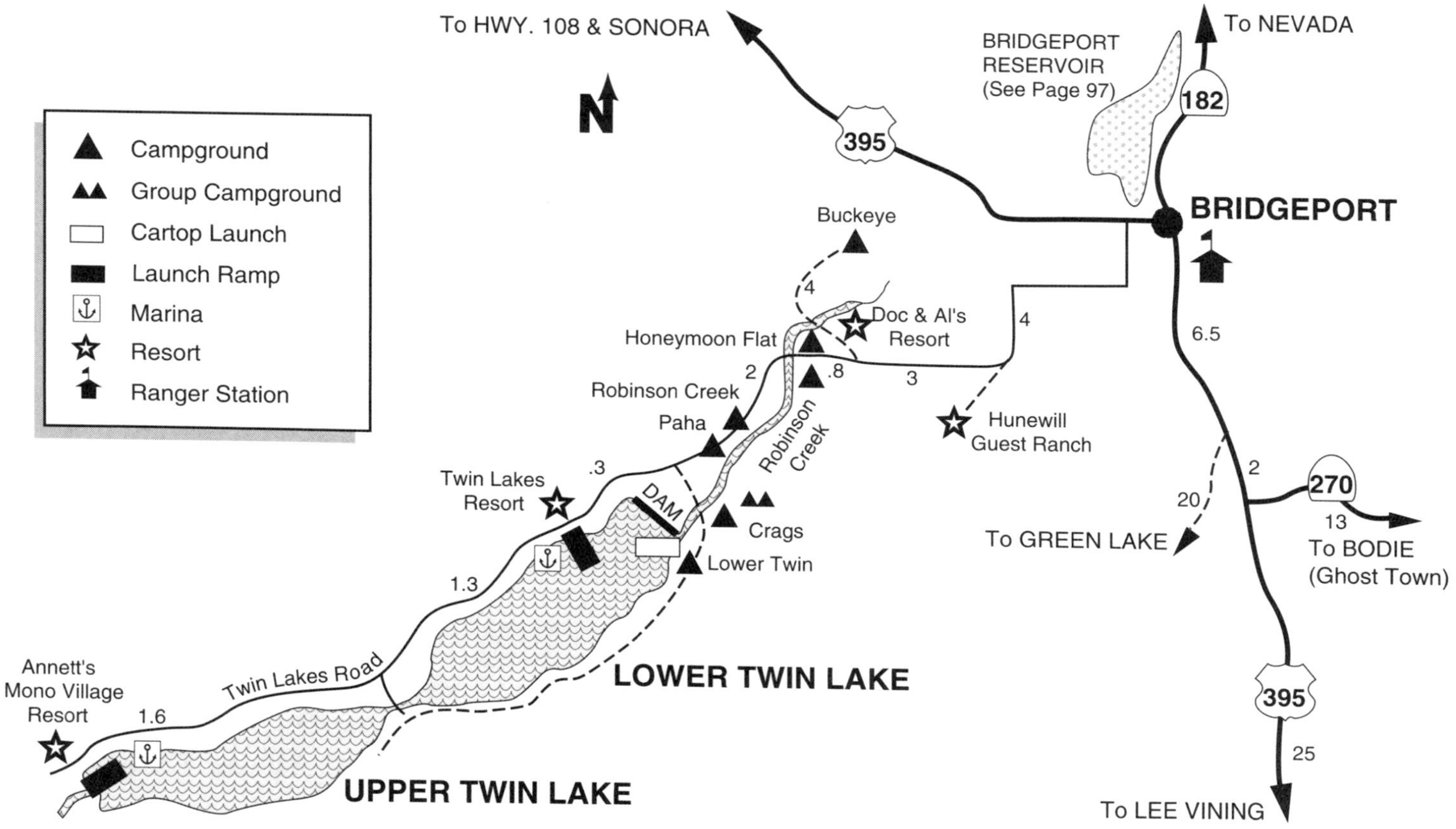

To HWY. 108 & SONORA
To NEVADA
BRIDGEPORT RESERVOIR (See Page 97)
182
395
N
Campground
Group Campground
Cartop Launch
Launch Ramp
Marina
Resort
Ranger Station
BRIDGEPORT
Buckeye
4
Doc & Al's Resort
4
Honeymoon Flat
6.5
2
.8
3
Robinson Creek
Paha
Robinson Creek
Hunewill Guest Ranch
.3
Twin Lakes Resort
DAM
2
270
20
Crags
13
To GREEN LAKE
To BODIE (Ghost Town)
Lower Twin
1.3
Annett's Mono Village Resort
Twin Lakes Road
LOWER TWIN LAKE
395
1.6
25
UPPER TWIN LAKE
To LEE VINING

INFORMATION: Bridgeport Ranger District, HC 62. Box 1000, Bridgeport 93517—Ph: (760) 932-7070

CAMPING	BOATING	RECREATION	OTHER
Dev. Sites for Tents/R.Vs Buckeye: 65 Sites Honeymoon Flat: 47 Sites Robinson Creek: 54 Sites Paha: 22 Sites Crags: 27 Sites Plus Group Camp Lower Twin: 15 Sites Fees: $15 - $17 Reservations: Ph: (877) 444-6777	Power, Row, Canoe, Sail & Inflatables Waterskiing at Upper Lake Only Full Service Marinas Launch Ramps Boat Rentals Docks	Fishing: Rainbow, German Brown, Eastern Brook & Kokanee Trout Picnicking Backpacking [Parking] Hoover Wilderness Hiking Trails Horseback Riding Trails	Annett's Mono Village Resort Ph: (760) 932-7071 300 Campsites, Cabins & Motel Units Full Resort Facilities Twin Lakes Resort Ph: (877) 932-7751 RV Sites & Cabins Full Resort Facilities Doc & Al's Resort Ph: (760) 932-7051 Hunewill Guest Ranch Ph: (760) 932-7710

VIRGINIA LAKES

Within the Virginia Lakes area, west of Highway 395, are numerous small Lakes at over 9,700 feet elevation. No swimming is allowed in these Lakes. Virginia Lake Resort, established in 1923, has a great variety of housekeeping cabins, a grocery store, fishing supplies and restaurant. The U. S. Forest Service operates campsites near Trumbull Lake. There is a Pack Station with horses available for scenic rides into the Hoover Wilderness and Yosemite National Park. A fisherman's paradise, the Lakes and many streams are within easy distance of the Resort. This is beautiful High Sierra country at its best.

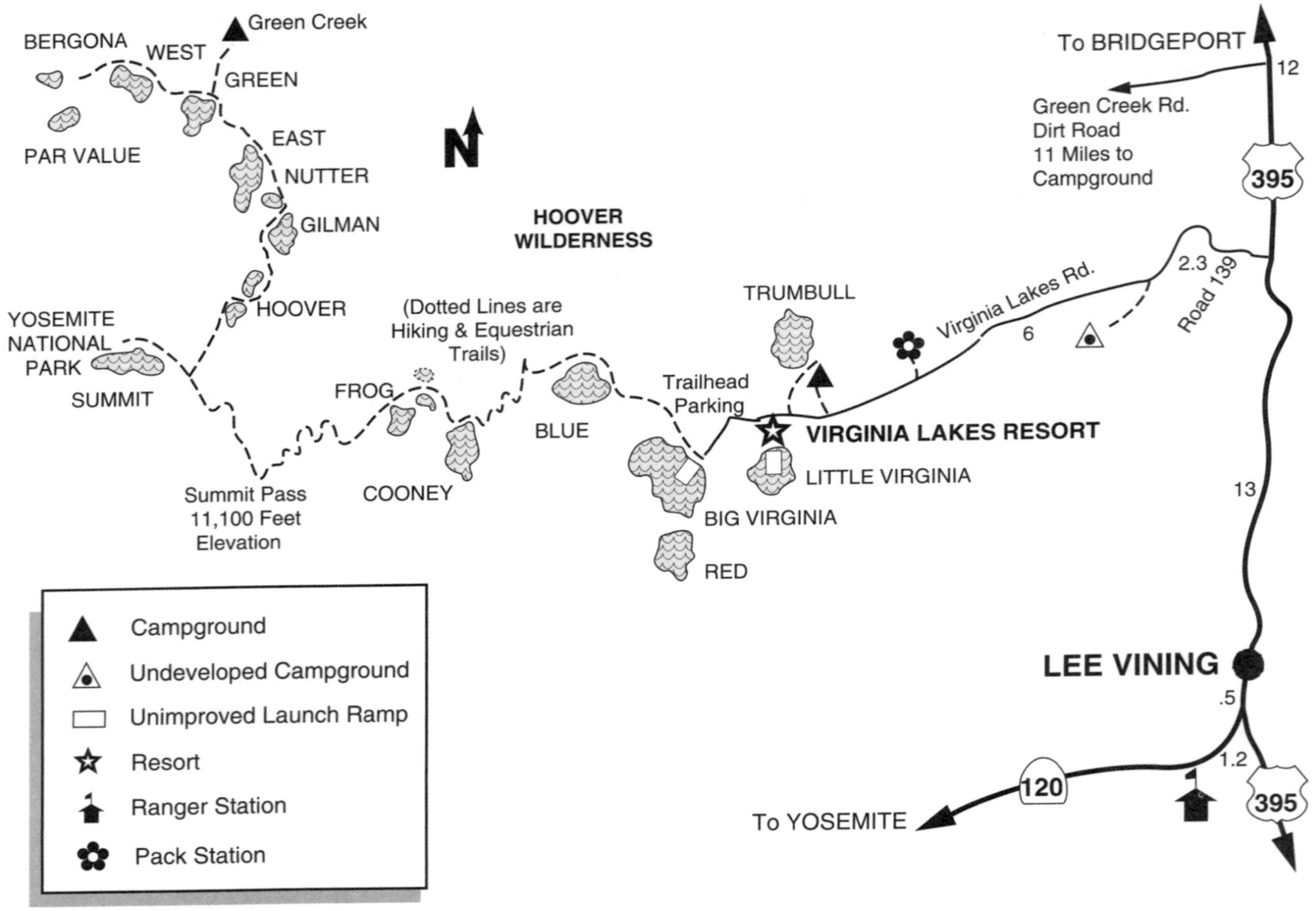

BERGONA
WEST
Green Creek
GREEN
PAR VALUE
EAST
NUTTER
GILMAN
HOOVER
N
HOOVER WILDERNESS
YOSEMITE NATIONAL PARK
SUMMIT
(Dotted Lines are Hiking & Equestrian Trails)
FROG
BLUE
COONEY
Summit Pass 11,100 Feet Elevation
TRUMBULL
Trailhead Parking
VIRGINIA LAKES RESORT
LITTLE VIRGINIA
BIG VIRGINIA
RED
Virginia Lakes Rd.
6
2.3
Road 139
To BRIDGEPORT
12
Green Creek Rd. Dirt Road 11 Miles to Campground
395
13
LEE VINING
.5
1.2
120
To YOSEMITE
395
Campground
Undeveloped Campground
Unimproved Launch Ramp
Resort
Ranger Station
Pack Station

INFORMATION: Bridgeport Ranger District, HC62, Box 1000, Bridgeport 93517—Ph: (760) 932-7070

CAMPING	BOATING	RECREATION	OTHER
Trumbull Lake: 45 Dev. Sites for Tents & R.V.s to 40 feet No Hookups Fee: $15 to $45 Green Creek: 11 Dev. Sites - Fee: $15 Plus 2 Group Sites 1 for 25 People - Fee: $52 1 for 30 People - Fee: $65 Reservations: Ph: (877) 444-6777	Electric Motors, Row, Canoe & Inflatables *No Gas Motors* 10 MPH Speed Limit Unimproved Launch Ramps Rentals: Fishing & Row Boats	Fishing: Rainbow, Golden, German Brown & Eastern Brook Trout Picnicking Hiking Trails 10 Lakes within a Mile of Resort Backpacking [Parking] Equestrian Trails All Expense Horse & Pack Camping Trips Day Rides & Group Tours	Virginia Lakes Resort HCR 62, Box 1065 Bridgeport 93517 Ph: (760) 647-6484 Cabins, Restaurant, Store, Bait & Tackle Virginia Lakes Pack Outfit Summer Phone: Ph: (760) 937-0326 Winter Phone: Ph: (925) 349-5074

Nestled in a high valley at an 7,800 feet elevation, Lundy Lake is at the trailhead to the 20 Lakes Basin. High, majestic mountains and a rocky, aspen and pine-covered shoreline provide spectacular scenery. The Lake is 1 mile long, 1/2 mile wide and covers 100 surface acres. The water is clear and cold. This is a popular fishing Lake for some very large brown trout. Miles of hiking trails include Lundy Canyon with beautiful waterfalls and wildflowers in Spring. Within the Inyo National Forest, the Lundy Canyon campground was originally the site of a sawmill and mining town in the 1880's. The rustic atmosphere is relaxed with good facilities at the Resort.

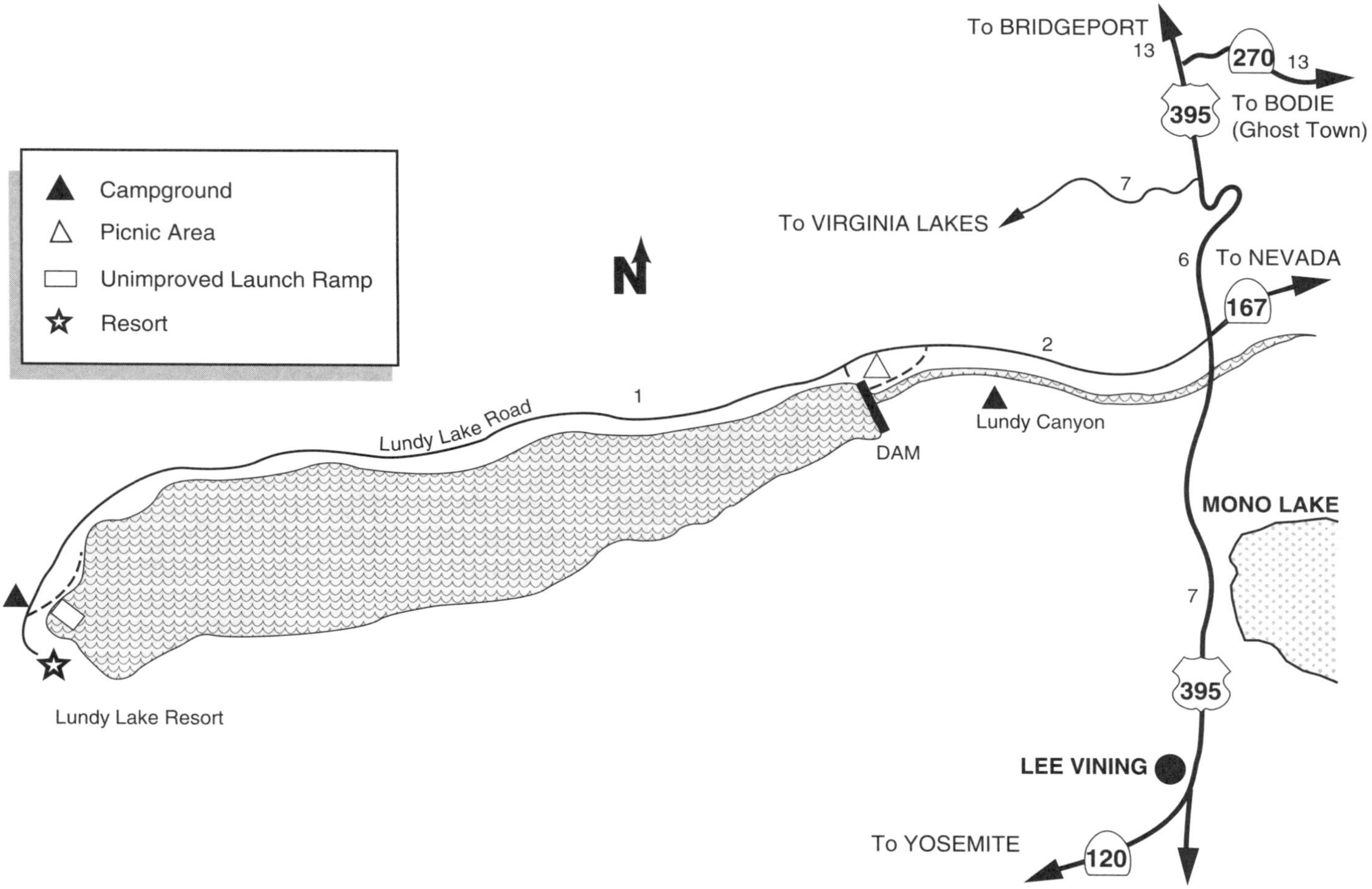
To BRIDGEPORT
13
270
13
395
To BODIE
(Ghost Town)
Campground
Picnic Area
Unimproved Launch Ramp
Resort
7
To VIRGINIA LAKES
N
6
To NEVADA
167
2
1
Lundy Lake Road
Lundy Canyon
DAM
MONO LAKE
7
395
Lundy Lake Resort
LEE VINING
To YOSEMITE
120

INFORMATION: Lundy Lake Resort, P.O. Box 550, Lee Vining 93541–Ph: (626) 309-0415

CAMPING	BOATING	RECREATION	OTHER
Lundy Lake Resort: 27 Tent Sites 3 Camp Huts 8 R.V. Sites with Full Hookups Mono County Parks Ph: (760) 932-5440 Lundy Canyon: 50 Tent & R.V. Sites No Hookups	Fishing Boats, Canoes & Inflatables Speed Limit - 10 MPH Hand Launch Only Rentals: Fishing Boats & Motors	Fishing: Rainbow, German Brown & Eastern Brook Trout Picnicking Hiking Trails Backpacking [Parking] Birdwatching	Housekeeping Cabins Grocery Store Bait & Tackle

MONO LAKE

Mono Lake, 6,380 feet elevation, is about 65 square miles in size with 15-1/2 miles of shoreline. The fascinating history of this expansive body of water is unique. Due to the efforts of dedicated groups, the Lake is open to dispursed camping, hiking trails and boating, especially kayaks and canoes. This is the nesting area of most of California's seagulls. During May each year, about 50,000 raise their young on the islands and along the shoreline. Brine shrimp and alkali flies thrive at the lake and provide food for thousands of migratory birds, including the amazing Wilson's Phalaropes that feed before their 3,000-mile, nonstop journey to South America. The International Shorebird Reserve, plus over 90 species of water birds and an incredible number of plants and animals, inhabit 14 different ecological zones. The million-year old ecosystem includes South Tufa Grove, one of the world's most beautiful natural sights. The towers, 200 to 900 years old, are calcium-carbonate spires formed by the interaction of alkaline lake water and freshwater springs. Mono Lake contains about 280 million tons of dissolved salts. The tufas are part of the State of California Natural Reserves. Various study programs and seminars are great examples of what people do to make a positive impact on the environment. The Mono Basin National Scenic Area Visitor Center has many displays, information and activity programs.

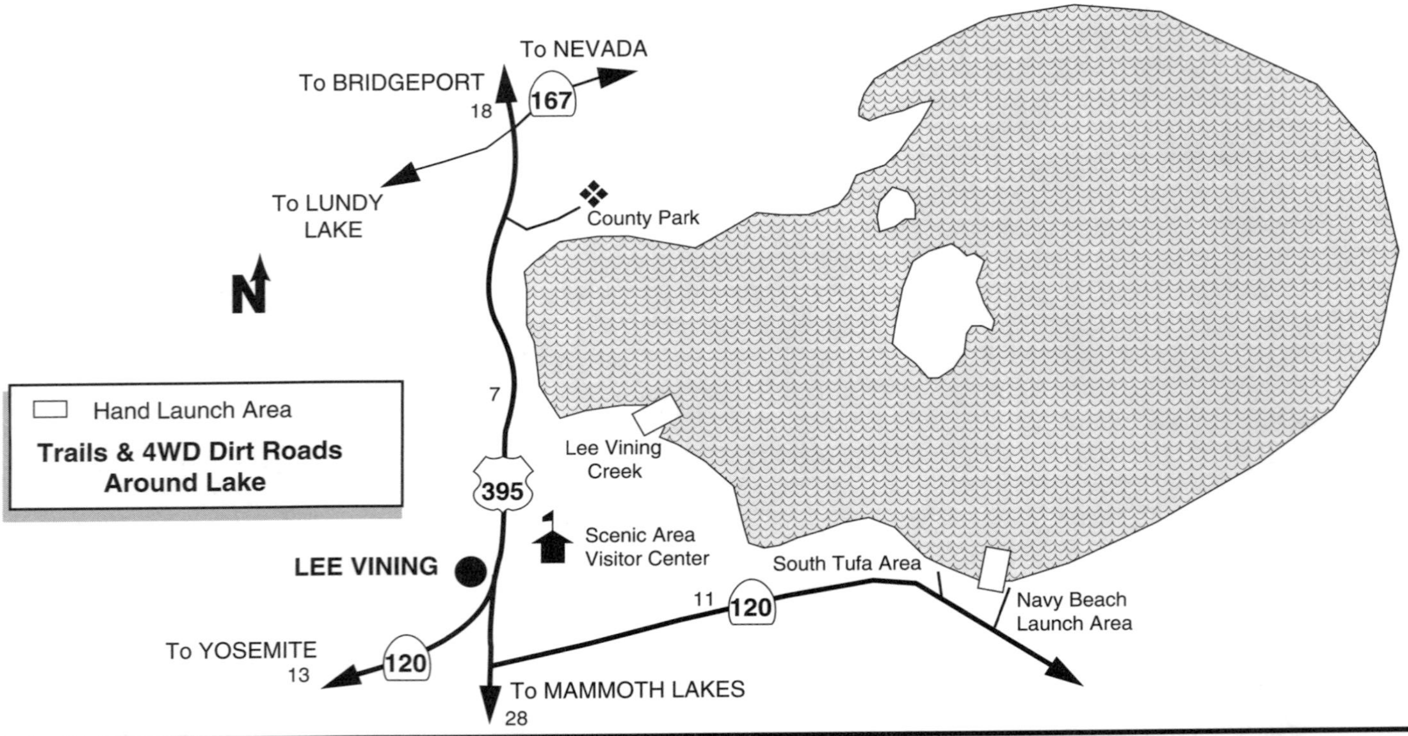
To NEVADA
To BRIDGEPORT
18
167
To LUNDY LAKE
County Park
N
7
Hand Launch Area
Trails & 4WD Dirt Roads Around Lake
Lee Vining Creek
395
Scenic Area Visitor Center
LEE VINING
South Tufa Area
11
120
Navy Beach Launch Area
To YOSEMITE
13
120
To MAMMOTH LAKES
28

INFORMATION: Mono Basin Scenic Area Visitor Center, Box 429, Lee Vining 93541–Ph: (760) 647-3044			
CAMPING	**BOATING**	**RECREATION**	**OTHER**
Dispersed Camping in Area for Boaters and Backpackers Shoreline & Islands are Closed April 1 through August 1 Contact Visitor Center for Authorization to Camp See Previous & Following Pages for Nearby Campgrounds	Open to Boating - Canoes & Kayaks Hand Launch Boats at Navy Beach Area 30 Yards from Parking Lot Unimproved Launch Ramp Near Lee Vining Creek High Afternoon Winds Restricted Access to Islands	No Fish in Mono Lake Picnicking Hiking Trails Birdwatching Environmental Study Interpretive Programs Summer Weekend Seminars Swimming: Lake's Salty Water Makes You More Buoyant	Mono Lake Tufa State Natural Reserve Ph: (760) 647-6331 Lee Vining Ranger Station Ph: (760) 647-3000 Mono Lake Committee & Guided Canoe & Kayak Tours - Reservations Ph: (760) 647-6595

Saddlebag Lake, at an elevation of 10,087 feet, is the highest Lake in California reached by public road. The 2-mile, partially paved road, north of Highway 120, is steep. Large R.V.s and trailers are not advised. The Lake is surrounded by rugged mountain peaks and the alpine setting is spectacular. Fishing from boat, bank or stream can be excellent. The boat taxi at Saddlebag Lake Resort is great for anglers. Located near the trailhead into the Hoover Wilderness Area, an hour or less of easy hiking from Saddlebag will bring you to the first lake and streams of the 20 Lakes Basin. This wilderness area is good for backpackers who can overnight with a permit obtained at the Visitors Center in Lee Vining. Open fires are prohibited so bring your own stove. Mt. Conness Glacier is a popular destination for experienced climbers.

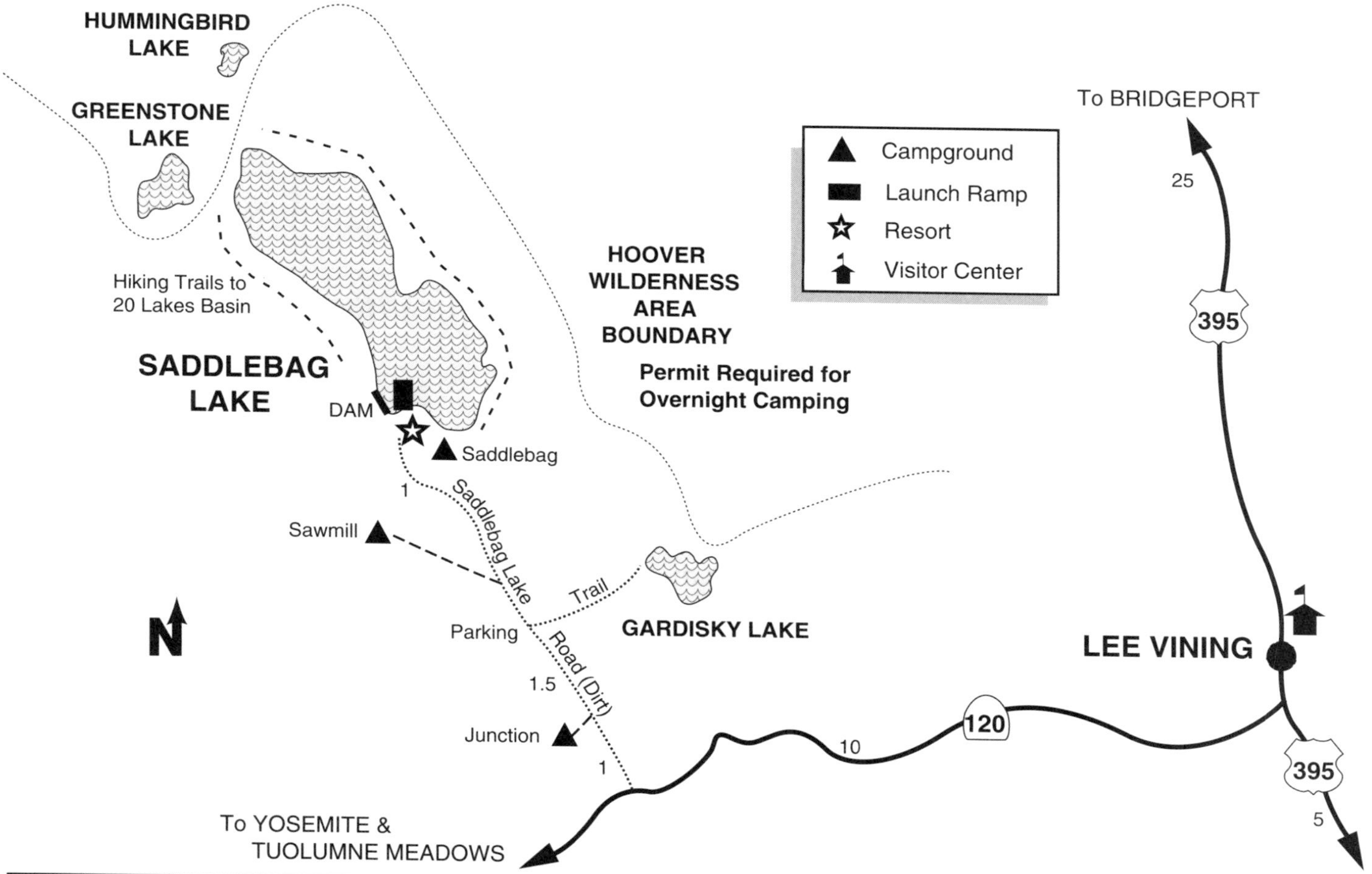
HUMMINGBIRD LAKE
GREENSTONE LAKE
Hiking Trails to 20 Lakes Basin
SADDLEBAG LAKE
DAM
Saddlebag
1
Sawmill
Saddlebag Lake Road (Dirt)
Trail
Parking
GARDISKY LAKE
1.5
Junction
1
HOOVER WILDERNESS AREA BOUNDARY
Permit Required for Overnight Camping
Campground
Launch Ramp
Resort
Visitor Center
To BRIDGEPORT
25
395
LEE VINING
120
10
395
5
To YOSEMITE & TUOLUMNE MEADOWS
N

INFORMATION: Mono Basin Visitor Center, Box 429, Lee Vining 93541—Ph: (760) 647-3044

CAMPING	BOATING	RECREATION	OTHER
Saddlebag Campground 20 Sites for Tents & Small R.V.s Fee: $17 1 Trailhead Group Site - Reservations Ph: (877) 444-6777 Sawmill: 12 Walk-In Sites Junction: 13 Sites Fee: $12	Fishing & Sail Boats, Canoes & Inflatables Unimproved Launch Ramp for Boats to 16 Feet Fees: Boats: $5 Inflatables: $2 Rentals: Fishing Boats & Motors	Fishing: Rainbow, Brook, Brown & Golden Trout Hiking Trails Backpacking [Parking] Mountain Climbing Nature Study Obtain Wilderness Permits at Mono Basin Visitor Center	Saddlebag Lake Resort P.O. Box 303 Lee Vining 93541 (No Phone) No Overnight Facilities Cafe Grocery Store Bait & Tackle Boat Taxi Across Lake for Hikers, Backpackers & Dogs on Leash Fees Charged

ELLERY, TIOGA and TENAYA

These Lakes are in the Eastern Sierra along Highway 120, west of Tioga Pass. Ellery and Tioga Lakes are within the Inyo National Forest and 2 miles outside the eastern entrance to Yosemite National Park. Tenaya is 15 miles inside the Park. There are many natural attractions in this scenic area and elevations range from 8,000 feet to over 13,000 feet. The Pacific Crest Trail passes by Ellery Lake. An interesting trip is the Bennettville mining site, a 20-minute hike from Junction Campground. The water in the Lakes is clear and cold, providing the angler with some good opportunities to catch trout. Numerous streams and small lakes are throughout this area. Bring a camera. The scenery is spectacular.

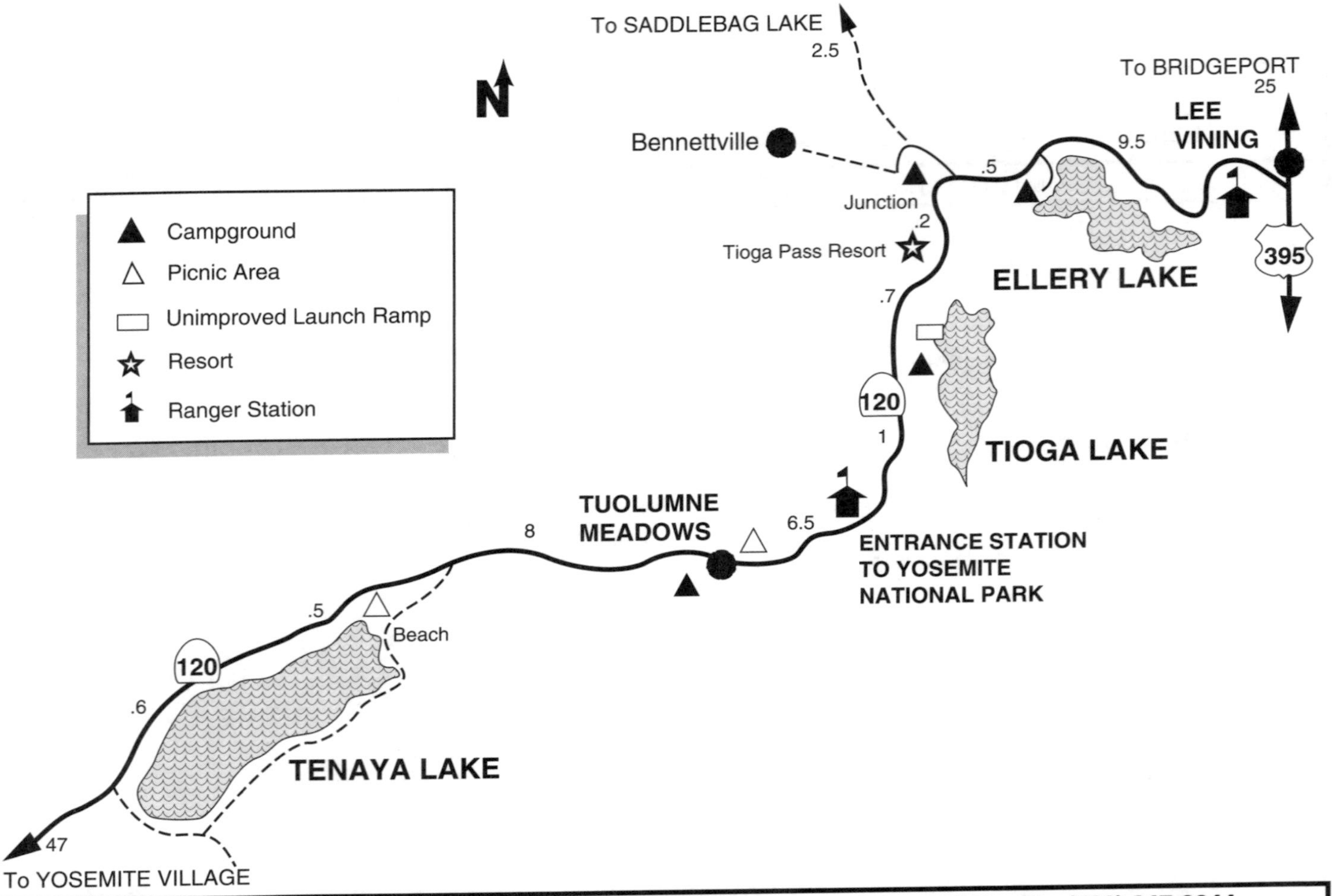
To SADDLEBAG LAKE
2.5
To BRIDGEPORT
25
LEE
VINING
9.5
N
Bennettville
.5
Junction
.2
Tioga Pass Resort
395
ELLERY LAKE
.7
Campground
Picnic Area
Unimproved Launch Ramp
Resort
Ranger Station
120
1
TIOGA LAKE
TUOLUMNE
MEADOWS
8
6.5
ENTRANCE STATION
TO YOSEMITE
NATIONAL PARK
.5
Beach
120
.6
TENAYA LAKE
47
To YOSEMITE VILLAGE

INFORMATION: Mono Basin Scenic Area Visitor Center, Box 429, Lee Vining 93541—Ph: (760) 647-3044

CAMPING	BOATING	RECREATION	OTHER
U.S.F.S. Ellery Lake: 21 Dev. Sites - Fee: $17 Tioga Lake (Small R.V.s): 13 Dev. Sites - Fee: $17 Junction Camp: 13 Dev. Sites - Fee: $12 No Reservations Yosemite National Park - Tuolumne Meadows: 304 Dev. Sites - Fee - $20 Some Reservations: Ph: 877-444-6777	Ellery and Tioga Lakes: Motors Permitted Hand Launch at Ellery Small Trailered Boats at Tioga Tenaya Lake: No Motors Hand Launch Only (No Camping)	Fishing: Rainbow, Brook, Brown & Golden Trout Picnicking Hiking Trails Mountain Bike Trails - Only in National Fores No Mountain Biking Allowed in Yosemit NP Rock Climbing Horseback Riding	Yosemite - Hotel & Lodging Reservations: Ph: (801) 559-5000 Tioga Pass Resort Box 7, Lee Vining 93541 (No Phone - email: reservations@ tiogapassresort. com) 10 Log Cabins & 4 Rooms Cafe, Groceries Bait & Tackle

The June Lake Loop includes 4 scenic mountain Lakes on the eastern slope of the high Sierras. At an elevation of 7,600 feet in the Inyo National Forest, these popular Lakes provide outstanding recreational opportunities. Grant is the largest Lake on the loop with 1,000 surface acres. Silver has 80 acres; Gull, the smallest, has 64 acres and June has 400 acres. Each Lake is interconnected by stream or creek and all are prime trout waters. Hikers, equestrians and backpackers can enjoy the nearby Ansel Adams Wilderness area with the spectacular scenery and many small lakes and streams. The June Lake Loop has numerous Forest Service campsites in addition to private facilities.

....Continued....

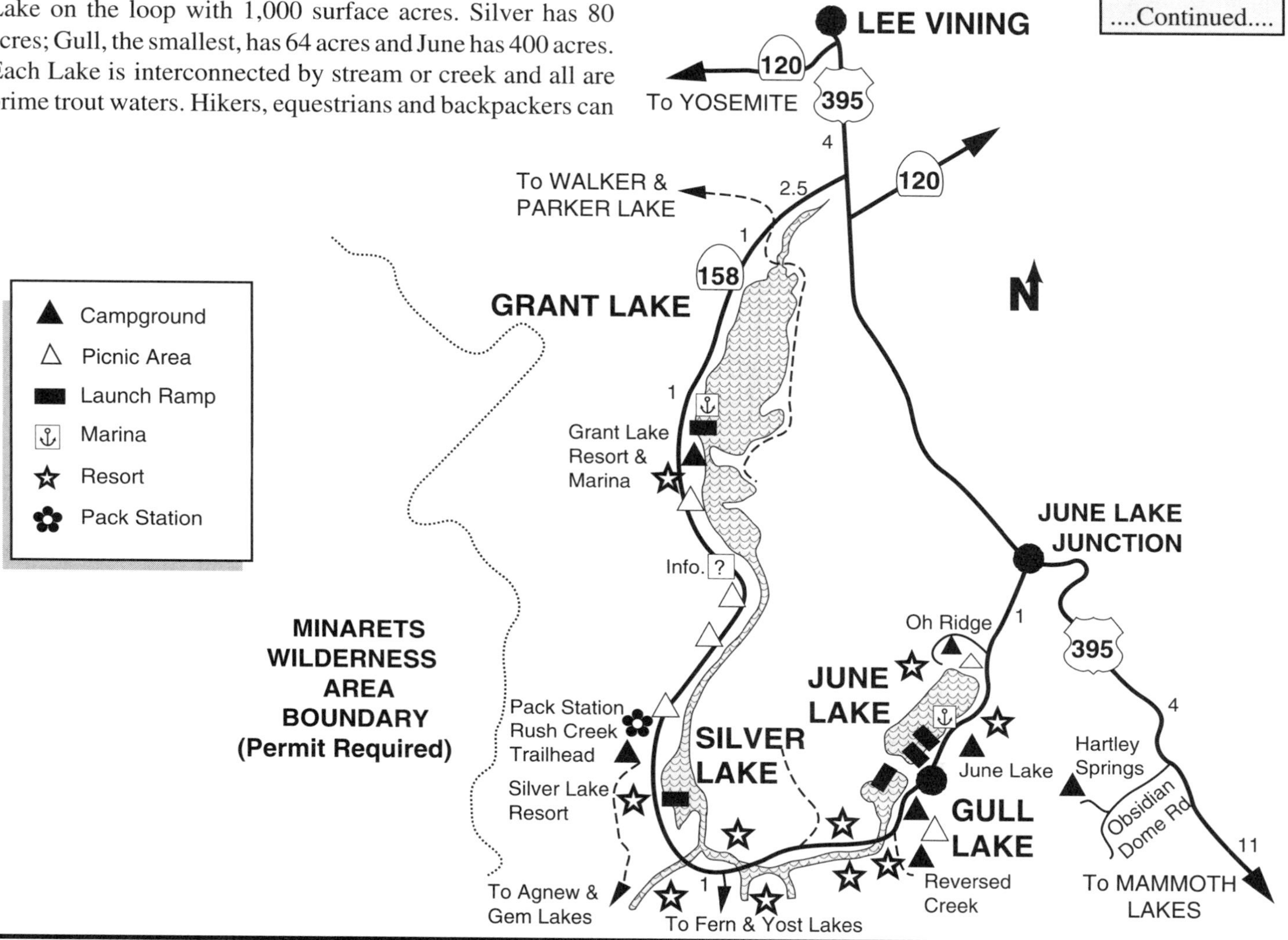
LEE VINING
120
To YOSEMITE
395
4
To WALKER &
PARKER LAKE
2.5
120
1
158
GRANT LAKE
Campground
Picnic Area
Launch Ramp
Marina
Resort
Pack Station
1
Grant Lake
Resort &
Marina
Info.
?
JUNE LAKE
JUNCTION
MINARETS
WILDERNESS
AREA
BOUNDARY
(Permit Required)
Oh Ridge
1
395
JUNE
LAKE
Pack Station
Rush Creek
Trailhead
SILVER
LAKE
4
Hartley
Springs
June Lake
Silver Lake
Resort
GULL
LAKE
Obsidian
Dome Rd
11
To Agnew &
Gem Lakes
1
To Fern & Yost Lakes
Reversed
Creek
To MAMMOTH
LAKES

INFORMATION: Mono Basin Scenic Area Visitor Center, P.O. Box 429, Lee Vining 93541—Ph: (760) 647-3044

CAMPING	BOATING	RECREATION	OTHER
U. S. Forest Service Campsites for Tents & R.V.s Numerous R.V. Parks & Resorts See Following Page for Details	Power, Row, Canoe, Sail, Windsurf & Inflatables Waterskiing at Grant Lake Only Other Lakes: 10 MPH Speed Limit Launch Ramps Rentals: Fishing Boats & Motors, Paddleboats, Canoes Docks, Gas, Repairs	Fishing: Rainbow, Brown, Cutthroat & Brook Trout Swimming - June Lake Backpacking [Parking] Equestrian Trails & Pack Station	Housekeeping Cabins Motels, Rental Condos Snack Bars Restaurants Grocery Stores Bait & Tackle Further Information: June Lake Chamber of Commerce P.O. Box 2 June Lake 93529

JUNE LAKE LOOP............Continued

GRANT LAKE

GRANT LAKE RESORT & MARINA, P.O. Box 627, June Lake 93529—Ph: (760) 648-7964
70 Developed Sites for Tents & R.V.s to 60 feet, Water & Sewer Hookups, Water, Fire Pits, Hot Showers, Disposal Station, Store, Cafe, Bait & Tackle, Beer & Wine, Ice, Propane, Launch Ramp, Boat Rentals & Dock Rental, Trailer Rentals. Waterskiing Approximately June - August - after 10 am.

SILVER LAKE

U. S. FOREST SERVICE CAMPGROUND - Reservations: Ph: (877) 444-6777
63 Developed Sites for Tents & R.V.s to 40 feet - *Fee: $18 Single, $30 Double.*

SILVER LAKE RESORT, P.O. Box 116, June Lake 93529—Ph: (760) 648-7525
R.V. Sites with Full Hookups - some to 40 feet, Housekeeping Cabins, General Store, Groceries, Bait & Tackle, Old-fashioned Country Cafe, Boat Gas, Launch Ramp, Rentals: Fishing Boats with Motors & Kayaks.

FRONTIER PACK TRAIN, P.O. Box 656, June Lake 93529—Summer Ph: (760) 648-7701
Winter Ph: (760) 873-7971
Horseback & Pack Trips to Remote Lakes & Streams in the Minaret Wilderness Plus Hour Rides & 1/2 Day Rides.

GULL LAKE

U. S. FOREST SERVICE CAMPGROUND - No Reservations
Gull Lake Campground -11 Sites for Tents & R.V.s to 30 feet - *Fee: $18.*
Reversed Creek Campground -17 Sites for Tents & R.V.s to 30 feet -*Fee: $18.*

GULL LAKE MARINA, P.O. Box 65, June Lake 93529—Ph: (760) 648-7539
Full Service Marina, Rental Boats & Motors, Canoes, Kayaks, Paddleboats, Pontoons, Docks, Free Launch Ramp, Bait & Tackle, Store
Gull Meadows Cartop Launch Ramp & Picnic Area

JUNE LAKE

U. S. FOREST SERVICE CAMPGROUNDS - Reservations: Ph: (877) 444-6777
Oh! Ridge - 144 Developed Sites for Tents & R.V.s to 30 feet. - *Fee: $18.*
June Lake - 28 Developed Sites for Tents & R.V.s to 20 feet. - *Fee: $18.*
Plus Hartley Springs - South on Highway 395 - 20 Sites for Tents & R.V.s - *No Water, No Fee, No Reservations*

JUNE LAKE MARINA, P.O. Box 26, June Lake 93529—Ph: (760) 648-7726
Full Service Marina, Boat Rentals: Canoes, Kayaks, Pontoons, Docks, Bait & Tackle, Launch Ramp, Gas, Repairs.

Numerous R.V. Parks, Cabins, Motels, Houses and Condos for Rent - Some Listed Here

Big Rock Resort	(800) 769-9831
Boulder Lodge	(800) 458-6355
Double Eagle Resort & Spa	(760) 648-7004
Fern Creek Lodge	(800) 621-9146
Four Seasons	(760) 648-7476
June Lake R.V. Park	(760) 648-7967
June Lake Motel	(800) 648-6835
Lake Front Cabins	(877) 648-7527
Reverse Creek Lodge	(800) 762-6440
Whispering Pines Resort	(800) 648-7762

Rainbow Ridge Realty and Reservations
Drawer C - 2603 Highway 158
June Lake 93529
Ph: (800) 462-5589 or (760) 648-7811

June Lake Properties Reservations
P. O. Box 606
June Lake 93529
Ph: (800) 648-5863 or (760) 648-7705

MAMMOTH LAKES BASIN

The Mammoth Lakes Basin is located in the high Sierras. These small glacial-formed Lakes range in elevation from 8,540 feet to 9,250 feet. They are easily accessible by road or pine-shaded trails. Fishing in the Lakes or streams is often excellent. (Lake Mary is one of our personal favorite lakes.)

The hiker and equestrian can enjoy the scenic landscape with trails leading into the John Muir or Ansel Adams Wilderness areas. Numerous resorts and campgrounds are available and complete facilities are located in the town of Mammoth Lakes. While Sotcher and Starkweather Lakes are outside the Lakes Basin, they share the same abundance of natural beauty and recreation.

....Continued....

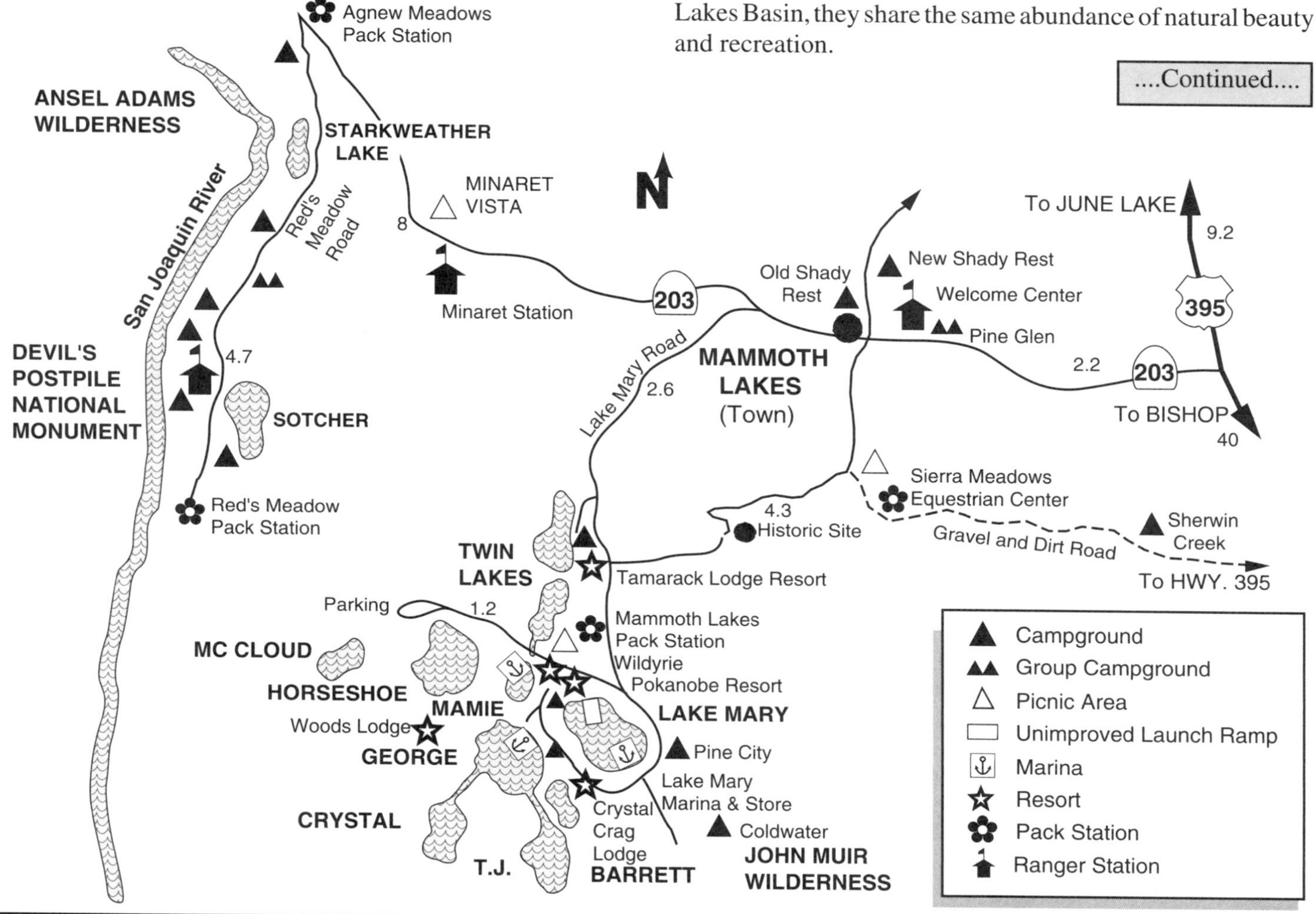
Agnew Meadows Pack Station
ANSEL ADAMS WILDERNESS
STARKWEATHER LAKE
San Joaquin River
Red's Meadow Road
MINARET VISTA
8
N
To JUNE LAKE
9.2
Minaret Station
203
Old Shady Rest
New Shady Rest
Welcome Center
395
Pine Glen
Lake Mary Road
2.6
MAMMOTH LAKES (Town)
2.2
203
To BISHOP
40
DEVIL'S POSTPILE NATIONAL MONUMENT
4.7
SOTCHER
Sierra Meadows Equestrian Center
4.3
Historic Site
Sherwin Creek
Gravel and Dirt Road
To HWY. 395
Red's Meadow Pack Station
TWIN LAKES
Tamarack Lodge Resort
Parking
1.2
Mammoth Lakes Pack Station
Wildyrie
Pokanobe Resort
MC CLOUD
HORSESHOE
MAMIE
LAKE MARY
Woods Lodge
GEORGE
Pine City
Lake Mary Marina & Store
CRYSTAL
Crystal Crag Lodge
Coldwater
T.J.
BARRETT
JOHN MUIR WILDERNESS
Campground
Group Campground
Picnic Area
Unimproved Launch Ramp
Marina
Resort
Pack Station
Ranger Station

INFORMATION: Mammoth Lakes Welcome Center, Box 148, Mammoth Lakes 93546—Ph: (760) 924-5500

CAMPING	BOATING	RECREATION	OTHER
See Following Pages Dev. Tent/R.V. and Group Sites - U.S.F.S. Numerous Resorts at Lakes Wilderness Permits Required for Overnight Stays in Ansel Adams and John Muir Wilderness Areas	Power, Row, Canoe & Sailboats 10 MPH Speed Limit Rentals: Fishing Boats & Motors Starkweather Lake & Sotcher Lake: Rowboats & Canoes Only	Fishing: Rainbow, Brown & Brook Trout Hiking Trails Equestrian Trails Nature Study Backpacking Picnicking Pack Stations & Horse Rentals	Resorts & Various Rentals Full Facilities In Town of Mammoth Lakes Guided Naturalist Activities Provided by Mammoth Lakes Welcome Center Throughout July & August Shuttle into Red's Meadow & Devil's Postpile Areas Transportation Fee

MAMMOTH LAKES BASIN............Continued

U.S. FOREST SERVICE CAMPGROUNDS
Reservations Required for Group Camps and Available for Some Individual Sites Shown Below: Ph: (877) 444-6777

NEW SHADY REST
92 Tent/R.V. Sites
Fee: $18

OLD SHADY REST
46 Tent/R.V. Sites
Fee: $18

SHERWIN CREEK
85 Tent/R.V. Sites
Fee: $18

TWIN LAKES
92 Tent/R.V. Sites
Fee: $19

LAKE GEORGE
16 Tent/R.V. Sites
Fee: $19
Boat Ramp and Rentals Nearby

REDS MEADOW
52 Tent/R.V. Sites
Fee: $16

PINE GLEN
17 Tent/R.V. Family-Group Sites - Fees Vary
Must Reserve: Ph (877) 444-6777
Plus Overflow as Needed - Fee: $18
Campers must obtain permission to use these Sites.

LAKE MARY
46 Tent/R.V. Sites
Fee: $19

COLDWATER
77 Tent/R.V. Sites
Fee: $19
Trailhead into the John Muir Wilderness

PINE CITY
10 Tent/R.V. Sites
Fee: $19

There are numerous other U.S. Forest Service Campgrounds in this Area
Contact the Welcome Center

For Further Information Contact:
Mammoth Lakes Welcome Center
P.O. Box 148 - Highway 203
Mammoth Lakes 93546
24 Hour Info: (760) 924-5500
Hearing Impaired: (760) 924-5531

Overnight visitors into the Sotcher Lake/Red's Meadow/Devil's Postpile Areas MUST obtain an access pass at Minaret Station between 6:30 am to 8:30 pm.
There is a mandatory shuttle bus system for all users from 7:00 a.m. to 7:00 p.m.
Inquire at the Welcome Center for further details. The Welcome Center also provides a number of interpretive programs.

Wilderness Permits are required year around for any overnight camping in the John Muir or Ansel Adams Wildernesses. Obtain Permits from the Welcome Center.

....Continued....

SOME PRIVATE FACILITIES NEAR THE LAKES:

TWIN LAKES:

TAMARACK LODGE RESORT - P.O. Box 69, Mammoth Lakes 93546—Ph: (760) 934-2442
34 Housekeeping Cabins, 11 Rooms in Historic Lodge, Lakeside Bar & Restaurant, Rentals: Boats & Canoes.

LAKE MAMIE:

WILDYRIE RESORT - P.O. Box 109, Mammoth Lakes 93546—Ph: (760) 934-2444
Housekeeping Cabins with Sundecks, Rooms in the Lodge, Snacks, Grocery Store, Bait & Tackle, Launch Ramp, Dock, Rentals: Boats & Motors.

LAKE GEORGE:

WOODS LODGE - P.O. Box 108, Mammoth Lakes 93546, Ph: (760) 934-2261
Housekeeping Cabins with Sundecks, Bait & Tackle, Launch Ramp, Dock, Rentals: Boats & Motors.

LAKE MARY:

CRYSTAL CRAG LODGE - P.O. Box 88, Mammoth Lakes 93546—Ph: (760) 934-2436
21 Housekeeping Cabins, All with Lake View, Most with Fireplace, Rentals: Boats & Motors, Family Size Party Boat.

POKONOBE MARINA RESORT - P.O. Box 3939, Mammoth Lakes 93546—Ph: (760) 934-2437
Grocery Store, Launch Ramp, Dock, Rentals: Boats & Motors, Pedal Boats, Canoes & Kayaks.

LAKE MARY MARINA & STORE - 482 Cottonwood Dr., Bishop 93514—Ph: (760) 934-5353
Grocery Store, Bait & Tackle, Hot Showers, Cafe, Launch Ramp, Docks, Rentals: Boats & Motors, Pontoons, Paddleboats, Canoes & Kayaks.

MAMMOTH MOUNTAIN R.V. PARK: P.O. Box 288, Mammoth Lakes 93546—Ph: (760) 934-3822
Reservations: Ph: (800) 582-4603
115 R.V. Sites, 47 Full Hookups, Disposal Stations, 17 Tent Sites, 2 Group Tent Sites, Cabins, Pool & Spa, Playground, Rec. Room.

Mammoth Lakes is a complete resort town. There are major grocery stores as well as small retail outlets. Gourmet restaurants, fast food chains, resorts, motels and condominiums are all too numerous to mention. Listed below are reservation services that can help find the best place to suit your needs.

Mammoth Reservation Bureau
P. O. Box 1608, Mammoth Lakes 93546
Ph: (800) 462-5571 or (760) 934-2528
Studios and up to 5 bedrooms
Over 200 Units Can Be Reserved

Town of Mammoth Lakes Tourism & Recreation
P. O. Box 48, Mammoth Lakes 93546
Ph: (888) GO-MAMMOTH (466-2666)
or (760) 934-2528
Visitor Information

CONVICT LAKE

Convict Lake is one of the most beautiful lakes in California (one of our personal favorites.) The crystal clear waters are surrounded by steep, rugged granite peaks. At an elevation of 7,583 feet, this small mountain Lake is 1 mile long and 1/2 mile wide. The 3 miles of shoreline are shaded by pine trees. A great trail goes all the way around the Lake. Boating is popular and the fishing can be excellent in both the Lake and creek. The backpacker and equestrian will find a trail leading through a rock-walled canyon to 9 lakes in the nearby John Muir Wilderness Area. The Inyo National Forest maintains the developed campground next to Convict Creek. The Resort includes cabins, deluxe rental houses for large groups and an excellent dinner house. Be sure to visit this Lake when you are travelling along Highway 395.

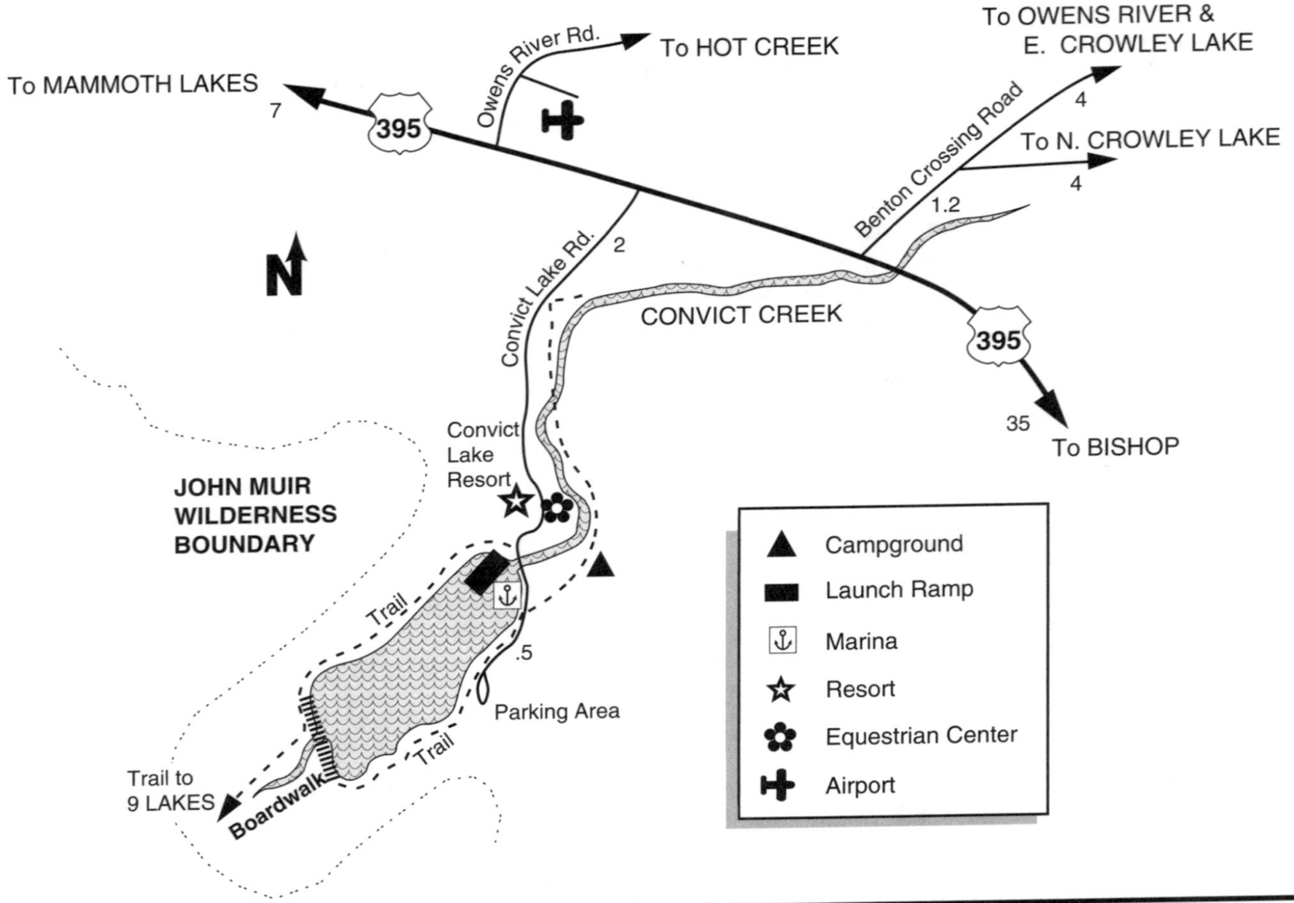

To HOT CREEK
Owens River Rd.
To OWENS RIVER &
E. CROWLEY LAKE
To MAMMOTH LAKES
7
395
4
Benton Crossing Road
To N. CROWLEY LAKE
4
1.2
Convict Lake Rd.
2
N
CONVICT CREEK
395
35
To BISHOP
Convict
Lake
Resort
JOHN MUIR
WILDERNESS
BOUNDARY
Trail
.5
Parking Area
Trail
Trail to
9 LAKES
Boardwalk
Campground
Launch Ramp
Marina
Resort
Equestrian Center
Airport

INFORMATION: Convict Lake Resort, HCR 79, Box 204, Mammoth Lakes 93546—Ph: (760) 934-3800

CAMPING	BOATING	RECREATION	OTHER
88 Dev. Sites for Tents & R.V.s No Hookups Fee: $18 25 Sites Can Be Reserved: Ph: (877) 444-6777 Disposal Station	Power, Row, Canoe, Sail & Inflatables Launch Ramp Rentals: Fishing Boats & Motors, Canoes, Kayaks, Pontoon Boat for up to 10 Adults Dry Storage	Fishing: Rainbow & German Brown Trout Picnicking Hiking Trails Backpacking [Parking] Bicycle Rentals Horse Rentals 2-Hour Scenic Ride	Housekeeping Cabins & Deluxe Houses Ph: (800) 992-2260 Gourmet Restaurant Reservations: Ph: (760) 934-3803 Special Events - Weddings Cocktail Lounge Grocery Store Bait & Tackle Airport with Auto Rentals - 5 Miles

Crowley Lake is one of California's most popular and productive fishing Lakes. At an elevation of 6,700 feet on the eastern side of the high Sierra, the Lake is situated in Long Valley surrounded by the Glass Mountains and the White Mountains. Anglers jam its shores and waters on opening weekends. This 650 surface-acre Lake has held State records for German brown trout and Sacramento perch. Trophy-sized fish are common. The Department of Fish and Game has an extensive planting season for Kamloop, Eagle Lake, Coleman and Cutt Trout. Guided fishing trips are available. Boating and waterskiing are also popular. Numerous resorts and other recreational facilities are nearby.

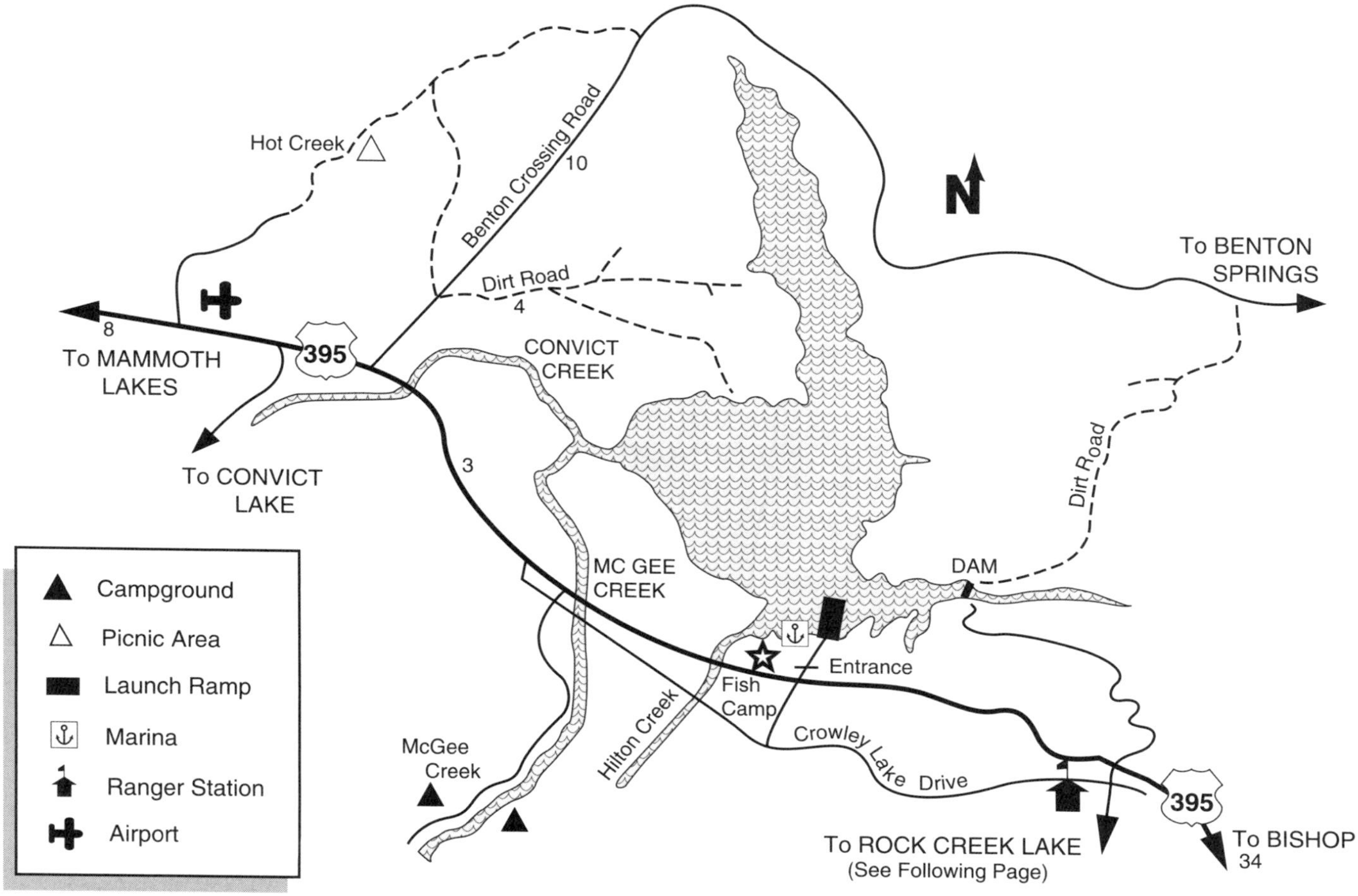
Hot Creek
Benton Crossing Road
10
N
To BENTON SPRINGS
Dirt Road
4
8
To MAMMOTH LAKES
395
CONVICT CREEK
To CONVICT LAKE
3
Dirt Road
DAM
MC GEE CREEK
Entrance
Fish Camp
Hilton Creek
Crowley Lake Drive
McGee Creek
To ROCK CREEK LAKE
(See Following Page)
395
To BISHOP
34
Campground
Picnic Area
Launch Ramp
Marina
Ranger Station
Airport

INFORMATION: Crowley Lake Fish Camp, P.O. Box 1268, Mammoth Lakes 93546—Ph: (760) 935-4301

CAMPING	BOATING	RECREATION	OTHER
Fish Camp: Dev. Sites for Tents & R.V.s - Fee: $15 Full Hookups: $40 Reservations in Season: Ph: (760) 935-4043 Inyo National Forest McGee Creek: 28 Dev. Sites for Tents & R.V.s Reservations: Ph: (877) 444-6777	Power, Waterskiing, Sail, Windsurf, Inflatable & PWCs - Check Season Strict Inspection of Boat, Trailer & Tow Vehicle to Prevent Spread of Mussels *All Craft Must Register-Fee* Launch Ramp Full Service Marina Boat Slips, Dry Storage Floating Gas Dock Rentals: Boats & Motors	Fishing: Rainbow & German Brown Trout, Sacramento Perch Check Restrictions: Barbless Lures & Flies Only Season Waterskiing Season Picnicking Hiking Trails Special Events Fishing Derbies No Swimming Day Use Fee	Grocery Store Bait & Tackle Guided Fly Fishing Service: Ph: (760) 937-3245 Full Facilities at Mammoth Lakes

ROCK CREEK LAKE

Rock Creek Lake, at an elevation of 9,682 feet, is one of the highest lakes in California. Located in the Rock Creek Canyon of Inyo National Forest, this area has over 60 lakes and streams for the equestrian, backpacker and angler. Snow-fed streams flow into Rock Creek, a natural Lake of 63 surface acres. Rainbow and German brown trout are planted throughout the season. Native Eastern brook and golden trout are found in the waters of the John Muir Wilderness. There are several U.S. Forest Service campgrounds along Rock Creek. The speed limit for boating is limited to 5 MPH. Rock Creek Pack Station has rental horses for a day or a variety of extended trips. This is a great way to see the incredible scenery of the John Muir Wilderness Area.

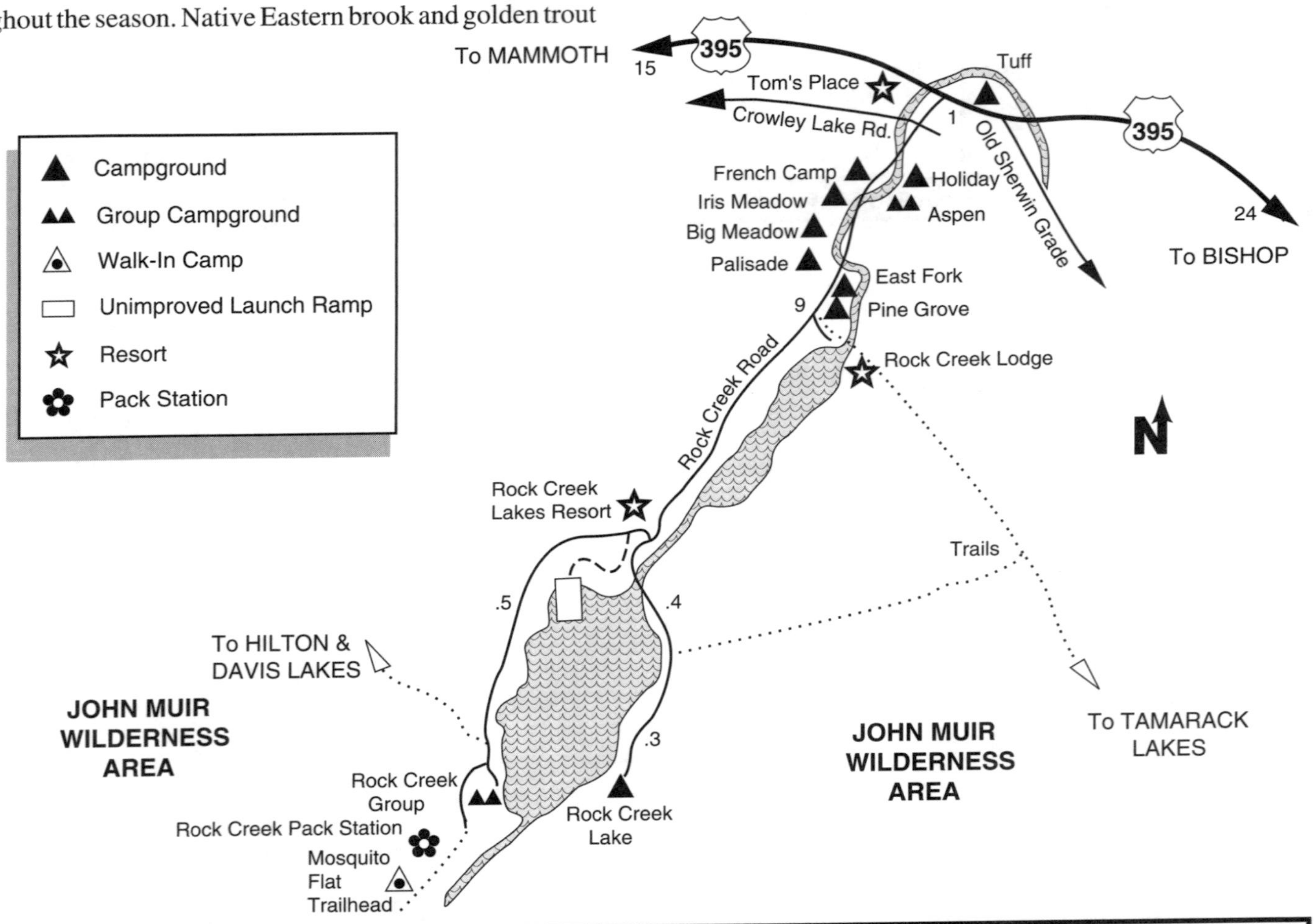

To MAMMOTH
395
15
Tom's Place
Tuff
Crowley Lake Rd.
1
Old Sherwin Grade
395
24
To BISHOP
French Camp
Holiday
Iris Meadow
Aspen
Big Meadow
Palisade
East Fork
9
Pine Grove
Rock Creek Lodge
Rock Creek Road
N
Campground
Group Campground
Walk-In Camp
Unimproved Launch Ramp
Resort
Pack Station
Rock Creek
Lakes Resort
Trails
.5
.4
To HILTON &
DAVIS LAKES
To TAMARACK
LAKES
JOHN MUIR
WILDERNESS
AREA
.3
JOHN MUIR
WILDERNESS
AREA
Rock Creek
Group
Rock Creek Pack Station
Rock Creek
Lake
Mosquito
Flat
Trailhead

INFORMATION: White Mountain Ranger District, 798 N. Main St., Bishop 93514—Ph: (760) 873-2500

CAMPING	BOATING	RECREATION	OTHER
Dev. Sites for Tents-Fee:$18 Tuff: 34, Iris Meadow: 14 Palisade: 5, Pine Grove: 8 Holiday: 35 Sites - Overflow Dev. Sites for Tents/R.V.s French Camp: 86, Big Meadow: 11, East Fork: 138 Group Sites - Aspen & Rock Creek Reservations for Some of Above: Ph: (877) 444-6777 Mosquito Flat Trailhead: 10 Walk-In Tent Sites	Power, Row, Canoe, Sail & Inflatables Speed Limit - 5 MPH Unimproved Launch Ramp Rentals at Rock Creek Lakes Resort: Fishing Boats & Motors	Fishing: Rainbow, Eastern Brook, German Brown & Golden Trout in Lake & Streams Picnicking Hiking Trails Equestrian Trails Horse Rentals John Muir Wilderness Permit Required	Rock Creek Lakes Resort Ph: (760) 935-4311 Cabins, Cafe, Store Boat Rentals Rock Creek Lodge Ph: (877) 935-4170 Cabins, Cafe, Store Tom's Place Resort Ph: (760) 935-4239 Lodge, Cabins, Cafe Rock Creek Pack Station Ph: (760) 935-4493 Trail Rides & Pack Trips

Bishop Creek Canyon is on the eastern slope of the Sierra Nevada at elevations ranging from 7,500 feet to 9,500 feet. This area is popular with backpackers and equestrians who can enjoy the nearby John Muir Wilderness Area. Lake Sabrina has a surface area of 150 acres. South Lake has 180 acres and North Lake is much smaller. These Lakes, along with Bishop Creek, are planted weekly with trout during the season. The U.S. Forest Service offers numerous campsites. In addition, there are private resorts with full facilities.

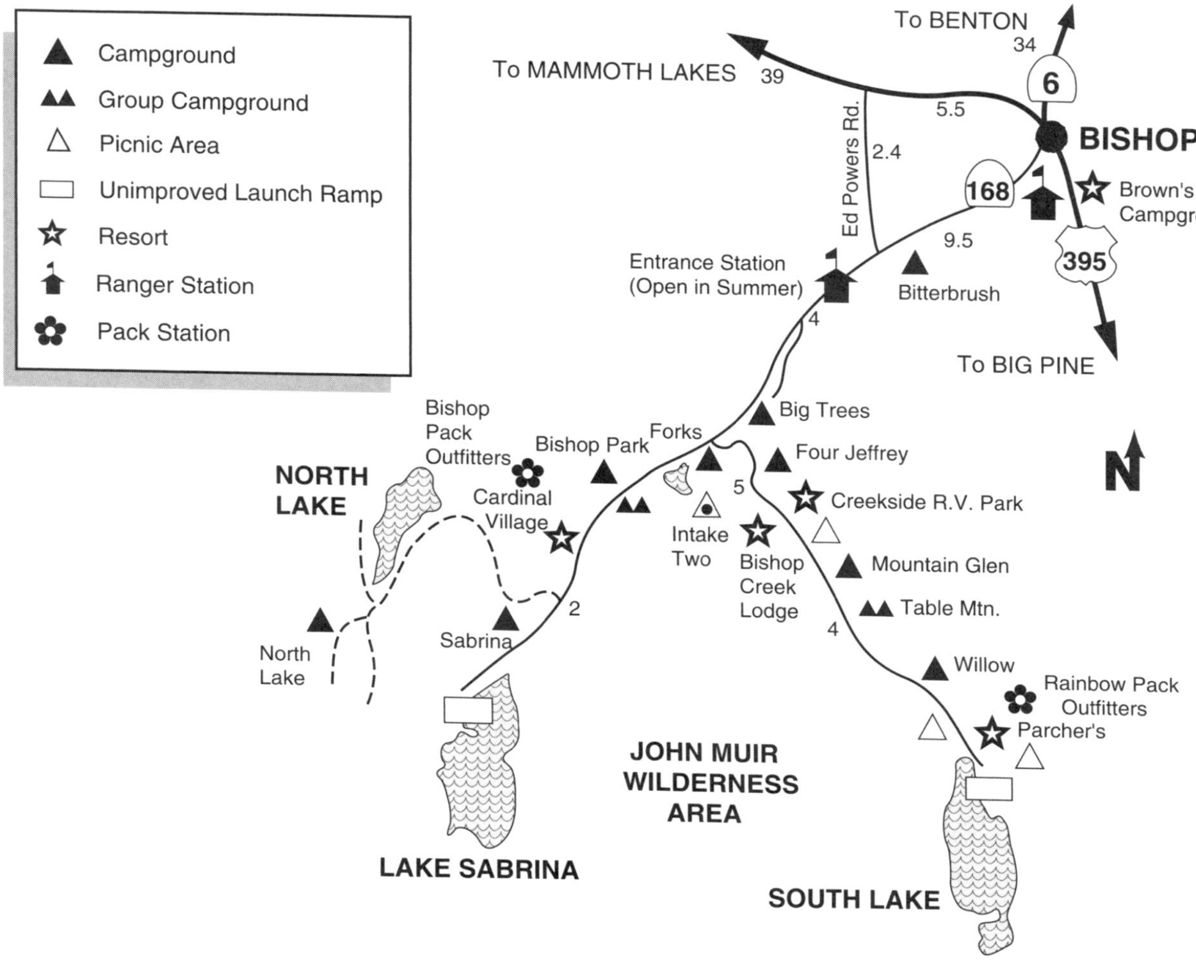
Campground
Group Campground
Picnic Area
Unimproved Launch Ramp
Resort
Ranger Station
Pack Station
To BENTON
34
To MAMMOTH LAKES
39
6
5.5
Ed Powers Rd.
2.4
BISHOP
168
Brown's Town Campground
9.5
395
Entrance Station (Open in Summer)
Bitterbrush
4
To BIG PINE
Big Trees
Bishop Pack Outfitters
Bishop Park
Forks
Four Jeffrey
NORTH LAKE
Cardinal Village
5
Creekside R.V. Park
Intake Two
Bishop Creek Lodge
Mountain Glen
Table Mtn.
2
North Lake
Sabrina
4
Willow
Rainbow Pack Outfitters
Parcher's
JOHN MUIR WILDERNESS AREA
LAKE SABRINA
SOUTH LAKE
N

INFORMATION: White Mountain Ranger District. 798 N. Main St., Bishop 93514—Ph: (760) 873-2500

CAMPING	BOATING	RECREATION	OTHER
Dev. Sites Tents/R.V.s: $19 Bitterbrush: 35 Sites Big Trees: 21, Forks: 9 Intake Two: 5 Walk-Ins Plus 8 Sites Bishop Park: 21 Sites Sabrina: 18 Sites North Lake: 11 Sites Mt. Glen: 5, Willow: 10 Four Jeffrey: 106 Sites Reserve (877) 444-6777: Groups: to 25 People Bishop Park & Table Mtn.	Power, Row, Canoe, Sail & Inflatables 5 MPH Speed Limit Unimproved Launch Ramps at South Lake and Sabrina Parcher's Resort - Rentals: Fishing and Motorboats Lake Sabrina Boat Landing: Ph: (760) 873-7425 Rentals: Fishing Boats. Motors, Canoes, Pontoon	Fishing: Rainbow & German Brown Trout Picnicking Hiking Trails Equestrian Trails Rainbow Pack Outfitters: Ph: (760) 872-8803 Bishop Pack Outfitters Ph: (760) 873-4785 John Muir Wilderness Permit Required	R.V. Sites With Hookups: Brown's Town Campground Ph: (760) 873-8522 Creekside R.V. Park Ph: (760) 873-4483 Cabins: Bishop Creek Lodge Ph: (760) 873-4484 Parcher's Resort Ph: (760) 873-4177 Cardinal Village Ph: (760) 873-4789

NEW MELONES LAKE

New Melones Lake is at an elevation of 1,100 feet in the Mother Lode Gold Country of Central California. Damming of the Stanislaus River has created the fifth largest Lake in California with 12,500 surface acres and over 100 miles of tree-covered shoreline. Extensive facilities have been developed under the management of the U. S. Bureau of Reclamation. There are 2 large campgrounds and recreational areas with complete facilities, Glory Hole to the north and Tuttletown to the south. Launch ramps and a full service marina are among the prime recreational facilities. Fishing is good for a variety of species, including small and largemouth bass. Over 800,000 people visit New Melones Lake each year.

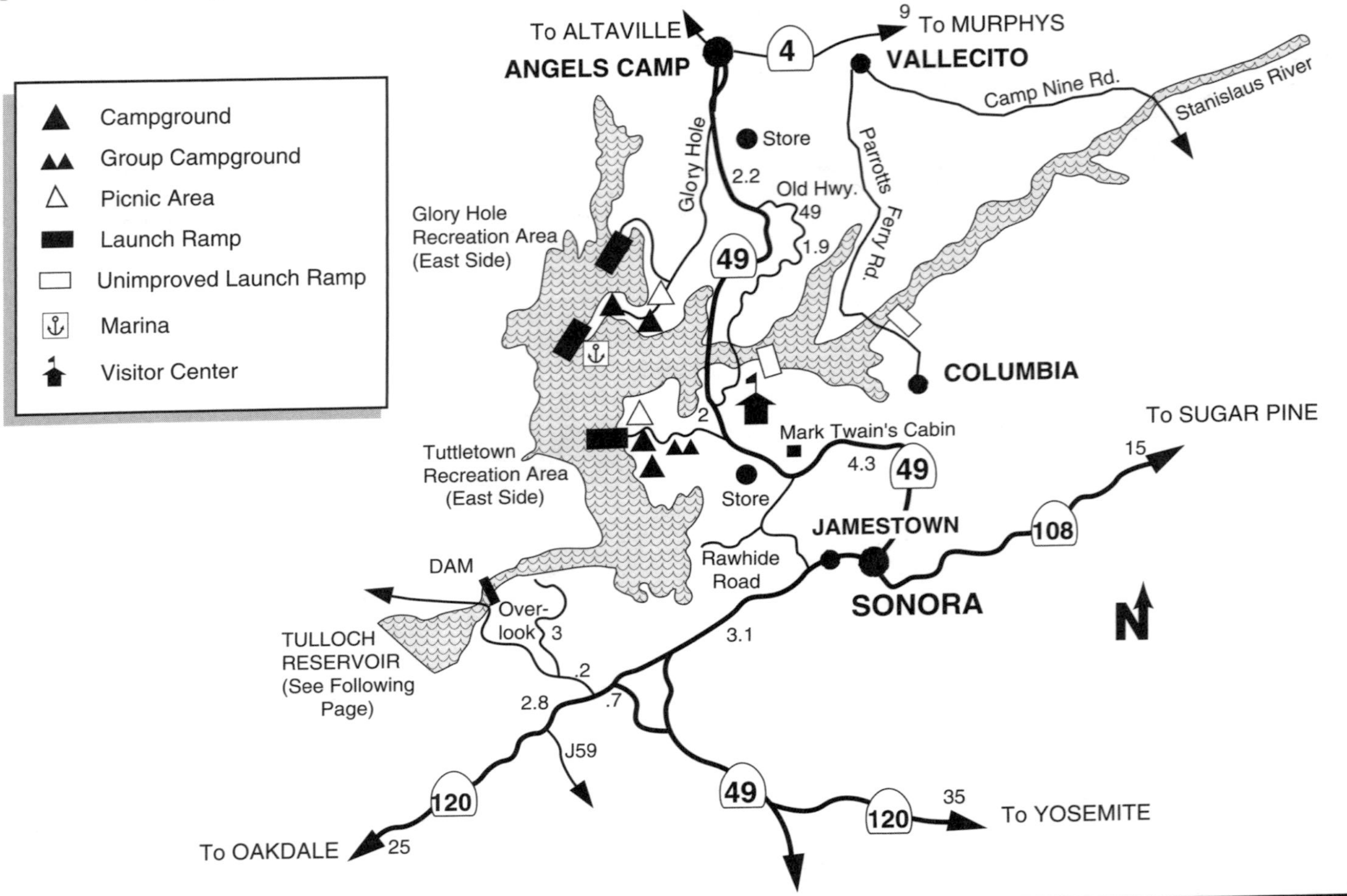

To ALTAVILLE
9 To MURPHYS
ANGELS CAMP
4
VALLECITO
Camp Nine Rd.
Stanislaus River
Campground
Group Campground
Picnic Area
Launch Ramp
Unimproved Launch Ramp
Marina
Visitor Center
Store
Glory Hole
2.2
Old Hwy. 49
1.9
Parrotts Ferry Rd.
Glory Hole Recreation Area (East Side)
49
COLUMBIA
To SUGAR PINE
15
2
Mark Twain's Cabin
4.3
Tuttletown Recreation Area (East Side)
Store
JAMESTOWN
108
Rawhide Road
DAM
SONORA
N
Over-look 3
TULLOCH RESERVOIR (See Following Page)
3.1
.2
2.8
.7
J59
120
To OAKDALE
25
35
To YOSEMITE

INFORMATION: Resource Manager, 6850 Studhorse Flat Road, Sonora 95370—Ph: (209) 536-9094			
CAMPING	**BOATING**	**RECREATION**	**OTHER**
Glory Hole: 124 Dev. Sites for Tents & R.V.s - Fee: $18 20 Walk-In Sites: $14 Tuttletown: 126 Dev. Sites for Tents & R.V.s - Fee: $18 20 Sites for Tents Only 2 Group Sites up to 60 People Fee: $100 to $120 Disposal Stations Reserve: (877) 444-6777	Open to All Boating Launch Ramps - Fee: $8 Full Service Marina Ph: (209) 785-3300 Fuel Dock Courtesy Docks Boat Pumpout Rentals: Fishing Boats, Canoes, Paddle Boats, Pontoons, Houseboats Check for Water Levels	Fishing: Rainbow & Brown Trout, Large & Smallmouth Bass, Kokanee, Bluegill, Catfish & Crappie Picnicking - Group Sites Swimming - Beaches Hiking Trails Bicycle Trails Equestrian Trails Amphitheater Programs Mark Twain's Cabin *No ORVs*	Visitors Center & Museum Ph: (209) 536-9543 Grocery Store at Glory Hole Marina Angels Camp R.V. & Camping Resort 3069 Hwy. 49 South Angels Camp 95222 Ph: (209) 736-0404 42 Dev. Sites for Tents & R.V.s - Full Hookups Rustic Cabins & Lodges

LAKE TULLOCH and SALT SPRINGS VALLEY RESERVOIR

Lake Tulloch, at an elevation of 510 feet, is on the western slope of the Sierras just east of Modesto. 55 miles of shoreline encompass two submerged valleys surrounded by rolling hills dotted with oak trees. This "Gold Country" Lake is open to all boating and has marine facilities. Fishing for trout can be good throughout the year because of the cold water flowing from New Melones Lake. Warm water fish and smallmouth bass are plentiful. Check water levels as they can drop late in the season. Salt Springs Valley Reservoir has a PWC course and a variety of boat races and fishing tournaments throughout the year. Bass fishing is a catch and release program.

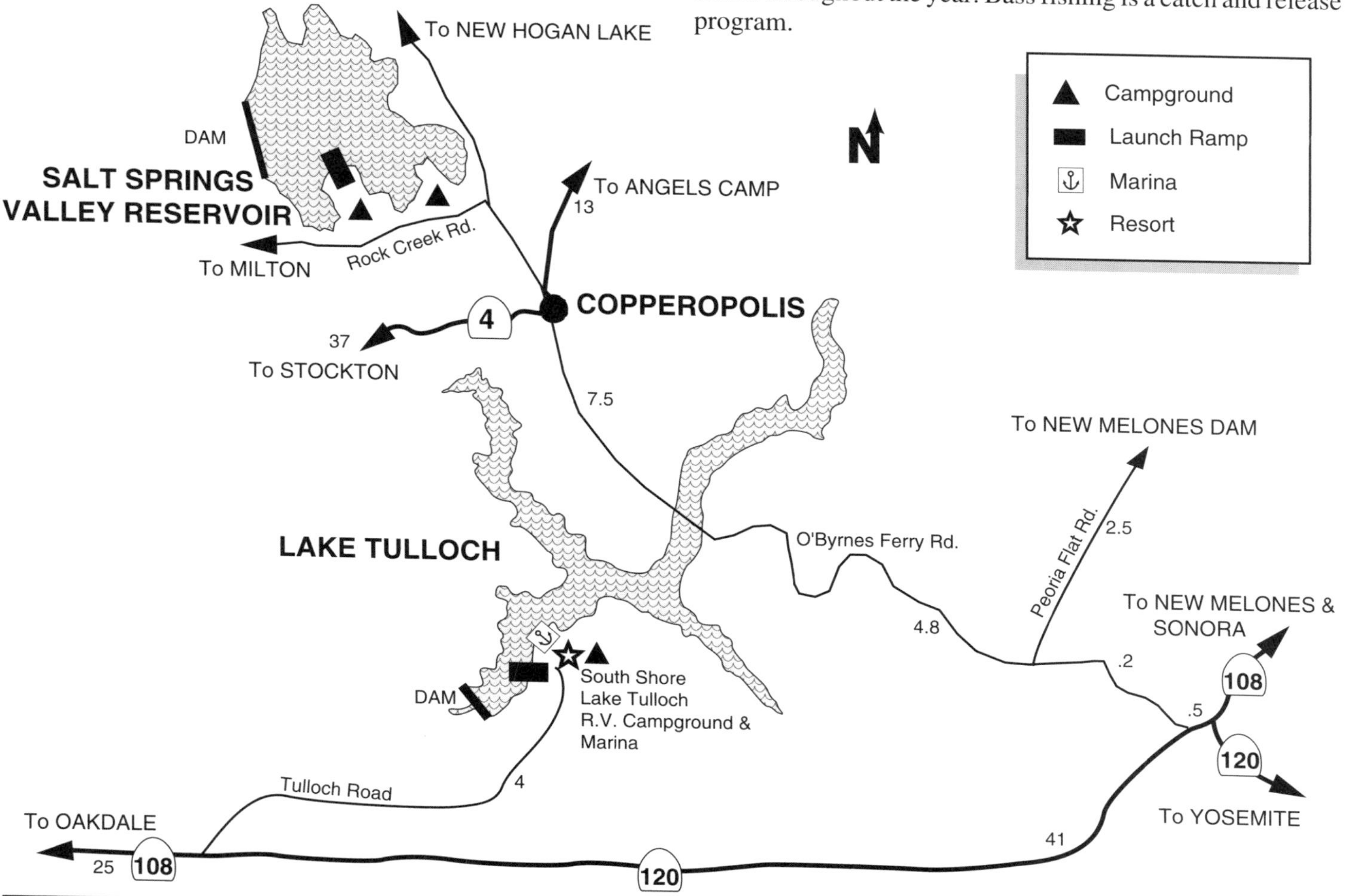

To NEW HOGAN LAKE
DAM
SALT SPRINGS VALLEY RESERVOIR
To MILTON
Rock Creek Rd.
To ANGELS CAMP
13
Campground
Launch Ramp
Marina
Resort
N
COPPEROPOLIS
4
37
To STOCKTON
7.5
To NEW MELONES DAM
LAKE TULLOCH
O'Byrnes Ferry Rd.
Peoria Flat Rd.
2.5
4.8
To NEW MELONES & SONORA
.2
108
.5
DAM
South Shore Lake Tulloch R.V. Campground & Marina
120
To YOSEMITE
Tulloch Road
4
To OAKDALE
25
108
120
41

INFORMATION: Tulloch R.V. Campground & Marina, 14448 Tulloch Rd., Jamestown 95327—Ph: (800) 894-2267

CAMPING	BOATING	RECREATION	OTHER
Lake Tulloch: 130 Dev. Sites for Tents & R.V.s Full Hookups Lakefront Cabins with Docks Overnight Boating Ph:(209) 881-0107 Salt Springs Valley: Dev. Sites for Tents & R.Vs. - $6 and up Day Use Fee: $15	Power, Row, Canoe, Sail, Waterski, PWCs, Windsurf & Inflatables Full Service Marina Launch Ramp Gas Dock Rentals: Fishing, Waterski & Patio Boats & Kayaks Ph: (209) 881-3410 Salt Springs Valley: No Waterskiing PWC Course Launch Ramp - Fee: $5	Fishing: Rainbow Trout, Small & Largemouth Bass, Bluegill, Catfish, Crappie Picnicking Swimming Pool & Beaches Hiking Trails Gold Panning Salt Springs Valley: Bass - Catch & Release	Lake Tulloch: Restaurant Grocery Store Group Packages for Special Events Salt Springs Valley Reservoir: 7422 Rock Creek Rd. Copperolpolis Ph: (209) 785-7787 Store Special Events

WOODWARD RESERVOIR

Woodward Reservoir, 2,900 surface acres, is at an elevation of 210 feet. It is located in the rolling foothills 6 miles north of Oakdale. This irrigation Reservoir is under the jurisdiction of Stanislaus County Department of Parks & Recreation. The 23 miles of shallow shoreline has many quiet coves and inlets for the boater and angler. The Lake is divided by speed limit restrictions with a few "No Boat" areas. Ample space allows all boaters to enjoy their sport. There is a good warm water fishery. The County maintains a campground on the edge of the Lake and a large overflow primitive camping area. This is a popular family park with approximately 3,240 acres of park land including a great radio control model plane area.

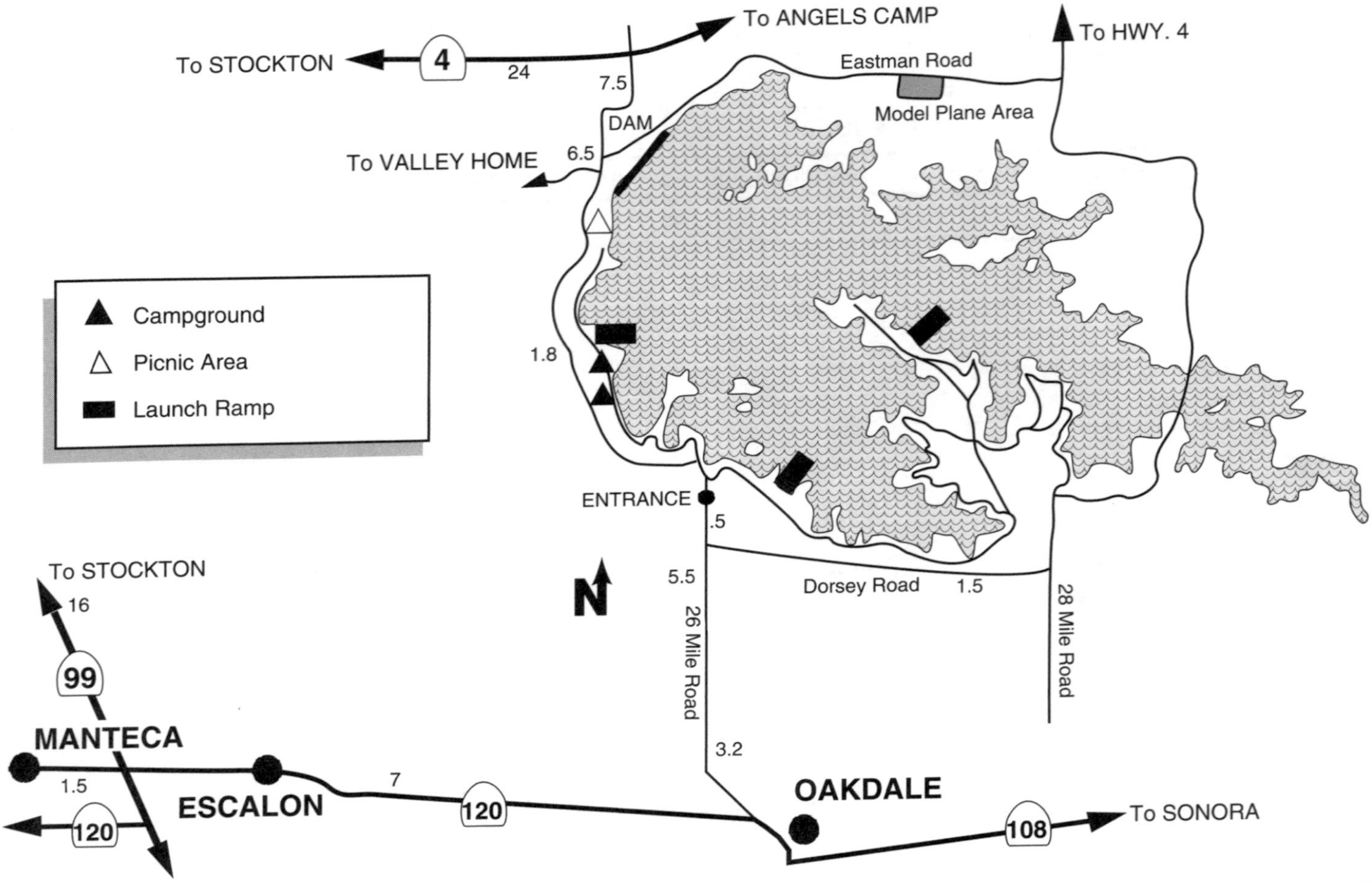

To ANGELS CAMP
To STOCKTON
4
24
7.5
To HWY. 4
Eastman Road
Model Plane Area
DAM
To VALLEY HOME
6.5
Campground
Picnic Area
Launch Ramp
1.8
ENTRANCE
.5
To STOCKTON
16
N
5.5
Dorsey Road
1.5
26 Mile Road
28 Mile Road
99
MANTECA
3.2
1.5
7
OAKDALE
ESCALON
120
120
108
To SONORA

INFORMATION: Woodward Reservoir, 14528 - 26 Mile Rd., Oakdale 95361—Ph: (209) 847-3304

CAMPING	BOATING	RECREATION	OTHER
155 Dev. Sites for Tents & R.V.s With 40 Full Hookups Fees: $17 - $23 Disposal Station No Reservations Undeveloped Sites in Designated Areas Fee: $15 Day Use Fee: $8	Power, Row, Canoe, Sail, Waterski, PWCs, Windsurf, Inflatables Restricted Speed Limit Areas Launch Ramps	Fishing: Rainbow Trout, Catfish, Sunfish, Bluegill & Largemouth Bass Swimming in Designated Areas Picnicking: Large Shelter Can Be Reserved Hiking Trails Equestrian Trails Radio Control Model Airplane Field No ORVs	Stanislaus County Dept. of Parks & Recreation 3800 Cornucopia Way #C Modesto 95358 Ph: (209) 525-6750 Full Facilities at Oakdale

DON PEDRO LAKE

Don Pedro Lake is at an elevation of 800 feet in the Sierra foothills of the southern region of the Gold Country. This huge Lake has a surface area of 13,000 acres with 160 miles of pine and oak-covered shoreline. The extensive facilities include three recreation areas and two full service marinas . The Lake is under the jurisdiction of Don Pedro Recreation Agency. The vast size and irregular shoreline provides a multitude of opportunities from boat-in camping to waterskiing. The angler will find a good varied fishery. Be aware, due to fluctuating water levels, emerging rocks and islands are potential boating hazards.

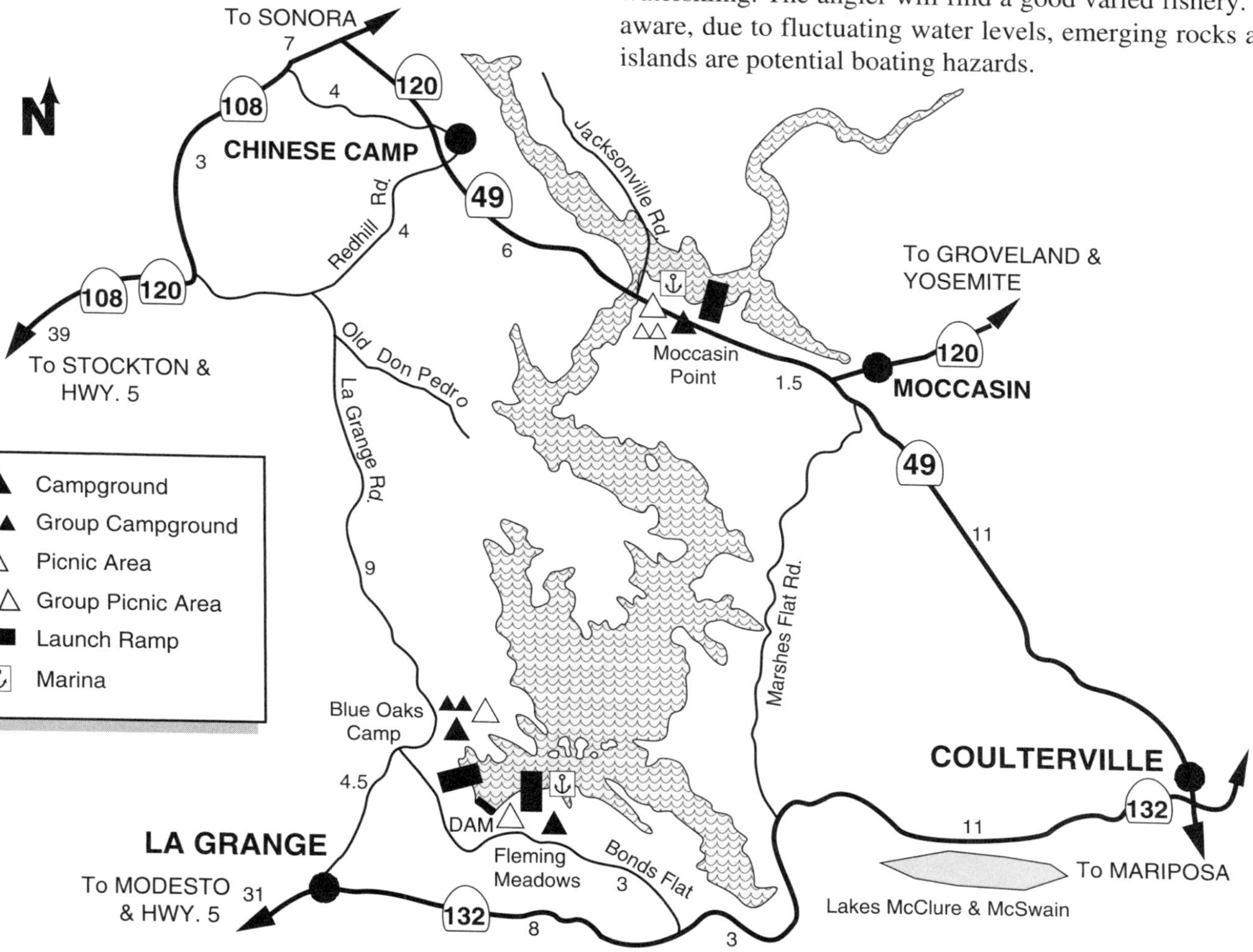

N
To SONORA
7
4
120
108
CHINESE CAMP
3
Redhill Rd.
4
49
6
Jacksonville Rd.
To GROVELAND &
YOSEMITE
108
120
39
To STOCKTON &
HWY. 5
Old Don Pedro
La Grange Rd.
Moccasin
Point
1.5
120
MOCCASIN
49
Campground
Group Campground
Picnic Area
Group Picnic Area
Launch Ramp
Marina
9
11
Marshes Flat Rd.
Blue Oaks
Camp
4.5
COULTERVILLE
132
11
DAM
LA GRANGE
Fleming
Meadows
Bonds Flat
3
To MARIPOSA
To MODESTO
& HWY. 5
31
132
8
3
Lakes McClure & McSwain

INFORMATION: Don Pedro Recreation Agency, 31 Bonds Flat Rd., La Grange 95329—Ph: (209) 852-2396

CAMPING	BOATING	RECREATION	OTHER
550 Dev. Sites for Tents & R.V.s Fees: $15 - $30 Full Hookups Group Camp to 200 People Reservation Fee: $7 Boat-in Camping - Fee: $5 *No Pets Allowed* Day Use Fee: $6	Power, Row, Canoe, Sail, Waterski, PWCs, Windsurf & Inflatable Full Service Marinas 3 Launch Ramps - $7 Rentals: Fishing & Ski Boats, Pontoons & PWCs Houseboat Rentals: Ph: (800) 255-5561 Docks, Berths, Moorings Dry Storage & Gas Private Houseboats Require Permit	Fishing: Trout, Catfish, Bluegill, Crappie, Salmon, Large & Smallmouth Bass Swimming Lagoon Handicap Access Picnicking Group Picnic Areas at Fleming Meadows & Moccasin Point Hiking Trails Softball & Volleyball Amphitheater	Snack Bars Cafe Grocery Stores Bait & Tackle Disposal Stations Gas Station Propane Lake Don Pedro Marina Ph: (209) 852-2369 Moccasin Point Marina Ph: (209) 989-2206

MODESTO RESERVOIR

Modesto Reservoir is at an elevation of 210 feet in the low hills and pasturelands northeast of Modesto. The Lake has a surface area of 2,800 acres with 31 miles of shoreline. The facilities are under the jurisdiction of the Stanislaus County Parks Department. This is a good boating Lake with westerly breezes for sailing and vast open water for the waterskier. Many coves are available for unlimited boat camping but there is a 5- mph speed limit near facilities and on the southern area of the Lake. There are also several no boating zones; refer to posted rules or ask a park attendant for specifics. Inlets and coves have submerged trees which provide for a good warm water fishery.

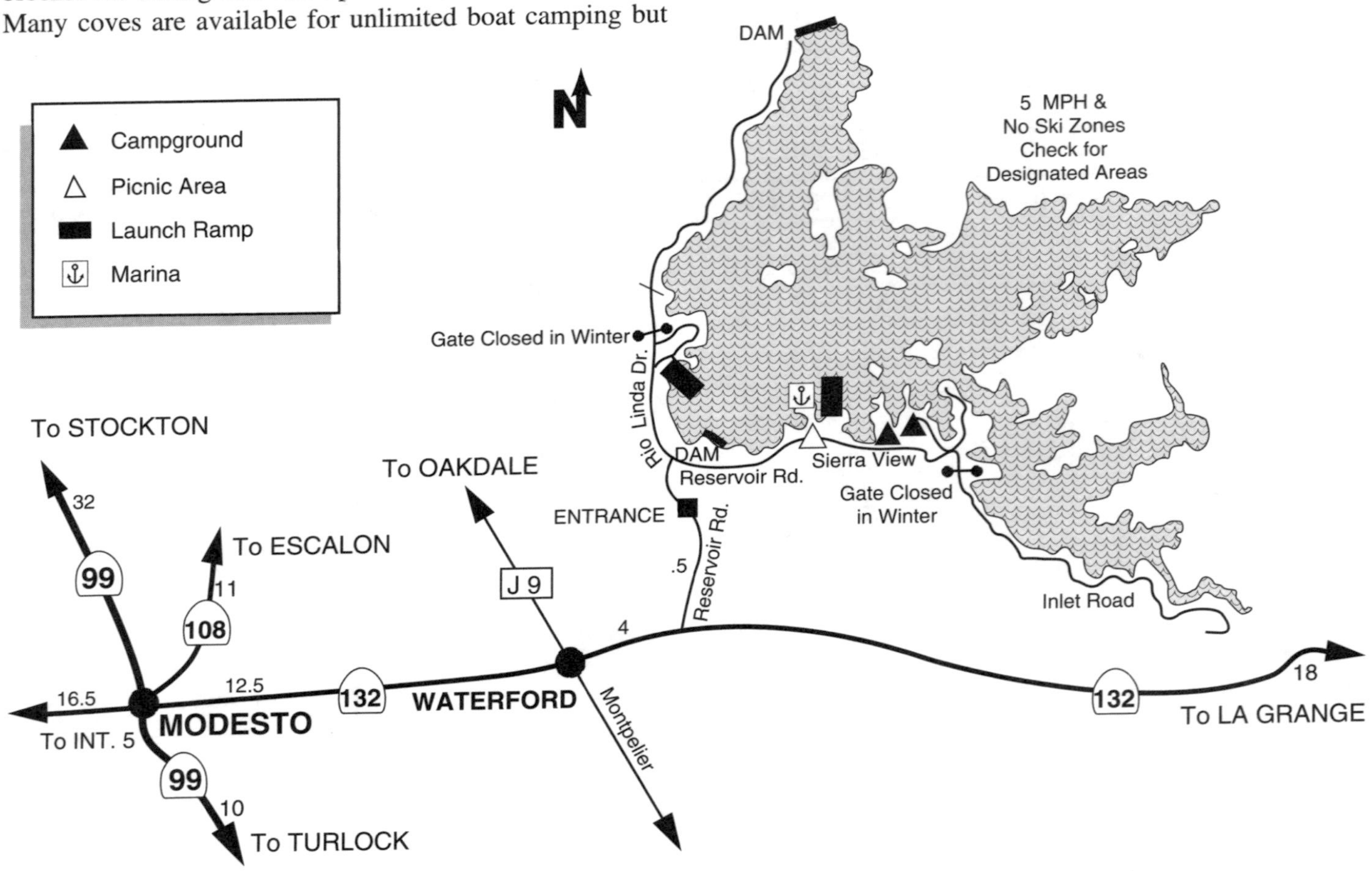

N
Campground
Picnic Area
Launch Ramp
Marina
DAM
5 MPH & No Ski Zones Check for Designated Areas
Gate Closed in Winter
Rio Linda Dr.
DAM
Reservoir Rd.
Sierra View
Gate Closed in Winter
ENTRANCE
.5
Reservoir Rd.
Inlet Road
To STOCKTON
32
99
To ESCALON
11
108
To OAKDALE
J 9
4
16.5
12.5
132
WATERFORD
MODESTO
To INT. 5
99
10
To TURLOCK
Montpelier
132
18
To LA GRANGE

INFORMATION: Modesto Reservoir, 18143 Reservoir Rd., Waterford 95386—Ph: (209) 874-9540

CAMPING	BOATING	RECREATION	OTHER
150 Dev. Sites for Tents & R.V.s Full Hookups Fees: $19 - $25 Disposal Station No Reservations Undeveloped Sites Fee: $15 Day Use Fee: $8	Power, Row, Canoe, Sail, Waterski, PWCs, Windsurfing & Inflatables Launch Ramps Docks 5 MPH and No Ski Zones Check Water Levels	Fishing: Large & Smallmouth Bass, Rainbow Trout, Catfish, Crappie Swimming - Beaches Picnicking Archery Range Radio Control Glider Field	Stanlislaus County Dept. of Parks & Recreation 3800 Cornucopia Way #C Modesto 95358 Ph: (209) 525-6750

TURLOCK LAKE

Turlock Lake, at an elevation of 250 feet, is nestled in the foothills 25 miles east of Modesto. The State Recreation Area is part of the California State Park System. The Lake has a surface area of 3,500 acres with 26 miles of shoreline. Open year around, this is a popular recreation area. The Lake is open to all types of boating. In late summer, low water levels can be a hazard. Trout are planted on a regular basis in season and there is a good warm water fishery. Swimming is popular and several beaches are available. The shaded campground is located along the Tuolomne River. Reservations are advised during summer months.

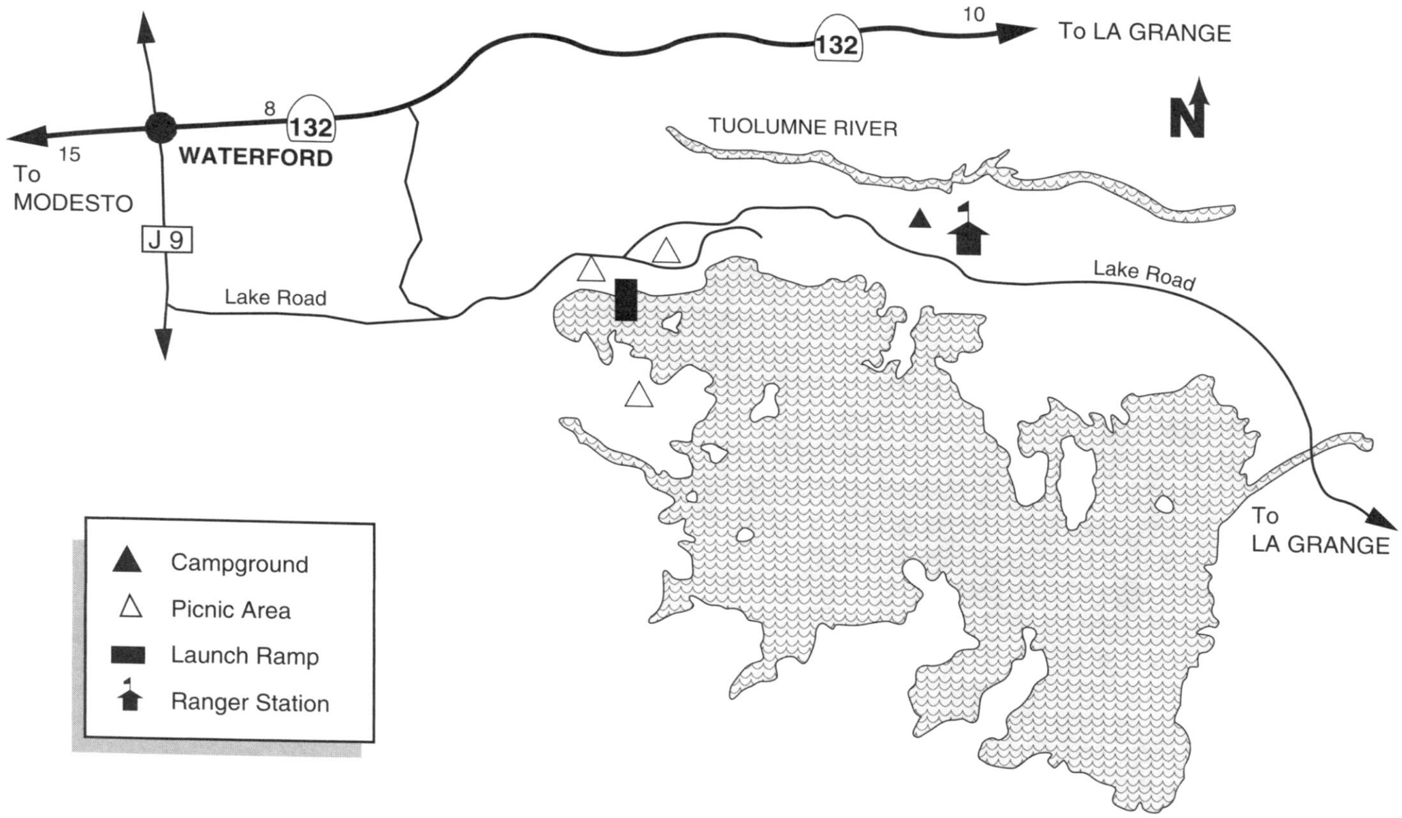

10
132
To LA GRANGE
N
8
132
15
WATERFORD
To
MODESTO
J 9
TUOLUMNE RIVER
Lake Road
Lake Road
To
LA GRANGE
Campground
Picnic Area
Launch Ramp
Ranger Station

INFORMATION: Turlock State Recreation Area, 22600 Lake Rd., La Grange 95329—Ph: (209) 874-2056

CAMPING	BOATING	RECREATION	OTHER
State Recreation Area: 66 Dev. Sites for Tents & R.V.s to 27 Feet Fees: $20 Reservations: Ph: (800) 444-7275 Day Use Fee: $6	Power, Row, Canoe, Sail, Waterski, PWCs, Windsurf & Inflatable Launch Ramp Boat Use Fee: $6 *Low Water Levels Late in Summer*	Fishing: Trout, Catfish, Bluegill, Crappie, Large & Smallmouth Bass Swimming - Beaches Picnicking Hiking Trails	Campfire & Junior Ranger Program Full Facilities at Waterford

LAKE MC CLURE and LAKE MC SWAIN

Located in the Mother Lode Country of the Sierra foothills, these Lakes are at an elevations of 400 to 1,000 feet. Lake McClure, with a surface area of 7,100 acres, has 82 miles of pine and oak-covered shoreline. Lake McSwain, 7-1/2 miles of shoreline, is the forebay of Lake McClure. Both these Lakes have full recreation facilities. Waterskiiers will find 26 miles of clear, open water. Many coves are popular for houseboats at Lake McClure. Very cold water flowing from the dam into Lake McSwain has created a good fishery with weekly trout plants in season. There is a 10 mph speed limit for boaters on Lake McSwain. This Lake is full year around. Waterskiing and houseboats are not allowed at McSwain.

....Continued....

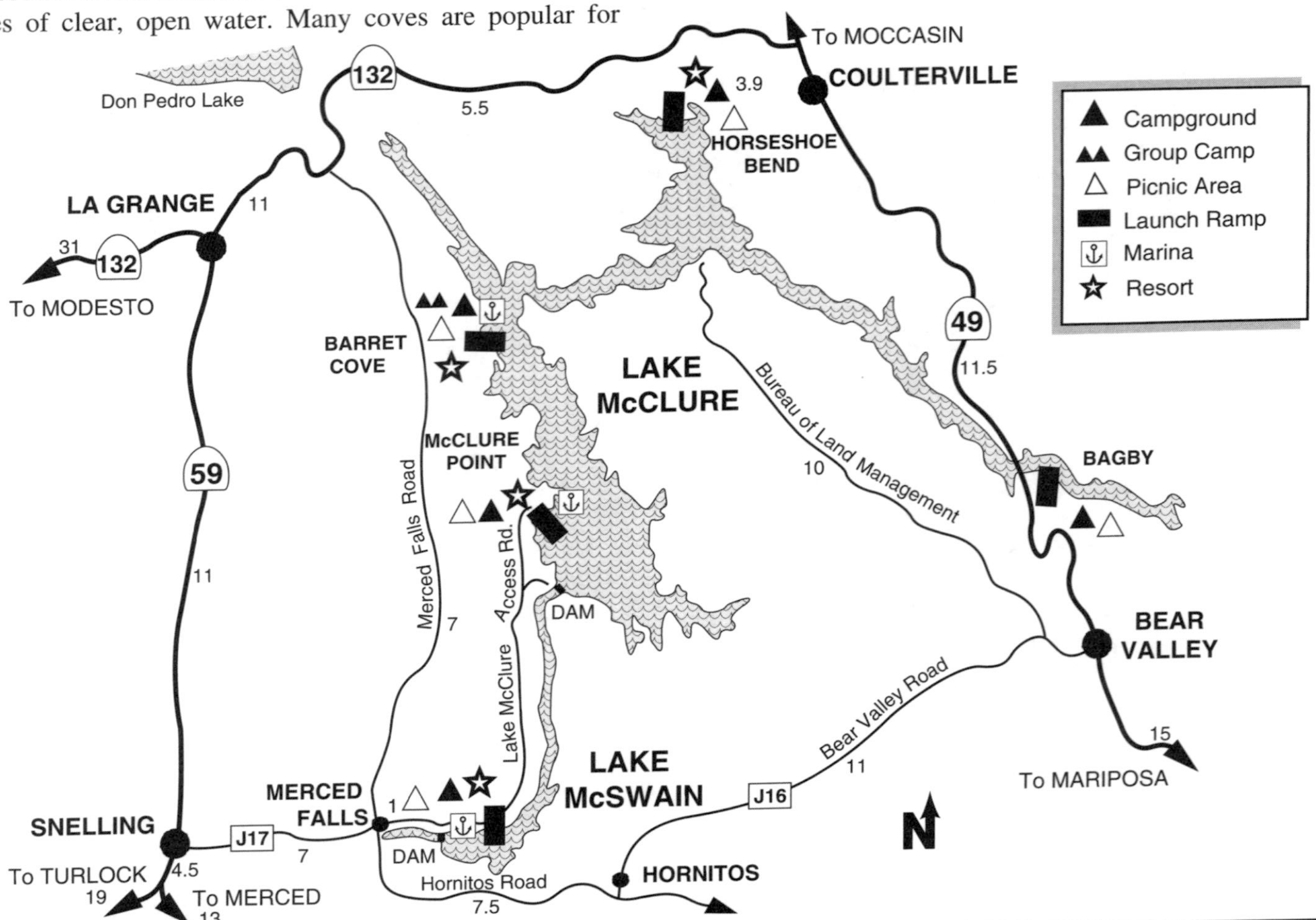

To MOCCASIN
COULTERVILLE
132
5.5
3.9
Don Pedro Lake
HORSESHOE BEND
Campground
Group Camp
Picnic Area
Launch Ramp
Marina
Resort
LA GRANGE
11
31
132
To MODESTO
49
BARRET COVE
LAKE McCLURE
11.5
Bureau of Land Management
10
McCLURE POINT
BAGBY
59
Merced Falls Road
Access Rd.
11
7
DAM
BEAR VALLEY
Lake McClure
Bear Valley Road
15
11
To MARIPOSA
LAKE McSWAIN
MERCED FALLS
1
J16
SNELLING
J17
7
DAM
N
To TURLOCK
19
4.5
To MERCED
13
Hornitos Road
7.5
HORNITOS

INFORMATION: Merced Irrigation District Parks Dept. - See Following Page for Recreation Areas			
CAMPING	**BOATING**	**RECREATION**	**OTHER**
600 Dev. Sites for Tents & R.V.s Fee: $20 With Full Hookups Fee: $26 Disposal Stations Reservations - Fee: $6 Ph: (800) 468-8889 Day Use Fee: $6 Pet Fee: $3	All Boating Allowed at Lake McClure No Waterskiing or Houseboats at Lake McSwain Full Service Marinas Launch Ramps - $6 Rentals: Fishing & Pontoon Boats, Houseboats Docks, Berths Moorings, Gas Boat Storage	Fishing: Trout, King Salmon, Catfish, Bluegill, Crappie & Largemouth Bass Swim Lagoons at Lake McClure Beaches Picnicking Group Picnic Shelters - Reservations Hiking Trails Playgrounds	Snack Bars Grocery Stores Bait & Tackle Gas Stations Propane

Merced Irrigation District Parks Department
9090 Lake McClure Road
Snelling 95369
Ph: (209) 378-2521

Campground Information: Ph: (209) 378-2521
Reservations: Ph: (800) 468-8889
Fess: Tent & R.V. Sites: $20
With Hookups: $26

McClure Point

100 Developed Campsites for Tents & R.V.
52 Water & Electric Hookups
30 Picnic Sites, Swim Lagoon,
Grocery Store, Laundromat, Showers
Full Service Marina - Ph: (209) 378-2441
2 Launch Ramps, Gas,
Docks, Berths, Houseboat Moorings, Storage
Rentals: Fishing & Patio Boats

Barrett Cove

275 Developed Campsites for Tents & R.V.
89 Water & Electric Hookups
Barrett Cove Ph: (209) 378-2611
50 Picnic Sites, Seasonal Swim Lagoon,
Children's Playground,
Grocery Store,
Full Service Marina - Ph: (209) 378-2441
5-Lane Launch Ramp, Gas,
Docks, Berths, Houseboat Moorings, Storage
Rentals: Fishing & Patio Boats
Houseboat Rentals: Ph: (877) 468-7326

Horseshoe Bend

110 Developed Campsites for Tents & R.V.
35 Water & Electric Hookups
Horseshoe Bend Ph: (209) 878-3452
32 Picnic Sites, Swim Lagoon,
Grocery Store,
2-Lane Launch Ramp

Lake McSwain

99 Developed Campsites for Tents & R.V.
65 Water & Electric Hookups
48 Picnic Sites, Swim Lagoon,
Children's Playground,
Grocery Store,
Full Service Marina - Ph: (209) 378-2534
2-Lane Launch Ramp, Gas,
Rentals: Fishing & Patio Boats

Bagby

30 Developed Campsites for Tents & R.V.
10 Water & Electric Hookups
5 Picnic Sites,
1-Lane Launch Ramp

LAKE YOSEMITE

Located in the rolling foothills of the Sierra Nevada, Lake Yosemite is east of Merced and under the jurisdiction of the County of Merced. This Lake has 387 surface acres and offers good boat launch facilities, beaches and shaded picnic sites for groups up to 200 people. All types of boating are allowed with designated areas for waterskiing, sailing and rowing. Fishing can be productive at this scenic Lake in the San Joaquin Valley. Merced County has an extensive network of bicycle paths which include Lake Yosemite. Facilities are for day use only except for Youth Group camping. Call for information and reservations.

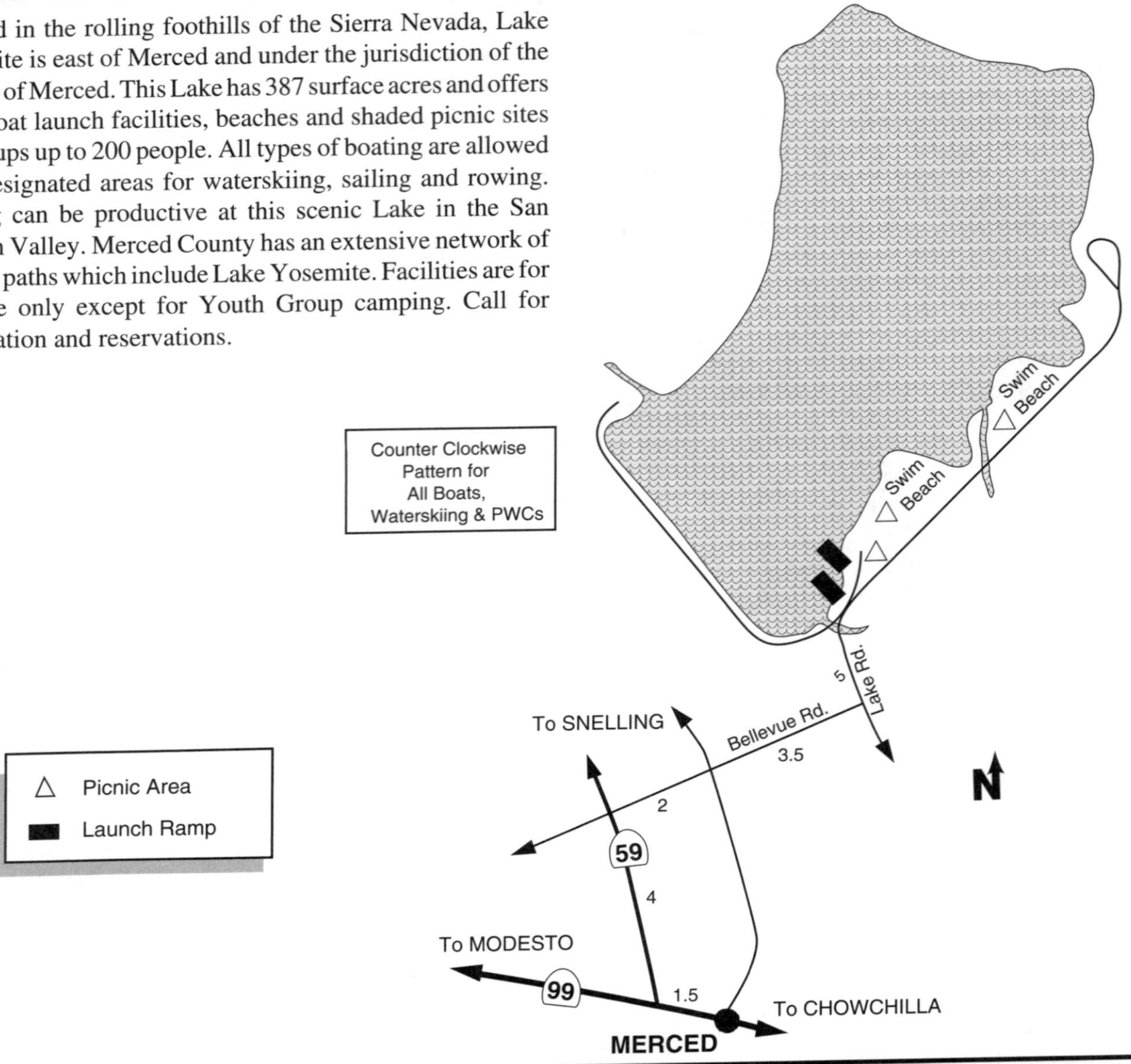
Counter Clockwise Pattern for All Boats, Waterskiing & PWCs
Swim Beach
Swim Beach
Lake Rd.
5
Bellevue Rd.
3.5
To SNELLING
N
Picnic Area
Launch Ramp
2
59
4
To MODESTO
99
1.5
To CHOWCHILLA
MERCED

INFORMATION: Merced County Parks & Recreation, 21st & N Sts., Merced 95340—Ph: (209) 385-7426

CAMPING	BOATING	RECREATION	OTHER
Youth Groups Only Reservations: Ph: (209) 385-7426 Day Use Fee: $6	All Boating Allowed with Designated Areas for Sailboats, Waterskiing, Rowboats, Powerboats & PWCs Launch Ramps Fee: $6 Docks and Marina Rentals: Paddle Boats	Fishing: Trout, Largemouth Bass, Bluegill & Catfish Swimming - Designated Areas Only Beaches Picnicking Group Picnic Facility with Covered Shelters Large Indoor Facility Bicycle Paths Volleyball Courts	Snack Bar Home to Lake Yosemite Sailing Club Summer Sailboat Races North Part of the Lake Channel for Kayakers during Summer Park is located at 5714 N. Lake Rd. Merced

SOULAJULE, NICASIO, PHOENIX, LAGUNITAS, BON TEMPE, ALPINE, KENT and STAFFORD LAKES

These Lakes, along the slopes of Mt. Tamalpais, are under the jurisdiction of the North Marin Municipal Water District except for Stafford Lake Park which is operated by the Marin County Department of Parks. There are numerous shaded hiking trails. Boating and swimming are not permitted at any Lake. Nicasio and Soulajule have warm water fisheries. Stafford Lake has largemouth bass. Lagunitas Lake has special restrictions including the use of artificial lures only with single barbless hooks and a limit of 2 fish.Stafford Lake Park, 139 acres, offers two large group picnic areas and other day use facilities. Samuel P. Taylor State Park campgrounds include single, group and horse campsites and a network of hiking, bicycling and equestrian trails.

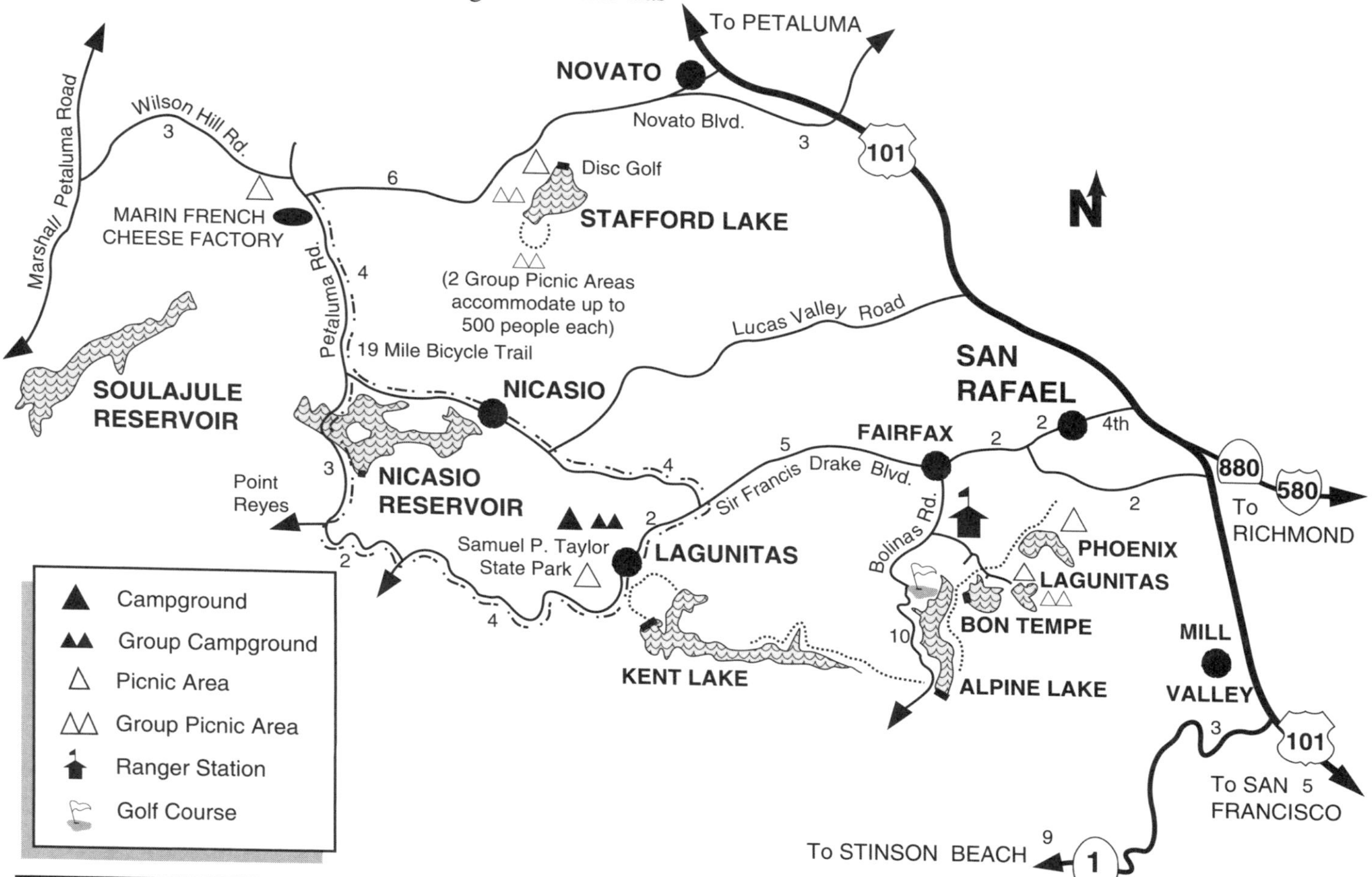

To PETALUMA
NOVATO
Novato Blvd.
Wilson Hill Rd.
Marshall Petaluma Road
Disc Golf
STAFFORD LAKE
MARIN FRENCH CHEESE FACTORY
Petaluma Rd.
(2 Group Picnic Areas accommodate up to 500 people each)
19 Mile Bicycle Trail
Lucas Valley Road
101
N
SAN RAFAEL
SOULAJULE RESERVOIR
NICASIO
NICASIO RESERVOIR
Point Reyes
FAIRFAX
4th
Sir Francis Drake Blvd.
Bolinas Rd.
880
580
To RICHMOND
Samuel P. Taylor State Park
LAGUNITAS
PHOENIX
LAGUNITAS
BON TEMPE
MILL VALLEY
KENT LAKE
ALPINE LAKE
To SAN FRANCISCO
To STINSON BEACH
1
Campground
Group Campground
Picnic Area
Group Picnic Area
Ranger Station
Golf Course

INFORMATION: Marin Municipal Water District, 220 Nellen Ave., Corte Madera 94925—Ph: (415) 945-1455

CAMPING	BOATING	RECREATION	OTHER
No Camping on Marin Water District Land Lakes: Day Use Only Vehicle Fee: $7 Nearby: Samuel P. Taylor Park Ph: (415) 488-9897 Developed Sites for Tents & R.V.s to 31 Feet Fees: $20 to $25 Group Camp Site Horse Camp Reserve Ph:(800) 444-7275	No Boating Allowed	Fishing: Trout, Bass, Bluegill, Catfish & Crappie Fishing Info: (415) 945-1194 Stafford: Largemouth Bass *No Live Bait (except worms)* Hiking & Equestrian Trails Bicycle Trails Picnicking Group Sites Group Picnic @ Lagunitas Reserve: (415) 945-1180 *No Swimming or Wading*	Stafford Lake: County of Marin Parks & Open Space 3501 Civic Center Dr. San Rafael 94903 Ph: (415) 499-6387 Picnic Areas up to 500 People Disc Golf Course Vehicle Fee: $5 to $8 Walk-In Fee: $2

LAKES ANZA, MERRITT and TEMESCAL, BERKELEY AQUATIC PARK

Lake Anza is a small Lake within the beautiful Charles Lee Tilden Regional Park, one of the most extensively developed facilities in the Bay Area. With over 2,077 acres, this Park includes a public golf course, botanical gardens, a carousel, pony rides and a scaled-down steam train. Temescal Recreation Area, 48 acres, includes a small 10-acre Lake. This facility is popular for swimming, fishing and picnicking. The City of Oakland administers the 160-acre brackish water Lake Merritt. The surrounding Lakeside Park has expansive shaded lawns, picnic areas, playground and North America's oldest bird sanctuary. Boating, bicycling and picnicking can be enjoyed at the Berkeley Aquatic Park along with a great playground for children.

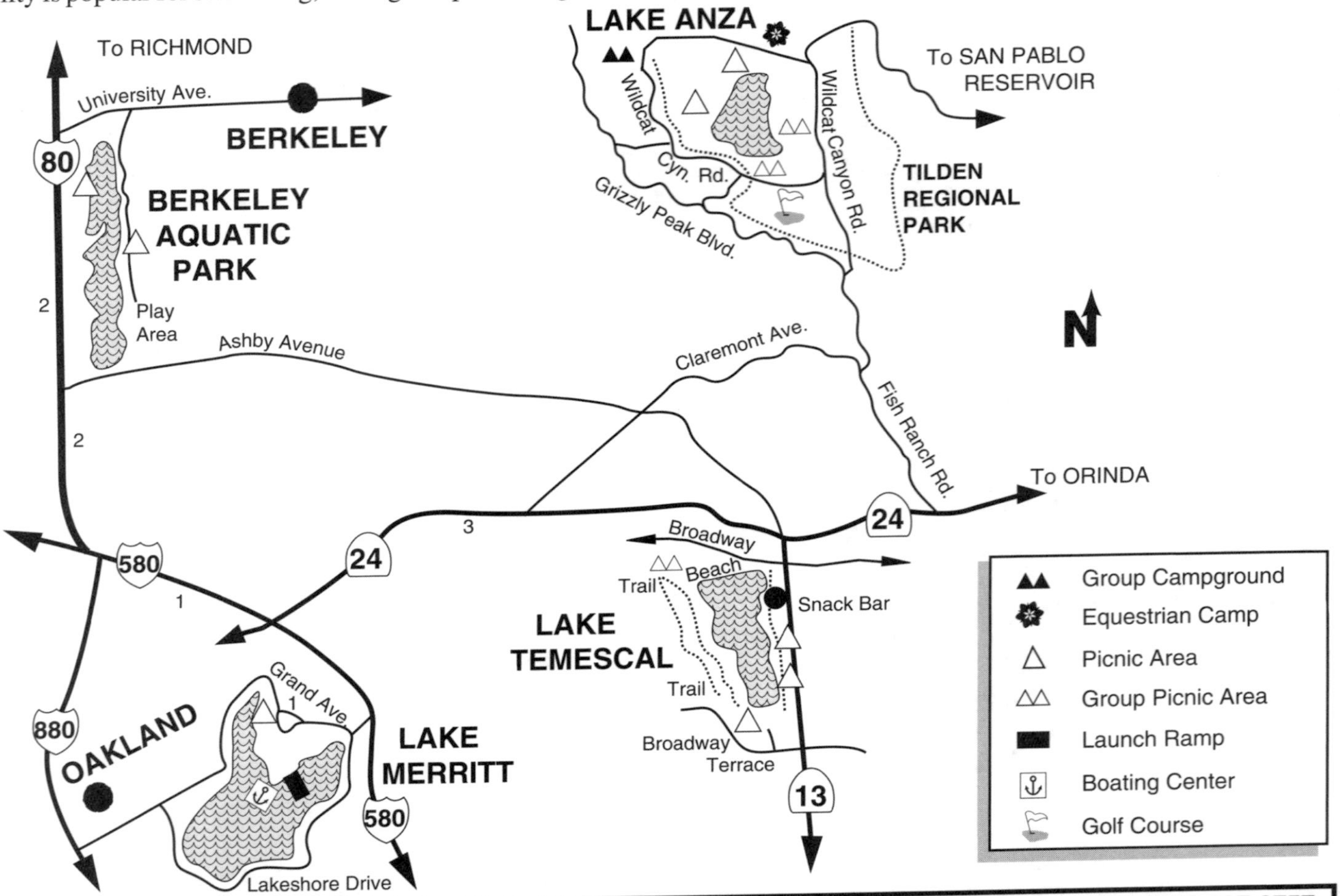
LAKE ANZA
To RICHMOND
University Ave.
BERKELEY
80
BERKELEY
AQUATIC
PARK
2
Play
Area
Ashby Avenue
2
Wildcat
Cyn. Rd.
Grizzly Peak Blvd.
Wildcat Canyon Rd.
TILDEN
REGIONAL
PARK
To SAN PABLO
RESERVOIR
N
Claremont Ave.
Fish Ranch Rd.
To ORINDA
24
580
1
3
24
Broadway
Beach
Trail
Snack Bar
LAKE
TEMESCAL
Trail
Broadway
Terrace
13
Grand Ave.
1
880
OAKLAND
LAKE
MERRITT
580
Lakeshore Drive
Group Campground
Equestrian Camp
Picnic Area
Group Picnic Area
Launch Ramp
Boating Center
Golf Course

INFORMATION:Anza & Temescal-East Bay Reg. Parks, 2950 Peralta Oaks, Oakland 94605—Ph: (888) 327-2757

CAMPING	BOATING	RECREATION	OTHER
Tilden Regional Park: Group Campground Reservations Ph: (888) 327-2757 Equestrian Campground Reservations Ph: (510) 636-1684 Temescal, Merritt & Berkeley Aquatic Park Day Use Only	Anza & Temescal: No Boating Berkeley Aquatic Park: Sail, Windsurf & Row Lake Merritt: Launch Ramp & Hoist Rentals: Sail, Row, Pedal Boats & Kayaks Sailing Instructions	Fishing: Trout, Bass, Catfish, Crappie & Sunfish Picnicking Group Picnic Sites Hiking & Bicycling Trails Equestrian Trails Playgrounds Swimming - Beaches: Anza & Temescal Only	Lake Merritt Boating Center: Oakland Office of Parks & Recreation 568 Bellevue Ave. Oakland 94610 Ph: (510) 238-2196 Bird Sanctuary Gardens & Bonsai Center Children's Fairyland Berkeley Aquatic Park Ph: (510) 981-5150

SAN PABLO RESERVOIR

East of the Berkeley hills, San Pablo Reservoir is located at an elevation of 314 feet. With 866 surface acres and 14 miles of shoreline, this Reservoir is under the jurisdiction of the East Bay Municipal Utility District. This is a popular boating Lake with good marine facilities. Afternoon winds are great for sailing. Windsurfing, waterskiing and swimming are not permitted. An extensive fishery habitat, along with an annual trout planting schedule, make this a good lake for anglers. There are 142 picnic sites with barbecues overlooking the water plus a children's play area. In addition, there is a large group picnic area which can be reserved. Hiking, bicycling and equestrian trails lead to Briones and Tilden Regional Parks. San Pablo Reservoir is closed in winter for migratory birds and the wildlife enchancement program.

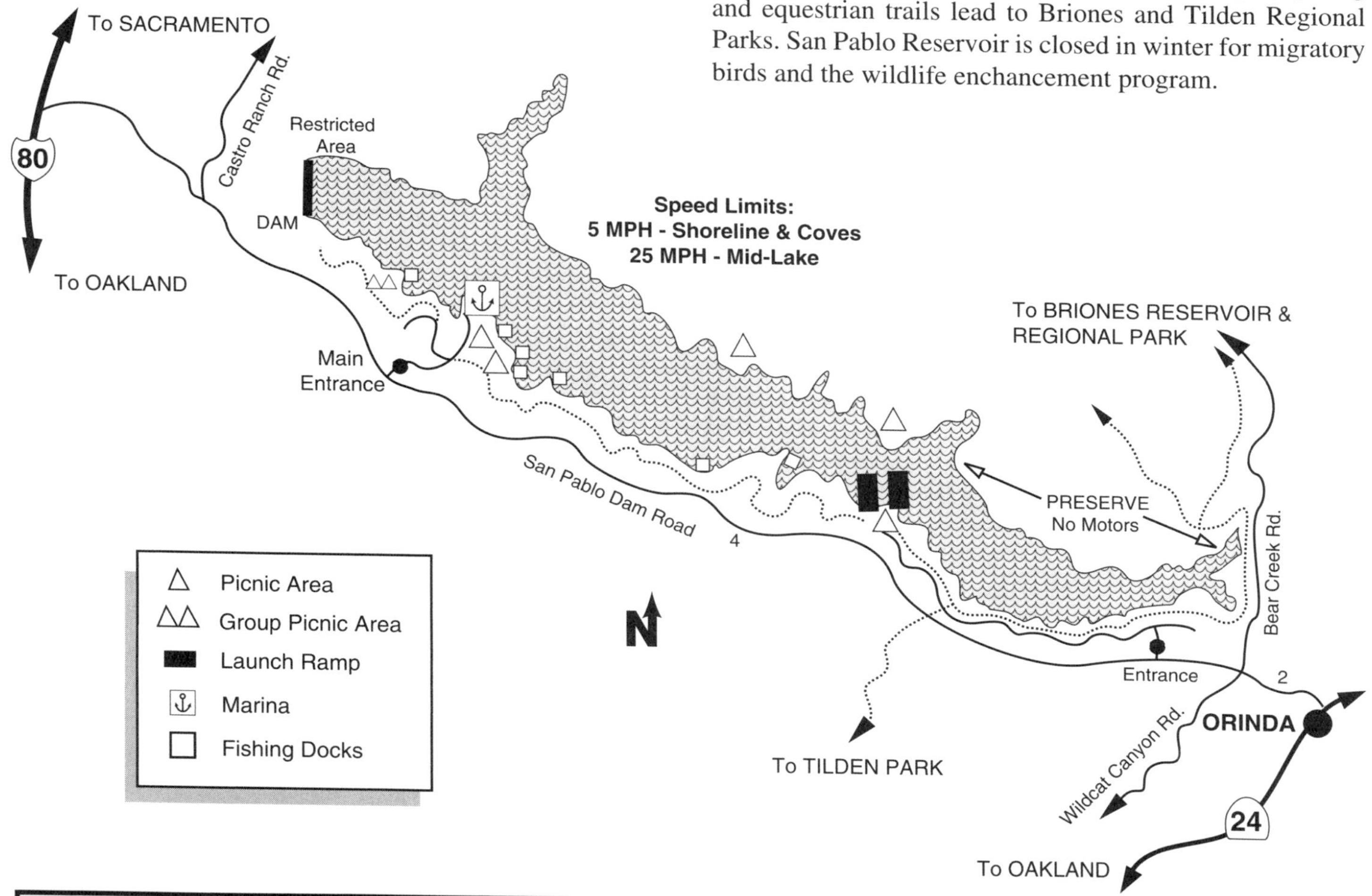

To SACRAMENTO
Castro Ranch Rd.
80
To OAKLAND
Restricted Area
DAM
Speed Limits:
5 MPH - Shoreline & Coves
25 MPH - Mid-Lake
Main Entrance
San Pablo Dam Road
4
To BRIONES RESERVOIR & REGIONAL PARK
PRESERVE
No Motors
Bear Creek Rd.
Entrance
2
ORINDA
To TILDEN PARK
Wildcat Canyon Rd.
24
To OAKLAND
N
Picnic Area
Group Picnic Area
Launch Ramp
Marina
Fishing Docks

INFORMATION: San Pablo Reservoir, 7301 San Pablo Dam Rd., El Sobrante 94803—Ph: (510) 223-1661

CAMPING	BOATING	RECREATION	OTHER
No Camping Day Use Only Fee: $6 Pets Fee: $2 No Dogs Allowed on Boats Group Picnic Area for up to 100 People By Reservation Only	Power, Row & Sail Boats *No Waterskiing or Windsurfing* Launch Ramp Fee: $7 Marina & Docks Rentals: Fishing, Row, Kayaks & Patio Boats	Fishing: Trophy Trout, Smallmouth Bass, Sturgeon, Catfish, Crappie & Bluegill Fishing Fee: $4 Fishing Docks Fishing Access Trail Picnic Areas Group Sites Hiking, Bicycle & Equestrian Trails Playground *No Swimming or Wading*	Restaurant Snack Bar Bait & Tackle Fish Cleaning Stations Briones Regional Park: Group Camping Group Picnic Sites For Information: East Bay Regional Parks Ph: (888) 327-2757

LAFAYETTE RESERVOIR

Lafayette Reservoir is a great scenic retreat from the urban areas that surround it. Amid the rolling, oak-covered hills of Contra Costa County and within the city limits of Lafayette, this popular Reservoir has 126 surface acres and is for day use only. Electric motors are permitted. You can hand launch small boats at the dock and rental boats are available. In addition to planted trout, the angler will find a warm water fishery. This is a good Lake for children to learn to fish and sail. Two group picnic areas can be reserved. A paved walking trail surrounds the Lake. At designated times, these trails can also be used by bicyclists, roller skaters and scooters. A self-guided nature trail goes through 925 acres of open space. The facilities are under the jurisdiction of the East Bay Municipal Utility District. No body contact with the water is permitted.

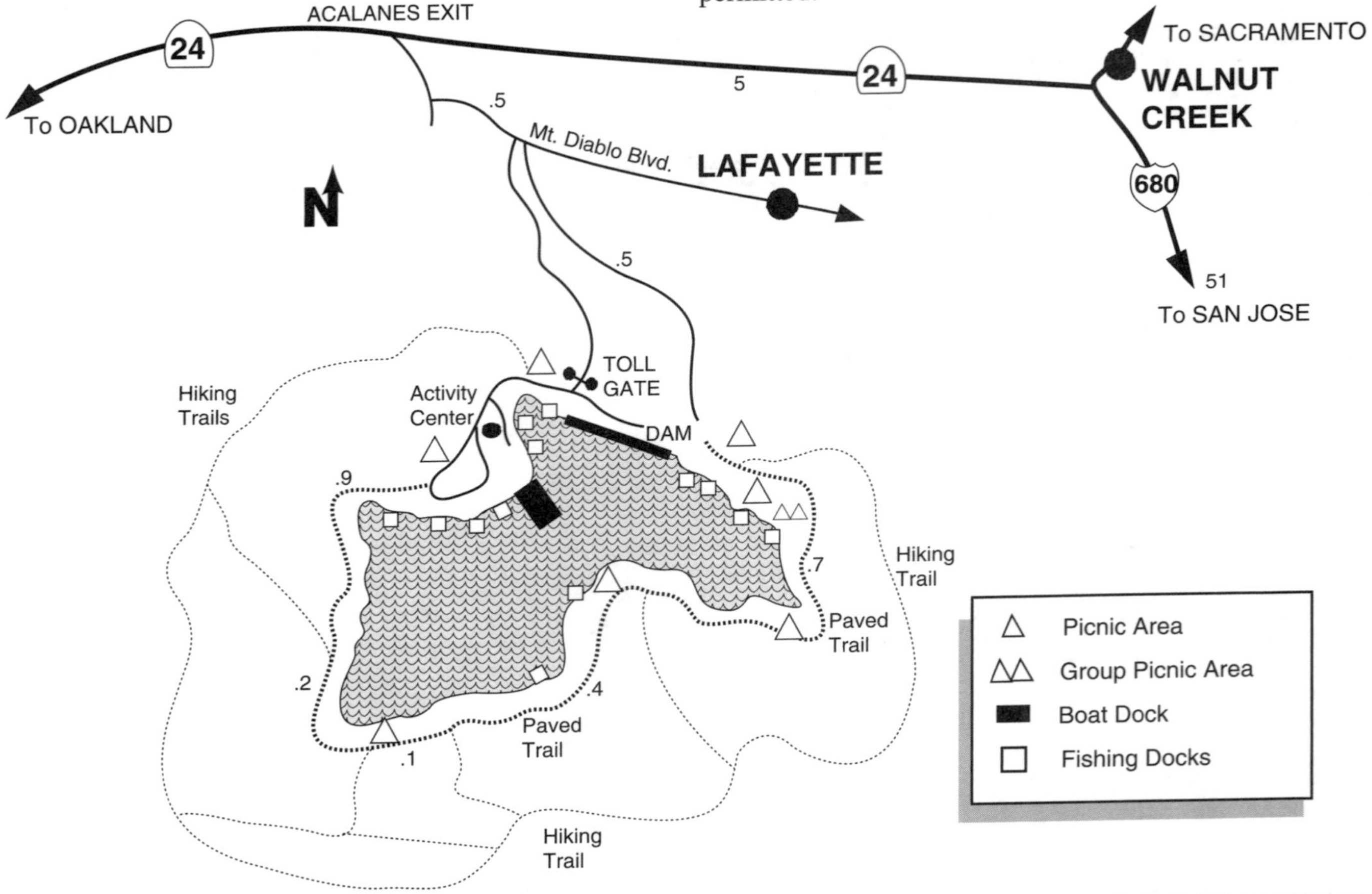
ACALANES EXIT
24
To OAKLAND
.5
Mt. Diablo Blvd.
5
24
To SACRAMENTO
WALNUT
CREEK
LAFAYETTE
680
51
To SAN JOSE
N
.5
TOLL
GATE
Activity
Center
DAM
Hiking
Trails
.9
.7
Hiking
Trail
Paved
Trail
.2
.4
.1
Paved
Trail
Hiking
Trail
Picnic Area
Group Picnic Area
Boat Dock
Fishing Docks

INFORMATION: East Bay Muni. Utility District. P.O. Box 24055, Oakland 94623—Ph: (925) 284-9669-Reservoir

CAMPING	BOATING	RECREATION	OTHER
No Camping Day Use Only Fee: $6 2 Group Picnic Areas By Reservation 50 & 250 People	Sail & Row Boats, Kayaks & Canoes Cartop Boats Only Hand Launch Electric Motors Only Launch Dock - Fee: $3 Rentals: Pedal & Row Boats	Fishing: Rainbow Trout, Largemouth Bass, Bluegill, Perch & Catfish Fishing Fee: $4 Fishing Docks Picnic Areas Group Picnic Sites Hiking Trails Bicycle Trails Children's Playground *No Swimming*	Bait & Tackle Fishing Licenses Fish Cleaning Stations Bicycles, Rollerskates & Scooters Permitted: Tues. & Thurs. Noon to Closing Sunday Opening to 11:00 am

CONTRA LOMA RESERVOIR

Located in the rolling hills of eastern Contra Costa County, Contra Loma Reservoir, 80 surface acres, is within the 775-acre Contra Loma Regional Park. Hiking, bicycling and equestrian trails run through the open grasslands of the Park into the adjoining Black Diamond Mines Regional Preserve. Large shaded lawns with picnic areas, group picnic sites and playgrounds are available. There is a sandy swim beach and a handicap accessible swim ramp. Row boats, electric powered boats and windsurfers are allowed. The angler will find catfish and bluegill along with a good striped bass population. This facility is under the jurisdiction of the East Bay Regional Park District.

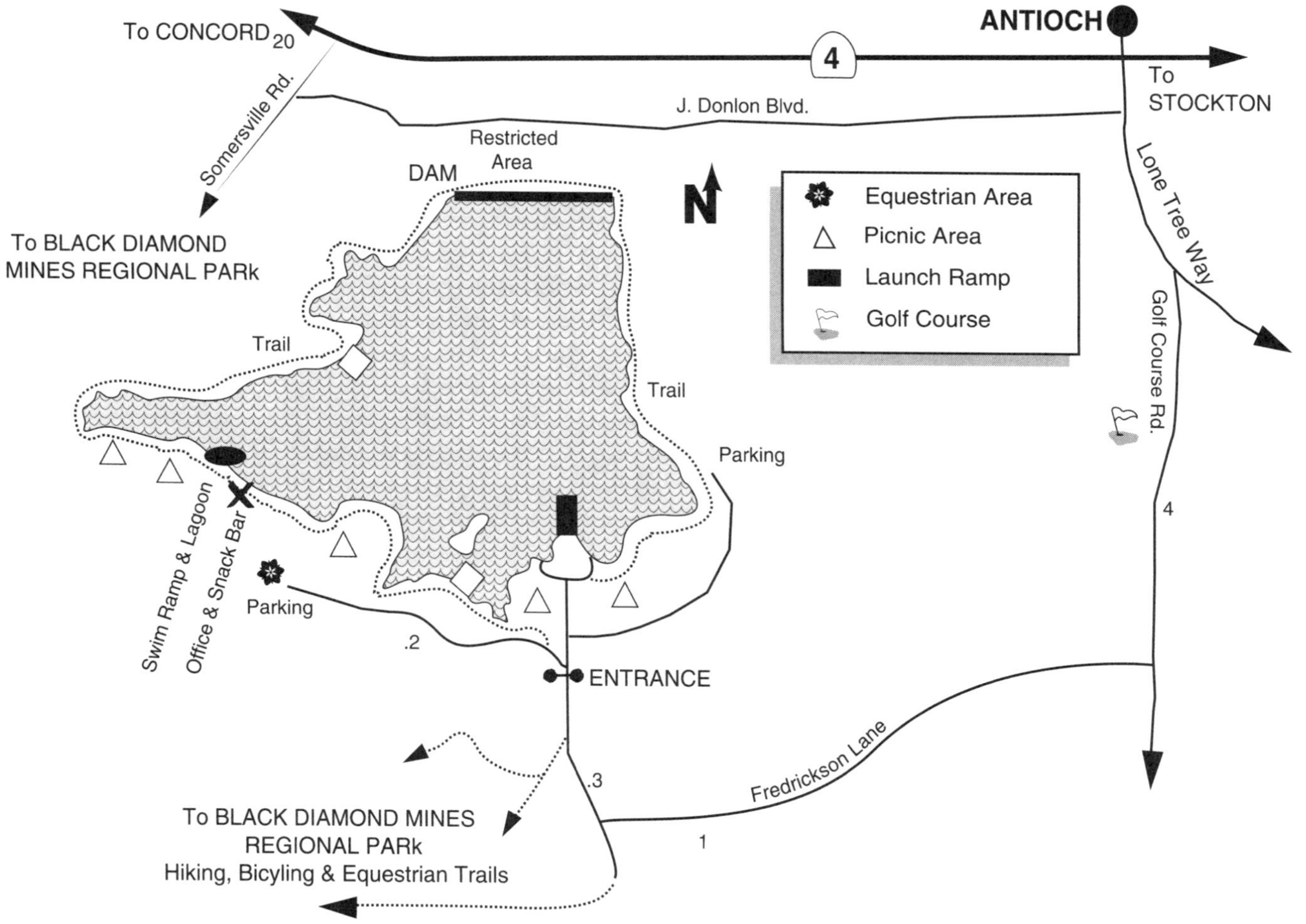

To CONCORD
20
ANTIOCH
4
To STOCKTON
J. Donlon Blvd.
Somersville Rd.
Restricted Area
DAM
To BLACK DIAMOND MINES REGIONAL PARk
Equestrian Area
Picnic Area
Launch Ramp
Golf Course
Lone Tree Way
Golf Course Rd.
Trail
Trail
Parking
Swim Ramp & Lagoon
Office & Snack Bar
Parking
.2
ENTRANCE
4
.3
Fredrickson Lane
1
To BLACK DIAMOND MINES REGIONAL PARk
Hiking, Bicyling & Equestrian Trails

INFORMATION: East Bay Regional Parks, 2950 Peralta Oaks Ct., Oakland 94605—Ph: (888) 327-2757

CAMPING	BOATING	RECREATION	OTHER
Day Use Only Fee: $5 Dog: $2 Park Ranger Headquarters Ph: (925) 757-0404	Electric Motors, Row, Sail & Windsurfing Boats up to 17 feet No Gas Motors Launch Ramp Fees: Cartop: $2 Trailer: $4	Fishing: Black & Striped Bass, Trout, Bluegill & Sunfish Fishing Fee: $4 Designated Hiking, Bicycling & Equestrian Trails Picnicnicking Group Picnic Reservations: Ph: (888) 327-2757 Swimming in Lagoon: $3 Playground	Snack Bar Bait & Tackle Golf Course Nearby

CHABOT, CULL CANYON, DON CASTRO and JORDAN POND

These four small Lakes are within the East Bay Regional Park District. The angler will find a warm water fishery at all of these facilities along with trout at Lake Chabot and Don Castro. Boating is limited to Lake Chabot 315 surface acres. Each of these Regional Parks provides numerous attractions along with picnic facilities. Anthony Chabot Regional Park, 4,972 acres, has campgrounds and hiking, equestrian and bicycle trails. Facilities at Cull Canyon include a swim complex with a sandy beach and picnic areas. The angler will find bass and catfish. Don Castro has a swim lagoon, numerous picnic areas and large lawns. This Lake is regularly stocked with trout and catfish. Jordan Pond is in the scenic 2,685 acre Garin Regional Park and has an interpretive center with interesting programs conducted by park naturalists.

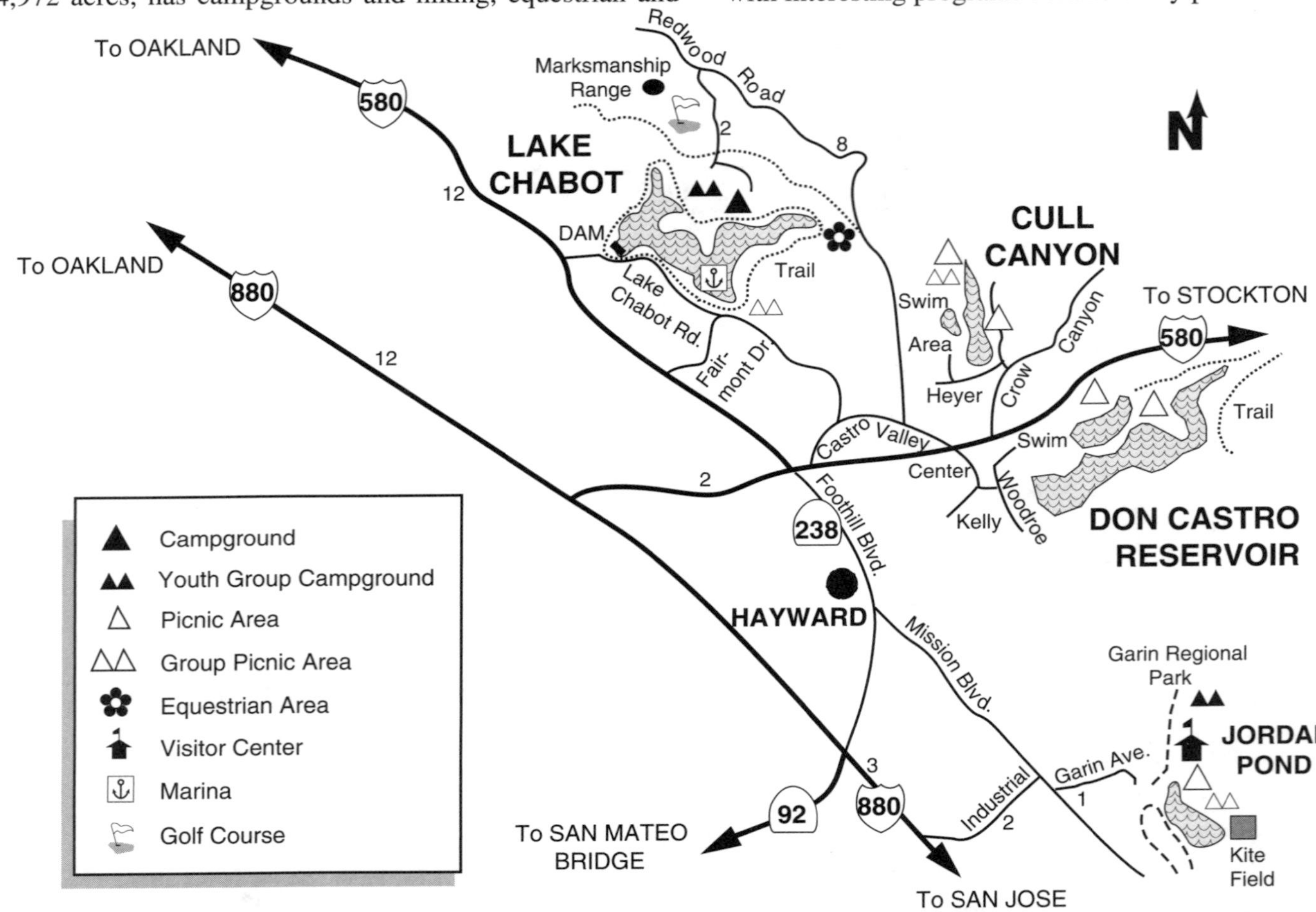

To OAKLAND
580
Marksmanship Range
Redwood Road
2
8
N
LAKE CHABOT
12
DAM
Trail
CULL CANYON
To OAKLAND
880
Lake Chabot Rd.
Swim Area
Heyer
Crow Canyon
To STOCKTON
580
12
Fair-mont Dr.
Castro Valley
Swim
Trail
Center
2
Kelly
Woodroe
DON CASTRO RESERVOIR
238
Foothill Blvd.
HAYWARD
Mission Blvd.
Garin Regional Park
JORDAN POND
Garin Ave.
1
Industrial
2
3
92
880
To SAN MATEO BRIDGE
To SAN JOSE
Kite Field
Campground
Youth Group Campground
Picnic Area
Group Picnic Area
Equestrian Area
Visitor Center
Marina
Golf Course

INFORMATION: East Bay Regional Parks, 2950 Peralta Oaks Ct., Oakland 94605—Ph: (888) 327-2757

CAMPING	BOATING	RECREATION	OTHER
Lake Chabot: 75 Tent & R.V. Sites Water & Sewer Hookups Plus Walk-In Sites Fees: $18 - $23 Group Camp Reservations Garin Regional Park: Youth Group Camp Don Castro & Cull Canyon: Day Use Only Parking Fees - $4 - $5	Lake Chabot: Cartop Canoes, Kayaks & Sculls to 20 feet Launch Fee: $2 Rentals: Row Boats, Pedal Boats, Canoes & Kayaks Marina Ph: (510) 247-2526 No Boating at Other Lakes	Fishing: Trout, Black Bass, Bluegill, Catfish & Crappie Fishing Fee: $4 Designated Hiking, Bicyling & Equestrian Trails Swim Lagoons: Don Castro & Cull Canyon Nature Study & Interpretive Center Group Picnic Reservations: Ph: (888) 327-2757 Playgrounds	Lake Chabot: Coffee Shop Bait & Tackle Golf Course Chabot Gun Club & Marksmanship Range Open to the Public Fri. through Mon. Equestrian Center Ph: (510) 569-4428

Within the greater Bay Area, these day-use Lakes have many different recreational opportunities. Bethany Reservoir is a State Recreation Area and is open to boating with a 5 mph speed limit. Shadow Cliffs Reservoir has a variety of activities throughout the 296-acre park including a swim beach for families with children. Quarry Lakes includes Horseshoe and Rainbow Lakes that have planted trout and catfish. A license is required. Lake Elizabeth is popular with boaters and anglers. Numerous activities are available including boat rentals and various sports fields. *See following page for detailed information.*

....Continued....

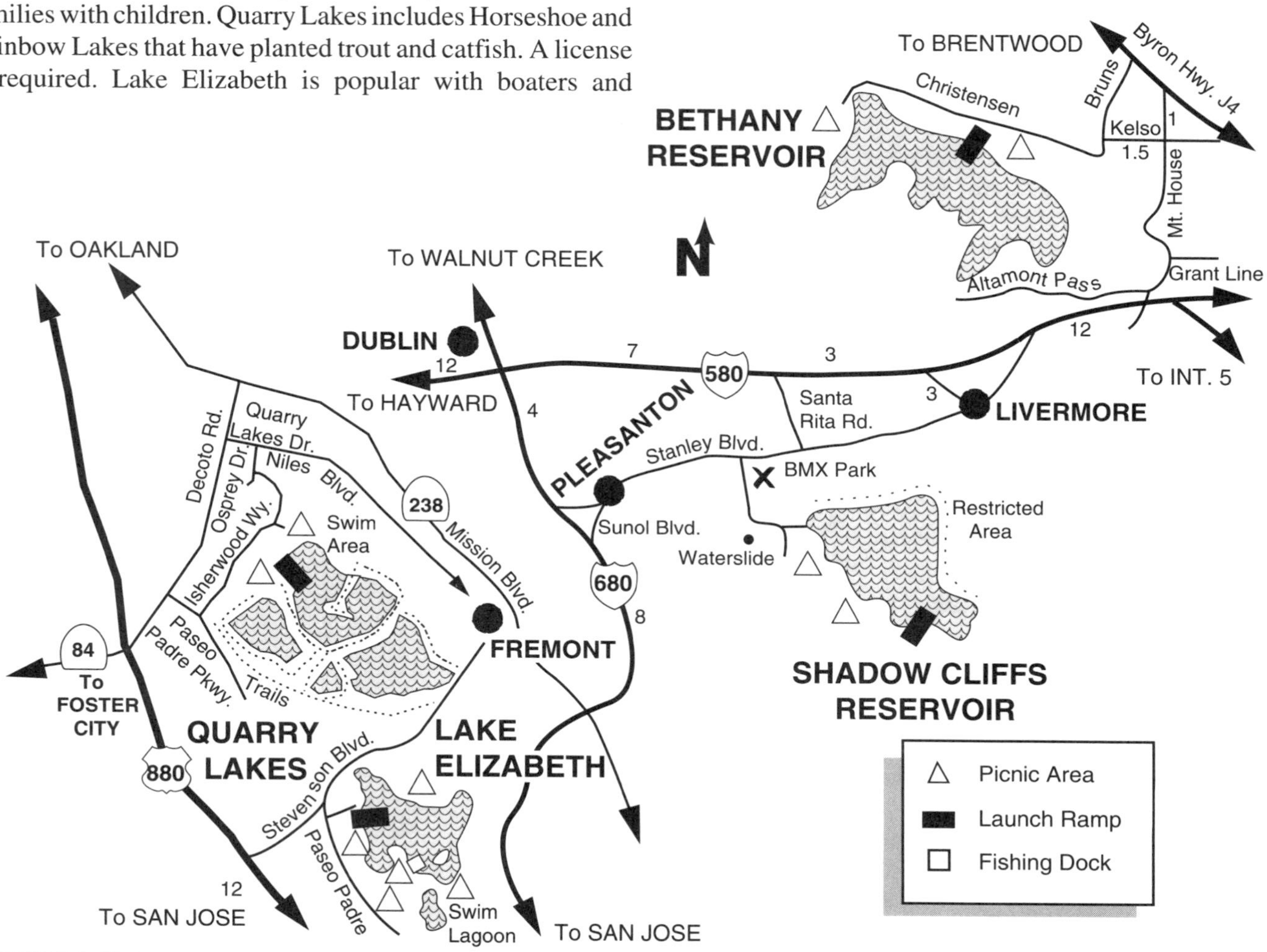

To BRENTWOOD
Byron Hwy. J4
Christensen
Bruns
BETHANY RESERVOIR
Kelso
1
1.5
Mt. House
Altamont Pass
Grant Line
N
To OAKLAND
To WALNUT CREEK
DUBLIN
12
7
580
3
12
To INT. 5
To HAYWARD
4
3
LIVERMORE
Santa Rita Rd.
PLEASANTON
Stanley Blvd.
BMX Park
Quarry Lakes Dr.
Decoto Rd.
Osprey Dr.
Niles Blvd.
238
Isherwood Wy.
Swim Area
Mission Blvd.
Sunol Blvd.
Waterslide
Restricted Area
680
8
84
To FOSTER CITY
Paseo Padre Pkwy.
Trails
FREMONT
SHADOW CLIFFS RESERVOIR
QUARRY LAKES
LAKE ELIZABETH
880
Stevenson Blvd.
Paseo Padre
12
To SAN JOSE
Swim Lagoon
To SAN JOSE
Picnic Area
Launch Ramp
Fishing Dock

INFORMATION: See Following Page for Individual Lake Information

CAMPING	BOATING	RECREATION	OTHER
Day Use Only *See Following Page*	Varies at Each Lake *See Following Page*	Fishing: Trout, Largemouth & Striped Bass, Catfish, Bluegill & Crappie Picnicking - Group Sites Hiking & Bicycle Trails Bethany Reservoir: California Aqueduct Bikeway Swimming Beaches & Lagoons Playgrounds Athletic Fields	Waterslide at Shadow Cliffs Concessions at Shadow Cliffs & Lake Elizabeth Full Facilities Near Each Lake

BETHANY and SHADOW CLIFFS RESERVOIRS, QUARRY LAKES, LAKE ELIZABETH...Cont.

BETHANY RESERVOIR

State Recreation Area
Mailing Address:
22600 Lake Rd.
La Grange 95329
Ph: (209) 874-2056
Park Ph: (209) 532-0150

Bethany Reservoir State Recreation Area is located in gently rolling, grass-covered hills overlooking the vast Delta of the Sacramento and San Joaquin Rivers. This 58-surface acre Reservoir is open to boating with a 5 MPH speed limit. Windsurfing is very popular. Strong winds can be a hazard at times. This is a good warm water fishery for striped bass and catfish. Bethany is the northern terminus for the California Aqueduct Bikeway. Around the Reservoir are hundreds of windmills generating electricity.

SHADOW CLIFFS RESERVOIR

East Bay Regional Park District
2500 Stanley Blvd.
Pleasanton 94556
Ph: (888) 327-2757

This facility has been transformed from a sand and gravel quarry to a complete 296-acre park with an 80 surface-acre Lake. Visitor's boats are limited to a maximum of 20 feet and only electric motors are permitted. Boat rentals include fishing and electric motorboats and paddle boats. The angler can fish for trout, black bass, channel and white catfish and bluegill. There is a sandy swim beach with a bathhouse, a snack bar and a four-flume waterslide in a separate area of the park. A BMX park is located on the west side of the reservoir. Picnic sites, lawn areas, hiking, bicycling and equestrian trails are available.

BEST LIVE BAIT
RECREATION LAKES
OF CALIFORNIA
"IT'S WERE THE ACTION IS."

QUARRY LAKES

East Bay Regional Park District
2100 Isherwood Way
Fremont 94535
Ph: (888) 327-2757

Horseshoe and Rainbow Lakes, along with nearby surrounding ponds and lagoons cover about 350 surface acres in this 450-acre park. Horseshoe Lake has easy access for swimming and fishing along with a launch ramp, handicap fishing area and a fish cleaning station. It is open to electric-powered boats, windsurfers, canoes and kayaks. Horseshoe and Rainbow Lakes have planted trout and catfish. Also the East Bay Regional Park District promotes the reproduction and growth of largemouth and smallmouth bass, bluegill, sunfish and crappie. No lead fishing weights are allowed. Fees are collected for parking, dogs, fishing, swimming and boat launching. Laga Los Osos is a natural preserve lake so no body contact or fishing is allowed. This is a good birdwatcing area. Hiking and bicycling trails, group picnic sites with BBQs, two sand-filled volleyball courts and a large white sandy beach make this park a great family facility.

LAKE ELIZABETH CENTRAL PARK

Visitor Services Center
40000 Paseo Padre Parkway
Fremont 94538
Ph: (510) 790-5541
Sports Fields Information Ph: (510) 791-4372
Fremont Sailing Club Ph: (510) 797-5524

Lake Elizabeth, 83 surface acres, is within Fremont Central Park. Complete facilities include ramps for non-powered boats, docks and storage. Rental sailboats, paddle boats and kayaks are available. This is a good sailing lake with westerly winds which can become strong in the afternoons. The Lake contains populations of black bass, bluegill and catfish. The Park, nearly 450 acres, has several recreational facilities with open lawn areas, snack bars, tennis courts, athletic fields, skate park, dog park and a golf driving range. There are dozens of picnic tables and ten group picnic sites which can accommodate up to 500 people. Group sites can be reserved. The 1.96 mile path around the Lake accommodates joggers, hikers and bicyclists. This Park and Lake are a great city recreational facility.

LOS VAQUEROS RESERVOIR

With 1,500 surface acres, Los Vaqueros Reservoir is one of California's prime fisheries. The Department of Fish and Game, Contra Costa County and the concessionaire plant rainbow trout and chinook salmon. Bass and kokanee are also established. Due to the tremendous amount of feed in the Lake, expect to catch some large fish. Body contact with the water is not allowed because this is a watershed for drinking water. Over 55 miles of open trails are available for hikers including miles of designated bicycle and equestrian trails. Oak trees and brush are scattered throughout the rolling grasslands surrounding the Reservoir. This well-maintained facility includes a marina, rental boats and a fish cleaning station. An Interpretive Center has a variety of interesting programs.

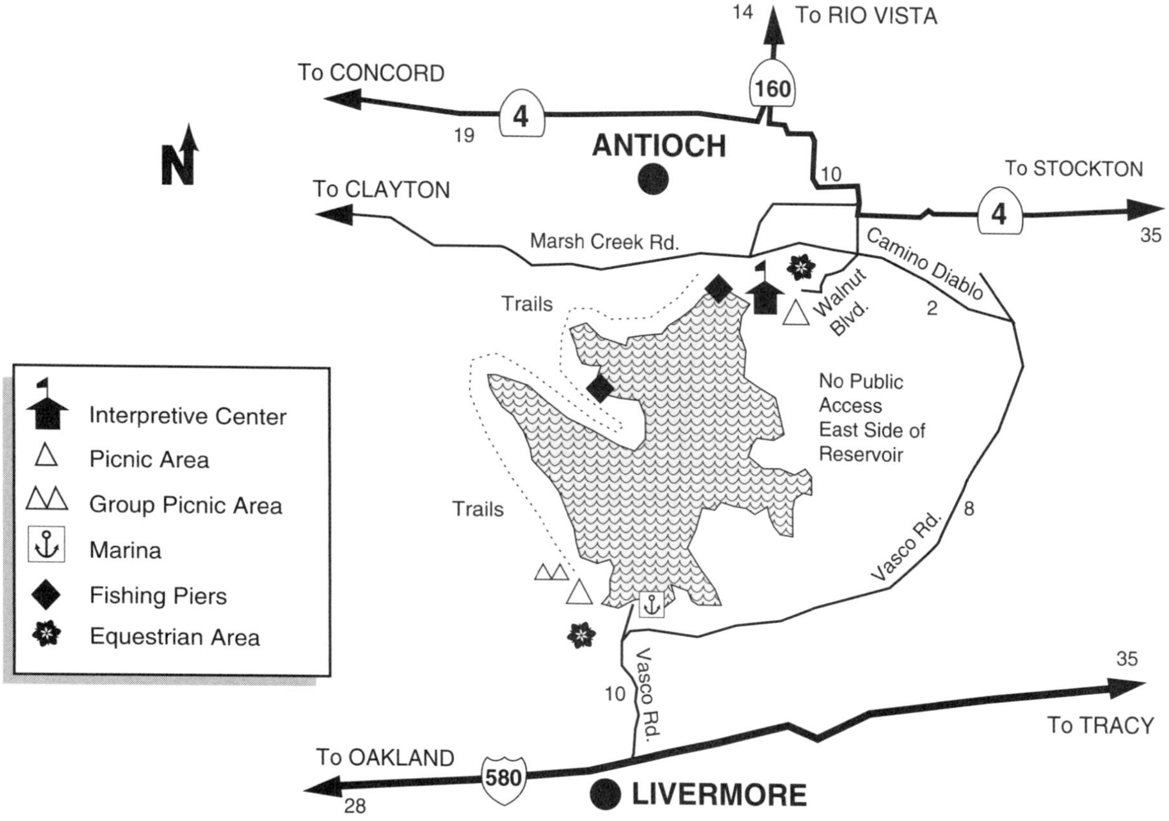

14
To RIO VISTA
160
To CONCORD
4
19
ANTIOCH
N
10
To STOCKTON
To CLAYTON
4
35
Marsh Creek Rd.
Camino Diablo
Walnut Blvd.
2
Trails
No Public Access East Side of Reservoir
Interpretive Center
Picnic Area
Group Picnic Area
Marina
Fishing Piers
Equestrian Area
Trails
8
Vasco Rd.
Vasco Rd.
10
35
To TRACY
To OAKLAND
580
28
LIVERMORE

INFORMATION: Contra Costa Water District, 1331 Concord Ave., Concord 94524—Ph: (925) 688-8000			
CAMPING	**BOATING**	**RECREATION**	**OTHER**
No Camping Day Use Only Parking Fee: $6 No Pets Allowed	Rental Boats: Fishing Boats with Electric Motors Pontoon Boats Marina Ph: (925) 371-2628 No Private Boats Allowed	Fishing: Rainbow Trout, Largemouth Black & Striped Bass, Kokanee, Chinook, Catfish, Perch & Sunfish Fishing Permit: $3.75 Covered Picnic Sites at North End Hiking, Bicycling & Equestrian Trails Horse Staging Area No Swimming or Body Contact	Located at North End: Interpretive Center Open Friday, Saturday, Sunday & Holidays Located at South End: Bait & Tackle Snack Bar Bird Watchers - Look for Bald Eagles, Golden Eagles & Hawks Group Picnic Site: Reserve Ph: (925) 426-3060

DEL VALLE RESERVOIR

Del Valle Reservoir, at an elevation of 700 feet, is located in oak-covered, rolling hills near Livermore. The Lake has a surface area of 750 acres with 16 miles of shoreline. Del Valle Park, 3,997 acres, is under the jurisdiction of the East Bay Regional Park District. In addition to the large tree-shaded campgrounds, there are group campsites, picnic areas, equestrian staging and marine facilities. Boating is limited to 10 mph. Westerly winds can be strong in the afternoon. This is a very popular windsurfing Lake. Miles of scenic trails are available for the hiker and equestrian. Del Valle is the eastern gateway to the 28-mile Ohlone Wilderness Trail.

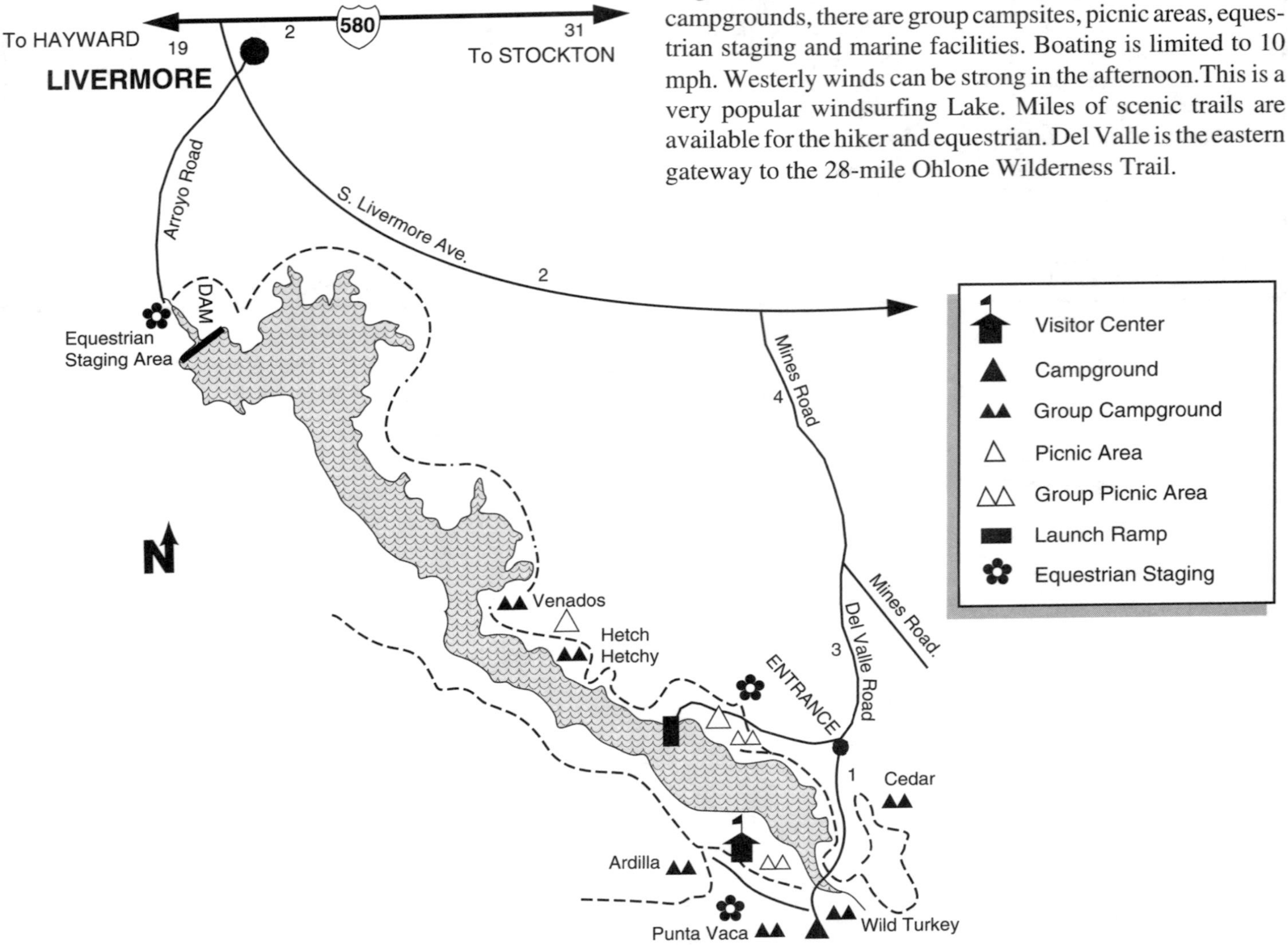

To HAYWARD
19
2
580
31
To STOCKTON
LIVERMORE
Arroyo Road
S. Livermore Ave.
2
DAM
Equestrian Staging Area
N
Mines Road
4
Venados
Hetch Hetchy
ENTRANCE
3
Del Valle Road
Mines Road.
1
Cedar
Ardilla
Punta Vaca
Wild Turkey
Visitor Center
Campground
Group Campground
Picnic Area
Group Picnic Area
Launch Ramp
Equestrian Staging

INFORMATION: Del Valle Park, 7000 Del Valle Rd., Livermore 94550—Ph: (888) 327-2757

CAMPING	BOATING	RECREATION	OTHER
150 Dev. Sites for Tents & R.V.s 21 with Water & Sewer Hookups Fees: $18 - $23 Disposal Station Youth Group Campgrounds Equestrian Group Camp Reservations: Ph: (888) 327-2757 Day Use Fee:$6 Dogs: $2	Power, Row, Canoe, Sail, Windsurf & Inflatables Speed Limit - 10 MPH Launch Ramp Fee: $2 - $4 Rentals: Fishing Boats with Motors, Row, Paddle & Patio Boats, Canoes & Kayaks Ph: (925) 449-5201	Fishing: Trout, Catfish, Bluegill, Large & Smallmouth Bass, Striped Bass Swimming - 2 Beaches Picnicking 12 Group Sites Hiking Trails Designated Bicycle & Equestrian Trails Summer Weekends: Campfire Program Boat Tour of Lake	Visitor Center Ph: (925) 373-0432 Snack Bar Bait & Tackle Store Full Facilities in Livermore

SHORELINE PARK, LAKE MERCED and STEVENS CREEK RESERVOIR

These three Lakes have a variety of recreational activities available. Shoreline Lake has a 50-acre expanse of saltwater for windsurfing and sailing. Protected wildlife areas can reached by paved trails. This is a popular windsurfing Lake with prevailing northwesterly winds. Also there are various boat and bicycle rentals. Lake Merced, adjacent to San Francisco, is actually two small lakes, surrounded by three golf courses. Stevens Creek Reservoir has 92 surface acres when full. Oak-shaded trails are great for the hiker and equestrian. Mountain bikers can use the multiple trail system which allows access to adjacent park lands. Family and group picnic sites are available.

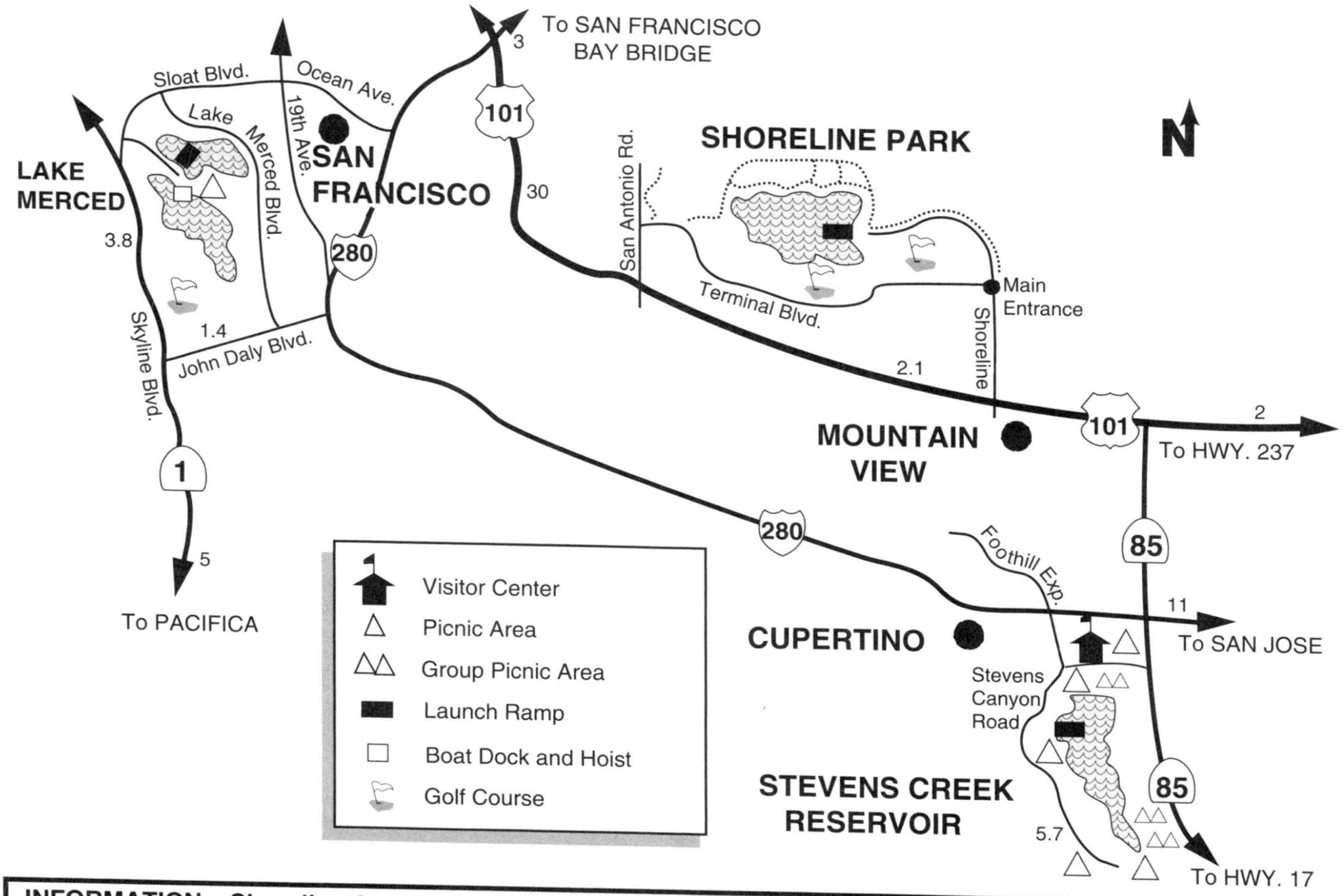

To SAN FRANCISCO BAY BRIDGE
3
101
30
Sloat Blvd.
Ocean Ave.
Lake
Merced Blvd.
19th Ave.
SAN FRANCISCO
LAKE MERCED
3.8
280
1.4
John Daly Blvd.
Skyline Blvd.
1
5
To PACIFICA
SHORELINE PARK
San Antonio Rd.
Terminal Blvd.
Main Entrance
Shoreline
2.1
101
2
To HWY. 237
MOUNTAIN VIEW
N
280
Foothill Exp.
85
11
To SAN JOSE
CUPERTINO
Stevens Canyon Road
STEVENS CREEK RESERVOIR
85
5.7
To HWY. 17
Visitor Center
Picnic Area
Group Picnic Area
Launch Ramp
Boat Dock and Hoist
Golf Course

INFORMATION: Shoreline Aquatic Center, 3160 N. Shoreline Blvd., Mountain View 94043—Ph: (650) 965-7474

CAMPING	BOATING	RECREATION	OTHER
Day Use Only - Fees No Camping Stevens Creek Park: County of Santa Clara 11401 Stevens Canyon Cupertino Ph: (408) 867-3654 Group Picnic Area Reservations	Shoreline Park: No Motors Launch Ramp: $4 - $5 Rentals: Windsurfers, Sail Boats, Canoes, Kayaks, Pedal Boats, Bicycles Sailing Lessons, Sales Stevens Creek: No Motors Allowed Launch Ramp - Fee	No Fishing at Shoreline Fishing at Stevens Creek & Lake Merced: Trout, Bass, Bluegill, Catfish & Crappie Picnicking - Group Sites No Swimming at Lakes Hiking, Bicycle & Equestrian Trails Golf Courses	Shoreline Park: Supplies - Store Events & Catering Services Ph: (650) 965-3779 Lakeside Cafe Ph: (650) 965-1745 Lake Merced: San Francisco Parks Ph: (415) 831-2773 Call for current info. on water level and conditions

VASONA, LEXINGTON and LOS GATOS CREEK PARK

Located off Highway 17, these Lakes are in the southwest corner of Santa Clara County and under the jurisdiction of the Parks and Recreation Department. Lexington, the largest, is popular with sailors, rowers, windsurfers and anglers. Only electric motors are allowed. Vasona is a 57-acre Lake surrounded by 94 acres of lawn areas, picnic sites, playgrounds and paved paths. Los Gatos Creek Park permits fishing and sail craft in the north pond. Remote control model boating is allowed in the middle pond. There is also a flycasting pond for practice only (no hooks). It is equipped with circular targets. Hikers, bicyclists and skaters can enjoy the Los Gatos Creek trail. This runs from Lexington along Los Gatos Creek through Vasona Lake Park and into nearby cities.

LOS GATOS CREEK PARK
To CUPERTINO
SAN JOSE
Winchester Ave.
Dell Ave.
Lark Ave.
DAM
85
12
To HIGHWAY 101
University Ave.
LAKE VASONA
LOS GATOS
DAM
Blossom Hill Rd.
N. Santa Cruz
To HIGHWAY 9
Black Rd.
To Skyline Blvd.
Hwy. 35
Bear Creek Rd.
Alma Bridge Rd.
N
Old Santa
Cruz Hwy.
LEXINGTON
RESERVOIR
17
To SANTA CRUZ
20
Picnic Area
Group Picnic Area
Launch Ramp

INFORMATION: Santa Clara County Parks & Rec., 298 Garden Hill Dr., Los Gatos 95032—Ph: (408) 355-2200

CAMPING	BOATING	RECREATION	OTHER
Day Use Only *No Camping* Vasona & Los Gatos Creek Parks: Entrance Fee: $6 per Vehicle Reservations for Group Picnics or Special Events Ph: (408) 355-2201	Lexington: Sail, Canoe, Row, Windsurfer, Paddleboats Electric Motors Only Launch Ramp - $5 *Check for Current Water Level Conditions & Construction* Vasona: Same as Lexington *except No Motors* Launch Ramp - $5 Docks, Dry Storage Rental Boats	Fishing: Trout, Bass, Bluegill, Catfish & Crappie Picnicking Group Sites Hiking & Bicycle Trails No Swimming Playground at Vasona Oak Meadow Park: Ph: (408) 354-6809 (Next to Vasona) Billy Jones Wildcat Railroad & Carousel	Los Gatos Creek Park: North Pond: Sail Craft Model Boat Area Fly Casting Pond Dog Park Full Facilities in Los Gatos & San Jose

Almaden Lake Regional Park is administered by the City of San Jose and includes a 32 surface acre Lake for sailing and fishing along with a swim beach, lagoon and picnic sites. Guadalupe and Almaden Reservoirs are 60 surface acres each. They are under the jurisdiction of Santa Clara County and are adjacent to Almaden Quicksilver Park, a popular hiking and equestrian area. Chesbro and Uvas, also under the jurisdiction of Santa Clara Parks, are primarily small fishing Lakes with picnic sites. Calero Reservoir, 349 surface acres, is a popular power-boating and waterskiing Lake with a sandy beach and picnic facilities. At low water, the ramp may be closed so call for information. Uvas Canyon Park has campgrounds and a beautiful waterfall loop nature trail.

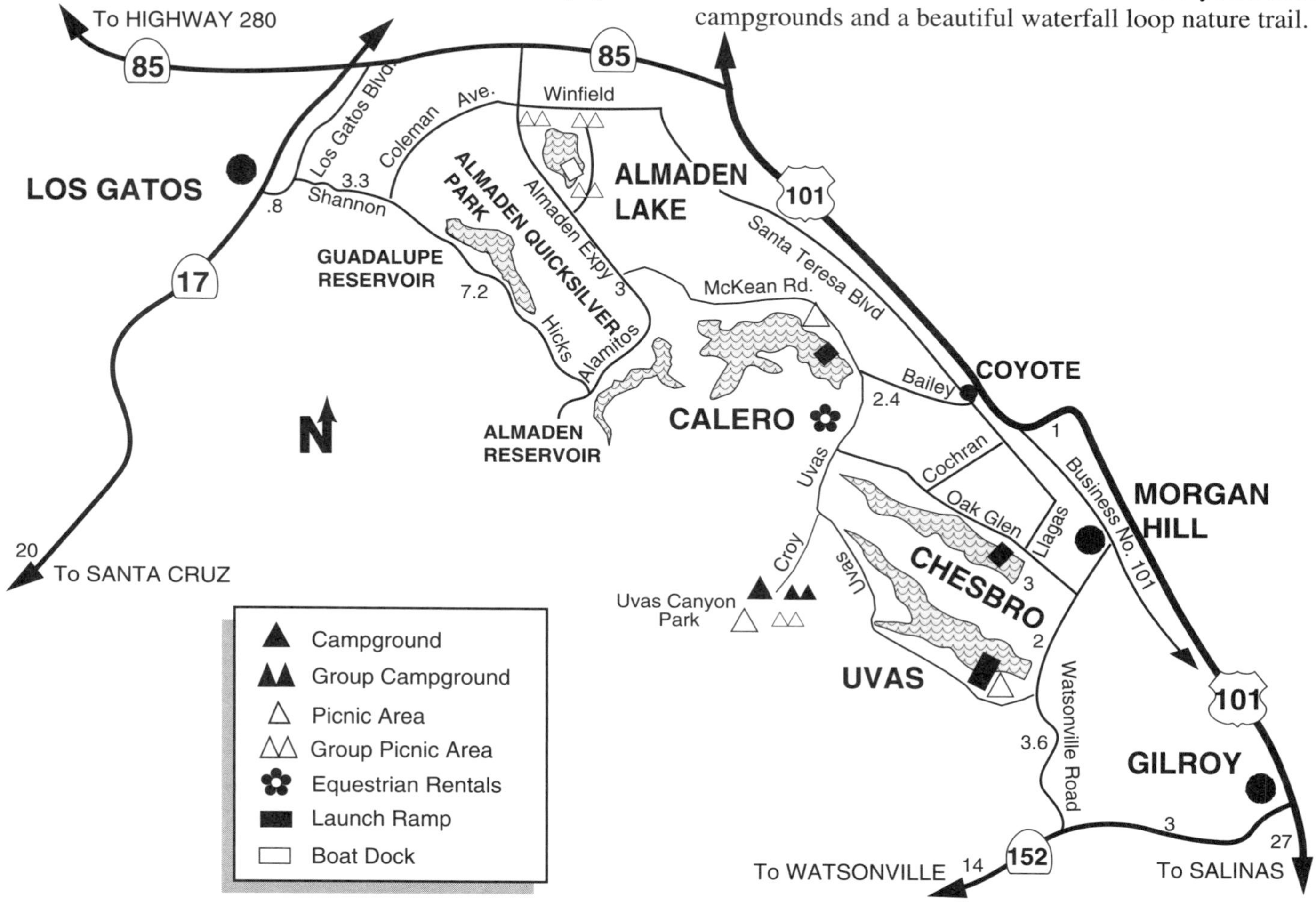

To HIGHWAY 280
85
85
Winfield
Los Gatos Blvd.
Coleman Ave.
LOS GATOS
3.3
.8
Shannon
ALMADEN QUICKSILVER PARK
Almaden Expy
ALMADEN LAKE
101
Santa Teresa Blvd
17
GUADALUPE RESERVOIR
7.2
3
McKean Rd.
Hicks
Alamitos
Bailey
COYOTE
2.4
N
ALMADEN RESERVOIR
CALERO
1
Uvas
Cochran
Business No. 101
MORGAN HILL
Oak Glen
Llagas
Croy
Uvas
CHESBRO
3
20
To SANTA CRUZ
Uvas Canyon Park
2
UVAS
101
Watsonville Road
3.6
GILROY
3
27
To WATSONVILLE
14
152
To SALINAS
Campground
Group Campground
Picnic Area
Group Picnic Area
Equestrian Rentals
Launch Ramp
Boat Dock

INFORMATION: Santa Clara County Parks & Rec., 298 Garden Hill Dr., Los Gatos 95032—Ph: (408) 355-2200

CAMPING	BOATING	RECREATION	OTHER
Uvas Canyon Park: Youth Group Camp to 40 People Max. Fee: $40 Plus 25 Campsites by Reservation Ph: (408) 779-9232 No Camping at Other Lakes & Reservoirs Entrance & Lake Use Fees	Almaden Lake: Sail & Row Boats up to 16 ft., Windsurfing No Power Boats Launch Ramp - Fee Rentals: Windsurf & Paddleboats Chesbro & Uvas: Sail, Row & Electric Motors Calero: Power & Sailboats, Waterski - Launch Ramp *Guadalupe & Almaden: No Boating Allowed*	Fishing: Bass, Catfish, Bluegill, Crappie, Carp *Warning: Mercury Contaminated Fish at Calero, Guadalupe & Almaden Reservoirs Do Not Eat Fish Catch & Release Only* Swimming - Beach: *Almaden Lake Only* Picnicking - Group Sites Hiking & Equestrian Trails	Almaden Lake Park: 15652 Almaden Expressway San Jose 95113 Ph: (408) 277-5130 Almaden Quicksilver Park Ph: (408) 268-3883

ED R. LEVIN, JOSEPH D. GRANT and HELLYER PARKS, LAKE CUNNINGHAM

The County of Santa Clara operates the Ed R. Levin, Hellyer and Joseph D. Grant Parks. Sandy Wool Lake at Ed R. Levin Park is stocked with fish and the Park also has a hang gliding club. Cottonwood Lake is located in Hellyer Park which has an Olympic-size velodrome. Coyote Creek Parkway includes a 15-mile long bicycle trail that runs from Hellyer Park in South San Jose to Anderson Lake Park in Morgan Hill. The rugged 9,560 acres of Joseph D. Grant Park has a 52-mile trail system for hikers and equestrians. Mountain bikes are allowed on nearly half of the Park's trails. Camping and picnic areas are included in this well-maintained County Park. Lake Cunningham Regional Park is under the jurisdiction of the City of San Jose. This 200-acre Park includes numerous picnic sites, walking and jogging paths and a 50-surface acre Lake for boating and fishing. Raging Waters has a variety of waterslides, activity pools, swim lagoon with beach, river rides and many other activities.

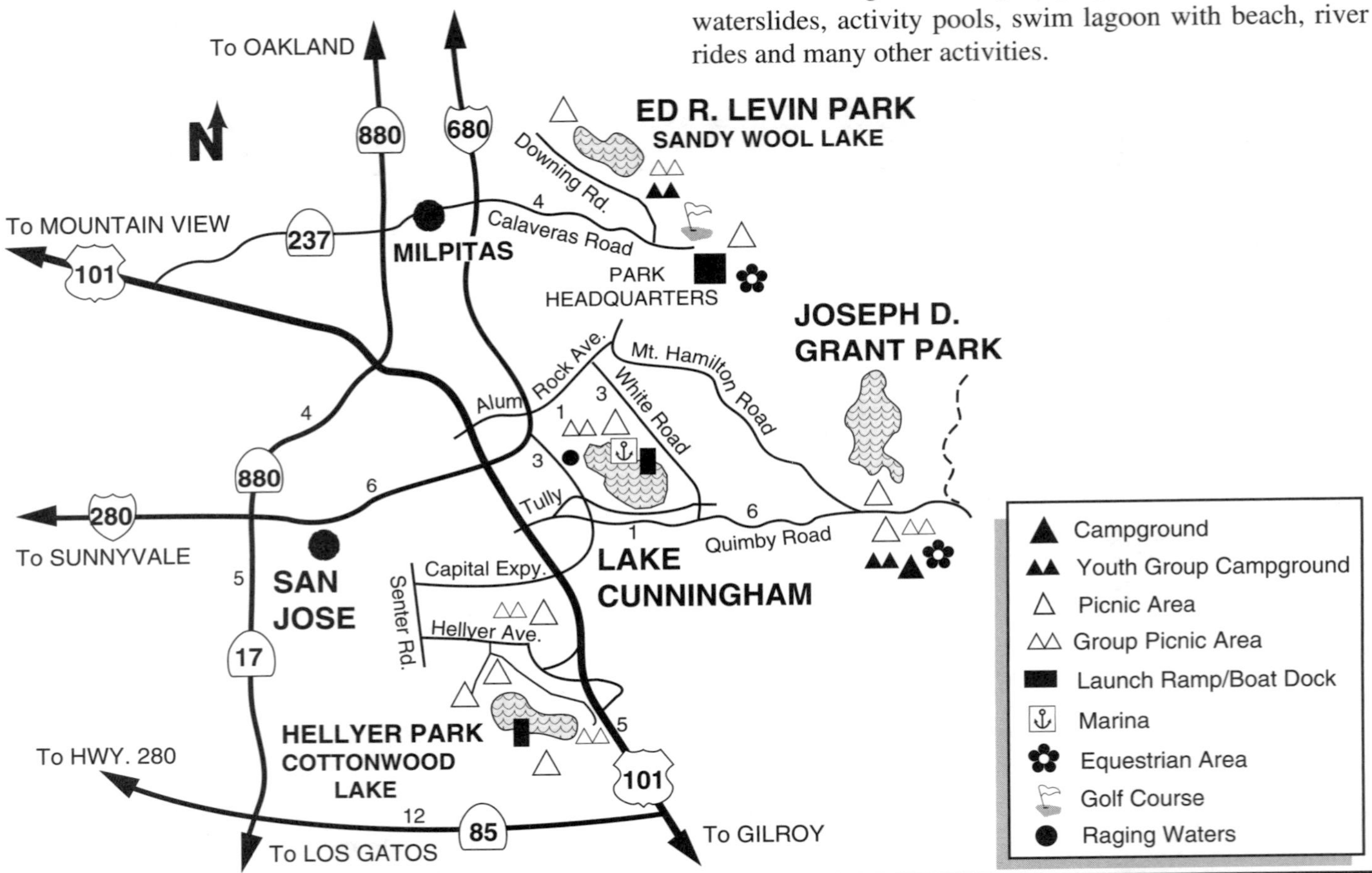
To OAKLAND
N
880
680
ED R. LEVIN PARK
SANDY WOOL LAKE
Downing Rd.
4
Calaveras Road
To MOUNTAIN VIEW
237
MILPITAS
101
PARK
HEADQUARTERS
JOSEPH D.
GRANT PARK
Mt. Hamilton Road
Rock Ave.
Alum
White Road
3
1
4
880
6
280
To SUNNYVALE
Tully
1
6
Quimby Road
5
SAN
JOSE
Capital Expy.
LAKE
CUNNINGHAM
Senter Rd.
Hellyer Ave.
17
HELLYER PARK
COTTONWOOD
LAKE
5
101
To HWY. 280
12
85
To LOS GATOS
To GILROY
Campground
Youth Group Campground
Picnic Area
Group Picnic Area
Launch Ramp/Boat Dock
Marina
Equestrian Area
Golf Course
Raging Waters

INFORMATION: Santa Clara County Parks, 298 Garden Hill Dr., San Jose 95032—Ph: (408) 355-2200

CAMPING	BOATING	RECREATION	OTHER
Youth Group Camping: Joseph D. Grant & Ed R. Levin Parks Fee: $40 Ph: (408) 355-2201 Joseph D. Grant Park: Family Campsites Equestrian Campground Day Use Only: Hellyer Park & Lake Cunningham	Ed R. Levin & Cottonwood: Row & Sail Boats, Lake Cunningham: Row & Sail Boats, Electric Motors Only Launch Ramp: $5 Marina Rentals: Sailboats, Kayaks & Pedal Boats Boat Dock *Joseph D. Grant:* *No Boating Allowed*	Fishing: Catfish, Trout Picnicking - Group Sites Walking & Jogging Paths Hiking & Equestrian Trails Mountain Biking Trails Bicycling - Velodrome at Hellyer Park Hang Gliding Golf Course & Horse Rentals at Ed R. Levin Off-Leash Dog Park Raging Waters Theme Park	Ed R. Levin: Ph: (408) 262-6980 Joseph D. Grant: Ph: (408) 274-6121 Hellyer Park: Ph: (408) 225-0225 Lake Cunningham 2305 S. White Rd. San Jose 95148 Ph: (408) 277-4319 Raging Waters: Ph: (408) 238-9900

ANDERSON and PARKWAY LAKES

The largest body of fresh water in Santa Clara County, Anderson Lake is 7 miles long with a surface area of 1,250 acres. This is a popular boating and waterskiing Lake and afternoon winds make for good sailing and windsurfing. There is a launch ramp and the angler will find a warm water fishery. The County of Santa Clara has picnic sites near the dam as well as a boat-in picnic area on the southeast shore. Anderson Park, over 3,100 acres, includes a multiple use 15-mile trail which follows Coyote Creek north to Hellyer County Park. An equestrian staging area leads to an 8-mile horseback riding trail. Parkway is a 35-acre fishing Lake. Planted year around with large trout, channel catfish and sturgeon, the Lake usually rewards the angler with a good catch. Henry Coe is a State Park with sites for campers and equestrians and an extensive trail system.

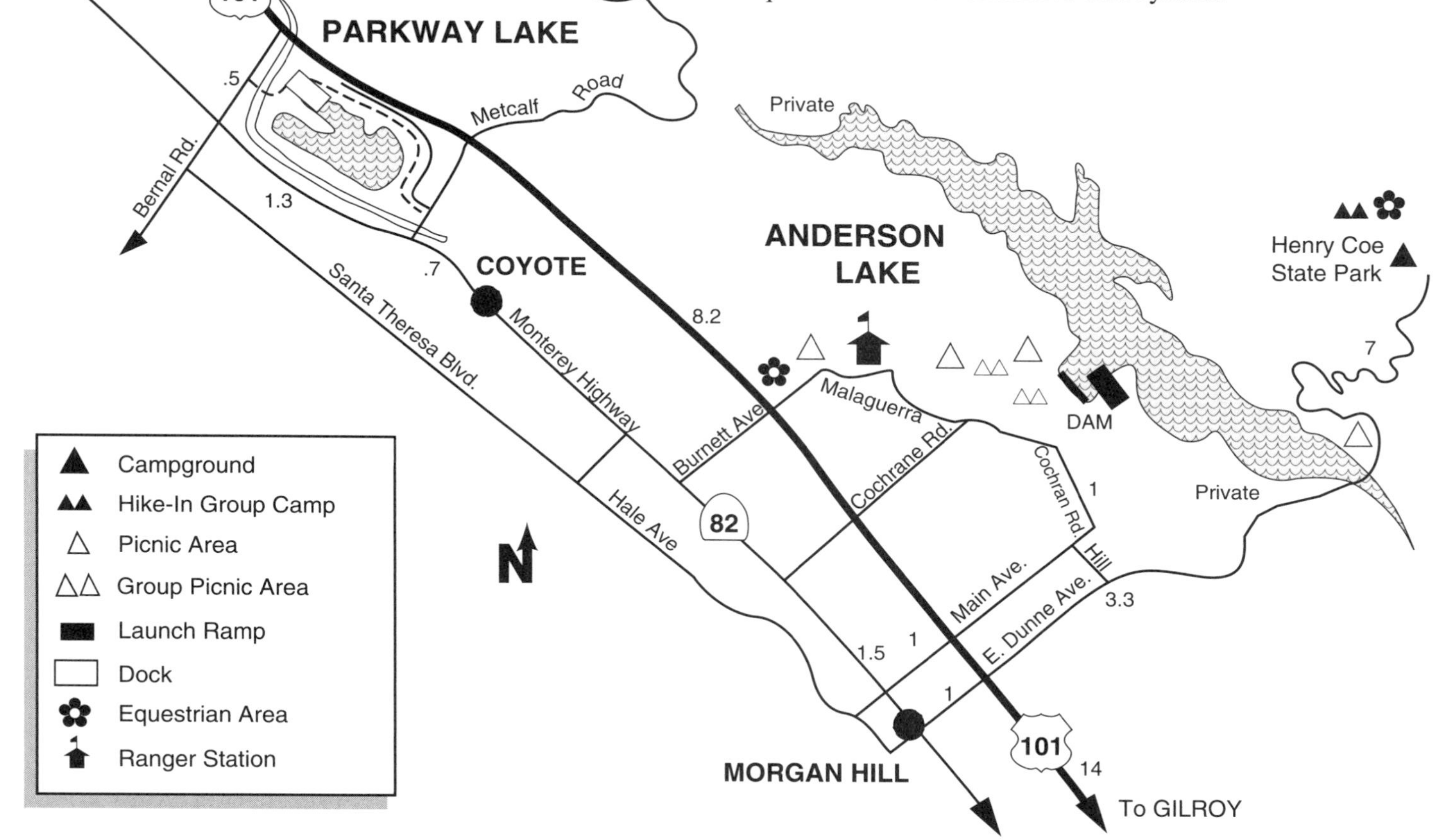

To SAN JOSE
101
PARKWAY LAKE
Metcalf Road
.5
Bernal Rd.
1.3
.7
COYOTE
Santa Theresa Blvd.
Monterey Highway
8.2
Private
ANDERSON
LAKE
Henry Coe
State Park
7
Malaguerra
Burnett Ave
Cochrane Rd.
Cochran Rd.
DAM
1
Private
Hale Ave
82
Hill
Main Ave.
E. Dunne Ave.
3.3
1.5
1
1
101
14
MORGAN HILL
To GILROY
N
Campground
Hike-In Group Camp
Picnic Area
Group Picnic Area
Launch Ramp
Dock
Equestrian Area
Ranger Station

INFORMATION: Santa Clara County Parks & Rec., 298 Garden Hill Dr., Los Gatos 95032—Ph: (408) 355-2200

CAMPING	BOATING	RECREATION	OTHER
Day Use Only Anderson Lake : Entrance Fee: $6 Nearby: Henry Coe State Park: Tent & R.V. Sites Fee: $12 Hike-In Group Sites Equestrian Campsites Ph: (408) 779-2728	Anderson: Open to All Boats, Waterskiing & PWCs Launch Ramp, Dock Boat Use Fee: $6 Launch Reservations in Summer Ph: (408) 355-2201 *Check for Current* *Water Level Conditions* Parkway: No Private Boats Rentals: Fishing Boats with Trolling Motors	Fishing: Largemouth Bass, Catfish, Crappie & Bluegill Plus Trout & Sturgeon in Parkway Picnicking Group Sites at Anderson Reservations: Ph: (408) 355-2201 Hiking, Bicycle & Equestrian Trails	Anderson Lake County Park Ph: (408) 779-3634 Parkway Lake: 101 Metcalf Road San Jose 95138 Ph: (408) 629-9111 Fishing Fee: $15 No License Required Bait & Tackle Snacks Rental Fishing Boats No Pets Allowed

LOCH LOMOND

Loch Lomond is located at an elevation of 577 feet in the Santa Cruz Mountains. This scenic 3-1/2 mile long Reservoir is under the jurisdiction of the City of Santa Cruz. Fishing is a main attraction and often productive. As a watershed for Santa Cruz drinking water, an aeration system enhances the fishery. Over 100 picnic sites are located around the shoreline. Hiking trails extend along the water and into a forest of oak, madrone, pine and redwood trees. In addition to nature programs, there is a self-guided Big Trees Nature Trail.

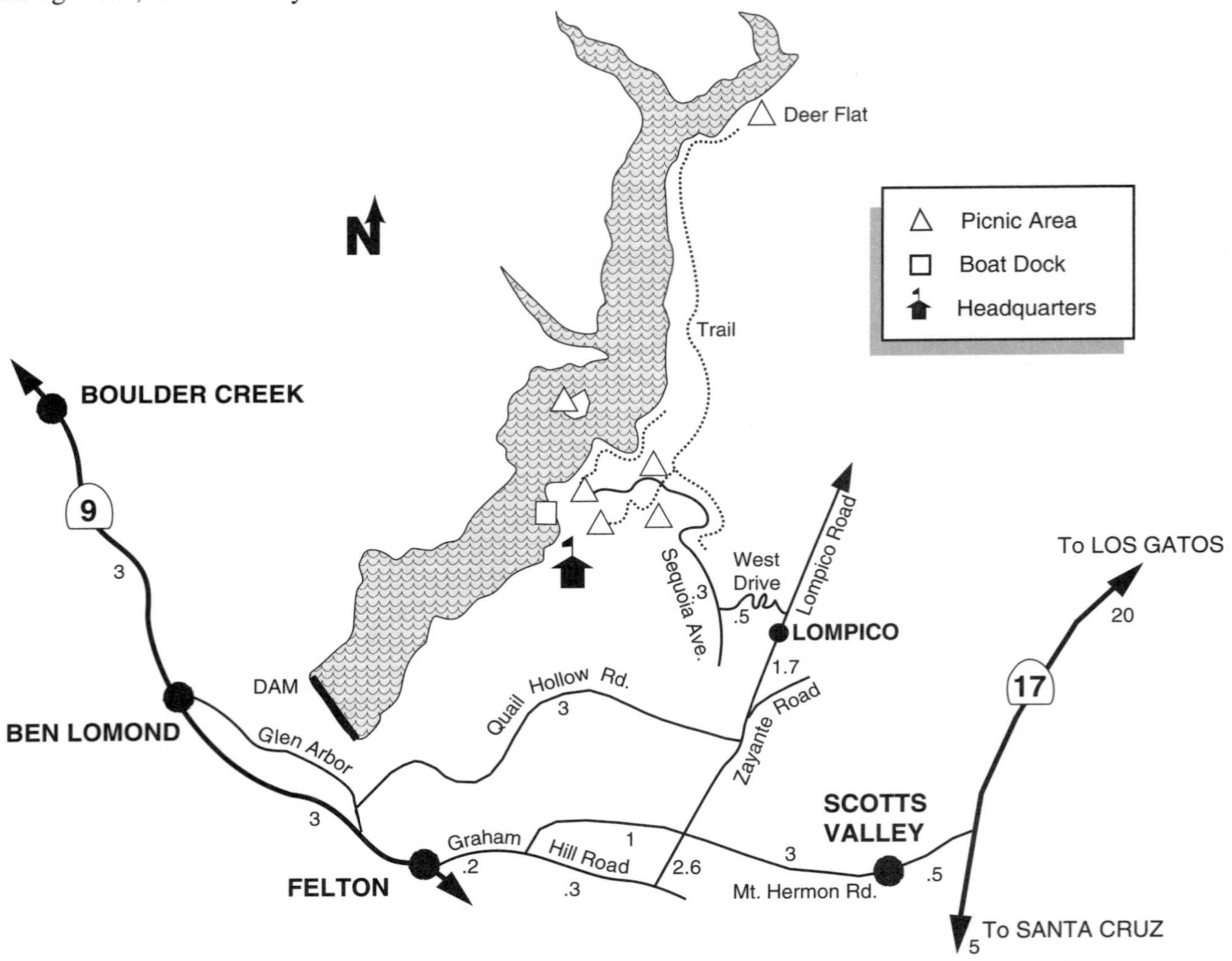
Deer Flat
N
Picnic Area
Boat Dock
Headquarters
Trail
BOULDER CREEK
9
3
West
Drive
Lompico Road
Sequoia Ave.
.3
.5
LOMPICO
To LOS GATOS
20
17
1.7
Zayante Road
DAM
Quail Hollow Rd.
3
BEN LOMOND
Glen Arbor
3
SCOTTS
VALLEY
Graham
Hill Road
1
3
2.6
.2
.3
.5
FELTON
Mt. Hermon Rd.
To SANTA CRUZ
5

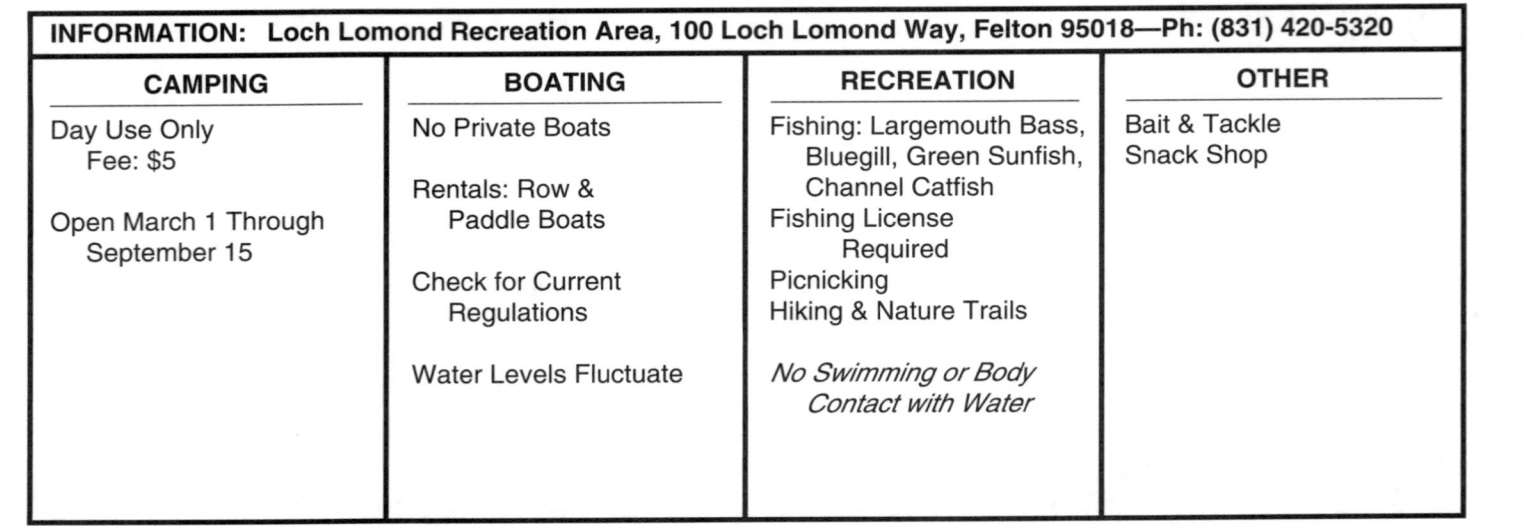

INFORMATION: Loch Lomond Recreation Area, 100 Loch Lomond Way, Felton 95018—Ph: (831) 420-5320			
CAMPING	**BOATING**	**RECREATION**	**OTHER**
Day Use Only Fee: $5 Open March 1 Through September 15	No Private Boats Rentals: Row & Paddle Boats Check for Current Regulations Water Levels Fluctuate	Fishing: Largemouth Bass, Bluegill, Green Sunfish, Channel Catfish Fishing License Required Picnicking Hiking & Nature Trails *No Swimming or Body Contact with Water*	Bait & Tackle Snack Shop

PINTO LAKE

Under the jurisdiction of the City of Watsonville, Pinto Lake Park is privately leased and managed. This facility has R.V. sites with full hookups, a picnic area, a group picnic site with a BBQ pavillion, large lawn areas and a softball field. With incoming Pacific breezes, the 92 surface-acre Lake is popular for sailing. There is a warm water fishery along with planted trout. In addition to a launch ramp and rental boats, there are also sports fields.

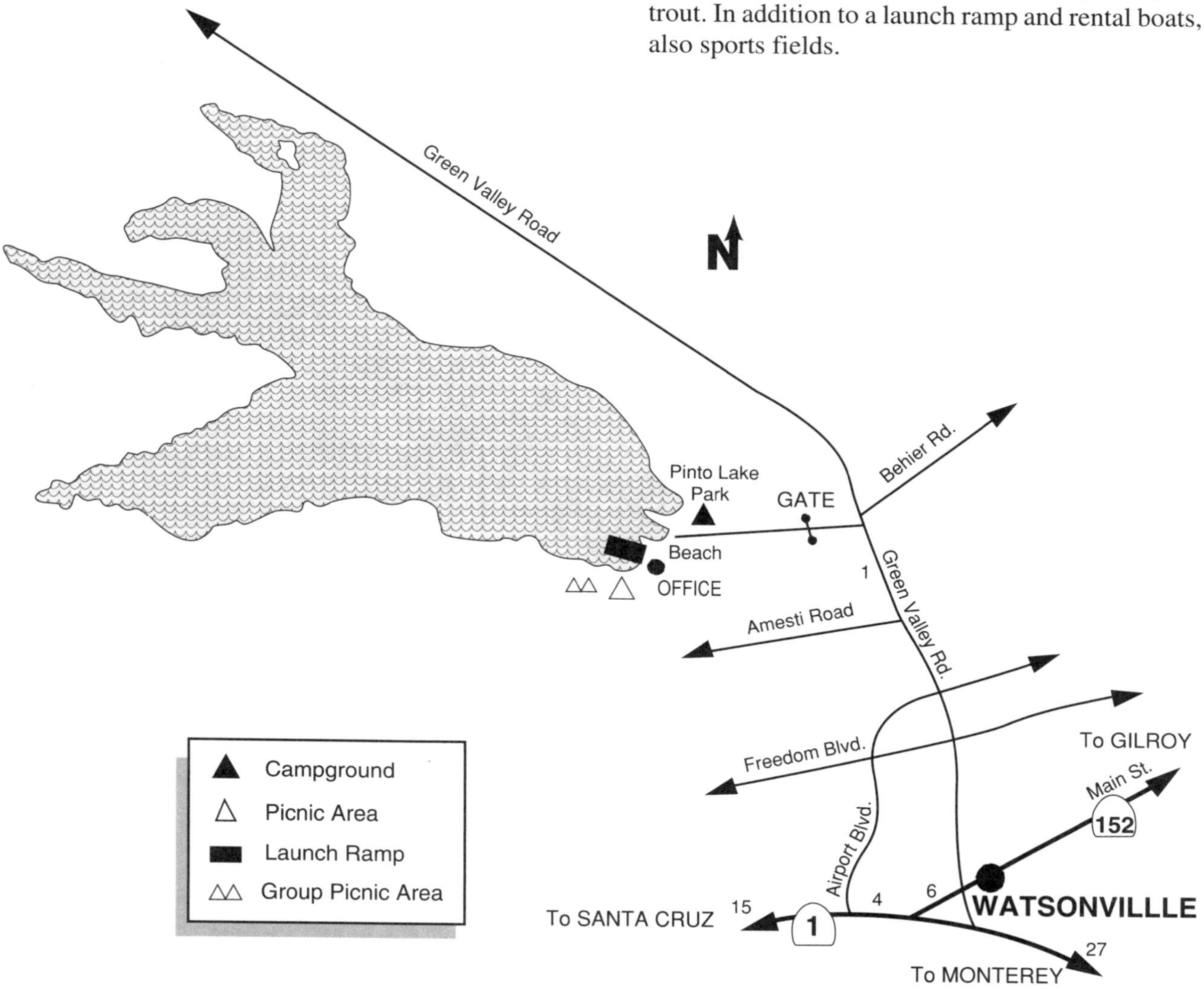

Green Valley Road
N
Pinto Lake Park
GATE
Behier Rd.
Beach
OFFICE
1
Green Valley Rd.
Amesti Road
Freedom Blvd.
Airport Blvd.
To GILROY
Main St.
152
Campground
Picnic Area
Launch Ramp
Group Picnic Area
To SANTA CRUZ
15
1
4
6
WATSONVILLLE
27
To MONTEREY

INFORMATION: Pinto Lake R.V. Campground, 451 Green Valley Rd., Watsonville 95076—Ph: (831) 722-8129

CAMPING	BOATING	RECREATION	OTHER
Pinto Lake Park: 28 R.V. Sites with Full Hookups Fee: $28	Power, Row, Canoe, Sail, Windsurf Speed Limit: 5 MPH Launch Ramp Rentals: Row & Pedal Boats	Fishing: Rainbow Trout, Largemouth Bass, Bluegill, Crappie & Catfish Picnicking Group Picnic Site Playground Softball Field Volleyball *No Swimming Allowed*	Full Facilities in Watsonville

COYOTE RESERVOIR

At an elevation of 777 feet, Coyote Reservoir is located in scenic, oak-covered hills near Gilroy. Santa Clara County Parks and Recreation has facilities for lakeside camping, picnicking, hiking, fishing and all types of boating. With 4,595 acres, the Coyote Lake-Harvey Bear Ranch County Park is within the Mount Hamilton Range. A network of trails are available for hiking, bicycling and horseback riding. The Lake, 635-surface acres, is open at the northwest end so the winds come down the length of the Lake for good sailing and windsurfing. Campers can fish from shore during the night but there is no night boating permitted.

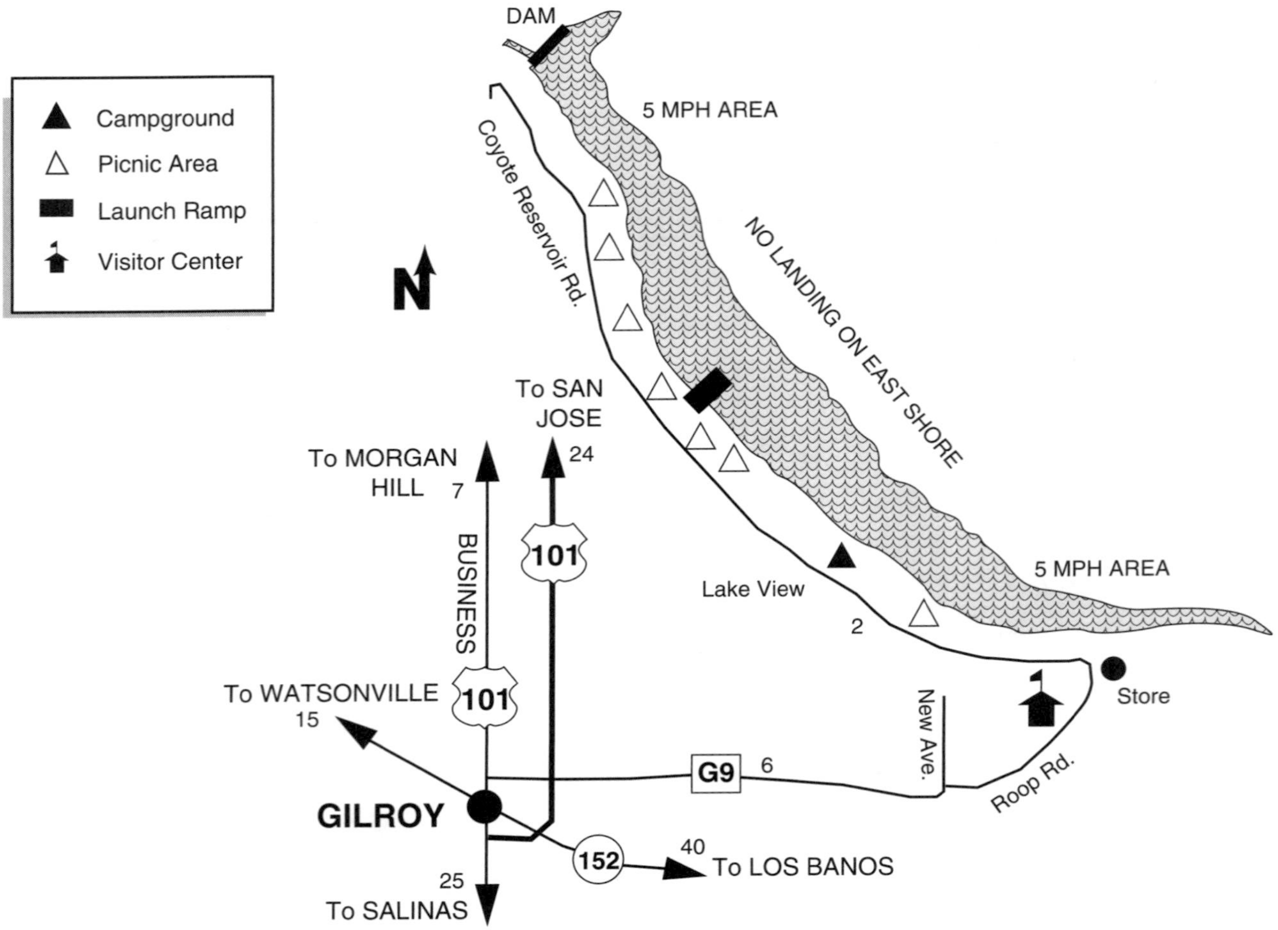
Campground
Picnic Area
Launch Ramp
Visitor Center
N
DAM
5 MPH AREA
Coyote Reservoir Rd.
NO LANDING ON EAST SHORE
To SAN JOSE
24
To MORGAN HILL
7
BUSINESS
101
Lake View
2
5 MPH AREA
Store
New Ave.
To WATSONVILLE
15
G9
6
Roop Rd.
GILROY
152
40
To LOS BANOS
25
To SALINAS

INFORMATION: Santa Clara County Parks, 298 Garden Hill Dr., San Jose 95032—Ph: (408) 355-2200

CAMPING	BOATING	RECREATION	OTHER
74 Dev. Sites for Tents & R.V.s Electric & Water Hookups Fees: $20 Reservations: Ph: (408) 355-2201 Day Use Fee: $6	Power, Row, Canoe, Sail, Waterski & PWC's Speed Limit - 35 MPH *Counter Clockwise Traffic Pattern* 5 MPH Some Areas Launch Ramp Fee: $6 *Call for Information on Low Water Levels*	Fishing: Rainbow Trout, Bluegill, Crappie & Black Bass, Carp Channel Catfish Picnicking Hiking, Bicycling & Equestrian Trails Ranger Interpretive Programs *No Swimming*	Coyote Lake-Harvey Bear Ranch County Park Ph: (408) 842-7800 Visitor Center Full Facilities at Gilroy

EL ESTERO, LAGUNA SECA, LOWER and UPPER ABBOTT LAKES

These three Recreation Parks in Monterey County range from a day-use City Park in Monterey to a Forest Service Campground at Arroyo Seco. The Laguna Seca Recreation Area includes a campground and a small 10 acre Lake (no fishing). Campsites overlook the famous race car track. El Estero is a scenic Lake in downtown Monterey with a children's play area, fishing dock, picnic facilities and athletic fields. The Abbott Lakes are in the Los Padres National Forest at 1,200 feet elevation. Family and group campgrounds and a warm water fishery are available. Trout fishing and swimming are popular in the Arroyo Seco River.

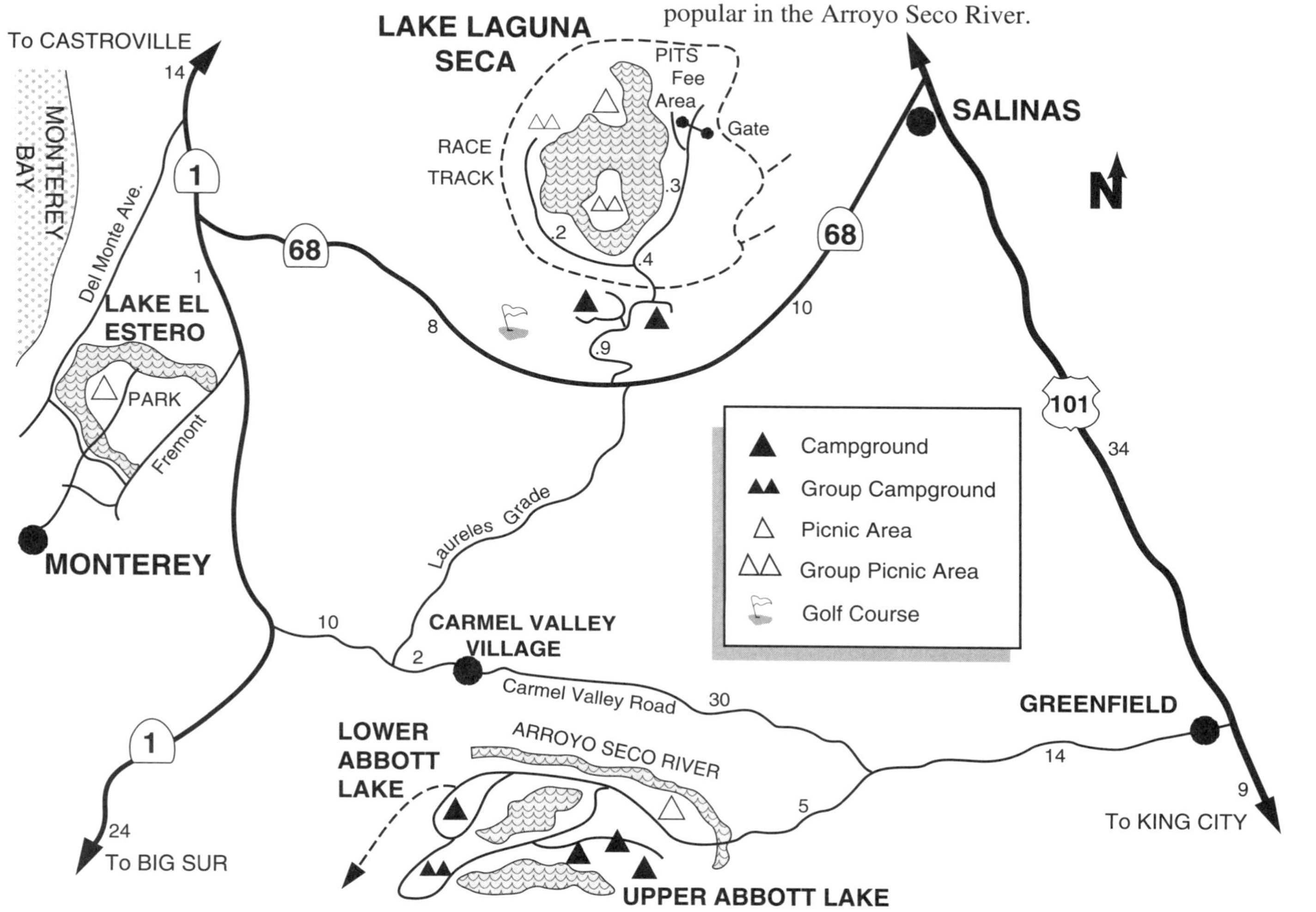

To CASTROVILLE
14
MONTEREY BAY
1
Del Monte Ave.
1
LAKE EL ESTERO
PARK
Fremont
MONTEREY
LAKE LAGUNA SECA
PITS
Fee Area
Gate
RACE TRACK
.3
.2
.4
68
8
.9
10
68
SALINAS
N
101
34
Campground
Group Campground
Picnic Area
Group Picnic Area
Golf Course
Laureles Grade
10
CARMEL VALLEY VILLAGE
2
Carmel Valley Road
30
GREENFIELD
14
9
To KING CITY
1
24
To BIG SUR
LOWER ABBOTT LAKE
ARROYO SECO RIVER
5
UPPER ABBOTT LAKE

INFORMATION: Laguna Seca Recreation Area, P.O. Box 5249, Salinas 93915—Ph: (831) 755-4899

CAMPING	BOATING	RECREATION	OTHER
Laguna Seca: Tent & R.V. Sites No Hookups: $25 Electric & Water Hookups: $30 Reserve: Ph: (888) 588-2267 U.S.F.S. Arroyo Seco Abbott Lakes: 49 Tent & R.V. Sites Group Site King City Ranger Station Reserve: Ph: (877) 444-6777	El Estero: Paddle Boat Rentals Ph: (831) 375-1484 Abbott Lakes: Canoes Laguna Seco: No Boating	Fishing: Trout, Bass & Catfish *No Fishing at Laguna Seca* Picnicking - Group Sites Reserve Laguna Seca Hiking & Bicycle Trails Playgrounds Laguna Seca: Race Track Events Race School Rifle & Pistol Range Motorcross Track Festivals, Concerts	El Estero Lake: City of Monterey Recreation & Community Services Department 546 Dutra St. Monterey 93940 Ph: (831) 646-3866 Full Facilities & Golf Courses in Monterey Monterey Jazz Festival Salinas Rodeo

SAN LUIS RESERVOIR and O'NEILL FOREBAY

San Luis Reservoir State Recreation Area is at an elevation of 544 feet in the eastern foothills of the Diablo Mountain Range, west of Los Banos. This huge Reservoir has 13,800 surface acres and 65 miles of grassy shoreline. In addition to good fishing, San Luis Reservoir is popular for boating, swimming and windsurfing but sudden strong winds can be a hazard. Warning lights are located at the Romero Overlook, Basalt campground and Quien Sabe Point at the Reservoir as well as the Medeiros launch ramp and San Luis Creek area at the Forebay. The O'Neill Forebay has a surface area of 2,000 acres with 14 miles of brush-covered shoreline. The 67-mile San Joaquin Section of the California Aqueduct Bikeway ends at the Forebay. Boating and fishing are popular. Waterfowl hunting is allowed at these Lakes in season.

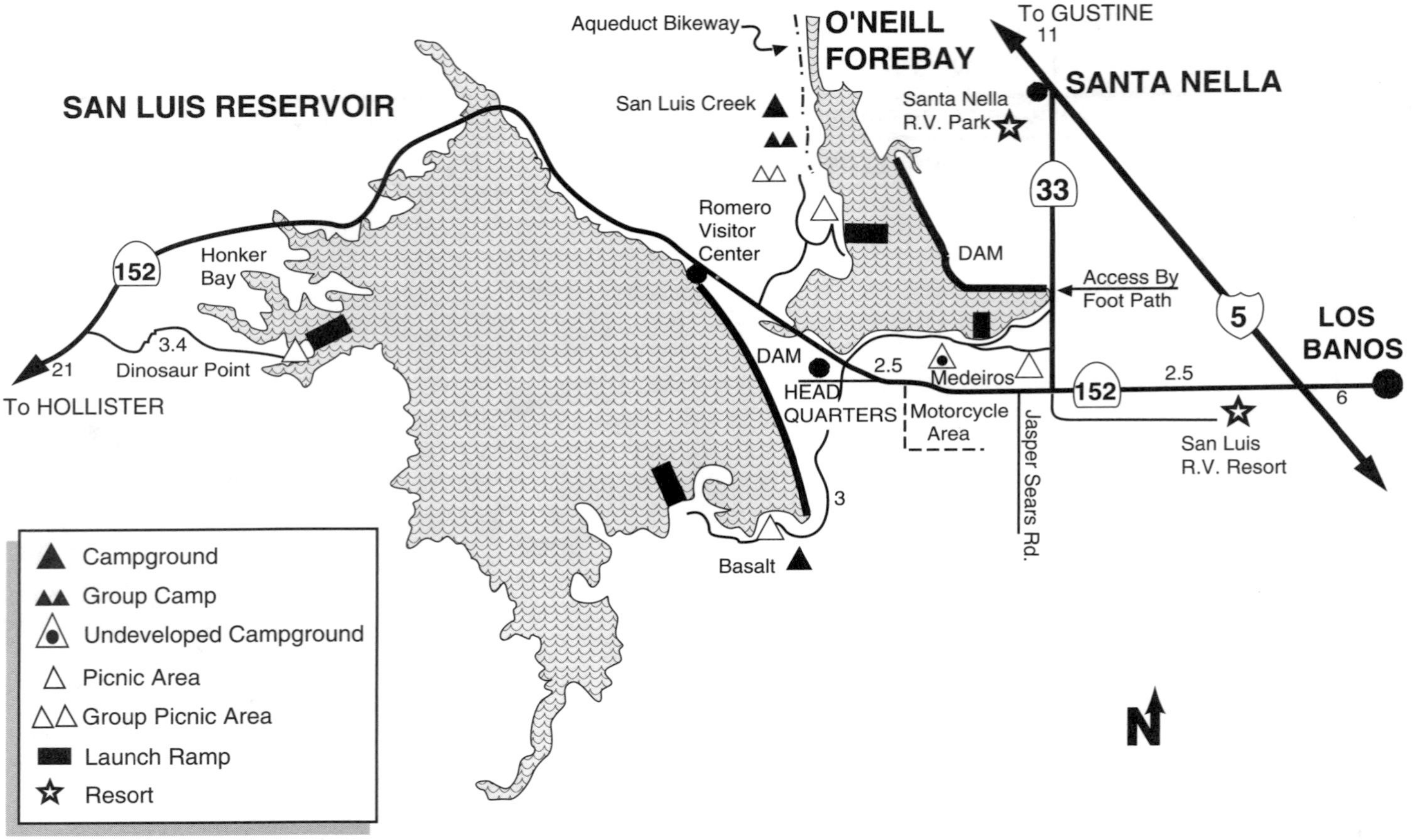

SAN LUIS RESERVOIR
O'NEILL FOREBAY
Aqueduct Bikeway
To GUSTINE
11
SANTA NELLA
Santa Nella R.V. Park
San Luis Creek
33
Romero Visitor Center
DAM
Access By Foot Path
5
LOS BANOS
152
Honker Bay
3.4
21
Dinosaur Point
To HOLLISTER
DAM
2.5
Medeiros
HEAD QUARTERS
Motorcycle Area
2.5
6
San Luis R.V. Resort
Jasper Sears Rd.
3
Basalt
N
Campground
Group Camp
Undeveloped Campground
Picnic Area
Group Picnic Area
Launch Ramp
Resort

INFORMATION: San Luis Reservoir State Rec. Area, 31426 Gonzaga Rd., Gustine 95322—Ph: (209) 826-1197

CAMPING	BOATING	RECREATION	OTHER
Basalt: 79 Dev. Sites for Tents & R.V.s to 30 ft. - No Hookups San Luis Creek: 53 Dev. Sites for Tents & R.V.s Water & Electric Hookups Fees: $15 to $25 Group Camps to 60 People Reserve:Ph:(800) 444-7275 Disposal Stations Medeiros: 500 Undev. Sites for Tents & R.V.s Day Use Only Fee: $6	Power, Row, Canoe, Sail, Waterski, PWCs, Windsurf & Inflatable Launch Ramps O'Neill Forebay: Counter-Clockwise Boating Pattern Only *Beware of Sudden Winds* 24 Hour Weather Conditions Updated Every 20 Min. Ph: (800) 805-4805 *Water May Fluctuate up to 200 Feet Annually*	Fishing: Catfish, Bluegill, Crappie, Largemouth & Striped Bass, Sturgeon, Shad Swimming - Beaches Picnicking - Group Sites 157-Acre Motorcycle Trail Area California Aqueduct Bikeway Visitor's Center at Romero Overlook	Santa Nella R.V. Park Full Hookups Ph: (209) 826-3105 San Luis R.V. Resort Full Hookups Ph: (209) 826-5542 Full Facilities in Los Banos and Santa Nella

LOS BANOS CREEK RESERVOIR

At an elevation of 328 feet, Los Banos Creek Reservoir is located in the hilly grasslands west of Los Banos. This Lake has 620 surface acres and 12 miles of shoreline. Los Banos is under the jurisdiction of the California State Parks system. There is a small undeveloped campground along with a horse camp and a paved launch ramp. There are several trees around the campgrounds along with shade ramadas. This Reservoir is primarily used as a warm water fishery and bass fishing derbies are held here. There are usually good winds for sailing and windsurfing.

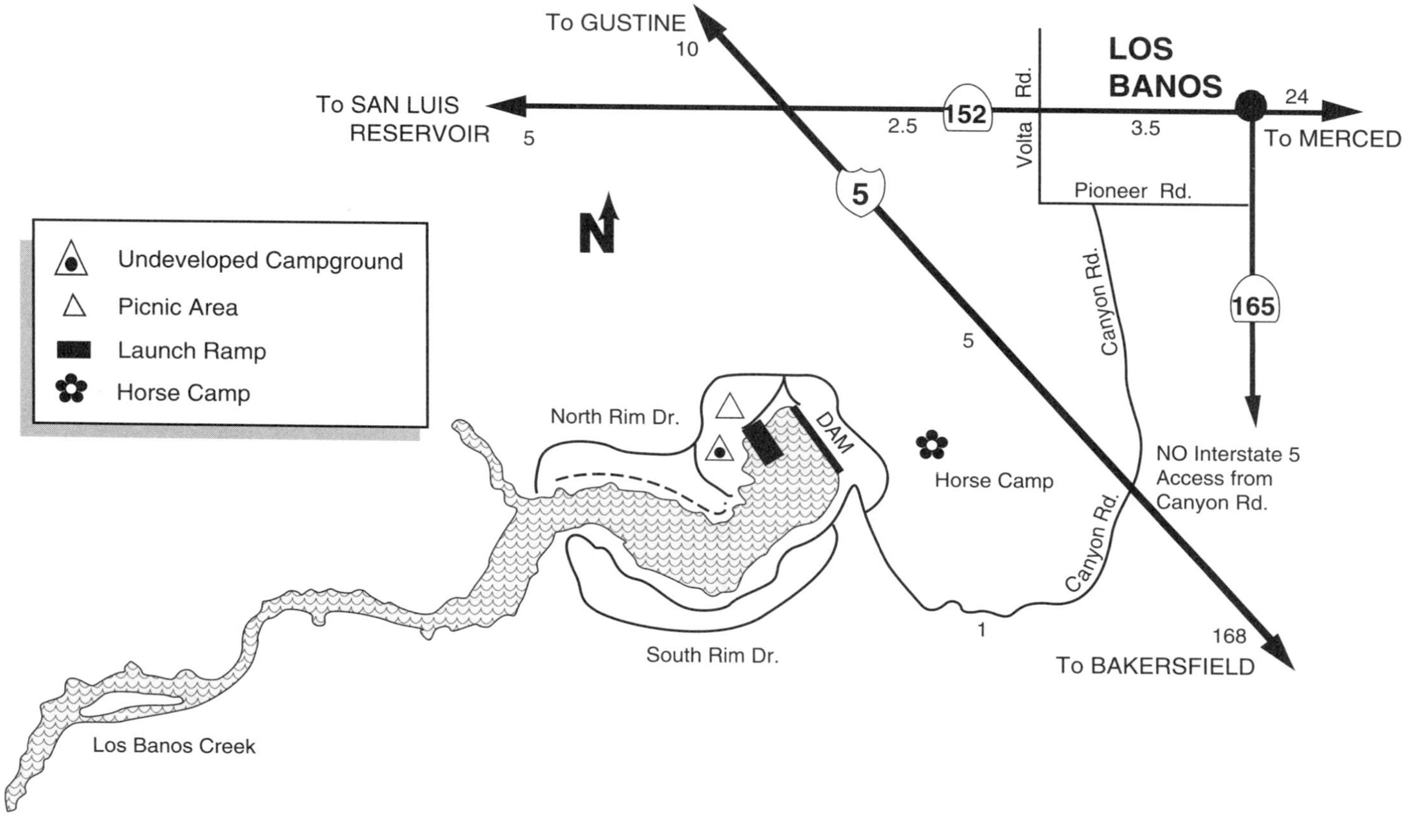

To GUSTINE
10
To SAN LUIS
RESERVOIR
5
2.5
152
Volta Rd.
LOS
BANOS
3.5
24
To MERCED
5
Pioneer Rd.
N
Undeveloped Campground
Picnic Area
Launch Ramp
Horse Camp
Canyon Rd.
165
5
North Rim Dr.
DAM
Horse Camp
NO Interstate 5
Access from
Canyon Rd.
Canyon Rd.
1
168
To BAKERSFIELD
South Rim Dr.
Los Banos Creek

INFORMATION: San Luis Reservoir State Rec. Area, 31426 Gonzaga Rd.,Gustine 95322—Ph: (209) 826-1197

CAMPING	BOATING	RECREATION	OTHER
20 Undev. Sites for Tents & R.V.s Fee: $12 Horse Camp Day Use: $6	Power, Row, Canoe, Sail, Windsurf & Inflatables Speed Limit - 5 MPH Launch Ramp	Fishing: Trout, Catfish, Bluegill, Largemouth Bass Swimming Picnicking Horses are Allowed but No Designated Trails	Full Facilities at Los Banos

EASTMAN LAKE

Located in oak-covered foothills 25 miles northeast of Chowchilla, Eastman Lake has 1,780 surface acres and is at 600 feet elevation. Winters are mild but summer temperatures can be in the 100's. Eastman is California's first designated trophy bass fishery with a limit of one bass per day, 22 inch minimum size. The upper Lake, including the Chowchilla River, is closed to boating and fishing to protect nesting eagles. Be aware of the "keep out" buoys as this area is closed to all water recreation. Berenda Reservoir, to the west, is a small day-use Lake with boating, swimming and fishing during the summer only.

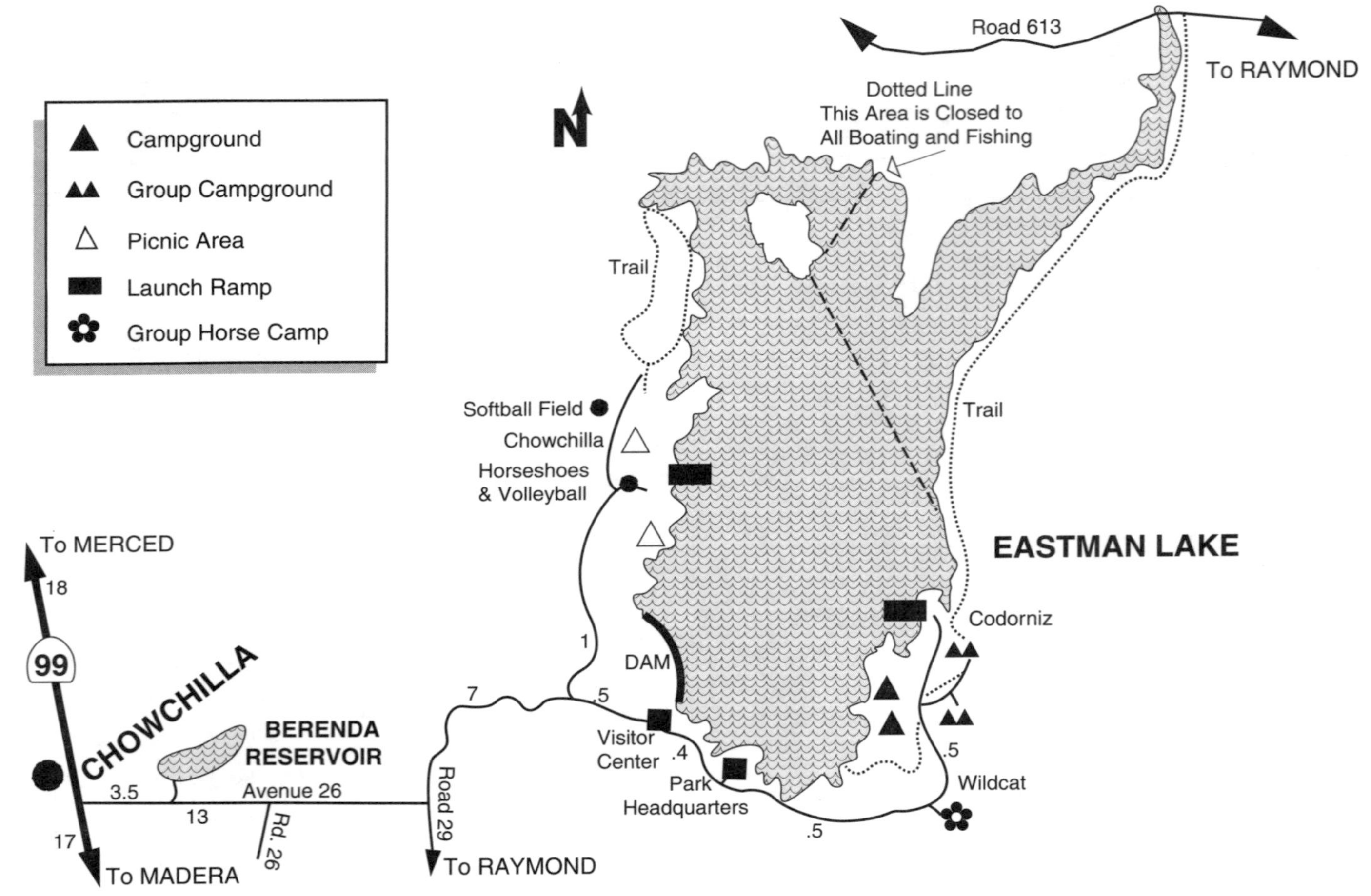
Campground
Group Campground
Picnic Area
Launch Ramp
Group Horse Camp
N
Road 613
To RAYMOND
Dotted Line
This Area is Closed to
All Boating and Fishing
Trail
Trail
Softball Field
Chowchilla
Horseshoes
& Volleyball
EASTMAN LAKE
To MERCED
18
99
CHOWCHILLA
BERENDA
RESERVOIR
3.5
Avenue 26
13
17
Rd. 26
To MADERA
Road 29
To RAYMOND
7
.5
1
DAM
Visitor
Center
.4
Park
Headquarters
.5
Codorniz
.5
Wildcat

INFORMATION: U.S. Army Corps of Engineers, Eastman Lake, Box 67, Raymond 93653—Ph: (559) 689-3255			
CAMPING	**BOATING**	**RECREATION**	**OTHER**
65 Dev. Sites for Tents & R.V.s - Fee: $14 Electric Hookups - $20 Full Hookups - $22 Group Areas to 100 People Fee: $55 - $75 Per Night Disposal Station Equestrian Group Camp Fee: $25 Reservations: Ph: (877) 444-6777 Day Use Fee: $3	Power, Row, Sail, Windsurf, Waterski & Inflatables Launch Ramps Berenda Reservoir: Limited to 15 Boats First Come Basis Open Summers Only Power, Waterskiing & PWCs Speed Limit 35 mph Drag Boat Racing	Fishing: Largemouth Bass, Catfish, Bluegill, Crappie, Trout in Winter Designated Trophy Bass Fishery - Limit: 1 per Day At least 22 Inches Long Swimming Picnicking - Shelters Hiking & Equestrian Trails Mountain Bike Trails Horseshoes, Softball Amphitheater Tours & Ranger Programs	Berenda Reservoir: Chowchilla Parks & Recreation Ph: (559) 665-8640 Swimming - Beaches BBQ Picnic Shelter Day Use Fee: $3 - $5 Full Facilities in Chowchilla & Madera

HENSLEY LAKE

Hensley Lake is at an elevation of 540 feet in the rolling foothills northeast of Madera. The surrounding area is covered with majestic oaks and granite outcroppings. The Lake has a surface area of 1,500 acres with 24 miles of shoreline. The U.S. Army Corps of Engineers has campgrounds, picnic areas and boating facilities. The expanse of open water and many secluded coves are good for all types of boating. The angler will find an abundant warm water fishery. Trails lead into the Wildlife Area where many birds, animals and native wildflowers can be observed.

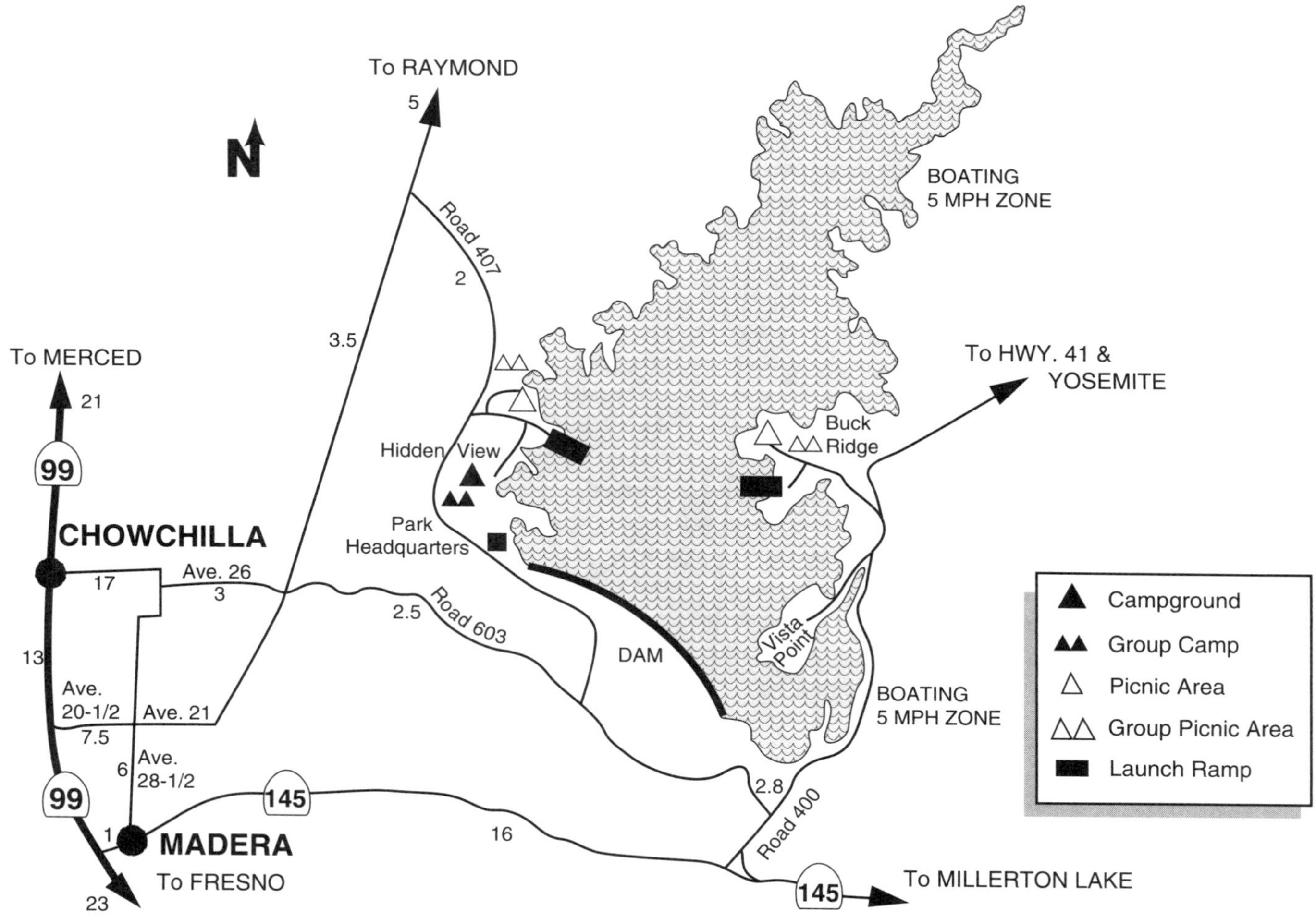

To RAYMOND
5
N
Road 407
2
3.5
BOATING
5 MPH ZONE
To MERCED
21
99
To HWY. 41 &
YOSEMITE
Buck
Ridge
Hidden View
CHOWCHILLA
Park
Headquarters
17
Ave. 26
3
2.5
Road 603
Vista Point
DAM
13
Ave.
20-1/2
Ave. 21
7.5
BOATING
5 MPH ZONE
6
Ave.
28-1/2
99
145
2.8
Road 400
1
MADERA
16
To FRESNO
23
145
To MILLERTON LAKE
Campground
Group Camp
Picnic Area
Group Picnic Area
Launch Ramp

INFORMATION: U.S. Army Corps of Engineers, Hensley Lake, P.O. Box 85, Raymond 93653—Ph: (559) 673-5151

CAMPING	BOATING	RECREATION	OTHER
55 Dev. Sites for Tents & R.V.s Fee: $16 With Electric Hookups: Fee: $22 Disposal Station 2 Group Camp Areas to 100 People Fee: $65 Reservations: Ph: (877) 444-6777 Day Use Fee: $4 Pets Allowed	Power, Row, Sail, Waterski, PWCs, Windsurf & Inflatable 2 Paved Launch Ramps Fees: $4 per Day $30 Annual Pass Courtesy Docks *Low Water Levels Submerged Hazards*	Fishing: Largemouth Bass, Bluegill, Catfish & Crappie, Trout in Winter, Night Fishing Allowed Swimming - Beach at Buck Ridge Picnicking Group Picnic Site Reserve: (877) 444-6777 Hiking, Mountain Bike & Equestrian Trails Amphitheater at Hidden View	Primitive Camping Area: Call Park Headquarters for Information Tours & Ranger Programs Full Facilities in Madera & Chowchilla

MILLERTON LAKE and LOST LAKE PARK

Millerton State Recreation Area, 8,000 acres, is located along the San Joaquin River and a part of the California State Park System. The popular 5,000 surface-acre Lake has over 40 miles of shoreline and has good boating facilities. The angler will find a warm water fishery. Sandy swim areas and picnic sites are located around the Lake. In winter, group tour boats are available to view bald and golden eagles.

Lost Lake Recreation Area is a separate facility under the jurisdiction of Fresno County Parks. This 305-acre park on the San Joaquin River, below Millerton, includes a small 38-acre Lake, a campground, picnic areas, including group sites, and beach volleyball. In addition, there is a 70-acre primitive nature study area.

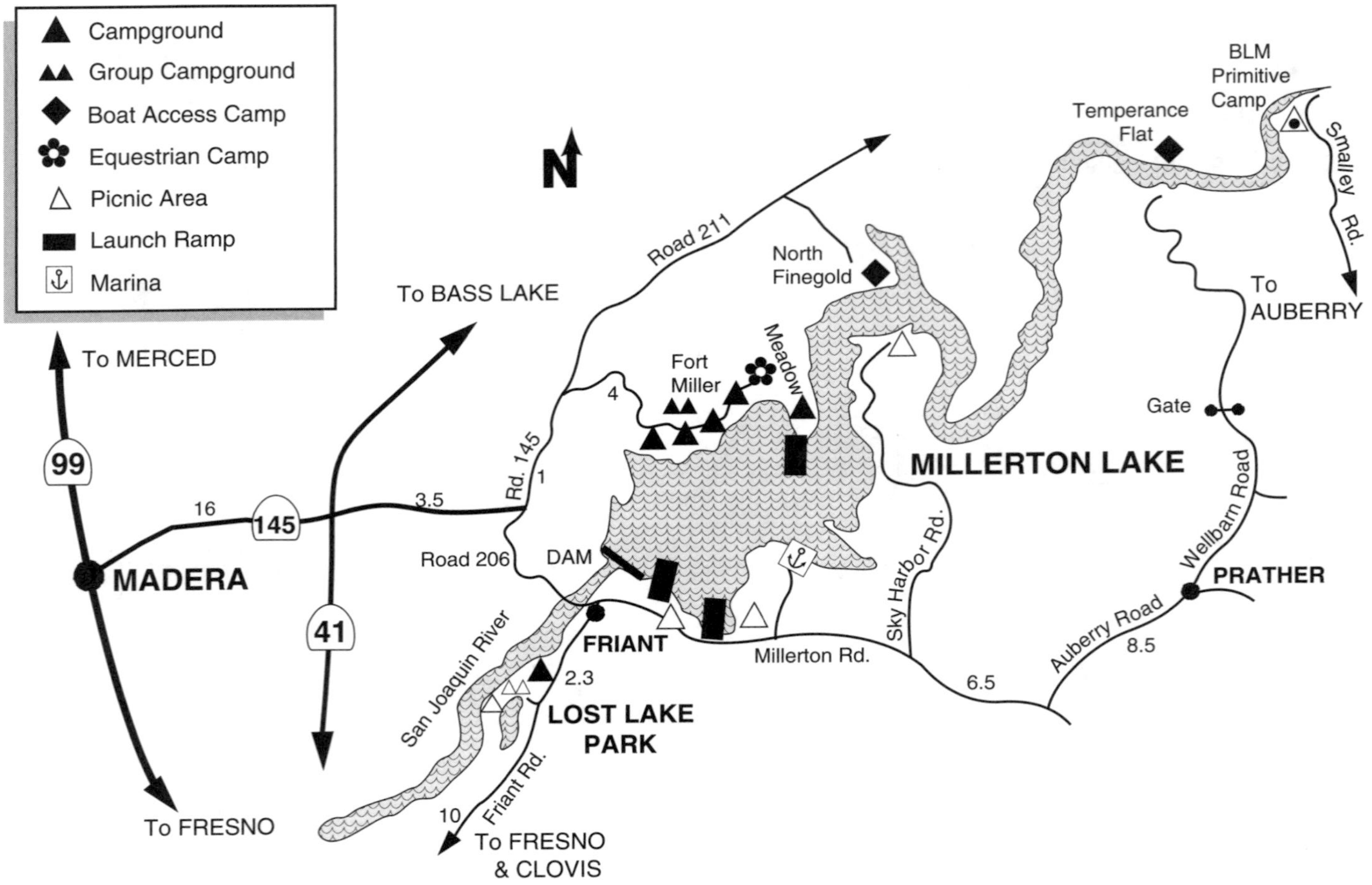
Campground
Group Campground
Boat Access Camp
Equestrian Camp
Picnic Area
Launch Ramp
Marina
N
To MERCED
99
16
145
MADERA
To FRESNO
41
To BASS LAKE
Road 211
North
Finegold
Fort
Miller
Meadow
4
Rd. 145
1
3.5
Road 206
DAM
FRIANT
2.3
LOST LAKE
PARK
San Joaquin River
Friant Rd.
10
To FRESNO
& CLOVIS
Millerton Rd.
Sky Harbor Rd.
6.5
MILLERTON LAKE
Auberry Road
8.5
PRATHER
Wellbarn Road
Gate
To
AUBERRY
Smalley Rd.
BLM
Primitive
Camp
Temperance
Flat

INFORMATION: Millerton Lake State Recreation Area, P.O. Box 205, Friant 93626—Ph: (559) 822-2332

CAMPING	BOATING	RECREATION	OTHER
Millerton Lake: 137 Dev. Sites for Tents & R.V.s to 36 Feet Fee: $29 Full Hookups: $34 Group Sites for 40 to 75 People - Fees: $90 - $169 Disposal Stations Reservations: Ph: (800) 444-7275 40 Boat Camp Sites Equestrian Camp Day Use Fee: $7	Millerton: Open to All Boating Full Service Marina Ph: (559) 822-2264 Launch Ramps: $7 Slips, Storage Rentals: Fishing Boats & Motors, Party Barge Lost Lake: Small Boats Electric Motors Only Hand Launch Only	Fishing: Trout, Striped, Spotted, Large & Smallmouth Bass, Catfish, Crappie Picnicking - Group Site Hiking & Equestrian Trails Bicycle Trails Swimming: Millerton Lake Birdwatching - Boat Tours Nature Study Area Wild Life Refuge Playground Beach Volleyball Court	Bait & Tackle Store Lost Lake Recreation Area Fresno County Parks 2220 Tulare St. Fresno 93721 Ph: (559) 488-3004 42 R.V. Sites First Come Basis Fee: $12 Group Picnic Sites Hiking Trails

Bass Lake is located in the Sierra National Forest at 3,500 feet elevation. This beautiful man-made Lake is in a forested area and recreational opportunities are numerous. Fishing and boating on the 1,165 surface-acre Lake is extremely popular. Water levels are generally maintained through Labor Day. Facilities on the South Shore are administered by the U. S. Forest Service and managed by California Land Management. There are numerous group sites for camping and picnicking at Crane Valley and Recreation Point. Luxury resorts, cabins and R.V. parks are available at privately owned areas around the Lake. Hikers can enjoy self-guided interpretive trails and a steep climb up to Goat Mountain Lookout. Bass Lake is a great place for old-fashioned family vacations.

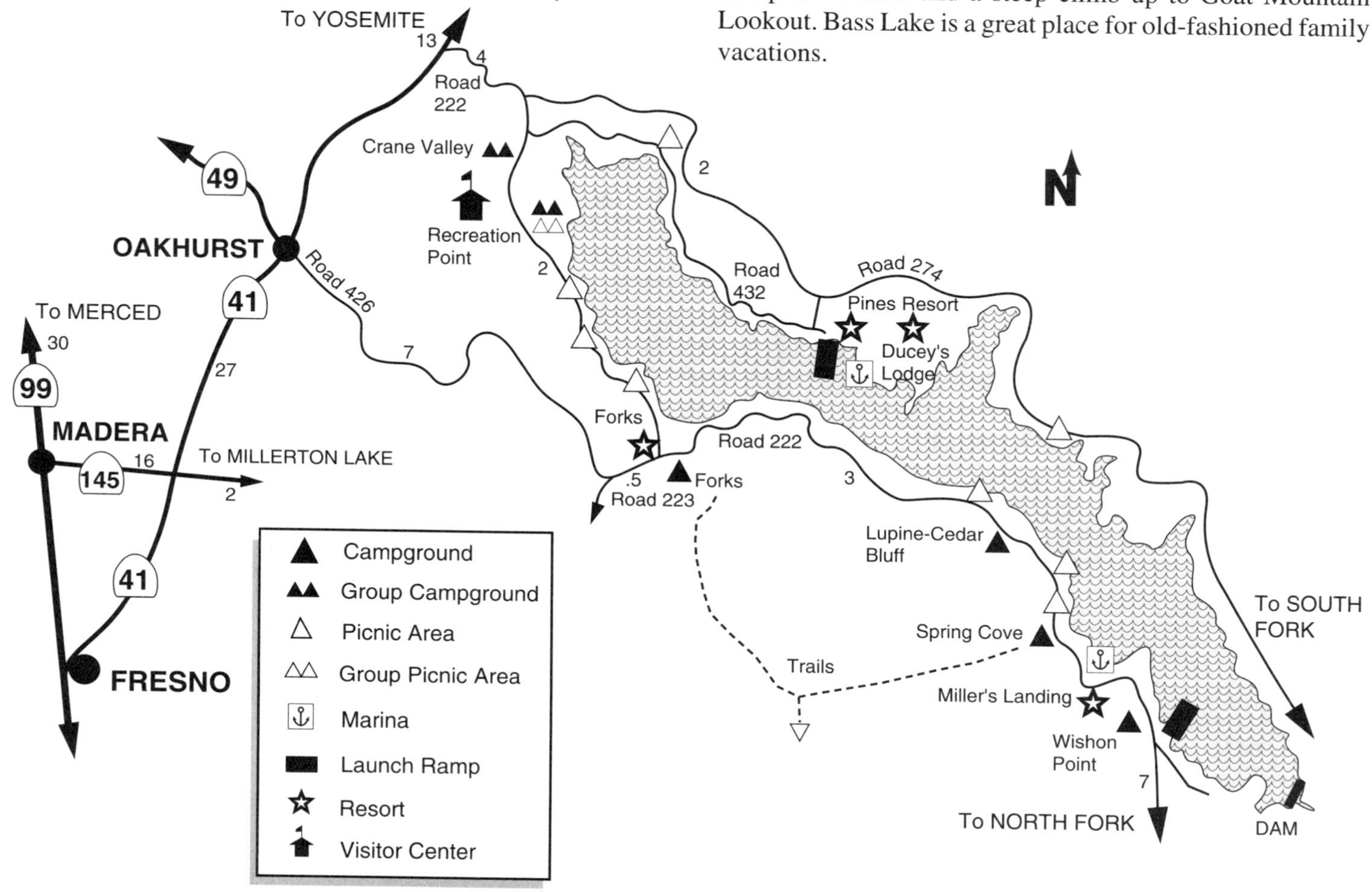
To YOSEMITE
13
4
Road 222
Crane Valley
2
N
49
OAKHURST
Recreation Point
Road 426
41
To MERCED
30
99
27
7
Road 432
Road 274
Pines Resort
Ducey's Lodge
MADERA
16
To MILLERTON LAKE
145
2
Forks
Road 222
.5
Road 223
Forks
3
41
FRESNO
Lupine-Cedar Bluff
Spring Cove
Trails
Miller's Landing
Wishon Point
7
To NORTH FORK
To SOUTH FORK
DAM
Campground
Group Campground
Picnic Area
Group Picnic Area
Marina
Launch Ramp
Resort
Visitor Center

INFORMATION: Bass Lake Ranger District, 57003 Road 225, North Fork 93643—Ph: (559) 877-2218

CAMPING	BOATING	RECREATION	OTHER
Dev. Sites for Tents & R.V.s - Fee: $21 No Hookups-No Showers Forks: 31 Sites Lupine-Cedar: 113 Sites Spring Cove: 63 Sites Wishon: 47 Sites Group Campgrounds Disposal Stations Reservations: Ph: (877) 444-6777	Power, Row, Canoe, Sail, Waterski, PWCs, Windsurfing & Inflatables Boats Must Be Registered Full Service Marinas Launch Ramps Moorings & Gas Summer Cruises Rentals: Fishing & Waterski Boats, Canoes & Party Barges	Fishing: Rainbow Trout, Catfish, Bluegill, Perch, Crappie, Black Bass & Kokanee Salmon Picnicking Group Picnic Sites Reservations: Ph: (877) 444-5777 Swimming - Beaches Hiking & Equestrian Trails Baseball & Volleyball Ranger Programs	The Pines Resort & Ducey's Lodge Ph: (800) 350-7463 or Ph: (559) 642-3131 Forks Resort Ph: (559) 642-3737 Miller's Landing Ph: (559) 642-3633 Rustic Cabins to Deluxe Resorts Snack Bars & Restaurants Groceries, Bait & Tackle Gas Station

REDINGER LAKE and KERCHKOFF RESERVOIR

Redinger Lake, in the Sierra National Forest, is at an elevation of 1,400 feet. Located in a narrow valley, the surrounding mountains rise more than 1,000 feet above the Lake. The Lake is 3 miles long and 1/4 mile wide. This area of digger pine and chaparral is intermingled with live and valley oak. Redinger is popular for waterskiing and PWCs and has numerous sandy beaches. Kerckhoff Reservoir, 172 surface acres, is located 6 miles to the west at 1,000 feet elevation and is operated by P.G.&E. Fishing for striped bass is the main activity and boating is limited to hand-launched boats. The town of North Fork is an interesting place to visit and enjoy the shops. It is the geographical center of California.

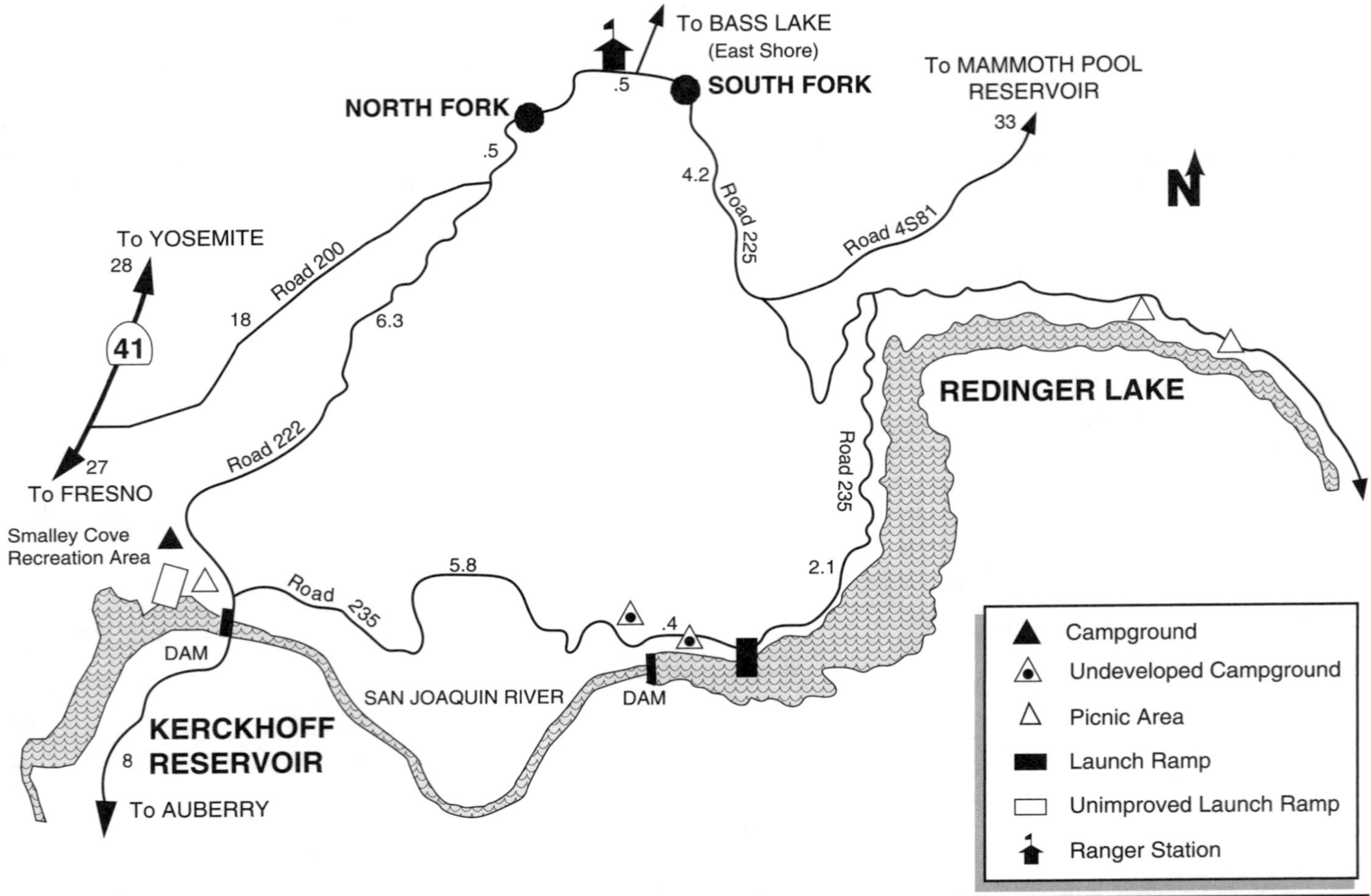
To BASS LAKE
(East Shore)
SOUTH FORK
NORTH FORK
To MAMMOTH POOL RESERVOIR
33
.5
.5
4.2
Road 225
Road 4S81
N
To YOSEMITE
28
Road 200
18
41
6.3
Road 222
27
To FRESNO
REDINGER LAKE
Road 235
Smalley Cove Recreation Area
Road 235
5.8
2.1
.4
DAM
SAN JOAQUIN RIVER
DAM
KERCKHOFF RESERVOIR
8
To AUBERRY
Campground
Undeveloped Campground
Picnic Area
Launch Ramp
Unimproved Launch Ramp
Ranger Station

INFORMATION: Bass Lake Ranger District, 57003 Road 225, North Fork 93643—Ph: (559) 877-2218

CAMPING	BOATING	RECREATION	OTHER
Redinger Lake: Primitive Camp Sites - 2 Designated Areas Only - No Water P.G.&E. Kerckhoff : Smalley Cove Recreation Area: 5 Campsites 5 Picnic Sites Ph: (916) 386-5164 *Extreme Fire Danger* *No Campfires*	Power, Row, Canoe, PWCs, Sail & Inflatables Speed Limit - 35 MPH 5 MPH Zones Launch Ramp at Redinger Lake Car Top Launch Only at Kerckhoff	Fishing: Trout, Smallmouth & Striped Bass, Catfish, Bluegill Swimming Picnicking Hiking Trails White Water Rafting from Redinger Lake to Kerckhoff Reservoir	North Fork Chamber of Commerce Ph: (559) 877-2410 Nearest Facilities at North Fork & Auberry

MAMMOTH POOL RESERVOIR

Mammoth Pool Reservoir is located on the San Joaquin River. Elevations range from 3,300 to 5,300 feet. The surface area of the Reservoir is 1,107 acres when full although water levels can drop 90 feet in the fall, closing the launch ramp. Southern California Edison Company completed the dam in 1959 to produce hydroelectric power. The Lake is nestled in a narrow valley of ponderosa pine, incense cedar, black and live oak with mountains rising 2,000 feet above the shoreline. The access road, part of the beautiful Sierra Vista Scenic Byway, is impassable when winter snow arrives. Mile High Vista Point offers 180 degree views of the Ansel Adams Wilderness, Mount Ritter and Mammoth Mountain.

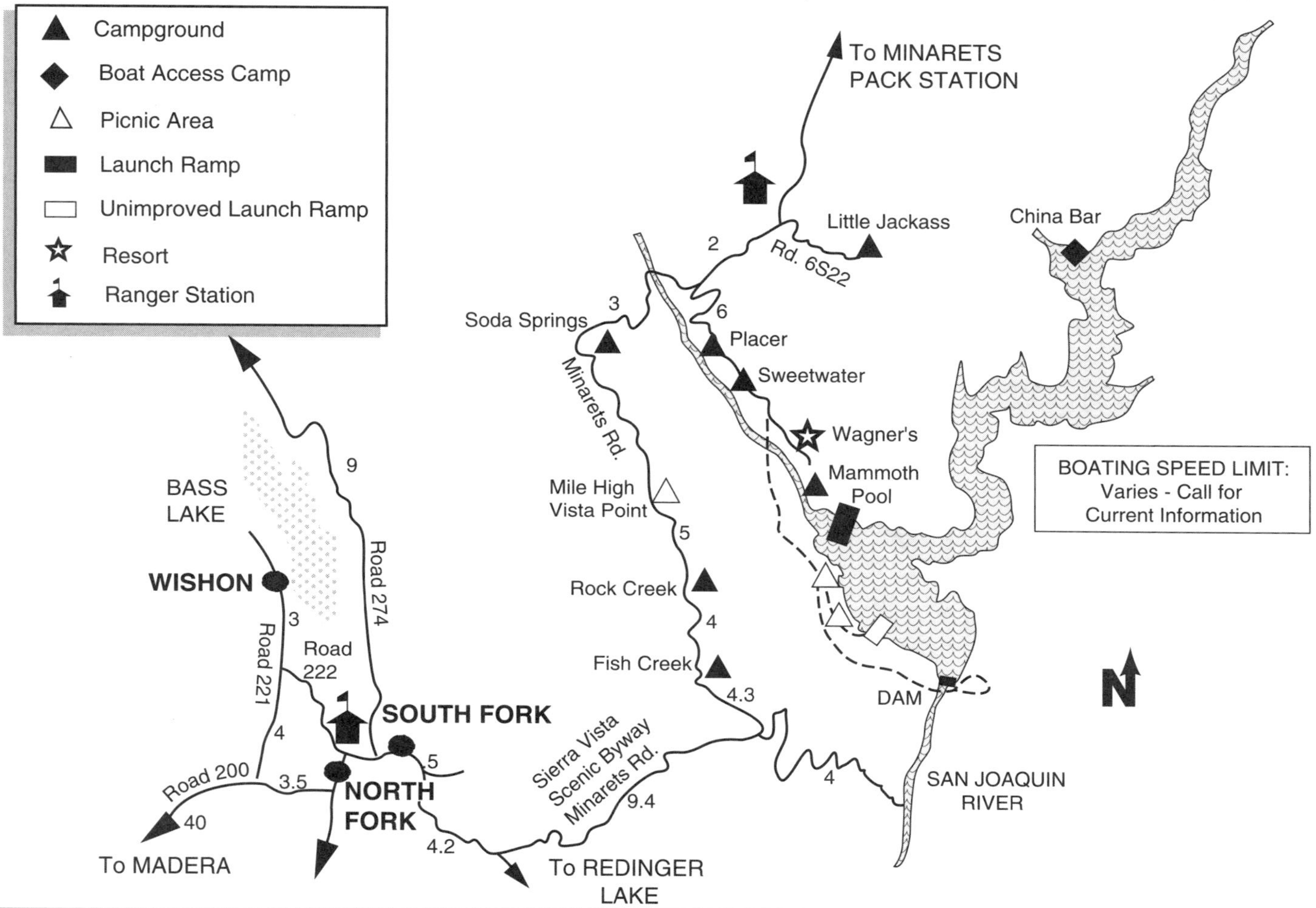
Campground
Boat Access Camp
Picnic Area
Launch Ramp
Unimproved Launch Ramp
Resort
Ranger Station
To MINARETS PACK STATION
Little Jackass
China Bar
2
Rd. 6S22
3
Soda Springs
6
Placer
Sweetwater
Minarets Rd.
Wagner's
Mammoth Pool
BOATING SPEED LIMIT: Varies - Call for Current Information
Mile High Vista Point
5
9
BASS LAKE
Road 274
WISHON
Rock Creek
4
3
Road 221
Road 222
Fish Creek
4.3
DAM
SOUTH FORK
4
5
Sierra Vista Scenic Byway Minarets Rd.
4
SAN JOAQUIN RIVER
N
Road 200
3.5
NORTH FORK
9.4
40
To MADERA
4.2
To REDINGER LAKE

INFORMATION: Bass Ranger District, 57003 Road 225, North Fork 93643—Ph: (559) 877-2218			
CAMPING	**BOATING**	**RECREATION**	**OTHER**
Mammoth Pool: 47 Dev. Sites for Tents & R.V.s Fee: $17 Placer: 8 Dev. Sites Sweetwater: 10 Dev. Sites Fees: $16 China Bar: 6 Boat-In or Hike-In Sites 48 Sites Along Minarets Rd. Reserve Some Sites: Ph: (877) 444-6777	Power, Sail, Row, Canoe, Windsurf & Inflatables Designated Areas Waterskiing - 35 MPH Speed Limit - Summer Launch Ramps No Large Boats *Check for Boating Speed* *Limits - Various* *Call for Current Lake* *Level Information*	Fishing: Rainbow, Eastern Brook & German Brown Trout Closed to Fishing & Boating May 1 to June 15 for Migrating Deer Picnicking Hiking & Equestrian Trails *Extreme Fire Danger*	Wagner's Resort Ph: (559) 841-3736 35 Dev. Sites for Tents & R.V.s - Fee: $17 Deli, Grocery Store Bait & Tackle Gas Station Open: End of May to Sept.15

COURTRIGHT, WISHON and BLACK ROCK RESERVOIRS

These Lakes range in elevation from 8,200 feet at Courtright, 6,600 feet at Wishon to 4,200 feet at Black Rock. They are all part of the Kings River System. Located in the Sierra National Forest, these Lakes offer good fishing for native trout. In addition, the angler can enjoy the Upper King's River. Wishon Village has resort facilities in this remote area. The Forest Service operates numerous campgrounds as shown on the map. Hikers and equestrians will find trailheads leading into the John Muir and Dinkey Lakes Wilderness Areas. This entire region has some of the most spectacular scenery in California. The Helms Creek Hydroelectric Project affects water levels daily at Wishon, Courtright and Black Rock.

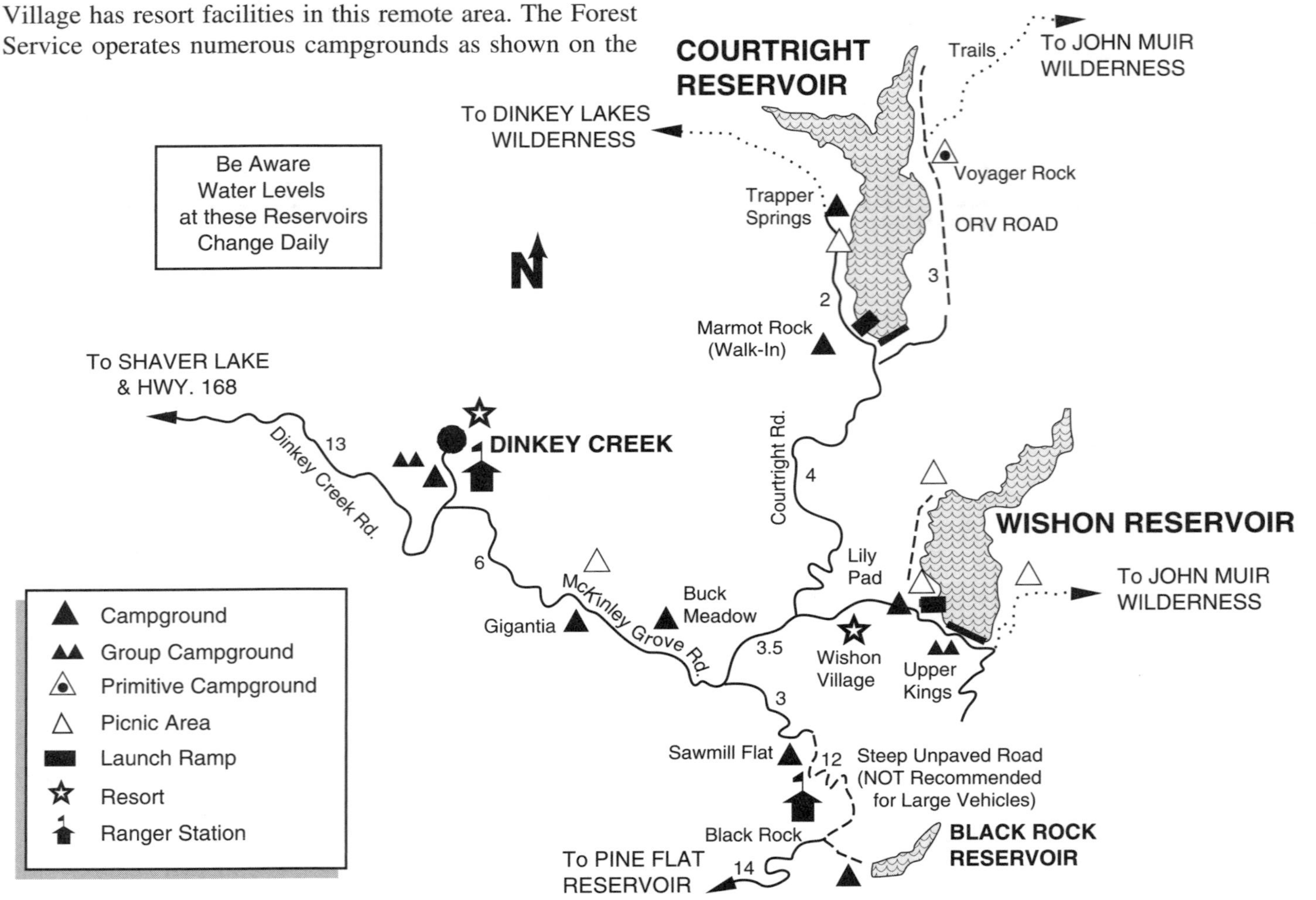
COURTRIGHT RESERVOIR
Trails
To JOHN MUIR WILDERNESS
To DINKEY LAKES WILDERNESS
Voyager Rock
Trapper Springs
ORV ROAD
Be Aware Water Levels at these Reservoirs Change Daily
N
3
2
Marmot Rock (Walk-In)
To SHAVER LAKE & HWY. 168
DINKEY CREEK
13
Dinkey Creek Rd.
Courtright Rd.
4
WISHON RESERVOIR
Lily Pad
6
McKinley Grove Rd.
Buck Meadow
To JOHN MUIR WILDERNESS
Gigantia
3.5
Wishon Village
Upper Kings
3
Sawmill Flat
12
Steep Unpaved Road (NOT Recommended for Large Vehicles)
Black Rock
BLACK ROCK RESERVOIR
To PINE FLAT RESERVOIR
14
Campground
Group Campground
Primitive Campground
Picnic Area
Launch Ramp
Resort
Ranger Station

INFORMATION: High Sierra Ranger District, 29688 Auberry Rd. P.O. Box 559, Prather 93651—Ph: (559) 855-5355

CAMPING	BOATING	RECREATION	OTHER
P.G.&E. Dev. Sites: TrapperSprings-75 Sites:$18 Marmot Rock-15 Sites: $18 Lily Pad-15 Sites: $18 Upper Kings Group: $150 - up to 50 People Reservations for Group Site Ph:(916) 386-5164 Black Rock-10 Sites: $10 USFS Dev. Sites Dinkey Creek-128 Sites: $22 Dinkey Group to 50 People Reserve Ph: (877) 444-6777	Courtright & Wishon: Open to All Boating *Except Waterskiing & PWC's* 15 MPH Speed Limit Launch Ramps Rentals at Wishon Village: Fishing & Patio Boats No Boating at Black Rock	Fishing: Rainbow, Brown & Brook Trout Swimming at Courtright & Wishon No Swimming at Black Rock Picnicking Hiking & Equestrian Trails Horse Rentals & Pack Services ORV Areas Calif. Land Management: Interpretive Programs in Summer at Dinkey Creek	Wishon Village Ph: (559) 865-5361 26 Tent Sites & 97 R.V. Sites - Full Hookups Fees: $23 to $38 Grocery Store Bait & Tackle Dinkey Creek Inn - Cabins Ph: (559) 841-3435 Full Facilities at Shaver Lake

HUNTINGTON LAKE

Huntington Lake is at an elevation of 7,000 feet in the Sierra National Forest. Resting in a forested natural basin, this man-made Lake is 6 miles long and 1/2 mile wide with 14 miles of shoreline. The Forest Service Campgrounds are operated by California Land Management. Many private resorts offer R.V. sites, cabins and restaurants. This is a great spot for family vacations. Sailing regattas are held in the summer to take advantage of the westerly winds. Hiking and equestrian trails surround Huntington Lake. Kaiser Wilderness Area, 22,750 acres, is nearby with permits required for entry. The angler will find good fishing from the shore, boat and nearby lakes and streams.

....Continued....

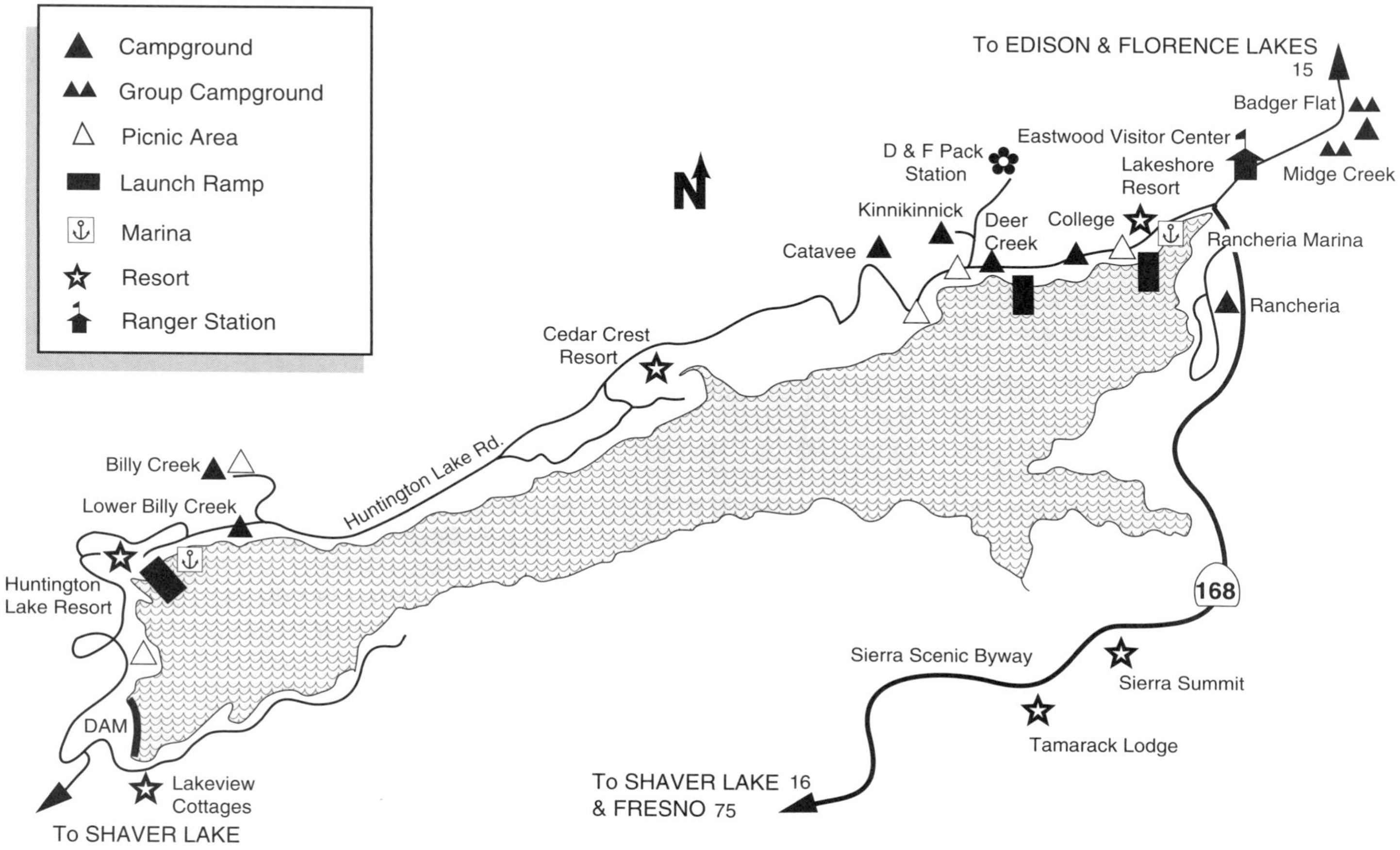

Campground
Group Campground
Picnic Area
Launch Ramp
Marina
Resort
Ranger Station
N
To EDISON & FLORENCE LAKES 15
Badger Flat
Eastwood Visitor Center
D & F Pack Station
Lakeshore Resort
Midge Creek
Kinnikinnick
Deer Creek
College
Catavee
Rancheria Marina
Rancheria
Cedar Crest Resort
Huntington Lake Rd.
Billy Creek
Lower Billy Creek
Huntington Lake Resort
DAM
Lakeview Cottages
To SHAVER LAKE
168
Sierra Scenic Byway
Sierra Summit
Tamarack Lodge
To SHAVER LAKE 16 & FRESNO 75

INFORMATION:High Sierra Ranger District, 29688 Auberry Rd. P.O. Box 559, Prather 93651—Ph: (559) 855-5355

CAMPING	BOATING	RECREATION	OTHER
Developed Sites for Tents & R.V.s to 40 Ft. Fees: $17 - $42 Lower Billy Creek: 15 Sites Upper Billy Creek: 44 Sites Catavee: 23 Sites Kinnikinnick: 27 Sites Deer Creek: 28 Sites College: 11 Sites Rancheria: 149 Sites Badger Flat: 15 Sites Group Camps to 100 People Reserve: Ph: (877) 444-6777	Power, Row, Canoe, Sail, Waterski Full Service Marinas Huntington Lake Marina Ph: (559) 893-6750 Rancheria Marina Ph: (559) 893-3234 Launch Ramps Rentals: Fishing & Sail Boats, Canoes, Paddleboats & Patio Boats Boat Slips	Fishing: Rainbow, Brown & Brook Trout, Kokanee Swimming Picnicking Hiking & Equestrian Trails Horses Permitted at Badger Flat Campgrounds Horse Rentals & Pack Trips Calif. Land Management: Interpretive Programs in Summer	Motels, Cabins & Condos Restaurants Grocery Stores Bait & Tackle Gas Station Eastwood Visitor Center Ph: (559) 893-6611 See Following Page

HUNTINGTON LAKE..............Continued

The following is a list of a variety of accommodations and facilities at or near Shaver Lake and Huntington Lake. This area is one of the top spots for family vacations. Advance reservations are usually necessary in season.
Call for Current Fees

HUNTINGTON LAKE

LAKESHORE RESORT - 61953 Huntington Lake Rd., Lakeshore 93634—Ph: (559) 893-3193
R.V.s to 35 feet, Full Hookups, 25 Housekeeping Cabins for 2 to 6 People, Store, Restaurant & Saloon, Launch Ramp, Marina, Slips, Rentals: Fishing & Sail Boats, Kayaks & Canoes, Summer Sailing Regattas, Pets Allowed.

CEDAR CREST RESORT - 61011 Cedar Crest Lane, P. O. Box 163, Lakeshore 93634—Ph: (559) 893-3233
R.V. Sites with Lake View, Full Hookups, 11 Tent Cabins, 14 Housekeeping Cabins, Store, Gourmet Restaurant & Bar, Dock, Rentals: Fishing Boats, Movies & Bonfires on Weekends, Pets Allowed.

HUNTINGTON LAKE RESORT - 58910 Huntington Lake Rd., Lakeshore 93634—Ph: (559) 893-6750 or 893-3226
10 Housekeeping Cabins for 2 to 8 People, Restaurant, Marina, Dock, Slips, Rentals: Fishing & Sail Boats, Kayaks & Canoes, Patio Boats & Paddle Boats, Sunset Cruises.

LAKEVIEW COTTAGES - 58374 Huntington Lodge Rd., P. O. Box 177, Lakeshore 93634—Ph: (559) 553-3550
12 Housekeeping Cabins for 2 to 6 People, Dock, Rentals: Fishing Boats & Canoes.

TAMARACK LODGE - 55380 Flintridge Rd., P. O. Box 175, Lakeshore 93634—Ph: (559) 893-3244 or (800) 268-0274
Motor Lodge Rooms with Kitchens & Fireplaces, Open Year Around.

RANCHERIA MARINA ENTERPRISES, P. O. Box 157, Lakeshore 93634—Ph: (559) 893-3234
Marina, Slips, Rentals: Fishing & Patio Boats, PWCs, Canoes & Kayaks, Pedal Boats, Boat Repairs, Store, Snacks, Bait & Tackle, Fishing Licenses.

SIERRA SUMMIT MOUNTAIN RESORT, 59265 Highway 168, P. O. Box 236, Lakeshore 93634—Ph: (559) 233-1200
Inn with Rooms & Suites, Restaurant & Bar, Groups, Special Events, Ski Resort and R.V. Sites in Winter.

D & F PACK STATION, P. O. Box 156, Lakeshore 93634—Ph: (559) 893-3220
Horseback Riding - 1 Hour, 2 Hours, 1/2 Day, All Day & Fishing Rides, Spot & Extended Pack Trips, Full Service Trips including Meals.

SHAVER LAKE

LAKESIDE AT THE POINT - 44185 Highway 168, Shaver Lake 93664—Ph: (559) 841-3326
21 Rustic Cabins for 2 to 6 People on the Lake, Restaurant & Bar, Weekend Entertainment, Gift Shop, Pets Allowed.

Other Accommodations in Town of Shaver Lake:

Elliott House Bed & Breakfast—Ph: (559) 841-8601

Knotty Pine Cabins—Ph: (559) 779-8426

Shaver Lake Village Hotel—Ph: (559) 841-8289

Shaver Stable - Ph: (559) 841-8500

SHAVER LAKE

Shaver Lake is at an elevation of 5,560 feet in the Sierra National Forest. The Lake has a surface area of 2,000 acres with a shoreline of 13 miles surrounded by tall pine trees and granite boulders. This is a popular boating Lake with good marine facilities. In addition to excellent fishing at Shaver, there are numerous trout streams nearby for the angler. The John Muir and Dinkey Lakes Wilderness Areas are available for the backpacker and equestrian. Both the U. S. Forest Service and Southern California Edison maintain campgrounds in this beautiful setting. Shaver Lake is one of our personal favorites.

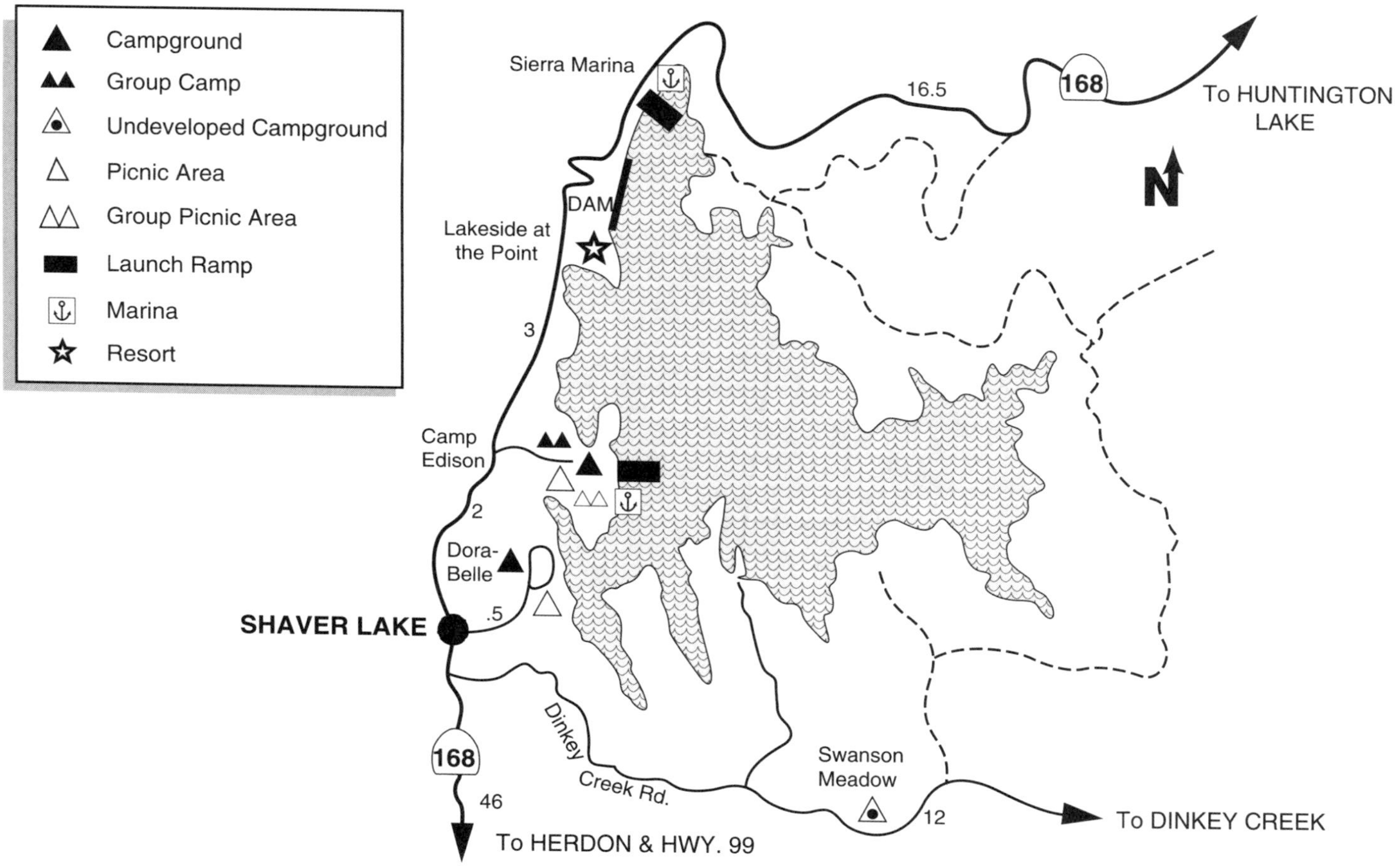
Campground
Group Camp
Undeveloped Campground
Picnic Area
Group Picnic Area
Launch Ramp
Marina
Resort
Sierra Marina
16.5
168
To HUNTINGTON LAKE
N
DAM
Lakeside at the Point
3
Camp Edison
2
Dora-Belle
.5
SHAVER LAKE
168
46
Dinkey Creek Rd.
Swanson Meadow
12
To DINKEY CREEK
To HERDON & HWY. 99

INFORMATION: High Sierra Ranger District, 29688 Auberry Rd. P.O.Box 559, Prather 93651—Ph: (559) 855-5355

CAMPING	BOATING	RECREATION	OTHER
U.S.F.S. - Dorabelle: 68 Dev. Sites for Tents & R.V.s to 40 Ft. No Hookups - Fee: $19 Reserve: (877) 444-6777 Swanson Meadows: 8 Undeveloped Sites Southern California Edison: 252 Dev. Sites for Tents & R.V.s - Fee: $25 - $50 Electric Hookups Group Sites to 60 People Reserve Ph: (559) 841-3134	Power, Row, Canoe, Sail, Waterski, PWCs, Windsurf & Inflatable Launch Ramps Sierra Marina Ph: (559) 841-3324 Shaver Lake Marina Ph: (559) 841-5331 Rental: Fishing Boats & Motors, Waterski Boats, PWCs, Pontoons Slips, Dry Storage, Gas	Fishing: Rainbow, Brown & Brook Trout, Kokanee, Large & Smallmouth Bass, Catfish & Sunfish Picnicking - Group Sites at Edison Swimming - Beaches Hiking & Equestrian Trails	Lakeside at the Point: Ph: (559) 841-3326 Motels Restaurants Grocery Stores Bait & Tackle Gas Station See Previous Page

EDISON and FLORENCE LAKES

Edison Lake, at 7,300 feet and Florence Lake, at 7,400 feet are both located in the scenic high Sierras bordering the John Muir and Ansel Adams Wilderness Areas. Granite boulders and sandy beaches are located around the timbered shorelines. Vermilion Valley Resort at Edison Lake has a motel, tent cabins, restaurant, store, boat rentals and launch ramp. Florence Lake has a store with supplies and a pack station.

Mono Hot Springs Resort has cabins and hot mineral baths. Although the roads are difficult and not suitable for larger R.V.s, these Lakes are so beautiful, the trip is very worthwhile. A water ferry service is available at both Lakes for backpackers going into the Wilderness Areas. Trout fishing can be excellent in these Lakes and many nearby streams.

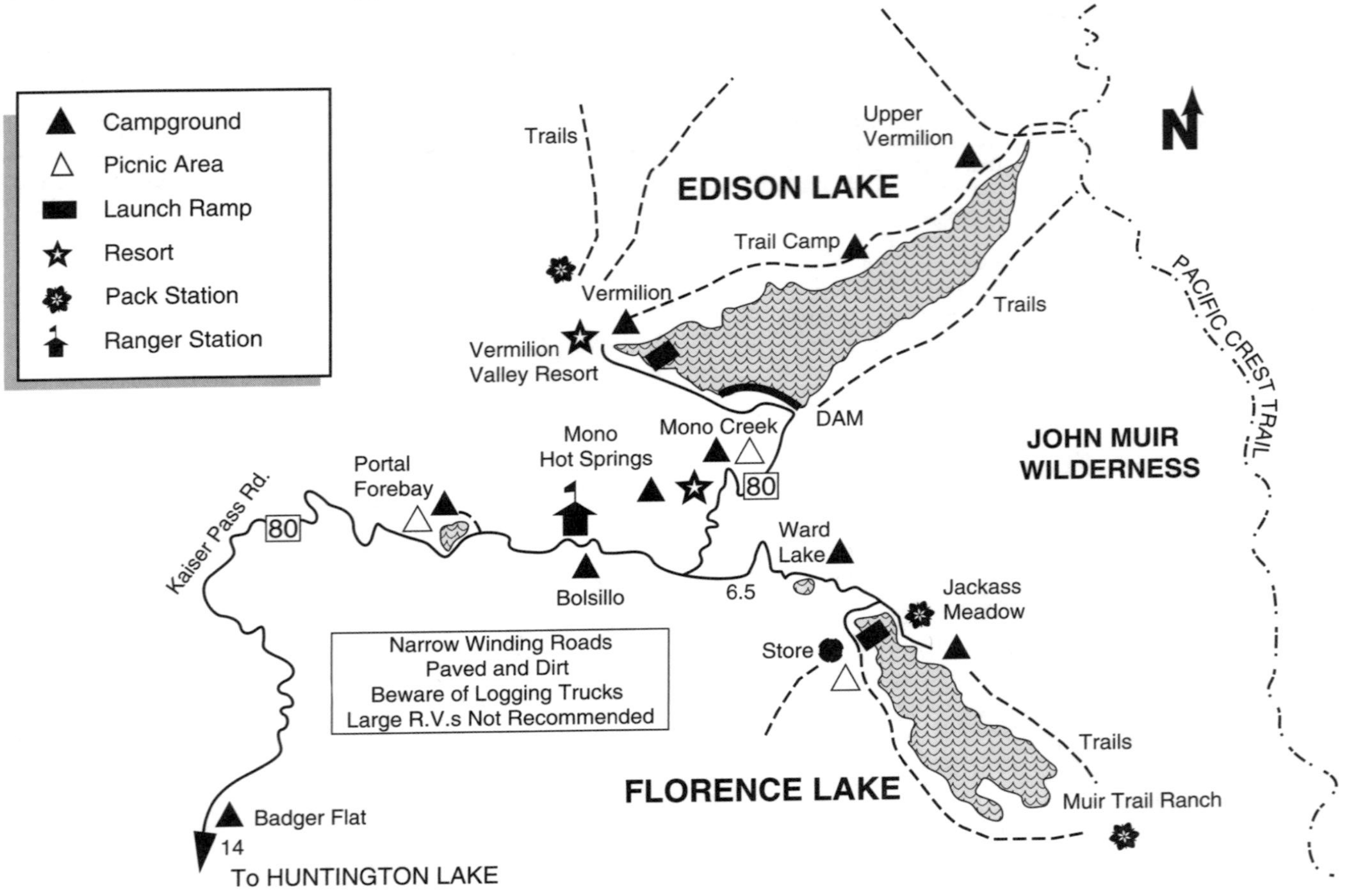
Campground
Picnic Area
Launch Ramp
Resort
Pack Station
Ranger Station
N
Trails
Upper Vermilion
EDISON LAKE
Trail Camp
Vermilion
Trails
Vermilion Valley Resort
PACIFIC CREST TRAIL
DAM
Mono Creek
Mono Hot Springs
JOHN MUIR WILDERNESS
Portal Forebay
Kaiser Pass Rd.
80
80
Ward Lake
Bolsillo
6.5
Jackass Meadow
Store
Narrow Winding Roads
Paved and Dirt
Beware of Logging Trucks
Large R.V.s Not Recommended
Trails
FLORENCE LAKE
Muir Trail Ranch
Badger Flat
14
To HUNTINGTON LAKE

INFORMATION: High Sierra Ranger District, 29688 Auberry Rd. P.O. Box 559, Prather 93651—Ph: (559) 855-5355

CAMPING	BOATING	RECREATION	OTHER
Dev. Sites for Tents & Small R.V.s: Vermilion: 31 Sites Mono Creek: 14 Sites Jackass Meadow: 44 Sites Ward Lake: 17 Sites Portal Forebay: 11 Sites Bolsillo: 3 Sites Fees: $13 - $28 Reserve: (877) 444-6777 Large R.V.s Not Recommended	Power, Row, Canoe & Inflatable Speed Limit - 15 MPH Launch Ramps Rentals: Fishing Boats & Kayaks at Vermilion Valley Resort	Fishing: Rainbow, Brown & Brook Trout Picnicking Hiking & Equestrian Trails High Sierra Pack Station Ph: (559) 285-7225 Water Ferry Service for Backpackers Entry Point to John Muir & Ansel Adams Wilderness Permit Required	High Sierra Visitor Center Ph: (559) 877-7173 Mono Hot Springs: Ph: (559) 325-1710 Cabins Hot Mineral Baths Cafe & Store Vermilion Valley Resort: Ph: (559) 259-4000 Motel, Cabins & Yurts Cafe & Store

PINE FLAT LAKE and AVOCADO LAKE PARK

Pine Flat Lake is at an elevation of 952 feet in the Sierra foothills east of Fresno. The Lake is 20 miles long with 67 miles of shoreline and over 5,500 surface acres in the spring and summer. Pine and oak trees grow throughout the area. The U. S. Army Corps of Engineers has jurisdiction over this very popular Lake. In addition to the public campgrounds, there are privately owned resorts which offer overnight lodging and R.V. accommodations. All boating is allowed. The angler will find a variety of fish including kokanee salmon. Fresno County maintains campgrounds between the dam and Avocado Lake Park. The Park, 210 acres, is on the Kings River below Pine Flat Dam. The small 83 surface-acre Lake is open to non-powered boating. There is a warm water fishery. There is no camping permitted in the Park but there are picnic areas, including group sites, and a swim beach.

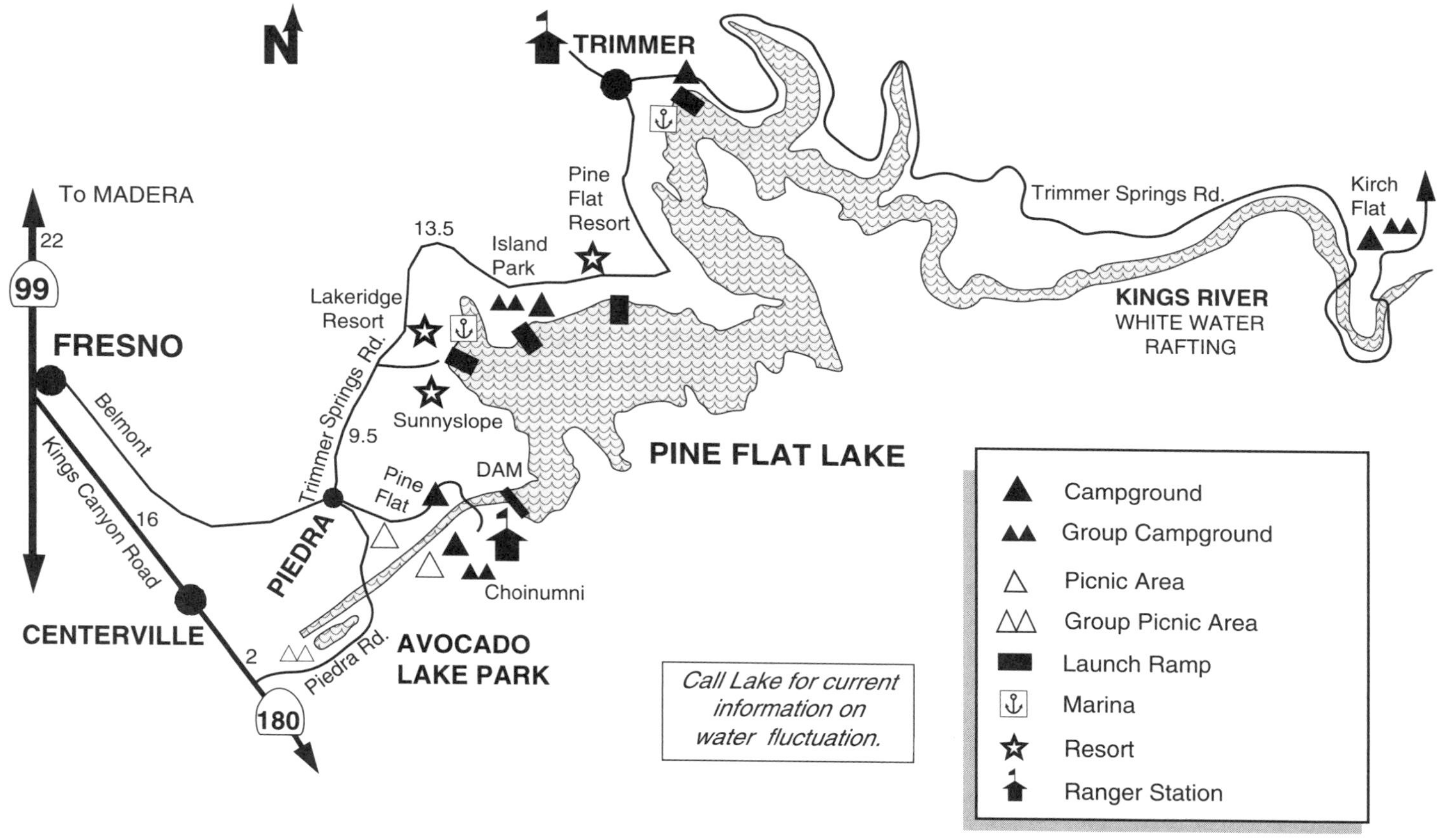
N
TRIMMER
To MADERA
22
99
FRESNO
13.5
Pine
Flat
Resort
Island
Park
Lakeridge
Resort
Trimmer Springs Rd.
Kirch
Flat
KINGS RIVER
WHITE WATER
RAFTING
Belmont
Kings Canyon Road
Sunnyslope
9.5
Trimmer Springs Rd.
Pine
Flat
DAM
PINE FLAT LAKE
16
PIEDRA
Choinumni
CENTERVILLE
2
Piedra Rd.
AVOCADO
LAKE PARK
180
Call Lake for current
information on
water fluctuation.
Campground
Group Campground
Picnic Area
Group Picnic Area
Launch Ramp
Marina
Resort
Ranger Station

INFORMATION: U.S. Army Corps of Engineers, Pine Flat Lake, P.O. Box 117, Piedra 93649—Ph: (559) 787-2589

CAMPING	BOATING	RECREATION	OTHER
Island Park: 97 Dev. Sites for Tents & R.V.s Fee: $16 2 Group Sites - Fee: $75 Reserve: (877) 444-6777 Fresno County Parks: Choinumni: 75 Dev.Sites for Tents & R.V.s Plus Group Site Pine Flat: 52 Dev. Sites USFS: Ph: (559) 855-8321 Kirch Flat: 17 Sites Plus Group Site - No Water	Pine Flat: Open to All Boats Including Houseboats Trimmer Marina & Camp: Ph: (559) 855-2039 Lakeridge Marina: Ph: (559) 787-2506 Launch Ramps - Fees Overnight Moorings, Slips Rentals: Fishing & Patio Boats, PWCs, Houseboats Avocado Lake Park: No Gas-Powered Boats Hand Launch Only	Fishing: Rainbow Trout, Large & Smallmouth Bass, Chinook & Kokanee, Catfish, Crappie, Bluegill Swimming Picnicking Hiking - Nature Trails Campfire Programs River Raft Trips	Motels, Cabins, Restaurants Snack Bars - Stores Bait, Tackle & Gas Disposal Station Avocado Lake Fresno Co. Parks Ph: (559) 488-3004 Pine Flat R.V. Resort-Motel Ph: (559) 787-2207 Lakeridge Resort Ph: (559) 787-2260 Sunnyslope Campground: Ph: (559) 787-2730

HUME and SEQUOIA LAKES

Hume Lake, at 5,200 feet elevation, and Sequoia, at 5,300 feet, are in the scenic Sequoia National Forest. Hume Lake, within the incredible Giant Sequoia National Monument, has 85 surface acres . The angler will find trout and the boater can hand launch small craft with electric motors. Sequoia Lake is operated by the YMCA and is open only to members. Early reservations are advised at this popular camp. Many of the roads in this area are only open during summer months. Be sure to bring your camera to this spectacular country of the Giant Sequoia trees, survivors of the Ice Age, and Kings Canyon National Park. This area is one of our greatest national treasures.

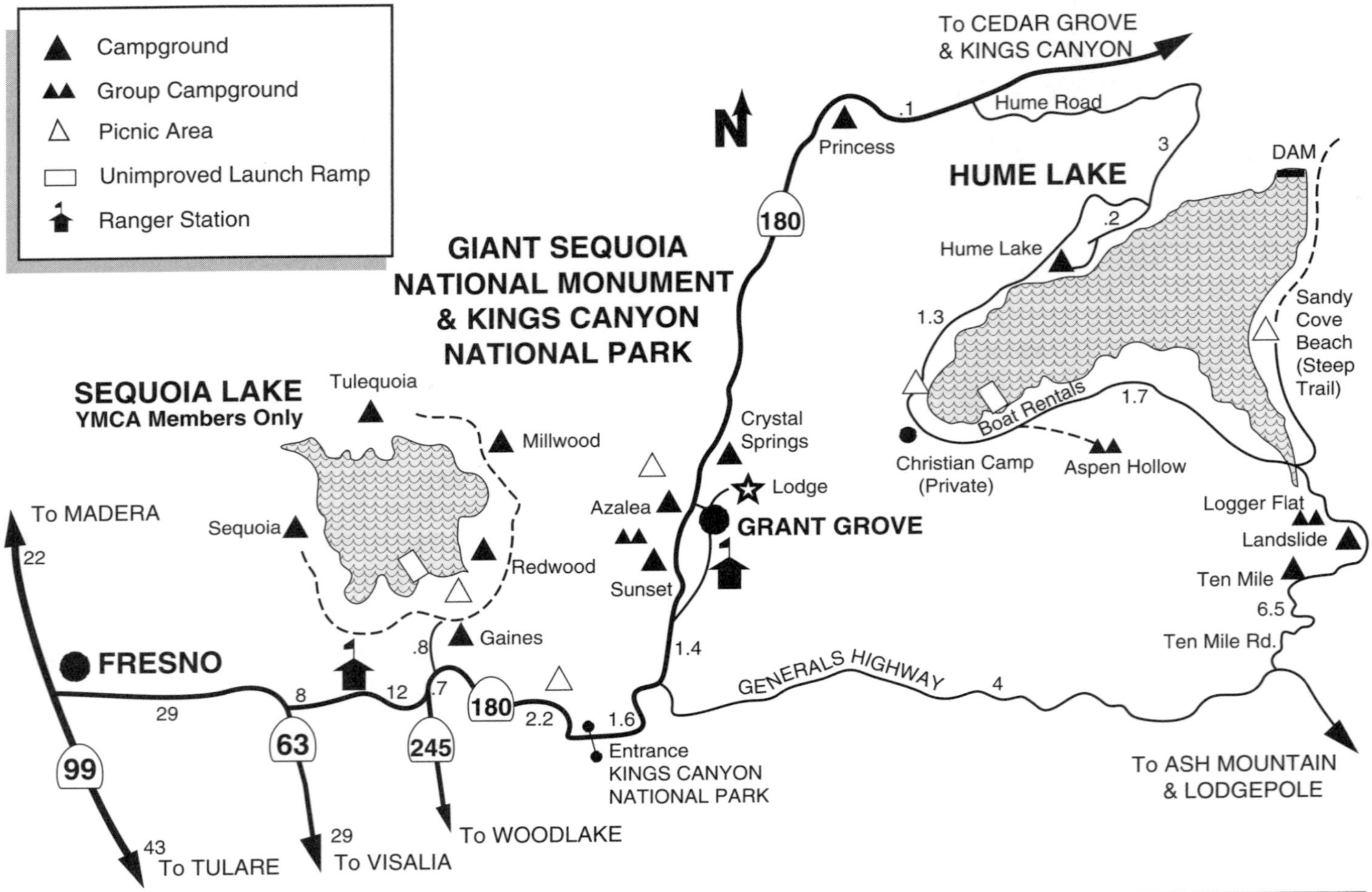

Campground
Group Campground
Picnic Area
Unimproved Launch Ramp
Ranger Station
GIANT SEQUOIA NATIONAL MONUMENT & KINGS CANYON NATIONAL PARK
SEQUOIA LAKE
YMCA Members Only
HUME LAKE
To CEDAR GROVE & KINGS CANYON
Hume Road
Princess
.1
3
DAM
180
Hume Lake
.2
1.3
Sandy Cove Beach (Steep Trail)
Boat Rentals
1.7
Christian Camp (Private)
Aspen Hollow
Crystal Springs
Lodge
GRANT GROVE
Logger Flat
Landslide
Ten Mile
6.5
Ten Mile Rd.
Tulequoia
Millwood
Azalea
Sunset
Redwood
Sequoia
Gaines
To MADERA
22
FRESNO
29
8
12
.8
.7
180
2.2
1.6
1.4
GENERALS HIGHWAY
4
Entrance KINGS CANYON NATIONAL PARK
To ASH MOUNTAIN & LODGEPOLE
99
63
245
43
To TULARE
29
To VISALIA
To WOODLAKE

INFORMATION: Hume Lake Ranger District, 35860 E. Kings Canyon Rd., Dunlap 93621—Ph: (559) 338-2251

CAMPING	BOATING	RECREATION	OTHER
Hume Lake: 74 Dev. Sites for Tents & R.V.s - No Hookups Fee: $18 Aspen Hollow Group Camp: To 100 People Reservations: Ph: (877) 444-6777 Grant Grove Area: 376 Dev. Sites for Tents & R.V.s Fee: $18 Group Sites: $50	Hume Lake: Fishing Boats with Electric Motors 5 MPH Speed Limit Hand Launch Sequoia Lake: YMCA Members Only	Fishing at Hume Lake: Rainbow & Brown Trout Picnicking Swimming - Beaches Hiking & Equestrian Trails Parks - Entrance Fees: $20 - Vehicle $10 - Bicyclists & Hikers Grant Grove Visitor Center: Ph: (559) 565-4307	Grant Grove Lodge: Ph: (559) 335-5500 Rustic Cabins & Modern Lodge Rooms Reservations: Ph: (866) 522-6966 Hume Lake Christian Camp: Ph: (559) 335-2881 Sequoia Family Camp: Ph: (559) 335-2382

PLEASANT VALLEY RESERVOIR and DIAZ LAKE

Inyo County operates several campgrounds along Highway 395. At 4,200 feet elevation, Pleasant Valley Reservoir is in a canyon along the Chalk Bluffs. Boating is not allowed. The angler can fish from shore or use a float tube. The campground is located along the Owens River, known for excellent trout fishing. Tinnemaha Reservoir, open for fishing year around, is located about two miles across highway 395 from the campground. Diaz Lake is at an elevation of 3,700 feet on the eastern side of the Sierras, 15 miles from the Mt. Whitney Trailhead. This 80-surface acre Lake is open to varied boating and is popular with waterskiers. There is both a trout and warm water fishery. Numerous ORV trails are throughout this entire area.

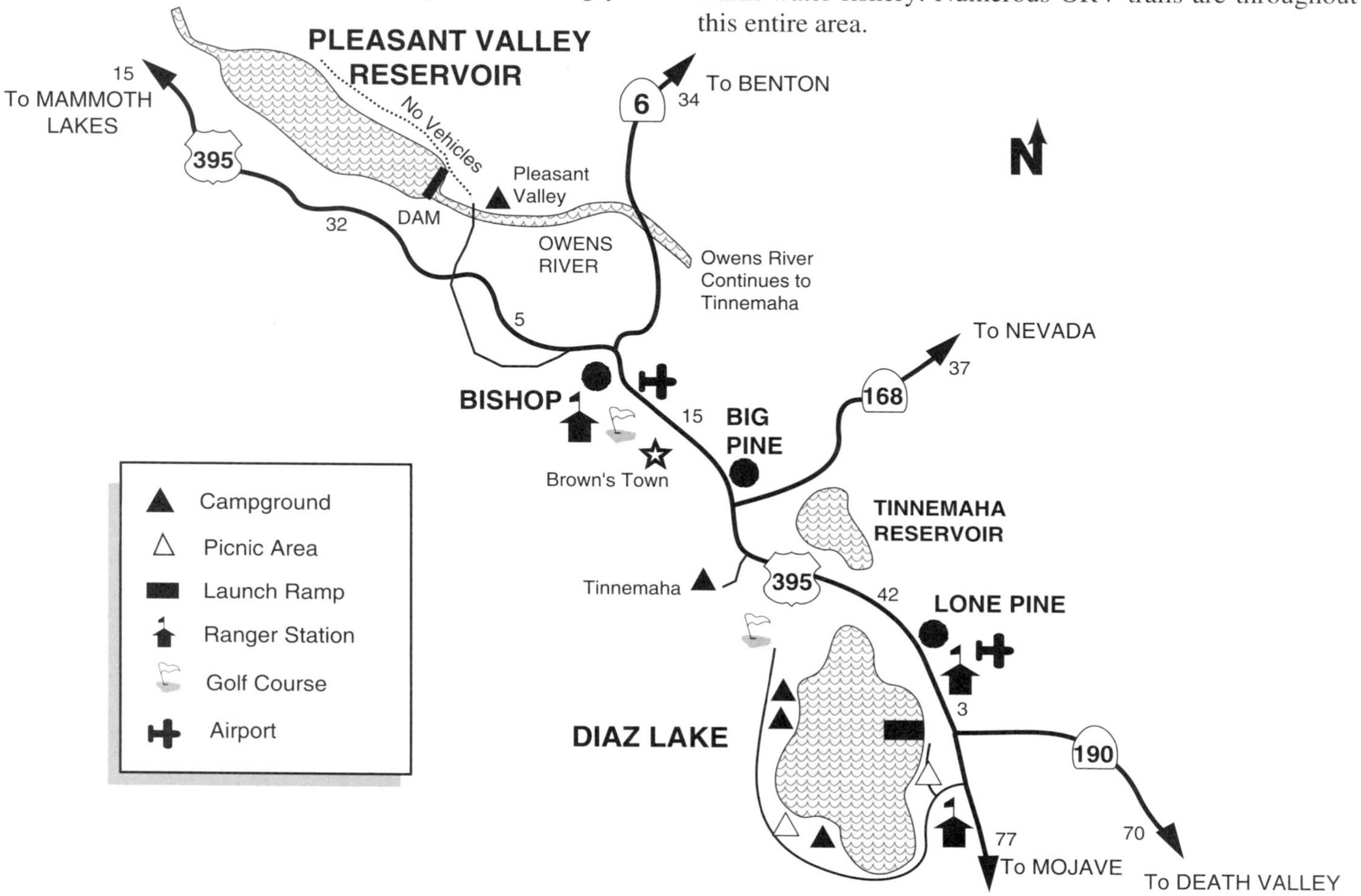

PLEASANT VALLEY RESERVOIR
No Vehicles
15
To MAMMOTH LAKES
395
32
DAM
Pleasant Valley
OWENS RIVER
6
34
To BENTON
N
Owens River Continues to Tinnemaha
5
To NEVADA
37
168
BISHOP
15
BIG PINE
Brown's Town
TINNEMAHA RESERVOIR
Tinnemaha
395
42
LONE PINE
3
DIAZ LAKE
190
77
To MOJAVE
70
To DEATH VALLEY
Campground
Picnic Area
Launch Ramp
Ranger Station
Golf Course
Airport

INFORMATION: Inyo County Parks & Recreation, 163 May St., Bishop 93514—Ph: (760) 873-5577

CAMPING	BOATING	RECREATION	OTHER
Pleasant Valley: 200 Tent & R.V. Sites No Hookups - Fee: $10 Tinnemaha: 55 Tent & R.V. Sites No Hookups - Fee: $10 Diaz Lake: 200 Tent & R.V. Sites No Hookups - Fee: $10 Reservations Ph:(760) 876-5656	Diaz Lake: Power, Row, Canoe, Sail, Waterski, PWCs & Inflatables Launch Ramp - $10 May 15 through Oct. 31 Speed Limit - 35 MPH Nov. 1 through May 14 Speed Limit - 15 MPH Maximum Boat Size: 22 Ft. *Noise Level Laws Enforced* No Boats at Pleasant Valley	Fishing: Rainbow & Brown Trout (Catch & Release on Sections of the Owens River), Smallmouth Bass, Bluegill & Catfish Swimming - Beaches Picnicking Hiking & Equestrian Trails ORV Trails	Brown's Town Campground Ph: (760) 873-8522 100 Tent & R.V. Sites Electric Hookups Fees: $20 - $27 Full Facilities at Bishop & Lone Pine

South Section   Lakes 151 - 199

Numbers around highways represent lakes in numerical order in this book. *See Index for complete listing.*

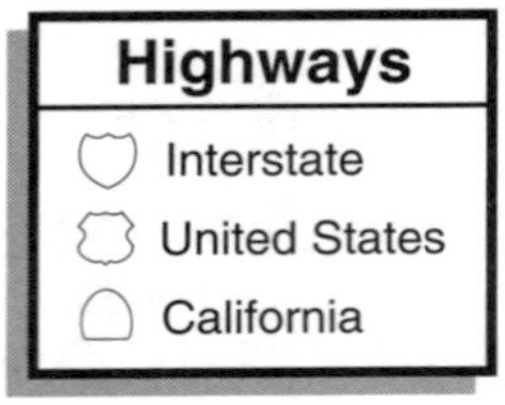
Highways
Interstate
United States
California

101
5
99
395
Bishop
Visalia
151
152
155
156
Paso Robles
157
46
Lone Pine
San Luis Obispo
154
153
178
158
159
Bakersfield
161
58
14
15
395
Santa Barbara
162
160
165
166
Lancaster
163
58
164
126
14
101
Los Angeles
15
175
174
168
172
173
167
169
170
171
San Bernardino
Needles
176
179
177
180
178
181
183
185
199
40
15
181
184
182
186
10
95
187
188
Escondido
192
193
191
Blythe
86
194
196
78
San Diego
195
189
10
197
78
El Cajon
198
190
86
El Centro
5
MEXICO
8

At an elevation of 650 feet, Lake Kaweah is in the rolling foothills below Sequoia National Park. The Lake is 6 miles long with 22 miles of shoreline surrounded by oak-studded hills. There is a total surface area of 2,154 acres when full but there can be a 100-foot water level drop late in the season. The U. S. Army Corps of Engineers maintain Terminus Dam, 250 feet high and 2,375 feet long, along with a campground, picnic areas and marina. Houseboating is popular with all the coves and inlets. The angler will find a broad variety of fish.

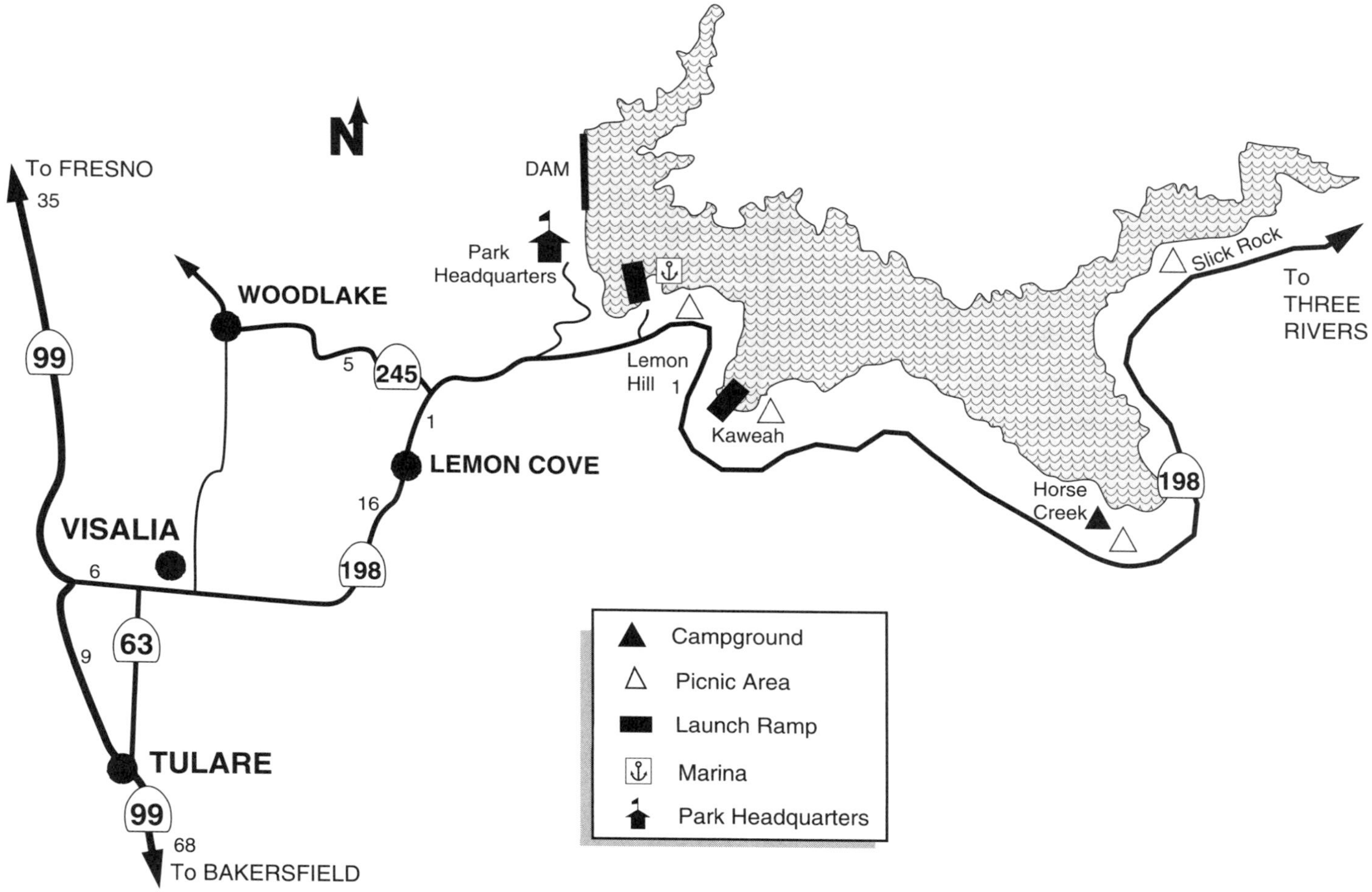
N
To FRESNO
35
99
WOODLAKE
5
245
1
LEMON COVE
16
198
VISALIA
6
63
9
TULARE
99
68
To BAKERSFIELD
DAM
Park
Headquarters
Lemon
Hill
1
Kaweah
Slick Rock
To
THREE
RIVERS
198
Horse
Creek
Campground
Picnic Area
Launch Ramp
Marina
Park Headquarters

INFORMATION: U.S. Army Corps of Engineers, P.O. Box 44270, Lemon Cove 93244—Ph: (559) 597-2301

CAMPING	BOATING	RECREATION	OTHER
Horse Creek: 80 Dev. Sites for Tents & R.V.s Fees: $16 Disposal Station Reserve: Ph: (877) 444-6777 Boat Camping Permitted Away From Shore Day Use Fee: $4	Power, Row, Canoe, Sail, Waterski & PWCs Full Service Marina Ph: (559) 597-2526 Launch Ramps Fee: $4 Rentals: Fishing Boats, Houseboats & Pontoons Slips, Gas *Low Water Late in Season* *Submerged Rock Hazards*	Fishing: Largemouth Bass, Bluegill, Channel Catfish, Black & White Crappie, Rainbow Trout in Season Picnicking Birdwatching Campfire Program Saturday Nights in Season	Visitors Center Snack Bar Bait & Tackle Full Facilities at Woodlake and Three Rivers

SUCCESS LAKE

Built in 1961 for flood protection and irrigation, Success Lake is at an elevation of 640 feet in the southern Sierra foothills. The Lake has 2,450 surface acres with 30 miles of shoreline. The dam spans 3,490 feet across the Tule River. The U.S. Army Corps of Engineers has jurisdiction over the camping, marine and recreation facilities. There is good fishing year around and all types of boating are permitted from houseboats to waterskiing. Summer temperatures often are over 100 degrees. The climate is mild the rest of the year. The birdwatcher may find several rare or endangered species, including the Bald Eagle.

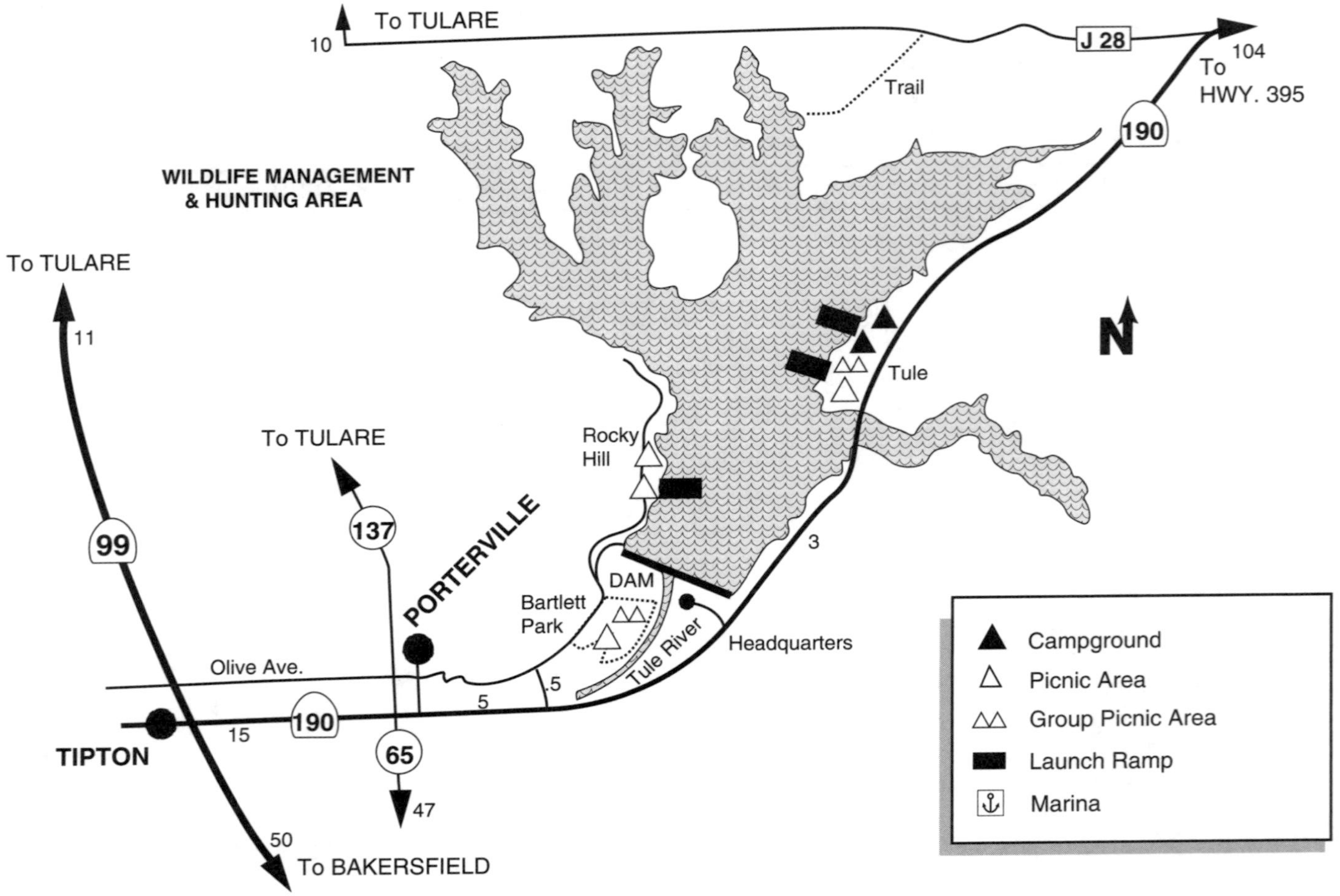

To TULARE
10
J 28
104
To
HWY. 395
190
Trail
WILDLIFE MANAGEMENT
& HUNTING AREA
To TULARE
11
N
Tule
To TULARE
Rocky
Hill
137
99
PORTERVILLE
3
DAM
Bartlett
Park
Headquarters
Tule River
Olive Ave.
.5
5
15
190
TIPTON
65
47
50
To BAKERSFIELD
Campground
Picnic Area
Group Picnic Area
Launch Ramp
Marina

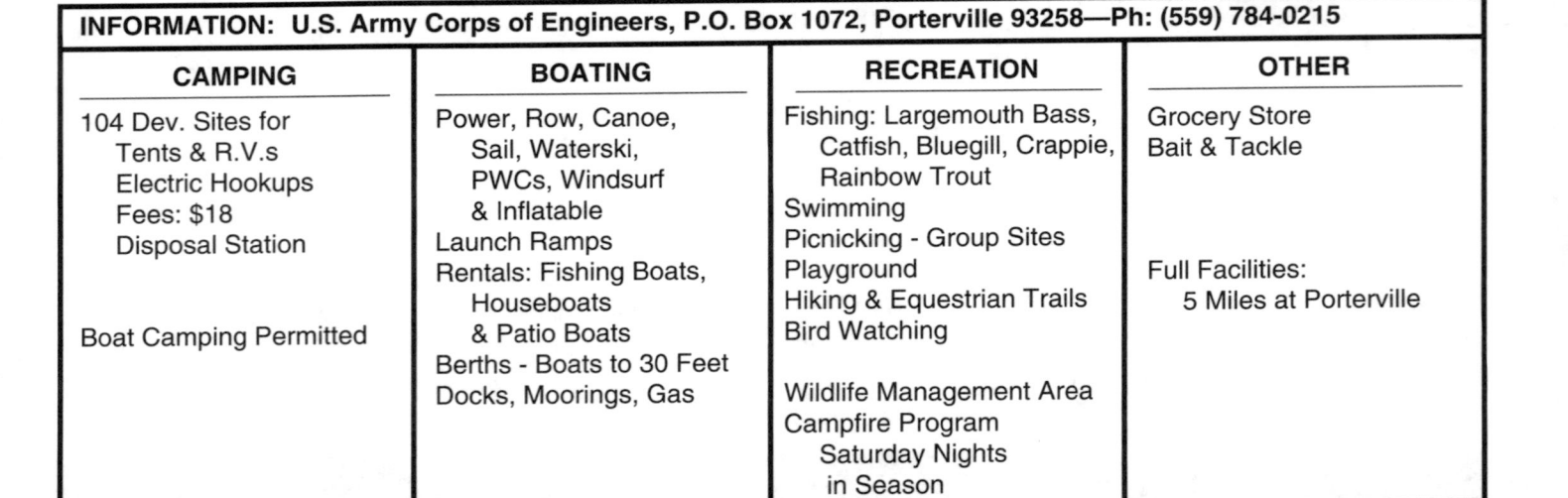

INFORMATION: U.S. Army Corps of Engineers, P.O. Box 1072, Porterville 93258—Ph: (559) 784-0215

CAMPING	BOATING	RECREATION	OTHER
104 Dev. Sites for Tents & R.V.s Electric Hookups Fees: $18 Disposal Station Boat Camping Permitted	Power, Row, Canoe, Sail, Waterski, PWCs, Windsurf & Inflatable Launch Ramps Rentals: Fishing Boats, Houseboats & Patio Boats Berths - Boats to 30 Feet Docks, Moorings, Gas	Fishing: Largemouth Bass, Catfish, Bluegill, Crappie, Rainbow Trout Swimming Picnicking - Group Sites Playground Hiking & Equestrian Trails Bird Watching Wildlife Management Area Campfire Program Saturday Nights in Season	Grocery Store Bait & Tackle Full Facilities: 5 Miles at Porterville

The facilities at Hart, Woollomes and Ming Lakes are under the jurisdiction of Kern County. The Kern River County Park has campsites and picnic areas within 1,445 acres. Lake Woollomes, 300 surface acres, and Hart Lake, 18 surface acres, allow non-powered boating and fishing. Lake Ming, 104 surface acres, is primarily a waterskiing and power boating Lake but sailing and fishing are scheduled as shown below. Brite Valley is under the jurisdiction of the Tehachapi Valley Recreation and Parks District. The 90-surface acre Lake is at an elevation of 4,000 feet.

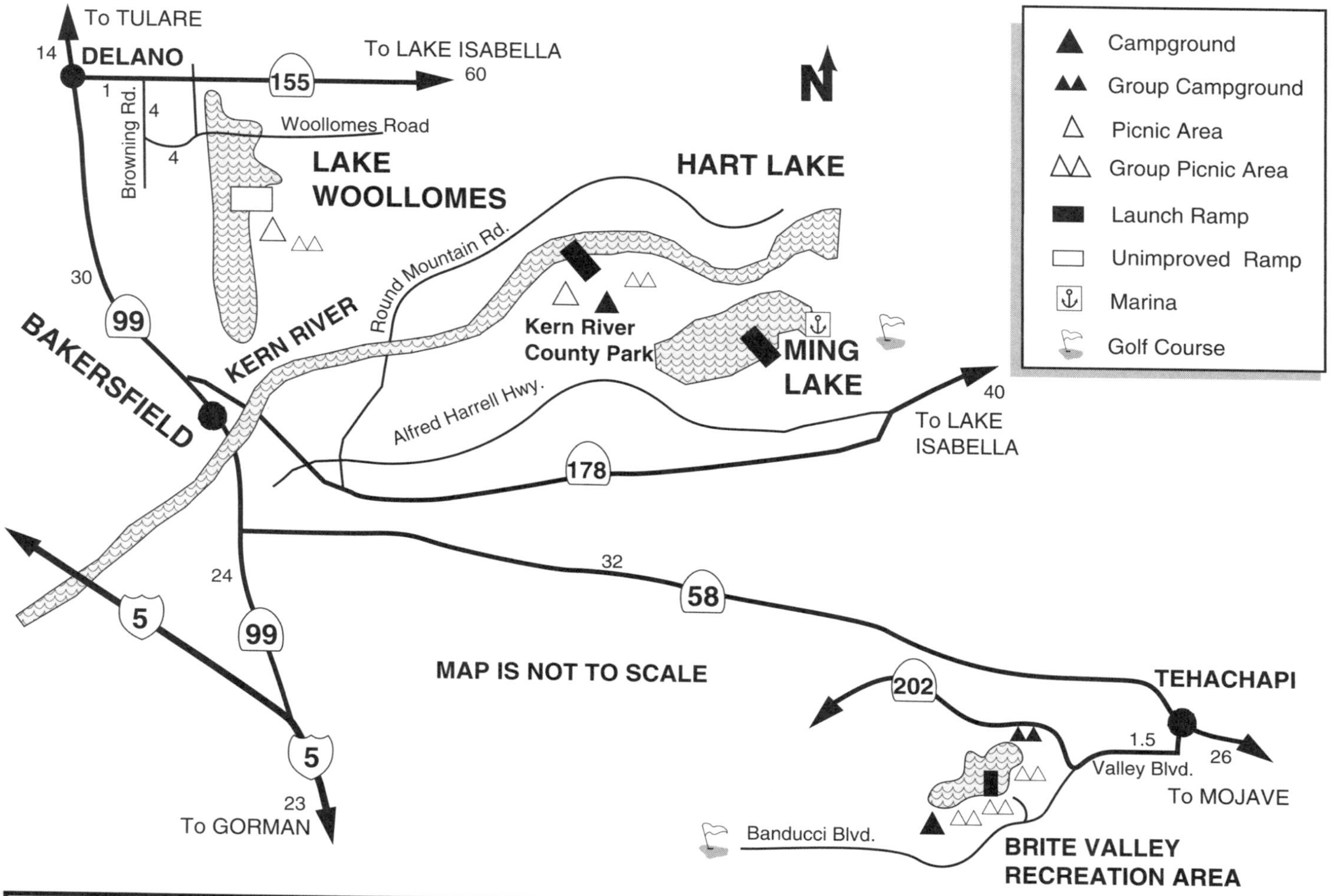
To TULARE
14
DELANO
1
4
4
Browning Rd.
155
To LAKE ISABELLA
60
Woollomes Road
LAKE WOOLLOMES
HART LAKE
N
Round Mountain Rd.
30
99
BAKERSFIELD
KERN RIVER
Kern River County Park
MING LAKE
Alfred Harrell Hwy.
40
To LAKE ISABELLA
178
32
58
24
5
99
MAP IS NOT TO SCALE
202
TEHACHAPI
1.5
26
Valley Blvd.
To MOJAVE
5
23
To GORMAN
Banducci Blvd.
BRITE VALLEY RECREATION AREA
Campground
Group Campground
Picnic Area
Group Picnic Area
Launch Ramp
Unimproved Ramp
Marina
Golf Course

INFORMATION: Kern County Parks, 1110 Golden State Ave., Bakersfield 93301—Ph: (661) 868-7000

CAMPING	BOATING	RECREATION	OTHER
Kern River County Park: 52 Dev. Sites for Tents & R.V.s - No Hookups Fees: March 15-Oct. 15: $22 Oct. 16-March 14: $11 No Reservations Disposal Station Brite Valley: 90 Dev. Sites for Tents & R.V.s - 12 Water & Electric Hookups	Woollomes & Hart: Sail, Canoe, Row & Pedal Boats Only Day Use: $3 Ming: Waterskiing, Power Boats & Drag Races Sailing Only - Allowed Tuesdays & Thursdays After 1:30 pm & the 2nd Full Weekend of Month Brite Valley: Electric Motors Only	Fishing: Largemouth Bass, Bluegill, Crappie & Catfish Hart & Ming: Trout Brite Valley: Trout, Catfish & Bass Picnicking - Group Sites Kern River County Park: Group Picnic Sites can Accommodate Thousands Hiking Trails Swimming-Woollomes Only Golf Courses	Brite Valley Aquatic Recreation Area Tehachapi Valley Recreation & Parks P.O. Box 373 Tehachapi 93581 Information: Ph: (661) 822-3228

ISABELLA LAKE

Isabella Lake is at 2,578 feet elevation in the foothills east of Bakersfield. The surface area of the Lake is over 11,200 acres with a shoreline of 38 miles. This is one of the largest reservoirs in Southern California. Campgrounds are numerous with over 800 developed sites and 6 group camp areas.

The main attractions at Isabella are boating, waterskiing, windsurfing and fishing. Other activities range from whitewater rafting to bird watching. A target shooting range is available and the Cyrus Canyon ORV Area is nearby. Annual Boat Permits are required for Lake use and can be obtained at any one of the Marinas.

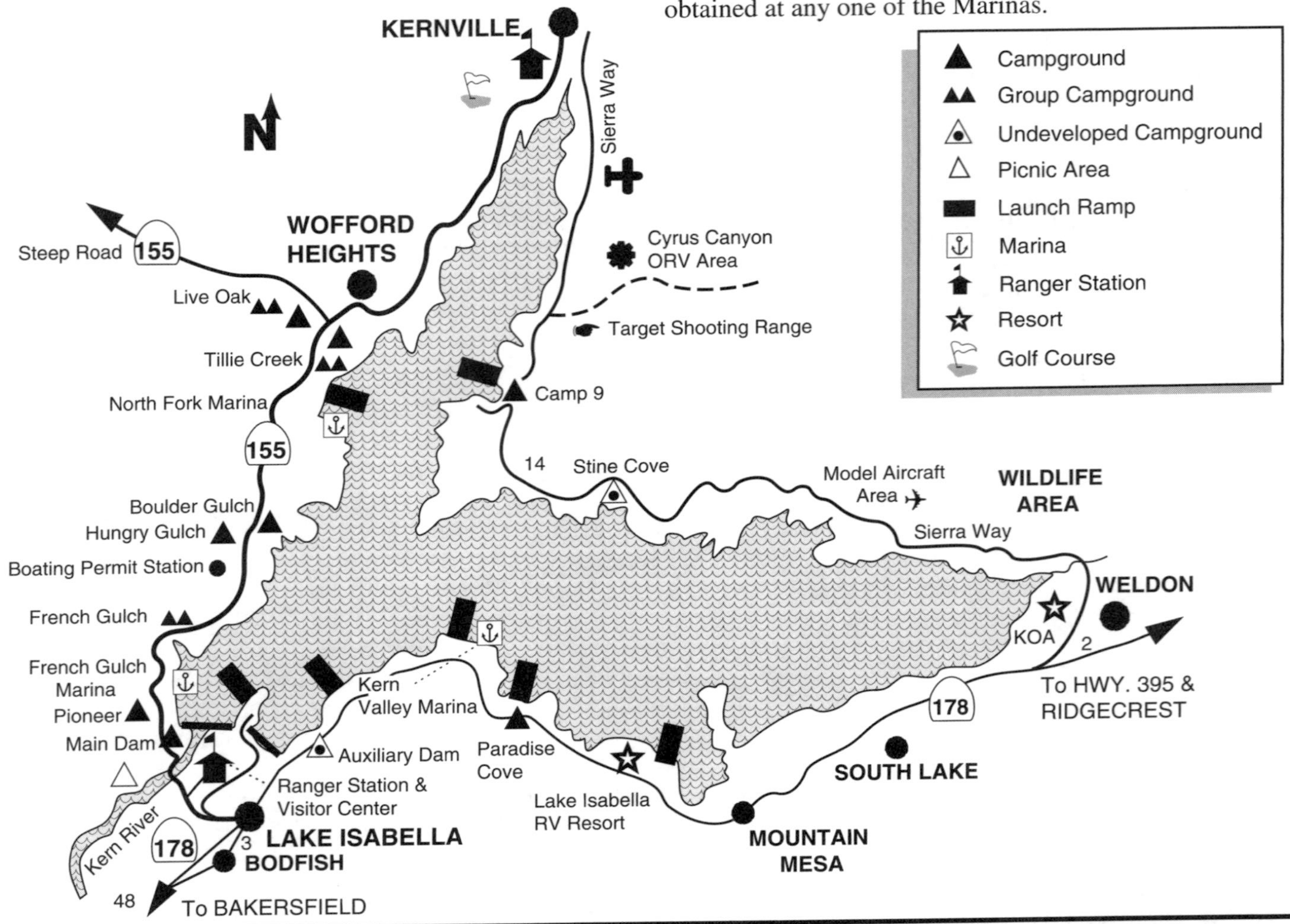
KERNVILLE
Sierra Way
N
WOFFORD HEIGHTS
Steep Road
155
Live Oak
Tillie Creek
North Fork Marina
Cyrus Canyon ORV Area
Target Shooting Range
Camp 9
14
Stine Cove
Model Aircraft Area
WILDLIFE AREA
Sierra Way
Boulder Gulch
Hungry Gulch
Boating Permit Station
French Gulch
French Gulch Marina
Pioneer
Main Dam
Kern Valley Marina
Auxiliary Dam
Paradise Cove
Ranger Station & Visitor Center
Lake Isabella RV Resort
KOA
2
WELDON
To HWY. 395 & RIDGECREST
178
SOUTH LAKE
MOUNTAIN MESA
Kern River
3
LAKE ISABELLA
BODFISH
48
To BAKERSFIELD
Campground
Group Campground
Undeveloped Campground
Picnic Area
Launch Ramp
Marina
Ranger Station
Resort
Golf Course

INFORMATION: Visitors Center, 4875 Ponderosa Dr., P.O. Box 3810, Lake Isabella 93240—Ph: (760) 379-5646

CAMPING	BOATING	RECREATION	OTHER
800 Dev. Sites for Tents & R.V.s Fee: $19 - $21 6 Group Camp Areas Disposal Stations Reservations: Ph: (877) 444-6777 Plus Undeveloped Campsites at Stine Cove No Fee Day Use Fee: $10	Power, Row, Canoe, Sail, Waterski, PWCs, Windsurf & Inflatables Check for Restrictions All Boats Must Have Permits Call for Current Fees: (661) 868-7000 Launch Ramps Full Service Marinas Rentals: Fishing & Waterski Boats Docks, Berths, Gas	Fishing: Trout, Catfish, Bluegill, Crappie & Largemouth Bass Fish Cleaning Stations Swimming Picnicking Playgrounds Hiking & Bicycle Trails Campfire Programs Birdwatching White Water Rafting: Kern River	Lake Isabella R.V. Resort Ph: (800) 787-9920 KOA Campground Ph: (760) 378-2001 ORV Use Area Target Shooting Range Golf Course Call Above for Current Water Levels Full Facilities at Towns Near Lake

San Antonio Lake is at an elevation of 900 feet in the rolling, oak-covered hills of southern Monterey County. The Lake has a surface area of 5,500 acres with 60 miles of shoreline. It is under the jurisdiction of the Monterey County Parks Department. There is an abundance of campsites, many with full hookups and some right on the Lake. With mild water temperatures and a length of 16 miles, this is an ideal Lake for waterskiing. The warm water fishery makes San Antonio a good year around angler's Lake. The Lake is open 24 hours so cat fishing at night is allowed. The popular facilities are open all year with complete services for vacation activities.

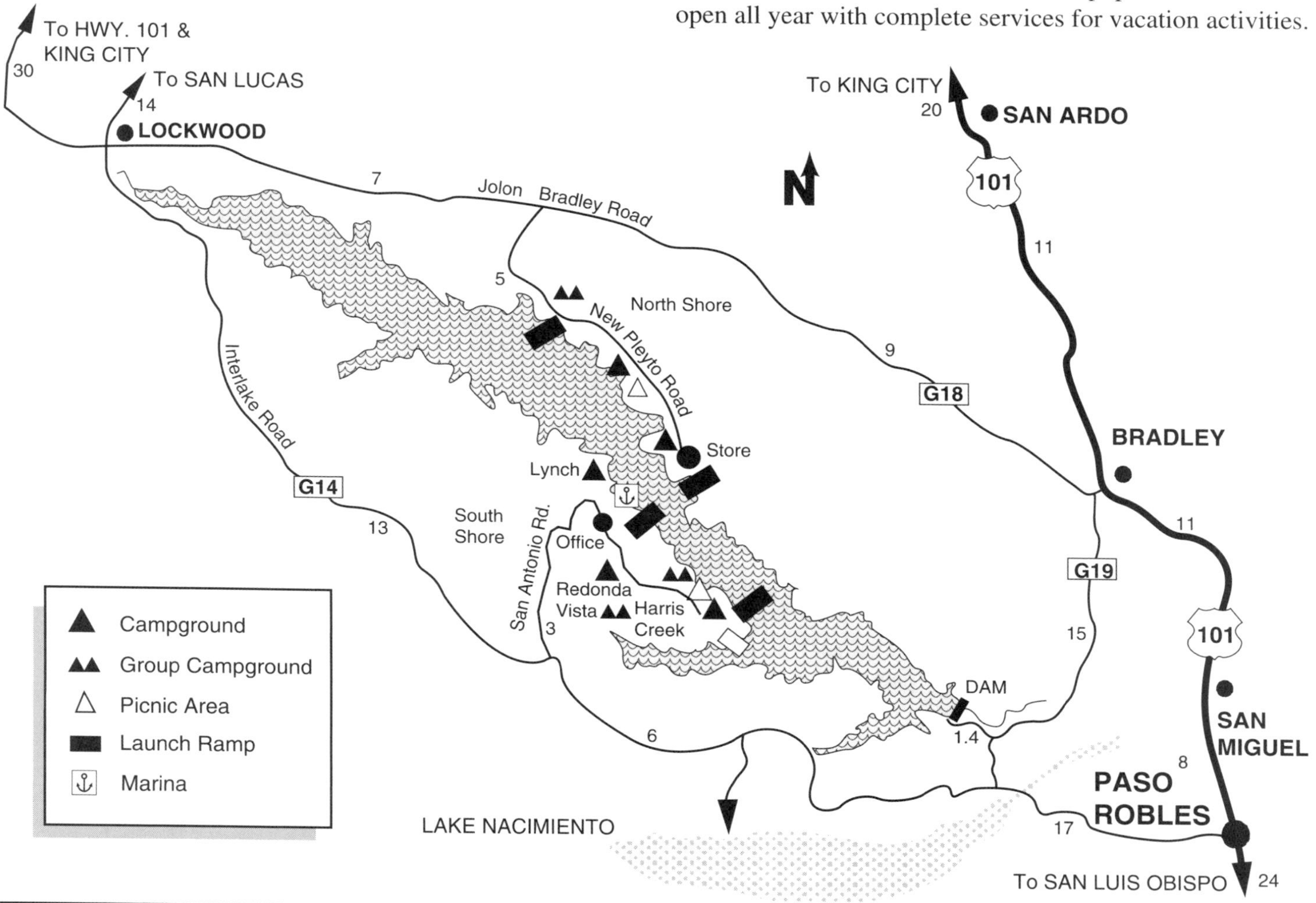
To HWY. 101 &
KING CITY
30
To SAN LUCAS
14
LOCKWOOD
7
Jolon Bradley Road
To KING CITY
20
SAN ARDO
N
101
11
5
North Shore
New Pleyto Road
9
G18
Interlake Road
Store
BRADLEY
Lynch
G14
South
Shore
San Antonio Rd.
Office
13
11
G19
Redonda
Vista
Harris
Creek
3
15
101
DAM
SAN
MIGUEL
6
1.4
8
PASO
ROBLES
LAKE NACIMIENTO
17
To SAN LUIS OBISPO
24
Campground
Group Campground
Picnic Area
Launch Ramp
Marina

INFORMATION: Lake San Antonio, 2610 San Antonio Rd., Bradley 93426—Ph: (805) 472-2311

CAMPING	BOATING	RECREATION	OTHER
767 Dev. Sites for Tents & R.V.s Full Hookups Fees: $22 - $27 Limited Reservations: Ph: (888) 588-2267 Group Camp Sites Overflow Camping Area Disposal Stations Day Use Fee: $7 Pets Allowed	Power, Row, Canoe, Sail, Waterski, Pontoon, PWCs, Windsurf & Inflatable Full Service Marina Launch Ramps - $6 Rentals: Fishing Boats, Pontoons & Ski Boats Information: Ph: (805) 472-2818 Slips, Gas, Dry Storage *Check for Current Water Level Conditions*	Fishing: Catfish, Bluegill, Large & Smallmouth Bass, Striped Bass, Redear Perch & Crappie Swimming - Beach Picnicking Hiking, Bicycling & Equestrian Trails Eagle Watching Tours in Summer Exercise Course Weekend Movies in Summer	Resort: Mobile Home Rentals Ph: (800) 310-2313 16 at South Shore 4 at North Shore Cafe Grocery Store Bait & Tackle Laundromat Gas Station Game Room Visitor Center

LAKE NACIMIENTO

Nestled in a valley of pine and oak trees, Lake Nacimiento is at an elevation of 800 feet and has 5,370 surface acres with 165 miles of shoreline. As the map shows, boaters and anglers can enjoy the innumerable coves. Fishing from shore or boat will usually produce largemouth, smallmouth or white bass.

Waterskiing is excellent on this 16-mile long Lake with water temperature about 68 degrees. Lake Nacimiento Resort has many campsites and complete marina facilities. There are lakeside lodge accommodations and a full array of activities. This is a great family recreation area year around and very popular during the summer.

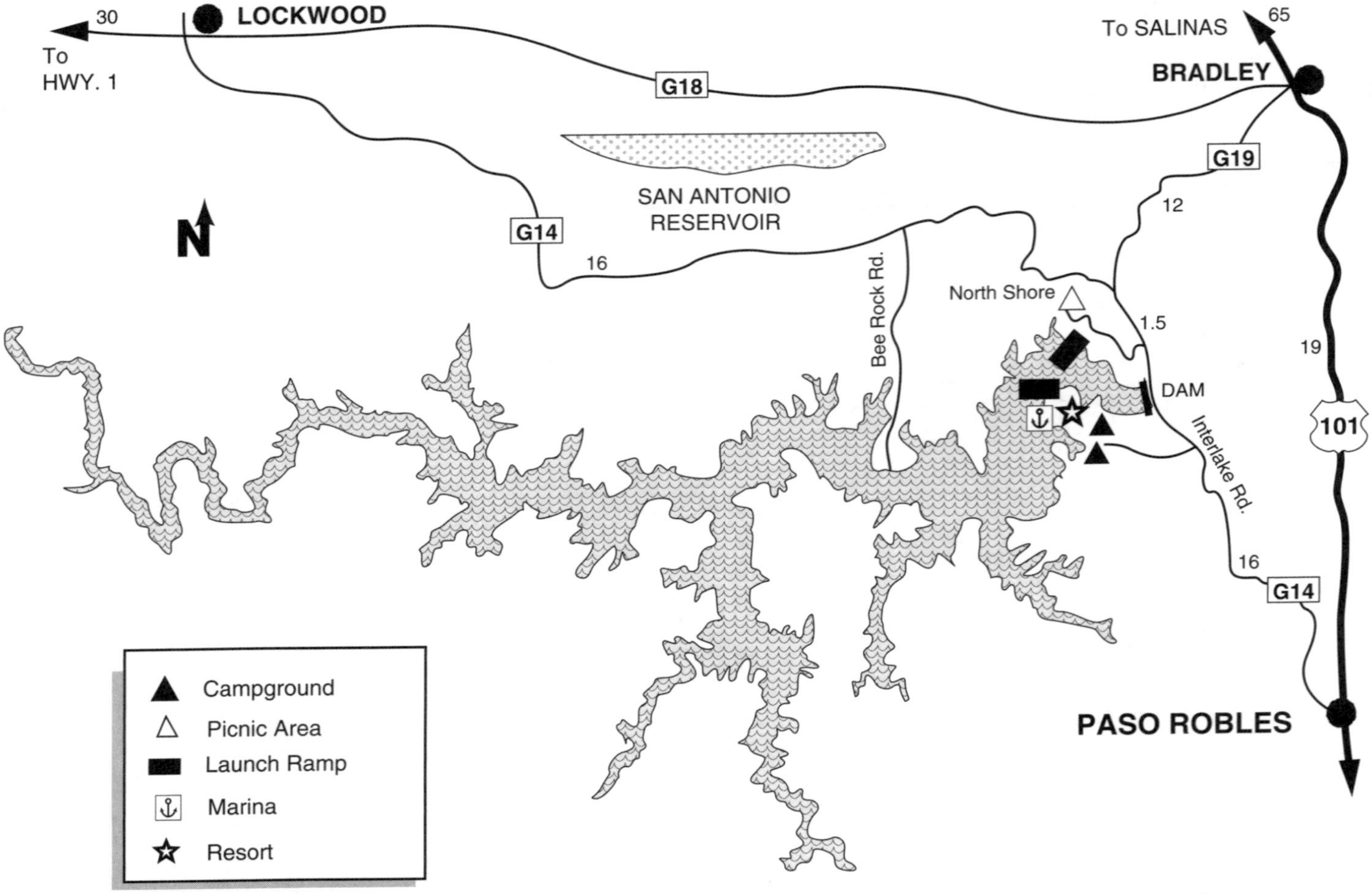
30
LOCKWOOD
To HWY. 1
G18
To SALINAS
65
BRADLEY
G19
12
SAN ANTONIO RESERVOIR
N
G14
16
Bee Rock Rd.
North Shore
1.5
19
DAM
101
Interlake Rd.
16
G14
PASO ROBLES
Campground
Picnic Area
Launch Ramp
Marina
Resort

INFORMATION: Resort, 10625 Nacimiento Lake Dr., Paso Robles 93426—Ph: (805) 238-3256 or (800) 323-3839

CAMPING	BOATING	RECREATION	OTHER
350 Dev. Sites for Tents & R.V.s Fees: $20 - $30 Full Hookups Fees: $25 - $40 Group Sites Available Oct. 1 - March 1 Overflow Camping Area Day Use: $12 - $15 Pets Allowed	Power, Row, Canoe, Sail, Waterski, PWCs, Windsurf & Inflatable Full Service Marina Launch Ramps - $7 Rentals: Fishing Boats, Ski Boats, Canoes, Pontoons & Peddle Boats Slips, Dry Storage	Fishing: Catfish, Bluegill, Crappie, White Bass, Large & Smallmouth Bass Swimming Picnicking Hiking Trails Day Use Fee: $10 & Up *No Motorcycles*	Lodge Accommodations & Mobile Home Rentals Restaurant Grocery Store Bait & Tackle Disposal Station Gas & Propane Playgrounds Volleyball & Horseshoes Swimming Pool in Summer - Fee: $3

SANTA MARGARITA LAKE, WHALE ROCK RESERVOIR and ATASCADERO LAKE

Located amid Central California's coastal range, Santa Margarita Lake has 1,070 surface acres under the jurisdiction of San Luis County Parks. This is a good warm water fishery with camping facilities and equestrian staging areas. Boats over 10 feet are allowed. Swimming, waterskiing and windsurfing are not permitted as this is a drinking water reservoir for the City of San Luis Obispo. Whale Rock Reservoir is under the jurisdiction of the City of San Luis Obispo. Trout fishing is limited to 5 per day. Boating or water contact are not permitted. This is a good area for birdwatching. Atascadero is a small city Lake with picnic sites, playgrounds and a zoo. The angler will find trout and bass.

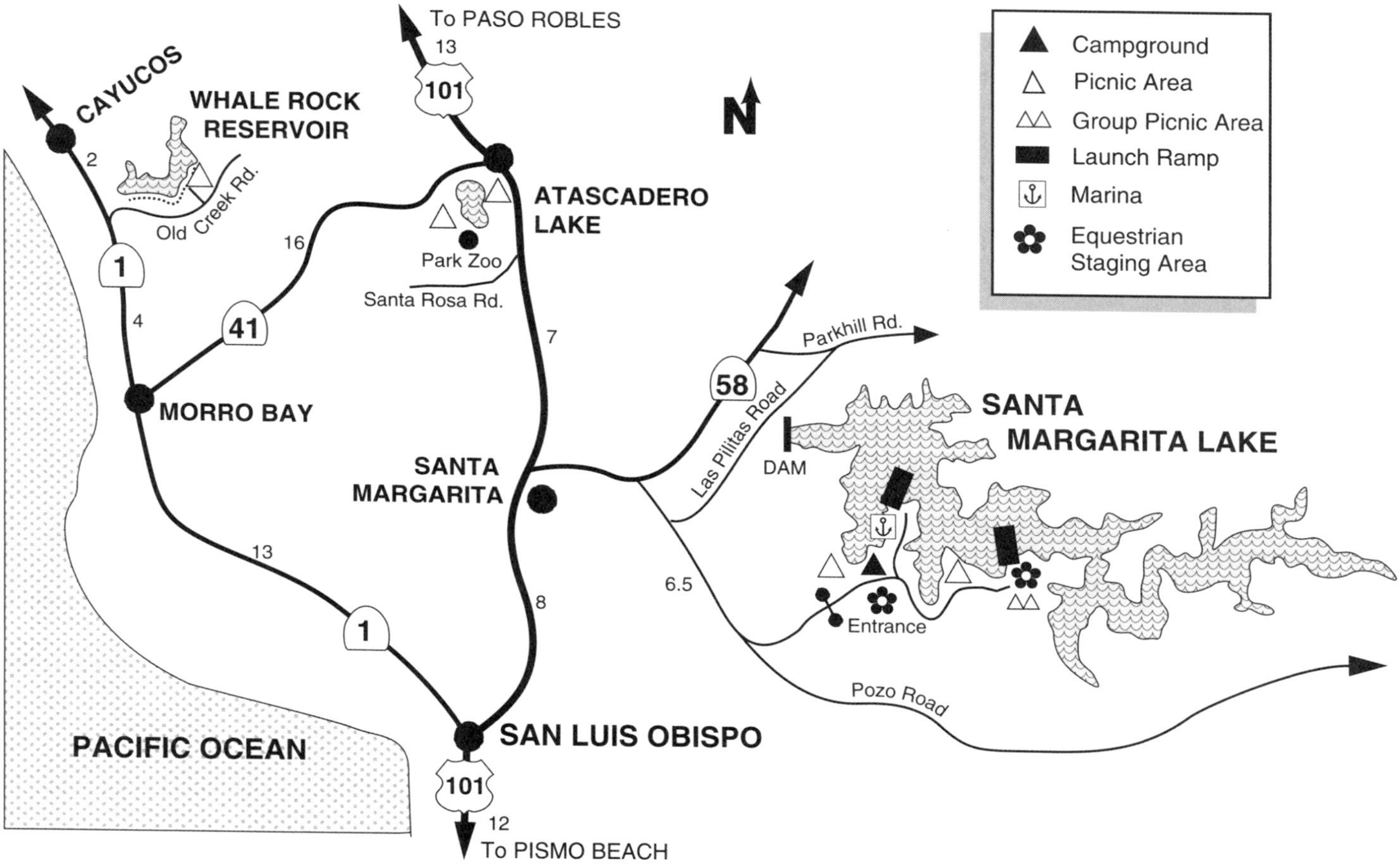

To PASO ROBLES
13
101
CAYUCOS
WHALE ROCK
RESERVOIR
2
Old Creek Rd.
16
ATASCADERO
LAKE
Park Zoo
Santa Rosa Rd.
1
4
41
7
MORRO BAY
N
Campground
Picnic Area
Group Picnic Area
Launch Ramp
Marina
Equestrian
Staging Area
Parkhill Rd.
58
Las Pilitas Road
SANTA
MARGARITA LAKE
DAM
SANTA
MARGARITA
13
6.5
8
1
Entrance
Pozo Road
SAN LUIS OBISPO
PACIFIC OCEAN
101
12
To PISMO BEACH

INFORMATION:San Luis Obispo County Parks, 1087 Santa Rosa St., San Luis Obispo 93408—Ph:(805) 781-5930

CAMPING	BOATING	RECREATION	OTHER
Santa Margarita Lake: 64 Sites for Tents & R.V.s - Fee: $22 No Hookups Group Sites Reservations: Ph: (805) 788-2401 Primitive Boat-In Sites Day Use: $8 Pets: $3	Santa Margarita Lake: Boats Over 10 Feet Only *No Waterskiing, PWCs or Windsurfing* Approved Inflatables Full Service Marina Ph: (805) 438-1522 Launch Ramps - $8 Rentals: Fishing Boats & Pontoons (Boat Decontamination: $10)	Fishing: Striped Bass, Rainbow Trout, Bluegill & Catfish Swimming : Santa Margarita Lake: Pool Only Picnicking - Group Site at Santa Margarita Lake: Ph: (805) 788-2401 Hiking Trails Equestrian Trails Bicycle Trails	Santa Margarita Lake: Snacks & Drinks Bait & Tackle Boat Tours Atascadero Lake Info: Ph: (805) 461-5000 Whale Rock Reservoir Info: Ph: (805) 781-7300

LOPEZ LAKE

Lopez Lake, with 22 miles of shoreline, is administered by the San Luis Obispo County Parks Department. The 950 surface acres are favored by westerly breezes coming off the Pacific making it a popular Lake for sailing and windsurfing. There are good marine facilities and special areas are set aside for sailing, windsurfing, waterskiing and PWCs. The angler will find a variety of game fish. In addition to the oak-shaded campsites listed below, there are overflow sites and a horse camp. This complete facility includes a naturalist program which can be enjoyed along trails, by boat or around the campfire. The Mustang Waterslides are a popular addition to this recreation area.

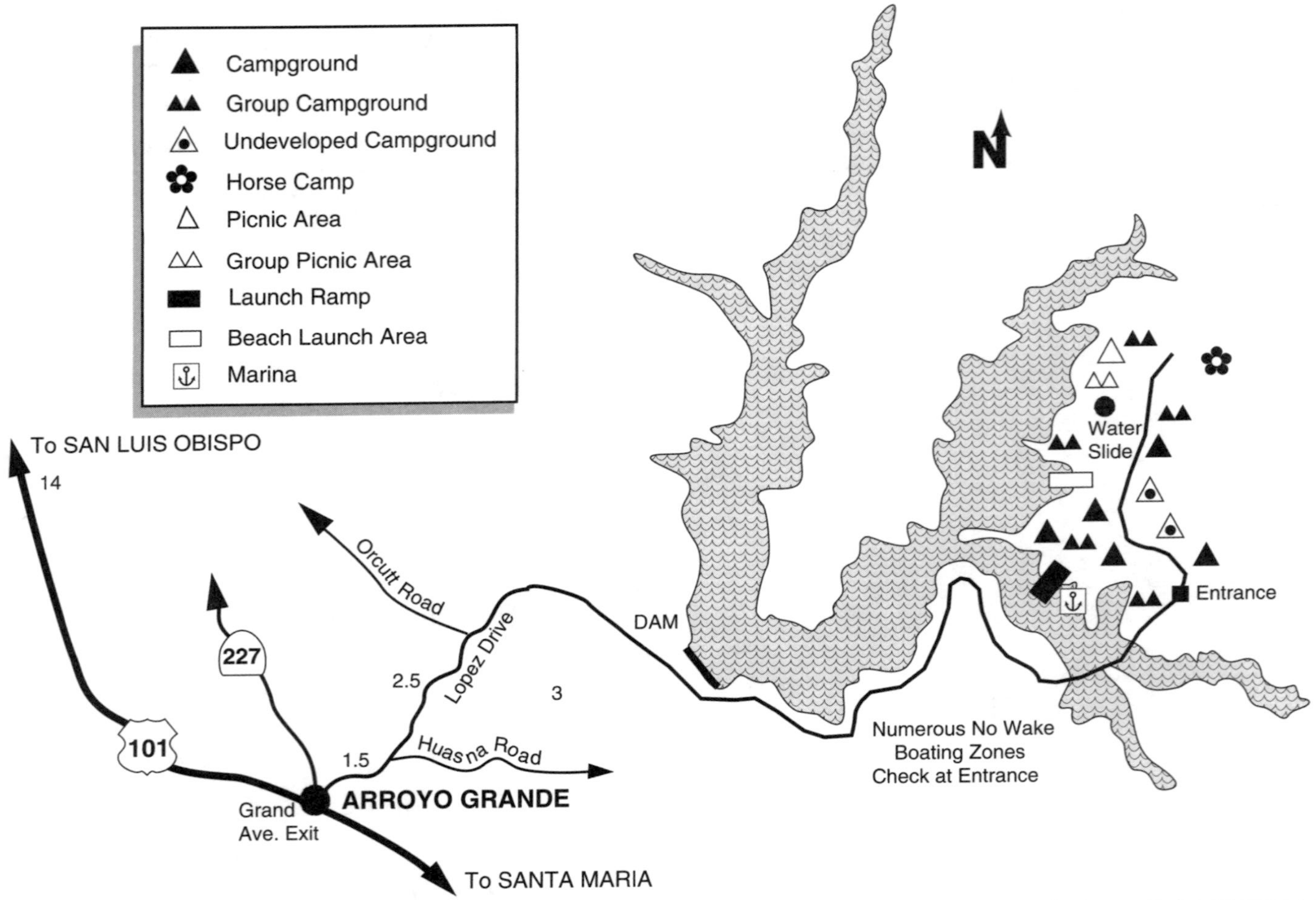
Campground
Group Campground
Undeveloped Campground
Horse Camp
Picnic Area
Group Picnic Area
Launch Ramp
Beach Launch Area
Marina
To SAN LUIS OBISPO
14
Orcutt Road
227
2.5
Lopez Drive
3
DAM
101
1.5
Huasna Road
Grand Ave. Exit
ARROYO GRANDE
To SANTA MARIA
N
Water Slide
Entrance
Numerous No Wake Boating Zones Check at Entrance

INFORMATION: Lopez Lake Recreation Area, 6800 Lopez Dr., Arroyo Grande 93420—Ph: (805) 788-2381

CAMPING	BOATING	RECREATION	OTHER
354 Dev. Sites for Tents & R.V.s Full Hookups Fee: $19 - $30 Group Camp Sites Disposal Station Reservations: Ph: (805) 788-2381 Undeveloped Sites Day Use Fee: $8	Open to All Boating Speed Limit: 40 MPH No Wake Zones Full Service Marina Launch Ramp - $4 - $8 Beach Launch Area Moorings, Boat Docks Boat & Trailer Storage Rentals: Fishing Boats, Waterski & Patio Boats, Kayaks	Fishing: Rainbow Trout, Catfish, Bluegill, Crappie, Redear Sunfish, Large & Smallmouth Bass Swimming: In Designated Areas Picnicking - Group Sites to 300 People Hiking & Equestrian Trails Boat Tours Nature Programs Campfire Programs	Marina & Store Ph: (805) 489-1006 Snack Bar Bait & Tackle Gas Station Pets Allowed Mustang Water Slides & Hot Spas Ph: (805) 489-8898

Lake Cachuma is at an elevation of 800 feet amid the oak-shaded hills of Santa Ynez Valley. Under the jurisdiction of Santa Barbara County, this is one of the most complete parks in California with camping, marine and many other recreation facilities. The 3,200 surface acre Lake is open to most boating but waterskiing, canoes, kayaks and rafts are not allowed. The angler will find a large variety of fish. There are hiking, bicyling and equestrian trails. Swimming pools can be enjoyed from June through Labor Day. Park naturalists conduct a variety of programs. In addition to the campgrounds at the Lake, the Cachuma Recreation Area includes Live Oak Camp which can be reserved for large group functions. During winter months, boat tours are available for eagle watching.

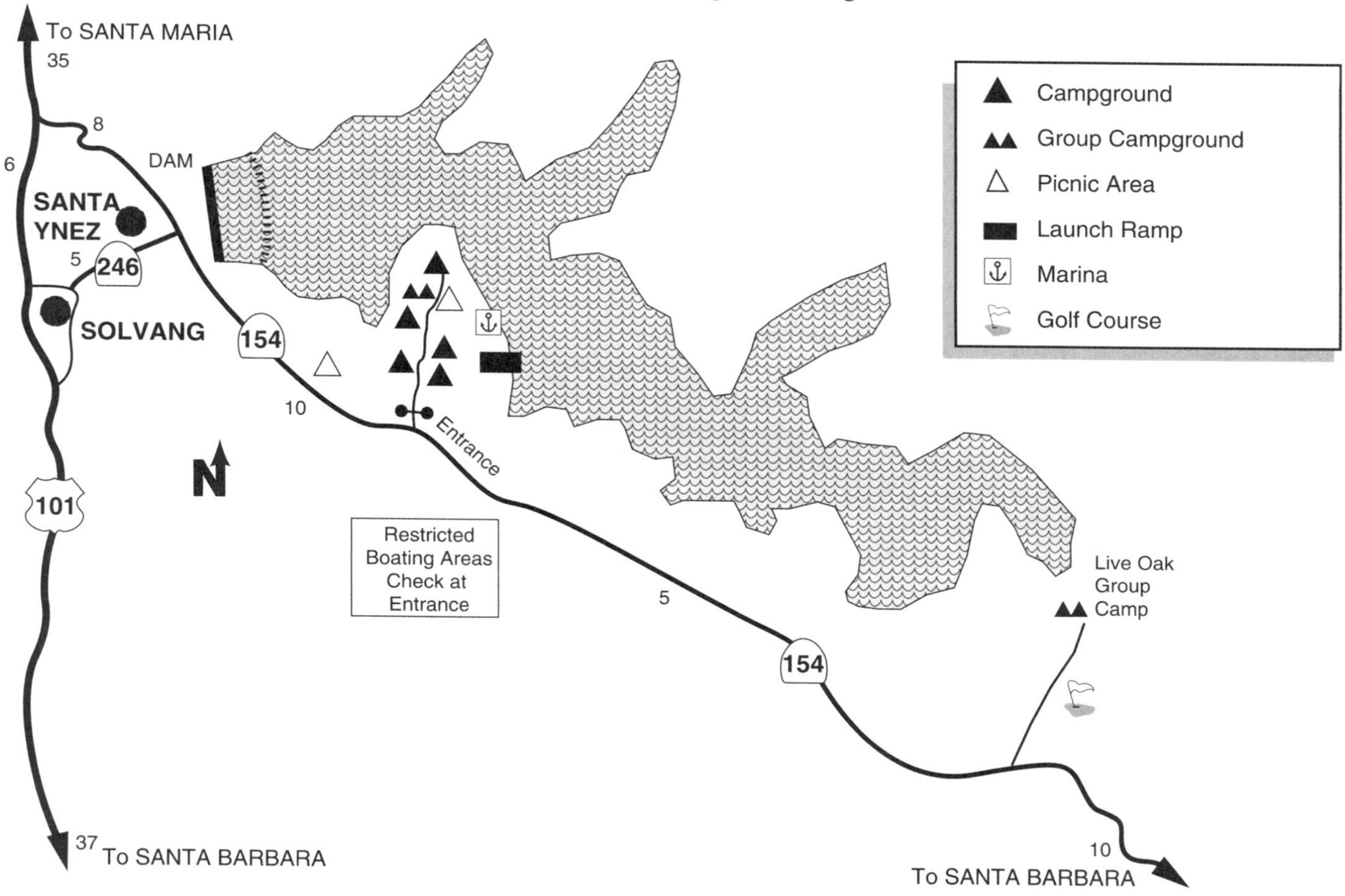
To SANTA MARIA
35
8
6
DAM
SANTA YNEZ
5
246
SOLVANG
154
10
Entrance
N
101
Restricted Boating Areas Check at Entrance
5
154
Live Oak Group Camp
37 To SANTA BARBARA
10
To SANTA BARBARA
Campground
Group Campground
Picnic Area
Launch Ramp
Marina
Golf Course

INFORMATION: Cachuma Lake Recreation Area, HC 59 - Hwy. 154, Santa Barbara 93105—Ph: (805) 686-5055

CAMPING	BOATING	RECREATION	OTHER
588 Dev. Sites for Tents & R.V.s Full & Partial Hookups Fees: $20 - $30 First Come Basis 9 Group Camps to 120 People Reservations: Ph: (805) 686-5050 Disposal Stations Yurt Tents: Heat, Light & Lockable Door Day Use Fee: $8	Most Boating Allowed Except No Canoes, Kayaks or Rafts & No Waterskiing Launch Ramp - Fee: $15 Full Service Marina Docks, Berths & Moorings Boat & Trailer Storage Rentals: Row Boats & Motors, Paddle & Patio Boats	Fishing: Channel Catfish, Bluegill, Crappie, Large & Smallmouth Bass, Sunfish, Redear, & Rainbow Trout Swimming: Pool Only Picnicking - Group Sites Hiking & Equestrian Trails Bicycle Trails Winter Eagle Watching Boat Tours Playgrounds Ball Fields	General Store Bait & Tackle Snack Bar Gas Station Recreation Center Nature Center Pets Allowed Fully Equipped Cabins with Kitchenettes Info Ph: (805) 934-1441 Live Oak Group Camp Info Ph: (805) 686-5076

LAKE CASITAS

Lake Casitas is at an elevation of 600 feet in the oak-covered rolling hills west of the Los Padres National Forest. Under the jurisdiction of the Casitas Municipal Water District, this very popular 2,700 surface-acre Lake has 32 miles of shoreline. No swimming or body contact with the water is allowed. Except for the main recreation area, the remainder of the shoreline is closed. Casitas is famous for big fish and holds State records for largemouth bass, catfish and redear sunfish. Night fishing is allowed one three-day weekend a month. The 6,200 acre tree-shaded recreation area offers extensive camping, boating and picnicking facilities.

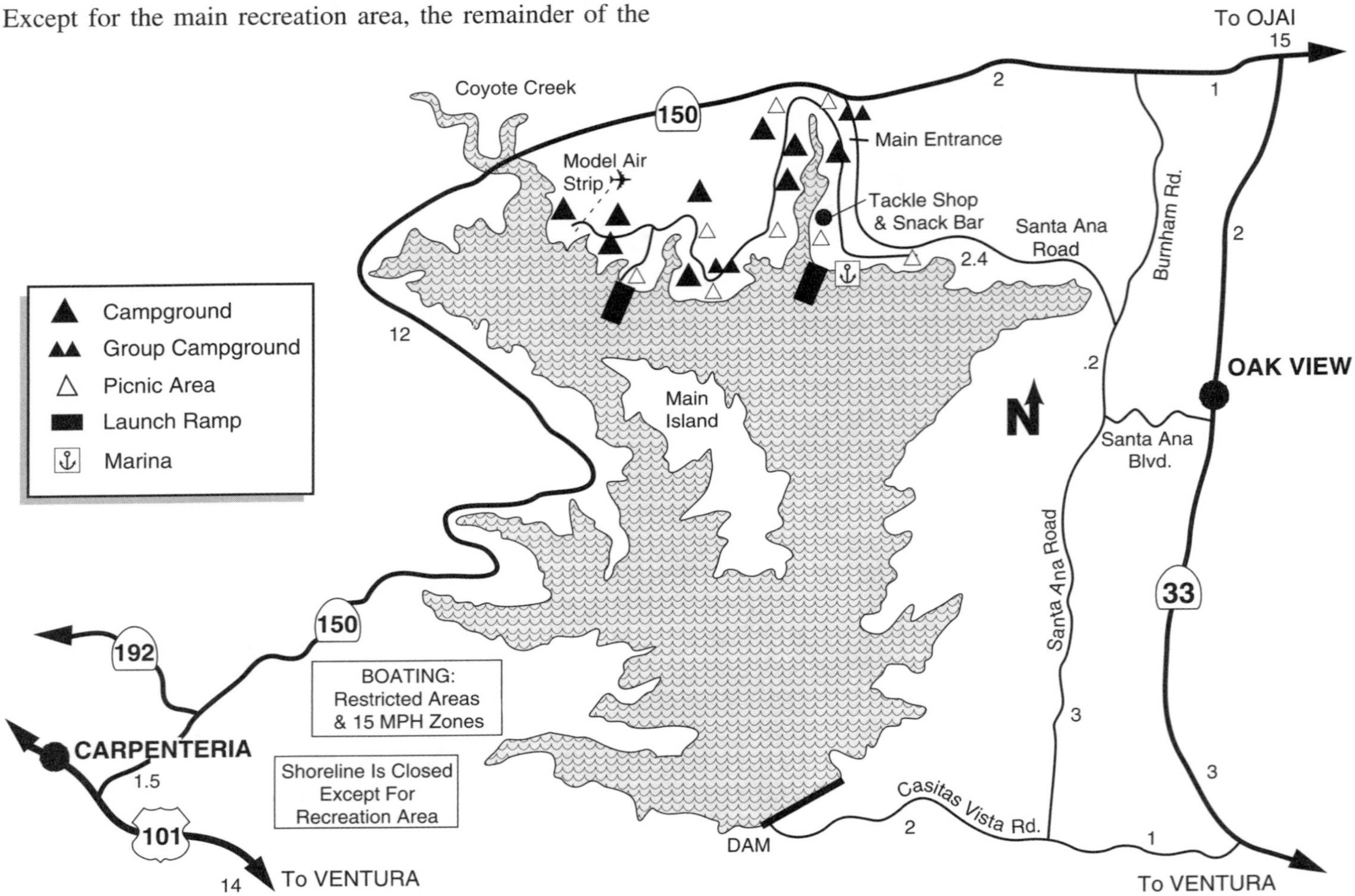

To OJAI
15
Coyote Creek
150
2
1
Main Entrance
Model Air Strip
Tackle Shop & Snack Bar
Santa Ana Road
2.4
Burnham Rd.
2
12
Campground
Group Campground
Picnic Area
Launch Ramp
Marina
Main Island
.2
OAK VIEW
N
Santa Ana Blvd.
Santa Ana Road
33
150
192
BOATING: Restricted Areas & 15 MPH Zones
CARPENTERIA
1.5
Shoreline Is Closed Except For Recreation Area
3
3
Casitas Vista Rd.
2
1
DAM
101
14
To VENTURA
To VENTURA

INFORMATION: Casitas Recreation Area, 11311 Santa Ana Rd., Ventura 93001—Ph: (805) 649-2233

CAMPING	BOATING	RECREATION	OTHER
Over 400 Dev. Sites for Tents & R.V.s Full & Partial Hookups Fee: $25 - $60 Group Camps Reservations: Ph: (805) 649-1122 Disposal Stations Day Use: $10 Pets Allowed	Power, Row, Sail & Canoe *Strict Regulations* *Call for Information* Speed Limit - 35 MPH Boat Permit: $10 Full Service Marina Launch Ramps Rentals: Row Boats & Pontoons Docks, Moorings, Berths, Gas, Storage	Fishing: Largemouth & Florida Bass, Catfish, Trout, Bluegill, Redear Sunfish & Crappie Night Fishing - Schedule Picnicking Hiking & Bicycle Trails Playgrounds Model Airplane Strip Bicycle Rentals Water Playground Disc Golf Course *No Swimming in Lake*	Snack Bar Marina Cafe Grocery Store Bait & Tackle Travel Trailer Rentals Info Ph: (805) 649-9170

LAKE EVANS and LAKE WEBB— BUENA VISTA AQUATIC RECREATION AREA

Buena Vista Recreation Area is located at an elevation of 350 feet in the south San Joaquin Valley. In Kern County, this recreation area consists of 1,586 acres and two Lakes with complete facilities for camping, picnicking, swimming and boating. Lake Evans has a surface area of 86 acres and Lake Webb has 873 acres. Trophy trout are stocked in the winter months at Lake Evans. Boating is allowed at both Lakes. Specific zones are designated for speed limits. Waterskiing and PWCs are permitted at Lake Webb in a counter-clockwise pattern. During busy summer months, Lake Evans is also open to PWCs.

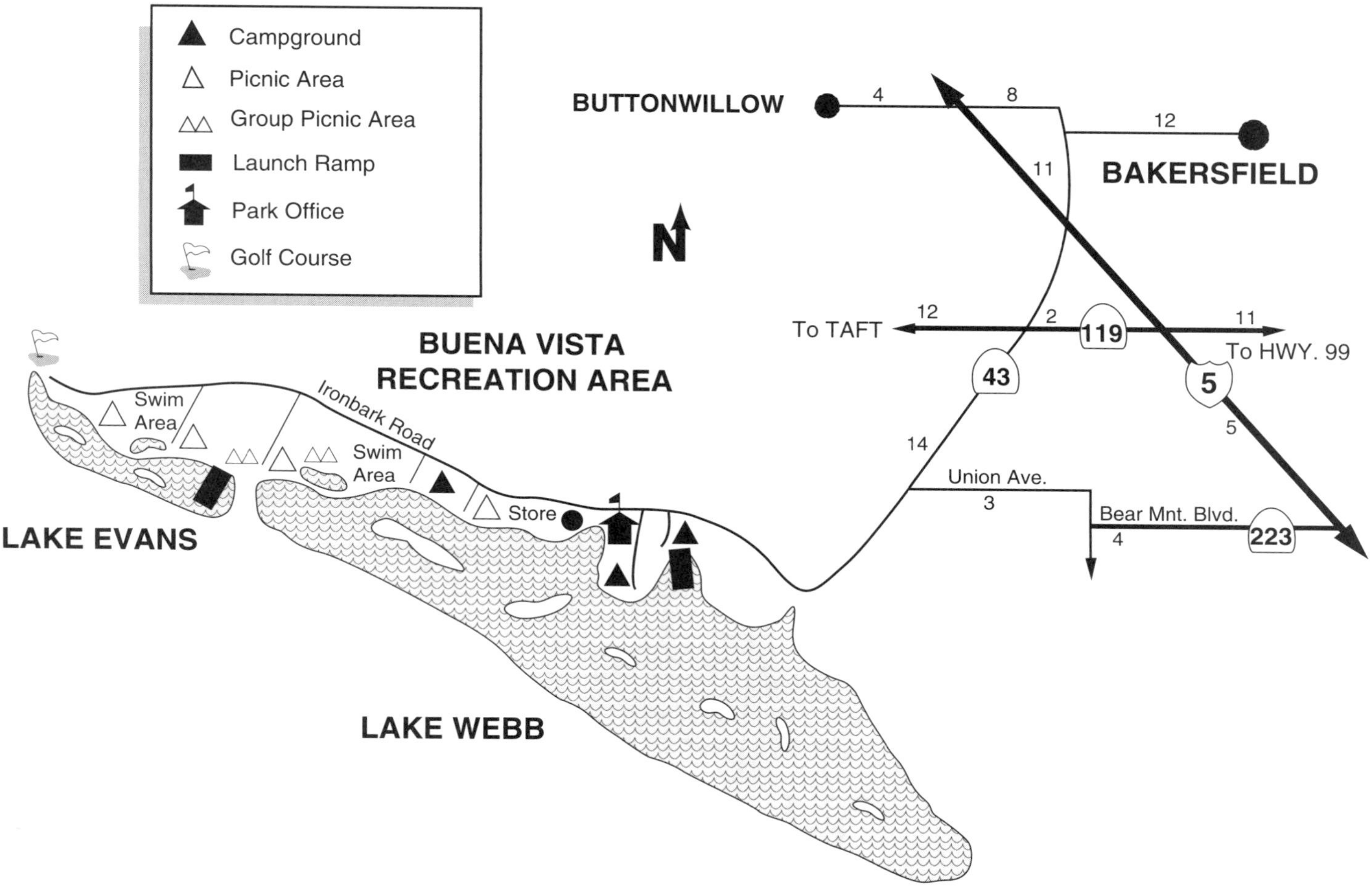
Campground
Picnic Area
Group Picnic Area
Launch Ramp
Park Office
Golf Course
BUTTONWILLOW
BAKERSFIELD
N
To TAFT
To HWY. 99
BUENA VISTA
RECREATION AREA
Ironbark Road
Swim Area
Swim Area
Store
Union Ave.
Bear Mnt. Blvd.
119
43
5
223
4
8
12
11
11
12
2
11
14
5
3
4
LAKE EVANS
LAKE WEBB

INFORMATION: Kern County Parks, 1110 Golden State Ave., Bakersfield 93301—Ph: (661) 868-7000

CAMPING	BOATING	RECREATION	OTHER
112 Dev. Sites for Tents & R.V.s Fees: $14 - $32 Full Hookups Fees: $21 - $39 Reservations: Ph:(661) 868-7050 Plus Overflow Area Disposal Station Day Use: $6 Pets Allowed: $4	Power, Row, Canoe, Sail, Windsurf, PWCs & Inflatable With Restrictions Designated Speed Limit Zones Launch Ramps: $7 Docks, Moorings, Gas	Fishing: Largemouth & Striped Bass, Catfish & Bluegill Lake Evans: Trout in Winter Fishing Fees Swimming: Lagoons Only Picnicking - Group Sites to 400 People Reservations: Ph: (661) 868-7050 Playgrounds	Grocery Store Bait & Tackle Gas Station Propane Buena Vista Golf Course Full Facilities 14 Miles at Taft

PYRAMID LAKE

Pyramid Lake, at an elevation of 2,600 feet, is in the Angeles National Forest in Northwestern Los Angeles County. This popular Lake has a surface area of 1,297 acres. Most of the 21 miles of rugged shoreline are accessible only by boat. There are boat-in picnic sites and restrooms scattered around the Lake. Spanish Point is a favorite spot with picnic sites and a beach. Pyramid is known as one of Southern California's prime striped bass waters. No camping is at the Lake but campgrounds are at Los Alamos under concession from the U.S. Forest Service.

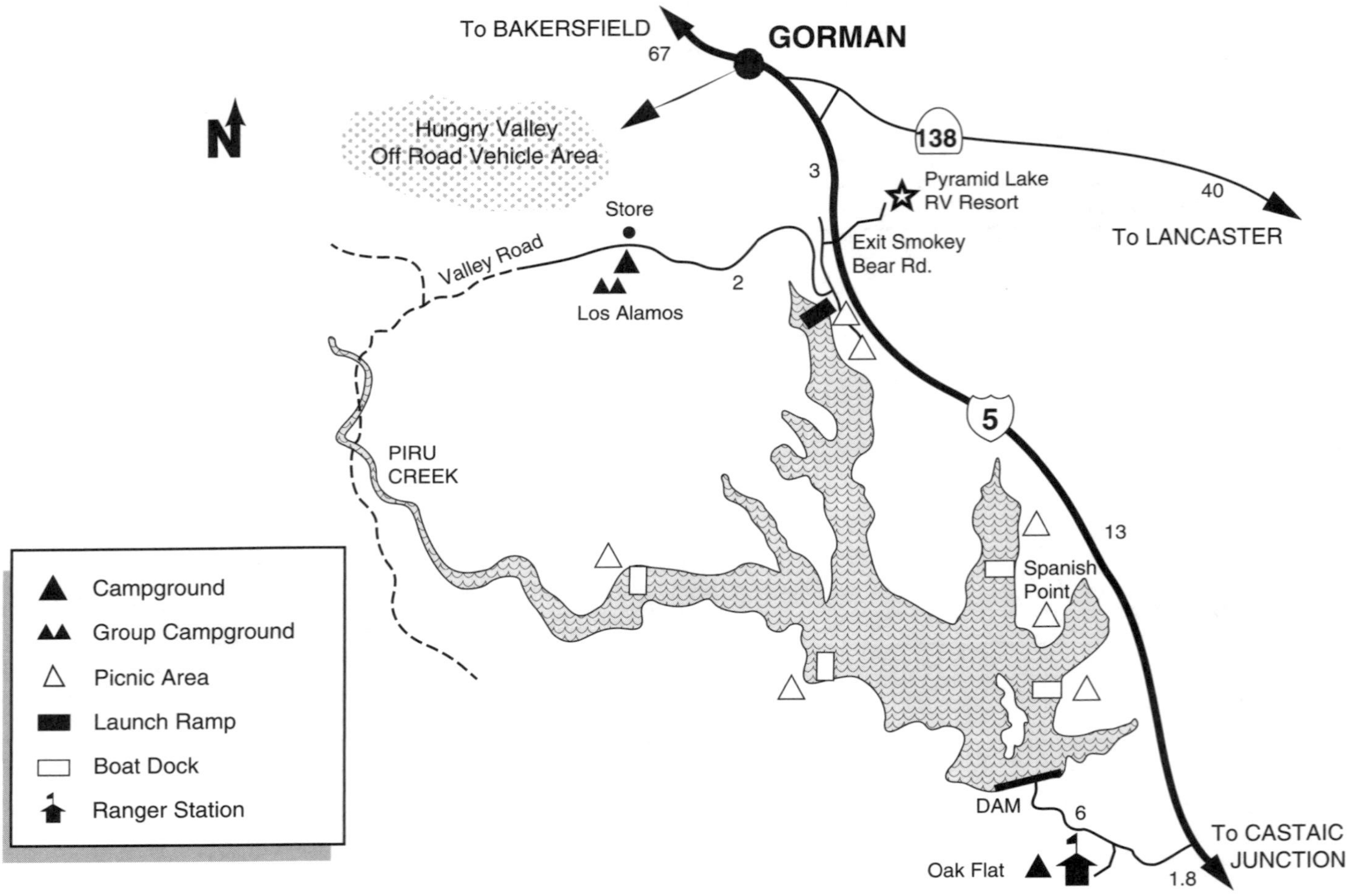
To BAKERSFIELD
67
GORMAN
N
Hungry Valley
Off Road Vehicle Area
138
3
Pyramid Lake
RV Resort
40
To LANCASTER
Store
Valley Road
Exit Smokey
Bear Rd.
2
Los Alamos
5
PIRU
CREEK
13
Spanish
Point
Campground
Group Campground
Picnic Area
Launch Ramp
Boat Dock
Ranger Station
DAM
6
To CASTAIC
JUNCTION
Oak Flat
1.8

INFORMATION: Pyramid Lake, Pyramid Lake Rd., Gorman 93243—Ph: (661) 257-2790			
CAMPING	**BOATING**	**RECREATION**	**OTHER**
No Camping at Lake Los Alamos: 93 Dev. Sites for Tents & R.V.s Fee: $12 3 Group Sites to 30 People Each Disposal Station Reservations: Ph: (800) 416-6992 Day Use Fee at Pyramid Lake: $3 - $28	Open to All Boating, Waterskiing, PWCs & Windsurfing Speed Limit 35 MPH Launch Ramp Limited Number of Boats & PWCs Allowed First-Come Basis Boat-In Day Use Area	Fishing: Striped Bass, Largemouth & Smallmouth Bass, Rainbow Trout, Channel Catfish, Bluegill, Crappie & Sunfish Swimming Beaches Picnicking 5 Boat-In Picnic Sites Off Road Vehicles: Only at Hungry Valley Designated Area	Santa Clara/Mojave River Ranger District 28245 Avenue Crocker Valencia 91355 Ph: (661) 296-9710 Pyramid Lake R.V. Resort Ph: (661) 248-0100 117 Dev. R. V. Sites Full Hookups Fee: $35 - $39

Castaic Lake and the Afterbay Lagoon are at an elevation of 1,500 feet and operated by the County of Los Angeles. The large, popular recreation area covers 8,800 acres. The Main Reservoir has 29 shoreline miles and the Afterbay Lagoon has 3 shoreline miles. Various events and fishing derbies are scheduled during the summer. The Lagoon is open to boating and swimming from mid-June through September but no gas motors are allowed. Fishing at the Main Reservoir is from sunrise to sunset. The Lagoon has 24-hour fishing on the east shoreline. There is a good warm water fishery and trout are stocked in the winter months.

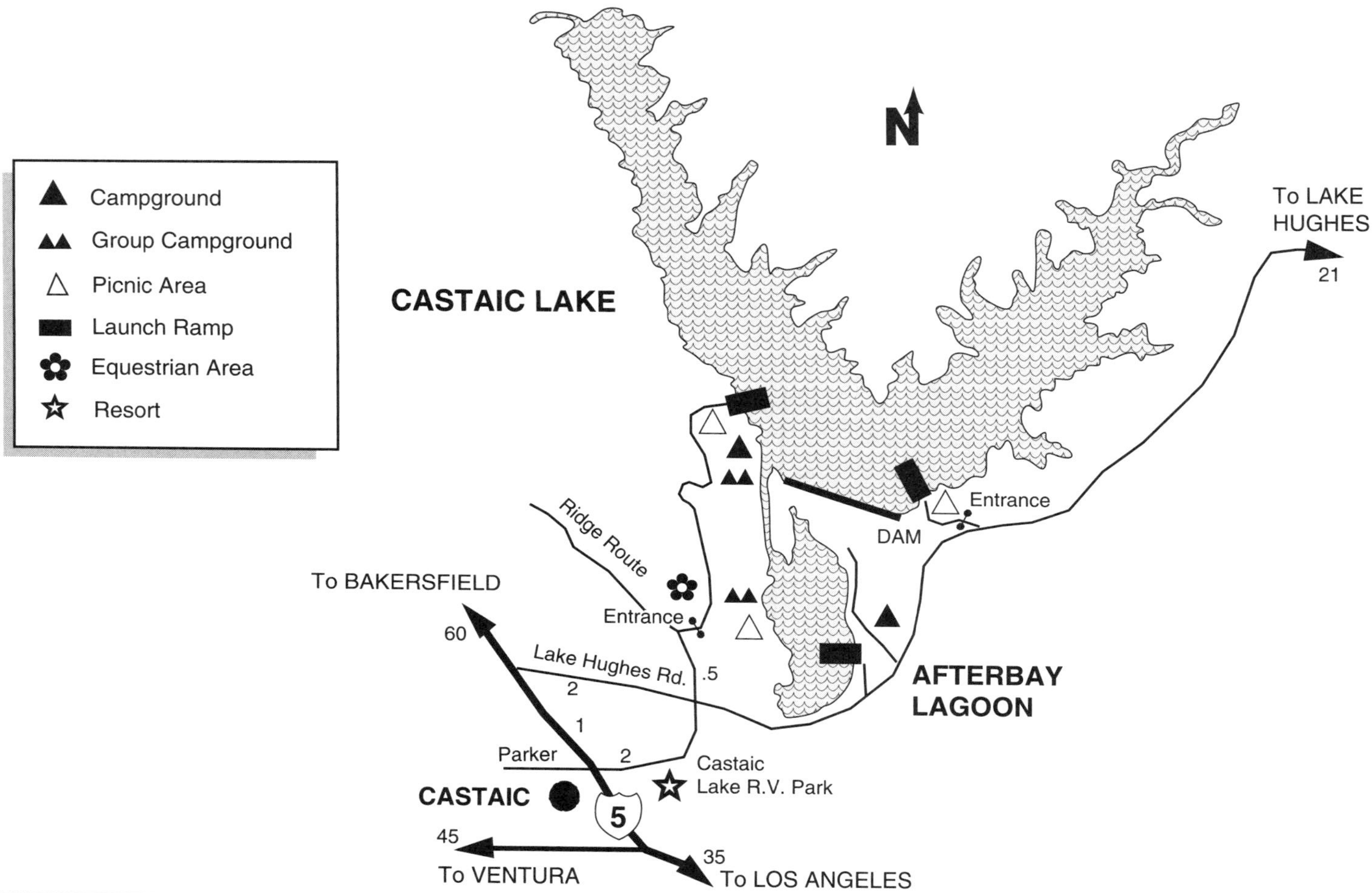
Campground
Group Campground
Picnic Area
Launch Ramp
Equestrian Area
Resort
CASTAIC LAKE
N
To LAKE HUGHES
21
Entrance
DAM
Ridge Route
To BAKERSFIELD
60
Entrance
Lake Hughes Rd.
.5
2
1
AFTERBAY LAGOON
Parker
2
Castaic Lake R.V. Park
CASTAIC
5
45
35
To VENTURA
To LOS ANGELES

INFORMATION: Castaic Lake State Recreation Area, 32132 Castaic Lake Dr., Castaic 91384—Ph: (661) 257-4050

CAMPING	BOATING	RECREATION	OTHER
60 Dev. Sites for Tent & R.V.s to 35 feet No Hookups Fee: $15 - $18 Tent Sites are Limited Group Camp Areas Disposal Station Reservations: Ph: (661) 257-4050 Day Use Fee: $11	Main Reservoir: All Boating Allowed Designated Speed Areas 35 MPH Speed Limit Launch Ramps: $6-$13 Plus $11 Vehicle Fee Boat Inspections at Entrance Rentals: Fishing Boats with Motors Afterbay: No Gas Motor Boats Launch Ramp: $6	Fishing: Rainbow Trout, Catfish, Largemouth & Striped Bass Afterbay Lagoon: 24-Hour Fishing Area Afterbay Lagoon: Swimming Beach No Swimming - Main Lake Picnicking - Group Areas to 500 People Hiking, Bicycle & Equestrian Trails Amphitheater	Snack Bar Bait & Tackle Castaic Lake R.V. Park 31540 Ridge Route Rd. Castaic 91384 Ph: (661) 257-3340

LAKE PIRU

Lake Piru is at an elevation of 1,055 feet in the Los Padres National Forest north of Los Angeles. The surface area of the Lake ranges from 750 surface acres to 1,200 surface acres depending on the season. Be sure to call for current water conditions. This is a warm water fishery and also trout are planted twice a week in season. Piru Lake has complete marina facilities including boat rentals. Be aware that special boating restrictions apply and boat inspections are necessary. The campgrounds are located amid oak and olive trees above the launch ramp.

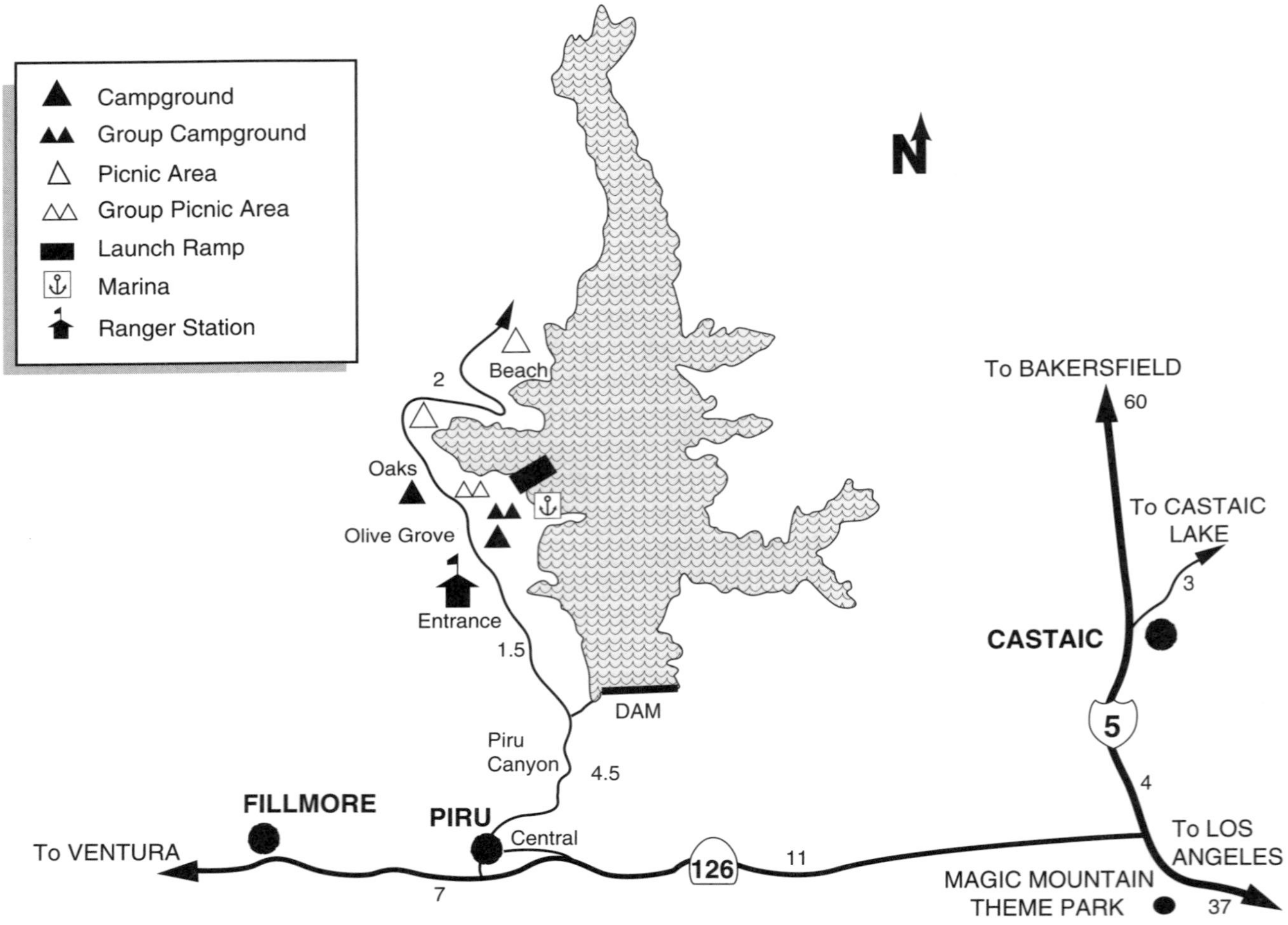
Campground
Group Campground
Picnic Area
Group Picnic Area
Launch Ramp
Marina
Ranger Station
N
2
Beach
Oaks
Olive Grove
Entrance
1.5
DAM
Piru
Canyon
4.5
FILLMORE
PIRU
Central
To VENTURA
7
126
11
To BAKERSFIELD
60
To CASTAIC
LAKE
3
CASTAIC
5
4
To LOS
ANGELES
MAGIC MOUNTAIN
THEME PARK
37

INFORMATION: Park Manager, P.O. Box 202, 4780 Piru Canyon Rd., Piru 93040—Ph: (805) 521-1500			
CAMPING	**BOATING**	**RECREATION**	**OTHER**
238 Dev. Sites for Tents & R.V.s - Fee: $19 - $27 Electric Hookups - Fee: $21 - $31 Full Hookups - Fee: $30 - $42 Group Camps Overflow Camping Area Disposal Stations Reservations: Ph: (805) 521-1500 Day Use Fee: $8 - $10 Pets Allowed	Power, Waterskiing, Sail, Canoe & Inflatables *Call for Specific Regulations* *No Windsurfing or PWCs* Speed Limit: 35 MPH Designated Boating Areas Full Service Marina Ph: (805) 521-1231 Launch Ramp: $8 - $10 Rentals: Fishing Boats & Pontoons Slips, Moorings, Dry Storage	Fishing: Rainbow Trout, Largemouth Bass, Catfish, Crappie, Bluegill Swim Beach Picnicking Groups to 120 People Hiking & Equestrian Trails in Los Padres National Forest Ojai Ranger District: Ph: (805) 646-4348	Snack Bar Restaurant Bait & Tackle Grocery Store Marine Supplies Dock, Moorings R.V. & Boat Storage Gas Full Facilities in Piru

LAKE HUGHES and ELIZABETH LAKE

Elizabeth Lake and Lake Hughes are at an elevation of 3,300 feet in the Angeles National Forest north of Los Angeles. These Lakes are within 5 miles of each other and are separated by a small private Lake. Lake Hughes has a 35 surface acres. Access is through the resort which is open to the public all year and offers camping, fishing and boating. The western half of Elizabeth Lake is owned and operated by the U.S. Forest Service which maintains picnic sites and swimming is permitted. The eastern half of the Lake is private. There are warm water fisheries at both Lakes and trout fishing can be good in season at Elizabeth Lake.

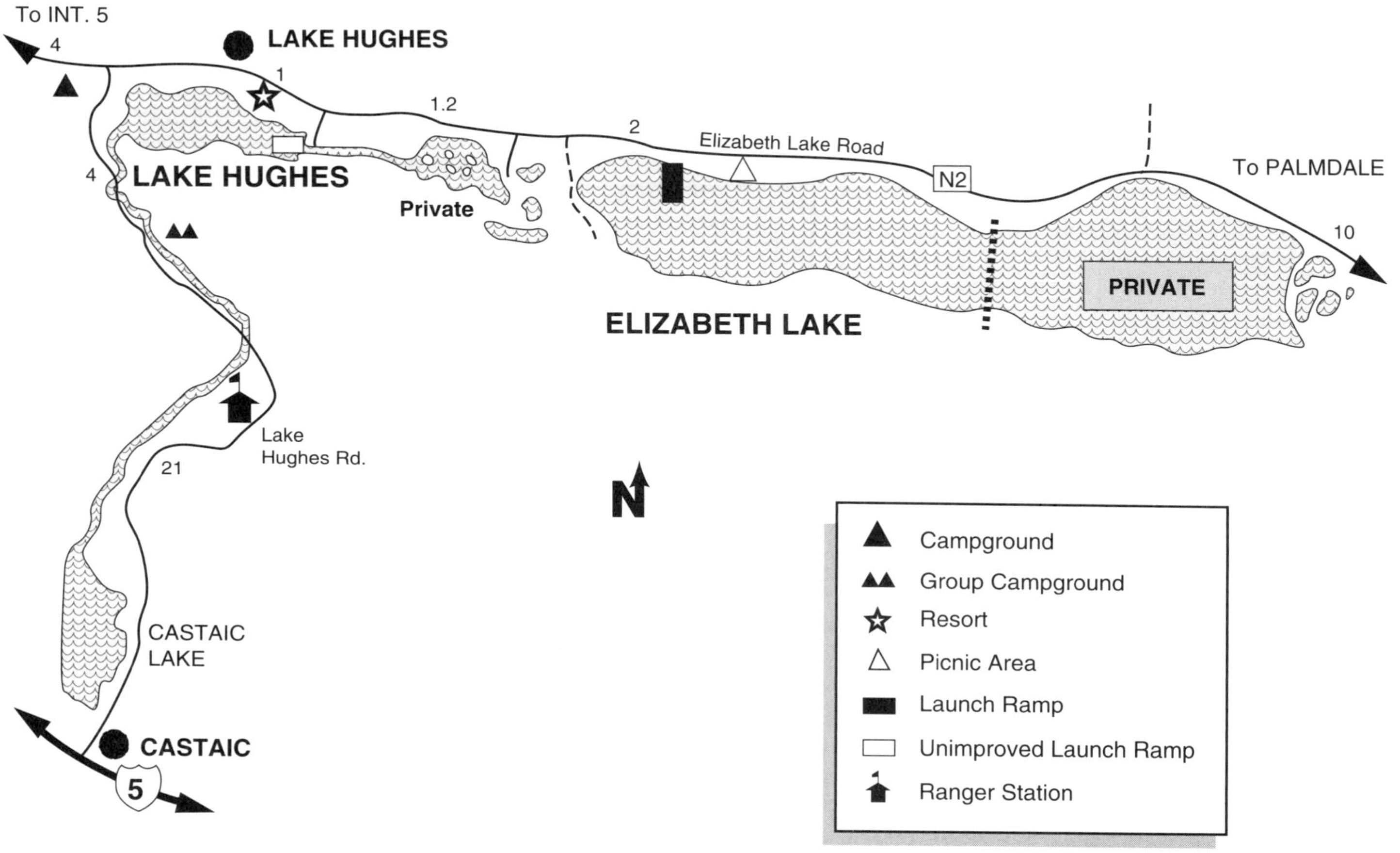
To INT. 5
4
LAKE HUGHES
1
1.2
2
Elizabeth Lake Road
N2
To PALMDALE
10
4
LAKE HUGHES
Private
PRIVATE
ELIZABETH LAKE
Lake
Hughes Rd.
21
N
CASTAIC
LAKE
CASTAIC
5
Campground
Group Campground
Resort
Picnic Area
Launch Ramp
Unimproved Launch Ramp
Ranger Station

INFORMATION: Santa Clara/Mojave Rivers Rang. Dist., 28245 Ave. Crocker, Valencia 91355—Ph: (661) 296-9710

CAMPING	BOATING	RECREATION	OTHER
Hughes Lake Shore Park 43677 Trail K Lake Hughes Ph: (661) 724-1845 44 Dev. Sites for Tents & R.V.s No Hookups Fees: $18 Pets Allowed Day Use Fee: $14 Elizabeth Lake: Day Use Only	Fishing and Sail Boats 10 HP Motors Max. Launch Ramps Check for Current Water Level Conditions	Fishing: Catfish, Bass, Bluegill & Crappie Plus Trout at Lake Elizabeth in Season Swimming at Elizabeth Lake Picnicking Hiking Trails	Lake Hughes: Snack Bar General Store

APOLLO PARK, QUAIL LAKE and LITTLEROCK RESERVOIR

Apollo County Park is a part of the Los Angeles County Regional Park System. The three Lakes, totaling 26 surface acres, are named for the astronauts of the Apollo flight that landed on the moon in 1969. There is a well-stocked catfish and trout fishery. Quail Lake, 290 surface acres, is a storage facility for the State Water Project. This shoreline is open to fishing for striped bass and catfish. Littlerock Reservoir, 150 surface acres, is located at 3,400 feet elevation in the Angeles National Forest. Fishing can be good for rainbow and brown trout.

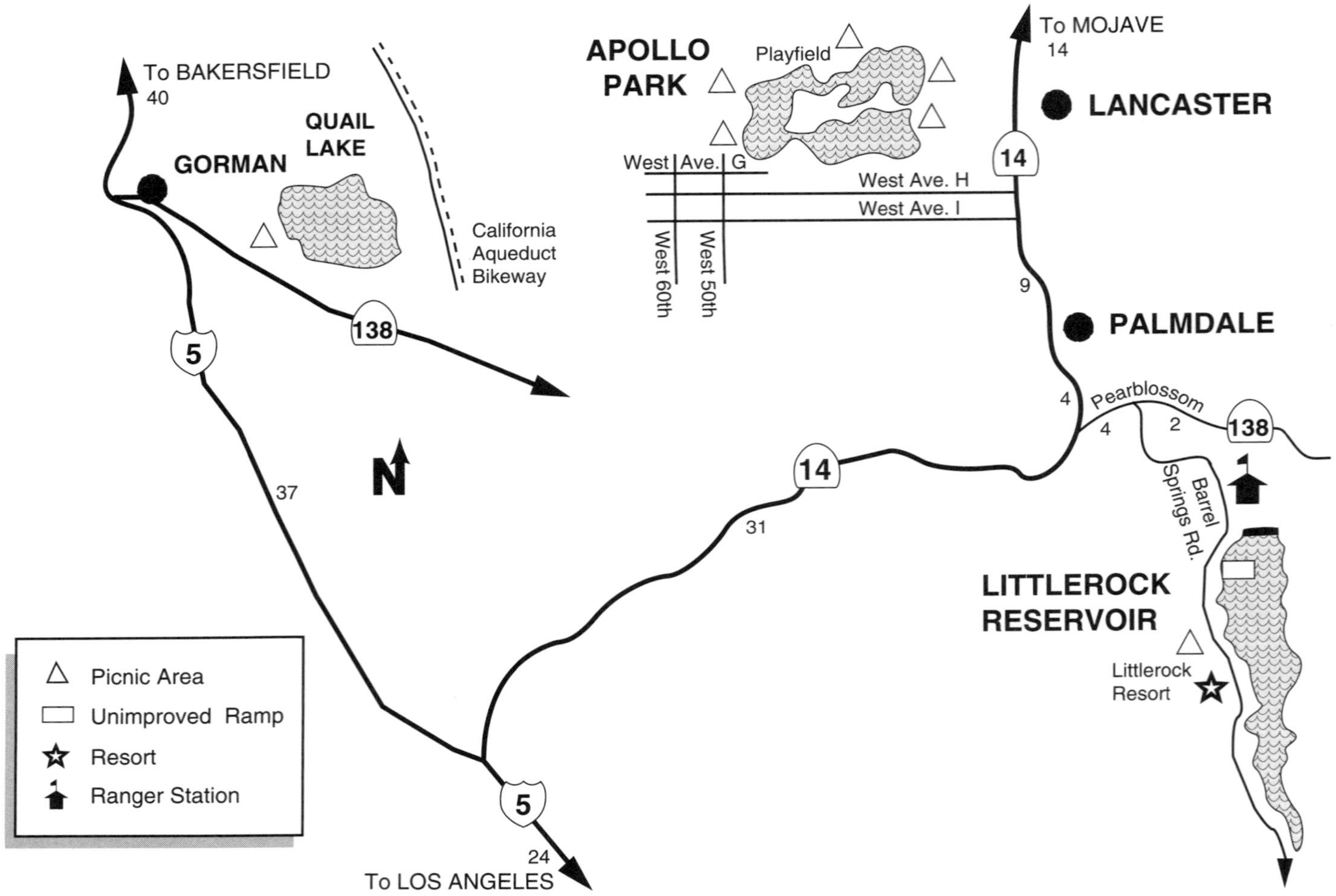

To BAKERSFIELD
40
GORMAN
QUAIL LAKE
California Aqueduct Bikeway
APOLLO PARK
Playfield
West Ave. G
West Ave. H
West Ave. I
West 60th
West 50th
To MOJAVE
14
LANCASTER
14
9
PALMDALE
5
138
4
Pearblossom
4
2
138
Barrel Springs Rd.
N
37
14
31
LITTLEROCK RESERVOIR
Littlerock Resort
Picnic Area
Unimproved Ramp
Resort
Ranger Station
5
24
To LOS ANGELES

INFORMATION: Santa Clara/Mojave Rivers Rang. Dist., 28245 Ave. Crocker, Valencia 91355—Ph: (661) 296-9710

CAMPING	BOATING	RECREATION	OTHER
No Camping at Any of These Facilities Call for Current Information Quail Lake: State Water Resources Ph: (805) 257-3610	Littlerock Reservoir: Fishing Boats Only Speed Limit: 5 MPH 10 HP Motors Max. Launch Area No Boating at Apollo Park, Quail Lake or Frazier Park	Fishing: Rainbow, German Brown and Kamloop Trout, Catfish Quail Lake: Striped Bass & Catfish Picnicking Hiking Trails Quail Lake: Aqueduct Bikeway Apollo Park: Fishing Derbies	Littlerock Lake Resort 32700 Cheseboro Rd. Palmdale 93552 Ph: (661) 533-1923 Day Use Only Grocery Store Cafe, Bait & Tackle Boat Rentals Apollo County Park 4555 W. Ave. G Lancaster 93534 Ph: (661) 940-7701

MOJAVE NARROWS PARK, GLEN HELEN PARK and JACKSON LAKE

Mojave Narrows Regional Park, an oasis in the high desert, is at an elevation of 2,700 feet. Glen Helen Regional Park is at 1,000 feet, just 15 minutes from downtown San Bernardino. Both Parks are under the jurisdiction of San Bernadino County Regional Parks. Campgrounds and many recreational facilities are located at these two facilities. Boating is limited but the angler will find trout, stocked in winter, bass and channel catfish at Glen Helen and Mojave Narrows. Jackson Lake, at an elevation of 6,500 feet, is in the Big Pines Recreation Area. Trout can be found in spring, summer and fall at Jackson Lake along with campgrounds, picnic areas, hiking and equestrian trails.

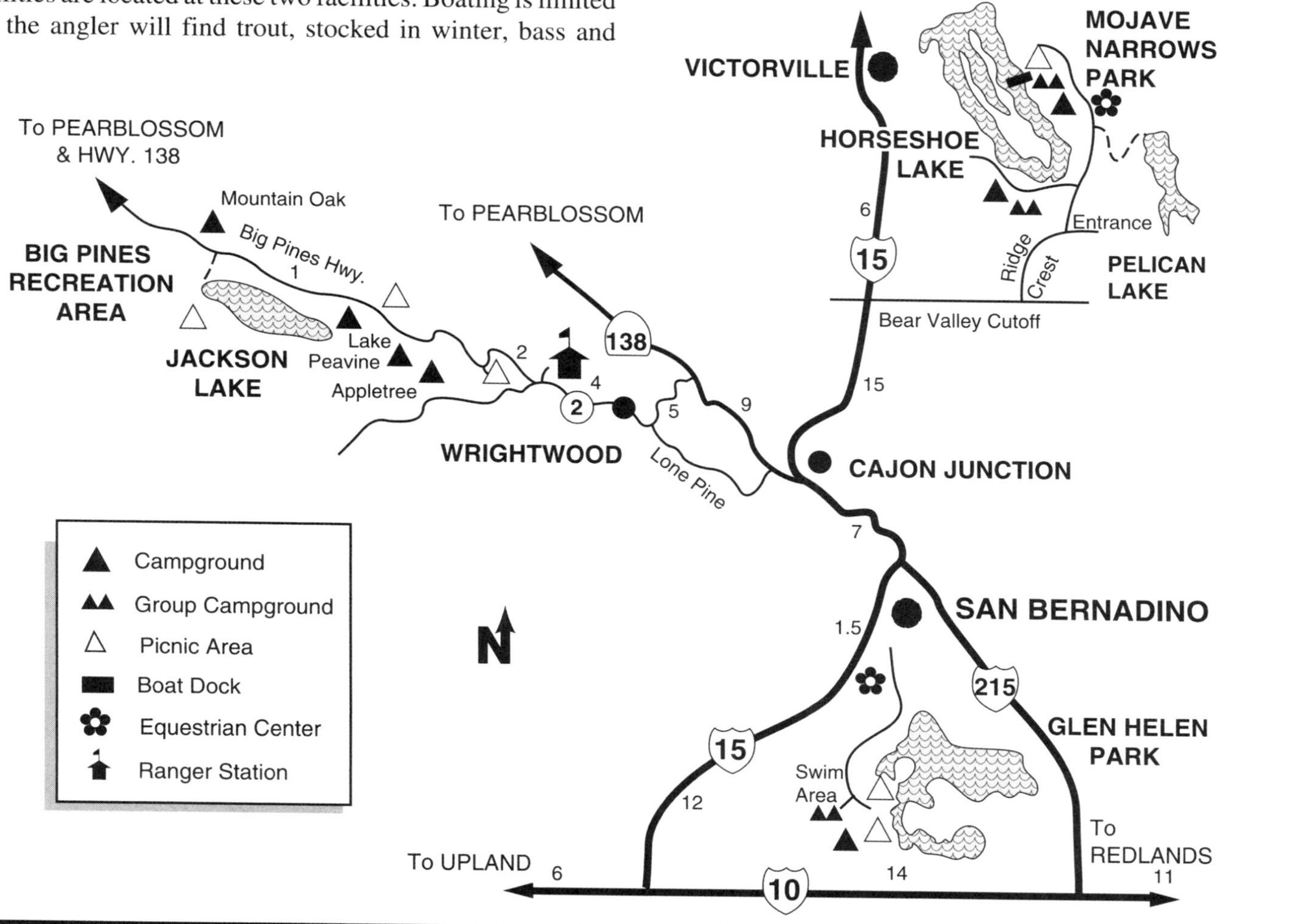

VICTORVILLE
MOJAVE NARROWS PARK
HORSESHOE LAKE
Entrance
PELICAN LAKE
Ridge Crest
Bear Valley Cutoff
To PEARBLOSSOM & HWY. 138
Mountain Oak
Big Pines Hwy.
BIG PINES RECREATION AREA
JACKSON LAKE
Lake Peavine
Appletree
To PEARBLOSSOM
138
WRIGHTWOOD
Lone Pine
CAJON JUNCTION
15
SAN BERNADINO
215
GLEN HELEN PARK
Swim Area
To UPLAND
To REDLANDS
10
Campground
Group Campground
Picnic Area
Boat Dock
Equestrian Center
Ranger Station
N

INFORMATION: San Bernadino County Reg. Parks, 777 E. Rialto, San Bernardino 92415—Ph: (909) 387-2757

CAMPING	BOATING	RECREATION	OTHER
Mojave Narrows: Ph: (760) 245-2226 85 Dev. Sites for Tents & R.V.s 38 Full Hookups Fees: $15 to $22 Group Camp Areas Glen Helen Regional Park: Ph: (909) 887-7540 Group Camp Areas Disposal Station Day Use Fee: $5 - $10 Pets Allowed	Mojave Narrows & Glen Helen: Rentals: Pedal Boats Jackson Lake: Hand Launch Only No Motor Boats	Fishing: Trout, Bass, Catfish Picnicking - Group Areas Glen Helen: Swim Lagoon, Waterslides Picnic Sites, Playgrounds ORV Park Nature Trails Mojave Narrows: Hiking & Equestrian Trails Horse Rentals: Ph: (760) 955-1913	Big Pines Recreation Area Jackson Lake: Santa Clara/Mojave Rivers Ranger District 28245 Ave. Crocker Valencia 91355 Ph: (661) 296-9710 Lake: 8 Campsites No Water at: Peavine: 4 Campsites Appletree: 8 Campsites Reservations: Ph: (877) 444-6777

CRYSTAL LAKE, SAN GABRIEL, MORRIS & SAN DIMAS RESERVOIRS

Be certain to check with the Forest Service for current conditions for this entire area - Ph: (626) 335-1251. At an elevation of 5,700 feet, Crystal Lake Recreation Area is located in the Angeles National Forest. The small 5-acre Lake can have good fishing and limited small craft boating. There are many miles of hiking trails ranging from self-guided nature trails to moderately strenuous hikes along the Pacific Crest Trail. The angler can fish along the North, East and West Forks of the San Gabriel River. The San Dimas and San Gabriel Reservoirs are open to shoreline fishing only. There are no boating facilities.

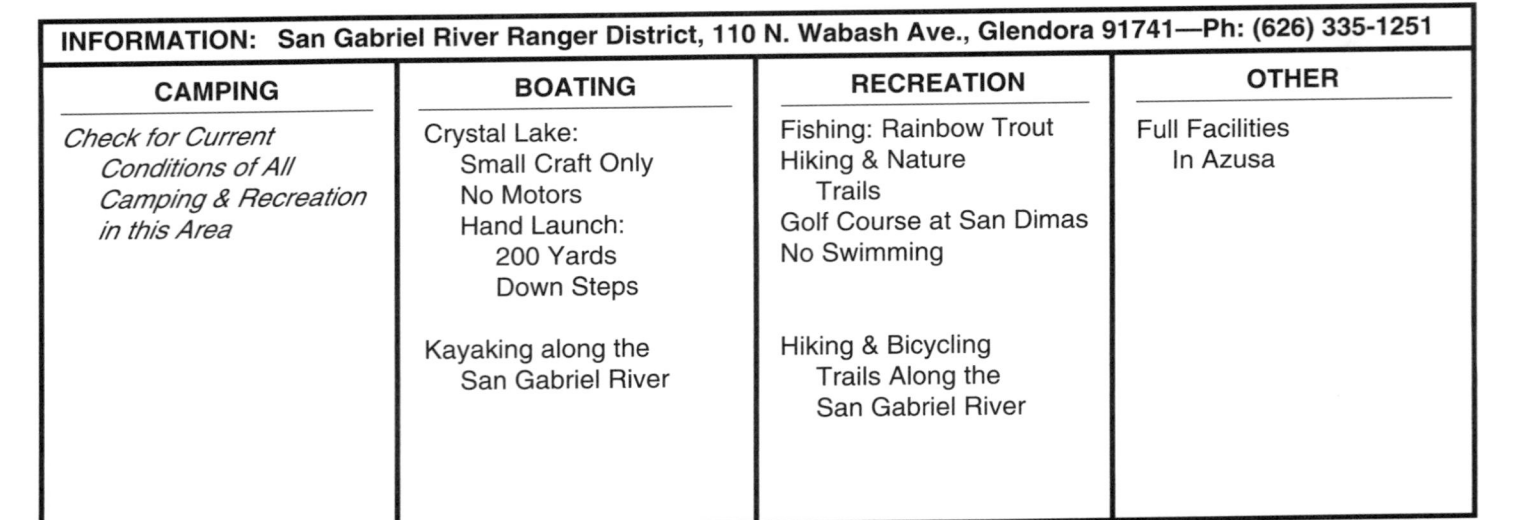

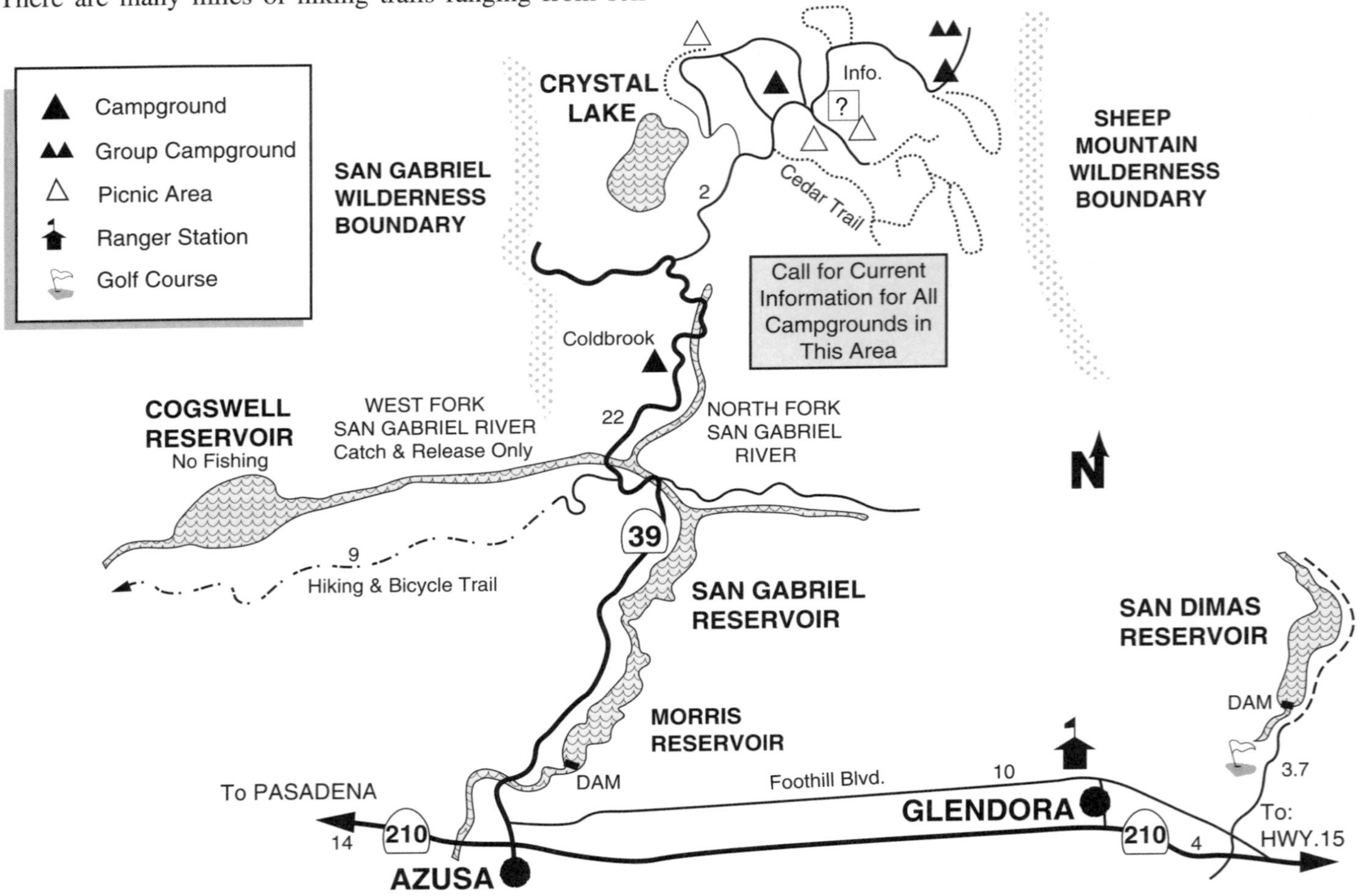
Campground
Group Campground
Picnic Area
Ranger Station
Golf Course
CRYSTAL LAKE
SAN GABRIEL WILDERNESS BOUNDARY
SHEEP MOUNTAIN WILDERNESS BOUNDARY
Info.
Cedar Trail
2
Call for Current Information for All Campgrounds in This Area
Coldbrook
22
COGSWELL RESERVOIR
No Fishing
WEST FORK SAN GABRIEL RIVER
Catch & Release Only
NORTH FORK SAN GABRIEL RIVER
N
39
9
Hiking & Bicycle Trail
SAN GABRIEL RESERVOIR
SAN DIMAS RESERVOIR
DAM
MORRIS RESERVOIR
DAM
3.7
Foothill Blvd.
10
To PASADENA
14
210
AZUSA
GLENDORA
210
4
To: HWY.15

INFORMATION: San Gabriel River Ranger District, 110 N. Wabash Ave., Glendora 91741—Ph: (626) 335-1251

CAMPING	BOATING	RECREATION	OTHER
Check for Current Conditions of All Camping & Recreation in this Area	Crystal Lake: Small Craft Only No Motors Hand Launch: 200 Yards Down Steps Kayaking along the San Gabriel River	Fishing: Rainbow Trout Hiking & Nature Trails Golf Course at San Dimas No Swimming Hiking & Bicycling Trails Along the San Gabriel River	Full Facilities In Azusa

ALONDRA PARK and HARBOR LAKE PARK

Alondra Park is an 84-acre urban park with a small 8-acre Lake for fishing and is under the jurisdiction of Los Angeles County. Boating is not allowed. There are picnic sites, community gardens and a playground. Ken Malloy Harbor Regional Park is under the jurisdiction of the City of Los Angeles. Boating is not allowed at this small lake. The angler can find largemouth bass, bluegill, perch and catfish. Picnic areas and a playground are part of the facilities. Harbor Lake Park is a wildlife sanctuary where a variety of plants, birds and animals can be observed in their natural habitats.

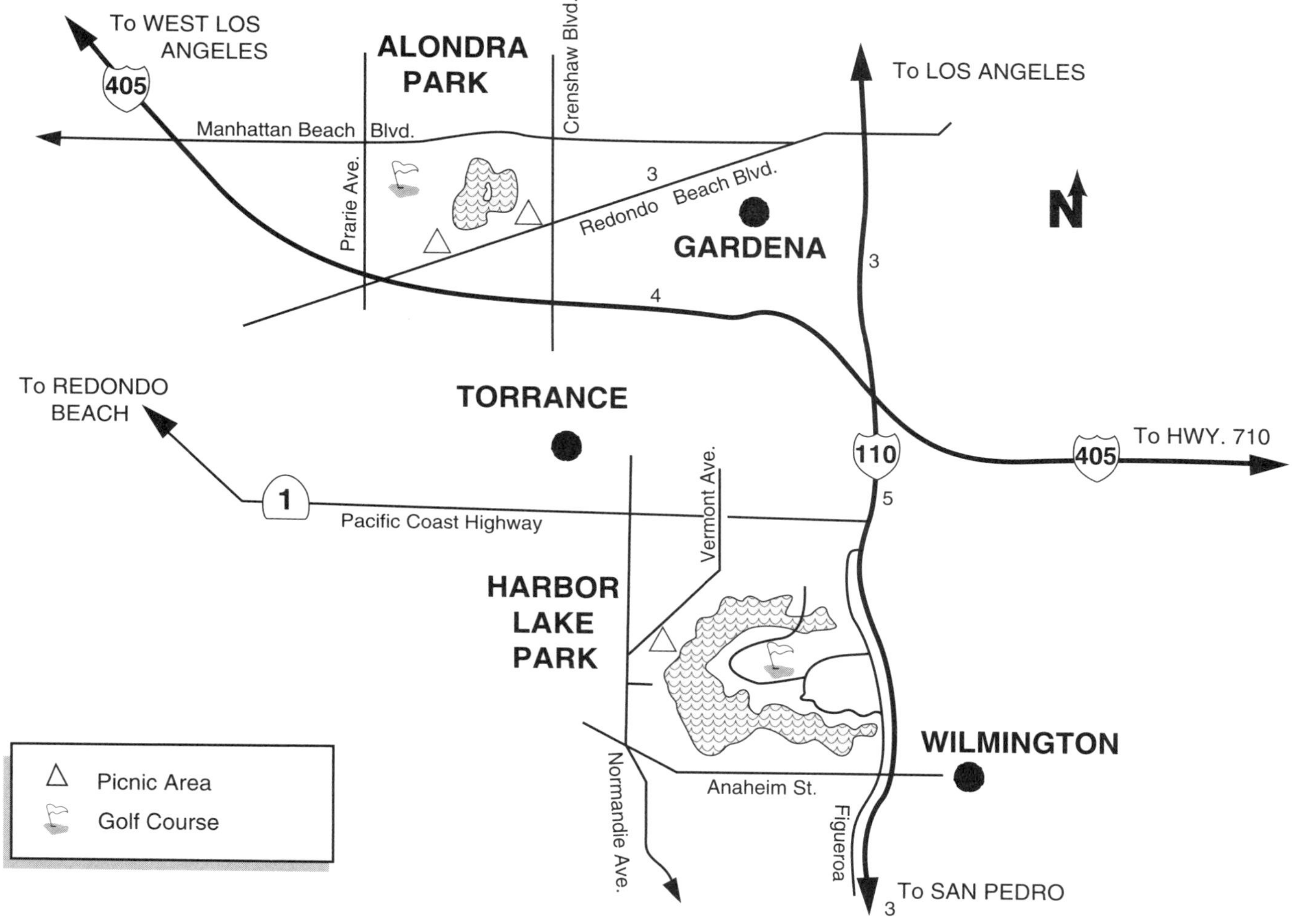

To WEST LOS ANGELES
405
ALONDRA PARK
Crenshaw Blvd.
To LOS ANGELES
Manhattan Beach Blvd.
Prarie Ave.
3
Redondo Beach Blvd.
GARDENA
N
3
4
To REDONDO BEACH
TORRANCE
110
405
To HWY. 710
1
Pacific Coast Highway
Vermont Ave.
5
HARBOR LAKE PARK
WILMINGTON
Anaheim St.
Normandie Ave.
Figueroa
To SAN PEDRO
3
Picnic Area
Golf Course

INFORMATION: Harbor Lake Park, 25820 S. Vermont Ave., Wilmington 90710—Ph: (310) 548-7728

CAMPING	BOATING	RECREATION	OTHER
Day Use Only No Camping Harbor Lake Park City of Los Angeles Alondra County Park 3850 W. Manhattan Beach Blvd. Lawndale 90260 Ph: (310) 217-8366	No Boating	Fishing: Largemouth Bass, Bluegill, Catfish & Perch Picnic Areas - Group Facilities Playgrounds Athletic Fields Nature Study Golf Courses Swimming Pools Only - Open in Summer Hiking & Bicycling Trails	Full Facilities Nearby

EL DORADO EAST REGIONAL PARK

El Dorado East is an urban park under the administration of the City of Long Beach. Nestled amid the rolling green hills of the park are 4 small Lakes totaling approximately 40 surface acres. There are no boats allowed except for rental boats and model boats. Fishing from the shore for trout and warm water species is often good. Individual and group picnic areas are available along with a network of paved trails for the bicycler and rollerskater. There is a fitness course for the casual jogger or serious runner. An 85-acre nature center with 2 miles of trails can also be enjoyed. The Olympic Archery Range is the finest in Southern California.

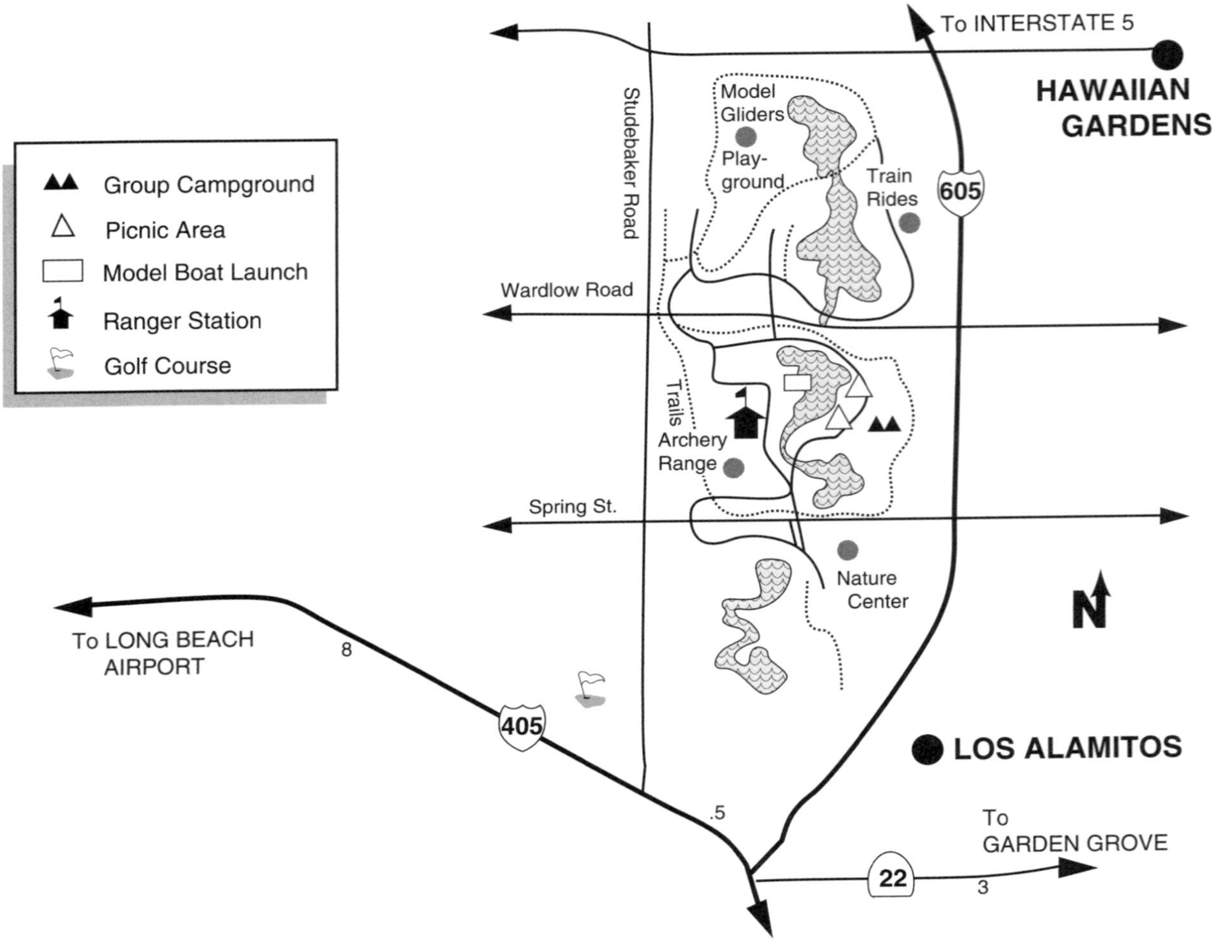

Group Campground
Picnic Area
Model Boat Launch
Ranger Station
Golf Course
To INTERSTATE 5
HAWAIIAN GARDENS
Studebaker Road
Model Gliders
Play-ground
Train Rides
605
Wardlow Road
Trails
Archery Range
Spring St.
Nature Center
N
To LONG BEACH AIRPORT
8
405
LOS ALAMITOS
.5
To GARDEN GROVE
22
3

INFORMATION: El Dorado East Regional Park, 7550 E. Spring St., Long Beach 90815—Ph: (562) 570-1773

CAMPING	BOATING	RECREATION	OTHER
Youth Group Camping Only Day Use Fees: Monday through Friday: $5 Saturday & Sunday: $7 Holidays: $8	No Private Boats Allowed Rentals: Pedal Boats Model Boats - Launch	Fishing: Trout in Winter, Bluegill, Catfish & Largemouth Bass, Picnicking - Group Sites Reservations: Ph: (562) 570-3111 Jogging, Skating & Bicycling Trails Fitness Course Playgrounds Nature Center & Trails *No Swimming*	Snack Bar Train Rides Pony Rides Petting Zoo Olympic Archery Range Full Facilities Nearby

PECK ROAD, SANTA FE and WHITTIER NARROWS

These three Los Angeles County Parks include fishing Lakes, picnic areas, hiking and bicycle trails. The 80-acre Lake at Peck Road Water Conservation Park has a fishing area and picnic tables but does not allow boating or swimming. Santa Fe Dam Park has a 70-acre Lake open to swimming and boats with no motors. There are also beaches, an equestrian staging area, a nature center and group picnic areas. Youth group camping is available at Santa Fe Dam. Three small Lakes, totaling 76.5 surface acres, are within Whittier Narrows Regional Park. This 1,400-acre multipurpose Park has a nature center, skeet and trap shooting range, archery range, model hobby areas, BMX track, athletic fields, equestrian area, golf course, lighted tennis courts and group picnic areas. There is no private boating or swimming at this Lake but you can rent pedal boats.

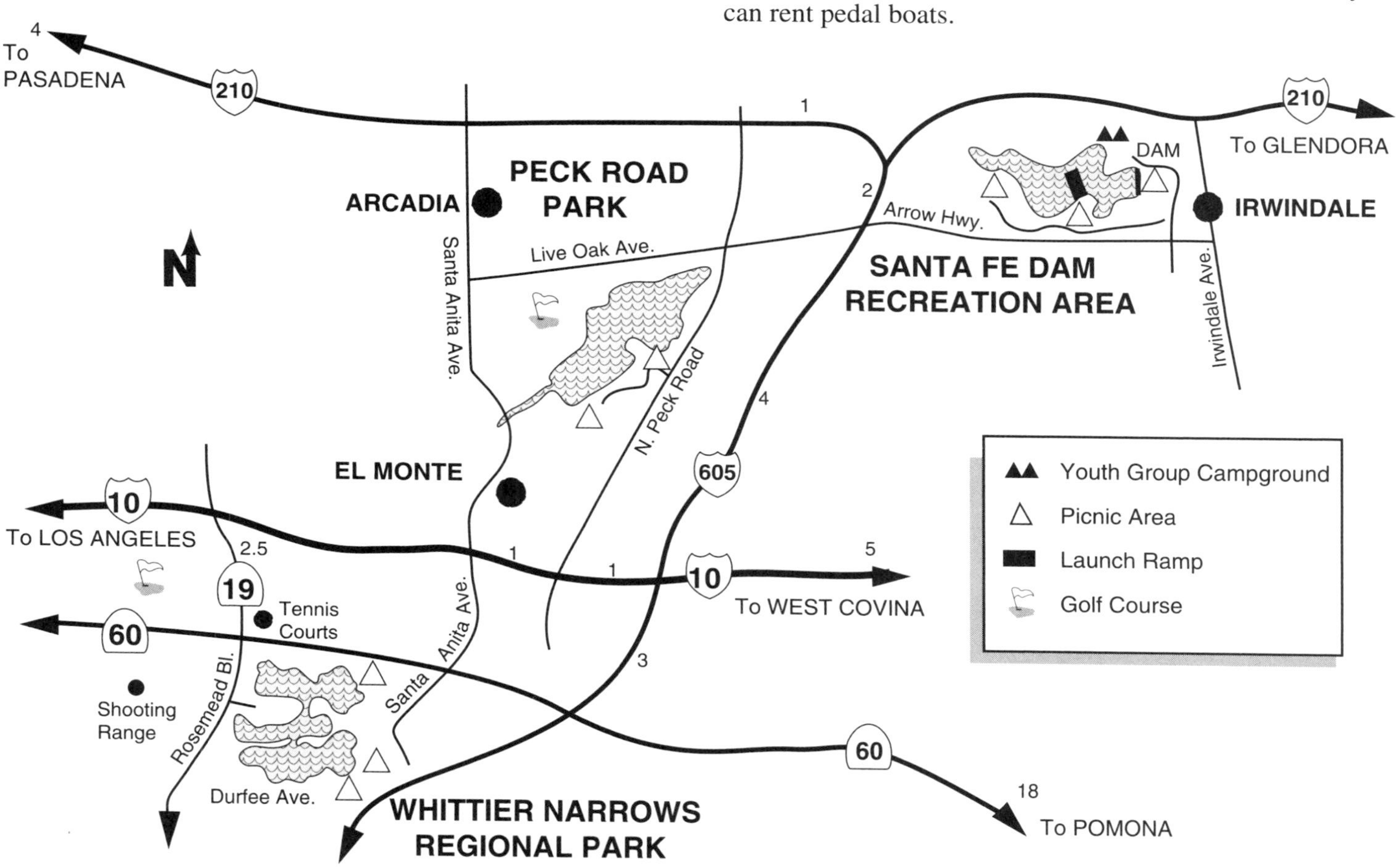

4
To PASADENA
210
1
210
To GLENDORA
DAM
PECK ROAD PARK
ARCADIA
2
Arrow Hwy.
IRWINDALE
Santa Anita Ave.
Live Oak Ave.
SANTA FE DAM RECREATION AREA
Irwindale Ave.
N
N. Peck Road
4
EL MONTE
605
Youth Group Campground
Picnic Area
Launch Ramp
Golf Course
10
To LOS ANGELES
2.5
1
1
10
5
To WEST COVINA
19
Tennis Courts
60
Anita Ave.
Shooting Range
Rosemead Bl.
Santa
3
60
Durfee Ave.
18
To POMONA
WHITTIER NARROWS REGIONAL PARK

INFORMATION: L. A. County Parks & Recreation, 433 S. Vermont, Los Angeles 90020—Ph: (213) 738-2961

CAMPING	BOATING	RECREATION	OTHER
Whittier Narrows 823 Lexington-Gallatin Rd. S. El Monte 91733 Ph: (626) 575-5525 Day Use: $4 Picnic Reservations: Ph: (626) 575-5600 Youth Group Camping: Santa Fe Dam Recreation Area	Peck Road: No Boating Santa Fe: Small Boats No Motors Launch Ramp Rental Boats Whittier Narrows: No Private Boats Rentals: Pedal Boats	Fishing: Trout in Winter, Largemouth Bass, Bluegill, Crappie & Catfish Picnicking Whittier Narrows & Santa Fe Group Picnic Areas Hiking, Bicycle & Equestrian Trails Athletic Fields Skeet & Trap, Archery Golf Courses, Tennis Courts Model Hobby Areas	Nature Center at Whittier Narrows Santa Fe Dam Rec. Area 15501 E. Arrow Hwy. Irwindale 91706 Ph: (626) 334-1065 Water Play Area Peck Road Park 5401 N. Peck Rd. Arcadia 91006 Ph: (626) 812-6377 Fishing Licenses Required at All Facilities

SILVERWOOD LAKE

Silverwood State Recreation Area is located in the San Bernardino Mountains at an elevation of 3,350 feet, making it the highest reservoir in the State Water Project. This is a popular recreation Lake with a surface area of 1,000 acres and 13 miles of shoreline. The Lake is open to all types of boating. Several brushy areas were left uncleared when filling the Lake which has provided a natural fish habitat. The angler will find a varied fishery with trophy-size largemouth and striped bass. 10 miles of paved trails are available for the hiker and bicyclist. The Pacific Crest Trail passes through this area. Reservations are highly recommended at this scenic facility. In addition to the oak-shaded campsites at Silverwood, the camper will find sites at nearby Mojave River Forks.

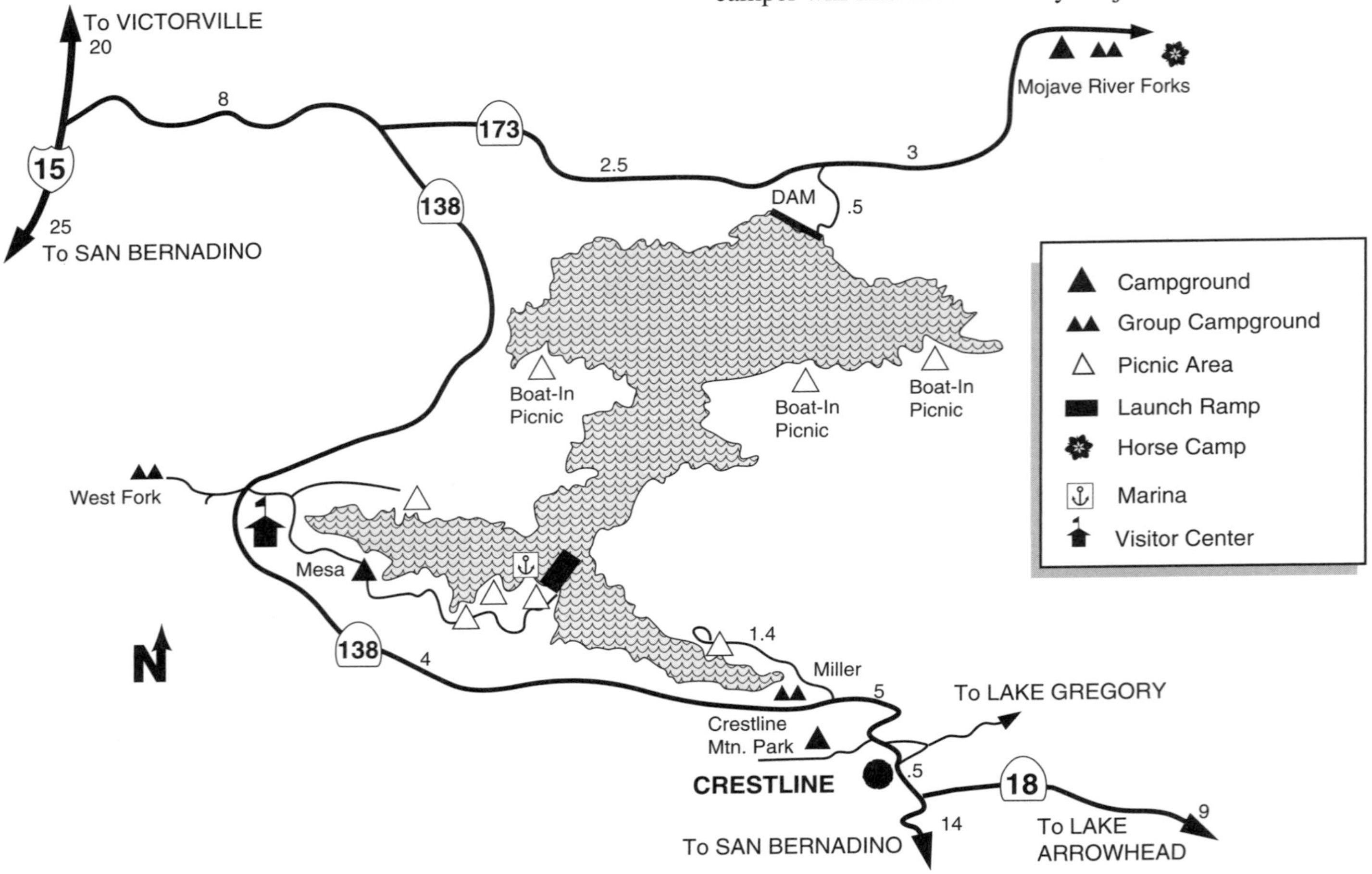
To VICTORVILLE
20
8
15
25
To SAN BERNADINO
173
138
2.5
3
Mojave River Forks
DAM
.5
Campground
Group Campground
Picnic Area
Launch Ramp
Horse Camp
Marina
Visitor Center
Boat-In
Picnic
Boat-In
Picnic
Boat-In
Picnic
West Fork
Mesa
N
138
4
1.4
Miller
5
To LAKE GREGORY
Crestline
Mtn. Park
CRESTLINE
.5
18
9
To LAKE
ARROWHEAD
14
To SAN BERNADINO

INFORMATION: State Recreation Area, 14651 Cedar Circle, Hesperia 92345—Ph: (760) 389-2303

CAMPING	BOATING	RECREATION	OTHER
136 Dev. Sites for Tents & R.V.s to 32 Feet Fee: $20 - $25 No Hookups Group Sites: To 120 People Disposal Station 7 Bike-In or Hike-In Sites Reserve: Ph: (800) 444-7275 Reservations Highly Recommended Summer Weekends Day Use Fee: $8	Power, Row, Canoe, Sail, Waterski, PWCs & Windsurf Speed Limit - 35 MPH Designated Boating Zones Boat Inspection Launch Ramp - Fee: $8 Rentals: Fishing Boats Docks, Berths Number of Boats Limited: Reservations Recommended	Fishing: Rainbow Trout, Catfish, Bluegill, Trophy Largemouth & Striped Bass Swimming - Beaches Picnicking Hiking & Bicycling Trails Visitor Center Campfire Programs Winter Bald Eagle Boat Tours: Contact Park for Reservations	Snack Bar Grocery Store Bait & Tackle Disposal Station Mojave River Forks R.V. Campground 18107 Highway 173 Hesperia 92345 Ph: (760) 389-2322 80 Dev. Sites for Tents & R.V.s Group Campground

Lake Gregory is part of the San Bernardino County Regional Park System. Located at an elevation of 4,520 feet in the San Bernardino Mountains near Crestline, this popular day-use area has a variety of water-related activities within the 150-acre Park. Sandy swim beaches, picnic areas, snack bars, a 300-foot waterslide and a boat house are included in these facilities. Boating is limited to rentals. The fish habitat is enhanced by an aeration system. In addition to the warm water species and rainbow trout, Lake Gregory is stocked with brown trout. This is a nice family park with full facilities in the village and nearby Crestline.

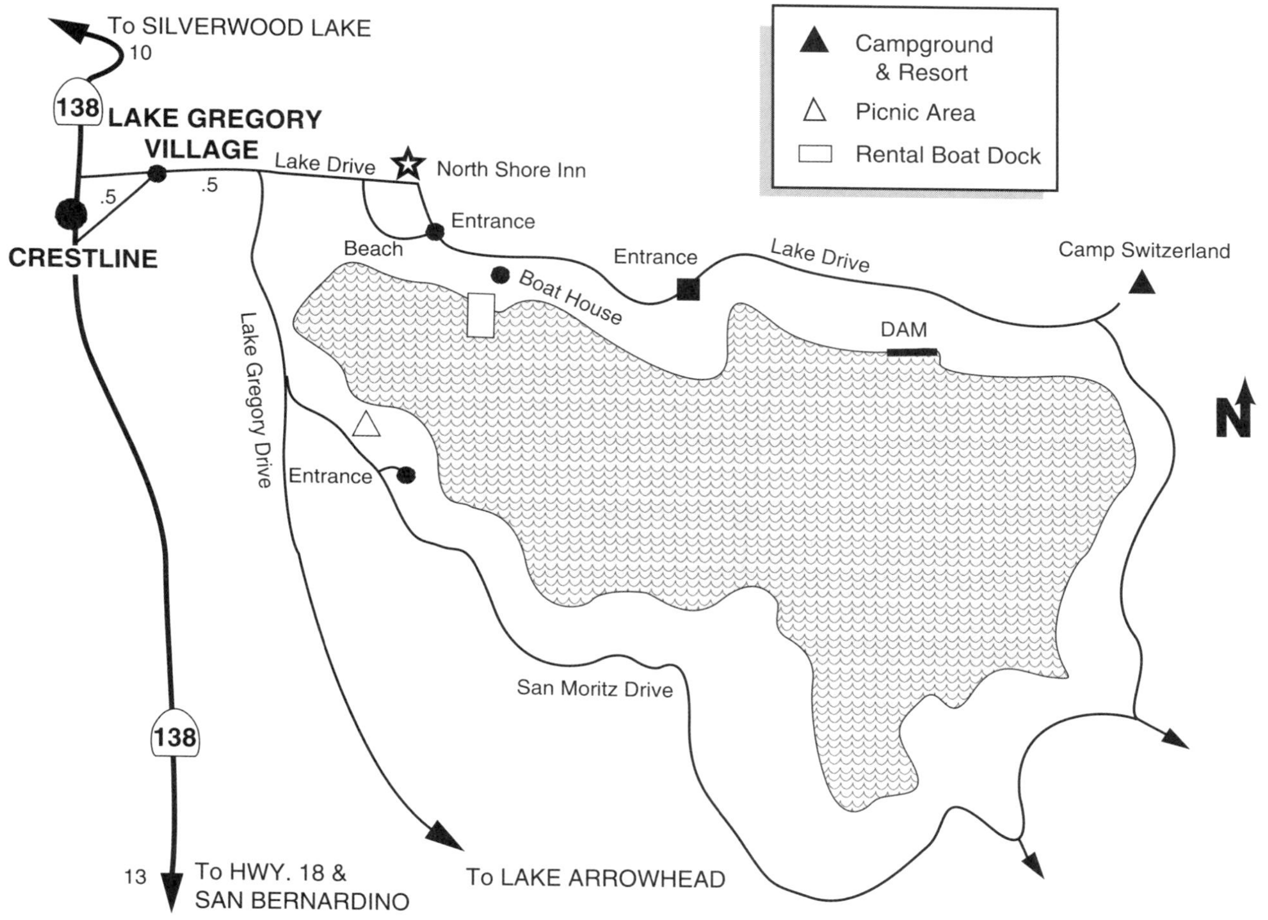
To SILVERWOOD LAKE
10
138
LAKE GREGORY VILLAGE
Lake Drive
North Shore Inn
.5
.5
CRESTLINE
Entrance
Beach
Boat House
Entrance
Lake Drive
Camp Switzerland
DAM
Lake Gregory Drive
Entrance
San Moritz Drive
138
13
To HWY. 18 &
SAN BERNARDINO
To LAKE ARROWHEAD
Campground & Resort
Picnic Area
Rental Boat Dock
N

INFORMATION: Lake Gregory, P.O. Box 656, 24171 Lake Dr., Crestline 92325—Ph: (909) 338-2233

CAMPING	BOATING	RECREATION	OTHER
Camp Switzerland P.O. Box 967 24558 Lake Dr. Crestline 92325 Ph: (909) 338-2731 40 Tent & R.V. Sites Full Hookups Cabins Call for Current Fees Reservations Advised	No Private Boats Rentals Only: Row Boats, Pedal Boats Water Bikes & Paddleboards You Can Bring Your Own Electric Motor For Use on Rental Boat	Fishing: Rainbow & Brown Trout, Largemouth Bass, Crappie, Bullhead & Channel Catfish Picnicking Swim Beaches in Season Fee: $3 Hiking Trails Volleyball Court Waterslide Fee: $6 All Day	Snack Bars Bait & Tackle Special Events Trout Derbies Conference Facilities Pets Allowed on Leash Except at Swim Beaches Full Facilities Nearby North Shore Inn: Ph: (909) 338-5230 Accommodations Overlooking Lake

ARROWHEAD, GREEN VALLEY, ARROWBEAR and JENKS LAKES

These Lakes are nestled high in the San Bernardino National Forest with elevations ranging from 5,100 feet at Lake Arrowhead to 7,200 feet at Green Valley Lake. Arrowhead Village is located in an alpine setting and has numerous accomodations. Arrowhead Lake is privately owned and not open to the public. The Forest Service has a number of campgrounds throughout this scenic area. There are many hiking and equestrian trails, especially near Jenks Lake and the San Gorgonio Wilderness Area. Green Valley is a small Lake for fishing, swimming and has non-powered rental boats. Arrowbear is a small fishing Lake which is stocked annually with trout.

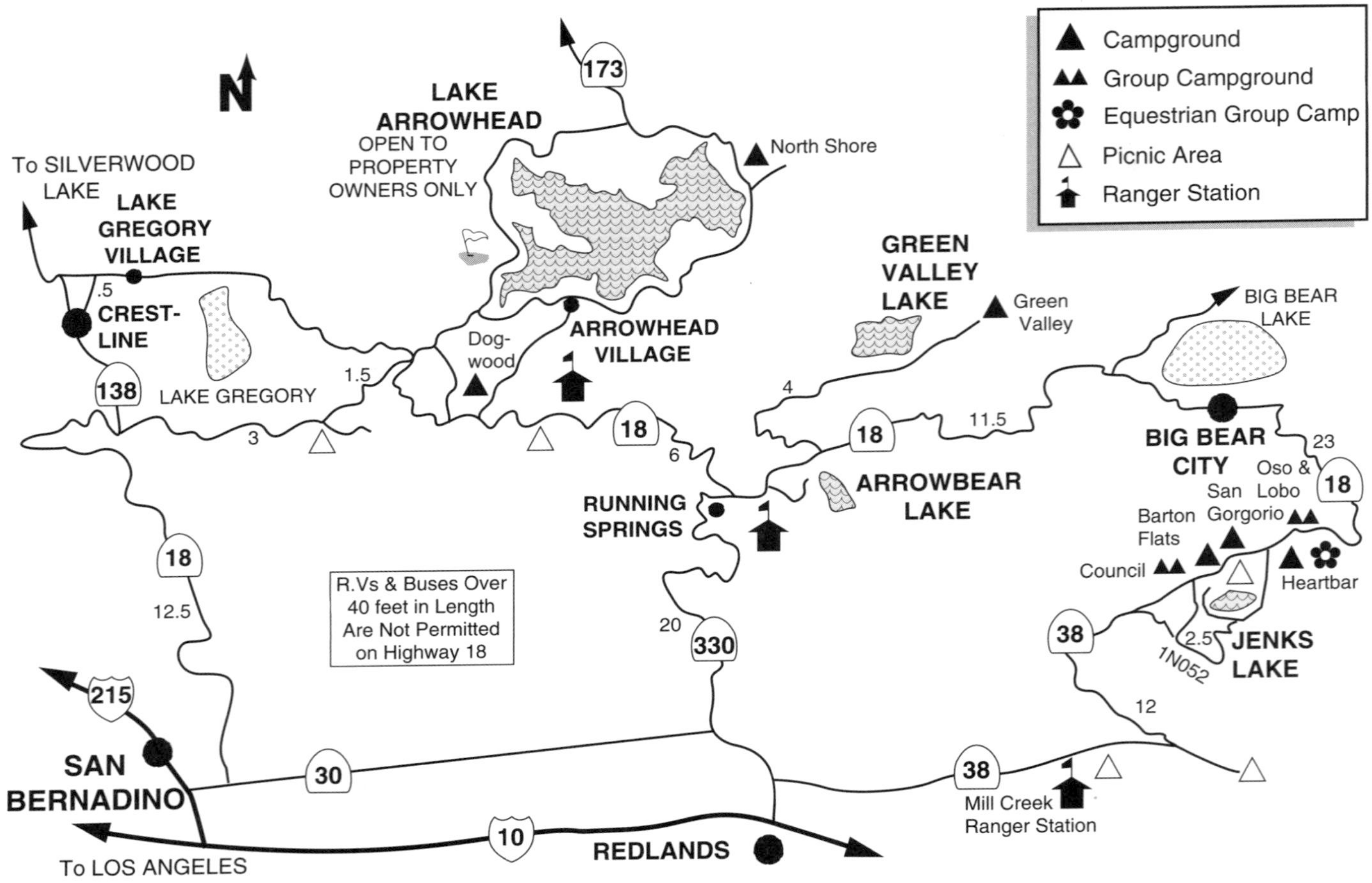
N
LAKE ARROWHEAD
OPEN TO PROPERTY OWNERS ONLY
North Shore
To SILVERWOOD LAKE
LAKE GREGORY VILLAGE
.5
CREST-LINE
LAKE GREGORY
138
1.5
3
Dog-wood
ARROWHEAD VILLAGE
18
6
173
GREEN VALLEY LAKE
Green Valley
4
18
11.5
ARROWBEAR LAKE
RUNNING SPRINGS
BIG BEAR LAKE
BIG BEAR CITY
23
Oso & Lobo
San Gorgonio
18
Barton Flats
Council
Heartbar
38
2.5
JENKS LAKE
1N052
12
18
12.5
R.Vs & Buses Over 40 feet in Length Are Not Permitted on Highway 18
20
330
215
SAN BERNADINO
30
38
Mill Creek Ranger Station
10
REDLANDS
To LOS ANGELES
Campground
Group Campground
Equestrian Group Camp
Picnic Area
Ranger Station

INFORMATION: Arrowhead Ranger District, 28104 Highway 18, Skyforest 92385—Ph: (909) 382-2782

CAMPING	BOATING	RECREATION	OTHER
Dev. Tent & R.V. Sites: Dogwood: 93 Sites North Shore: 27 Sites Green Valley: 36 Sites Barton Flats: 52 Sites San Gorgonio: 54 Sites Fees: $17 to $31 Group Sites at: Council, Oso, Lobo Heartbar Equestrian Camp Reservations: Ph: (877) 444-6777	Arrowhead: Closed to the Public - Property Owners Only Green Valley: Non-Power Rentals Arrowbear: No Boating Jenks: Non-Power Hand Launch Down Stairs Check All Lakes for Current Conditions	Fishing: Rainbow & Brown Trout, Smallmouth Bass, Kokanee Salmon, Catfish & Bluegill Picnicking Swimming - Beaches Hiking & Equestrian Trails Horse Rentals	Lake Arrowhead Resort & Spa Ph: (909) 336-1511 Luxury Rooms, Restaurant, Pool, Private Beach Special Events Resorts & Other Facilities Nearby

BIG BEAR LAKE

Big Bear Lake is one of California's most popular recreation Lakes. Located in the San Bernardino National Forest at an elevation of 6,743 feet, this beautiful mountain Lake is just two hours from downtown Los Angeles. Originally created in 1884 by a single arch dam and enlarged by the 1911 multiple arch dam, Big Bear Lake now covers 3,000 surface acres. The Lake is over 7 miles long and has a shoreline of 22 miles. Lake management is maintained by the Big Bear Municipal Water District. All types of boating are permitted, subject to size restrictions and a valid Lake Use permit which can be obtained at most marinas. In addition to the many Forest Service campsites, there are extensive private facilities at this complete destination resort area.

....Continued....

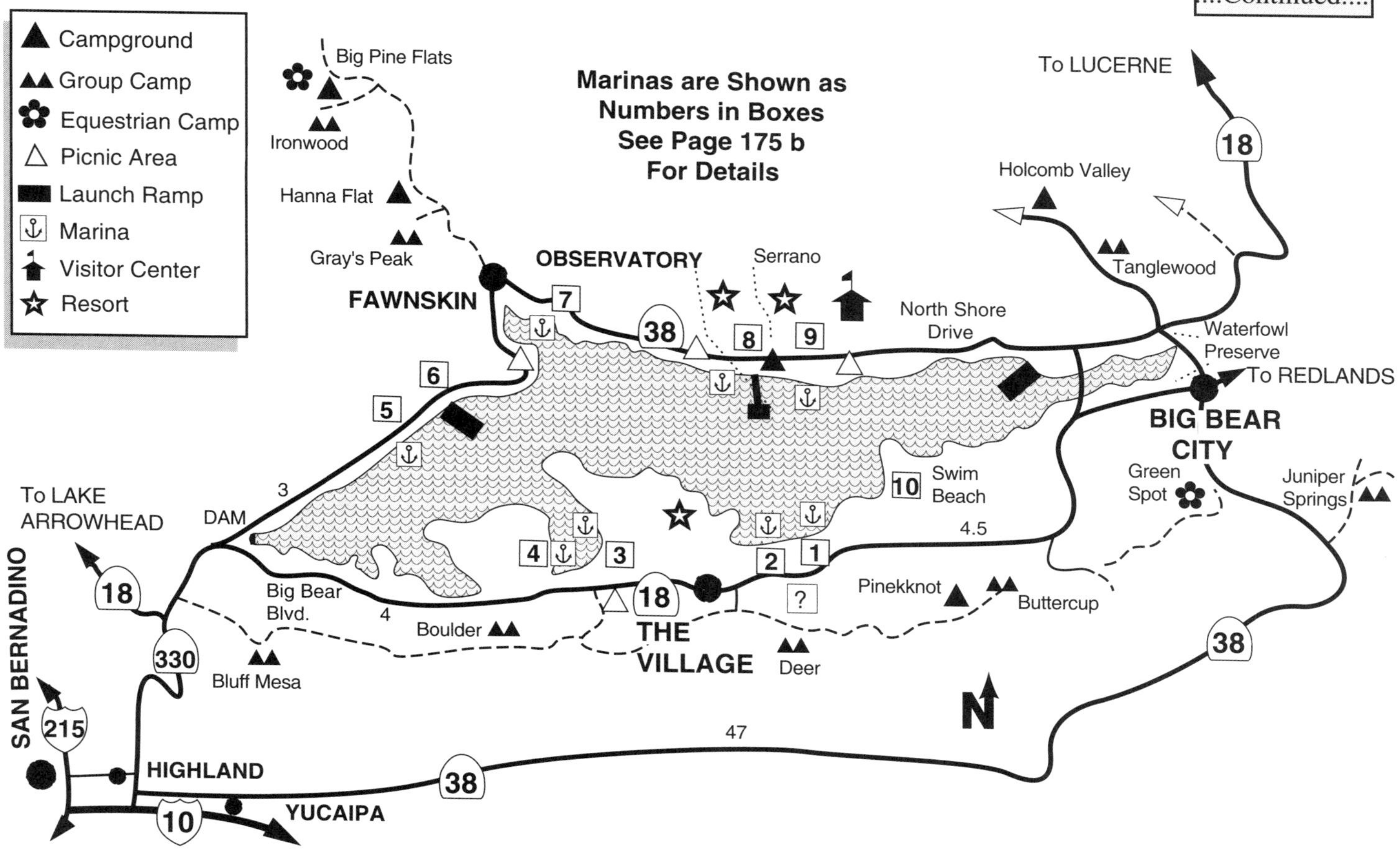

Campground
Group Camp
Equestrian Camp
Picnic Area
Launch Ramp
Marina
Visitor Center
Resort
Big Pine Flats
Ironwood
Hanna Flat
Gray's Peak
FAWNSKIN
Marinas are Shown as Numbers in Boxes See Page 175 b For Details
To LUCERNE
18
Holcomb Valley
Tanglewood
OBSERVATORY
Serrano
North Shore Drive
Waterfowl Preserve
To REDLANDS
BIG BEAR CITY
Green Spot
Juniper Springs
Swim Beach
To LAKE ARROWHEAD
DAM
Big Bear Blvd.
Boulder
Pinekknot
Buttercup
THE VILLAGE
Deer
Bluff Mesa
SAN BERNADINO
HIGHLAND
YUCAIPA
330
215
10
38
47
4.5
N

INFORMATION: Mountaintop Ranger District, 41397 North Shore Dr., Fawnskin 92333—Ph (909) 382-2790			
CAMPING	**BOATING**	**RECREATION**	**OTHER**
U.S. Forest Service: Numerous Sites for Tents & R.V.s Group Camp Sites Equestrian Camps Remote Area Camping *See Following Pages*	Open to All Boating Subject to Length Maximum 26 Feet Valid Lake Permit Required - Check at Marinas 35 MPH Speed Limit Full Service Marinas Launch Ramps Berths, Docks, Storage Rentals: Power, Sail, Waterski, Fishing, Sailboard & PWCs	Fishing: Trout, Bass, Channel Catfish, Bluegill, Carp & Crappie Swimming Picnicking Hiking, Bicycling & Equestrian Trails Horse Rentals Boat Tours	Golf & Tennis Complete Resort Facilities *See Following Pages for Information*

BIG BEAR LAKE............Continued

U.S. FOREST SERVICE
FAMILY CAMPGROUNDS
Some Road Diversions-Check for Current Information

BIG PINE FLATS - 7 Miles NW of Fawnskin on Forest Service Rd. 3N14 - 19 Tent & R.V. Sites to 30 ft. - *Fee: $18.*

HOLCOMB VALLEY - 4 Miles North on 2N09 to 3N16 East for 3/4 Mile - 19 Tent & R.V. Sites to 25 ft., Pack-In, Pack-Out, No Water - *Fee: $14*

The Following Sites can be Reserved: - Ph: (877) 444-6777

HANNA FLAT - 2-1/2 Miles NW of Fawnskin on Forest Service Rd. 3N14 - 88 Tent & R.V. Sites to 40 ft. - *Fee: $22.*

PINEKNOT - South on Summit Blvd., off Big Bear Blvd. - 52 Tent & R.V. Sites to 45 ft. - *Fee: $21.*

SERRANO - North Shore Lane off Highway 38 - 2 Miles East of Fawnskin - 132 Tent & R.V. Sites to 55 ft. - Disposal Station - *Fees: $26 - $36.*

GROUP CAMPGROUNDS for Tents & R.V.s
(Some Dirt Roads)

BLUFF MESA - Off 2N10 - 40 People, 8 Vehicles Max., No Water - *Fee: $66.*
BOULDER - Off 2N10 - 40 People, 8 Vehicles Max., No Water - *Fee: $66.*
BUTTERCUP - Near Pine Knot - 40 People, 8 Vehicles Max., - *Fee: $99.*
DEER - Off 2N10 - 40 People, 8 Vehicles Max., No Water - *Fee: $66.*
GRAY'S PEAK - Off 3N14 - 40 People, 10 Vehicles Max., No Water - *Fee: $75.*
IRONWOOD - Off 3N97 - 25 People, 5 Vehicles Max., No Water, *Fee: $75.*
JUNIPER SPRINGS - Off 2N01 - 40 People, 8 Vehicles Max., - *Fee: $60.*
ROUND VALLEY - Off 2NO1 - 15 People, 3 Vehicles Max., - *Fee: Free.*
TANGLEWOOD - Off 3N15 - 40 People, 8 Vehicles Max., No Water - *Fee: $75.*

EQUESTRIAN CAMPGROUNDS
BIG PINE FLAT - Near Fawnskin -To 25 People, Water - *Fee: $75.*
GREEN SPOT - Off 2N93 -To 25 People, No Water - *Fee: $50.*

LAKE INFORMATION
Big Bear Municipal Water District
40524 Lakeview Dr.
P. O. Box 2863
Big Bear Lake 92315
Ph: (909) 866-5796

GENERAL INFORMATION
Big Bear Chamber of Commerce
P. O. Box 2860
Big Bear Lake 92315
Ph: (909) 866-4607

VISITOR & LODGING INFORMATION:
Big Bear Lake Resort Association
630 Bartlett Rd.
Big Bear Lake 92315
Ph: (800) 4-BIGBEAR

CAMPING/HIKING INFORMATION:
Big Bear Discovery Center
40971 North Shore Dr.
P. O. Box 66
Fawnskin 92333
Ph: (909) 866-3437

....Continued....

PRIVATE CAMPGROUNDS - *Phone for Current Fees*

LIGHTHOUSE TRAILER RESORT AND MARINA
(Also See Marine Facilities)
40545 North Shore Drive - Adjacent to the Observatory Access
Ph: (909) 866-9464 - 88 R.V. Sites, Full Hookups, Store.

BIG BEAR SHORES R.V. RESORT & YACHT CLUB
(Also See Marine Facilities)
East of Lighthouse Marina
Ph: (909) 866-4151 - 170 Deluxe R.V. Sites, Full Hookups, Lodge, Pool, Spa.

HOLLOWAY'S MARINA AND R.V. PARK
(Also See Marine Facilities)
398 Edgemoor Road in Metcalf Bay - Ph: (800) 448-5335 or (909) 866-5706
66 Sites for Tents & R.V.s, Full Hookups, Store.

MUNICIPAL WATER DISTRICT R.V. PARK
West of "The Village" on Lakeview Drive
Ph: (909) 866-5796 - 25 R.V. Sites, Full Hookups, Walking Distance to Shops.

MARINE FACILITIES - Boxed Numbers Shown on Map - BOAT PERMITS REQUIRED FOR LAKE USE

1. **PINE KNOT LANDING MARINA** - Ph: (909) 866-2628 or 866-9512
Docks, Moorings, Ramp, Storage, Bait & Tackle, Store, Tours. Rentals: Fishing Boats, Pontoons, Canoes & Kayaks.

2. **BIG BEAR MARINA** - Ph: (909) 866-3218
Docks, Moorings, Ramp, Gas, Storage, Bait & Tackle, Permits. Rentals: Fishing Boats, Waterski, Canoes, Kayaks, Pontoons, PWCs - Big Bear Queen Lake Tours.

3. **HOLLOWAY'S R.V. PARK & MARINA** - Ph: (800) 448-5335 or (909) 866-5706
Docks, Moorings, Ramp, Gas, Bait & Tackle, Groceries, Permits. Rentals: Fishing & Paddle Boats, Waterski, Canoes & Kayaks, Pontoons, PWCs.

4. **PLEASURE POINT LANDING** - Ph: (909) 866-2455
Docks, Moorings, Ramp, Gas, Bait & Tackle, Boat Permits, Boat Storage, Snack Bar, Rentals: Fishing Boats, Pontoons & Canoes, Pirate Ship Boat Tours..

5. **NORTH SHORE LANDING** - Ph: (909) 878-4386
Moorings, Dock, Snacks, Bait & Tackle. Rentals: Fishing Boats, Sailboats, Waterski, Wakeboards, PWCs.

6. **MWD EAST & WEST LAUNCH** - Ph: (909) 866-5796
Boat Permits, Free Launch Ramp, Day Use Area.

7. **CAPTAIN JOHN'S FAWN HARBOR** - Ph: (909) 866-6478
Moorings, Snacks, Bait & Tackle. Rentals: Fishing Boats, Sailboats, Canoes & Kayaks, Pontoons.

8. **LIGHTHOUSE TRAILER RESORT & MARINA**- Ph: (909) 866-9464
Docks, Moorings, Snacks, Bait & Tackle, Propane. Rentals: Fishing Boats, Pontoons.

9. **BIG BEAR SHORES & R.V. RESORT**- Ph: (909) 878-4386
Launch Ramp, Moorings, Docks, Rentals: Fishing Boats, Pontoon Boats.

10. **MEADOW PARK SWIM BEACH** - Ph: (909) 866-9700
Park Avenue Near Knight Ave., Public Swimming Area with Slide & Raft, Snack Bar, Picnic Tables, BBQ's.

PUDDINGSTONE LAKE

Puddingstone Lake is at an elevation of 940 feet within the 2,000 acre Frank G. Bonelli Regional Park. This complete recreation facility is administered by the Department of Parks and Recreation of Los Angeles County. The 250 surface acre Lake has good marina facilities and is open to all boating. The angler will find trout and a warm water fishery. This well landscaped park has picnic areas, a swim beach and multi-purpose trails. There is an Equestrian Center and riding trails throughout the park. Raging Waters is a large water theme park near the dam at Puddingstone Lake. The East Shore R.V. Park and Campground is a complete facility with extensive services and recreation activities.

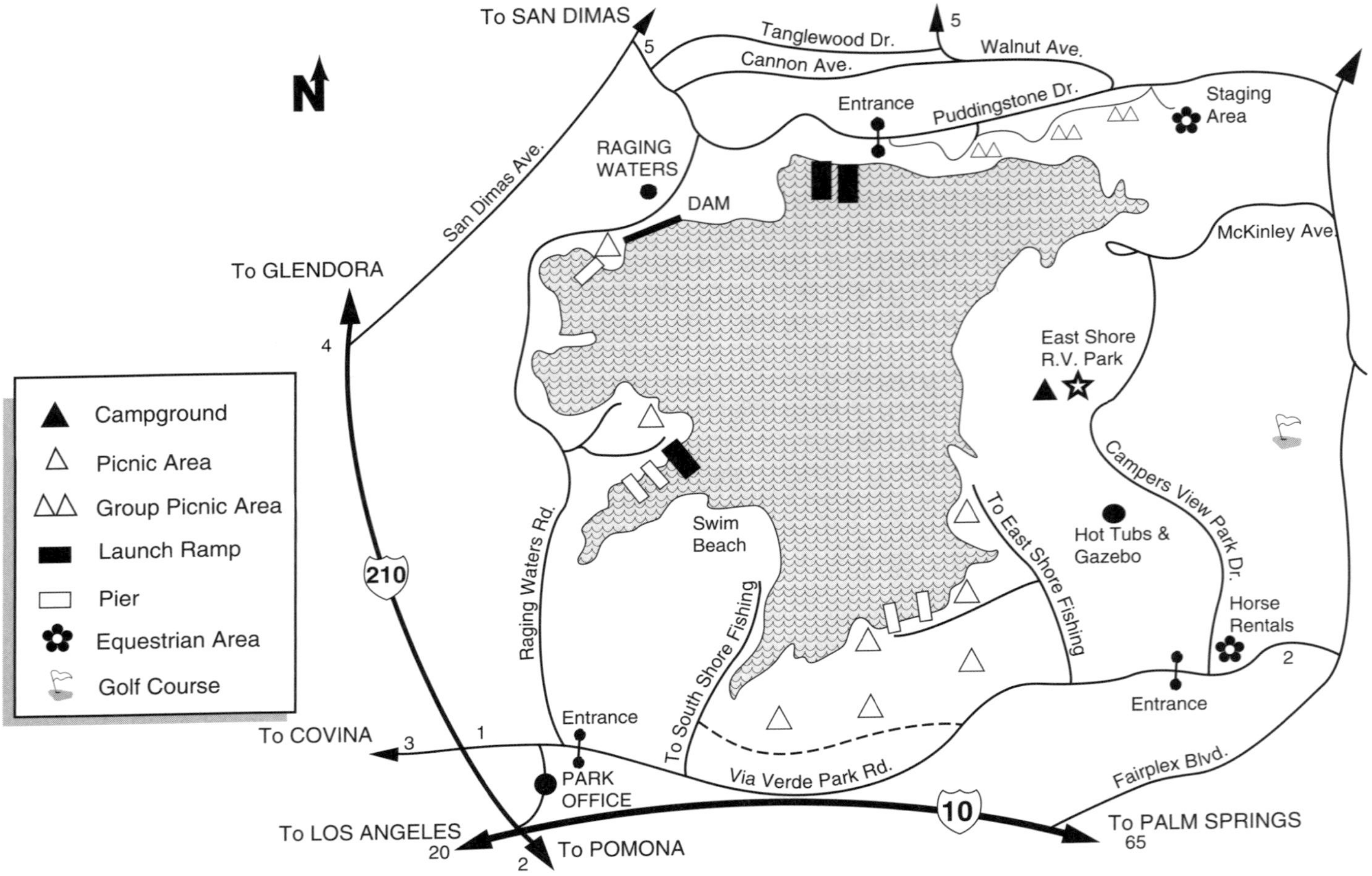
To SAN DIMAS
5
Tanglewood Dr.
5
Walnut Ave.
Cannon Ave.
Entrance
Puddingstone Dr.
Staging Area
N
RAGING WATERS
DAM
San Dimas Ave.
To GLENDORA
4
McKinley Ave.
East Shore R.V. Park
Campground
Picnic Area
Group Picnic Area
Launch Ramp
Pier
Equestrian Area
Golf Course
Campers View Park Dr.
Swim Beach
Raging Waters Rd.
210
To East Shore Fishing
Hot Tubs & Gazebo
Horse Rentals
To South Shore Fishing
2
Entrance
To COVINA
3
1
Entrance
PARK OFFICE
Via Verde Park Rd.
Fairplex Blvd.
10
To LOS ANGELES
20
2
To POMONA
To PALM SPRINGS
65

INFORMATION: Frank R. Bonelli Regional County Park, 120 E. Via Verde, San Dimas 91773—Ph: (909) 599-8411

CAMPING	BOATING	RECREATION	OTHER
East Shore R.V. Park 1440 Camper View Rd. San Dimas 91773 Ph: (909) 599-8355 519 Dev. Sites for R.V.s with Full Hookups $39 to $47 Group Camp Sites 25 Dev. sites for Tents Disposal Station Swimming Pool, Rec. Room Store, Bait & Tackle Reservations Accepted	Open to All Boating All Boats Must be 8 Feet Minimum to 26 Feet Maximum Power Boats Must be 12 Feet Minimum Call for Designated Boat Use Days Launch Ramps Boat Permits: $6 - $10 Rentals: Fishing Boats	Fishing: Trout, Bass, Bluegill, Crappie, Perch & Caffish Picnicking Day Use - $8 Group Picnic Areas by Reservation Hiking & Equestrian Trails Equestrian Center: Ph: (909) 599-8830 Horse Boarding Roping Arena Golf Course Nearby	Snack Bar Hot Tubs: 1 - 100 People & Gazebo Area for Private Parties Ph: (909) 592-2222 Raging Waters: Ph: (909) 802-2200 Water Slides, Wave Pool, Rapids, Kiddy Pool

Lake Perris State Recreation Area is the southern terminus of the California Water Project. The Lake's 2,200 surface acres are surrounded by rocky mountains towering to more than a thousand feet above the water's surface. Alessandro Island, rising to 230 feet, is a favorite boat-in picnic area. The complete recreation park provides an enormous number of activities and facilities. Fishing is good from boat or shore. This is a popular Lake for waterskiing, windsurfing, sailing and fishing. Speed zones are designated. The hiker, bicycler and equestrian will find extensive trails. There are also rock climbing and scuba diving areas. Camping reservations are recommended.

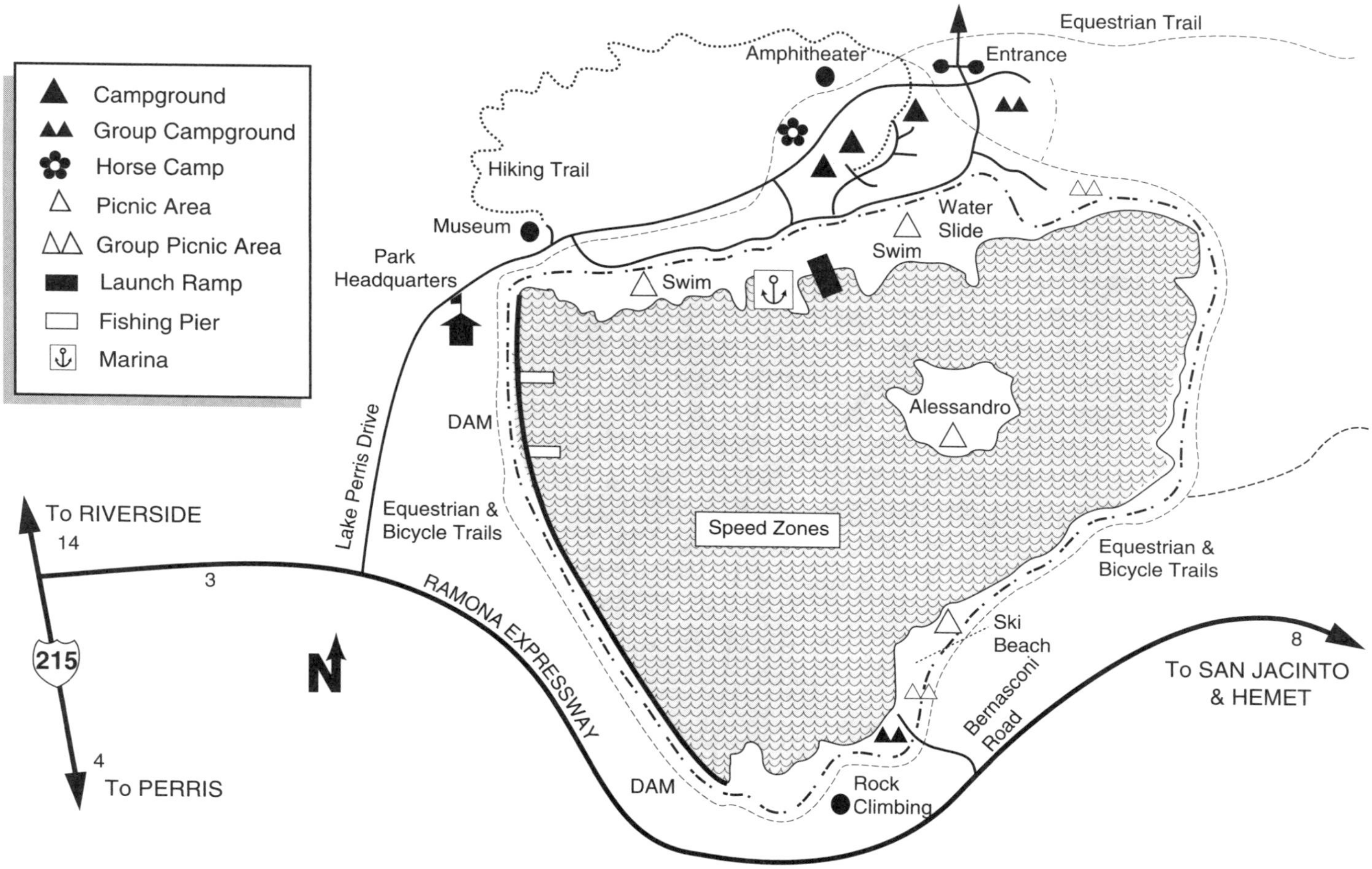
Campground
Group Campground
Horse Camp
Picnic Area
Group Picnic Area
Launch Ramp
Fishing Pier
Marina
Equestrian Trail
Entrance
Amphitheater
Hiking Trail
Museum
Park Headquarters
Water Slide
Swim
Swim
DAM
Alessandro
Lake Perris Drive
Equestrian & Bicycle Trails
Speed Zones
To RIVERSIDE
14
3
215
RAMONA EXPRESSWAY
N
Equestrian & Bicycle Trails
Ski Beach
8
To SAN JACINTO & HEMET
Bernasconi Road
4
To PERRIS
DAM
Rock Climbing

INFORMATION: State Recreation Area, 17801 Lake Perris Dr., Perris 92571—Ph: (951) 940-5600

CAMPING	BOATING	RECREATION	OTHER
167 Dev. Sites for Tents & R.V.s Fee: $20 - $25 264 R.V. Sites to 31 Feet with Water & Electric Hookups - Fee: $29 - $34 Disposal Station Pets Allowed Reservations: Ph: (800) 444-7275 6 Group Campgrounds - 25 to 100 People Each Horse Camps - Fee: $21	Open to All Boating 5 MPH & 35 MPH Designated Zones Reservations for Boating Suggested in Peak Season Check for Boat Restrictions Boat Inspections Full Service Marina: Ph: (951) 657-2179 Launch Ramps Storage, Slips, Gas, Docks Rentals: Fishing Boats	Fishing: Trout, Alabama Spotted & Largemouth Bass, Bluegill, Channel Catfish, Sunfish Picnicking 3 Group Sites Swimming, Scuba Diving Beaches & Waterslide Hiking, Bicycle & Equestrian Trails Horse Rentals Rock Climbing Area	Snack Bar Bait & Tackle Full Facilities Nearby

ORANGE COUNTY REGIONAL PARKS: CARBON CANYON, CRAIG, RALPH B. CLARK, YORBA, IRVINE, MILE SQUARE, WILLIAM R. MASON AND LAGUNA NIGUEL

The millions of residents and visitors to Orange County will find an abundance of regional parks, harbors and beaches. We have included only those regional parks that include a Lake. For those who are interested in the many other facilities, contact Orange County as listed on the following page.

Laguna Niguel Regional Park Lake is run by a private concession so no State fishing license is required. Rental boats are available but private boats are not allowed at this facility. Details for Irvine Lake are included on the following Lake page.

....Continued....

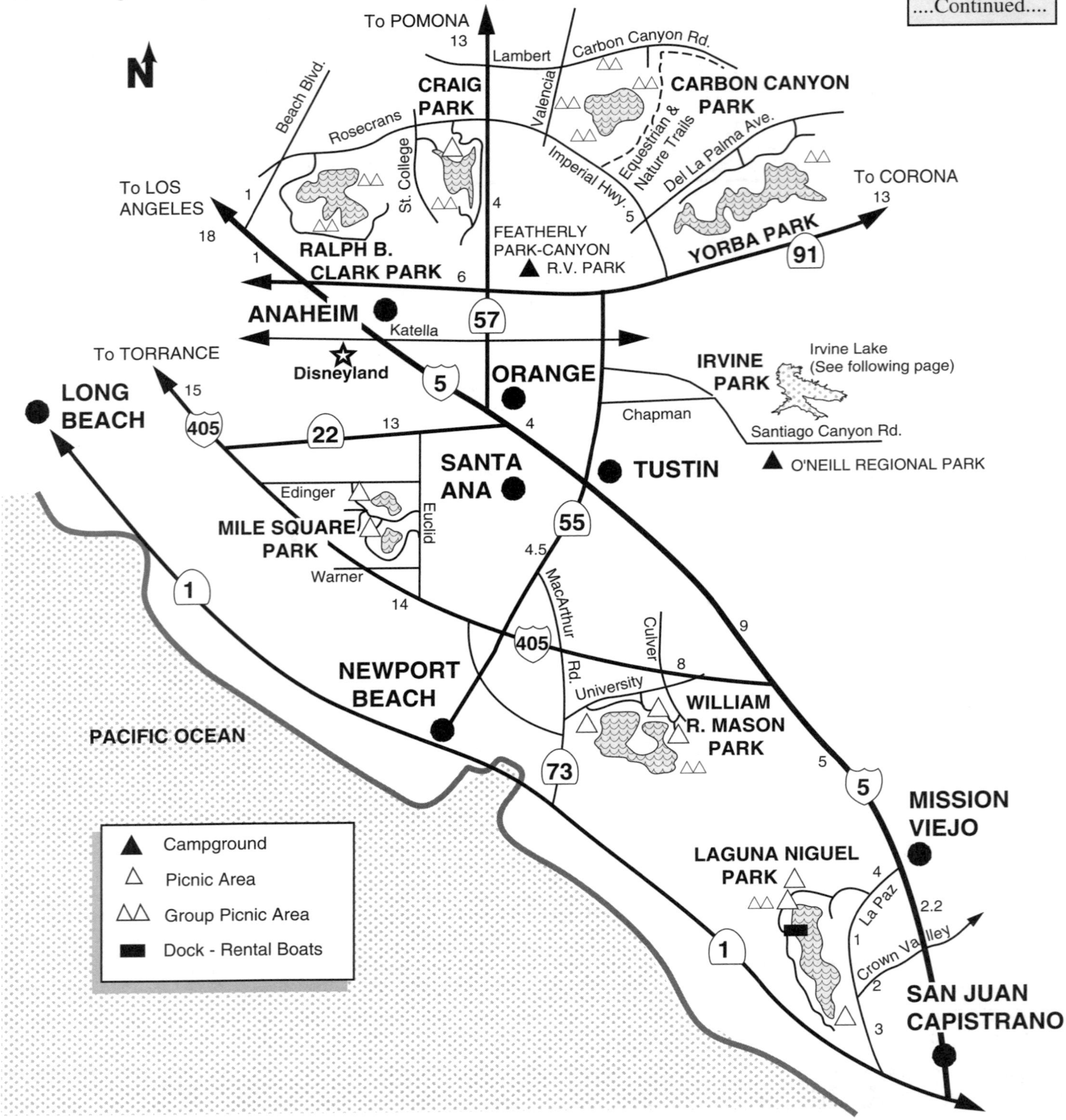
To POMONA
13
Lambert
Carbon Canyon Rd.
N
Beach Blvd.
CRAIG PARK
Valencia
CARBON CANYON PARK
Rosecrans
St. College
Imperial Hwy.
Equestrian & Nature Trails
Del La Palma Ave.
To CORONA
13
To LOS ANGELES
18
1
4
5
RALPH B. CLARK PARK
6
FEATHERLY PARK-CANYON R.V. PARK
YORBA PARK
91
ANAHEIM
57
Katella
To TORRANCE
15
Disneyland
5
ORANGE
IRVINE PARK
Irvine Lake (See following page)
LONG BEACH
405
22
13
4
Chapman
Santiago Canyon Rd.
SANTA ANA
TUSTIN
O'NEILL REGIONAL PARK
Edinger
MILE SQUARE PARK
Euclid
55
4.5
Warner
14
MacArthur Rd.
Culver
9
8
NEWPORT BEACH
University
WILLIAM R. MASON PARK
PACIFIC OCEAN
73
MISSION VIEJO
LAGUNA NIGUEL PARK
La Paz
2.2
Crown Valley
SAN JUAN CAPISTRANO
3
2
Campground
Picnic Area
Group Picnic Area
Dock - Rental Boats

CARBON CANYON, 4442 Carbon Canyon Rd., Brea 92823—Ph: (714) 973-3160

With 124 acres, this park is located in the foothills upstream from Carbon Canyon Dam. The park includes a 10-acre grove of coastal redwoods amid sycamore, pepper, eucalyptus and pine trees. There is a fishing Lake with 4 surface acres and 2 piers. Hiking, bicycle and equestrian trails, group picnic areas, playgrounds, tennis, volleyball, softball and athletic fields are also available.

CRAIG, 3300 State College Blvd., Fullerton 92835 Ph: (714) 973-3180

This very popular 124-acre park has picnic shelters, softball and baseball fields, horseshoe pits and a sports complex housing volleyball, racquetball, handball and a basketball court. Along with hiking, bicycling and equestrian trails, there is a 3 surface-acre Lake open for fishing and model sailboats.

RALPH B. CLARK, 8800 Rosecrans Ave., Buena Park 90621—Ph: (714) 973-3170

Acquired by the County of Orange in 1974 to preserve rich fossil beds, this 105-acre park has picnic areas, playgrounds, athletic fields, tennis and volleyball courts. Trails for hikers and bicyclists are also available. The small Lake has fishing for largemouth bass, channel catfish and bluegill.

YORBA, 7600 E. La Palma Ave., Anaheim 92807 Ph: (714) 973-6615

Adjacent to the Santa Ana River, this 175-acre park has a series of 4 Lakes with connecting streams that are great for fishing or sailing model boats. There are group picnic shelters and BBQs provided. 20 miles of hiking, bicycling and equestrian trails lead to the Pacific Ocean. Playgrounds, volleyball, horseshoe pits, ball diamonds and a physical fitness course are also available.

IRVINE, 1 Irvine Park Rd., Orange 92862 Ph: (714) 973-6835

This park is amid oaks and sycamores on the hillside of Santiago Canyon. California's oldest regional park, the 447 acres include two small lagoons, group picnic areas, BBQs, snack shop, stage, playgrounds, athletic fields, train rides and pony rides. Trails for walkers, bicyclists and equestrians are available. Bicycles can be rented. The Park Ranger conducts interpretive programs. The Orange County Zoo, barnyard and historic boathouse are also popular. See the following page for details on Irvine Lake.

MILE SQUARE, 16801 Euclid St., Fountain Valley 92708—Ph: (714) 973-6600

This 640-acre park has a golf course, driving range and restaurant. A variety of athletic fields, basketball courts, archery range, tennis and sheltered picnic areas are available. There are 4 miles of bicycling and jogging trails along with several playgrounds. In addition, there is a community center building and interpretive programs . Swimming is not allowed in the 2 Lakes but the angler will find stocked trout.

WILLIAM R. MASON, 18712 University Dr., Irvine 92612—Ph: (949) 923-2220

Throughout this 345-acre park, there are picnic shelters, playgrounds, a golf course and areas for softball and volleyball. Hiking, bicycling and equestrian trails can be enjoyed along with an amphitheater and physical fitness course. The park includes a 123-acre wilderness area. A large group picnic shelter can be reserved. The 9-surface acre Lake is open to fishing.

LAGUNA NIGUEL PARK, 28241 La Paz Rd. Laguna Niguel 92677—Ph: (949) 923-2240

The 236-acre park includes a 44 surface-acre Lake. The many facilities include picnic areas and shelters for large groups, bicycling and walking trails, horseshoes, golf, volleyball and tennis. Rental boats only.

INFORMATION: OC Parks, 13042 Old Myford Rd., Irvine 92602—Ph: (866) OC-PARKS or (714) 973-6865

CAMPING	BOATING	RECREATION	OTHER
Featherly Regional Park: Canyon R.V. Park 24001 Santa Ana Cyn. Rd. Anaheim 92808 Ph: (714) 637-0210 119 Dev. Sites for Tents & R.V.s Group Camp Sites Samll Cabins	No Boating Except Model Boats Rental Boats: Laguna Niguel Only	Fishing: Largemouth Bass, Bluegill, Channel Catfish, Trout Picnic Areas Playgrounds Lighted Athletic Fields Hiking & Equestrian Trails Bicycle Paths Interpretive Programs Group Facilities: Permits at Least 15 Days in Advance Dogs on Leash Allowed	O'Neill Regional Park 30992 Trabuco Canyon, Trabuco Canyon 92678 Ph: (949) 923-2260 Dev. Sites for Tents & R.V.s Group Camp Sites Equestrian Camp Sites

IRVINE, CORONA and SANTA ANA RIVER LAKES

These Lakes in Southern California are grouped together because they are all an angler's dream. Irvine Lake, 750 surface acres with 10 miles of shoreline, is located near the city of Orange and offers some of the best bass fishing in California. Limits for trophy-sized trout and catfish are often caught . Santa Ana River Lakes, a private facility, consists of three Lakes including a Kids Lake and Catfish Pond. This is an ideal spot for children to learn how to fish. Corona Lake, about 56 surface acres, is off Highway 15 south of Riverside. Fishing is great at this privately owned facility. Float tube fishing is permitted at all these very popular fishing Lakes. Major trout, bass and catfish tournaments are held throughout the year. Special fishing fee required for a minimum of 2 days.

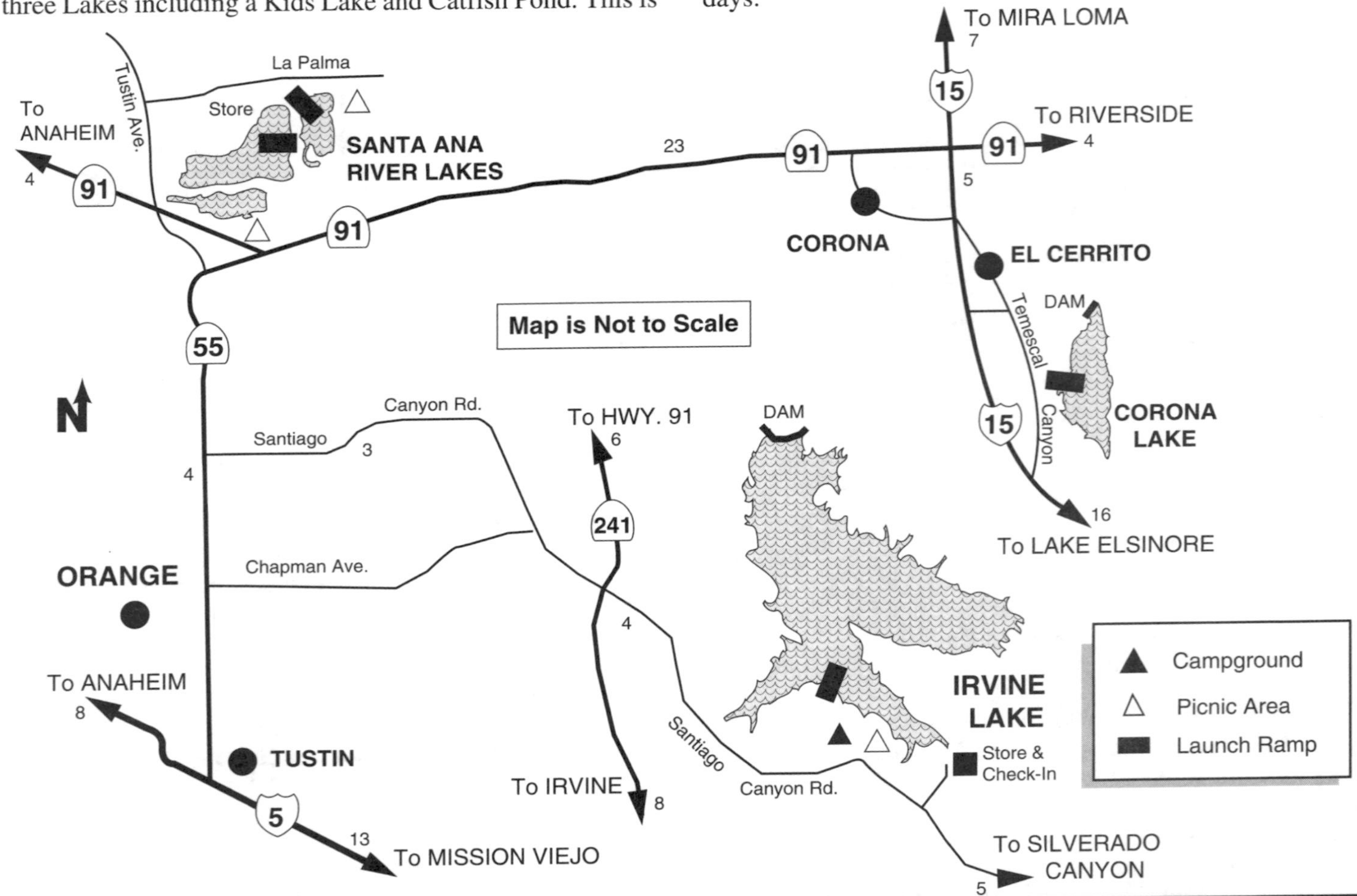

To MIRA LOMA
7
15
To RIVERSIDE
91
4
La Palma
Tustin Ave.
Store
To ANAHEIM
SANTA ANA RIVER LAKES
23
91
5
4
91
91
CORONA
EL CERRITO
DAM
Temescal
Canyon
CORONA LAKE
Map is Not to Scale
55
N
Canyon Rd.
Santiago
3
To HWY. 91
6
DAM
15
16
To LAKE ELSINORE
241
4
Chapman Ave.
ORANGE
4
To ANAHEIM
8
Santiago
IRVINE LAKE
Store & Check-In
Campground
Picnic Area
Launch Ramp
TUSTIN
To IRVINE
8
Canyon Rd.
5
13
To MISSION VIEJO
To SILVERADO CANYON
5

INFORMATION: ***Only*** **Irvine Lake: 4621 Santiago Canyon Rd., Silverado 92676—Ph: (714) 649-9111**

CAMPING	BOATING	RECREATION	OTHER
Irvine Lake: Upper Level - 24 Tent & Small R.V. Sites Lower Level - Can Accommodate Large R.V.s & Groups Fees: $15 Ph. (714) 649-9111 Santa Ana River Lakes & Corona Lake No Camping	Irvine Lake: Launch Fee: $10 5 MPH Limit Rentals: Row, Motor & Bass Boats & Pontoons, Santa Ana Rivers Lakes & Corona Lake Electric Motors Only Launch Fee: $8 Float Tubes: $5 Rentals: Row & Motor Boats	Fishing: Trout, Catfish, Striped Bass, Crappie, Bluegill, Sunfish, Sturgeon, Tilapia Irvine Lake: Group Facilities for Picnicking Kid's Fish'n Hole Volleyball, Horseshoes, Hiking Trails Santa Ana & Corona: Night Fishing Available *Fishing Fees Required*	Irvine Lake: Cafe & Store Fish Report - Ph: (714) 649-2168 Santa Ana River Lakes: Store, Bait & Tackle Fish Report - Ph: (714) 632-7830 Corona Lake : Store, Bait & Tackle Fish Report - Ph: (951) 277-4489

CUCAMONGA-GUASTI, YUCAIPA PARK, PRADO PARK and FAIRMOUNT PARK

These small Lakes and surrounding parks have an abundance of recreational activities with limited boating. Cucamonga-Guasti, Yucaipa Park and Prado Park are a part of the San Bernardino County Regional Park System. Fairmount Park is administered by the City of Riverside. Fishing is popular year around for bass and channel catfish and in winter months, the angler will find planted trout. In addition to campgrounds, Prado has equestrian trails and staging areas. There is a variety of activities unique to each park from trap shooting to waterslides.

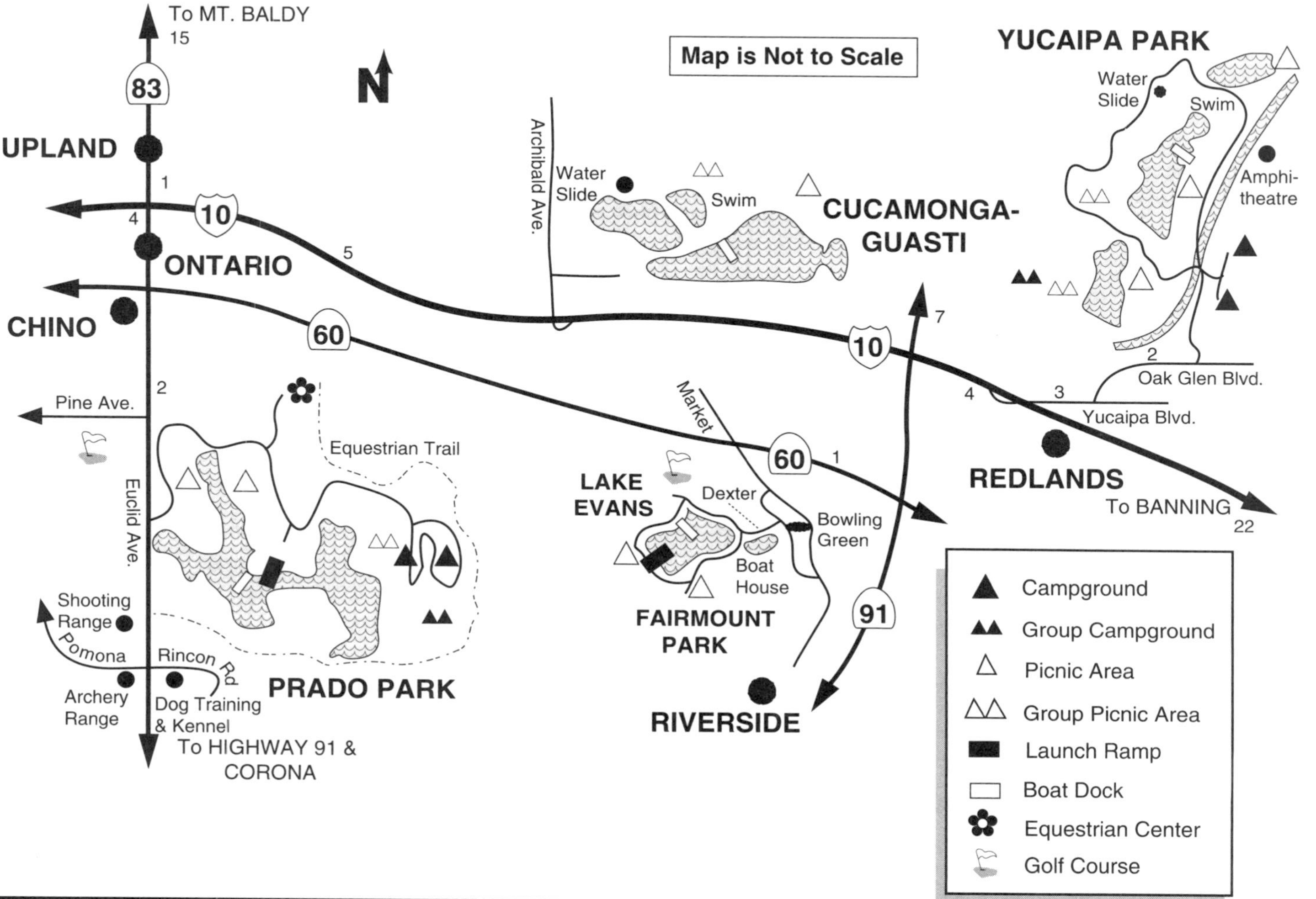

To MT. BALDY
15
83
UPLAND
1
4
10
ONTARIO
5
CHINO
60
2
Pine Ave.
Euclid Ave.
Equestrian Trail
Shooting Range
Pomona
Rincon Rd
Archery Range
Dog Training & Kennel
PRADO PARK
To HIGHWAY 91 & CORONA
N
Map is Not to Scale
Archibald Ave.
Water Slide
Swim
CUCAMONGA-GUASTI
YUCAIPA PARK
Water Slide
Swim
Amphi-theatre
7
10
2
Oak Glen Blvd.
4
3
Yucaipa Blvd.
REDLANDS
To BANNING
22
Market
60
1
LAKE EVANS
Dexter
Bowling Green
Boat House
FAIRMOUNT PARK
91
RIVERSIDE
Campground
Group Campground
Picnic Area
Group Picnic Area
Launch Ramp
Boat Dock
Equestrian Center
Golf Course

INFORMATION:San Bernadino County Regional Parks, 777 E. Rialto, San Bernardino 92415—Ph: (909) 387-2757

CAMPING	BOATING	RECREATION	OTHER
Yucaipa Park: Dev. Sites for Tents & R.V.s - 42 Full Hookups 9 Group Sites Prado Park: Dev. Sites for Tents & R.V.s - 75 Full Hookups 9 Group Sites Fees: $18 - $35 Disposal Stations Day Use Only: Cucamonga-Guasti & Fairmount Park	Yucaipa Park: Rentals Only: Pedal Boats & Aqua Cycles Prado: Non-Power Boats Launch Ramp Cucamonga-Guasti: Rentals: Pedal Boats & Aqua Cycles Fairmount Park: Launch Ramp for Rowboats Only With Permit Rentals: Pedal Boats	Fishing: Trout - Winter, Bass & Catfish Swimming & Picnicking Group Picnic Areas Yucaipa & Guasti: Waterslides Hiking & Equestrian Trails Prado Park: Athletic Fields Equestrian Center & Horse Rentals Shooting-Archery Ranges Golf Courses	Cucamonga-Guasti Ph: (909) 481-4205 Yucaipa Park Ph: (909) 790-3127 Prado Park: Ph: (909) 597-4260 Fairmount Park: City of Riverside Park & Rec. Dept. 3936 Chestnut St. Riverside 92501 Ph: (951) 826-2000

LAKE ELSINORE

Lake Elsinore is a very large, natural freshwater lake in Southern California with over 3,000 surface acres. The Lake, with 14 miles of shoreline, is popular for a variety of watersports including fishing and waterskiing. A channel is available for professional waterski instruction and pro-competition. Skydiving is another popular sport. Lake Elsinore Recreation Area, owned by the City of Lake Elsinore, has numerous quiet, shaded campsites close to the water. Extensive additions are planned for the future. The city's boat launch facility is an easy way to launch your watercraft. Campgrounds and resorts are available.

....Continued....

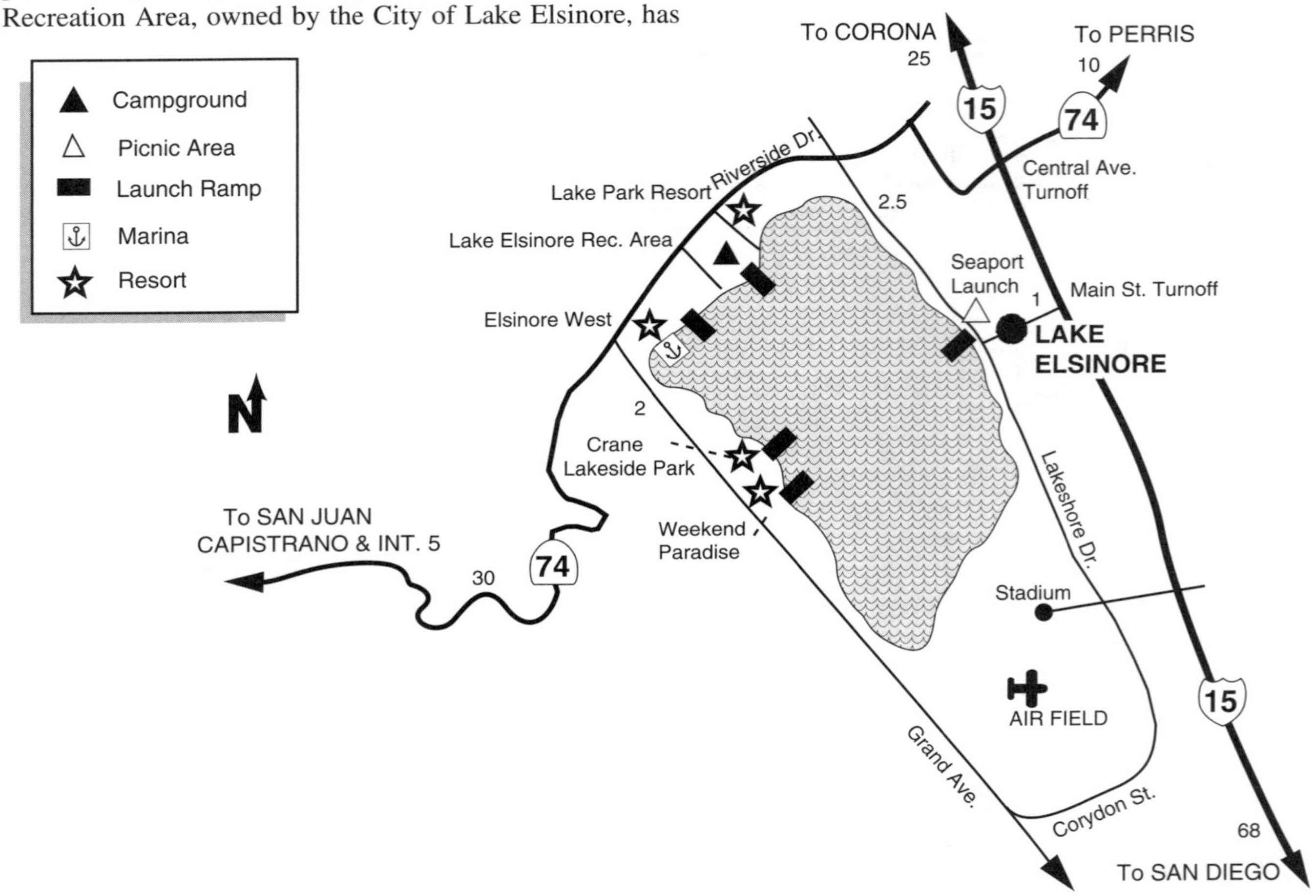

Campground
Picnic Area
Launch Ramp
Marina
Resort
N
To CORONA
25
To PERRIS
10
15
74
Riverside Dr.
Central Ave. Turnoff
Lake Park Resort
2.5
Lake Elsinore Rec. Area
Seaport Launch
1
Main St. Turnoff
Elsinore West
LAKE ELSINORE
2
Crane Lakeside Park
Lakeshore Dr.
Weekend Paradise
To SAN JUAN CAPISTRANO & INT. 5
30
74
Stadium
AIR FIELD
15
Grand Ave.
Corydon St.
68
To SAN DIEGO

INFORMATION: Lake Elsinore Recreation Area, 32040 Riverside Dr., Lake Elsinore 92530—Ph: (951) 471-1212

CAMPING	BOATING	RECREATION	OTHER
120 Dev. Sites for R.V.s with Partial Hookups Plus 10 Full Hookups 51 Dev. Sites for Tents 11 Group Camp Sites Disposal Station Reservations: Ph: (800) 416-6992 Day Use: Fees: $5 - Vehicle $2 - Walk-in	Power, Row, Canoe, Sail, Windsurf Waterski & PWCs 35 MPH Speed Limit Plus High Speed Designated Areas Lake Use Fee: $10 Launch Ramp Fee: $10 Boat Rentals	Fishing: Bass, Crappie, Carp, Bluegill & Catfish Picnicking Hiking, Bicycling & Equestrian Trails Skydiving Ph: (951) 245-9939 Golf Nearby	Full Facilities in Lake Elsinore *See Following Page for Some Resorts & Marine Facilities*

Some of the R.V. Parks & Resorts at Lake Elsinore
Check for Current Fees

LAKE PARK RESORT
32000 Riverside Dr., Lake Elsinore 92530
Ph: (951) 674-7911 or (888) 505-2537
121 R.V. Sites, Full Hookups - 28 Motel Rooms + Permanent Sites, Olympic Size Pool, Picnic Area, Rec. Room.

ELSINORE WEST MARINA
32700 Riverside Dr.
Lake Elsinore 92530
Ph: (951) 678-1300 or (800) 328-6844
197 R.V. Sites, Full Hookups Campsites for Tents, Open Tent & R.V. Camp Area, Hot Showers, Cable T.V.

CRANE LAKESIDE PARK and RESORT
15980 Grand Ave., Lake Elsinore 92530
Ph: (951) 678-2112
18 Tent & R.V. Sites on the Waterfront, Water & Electric Hookups
Weekly & Monthly Rates Available, 100 Permanent Sites,
Disposal Station, Hot Showers, Laundry Room, Sports Bar & Restaurant, Meeting Room, Launch Ramp.

WEEKEND PARADISE R.V. PARK
16006 Grand Ave., Lake Elsinore 92530
Ph: (951) 678-3715
R.V. Sites, Water & Electric Hookups - *Fee: $21*, Hot Showers, Disposal Station, Launch Ramp.

SEAPORT BOAT LAUNCH and ELM GROVE BEACH
500 W. Lakeshore Dr., Lake Elsinore 92530
Ph: (951) 245-9308
Launch, Beach and Shaded Picnic Areas
Day Use and Boat Lauch Fees

FOR OTHER FACILITIES AND ACCOMMODATIONS CONTACT:
Lake Elsinore Visitor Center
132 West Graham Ave.
Lake Elsinore 92530
Ph: (951) 245-8848

DIAMOND VALLEY LAKE

Located at an elevation of 1,756 feet, Diamond Valley Lake is the largest reservoir in Southern California. This huge body of water has 4,500 surface acres and is more than 2 miles wide and 4-1/2 miles long when full. Check for current water level conditions. It is controlled by the Metropolitan Water District of Southern California. Facilities are continuing to develop which will include campgrounds and additional trails. At this time, the area is for day use only. A 22-mile trail for hikers and bicyclists goes all the way around the Lake. Also a trail is available for hikers and equestrians. Near the marina, there is a designated area for shoreline fishing. As of now, no private boats are allowed due to low water levels. Rentals boats are available. Black bass, trout and a variety of other fish have been stocked and fishing can be excellent. The Visitor Center is very interesting and is home to the largest adult mastodon to be uncovered in the western United States.

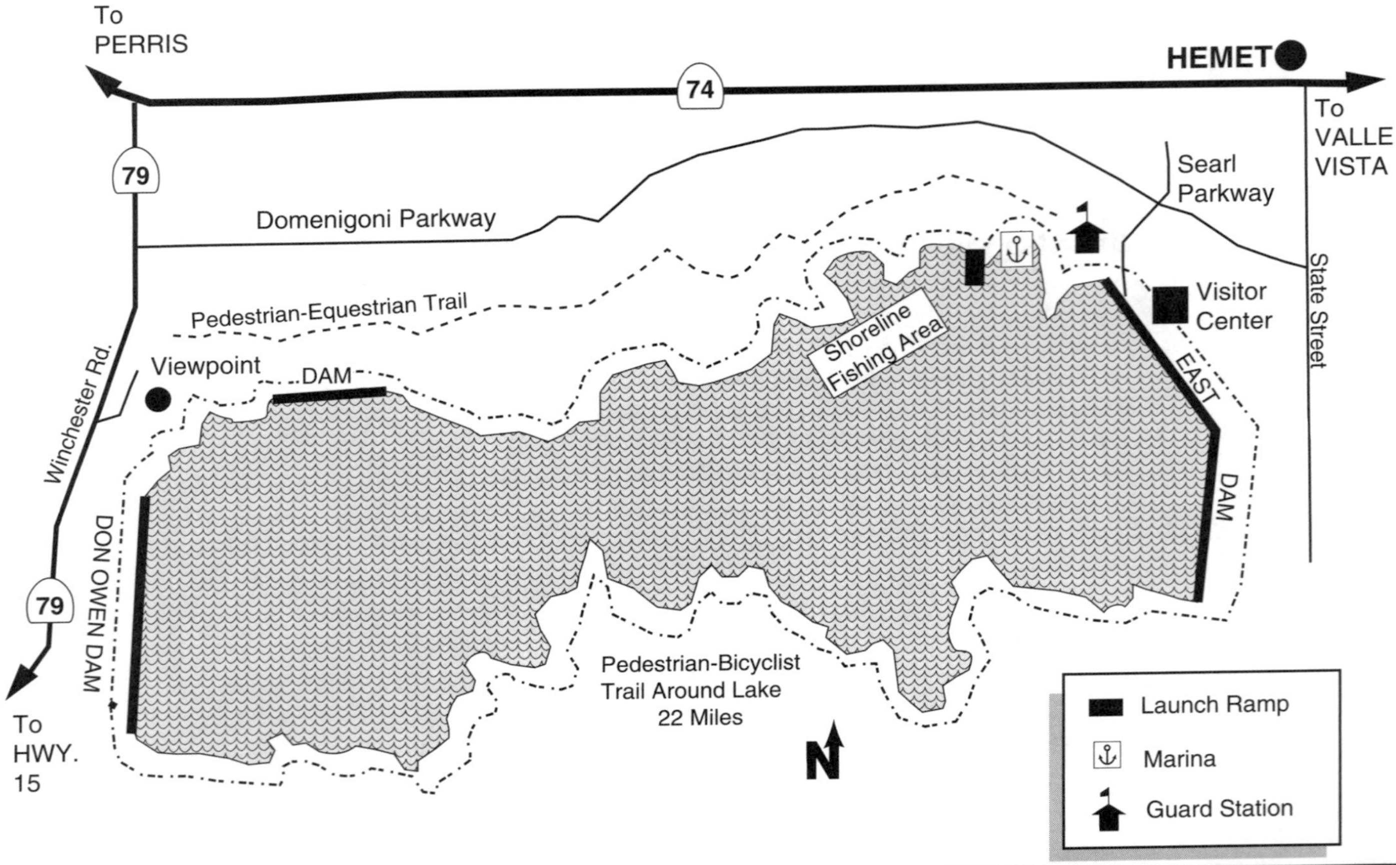
To PERRIS
HEMET
74
To VALLE VISTA
79
Searl Parkway
Domenigoni Parkway
Visitor Center
State Street
Pedestrian-Equestrian Trail
Shoreline Fishing Area
Winchester Rd.
Viewpoint
DAM
EAST
DAM
DON OWEN DAM
79
To HWY. 15
Pedestrian-Bicyclist Trail Around Lake 22 Miles
N
Launch Ramp
Marina
Guard Station

INFORMATION: Diamond Valley Lake, 2615 Angler Ave., Hemet 92545—Ph: (951) 926-7201or (800) 590-5253

CAMPING	BOATING	RECREATION	OTHER
Day Use Only Entrance Fee: $7 Campgrounds to be Constructed in Future	No Private Boats - Check for Current Water Level Canoes & Kayaks May Be Allowed Full Service Marina Launch Ramps - Check for Current Conditions Rental Boats: Bass Boats, Pontoons & Basic Fishing Boats - Reservations Dry Storage for Boats	Fishing: Black, Largemouth & Smallmouth Bass, Trout, Catfish, Bluegill, Sunfish & Perch Fishing Permit: $3 No Lake Swimming Swimming in Pool Only During Summer Picnicking Hiking, Bicycling & Equestrian Trails Nature Study	Visitor's Center 2325 Searl Parkway Hemet 92545 Ph: (951) 765-2612 Open Thursday-Sunday Water Play Area Ph: (951) 929-0047 Floating Restrooms

LAKE SKINNER and VAIL LAKE

Located at an elevation of 1,500 feet, Lake Skinner is amid rolling hills of wildflowers and oak trees. The Lake has a surface area of 1,200 acres with14 miles of shoreline within the 6,040-acre Lake Skinner Park. This facility is operated by Riverside County Parks Department. There are a number of trails throughout this area. Vail Lake has 1,100 surface acres. The Village and R.V. Resort, privately operated, is open to the public. Boating, however, is restricted to club members only. Visitors can fish from the shoreline. Full vacation facilities are available with miniature golf, a waterslide, fishing pond and special events including live entertainment and bike races.

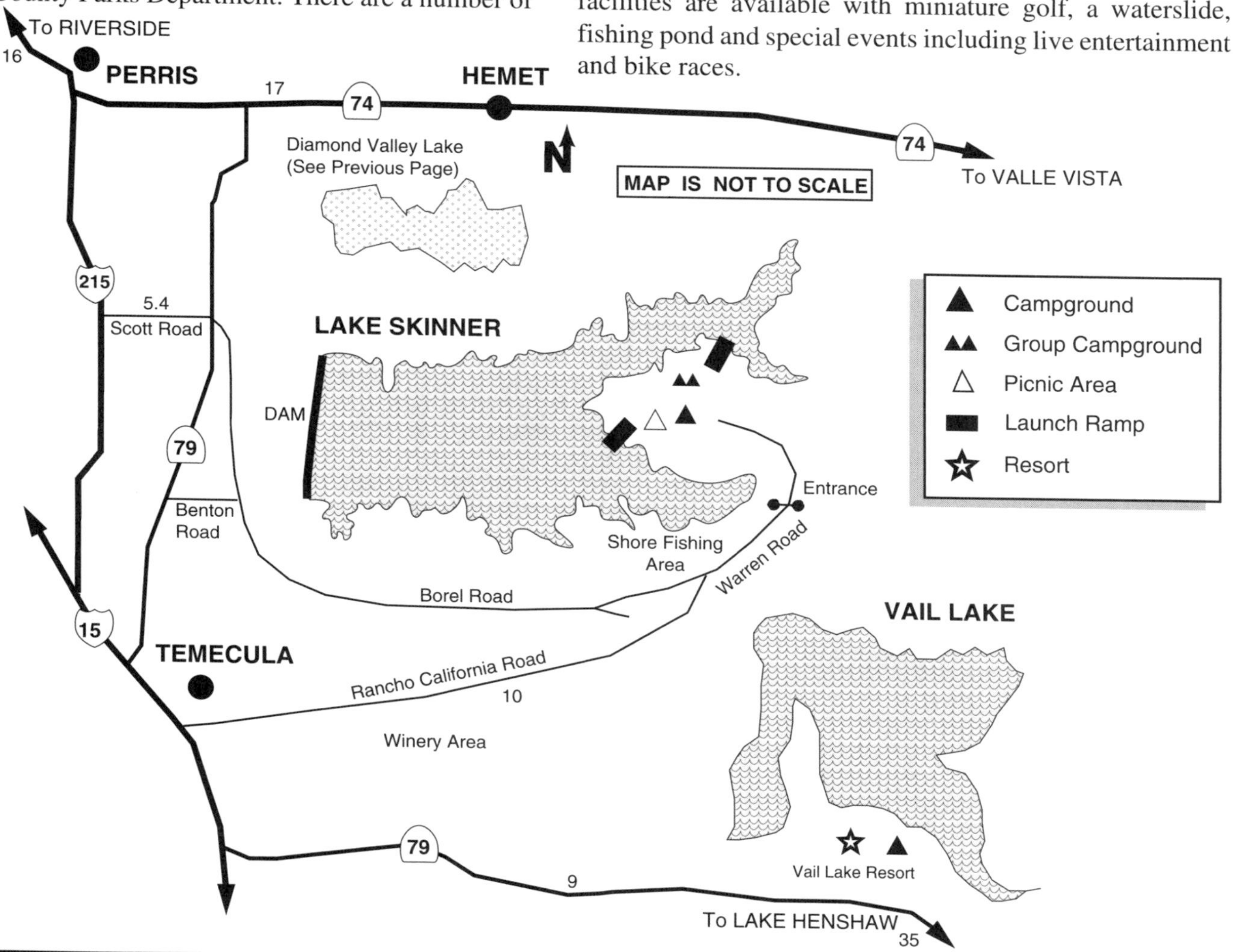

To RIVERSIDE
16
PERRIS
17
74
HEMET
74
To VALLE VISTA
Diamond Valley Lake
(See Previous Page)
N
MAP IS NOT TO SCALE
215
5.4
Scott Road
LAKE SKINNER
DAM
79
Benton Road
Entrance
Shore Fishing Area
Warren Road
Borel Road
15
TEMECULA
Rancho California Road
10
Winery Area
VAIL LAKE
79
9
Vail Lake Resort
To LAKE HENSHAW
35
Campground
Group Campground
Picnic Area
Launch Ramp
Resort

INFORMATION: Lake Skinner Park, 37701 Warren Rd., Temecula 92596—Ph: (951) 926-1541

CAMPING	BOATING	RECREATION	OTHER
Lake Skinner: 300 Dev. Sites for Tents & RVs 158 Full Hookups 16 Water & Electric 38 Water Only Fees: $17 - $20 Group Camp Reservations: Ph: (800) 234-7275	All Boats Must Be a Minimum of 12 Feet Long, 42 Inches Wide Sailboats Must be 10 Feet Long & 12 Inches of Freeboard Canoes, Kayaks, Multihulls Must Have Solid & Fixed Decking Speed Limit - 10 MPH Launch Ramp - Fee Rentals: Row & Motor Boats	Fishing: Striped Bass, Trout, Catfish, Bluegill, Crappie, Perch, Carp Fishing Permit - Fee Swimming in Pool Only Memorial Day through Labor Day Picnicking - Group Sites Hiking & Equestrian Trails Restaurant, Store Bait & Tackle	Vail Lake Resort 38000 Highway 79 South Temecula 92589 Ph: (951) 303-0173 or (866) 824-5525 Dev. Sites for R.V.s & Tents Full Hookups Fees: $50 - $65 & Up Restaurant, Store Bait & Tackle Waterslide, Minature Golf, Boat Use - Members Only

REFLECTION LAKE and LAKE FULMOR

Reflection Lake, at 1,600 feet elevation, is a privately owned, small fishing Lake. A developed campground for tents and R.V.s is available. Boating is limited to rowboats, canoes and inflatables. Electric motors are allowed. Trout and channel catfish are planted on a regular basis. State fishing licenses are not required at this private facility. Lake Fulmor is at an elevation of 5,300 feet near the scenic mountain resort community of Idyllwild. Although facilities are limited to day use at this small scenic Lake, the visitor will find many campsites at the Mt. San Jacinto State Park, Idyllwild County Park and McCall Equestrian Camp. There are also numerous campgrounds within the San Bernadino National Forest. The Pacific Crest Trail runs through this area.

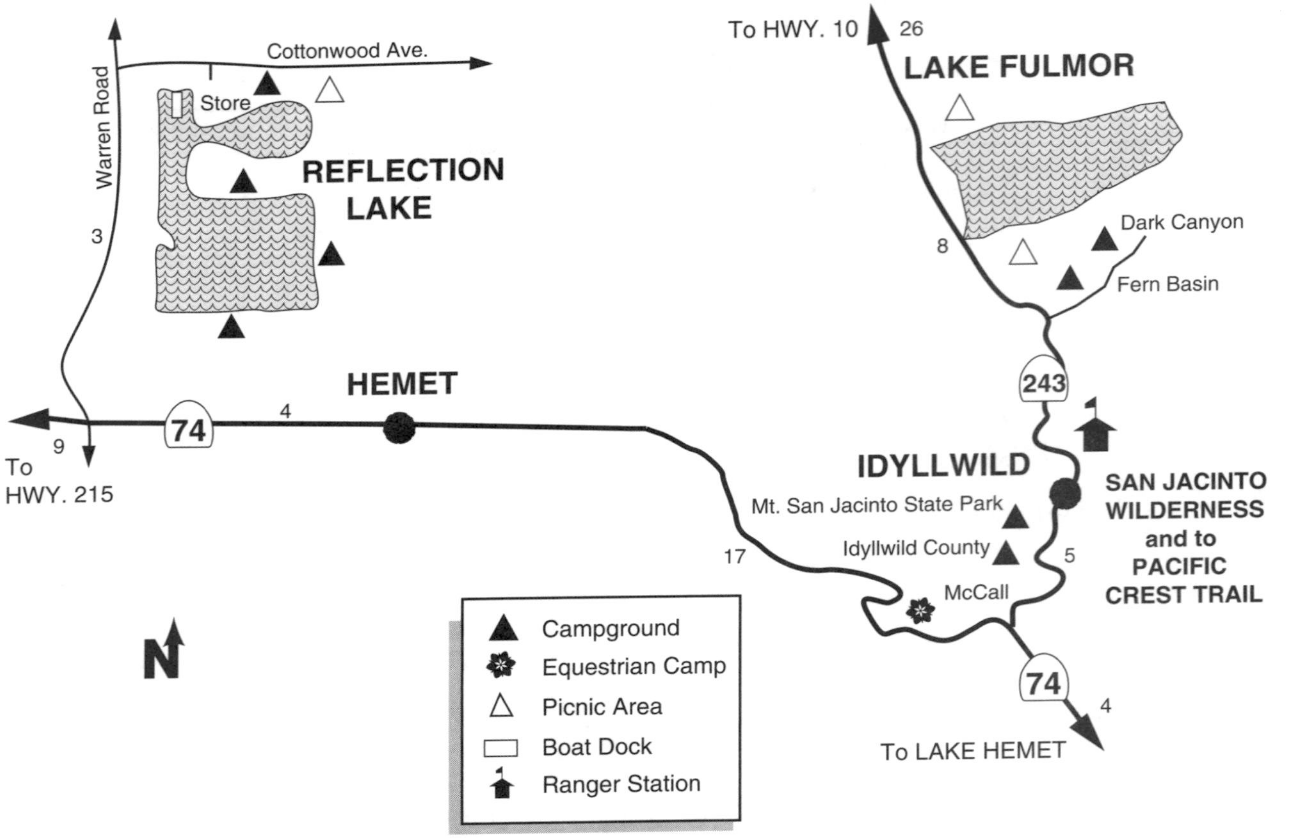

Cottonwood Ave.
Warren Road
Store
REFLECTION LAKE
3
HEMET
74
4
9
To HWY. 215
To HWY. 10
26
LAKE FULMOR
Dark Canyon
Fern Basin
8
243
IDYLLWILD
Mt. San Jacinto State Park
Idyllwild County
McCall
17
5
SAN JACINTO WILDERNESS and to PACIFIC CREST TRAIL
74
4
To LAKE HEMET
N
Campground
Equestrian Camp
Picnic Area
Boat Dock
Ranger Station

INFORMATION: Reflection Lake, 3440 Cottonwood Ave., San Jacinto 92582—Ph: (951) 654-7906

CAMPING	BOATING	RECREATION	OTHER
Reflection Lake: 121 Dev. Sites for Tents & R.V.s Water & Electric Hookups Fee: $25 - $40 Disposal Station Reservations Accepted Day Use: $8 Lake Fulmor: Day Use Only	Reflection Lake: Rowboats, Canoes & Inflatables, Electric Motors Only Lake Fulmor: No Boating *Check for Current Water Levels*	Fishing: Trout, Bass, Bluegill & Catfish Fishing Fees: Reflection Lake: $10 - $20 No Limits Picnicking Group Picnic Sites at Reflection Lake Hiking Trails - Pacific Crest Trail No Swimming in Lakes Swimming Pool at Reflection	Lake Fulmor: Idyllwild Ranger Station 54270 Pine Crest Idyllwild 92549 Ph: (909) 382-2921 Mt. San Jacinto State Park Ph: (951) 659-2607 Dev. Sites for Tents/RVs Idyllwild County Park Ph: (800) 234-7275 Dev. Sites for Tents/RVs McCall Equestrian Camp Ph: (951) 659-2311

LAKE HEMET

Lake Hemet, at an elevation of 4,340 feet, is located in a mountain meadow within the San Bernardino National Forest. Chaparral-covered hills surround the Lake. With 420 surface-acres and over 4 miles of shoreline, it is owned and operated by the Lake Hemet Municipal Water District. Only fishing boats with motors are allowed. Large trout are caught throughout the year. In addition, the angler will find a good bass and catfish population. A developed campground is available. Nearby Hurkey Creek also has a campground operated by Riverside County Regional Park District.

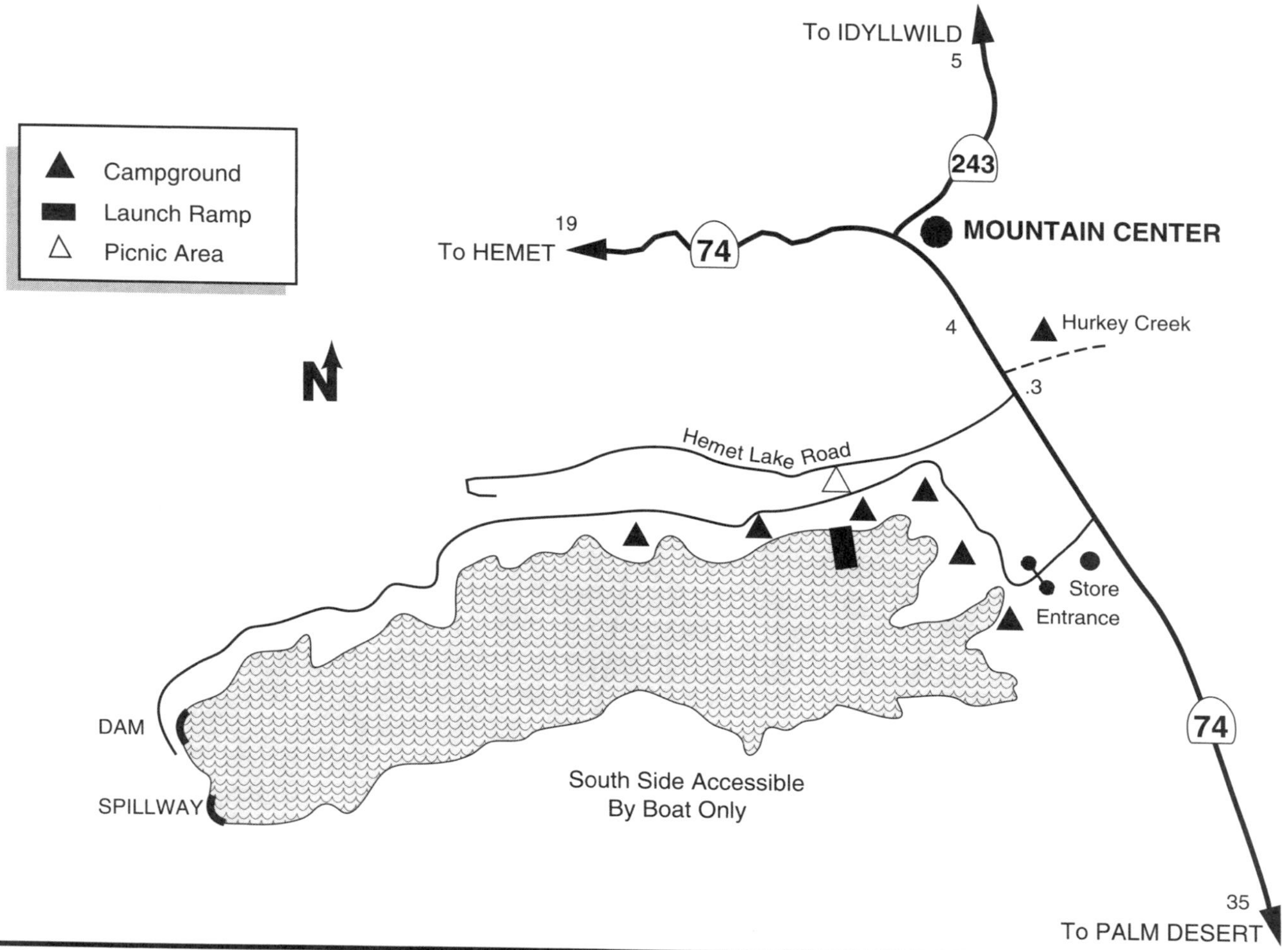

Campground
Launch Ramp
Picnic Area
N
To IDYLLWILD
5
243
MOUNTAIN CENTER
19
To HEMET
74
4
Hurkey Creek
.3
Hemet Lake Road
Store
Entrance
DAM
SPILLWAY
South Side Accessible
By Boat Only
74
35
To PALM DESERT

INFORMATION: Lake Hemet, 56570 Highway 74, Mountain Center 92561—Ph: (951) 659-2680

CAMPING	BOATING	RECREATION	OTHER
Lake Hemet: 74 Dev. Sites for Tents & R.V.s Electric & Full Hookups Fee: $20 - $25 Disposal Station No Reservations Pets Allowed Day Use: $10	Fishing Boats with Motors Boats Must Be At Least 10 Feet Long Restrictions for Kayaks No Sailboats, Canoes or Inflatables Rentals: Fishing Boats & Motors 10 MPH Speed Limit Launch Ramp Fee: $6	Fishing: Rainbow Trout, Largemouth Bass, Bluegill & Catfish Picnicking Hiking No Swimming Playgrounds Special Events No Motorcycles	General Store: Ph: (951) 659-2350 Food, Supplies Bait & Tackle Propane Riverside County of Parks Ph: (951) 659-2050 Hurkey Creek: 170 Sites for Tents & R.V.s to 40 ft. No Hookups Group Sites Reserve Ph: (800) 234-7275

LAKE CAHUILLA

Lake Cahuilla is at an elevation of 44 feet, southwest of Indio. The 135-surface acre Lake is owned by the Coachella Valley Water District. The palm-shaded park, a total of 710 acres, is operated by Riverside County. Temperatures can climb to over 100 degrees in summer but in winter months are often about 75 degrees attracting campers and anglers. There are campsites and a shaded picnic area. A swimming pool with sandy beach is open from April to October. Trails and corrals are available for the equestrian. Lake Cahuilla has a fascinating history. In prehistoric times, it covered over 2,000 square miles. Fossils, high water marks and other evidence of its original size remain throughout this area.

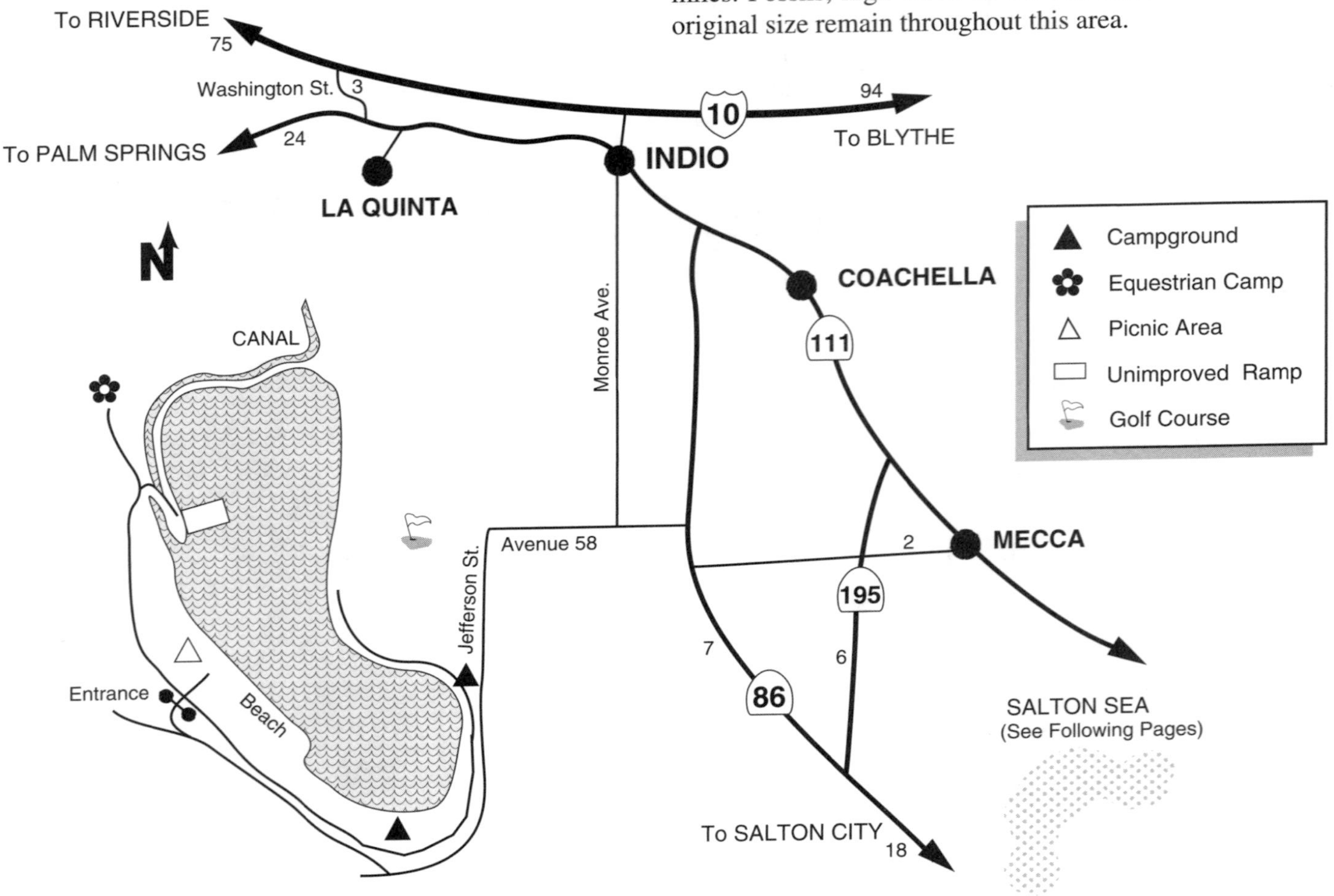
To RIVERSIDE
75
Washington St.
3
10
94
To BLYTHE
To PALM SPRINGS
24
INDIO
LA QUINTA
N
Campground
Equestrian Camp
Picnic Area
Unimproved Ramp
Golf Course
COACHELLA
111
Monroe Ave.
CANAL
Avenue 58
Jefferson St.
2
MECCA
195
7
6
86
Entrance
Beach
SALTON SEA
(See Following Pages)
To SALTON CITY
18

INFORMATION: Lake Cahuilla, 58075 Jefferson St., La Quinta 92253—Ph: (800) 234-7275 or (760) 564-4712

CAMPING	BOATING	RECREATION	OTHER
56 Dev. Sites for R.V.s 46 Water & Electric Hookups 10 Water Only Hookups Fees: $18 and up Equestrian Group Site Disposal Station Reservations: Riverside County Park District Ph: (800) 234-7275	No Private Boats Speed Limit: 10 MPH Rentals: Fishing Boats	Fishing: Rainbow Trout in Winter, Channel Catfish, Striped & Largemouth Bass No Swimming in Lake Swimming Pool Open April - October Picnicking Group Area Hiking & Bicycling Trails Equestrian Trails & Horse Corrals	Full Facilities at Indio

These 7,929 acres of the Imperial Wildlife Area is one of Southern California's most abundant wildlife habitats. The Wister Unit consists of a series of deep and shallow water ponds, good for sightseeing and nature study. This is the remarkable home of a variety of birds, fish, amphibians, reptiles and mammals. With prime waterfowl hunting available, there are restrictions which apply to the number of hunters along other regulations; contact the Wildlife Headquarters for details. Located below sea level in the hot desert climate of the Imperial Valley, the temperature is often over 100 degrees in the summer months. A milder climate of 70 degrees prevails in fall, winter and spring.

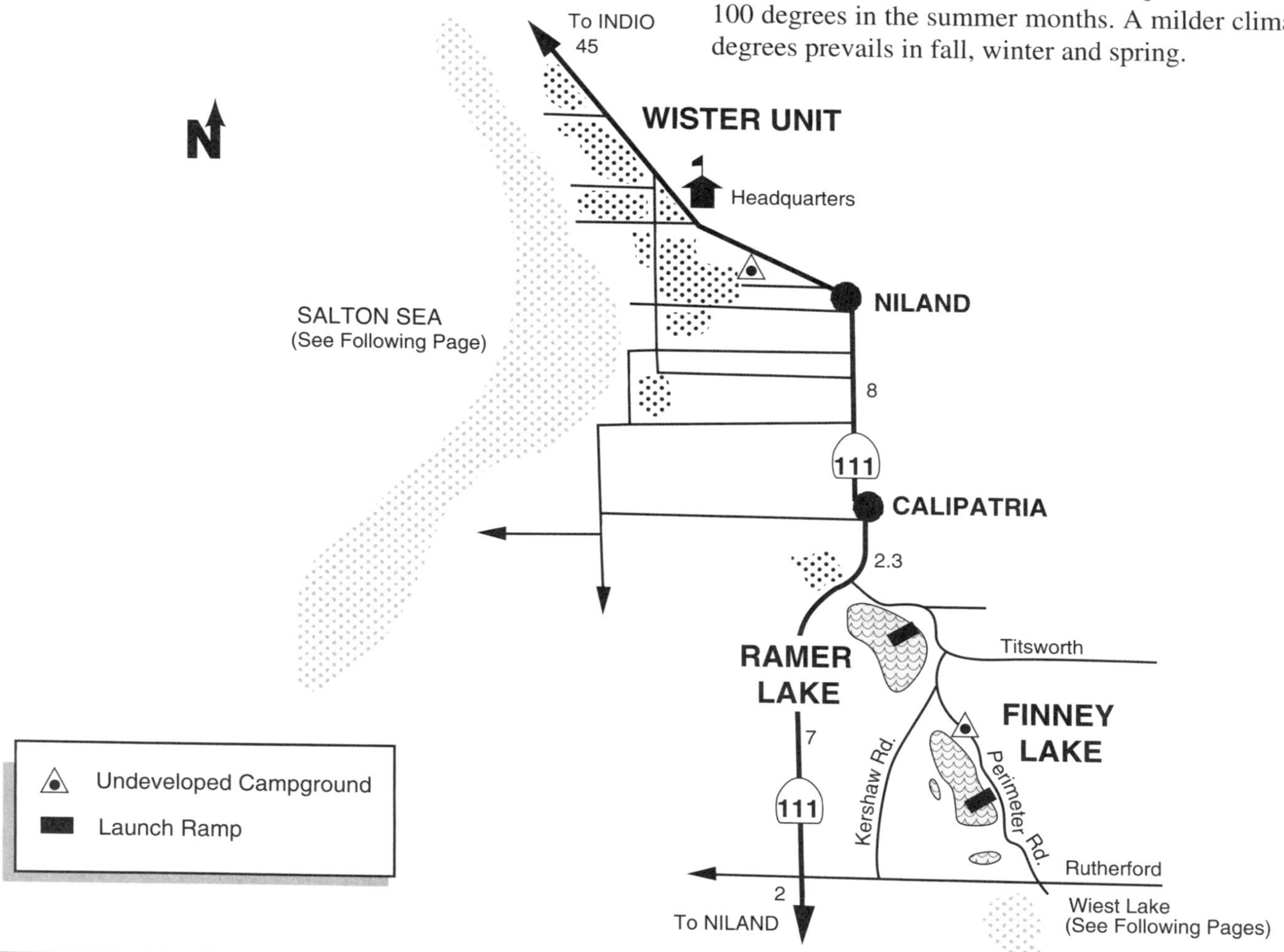
To INDIO
45
N
WISTER UNIT
Headquarters
NILAND
SALTON SEA
(See Following Page)
8
111
CALIPATRIA
2.3
Titsworth
RAMER
LAKE
FINNEY
LAKE
7
Kershaw Rd.
Perimeter Rd.
111
Rutherford
2
To NILAND
Wiest Lake
(See Following Pages)
Undeveloped Campground
Launch Ramp

INFORMATION: Imperial Wildlife Area, 8700 Davis Rd., Niland 92257—Ph: (760) 359-0577

CAMPING	BOATING	RECREATION	OTHER
Primitive Open Camping with Fire Rings Day Use Permit Required Wister Unit Entrance Fee: $3	Finney-Ramer: Electric Motors Only Wister Ponds: No Boating *Call for Current Water Level Conditions*	Fishing: Largemouth Bass, Bluegill Crappie, Catfish & Carp Picnicking Hiking Birdwatching Nature Study Hunting - Shotguns Only Duck, Geese, Dove Quail, Pheasant & Rabbit *Check Restrictions*	Nearest Facilities in Niland

SALTON SEA

The Salton Sea, located in a desert valley 226 feet below sea level, is surrounded by mountains reaching to 10,000 feet. It is one of the world's largest inland bodies of salt water with a surface area of 370 square miles. Summer temperatures are over 100 degrees. Fall, winter and spring temperatures are in the 70's. Tilapia, imported from Africa, is now believed to be the only fish found in the Salton Sea. More than 400 species of migrating birds pass through this area each year. Many problems have arised over time but future plans may include reducing the size of the Sea by constructing barriers and perimeter dikes. The hope is to restore the eco-system and revitalize the entire area. *Very strong winds can come up at times so caution is advised.*

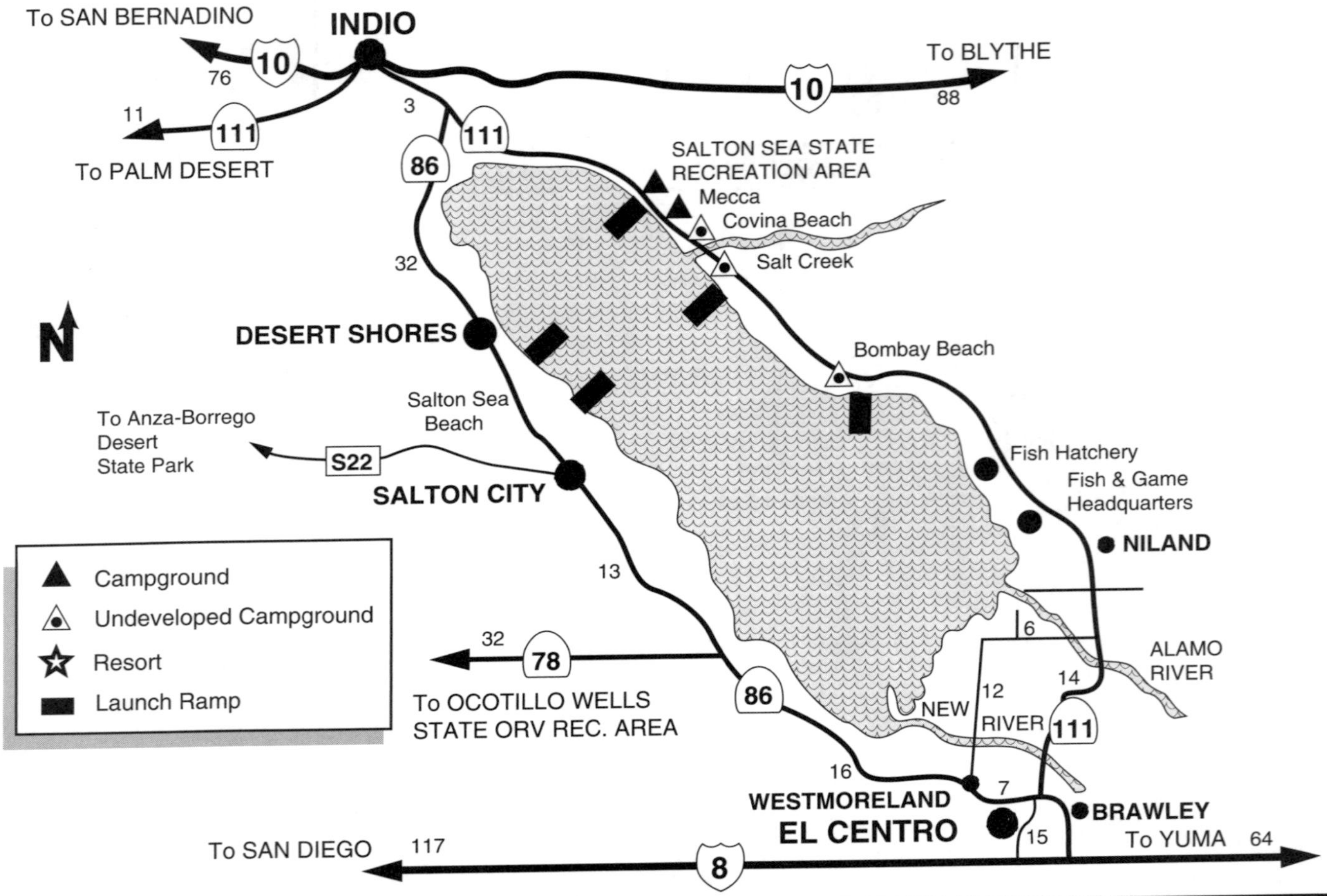
To SAN BERNADINO
INDIO
10
76
11
111
To PALM DESERT
3
111
86
10
To BLYTHE
88
SALTON SEA STATE
RECREATION AREA
Mecca
Covina Beach
Salt Creek
32
N
DESERT SHORES
Bombay Beach
Salton Sea
Beach
To Anza-Borrego
Desert
State Park
S22
SALTON CITY
Fish Hatchery
Fish & Game
Headquarters
NILAND
13
Campground
Undeveloped Campground
Resort
Launch Ramp
32
78
6
ALAMO
RIVER
To OCOTILLO WELLS
STATE ORV REC. AREA
86
NEW
12
RIVER
14
111
16
7
WESTMORELAND
EL CENTRO
BRAWLEY
15
To YUMA
64
To SAN DIEGO
117
8

INFORMATION: Salton Sea State Rec. Area, 100-225 State Park Rd., North Shore 92254—Ph: (760) 393-3059

CAMPING	BOATING	RECREATION	OTHER
6 Campgrounds with 1,500 Campsites Sites for Tents & R.V.s Some Hookups - Fee: $12 - $23 Day Use: $6 Call for Current	Information Open to All Boating Launch Ramps Docks Dry Storage Gas Call for Current Information *Sudden Strong Winds at Times*	Fishing: Tilapia Picnicking - Shade Ramadas Nature Trails Birdwatching 9-Hole Golf Course Sony Bono Salton Sea National Wildlife Refuge	Visitor Center Full Facilities at Indio & El Centro

WIEST LAKE

Wiest Lake, the park and campground are located approximately 4 miles northeast of Brawley in the heart of the rich agricultural Imperial Valley. The Lake, owned and operated by Imperial County, about 50 surface acres, is surrounded by a public park that has R.V. and tent spaces. Wiest Lake is open to all kinds of boating from fishing boats to waterskiing and PWCs. Picnic sites, a swim beach and hiking trails are available. Although there is no hunting allowed in the park, the valley and nearby Imperial Wildlife Area permits hunting at various times. The temperatures in the summer are hot with moderate climate for fall, winter and spring. This is a good area for "snowbirds" to stay for extended periods.

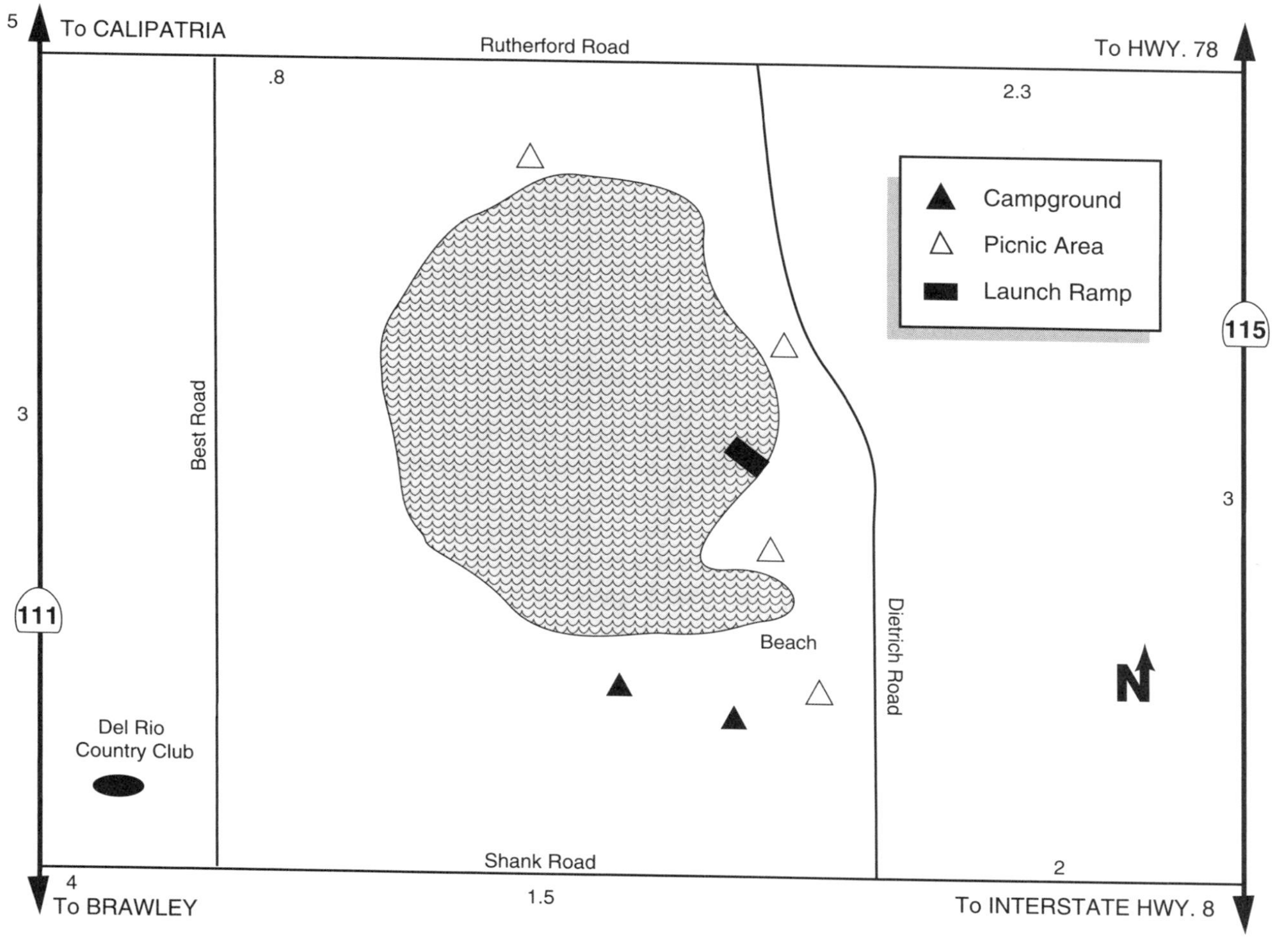

5
To CALIPATRIA
Rutherford Road
To HWY. 78
.8
2.3
Campground
Picnic Area
Launch Ramp
115
3
Best Road
3
111
Beach
Dietrich Road
N
Del Rio
Country Club
Shank Road
2
4
To BRAWLEY
1.5
To INTERSTATE HWY. 8

INFORMATION: Wiest Lake, 5351 Dietrich Rd., Brawley 92227—Ph: Imperial County: (760) 482-4236 - Ext. 1

CAMPING	BOATING	RECREATION	OTHER
10 Tent Sites Fee: $7 30 R.V. Sites Full Hookups - Fee: $35 Electric & Water Hookups - Fee: $25 Monthly Rates Available Disposal Station	Open to All Boating Paved Launch Ramp Docks	Fishing: Largemouth Bass, Bluegill, Catfish & Carp Picnicking Hiking Nature Study Swimming - Beach	Imperial County Planning & Development Services Parks & Recreation 801 Main St. El Centro 92243 Full Facilities in Brawley & Calipatria

SUNBEAM LAKE

Sunbeam Lake, with more than 25 surface acres, has been completely renovated. The Lake was enlarged, a swimming lagoon added along with a large playground. The lagoon has 12 surface acres. Owned and operated by Imperial County, the park has a variety of recreational opportunities. Boating is allowed on both the Lake and the Lagoon but no motors are permitted at the Lagoon. The angler will find a variety of warm water fish. These Lakes are 43 feet below sea level where summer temperatures average over 100 degrees. Fall, winter and spring are moderate. Surrounded by palm trees, Sunbeam Lake is a refreshing oasis located near Highway 8. Sunbeam Lake R.V. Resort, a 35-acre lake front property, is a full vacation facility including special events.

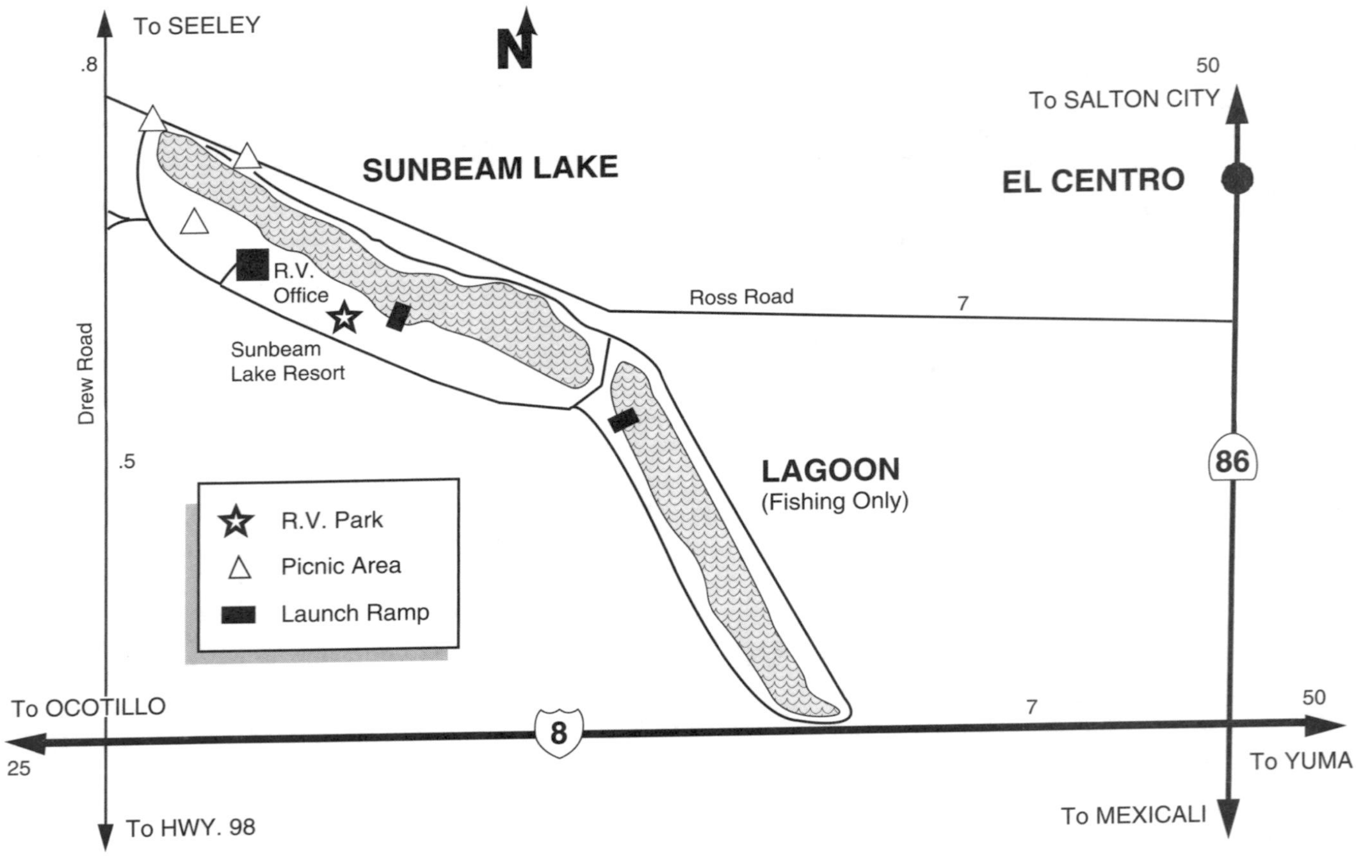
To SEELEY
.8
N
50
To SALTON CITY
SUNBEAM LAKE
EL CENTRO
R.V.
Office
Ross Road
7
Sunbeam
Lake Resort
Drew Road
.5
86
LAGOON
(Fishing Only)
R.V. Park
Picnic Area
Launch Ramp
To OCOTILLO
7
50
8
25
To YUMA
To HWY. 98
To MEXICALI

INFORMATION: Sunbeam Lake, 1750 Drew Rd., Seeley 92273—Ph: Imperial County: (760) 482-4236 - Ext. 1

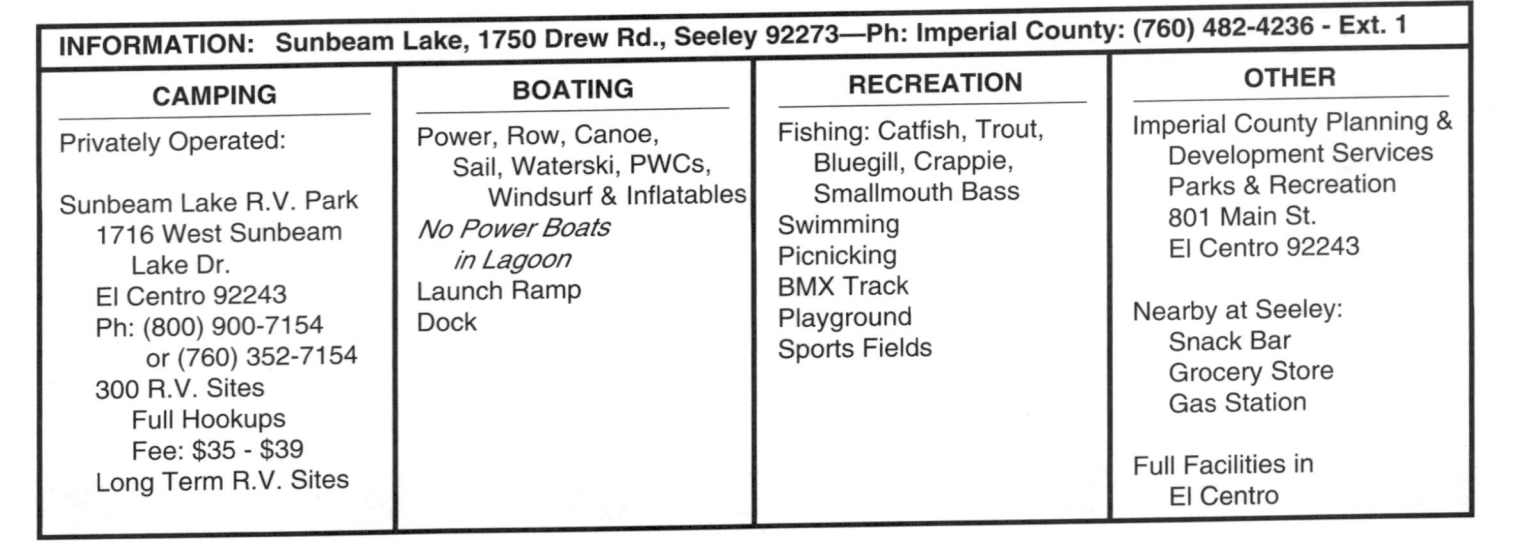

CAMPING	BOATING	RECREATION	OTHER
Privately Operated: Sunbeam Lake R.V. Park 1716 West Sunbeam Lake Dr. El Centro 92243 Ph: (800) 900-7154 or (760) 352-7154 300 R.V. Sites Full Hookups Fee: $35 - $39 Long Term R.V. Sites	Power, Row, Canoe, Sail, Waterski, PWCs, Windsurf & Inflatables *No Power Boats* *in Lagoon* Launch Ramp Dock	Fishing: Catfish, Trout, Bluegill, Crappie, Smallmouth Bass Swimming Picnicking BMX Track Playground Sports Fields	Imperial County Planning & Development Services Parks & Recreation 801 Main St. El Centro 92243 Nearby at Seeley: Snack Bar Grocery Store Gas Station Full Facilities in El Centro

DIXON LAKE

Nestled in chaparral and avocado-covered foothills, Dixon Lake is at an elevation of 1,045 feet. It has a surface area of 70 acres and 2 miles of shoreline within the 527-acre park. The Dixon Lake Recreation Area is operated by the City of Escondido Parks and Recreation Department. The facilities include camping, fishing and picnicking. Private boats are not allowed but rental boats are available. Fishing can be excellent and many large bass and catfish await the angler. Trout are stocked at Dixon Lake from November through May and catfish from June through August.

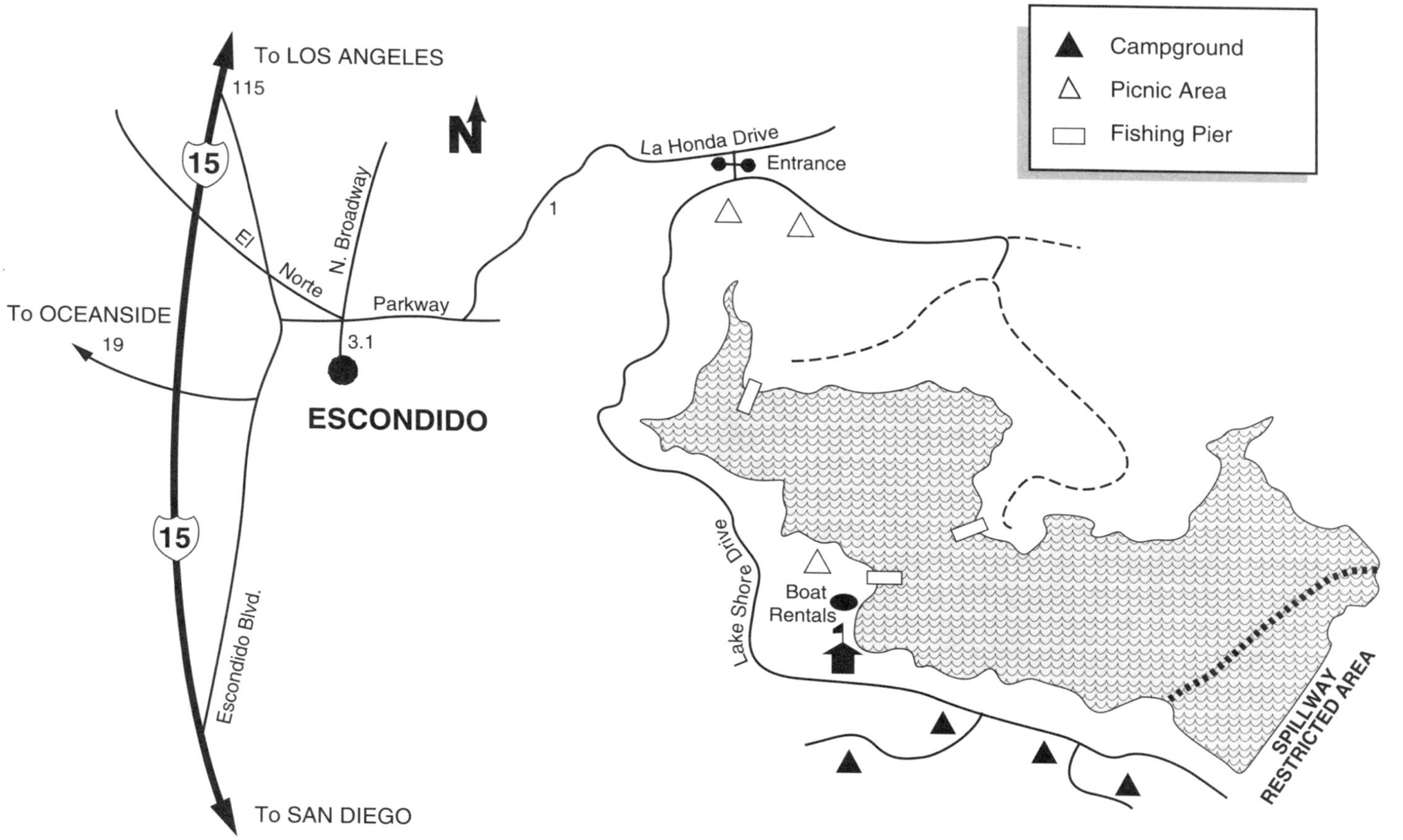

Campground
Picnic Area
Fishing Pier
To LOS ANGELES
115
15
N
La Honda Drive
Entrance
1
El Norte Parkway
N. Broadway
To OCEANSIDE
19
3.1
ESCONDIDO
15
Escondido Blvd.
Lake Shore Drive
Boat Rentals
SPILLWAY RESTRICTED AREA
To SAN DIEGO

INFORMATION: Dixon Lake, 1700 North La Honda Dr., Escondido 92027—Ranger Ph: (760) 839-4680

CAMPING	BOATING	RECREATION	OTHER
45 Tent & R.V. Sites Fee: $25 Full Hookups Fee: $35 Group Camping Disposal Station Reservations: Ph: (760) 741-3328 Day Use: $5 No Pets Allowed	No Private Boats Rentals: Rowboats with Electric Motors, Paddle Boats	Fishing: Rainbow Trout, Catfish, Bluegill, Largemouth Bass, Fishing Fee: $5 - $7 Fishing Piers Night Fishing Weekends in Summer Months No Swimming or Wading Picnicking - Shelters Nature Trails Campfire Programs Rock Climbing Wall	Snack Bar Bait & Tackle Annual Trout Derby Cabin Available for People With Special Physical Needs Public Works Dept. 201 North Broadway Escondido 92025 Full Facilities in Escondido

LAKE HENSHAW

Lake Henshaw is at an elevation of 2,740 feet in a valley on the southern slopes of Mt. Palomar. With up to 25 miles of shoreline, water levels vary depending on the season. Large oak trees around the resort create a pleasant contrast to semi-arid mountains surrounding the area. The resort has a campground with good support facilities. Housekeeping cabins are also available. No swimming is permitted in the Lake but there is a pool. Lake Henshaw is known for good fishing for bass, crappie, bluegill and channel catfish.

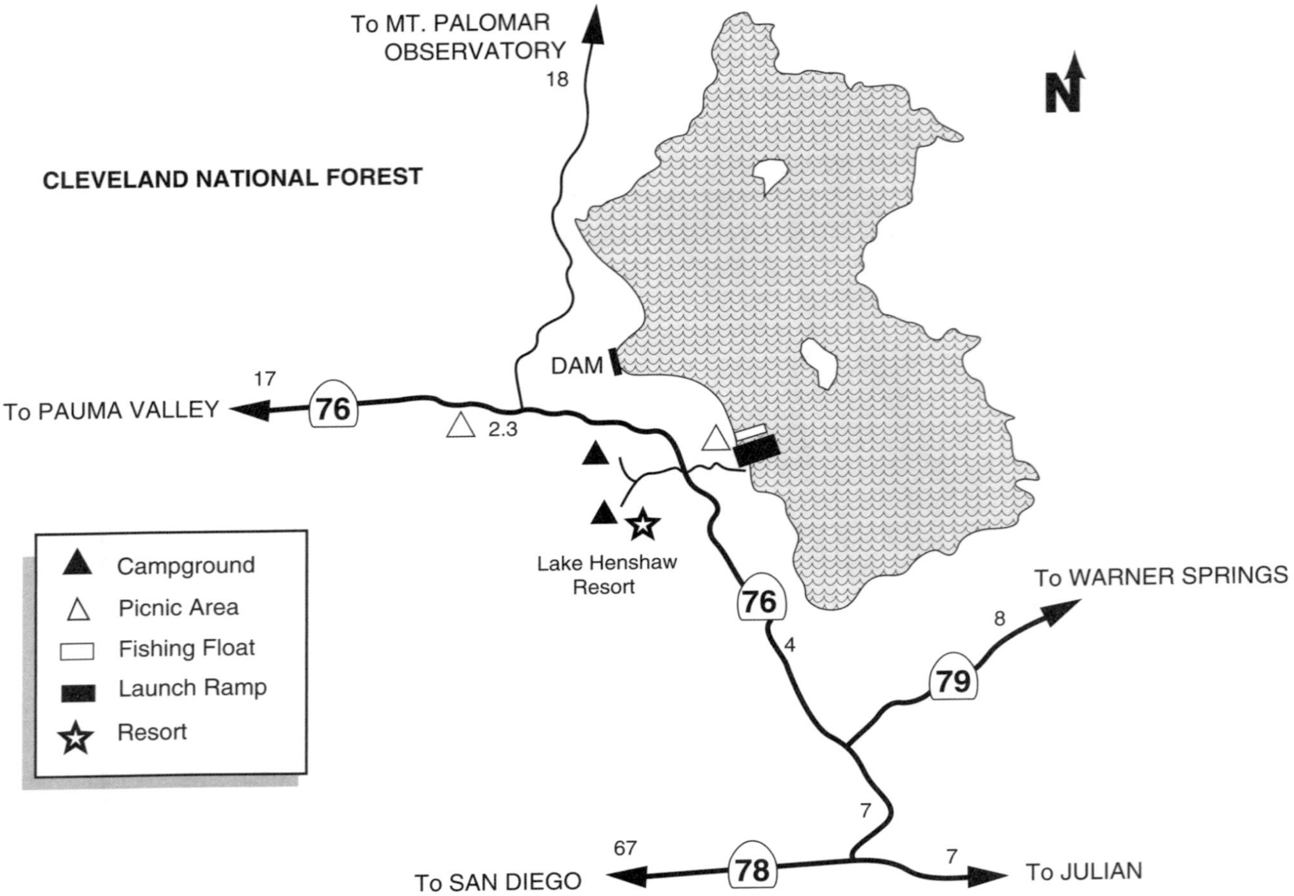
To MT. PALOMAR
OBSERVATORY
18
N
CLEVELAND NATIONAL FOREST
DAM
17
To PAUMA VALLEY
76
2.3
Lake Henshaw
Resort
Campground
Picnic Area
Fishing Float
Launch Ramp
Resort
76
4
To WARNER SPRINGS
8
79
7
67
To SAN DIEGO
78
7
To JULIAN

INFORMATION: Lake Henshaw Resort, 26439 Hwy. 76, Santa Ysabel 92070—Ph: (760) 782-3501

CAMPING	BOATING	RECREATION	OTHER
Dev. Sites for Tents & R.V.s - Fee: $20 - $25 Full Hookups (Available at Times - Several Permanent Residents - Call for Details) Disposal Station Pets Allowed	Power & Row Boats 12 Feet Minimum Length *NO Canoes, Kayaks or Rafts* 10 MPH Speed Limit Launch Ramp: $5 Rentals: Fishing Boats with Motors Lake Use Permit: $7.50 per Person per Day	Fishing : Bass, Catfish, Bluegill & Crappie Fishing Float Swimming - *Pool Only* Picnicking Hiking Trails Playground Special Events	Full Equipped Housekeeping Cabins for 2 to 7 People Reservations Accepted Restaurant Clubhouse Grocery Store Bait & Tackle

LAKE WOHLFORD, AGUA HEDIONDA LAGOON and PALOMAR PARK (DOANE POND)

From a saltwater lagoon to a coniferous mountain meadow pond at 5,500 feet, the Lakes on this page have a striking contrast. Lake Wohlford, at 1,500 feet elevation, is a good fishing Lake for trout in season. With about 145 surface acres, Wohlford is famous for trophy-size largemouth bass. Private boats are not permitted but there are rental fishing boats. Agua Hedionda Lagoon is a large saltwater lagoon off Interstate Highway 5. Designated areas are for all types of boating. This is a popular waterskiing and kayaking facility. There is a water ski school and personal watercraft rentals, a pro shop, 3-lane paved launch ramp, dry storage and a concession. Doane Pond, a separate facility, is in the Palomar Mountain State Park with spectacular views of the Pacific Ocean. Numerous hiking trails, picnic sites and campgrounds are available within the 1,862 acres of parkland. Anglers can catch trout with the best months being November through June.

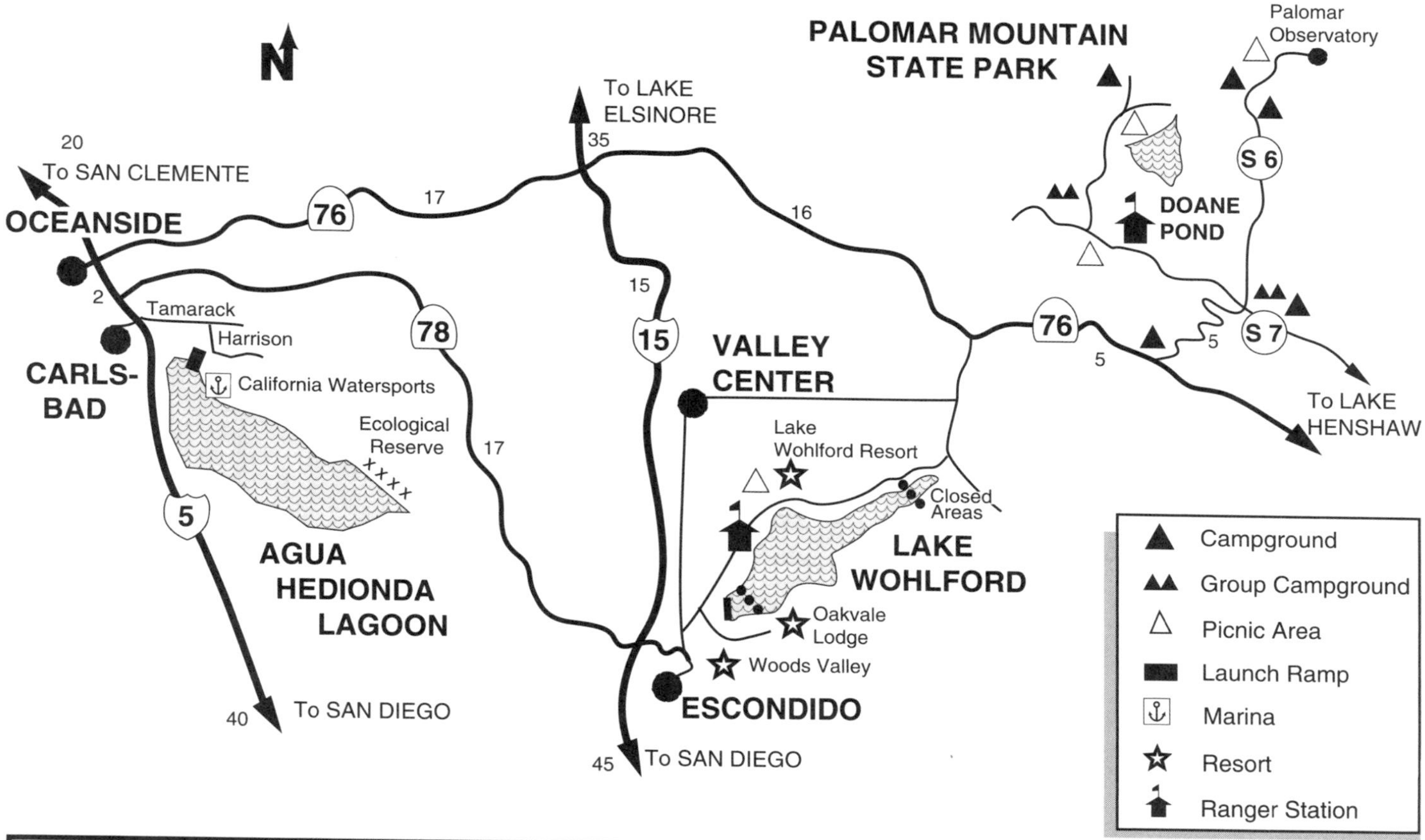

PALOMAR MOUNTAIN STATE PARK
Palomar Observatory
N
To LAKE ELSINORE
35
20
To SAN CLEMENTE
OCEANSIDE
76
17
16
S 6
DOANE POND
2
Tamarack
Harrison
California Watersports
78
15
15
VALLEY CENTER
76
5
S 7
5
To LAKE HENSHAW
CARLS-BAD
Ecological Reserve
17
Lake Wohlford Resort
Closed Areas
LAKE WOHLFORD
5
AGUA HEDIONDA LAGOON
Oakvale Lodge
Woods Valley
40
To SAN DIEGO
ESCONDIDO
45
To SAN DIEGO
Campground
Group Campground
Picnic Area
Launch Ramp
Marina
Resort
Ranger Station

INFORMATION: Lake Wohlford, 25453 Lake Wohlford Rd., Escondido 92027—Ph: (760) 839-4346

CAMPING	BOATING	RECREATION	OTHER
Dev. Sites for Tents & R.V.s - Hookups: Lake Wohlford Resort Ph: (760) 749-2755 Oakvale Park Ph: (760) 749-2895 Woods Valley Campground Ph: (760) 749-2905 Doane Valley Campground: Dev. Sites for Tents & R.V.s - Fee: $15 - $20 Reservations:(800) 444-7275	Lake Wohlford: No Private Boats Rentals: Fishing Boats & Motors, Bass Boats Agua Hedionda: California Watersports Ph: (760) 434-3089 Open to All Boats Designated Areas Speed Limit: 45 MPH Rentals: PWCs, Canoes & Kayaks Doane Pond: No Boating	Trout, Largemouth Bass, Catfish, Crappie & Bluegill Fishing Fee at Lake Wohlford Picnicking Hiking Trails Lake Wohlford: No Swimming Doane Pond: No Swimming California Watersports: Waterski School	Full Facilities and Other R.V. Parks in Valley Center & Escondido

SANTEE LAKES and LAKE POWAY

With seven different Lakes, the Santee Recreational Area, has 300 campsites with full hook-ups. A swimming pool, picnic facilities, playgrounds and volleyball courts are also available. Lake Poway has undeveloped, walk-in campsites along with picnic areas, nature walks and equestrian trails. The 60-surface acre Lake is open to night fishing on weekends during summer months. Both Poway and Santee Lakes are closed to private boating but rentals are available.

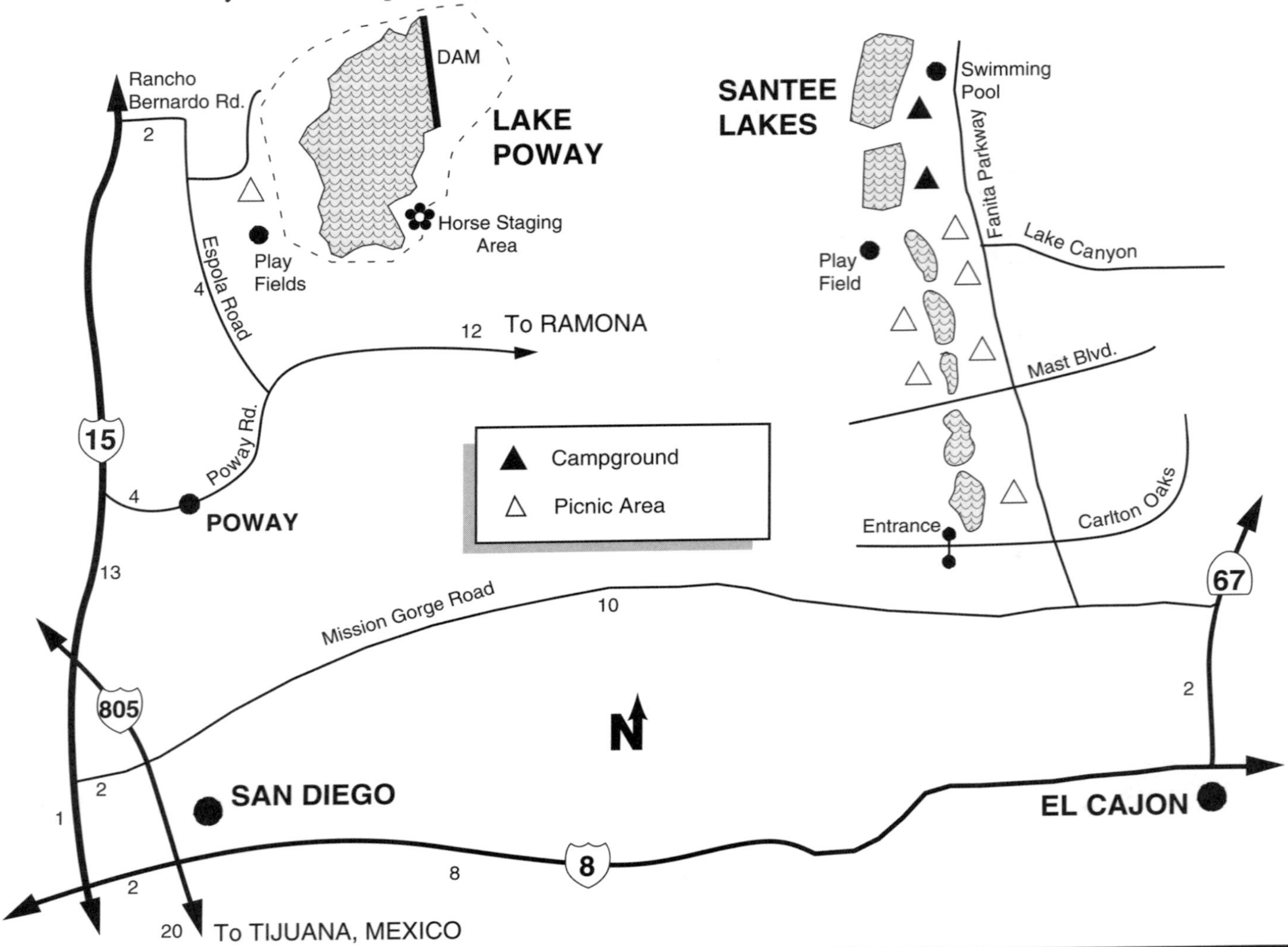

Rancho Bernardo Rd.
DAM
LAKE POWAY
Horse Staging Area
Play Fields
Espola Road
To RAMONA
Poway Rd.
POWAY
SANTEE LAKES
Swimming Pool
Fanita Parkway
Lake Canyon
Play Field
Mast Blvd.
Campground
Picnic Area
Entrance
Carlton Oaks
Mission Gorge Road
N
SAN DIEGO
EL CAJON
To TIJUANA, MEXICO
15
805
8
67
2
4
12
13
10
1
20

INFORMATION: Santee Lakes, 9310 Fanita Parkway, Santee 92071—Ph: (619) 596-3141			
CAMPING	**BOATING**	**RECREATION**	**OTHER**
Santee Lakes: 300 R.V. Sites Full Hookups Fees: $33 - $46 Disposal Station Grocery Store Swimming Pool Special Events Lake Poway: No Camping Picnic Sites Only	Lake Poway: *No Private Boats* Rentals: Row & Motor Boats, Pedal Boats No Boating Mon./Tues. Santee Lakes: *No Private Boats* Rentals: Rowboats, Pedal Boats, Kayaks & Canoes	Fishing: Rainbow Trout Largemouth Bass, Bluegill & Catfish Poway: Fishing Wed./Sun. Fishing Tournaments Picnicking Group Sites Hiking, Equestrian & Nature Trails - Poway Santee Lakes: Fishing Fee: $5 - $8 Playgrounds Volleyball Courts	Lake Poway 14644 Lake Poway Rd. Poway 92064 Ph: (858) 668-4772 Snack Bar Bait & Tackle Playgrounds Volleyball Courts, Horseshoes, Softball - Night Lights 15-Acre Grass Picnic Area

Lake Cuyamaca is at an elevation of 4,600 feet in a mountain setting of oak and pine trees. The dam was originally built in 1887. There is a minimum pool of 110 surface acres. Rainbow trout are stocked each year and there is also excellent fishing for warm water species. Check for specific boating regulations for lake use. Cuyamaca Rancho State Park, which borders Lake Cuyamaca, covers 25,000 acres and has over 100 miles of scenic equestrian and hiking trails. Paso Picacho has a developed campground. Los Caballos Horse Camp has developed sites including corrals for horses. This area is a great spot for viewing native wildlife.

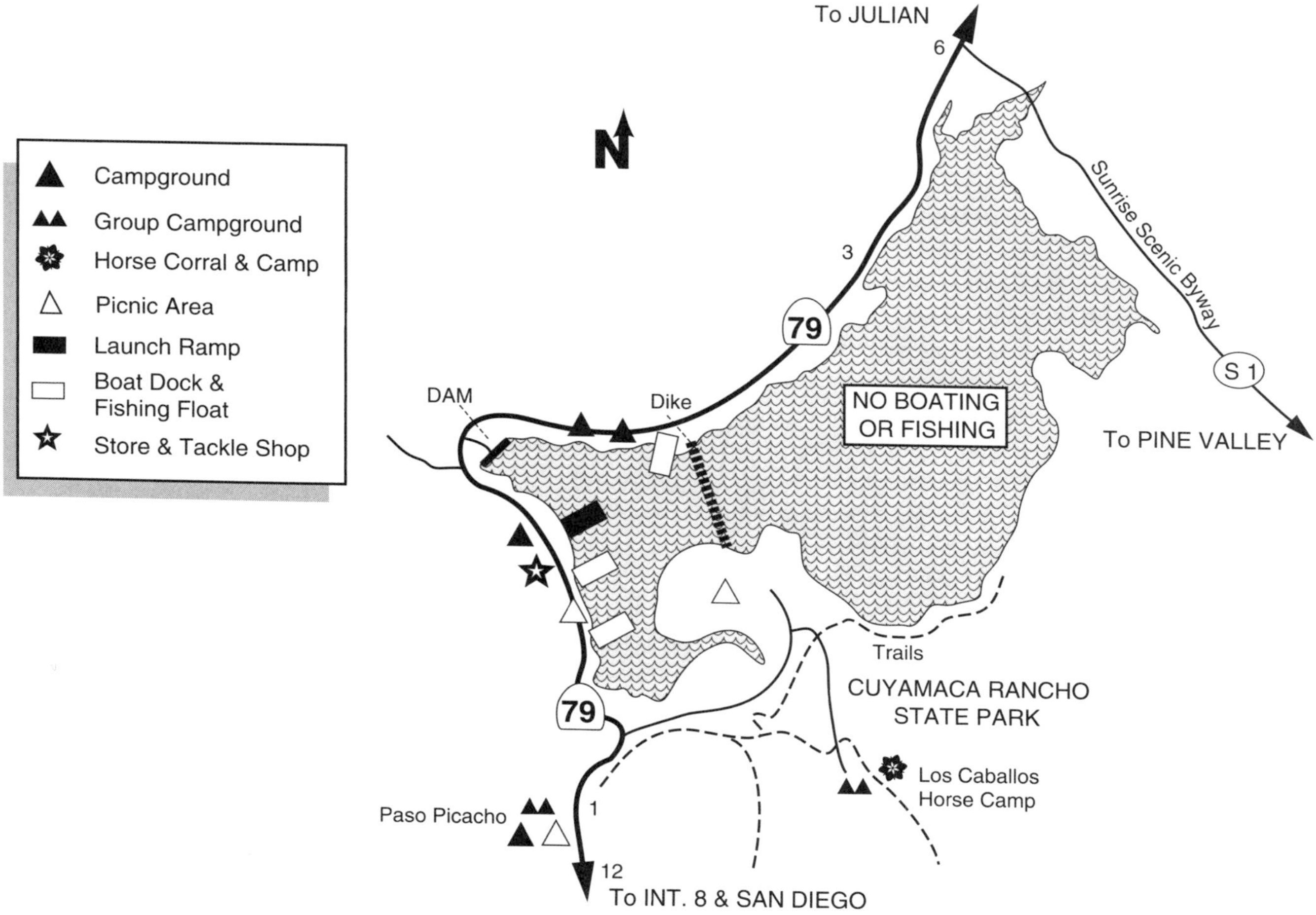
Campground
Group Campground
Horse Corral & Camp
Picnic Area
Launch Ramp
Boat Dock & Fishing Float
Store & Tackle Shop
N
To JULIAN
6
3
79
Sunrise Scenic Byway
S 1
To PINE VALLEY
DAM
Dike
NO BOATING OR FISHING
Trails
CUYAMACA RANCHO STATE PARK
79
Los Caballos Horse Camp
Paso Picacho
1
12
To INT. 8 & SAN DIEGO

INFORMATION: Lake Cuyamaca, 15027 Highway 79, Julian 92036—Ph: (760) 765-0515 or (877) 581-9904

CAMPING	BOATING	RECREATION	OTHER
19 Dev. R.V. Sites Water & Electric Hookups 21 Dev. Tent Sites Fees: $18 - $25 Group Site for 8 R.V.s 2 Fully Equipped Cabins 3 Sleeping Cabins	Power & Row Boats, Canoes & Kayaks, Inflatables & Float Tube Check for Specific Regulations Speed Limit - 10 MPH Launch Ramp - Fee: $5 Rentals: Boats & Motors & Paddle Boats	Fishing: Trout, Crappie, Catfish, Bluegill, Sturgeon, Smallmouth Bass Fishing Fee: $3.50 - $6 Free Fishing Class Sat. @ 10 am No Swimming or Body Contact with Water Picnicking Hiking & Equestrian Trails Bicycling Trails Bird & Wildlife Watching	Cuyamaca Rancho State Park - Ph: (760) 765-3020 85 Dev. Sites for Tents & R.V.s No Hookups Fee: $15 - $20 Equestrian Group Sites Including Corrals 5 Cabins Reservations: Ph: (800) 444-7275 Day Use Fee: $6

SAN DIEGO CITY LAKES: HODGES, SUTHERLAND, MIRAMAR, EL CAPITAN, MURRAY, UPPER and LOWER OTAY and BARRETT

These popular Lakes provide some of the best bass fishing in America. They are operated by the City of San Diego.

See the following page for details on each Lake.

....Continued....

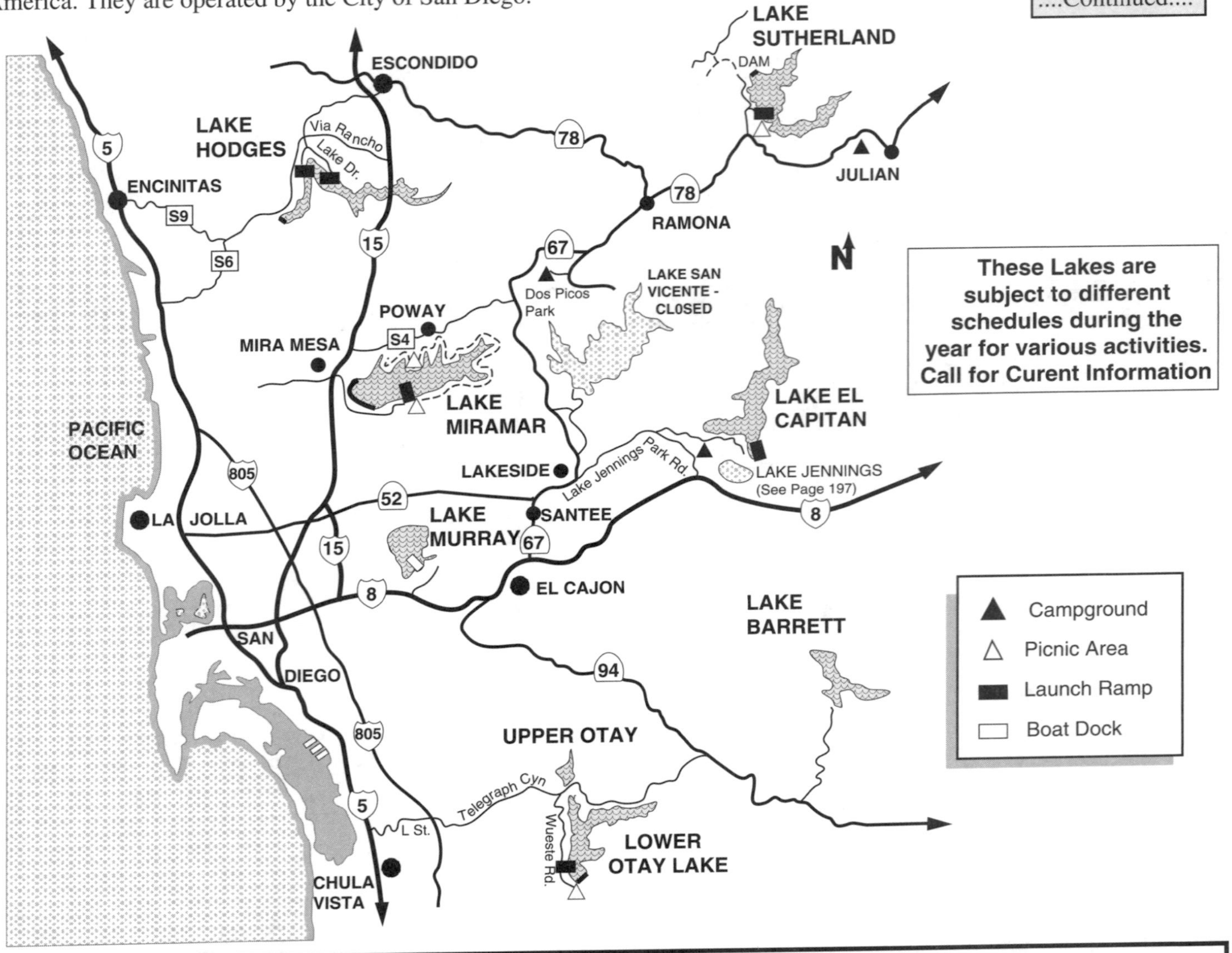
LAKE SUTHERLAND
DAM
ESCONDIDO
LAKE HODGES
Via Rancho
Lake Dr.
5
78
ENCINITAS
S9
S6
15
JULIAN
RAMONA
67
N
Dos Picos Park
LAKE SAN VICENTE - CLOSED
POWAY
S4
MIRA MESA
LAKE MIRAMAR
LAKE EL CAPITAN
PACIFIC OCEAN
805
LAKESIDE
Lake Jennings Park Rd.
LAKE JENNINGS (See Page 197)
52
LA JOLLA
SANTEE
LAKE MURRAY
8
EL CAJON
LAKE BARRETT
SAN DIEGO
94
Campground
Picnic Area
Launch Ramp
Boat Dock
UPPER OTAY
Telegraph Cyn
L St.
Wueste Rd.
LOWER OTAY LAKE
CHULA VISTA

These Lakes are subject to different schedules during the year for various activities. Call for Curent Information

INFORMATION: San Diego City Lakes—Ph: (619) 668-2050 or 24-Hour Recorded Information: (619) 465-3474

CAMPING	BOATING	RECREATION	OTHER
There is No Camping at Any of These San Diego City Lakes See Following Page for Nearest Camping Lake San Vicente is Closed to All Recreation	Power, Row, Sail, Kayaks & Inflatables Boat Inspections Fees: $7 Any Private Boat Use Including Canoes & Kayaks Speed Limits Vary Rentals: Rowboats, Motorboats & Kayaks	Fishing: Bass, Trout, Crappie, Bluefill, Catfish Fishing Permits: Adults: Fee $4 - $8 Juniors: 8-15 years: Fee $2.50 Picnicking Hiking & Bicycling Trails Water Contact Activities: Adults: Fee - $10 Juniors 8-15 years: Fee - $5	Bass Tournaments Full Facilities at Nearby Towns

The following Lakes are open from Sunrise to Sunset - Various Schedules for Activities.

HODGES at an elevation of 330 feet, is located approximately 31 miles north of San Diego and five miles south of Escondido. This reservoir has a maximum surface area of 1,234 acres with 27 miles of chaparral-covered shoreline. The reservoir is open from February through October on Wednesdays, Saturdays and Sundays for picnicking, boating and fishing for bass, crappie, bluegill, channel catfish and carp. Hiking and equestrian trails are around much of the reservoir. Rentals of rowboats, motorboats and kayaks are available Saturdays and Sundays.

SUTHERLAND at an elevation of 2,074 feet, is located 45 miles northeast of San Diego between Ramona and Julian. This reservoir has a maximum surface area of 557 acres with 11 miles of oak and chaparral-covered shoreline. Currently the water level is very low so check for conditions. The reservoir is open Saturdays and Sundays for picnicking, hiking, boating and fishing for bass, bluegill, sunfish, crappie, channel catfish and blue catfish. There are no rental boats. The nearest camping is at William Heise County Park or Dos Picos County Park. Sutherland also has wild turkey hunting during the spring season.

MIRAMAR at an elevation of 714 feet, is located about 18 miles north of San Diego. This small reservoir has a maximum surface area of 162 acres and four miles of shoreline. The reservoir is open 7 days a week for boating and fishing for bass, bluegill, sunfish, channel catfish, and trout. Float tubes and shore fishing are allowed. Miramar is also open 7 days a week for picnicking, walking, jogging, bicycling or skating. Rentals include rowboats, motorboats and kayaks on Saturdays and Sundays only.

EL CAPITAN at an elevation of 750 feet, is located in the foothills of Lakeside approximately 30 miles northeast of San Diego. There is a maximum surface area of 1,562 acres with 22 miles of shoreline. The reservoir is closed Tuesdays and Wednesdays. On Thursdays, Fridays, Saturdays and Sundays, it is open to fishing, general boating, waterskiing, PWCs and wakeboarding. Sunday there is no fishing but there is water contact boating only. Monday the reservoir is open to fishing and general boating but no waterskiing, PWCs or wakeboarding. Kayaks are allowed on Thursdays, Fridays, Saturdays and Mondays. Picnicking, hiking and fishing for bass, bluegill, blue and channel catfish, crappie and sunfish are available. Rowboats and motorboats can be rented on Saturdays. Nearest camping is at Lake Jennings County Park.

MURRAY, the "in town" reservoir, is located between San Diego and La Mesa at the base of Cowles Mountain. The reservoir has a maximum surface area of 172 acres with four miles of shoreline. It is open seven days a week for boating and fishing for bass, crappie, bluegill, channel catfish and trout. Picnicking, walking, jogging, bicycling and skating can be enjoyed all week. Rentals include rowboats, motorboats and kayaks and are available Saturdays and Sundays.

LOWER OTAY is in the rolling chaparral-covered hills east of Chula Vista, approximately 20 miles southeast of San Diego. The maximum surface area is 1,100 acres with 25 miles of shoreline. The reservoir is open Wednesdays, Saturdays and Sundays for picnicking, hiking, boating and fishing for bass, crappie, bluegill and channel, blue and white catfish and trout. Rowboats, motorboats and kayaks are available for rent. Nearest camping is at Sweetwater Summit County Park.

UPPER OTAY is located just north of Lower Otay. The maximum surface area is 20 acres with five miles of shoreline. The reservoir is open on Wednesdays, Saturdays and Sundays for fishing for bass, bluegill and bullhead. This is a catch and release fishery with use of barbless hooks on artificial lures only. No boats are allowed so fishing is from shore, waders or float tubes. Permits can be purchased at the Iron Ranger pay station.

BARRETT is located in a remote area 35 miles east of San Diego. The maximum surface area is 861 acres with 12 miles of shoreline. The reservoir is open Wednesdays, Saturdays and Sundays from May through September. This is a catch and release fishery with use of barbless hooks on artificial lures only. During the season (October through January), this Lake also has waterfowl hunting on Wednesdays and Saturdays. Call for information - Ph: (619) 668-2050.

Since schedules change, it is important to call first to confirm days and activities allowed.

Fluctuating water levels may cause closure of launch ramps and boat docks. All schedules are subject to change. Please call 24-hour recording (619) 465-3474 or check the City's website www.sandiego.gov to verify status before going to any San Diego City Lake.

LAKE JENNINGS

Lake Jennings is east of El Cajon at an elevation of 690 feet. Helix Water District administers this reservoir of 180 surface acres. The fairly steep shoreline is semi-arid and dotted with sumac trees and a few pines. Open year around, this is a very popular fishing lake so camping reservations are advised. The Lake is stocked with trout from mid-October into April. Catfish are stocked mid-May to mid-August. Lake Jennings holds records for catching big fish. This is a good facility for children and free fishing lessons are given on Sundays. Boating is limited to 10 mph and rentals are available. No swimming or wading is permitted at this Lake as it is a domestic water supply.

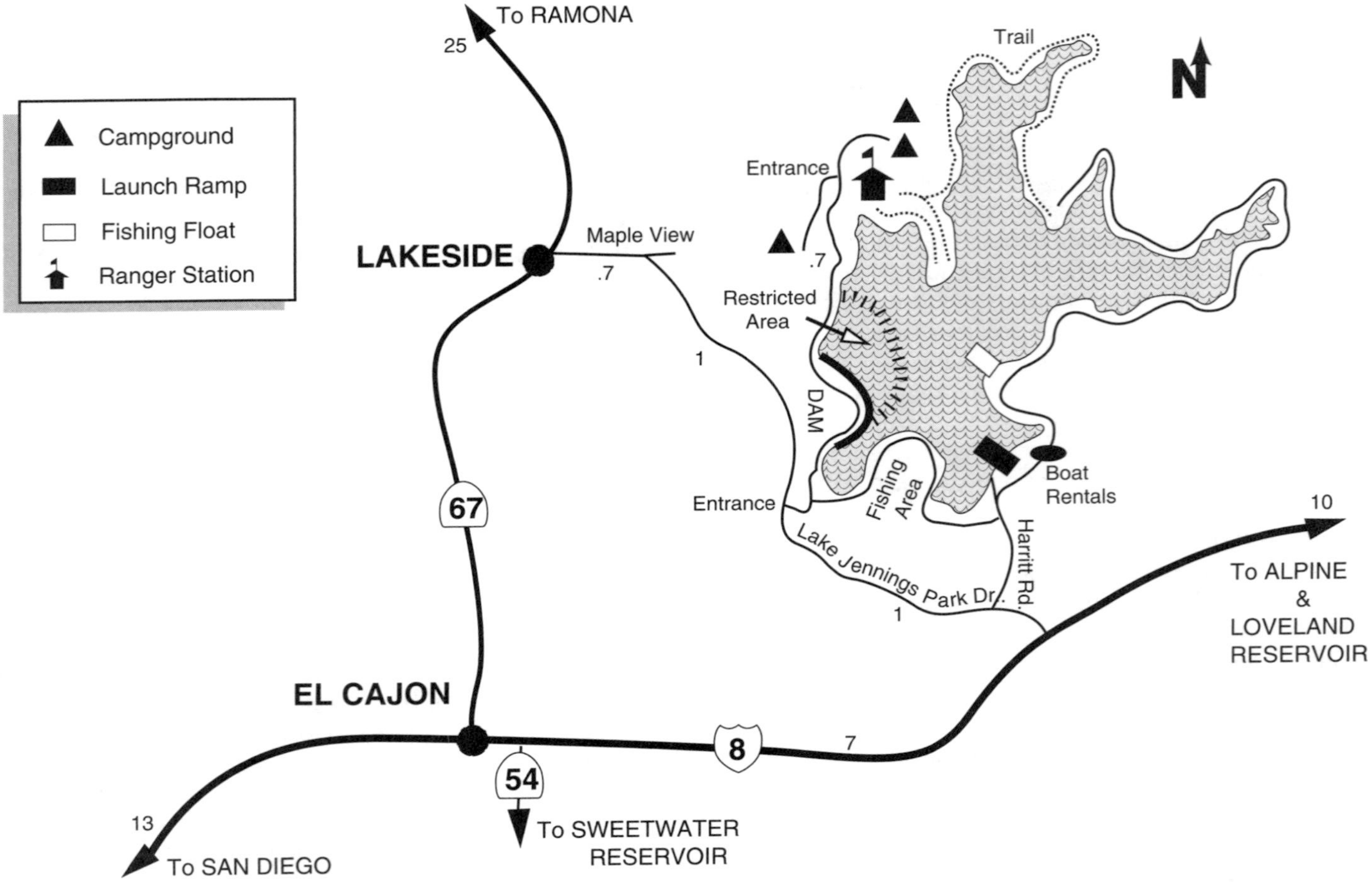
To RAMONA
25
Campground
Launch Ramp
Fishing Float
Ranger Station
LAKESIDE
Maple View
.7
1
Trail
N
Entrance
.7
Restricted
Area
DAM
Fishing
Area
Boat
Rentals
Entrance
Lake Jennings Park Dr.
1
Harritt Rd.
67
10
To ALPINE
&
LOVELAND
RESERVOIR
EL CAJON
8
7
54
13
To SAN DIEGO
To SWEETWATER
RESERVOIR

INFORMATION: Helix Water District, 7811 University Ave., La Mesa 91941—Ph: (619) 466-0585

CAMPING	BOATING	RECREATION	OTHER
96 Dev. Sites for Tents & R.V.s - Full & Partial Hookups Fees: $23 - $30 Group Campground - $75 Reservations Advised: Ph: (619) 390-1623 Youth Group Camp - $50 Ph: (619) 390-1300 Disposal Station Day Use: $1	Fishing Boats Only 10 MPH Speed Limit Launch Ramp- Fee: $6 Rentals: Fishing Boats & Motors, Paddle Boat	Fishing: Trout, Catfish, Bluegill, Bass Fees: $3 - $8 Plus California Fishing License Fishing Float Hiking Trails Playground Birdwatching No Swimming or Wading	Snack Bar Bait & Tackle Free Fishing Classes Information: Ph: (619) 443-2510 Sweetwater Authority: Sweetwater Reservoir Ph: (619) 409-6777 Loveland Reservoir Ph: (619) 409-6776 Hike-In Shoreline Fishing Only

Lake Morena, at an elevation of 3,000 feet, is located in the Cleveland National Forest east of San Diego. Surrounded by chaparral, oaks and grassland, the Lake is in the center of 3,250 acres of parkland maintained by San Diego County.

Lake Morena has a surface area of over 1,500 acres when full. Check for current water levels. There are warm water fish including the Florida strain of largemouth bass. Trout are planted during the winter months and fishing is the primary activity. Boating is limited to 10 MPH and inflatables are subject to strict standards. Hikers, backpackers and equestrians can enjoy the nearby Pacific Crest Trail. In Campo, you can take a train ride through the backcountry and visit the local Railway Museum.

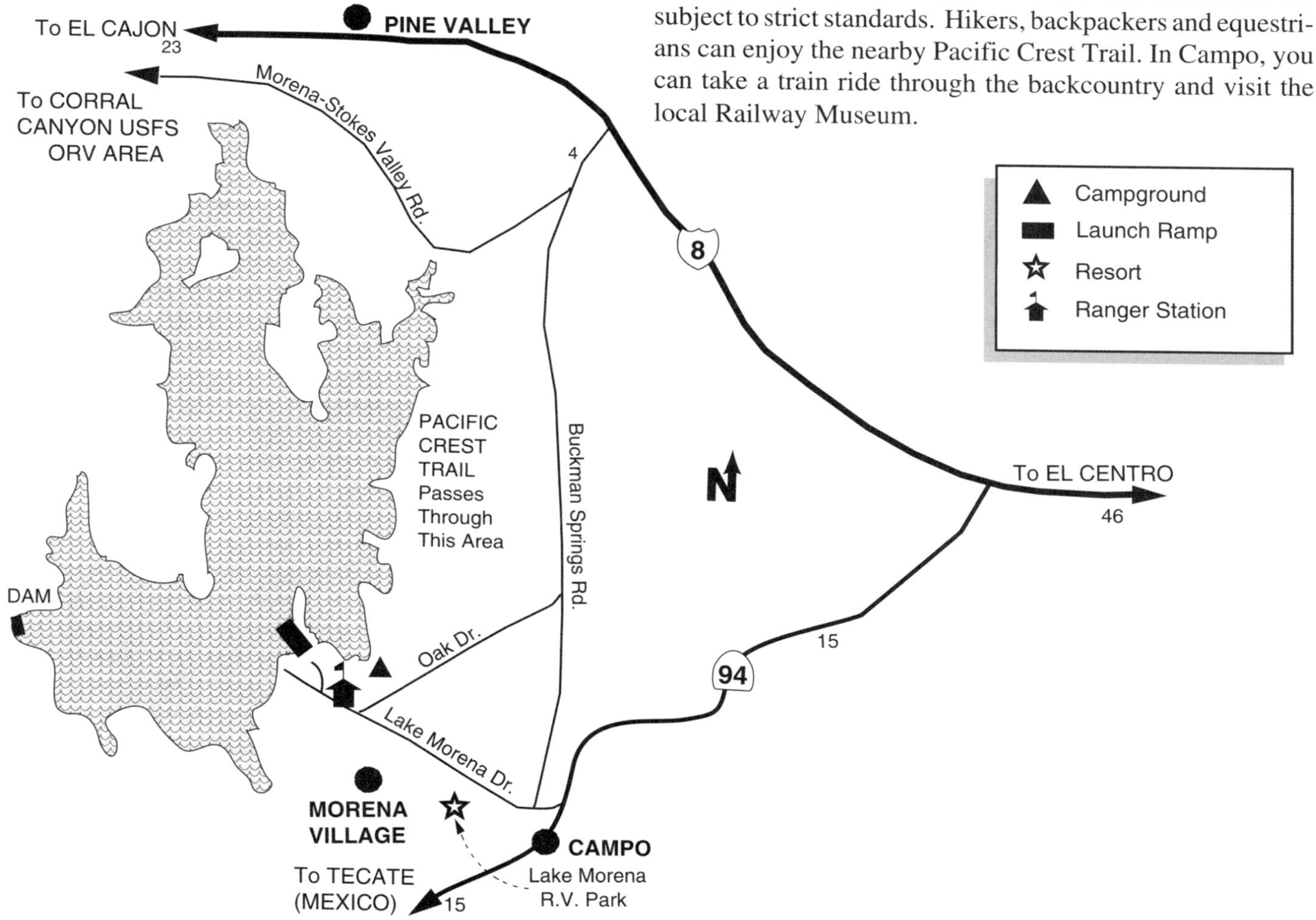
To EL CAJON
23
PINE VALLEY
To CORRAL CANYON USFS ORV AREA
Morena-Stokes Valley Rd.
4
8
Campground
Launch Ramp
Resort
Ranger Station
PACIFIC CREST TRAIL Passes Through This Area
Buckman Springs Rd.
N
To EL CENTRO
46
DAM
Oak Dr.
15
94
Lake Morena Dr.
MORENA VILLAGE
CAMPO
Lake Morena R.V. Park
To TECATE (MEXICO)
15

INFORMATION: Lake Morena County Park, 2550 Lake Morena Dr., Campo 91906—Ph: (619) 579-4101

CAMPING	BOATING	RECREATION	OTHER
86 Dev. Sites for Tents & R.V.s - 58 With Water & Electric Hookups Fees: $19 - $24 Youth Group Camp: $40 10 Wilderness Cabins No Water or Electricity - Fee: $30 Reservations Required: Ph: (858) 565-3600	Power, Row & Sail Boats, Kayaks & Inflatables Regulations - Call for Information 10 MPH Speed Limit Launch Ramp Lake Use Fee for Private Boats: $6 Rentals: Fishing, Motor & Row Boats *Check for Current Water Levels*	Fishing: Laregmouth Bass, Bluegill, Catfish, Crappie & Trout Fishing Fee: $2 - $5 Picnicking Hiking Trails Pacific Crest Trail Equestrian Trails Playground Interpretive Programs No Swimming Allowed	Lake Morena R.V. Park 2330 Lake Morena Dr. Campo 91906 Ph: (619) 478-5677 41 R.V. Sites to 40 Ft. 26 With Full Hookups Fee: $28 - $30 Disposal Station Morena Village: Gas, Store Campo: Railway Museum Train Ride

LAKE HAVASU

Lake Havasu is at an elevation of 482 feet in the desert between Arizona and California. Flowing out of Topock Gorge, the Colorado River becomes Lake Havasu. This 19,300 acre Lake of secluded coves, quiet inlets and open water backs up 45 miles behind Parker Dam. Famed for its outstanding fishery and excellent boating waters, Lake Havasu attracts thousands of visitors. Major fishing, powerboating and waterskiing tournaments are held each year. Numerous campgrounds, resorts and marinas are located around the Lake. The hub of the area is Lake Havasu City and Pittsburg Point which offer complete facilities.

....Continued....

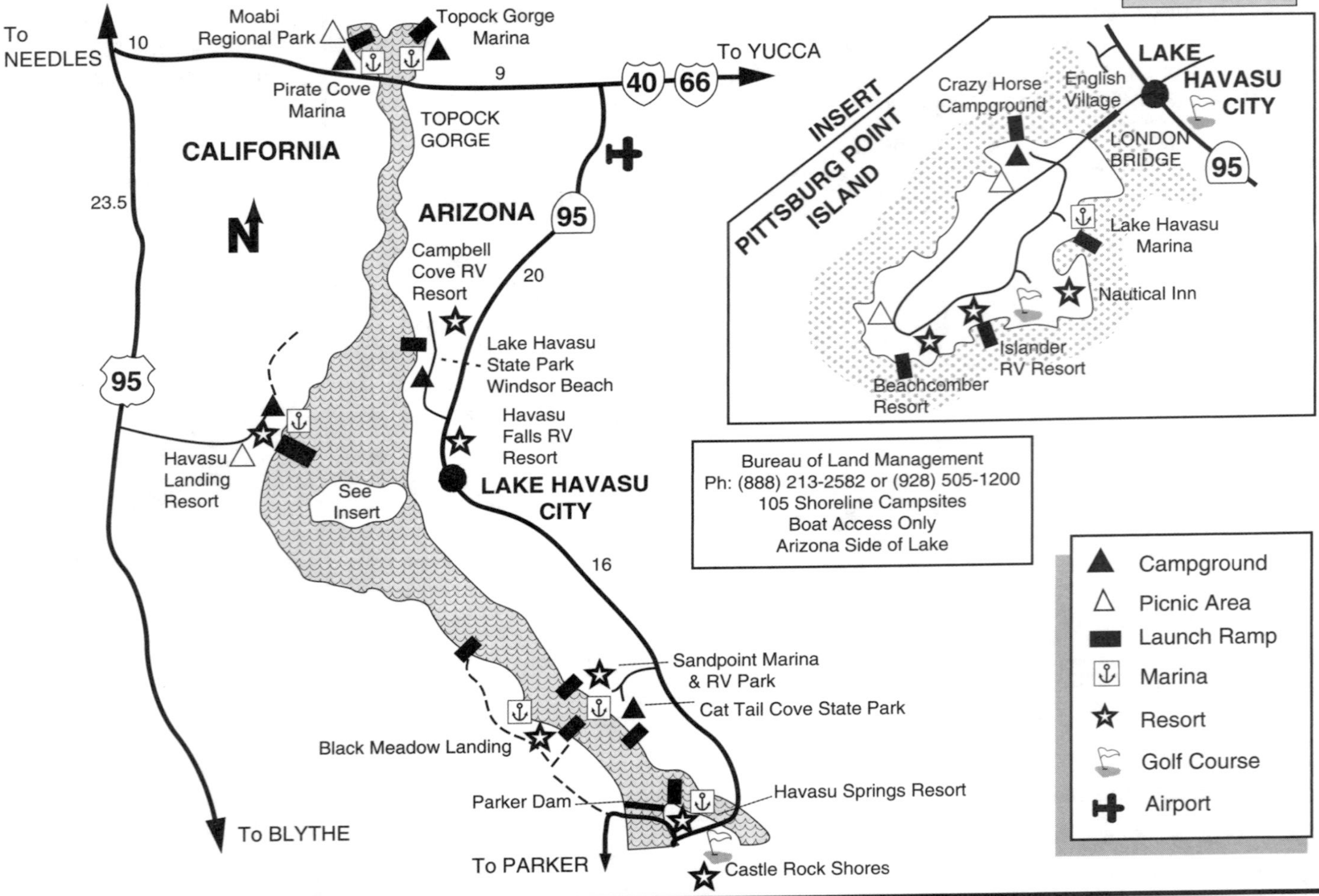

To NEEDLES
10
Moabi Regional Park
Topock Gorge Marina
To YUCCA
9
40
66
Pirate Cove Marina
TOPOCK GORGE
CALIFORNIA
23.5
N
ARIZONA
95
Campbell Cove RV Resort
20
Lake Havasu State Park Windsor Beach
95
Havasu Falls RV Resort
Havasu Landing Resort
See Insert
LAKE HAVASU CITY
16
Sandpoint Marina & RV Park
Cat Tail Cove State Park
Black Meadow Landing
Parker Dam
Havasu Springs Resort
To BLYTHE
To PARKER
Castle Rock Shores
INSERT
PITTSBURG POINT ISLAND
Crazy Horse Campground
English Village
LAKE HAVASU CITY
LONDON BRIDGE
95
Lake Havasu Marina
Nautical Inn
Islander RV Resort
Beachcomber Resort
Bureau of Land Management
Ph: (888) 213-2582 or (928) 505-1200
105 Shoreline Campsites
Boat Access Only
Arizona Side of Lake
Campground
Picnic Area
Launch Ramp
Marina
Resort
Golf Course
Airport

INFORMATION: Tourism Bureau, 314 London Bridge Rd., Lake Havasu City, AZ 86403—Ph: (928) 453-3444

CAMPING	BOATING	RECREATION	OTHER
Numerous Campgrounds Around Lake See Following Pages	Power, Row, Canoe, Sail, Waterski, PWCs, Windsurf & Inflatable Full Service Marinas Rentals: Fishing, Power, Pontoons & Houseboats *High Winds can be a Hazard*	Fishing: Catfish, Bluegill, Crappie, Largemouth & Striped Bass Swimming Picnicking Hiking Trails Nature Study River Rafting	Full Resort Facilitles Airport Golf Courses Tennis Courts Boat Excursions Casino Trips Home of the London Bridge

SOME CAMPGROUNDS & R. V. RESORTS AS SHOWN ON MAP - *Call for Fees*

CALIFORNIA

MOABI REGIONAL PARK

100 Park Moabi Rd., Needles 92363, Ph: (760) 326-3831

35 R.V. Sites with Full Hookups, 120 R.V. Sites with Water & Electric Hookups, Disposal Station
Unlimited Tent Sites, 24 Group Camp Areas
2-1/2 Miles of Shoreline, Picnic Sites with Tables & BBQs, Equestrian Trails,
7-Lane Launch Ramp, Boat Slips, Canoe Rentals, General Store.

PIRATE COVE MARINA

Ph: (760) 326-9187

Beachside Cabin Rentals, Bar & Grill,
Rentals: Pontoon Boats, Ski & Fishing Boats, Kayaks & PWCs, Courtesy Dock, Bait & Tackle.

HAVASU LANDING RESORT & CASINO

Box 1707, Havasu Lake 92363, Ph: (760) 858-4593 or (800) 307-3610

181 R.V. Sites with Full Hookups, 4 Large Tent Campsite Areas, Mobile Home Park,
Unlimited Boat Access Camping Along the Shoreline, Air Strip, Snack Bars,
Grocery Store, Restaurant & Lounge, Casino, Full Service Marina, 3 Launch Ramps, Boat Slips,
Courtesy Dock, Tour Boat with Hourly Trips to Lake Havasu City.

BLACK MEADOW LANDING

156100 Black Meadow Rd., Parker Dam 92267, Ph: (760) 663-4901 or (800) 742-8278

350 R.V. Sites with Full Hookups, Disposal Station, Tent Camping Plus 75 Motel Rooms,
Restaurant, Launch Ramp, 160 Boat Slips, Grocery Store, Tackle Shop, Swim Beach, 5-Hole Golf Course.

ARIZONA

TOPOCK GORGE MARINA

14999 Highway 95. Topock, AZ 86436, Ph: (928) 768-2325

Full Service Marina, Fuel Dock & Launch Ramp, Courtesy Dock, 50 Boat Slips
General Store, Restaurant, Bar.

CAMPBELL COVE R.V. RESORT

1523 Industrial Blvd., Lake Havasu City, AZ 96403, Ph: (928) 854-7200

109 R. V. Sites with Full Hookups, Tent Camping March Through October,
Boat Storage, Swimming Pool, BBQs, Clubhouse, Next to Windsor Beach

LAKE HAVASU STATE PARK- WINDSOR BEACH

2 Miles North of London Bridge. 699 London Beach Rd., Lake Havasu City, AZ 96403
Ph: (928) 855-2784

47 Sites for Tents & R.V.s, BLM Boat-In Camps, Disposal Station, 3 Launch Ramps, Picnic Area, Walking Trail.

HAVASU FALLS R.V. RESORT

3493 Highway 95, North Lake Havasu City, AZ 96404, Ph: (877) 843-3255 or (928) 764-0050

169 R.V. Sites with Full Hookups, Dry Storage, Swimming Pool, Clubhouse.

SANDPOINT MARINA AND R.V. PARK

P.O.Box 1469, Lake Havasu City, AZ 86405, Ph: (928) 855-0549

173 Sites R.V.s with Full Hookups, Tent Camping, Disposal Station,
Grocery Store & Tackle Shop, Gas Dock, Boat & R.V. Storage, Launch Ramp, 107 Boat Slips.

....Continued....

LAKE HAVASU............Continued

CATTAIL COVE STATE PARK
Box 1990, Lake Havasu City, AZ 86405, Ph: (928) 855-1223
61 Tent & R.V. Sites, Electric & Water Hookups, Disposal Station, Tent Camping, 28 Boat-In Camps, Launch Ramps, Picnic Areas, Swim Beach, Hiking Trail, 2,000 acres of Parkland.

HAVASU SPRINGS RESORT
2581 Highway 95, Parker, AZ 85344, Ph: (928) 667-3361
136 R.V. Sites with Full Hookups, 44 Motel Rooms, Restaurant & Lounge, Grocery Store, Swimming Pool & Beach, Launch Ramp, 250 Boat Slips, Fishing Dock, Tennis Courts, Golf Course.

CASTLE ROCK SHORES RESORT
5220 Highway 95, Parker, AZ 85344, Ph: (928) 667-2344 or (800) 701-1277
200 Tent & R.V. Sites with Full Hookups, Bungalow Units, Grocery Store, Launch Ramp, Boat Storage, Clubhouse, Golf Course.

BUREAU OF LAND MANAGEMENT SHORELINE CAMPSITES
Field Office - 2610 Sweetwater Ave., Lake Havasu City, AZ 96406, Ph: (928) 505-1200 or (888) 213-2582
105 Shoreline Campsites on Arizona Side of Lake Havasu from Lake Havasu City South to Park Dam. These Sites are Accessible by Boat Only, No Reservations

PITTSBURG POINT ISLAND

CRAZY HORSE CAMPGROUND
1534 Beachcomber Blvd., Lake Havasu City, AZ 86403, Ph: (928) 855-4033
632 Tent & R.V. Sites, Full & Partial Hookups, Disposal Station, R.V. Storage, Grocery Store, Launch Ramp, Boat & PWC Rentals, Beach, Swimming Pool, Clubhouse.

LAKE HAVASU MARINA
1100 McCulloch Blvd., Lake Havasu City, AZ 86403, Ph: (928) 855-2159
7-Lane Launch Ramp, Permanent Docks, Gas Dock, Boat Slips, Pumpouts & Repairs for Boats, Boat Cleaning, Grocery Store, Marine Supplies, Dry Storage.

NAUTICAL INN RESORT
1000 McCulloch Blvd. Lake Havasu City, AZ 86403, Ph: (928) 855-2141
170 Rooms - Suites and Condos Overlooking the Lake, Private Beach, Dock, Swimming Pool, 18-Hole Golf Course, Conference Center, Restaurant & Cocktail Lounge, Store.

ISLANDER R.V. RESORT
751 Beachcomber Blvd., Lake Havasu City, AZ 86403, Ph: (928) 680-2000
500 R.V. Sites with Full Hookups, Swim Beach, 2 Swimming Pools, Grocery Store, Storage, Launch Ramp, Boat Slips, Courtesy Dock, Adjacent to 18-Hole Golf Course.

BEACHCOMBER RESORT
601 Beachcomber Blvd., Lake Havasu City, AZ 86403, Ph: (928) 855-2322
500 R.V. Sites with Full Hookups. Showers, Laundromat, Ice, Launch Ramp, Swimming Pool, Recreation Hall, Courtesy Docks.

FOR ADDITIONAL ACCOMMODATIONS AND FACILITIES CONTACT:
Lake Havasu Tourism Bureau
314 London Bridge Road
Lake Havasu City, AZ 86403
Ph: (800) 242-8278 or (928) 453-3444

KEEP THIS CHECK LIST HANDY

This is a good basic list but your own personal needs will largely influence your equipment selection. The available space in your vehicle should also be a factor in your preparation. *Courtesy of The Coleman Company*

- Air Mattress
- Batteries
- Camera and Film
- Radiant Heater (in cold weather)
- Coffee Pot
- Compass
- Cooking Utensils
- Cooler
- Cups and Dishes
- Dishpan and Pot Scrubbers
- Eating Utensils
- First Aid Kit
- Flares/Mirror-Emerg. Devices
- Flashlights
- Folding Chair or Camp Stool
- Fuel
- Ground Cloth
- Hammer/Axe
- Hat
- Human Waste Bags
- Ice or Ice Substitutes
- Insect Repellent
- Jug of Water
- Knife
- Lantern & Mantle
- Lighter-Disposable Butane
- Maps
- Matches in Waterproof Container
- Pen & Paper
- Prescription Medicine
- Ropes
- Shovel-Small Folding Type
- Sleeping Bag or Blankets
- Snakebite Kit
- Soap-Biodegradable
- Stove & Propane
- Sunglasses
- Sun Block
- Tablecloth
- Tent, Poles & Stakes
- Toilet Paper
- Toiletries - Toothbrush & Paste
- Towels-Paper & Bath
- Trash Bags
- Water Purification Tablets
- Whistle

Food Storage Containers

Bear-Resistant Food Canisters are now a must for backpackers and campers. Storage lockers are available at most campgrounds and Trailheads although space is often very limited.

You cannot leave most items in your car or tent. These include trash, wrappers, grocery bags, boxes, ice chests, bottles, cans and even cosmetics. Bears will break in to obtain them. They can cause extensive damage. Cannisters and lockers are not only for your safety but the health and well-being of the bears and their environments.

Ranger Stations will rent bear cansiters by the day or week. You can also buy these canisters at some visitor centers or many local retailers.

Be sure to bring along *RECREATION LAKES OF CALIFORNIA*

Happy Camping!
Don't forget to tread lightly and pack out all your trash.

MT. TOP

QUAGGA AND ZEBRA MUSSEL PREVENTION PROGRAM

Quagga and Zebra Mussels are very invasive mollusks threatening the boating and fishing lakes and reservoirs of California. The massive ramifications of these destructive mussels affect lakes, reservoirs, streams, rivers, fisheries, water recreation, water systems, agriculture and the entire environment of California.

The mussels remove substantial amounts of plankton from the water reducing food sources for small fish. Water clarity can increase, affecting oxygen levels so fish die off.

Small mussels are invisible to the eye and feel like sandpaper. Adults cluster in huge numbers and are one to two inches in length with dark and light stripes on their shells. They clog water intake structures and reside on docks, buoys, boats and beaches. They can glue themselves to almost any hard surface including boat trailers, hulls, anchors, motors and waders. It is important that water containing these mussels is not emptied into drains, streams or any water system.

Boat and vehicle inspection programs are in force at many lakes and reservoirs included in this book. Some lakes have boat wash stations that will help you to clean before inspection. These programs are undoubtedly the best protection against Quagga and Zebra Mussels but all of us can help this problem by using extreme care and cleaning of any vessel, trailer or accessory that goes near the waters of lakes and reservoirs. Hot water and a power sprayer are not adequate for complete cleaning.

The most effective mussel-killing solution is 2 gallons of a 200 parts per million (ppm) of potassium chloride (KCL). This is harmless to humans and to the environment. Thoroughly mix one teaspoon of dry KCL salt crystals in 2 gallons of water. These crystals can be purchased at most hardware and garden stores. The most important thing is to thoroughly clean everything that touches the water including all boats, canoes, kayaks and float tubes, trailers, motors, ropes, nets, waders, fishing gear and clothing.

Information and Assistance - Phone Numbers:

Department of Fish & Game	(866) 440-9530
Department of Boating & Waterways	(888) 326-2822
Department of Water Resources	(916) 653-9712
Department of Parks & Recreation	(916) 654-7538

Website for Department of Fish & Game - http://www.dfg.ca.gov/invasives/quaggamussel/

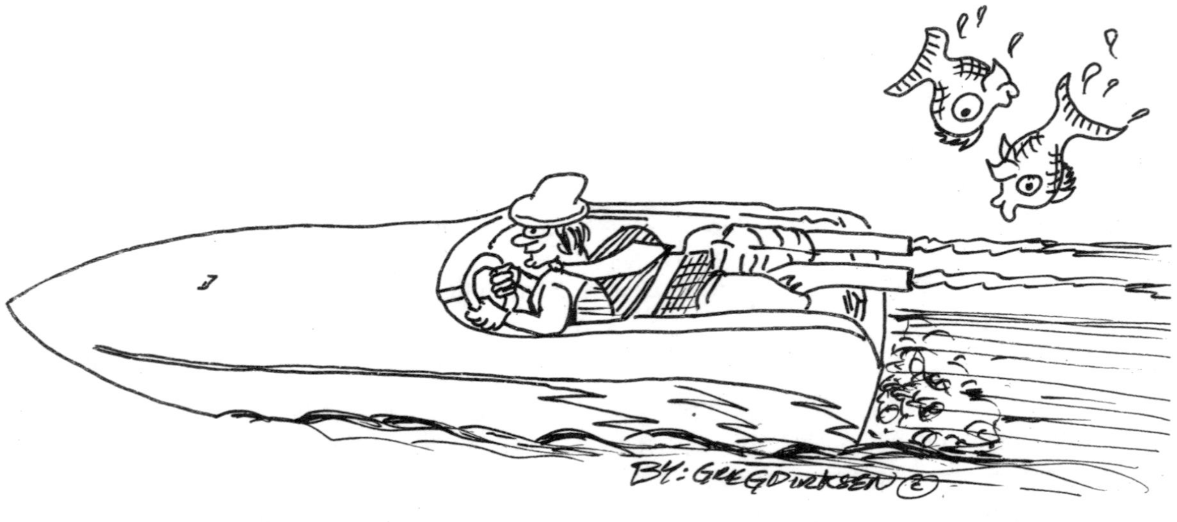
BY: GREG DIRKSEN ©

GIARDIASIS

Is the water safe?
Unless it is piped, it usually is not.

A microscopic organism, Giardia Lambia, is polluting most of our lakes and streams. By drinking this contaminated water, a severe intestinal disease is passed on to you. Giardiasis can cause extreme discomfort and must be treated by a doctor. Medication is the only way to get rid of this problem.

Unless you are certain there is clean drinking water, you need to bring your own. There are several methods for purifying water. Although water purification tablets kill bacteria, they are not reliable when it comes to Giardiasis. Portable filtration systems are fast and effective. A sure protection is to boil the water for at least ten minutes or longer at higher altitudes.

Giardia is very easily transmitted between animals and humans. All feces, human and animal, must be buried at least eight inches deep and one hundred feet away from natural water. ***Protect against Giardiasis by keeping our lakes, rivers and streams free of contamination.***

WATER

PETS

BY: GREG DIRKSEN
©

Dogs are welcome at most recreation facilities. A nominal fee is charged and there are some specific requirements. The dog must have a valid license and proof of a current rabies vaccination. There is a leash rule - the dog must be restrained by a leash no longer than ten feet. Be certain to call the campground or facility for full information before you take your pet with you.

Dogs must not be allowed to contaminate the water. As a rule, they are not permitted in public areas such as beaches and hiking trails. They are permitted in Wilderness Areas only when they are under your direct control. Keep your dog next to you and be sure to pick up after it.

USE LOW-IMPACT CAMPING TECHNIQUES TO PROTECT OUR NATURAL RESOURCES.

BOATING and SWIMMING

Boating is a popular activity at California Lakes. Many of these Lakes permit boating of all types from sailboats to jet skis. All are subject to specific rules and regulations which vary from Lake to Lake. ***Particular restrictions often apply to inflatable boats or boats that you assemble yourself.***

The type of boating permitted varies at each Lake. ***Although RECREATION LAKES OF CALIFORNIA lists what type of boats are allowed, it is always wise to check for regulations by calling the information number to confirm your particular boat can be launched. Don't be disappointed by arriving at your destination only to find you cannot enjoy your boat. Also be sure to check out Page B regarding the Quadra-Zebra Mussel infestion and mandatory inspections.***

Before launching a boat, check the local laws. The speed limit is specific at each Lake. ***There are always 5 MPH speed limits in certain areas such as near swimmers, docks or congested areas.*** There are often restricted areas or specific areas for waterskiing, sailing or fishing. The local ranger or manager will usually give you a copy of the rules and regulations.

For California State Boating Regulations, see "ABC's of California Boating Laws." This booklet may be obtained at your DMV Office.

Swimming in some California Lakes is very popular but there are potential hazards that can be minimized by using common sense and following some basic rules. ***Never swim alone;*** always have a partner. Never venture beyond your swimming and physical ability. Always ***swim in designated areas and obey the local regulations.*** Know the water conditions and environment prior to taking unnecessary risks such as diving. ***In high mountain Lakes were the water is very cold, hypothermia takes over quickly.***

WATER SKIER HAND SIGNALS

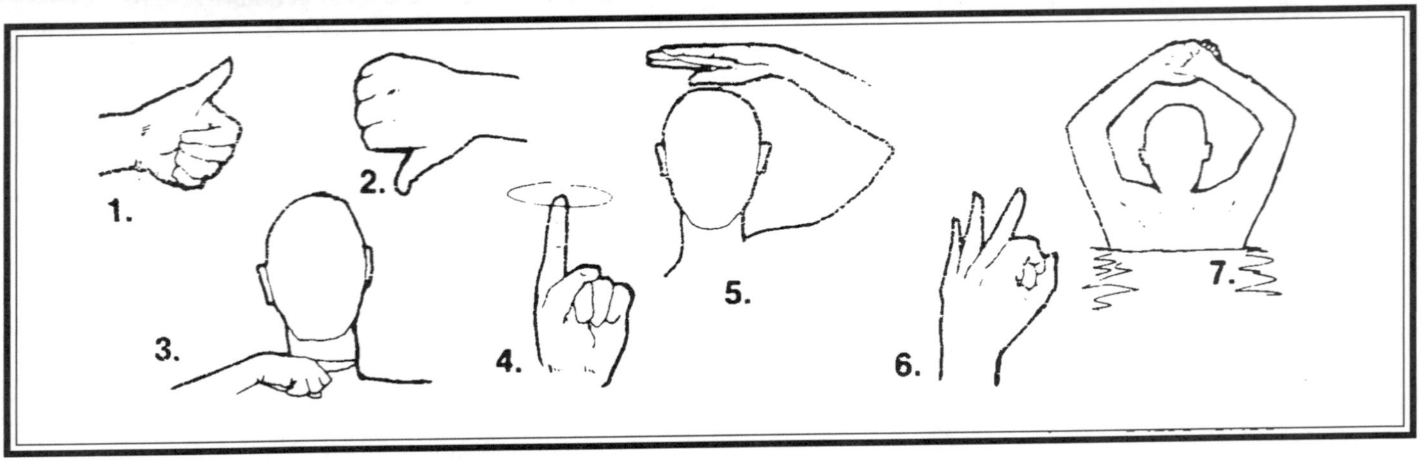
1.
2.
3.
4.
5.
6.
7.

1. **Thumb Up:** Speed up the boat.
2. **Thumb Down:** Slow down the boat.
3. **Cut Motor/Stop:** Immediately stop boat. Slashing motion over neck (also used by driver or observer).
4. **Turn:** Turn the boat (also used by driver). Circle motion—arms overhead. Then point in desired direction.
5. **Return to Dock:** Pat on the head.
6. **OK:** Speed and boat path OK. Or, signals understood.
7. **I'm OK**: Skier OK after falling.

Courtesy of the American Water Ski Association

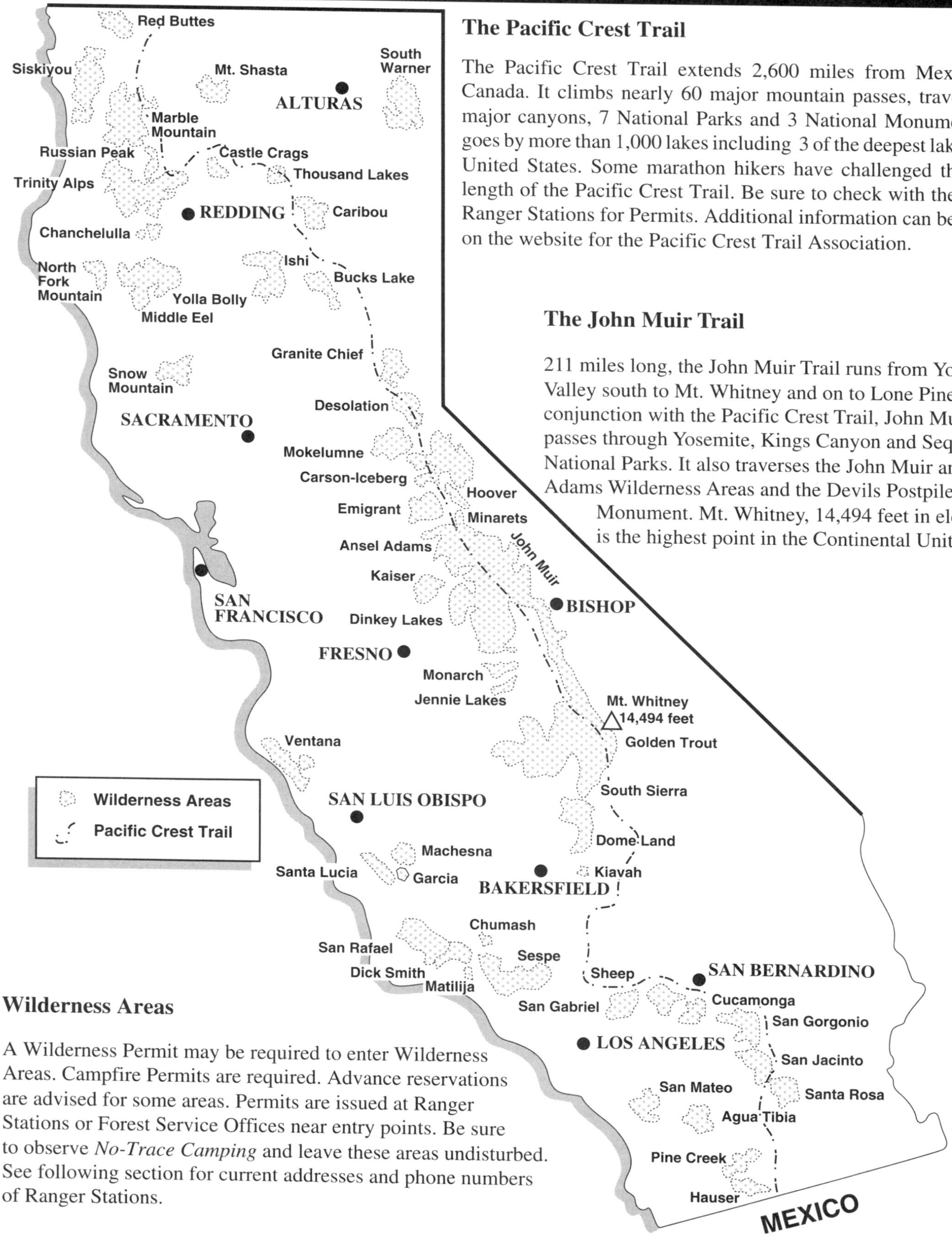
Red Buttes
Siskiyou
Mt. Shasta
South Warner
ALTURAS
Marble Mountain
Russian Peak
Castle Crags
Thousand Lakes
Trinity Alps
REDDING
Caribou
Chanchelulla
Ishi
North Fork Mountain
Bucks Lake
Yolla Bolly
Middle Eel
Granite Chief
Snow Mountain
Desolation
SACRAMENTO
Mokelumne
Carson-Iceberg
Hoover
Emigrant
Minarets
Ansel Adams
John Muir
Kaiser
SAN FRANCISCO
BISHOP
Dinkey Lakes
FRESNO
Monarch
Jennie Lakes
Mt. Whitney
14,494 feet
Golden Trout
Ventana
South Sierra
Wilderness Areas
Pacific Crest Trail
SAN LUIS OBISPO
Dome Land
Machesna
Santa Lucia
Garcia
BAKERSFIELD
Kiavah
Chumash
San Rafael
Sespe
Dick Smith
Matilija
Sheep
SAN BERNARDINO
Cucamonga
San Gabriel
San Gorgonio
LOS ANGELES
San Jacinto
San Mateo
Santa Rosa
Agua Tibia
Pine Creek
Hauser
MEXICO

The Pacific Crest Trail

The Pacific Crest Trail extends 2,600 miles from Mexico into Canada. It climbs nearly 60 major mountain passes, traverses 19 major canyons, 7 National Parks and 3 National Monuments and goes by more than 1,000 lakes including 3 of the deepest lakes in the United States. Some marathon hikers have challenged the entire length of the Pacific Crest Trail. Be sure to check with the nearest Ranger Stations for Permits. Additional information can be viewed on the website for the Pacific Crest Trail Association.

The John Muir Trail

211 miles long, the John Muir Trail runs from Yosemite Valley south to Mt. Whitney and on to Lone Pine. In conjunction with the Pacific Crest Trail, John Muir Trail passes through Yosemite, Kings Canyon and Sequoia National Parks. It also traverses the John Muir and Ansel Adams Wilderness Areas and the Devils Postpile National Monument. Mt. Whitney, 14,494 feet in elevation, is the highest point in the Continental United States.

Wilderness Areas

A Wilderness Permit may be required to enter Wilderness Areas. Campfire Permits are required. Advance reservations are advised for some areas. Permits are issued at Ranger Stations or Forest Service Offices near entry points. Be sure to observe *No-Trace Camping* and leave these areas undisturbed. See following section for current addresses and phone numbers of Ranger Stations.

NATIONAL FORESTS and STATE PARKS of CALIFORNIA

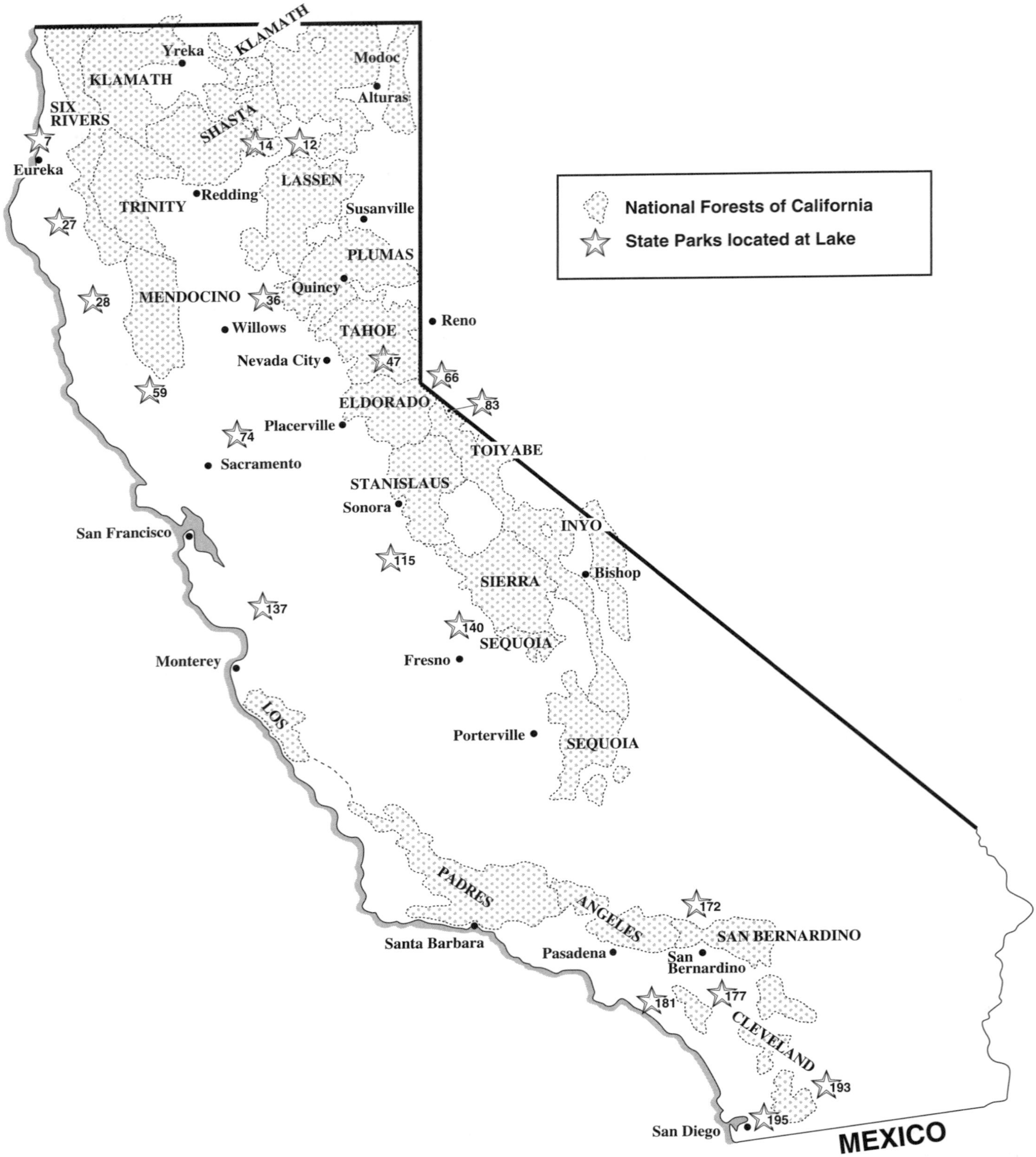

KLAMATH
Yreka
Modoc
KLAMATH
Alturas
SIX RIVERS
SHASTA
7
14
12
Eureka
LASSEN
Redding
TRINITY
Susanville
27
PLUMAS
Quincy
MENDOCINO
28
36
Reno
Willows
TAHOE
Nevada City
47
66
59
ELDORADO
83
Placerville
74
TOIYABE
Sacramento
STANISLAUS
Sonora
INYO
San Francisco
115
Bishop
SIERRA
137
140
SEQUOIA
Fresno
Monterey
LOS
Porterville
SEQUOIA
PADRES
172
ANGELES
SAN BERNARDINO
Santa Barbara
Pasadena
San Bernardino
181
177
CLEVELAND
193
195
San Diego
MEXICO
National Forests of California
State Parks located at Lake

CAMPGROUND RESERVATIONS

Campsites are by reservation or on a first-come, first-served basis. Reservations are not required at some campgrounds but they are often advised. Group campsites always require reservations. For specific information on public and private facilities listed in this guide, there is an information phone number and address on each page.

Reservations are particularly advised during summer months.

U S FOREST SERVICE RESERVATION SYSTEM
Toll Free Ph: (877) 444-6777
TDD Ph (877) 833-6777
Customer Service:Ph: (888) 448-1474
Website: http://www.recreation.gov

Individual Reservations can be made up to 6 months in advance
Group Reservations can be made up to 12 months in advance
$9 Fee for Reservation on the Website
$10 Fee for Reservation by Phone

Campsites at National Forest Service Facilities are Limited to:
Developed Sites: 14 Days Maximum
Unimproved Dispersed Camping: 30 Days Maximum within a 1 year period
Fees vary for family campground sites and group sites.
There is usually an additional fee for a second vehicle at family sites.
Fee changes can occur at any time.
Campfire Permits are required outside designated sites and are free of charge.

Various recreation facilities are open during summer months only and close at the first snow.
Be certain to check when campsites are open.

CALIFORNA STATE PARK SYSTEM CAMPGROUNDS
RESERVATIONS - Ph: (800) 444-7275 (PARK)

NATIONAL PARK SERVICE CAMPGROUNDS -
RESERVATIONS - Ph: (800) 365-2267 (CAMP)

*****ALL FEES ARE SUBJECT TO CHANGE*****
RESERVATION PHONE NUMBERS LISTED ABOVE ARE ALSO SUBJECT TO CHANGE.

FEDERAL and STATE RECREATION PASSES

NATIONAL PARKS & FEDERAL RECREATIONAL LANDS PASSES

AMERICA THE BEAUTIFUL PASS - Persons Age 16 to 61 - $80
This is an annual entrance pass to Parks and Lands that charge ENTRANCE FEES.
The Permit Holder and up to 3 passengers in a noncommercial vehicle are admitted. These passes do NOT cover use fees such as camping or parking.
Non-refundable - Non-transferable
Purchase at any National Parks & Federal Recreational Lands Entrance or
Website: http://store.usgs.gov/pass
email: fedrecpass@usgs.gov
Information: Ph: (888) ASK USGS (275-8747)

National Parks and Federal Recreational Lands include the U.S. Forest Service, National Park Service, Bureau of Land Management, Bureau of Reclamation, Fish and Wildlife Services and most Corps of Engineers Services.

ACCESS PASS - Persons with proof of permanent disability. These are free and must be obtained in person.

SENIOR ACCESS PASS - Persons 62 and older with proof of age - a State driver's license, birth certificate or passport plus a one-time fee of $10 . These must be obtained in person. If you already have a Golden Age Passport, it is valid for a lifetime and you do not have to purchase a Senior Access Pass.

These two above passports are lifetime entrance passes to federally operated National Parks, monuments, historic sites, recreation areas and national wildlife refuges that charge ENTRANCE FEES. Inquire in advance if you think there may be discounts for facilities and services such as camping, boat launching and parking. Admits Permit Holder and up to 3 accompanying passengers in a single, noncommercial vehicle.

CALIFORNIA STATE PARKS - PASSES AND DISCOUNTS

Department of Parks and Recreation
1416 - 9th Street
Sacramento 95814
Ph: (800) 777-0369 or (916) 653-6995
Website: www.parks.ca.gov
Annual Vehicle Day Use Pass - Fees: $90 - $125
Valid for passenger vehicles with a capacity of 9 people or less and for motorcycles.
Some State Parks will accept these passes at Parks where day use fees are collected.
Boat Use Pass: $75 for Launching Boats over 8 feet accepted where Launch Fees are collected.
OHV Vehicle Day Use: $50 for OHVs where Entrance Fees are collected.
Please phone or check the website for full information on all Passes and Discounts and where they are accepted.
Discounts for Disabled People, Veterans and Seniors 62 years or older - Applications:
Ph: (800) 777-0369 or (916) 375-8040

Bait
COLA

DEPARTMENT OF FISH & GAME OFFICES
HEADQUARTERS
1416 9th Street - 12th Floor
Sacramento 95814
Ph: (916) 445-0411

REGIONAL OFFICES:

Northern Region
601 Locust Street
Redding 96001
Ph: (530) 225-2300

North Central Region
1701 Nimbus Rd.
Rancho Cordova 95670
Ph: (916) 358-2900

Bay Delta Region
7329 Silverado Trail
Napa 94558
Ph: (707) 944-5500

Central Region
1234 E. Shaw Ave.
Fresno 93710
Ph: (559) 243-4005

South Coast Region
4949 Viewridge Ave.
San Diego 92123
Ph: (858) 467-4201

Inland Deserts Region
3602 Inland Empire Blvd.
Ontario 91764
Ph: (909) 484-0167

Marine Region
20 Lower Ragsdale Dr. #100
Monterey 93940
Ph: (831) 649-2870

CALIFORNIA STATE PARKS SYSTEM
1416 9th Street
Sacramento, CA 95814
Information Ph: (916) 653-6995

Publications Office
1416 Ninth Street - Room 118
Sacramento, CA 95814
Information Ph: (916) 653-4000

CALIFORNIA TOURISM

For Tourist Information Publications
Ph: (916) 444-4429 or (800) 862-2543

RANGER STATIONS and FOREST SERVICE OFFICES

CALIFORNIA REGION OF THE U.S. FOREST SERVICE

General Information, Maps and Wilderness Permits may be obtained at the following locations:

Pacific Southwest Region
USDA Forest Service
1323 Club Drive
Vallejo 94592
Ph: (707) 562-8737

ANGELES NATIONAL FOREST

Forest Supervisor's Office
701 N. Santa Anita Avenue
Arcadia 91006
Ph: (626) 574-5200

Santa Clara/Mojave Rivers Ranger District
28245 Avenue Crocker Suite 220
Valencia 91355
Ph: (661) 296-9710

LA River Ranger District
12371 N. Little Tujunga Cyn. Rd.
San Fernando 91342
Ph: (818) 899-1900

San Gabriel River Ranger District
110 N. Wabash Avenue
Glendora 91741
Ph: (626) 335-1251

CLEVELAND NATIONAL FOREST

Forest Supervisor's Office
10845 Rancho Bernardo Rd.
San Diego 92127
Ph: (859) 673-6180

Decanso Ranger District
3348 Alpine Boulevard
Alpine 91901
Ph: (619) 445-6235

Palomar Ranger District
1634 Black Canyon Road
Ramona 92065
Ph: (760) 788-0250

Trabuco Ranger District
1147 E. Sixth Street
Corona 92879
Ph: (951) 736-1811

ELDORADO NATIONAL FOREST

Forest Supervisor's Office
100 Forni Road
Placerville 95667
Ph: (530) 622-5061

Amador Ranger District
26820 Silver Drive & Hwy. 88
Pioneer 95666
Ph: (209) 295-4251

Georgetown Ranger District
7600 Wentworth Springs Rd.
Georgetown 95634
Ph: (530) 333-4312

Information Center
3070 Camino Heights Drive
Camino 95709
Ph: (530) 644-6048

Pacific Ranger District
7887 Highway 50
Pollock Pines 95726
Ph: (530) 644-2349

Placerville Ranger District
4260 Eight Mile Road
Camino 95709
Ph: (530) 644-2324

Placerville Nursery
2375 Fruitridge Road
Camino 95709
Ph: (530) 622 9600

INYO NATIONAL FOREST

Wilderness Permit Office
351 Pacu Lane, Suite 200
Bishop 93514
Ph: (760) 873-2485

Mono Basin Scenic Area
Ranger Station
Post Office Box 429
Lee Vining 93541
Ph: (760) 647-3044

Mammoth Ranger District
Post Office Box 148
Mammoth Lakes 93546
Ph: (760) 924-5500

Mt. Whitney Ranger District
Post Office Box 8
Lone Pine 93545
Ph: (760) 876-6200

White Mountain Ranger District
798 North Main Street
Bishop 93514
Ph: (760) 873-2500

KLAMATH NATIONAL FOREST

Forest Supervisor's Office
1312 Fairlane Road
Yreka 96097
Ph: (530) 842-6131

Goosenest Ranger District
37805 Highway 97
Macdoel 96058
Ph: (530) 398-4391

Happy Camp & Oak Knoll
Ranger District
63822 Highway 96
P O Box 377
Happy Camp 96039
Ph: (530) 493-2243

Salmon and Scott River
Ranger District
11263 N. Highway 3
Fort Jones 96032
Ph: (530) 468-5351

Ukonom Ranger District
Highway 96 & Ishi Pishi Road
Post Office Drawer 410
Orleans 95556
Ph: (530) 627-3291

LAKE TAHOE BASIN MANAGEMENT UNIT

Forest Supervisor's Office
35 College Drive
South Lake Tahoe 96150
Ph: (530) 543-2600

Management Unit Office
for North Tahoe
3080 North Lake Blvd.
Tahoe City, 96145
Ph: (530) 583-3593

LASSEN NATIONAL FOREST

Forest Supervisor's Office
2550 Riverside Drive
Susanville 96130
Ph: (530) 257-2151

Almanor Ranger District
900 East Highway 36
Post Office Box 767
Chester 96020
Ph: (530) 258-2141

Eagle Lake Ranger District
477-050 Eagle Lake Rd.
Susanville 96130
Ph: (530) 257-4188

Hat Creek Ranger District
43225 East Highway 299
Post Office Box 220
Fall River Mills 96028
Ph: (530) 336-5521

Continued...

Los Padres National Forest

Forest Supervisor's Office
6755 Hollister Ave., Suite 150
Goleta 93117
Ph: (805) 968-6640

Ojai Ranger District
1190 E. Ojai Avenue
Ojai 93023
Ph: (805) 646-4348

Monterey Ranger District
406 S. Mildred
King City 93930
Ph: (831) 385-5434

Santa Barbara Ranger District
3505 Paradise Road
Santa Barbara 93105
Ph: (805) 967-3481

Mt. Pinos Ranger District
34580 Lockwood Valley Road
Frazier Park 93225
Ph: (661) 245-3731

Santa Lucia Ranger District
1616 N. Carlotti Drive
Santa Maria 93454
Ph: (805) 925-9538

Mendocino National Forest

Forest Supervisor's Office
825 N. Humboldt Avenue
Willows 95988
Ph: (530) 934-3316

Stonyford Ranger District
5171 Stonyford-Elk Creek Road
Post Office Box 160
Stonyford 95979
Ph: (530) 963-3128

Covelo Ranger District
78150 Covelo Road
Covelo 95428
Ph: (707) 983-6118

Upper Lake Ranger District
10025 Elk Mountain Road
Upper Lake 95485
Ph: (707) 275-2361

Grindstone Ranger District
725 North Humboldt Avenue
Willows 95988
Ph: (530) 934-3316

Genetic Resource
and Conservation Center
2741 Cramer Lane
Chico 95928
Ph: (530) 895-1176

Modoc National Forest

Forest Supervisor's Office
800 West 12th Street
Alturas 96101
Ph: (530) 233-5811

Big Valley Ranger District
Post Office Box 159
Adin 96006
Ph: (530) 299-3215

Devil's Garden Ranger District
800 West 12th Street
Alturas 96101
Ph: (530) 233-5811

Doublehead Ranger District
Post Office Box 369
Tulelake 96134
Ph: (530) 667-2246

Warner Mountain Ranger District
Post Office Box 220
Cedarville 96104
Ph: (530) 279-6116

Plumas National Forest

Forest Supervisor's Office
159 Lawrence Street
Post Office Box 11500
Quincy 95971
Ph: (530) 283-2050

Feather River Ranger District
875 Mitchell Avenue
Oroville 95965
Ph: (530) 534-6500

Beckworth Ranger District
23 Mohawk Road
Post Office Box 7
Blairsden 96103
Ph: (530) 836-2575

Greenville Work Center
122 Hot Springs Road
Greenville 95947
Ph: (530) 284-7126

Challenge Visitor's Center
18050 Mulock Road
Challenge 95925
Ph: (530) 675-1146

Mt. Hough Ranger District
39696 Highway 70
Quincy 95971
Ph: (530) 283-0555

San Bernardino National Forest

Forest Supervisor's Office
602 South Tuppecanoe Ave.
San Bernardino 92408
Ph: (909) 382-2600

Arrowhead Ranger District
28104 Highway 18
Post Office Box 350
Skyforest 92385
Ph: (909) 382-2782

Big Bear Ranger District
41397 North Shore Drive
Post Office Box 290
Fawnskin 92333
Ph: (909) 382-2790

Cajon Ranger District
1209 Lytle Creek Road
Lytle Creek 92358
Ph: (909) 382-2851

Idyllwild Ranger District
54270 Pinecrest Ave.
Post Office Box 518
Idyllwild 92549
Ph: (909) 382-2921

San Gorgonio Ranger District
34701 Mill Creek Road
Mentone 92359
Ph: (909) 382-2881

Sequoia National Forest

Forest Supervisor's Office
1839 South Newcomb Street
Porterville 93257
Ph: (559) 784-1500

Kern River Ranger District
105 Whitney Road
Post Office Box 9
Kernville 93238
Ph: (760) 376-3781

Kern River Ranger District
Lake Isabella Office
4875 Ponderosa Drive
Post Office Box 3810
Lake Isabella 93240
Ph: (760) 379-5646

Hume Lake Ranger District
35860 E. Kings Canyon Rd.
Dunlap 93621
Ph: (559) 338-2251

Western Divide Ranger District
32588 Highway 190
Springville 93265
Ph: (559) 539-2607

Shasta-Trinity National Forest

Forest Supervisor's Office
3644 Avtech Parkway
Redding 96002
Ph: (530) 226-2500

Big Bar Ranger District
Star Route 1, Box 10
Big Bar 96010
Ph: (530) 623-6106

Hayfork Ranger District
Post Office Box 159
Hayfork 96041
Ph: (530) 628-5227

McCloud Ranger District
Post Office Box 1620
McCloud 96057
Ph: (530) 964-2184

Mt. Shasta Ranger District
204 West Alma
Mt. Shasta 96067
Ph: (530) 926-4511

Shasta Lake Ranger District
14225 Holiday Road
Redding 96003
Ph: (530) 275-1587

Weaverville Ranger District
Post Office Box 1190
Weaverville 96093
Ph: (530) 623-2121

Yolla Bolla Ranger District,
HC 01, Box 400
2555 State Highway 36
Platina 96076
Ph: (530) 352-4211

Sierra National Forest

Forest Supervisor's Office
1600 Tollhouse Road
Clovis 93611
Ph: (559) 297-0706

Bass Lake Ranger District
57003 Road 225
North Fork 93643
Ph: (559) 877-2218

Dinkey Creek Visitor Center
Shaver Lake 93664
Ph: (559) 841-3404 (Summer Only)

High Sierra Ranger District
29688 Auberry Road
Post Office Box 559
Prather 93651
Ph: (559) 855-5355

Yosemite/Sierra Visitors Bureau
43060 Highway 41
Oakhurst 93644
Ph: (559) 683-4665

Continued...

Six Rivers National Forest

Forest Supervisor's Office
1330 Bayshore Way
Eureka 95501
Ph: (707) 442-1721

Lower Trinity Ranger District
Post Office Box 68
Willow Creek 95573
Ph: (530) 629-2118

Mad River Ranger District
741 State Highway 36
Bridgeville 95526
Ph: (707) 574-6233

Orleans/Ukonom Ranger District
Post Office Box 410
Orleans 95556
Ph: (530) 627-3291

Smith River NRA
Highway 199
Post Office Box 228
Gasquet 95543
Ph: (707) 457-3131

Stanislaus National Forest

Forest Supervisor's Office
19777 Greenley Road
Sonora 95370
Ph: (209) 532-3671

Calaveras Ranger District
5519 Highway 4
Post Office Box 500
Hathaway Pines 95233
Ph: (209) 795-1381

Groveland Ranger District
24545 Highway 120
Groveland 95321
Ph: (209) 962-7825

Mi-Wok Ranger District
24695 Highway 108
Post Office Box 100
Mi-Wok Village 95346
Ph: (209) 586-3234

Summit Ranger District
#1 Pinecrest Lake Road
Pinecrest 95364
Ph: (209) 965-3434

Tahoe National Forest

Forest Supervisor's Office
631 Coyote Street
Nevada City 95959
Ph: (530) 265-4531

American River Ranger District
22830 Foresthill Road
Foresthill 95631
Ph: (530) 367-2224

Sierraville Ranger District
317 South Lincoln St.
Post Office Box 95
Sierraville 96126
Ph: (530) 994-3401

Truckee Ranger District
9646 Donner Pass Road
Truckee 96161
Ph: (530) 587-3558

Yuba River Ranger District
15924 Highway 49
Camptonville 95922
Ph: (530) 288-3231

National Parks

Lassen Volcanic National Park
Post Office Box 100
Mineral 96063
Ph: (530) 595-4480

Sequoia-Kings Canyon National Park
37050 Generals Highway
Three Rivers 93271
Ph: (209) 565-3341

Yosemite National Park
Post Office Box 577
Yosemite National Park 95389
Ph: (209) 372-0200